PRAIS

MILTON FRIEDMAN

THE LAST CONSERVATIVE

"Burns had full access to Friedman's papers stored at Stanford's Hoover Institution; she has interviewed many of Friedman's friends, colleagues and competitors; and she is plainly an authority on the at times highly abstruse subjects of economic theory and monetary policy. [*Milton Friedman: The Last Conservative*] is a tremendous scholarly accomplishment."

—Barton Swaim, *The Wall Street Journal*

"Burns has a rare ability to wield economic terms and concepts clearly and precisely, without either dumbing them down or resorting to phony erudition. Rather than simply tell us that Friedman was marked by an early reading of Alfred Marshall, she will tell us what is *in* Alfred Marshall and where it shows up in Friedman's work. In explaining how Friedman's ideas of the Fed's role differed from those of his rivals, she explains what 'open market operations' are, what a 'primary dealer' is, what the 'federal funds rate' is, and so on. The arguments are both sophisticated and easy to follow."

—Christopher Caldwell, *First Things*

"[Burns] presents not only a well-researched and nuanced biographical sketch of Milton Friedman, but also, in tracing his influence, a riveting tour de force of economic history across the twentieth century."

—Robert Steven Mack, *The New Criterion*

"Enriched by access to Friedman's papers . . . , Burns pulls together in satisfying fashion details of Friedman's life that formerly lay scattered. She also provides the academic background with a compelling portrait of Friedman's first revolution, [at] the University of Chicago. Her analysis of how Friedman and his allies made price theory king at Chicago is not to be missed. Nor are the stories."

—Amity Shlaes, *National Review*

"A most delightful and informative biography . . . If one has a yen for matters political economic, [this book is] beautifully researched candy."
—Brian Domitrovic, *Forbes*

"A testament to the power of ideas . . . Friedman's life never drags. Although large sections of the book deal with abstract economic theory and complicated technical matters that were the subject of immense debate between Friedman and various academic and professional economists, Burns manages to make them compelling to a lay reader because she puts them in human terms."
—Max Blaisdell, *Chicago Reader*

"Jennifer Burns manages in her new biography the near-impossible feat of doing justice to Friedman, both as an economist and more widely as—to quote the book's title in a nod to how US conservatism has been degraded in the era of Trump—'the last conservative' . . . Burns is superb at explaining complicated economic ideas . . . Burns has written a wonderful biography, but it is more than that. It is an intellectual history of the US in the last seventy years of the twentieth century and, as such, is an important read."
—Stephen Pollard, *The Jewish Chronicle*

"[A] definitive biography . . . Burns does a wonderful job of explaining the methodological importance of Friedman's thought . . . Burns' masterful biography of Milton Friedman is more than an intellectual portrait. It's a rich reminder of how ideas, historical context, and personal relationships shape the world we make."
—Michael N. Peterson, *Daily Economy*

"The first full-scale account of [Friedman's] personal and professional life, impact and legacy. Richly detailed, well-informed and informative, judicious and accessible, Burns' book is also, in essence, a primer on economics over the last century . . . Burns makes a compelling case that Friedman continues to cast a long shadow on economic and social policy."
—Glenn Altschuler, *The Messenger*

"Deeply researched and beautifully written, [*Milton Friedman*] makes the personal and intellectual life of Friedman jump off the page. Burns not only captures Friedman's life but conveys in her telling of that story the broader intellectual life of America and the global political and economic order of the twentieth century . . . A brilliant book, written by a first-rate scholar in accessible and graceful prose."

—Peter Boettke, *National Review*

"[An] excellent new biography . . . *Milton Friedman: The Last Conservative* shines as an exploration of Friedman's ideas and accomplishments."

—Brian Doherty, *Reason*

"A marvelous new biography . . . The book can also be read as a tour of the broader debate about capitalism, as seen through the eyes of a man who had an unwavering view from the start . . . Thanks to Burns . . . we have the building blocks for a less reductive narrative about the marketplace of ideas and ideas about the market." —Jeremy Adelman, *Project Syndicate*

"To call this book merely a biography of Milton Friedman is a disservice. It would be difficult to imagine a more comprehensive portrait of the influences, hard economics, and personal struggles and triumphs that shaped his life . . . [Burns] is evenhanded throughout and unafraid to critique . . . Sharp and illuminating . . . A masterful profile of a most consequential American." —*Kirkus Reviews* (starred review)

"One of the most brilliant biographies of Friedman to date. For both general readers and economics scholars."

—Claude Ury, *Library Journal* (starred review)

"Robust . . . A comprehensive accounting of Friedman's legacy."

—*Publishers Weekly*

"How did Milton Friedman become Milton Friedman? Jennifer Burns offers a definitive answer to this question, deftly blending the personal and professional sides of Friedman's life to paint a portrait of the man, his ideas, his times, and his enduring influence. She gives us the man in full: a husband, father, friend, scholar, policy adviser, public intellectual, and debater." —Bruce Caldwell, coauthor of *Hayek: A Life*

"Jennifer Burns has written what will stand as the definitive biography of Milton Friedman. It is full of insight and excitement, and I learned many new things from it."

—Tyler Cowen, coauthor of *Talent* and author of *Big Business*

"This is biography at its best: a probing, revelatory, and engrossing account of Milton Friedman's life. Any reckoning with this towering and divisive figure must start with Jennifer Burns's brilliant book."

—Gary Gerstle, author of *The Rise and Fall of the Neoliberal Order*

"Jennifer Burns has not just written an elegantly crafted and unfailingly perceptive biography of the most influential and controversial American economist who ever lived. In narrating the long life of Milton Friedman, she has also given us a lucid history of economic thought and its outsize influence on the politics of the United States—and the world. This is a book that anyone who cares about the role of ideas in the making of the twentieth century should read and enjoy."

—Michael Kazin, author of *What It Took to Win: A History of the Democratic Party*

"Jennifer Burns's *Milton Friedman: The Last Conservative* is a stunning achievement. In addition to a beautifully crafted and deeply researched biography of Friedman, Burns has given us an education in economic history and a tour of American beliefs, fears, and hopes throughout the tumultuous twentieth century. She tells the stories of the hidden figures, too: the women and men whose ideas shaped Friedman's own, but whose identities were hidden by the prejudices of their day. And she wraps this all into a complete page-turner of a book."

—Debora L. Spar, author of *Work Mate Marry Love* and *Wonder Women*

"If you love Milton Friedman, as I do, for his intellectual honesty and devotion to liberty, you won't be able to stop reading this graceful, balanced life of the man. If you think you hate him, I bet you also won't be able to stop reading. You'll emerge from the experience respecting him, and seeing him not as a 'conservative' but as the truest liberal of modern economics."

—Deirdre Nansen McCloskey, author of *Bourgeois Equality*

"Brilliantly researched and elegantly balanced, Jennifer Burns's book shows how Milton Friedman—argumentative, stubbornly out of step, frequently wrong and sometimes brilliantly right—became the most influential public economist of his age."

—Daniel T. Rodgers, author of *Age of Fracture*

"*Milton Friedman: The Last Conservative* is a lively, readable, and informative biography of an economist who, for good or ill, helped shape the world in which we now live."

—Roger E. Backhouse, author of *Founder of Modern Economics: Paul A. Samuelson*

Katya Mizrahi Photography

JENNIFER BURNS

MILTON FRIEDMAN

THE LAST CONSERVATIVE

Jennifer Burns is an associate professor of history at Stanford University, a research fellow at the Hoover Institution, and the author of *Goddess of the Market: Ayn Rand and the American Right*. She has written for *The New York Times*, the *Financial Times*, *Bloomberg*, and *Dissent*, and has discussed her work on *The Daily Show*, *The Colbert Report*, and other programs.

ALSO BY JENNIFER BURNS

Goddess of the Market: Ayn Rand and the American Right

MILTON FRIEDMAN

MILTON FRIEDMAN

THE LAST CONSERVATIVE

JENNIFER BURNS

PICADOR
FARRAR, STRAUS AND GIROUX
NEW YORK

Picador
120 Broadway, New York 10271

Copyright © 2023 by Jennifer Burns
All rights reserved
Printed in the United States of America
Originally published in 2023 by Farrar, Straus and Giroux
First paperback edition, 2024

Illustration credits can be found on pages 577–578.

The Library of Congress has cataloged the Farrar, Straus and Giroux hardcover edition as follows:
Names: Burns, Jennifer, 1975– author.
Title: Milton Friedman : the last conservative / Jennifer Burns.
Description: First edition. | New York : Farrar, Straus and Giroux, [2023] | Includes bibliographical references and index.
Identifiers: LCCN 2023018751 | ISBN 9780374601140 (hardcover)
Subjects: LCSH: Friedman, Milton, 1912–2006. | Economists—United States—Biography. | Economics—History.
Classification: LCC HB119.F84 B87 2023 | DDC 330.092 [B]—dc23/eng/20230420
LC record available at https://lccn.loc.gov/2023018751

Paperback ISBN: 978-1-250-33820-4

Designed by Patrice Sheridan

Our books may be purchased in bulk for promotional, educational, or business use. Please contact your local bookseller or the Macmillan Corporate and Premium Sales Department at 1-800-221-7945, extension 5442, or by email at MacmillanSpecialMarkets@macmillan.com.

Picador® is a U.S. registered trademark and is used by Macmillan Publishing Group, LLC, under license from Pan Books Limited.

For book club information, please email marketing@picadorusa.com.

picadorusa.com • Follow us on social media at @picador or @picadorusa

1 3 5 7 9 10 8 6 4 2

For Nick

The ideas of economists and political philosophers, both when they are right and when they are wrong, are more powerful than is commonly understood. Indeed the world is ruled by little else. Practical men, who believe themselves to be quite exempt from any intellectual influences, are usually the slaves of some defunct economist.

—John Maynard Keynes, 1936

Only a crisis—actual or perceived—produces real change. When that crisis occurs, the actions that are taken depend on the ideas that are lying around. That, I believe, is our basic function: to develop alternatives to existing policies, to keep them alive and available until the politically impossible becomes politically inevitable.

—Milton Friedman, 1982

CONTENTS

PART V: THE GREAT INFLATION

PART VI: THE AGE OF MONETARISM

A photographic insert follows page 274.

MILTON FRIEDMAN

INTRODUCTION

> In many ways Milton Friedman was a devil figure in my youth . . . I grew to see the issue as more nuanced.
>
> —LARRY SUMMERS, 2001

Rumpled and unpretentious, standing barely five feet tall, peering through thick glasses with an expression of amusement and wonder, Milton Friedman seemed an unlikely figure to inspire awe or rage. But love him and hate him they did. In Wisconsin there were picket lines to protest his firing; in Louisiana, picket lines to welcome him to town (also to urge that the post office be privatized); in Stockholm, picket lines to chase him away. There was even a picket line at his granddaughter's nursery school. Friedman was an economist in a century that gave economists extraordinary power, which accounts for some of the reaction. But for a time—and even today—Friedman's name conjured not just a person, but an entire constellation of ideas. On the 1980s TV show *Family Ties*, the smarmy Republican son of ex-hippie parents, Alex P. Keaton, loves Milton Friedman. Nearly fifteen years after Friedman's death, on the campaign trail in 2020 Joe Biden declared, "Milton Friedman isn't running the show anymore!" Both references point to one of Friedman's major legacies: crafting the basic intellectual consensus about free markets and limited government that powered twentieth-century American conservatism. It is true that Friedman was there on the ground for major developments in Republican politics.

He advised the presidential candidate Barry Goldwater, took to the ski slopes with *National Review*'s founder, William F. Buckley Jr., set up a back channel to allies in the Nixon White House, and cheered as Ronald Reagan folded his ideas about the "magic of the market" into a new establishment. As an economist, Friedman led a successful intellectual movement against Keynesian economics, which was closely linked with the Democratic Party. By the end of his career, as one rival admitted, "the age of John Maynard Keynes gave way to the age of Milton Friedman."[1] Yet as scholars increasingly recognize, although Friedman's political allegiances lay firmly with the Republican Party, his ideas shaped thinking across the partisan divide.[2]

Friedman was more than an economist; he offered a philosophy of freedom that made a tremendous political impact in a liberty-loving country. Many aspects of our contemporary world that today seem commonplace have their origins in one of Friedman's seemingly crazy ideas. If you've had taxes withheld from a paycheck, planned or postponed a foreign holiday due to the exchange rate, considered the military as a career, wondered if the Federal Reserve really knows what it's doing, worked at or enrolled your child in a charter school, or gotten into an argument about the pros and cons of universal basic income, you've had a brush with Friedman. Nor does it matter if you are an American. Friedman's ideas about capitalism, limited government, and inflation were taken up across the globe, from London to Santiago to Shanghai. He was a prime mover in the central economic transitions of the century: the decline of New Deal liberalism, the fall of the postwar currency regime of Bretton Woods, the shift to free trade, and the battle against inflation that gripped industrialized nations in the 1970s and 1980s. Friedman's monetarism, which he summarized with the dictum "Inflation is always and everywhere a monetary phenomenon," became a guiding philosophy of central banks across the world, despite its checkered record as a detailed guide for policy-makers. Applied as a broader statement of political economy, monetarism contributed to decades of low inflation, which persisted through 2020. Friedman himself became a major symbol of the hope for a more prosperous, free, and open world after the fall of Communism in the 1990s.

Friedman was born in 1912 and died in 2006, and thus his life tracks major events of the twentieth century. He became an economist as a young man living through the Great Depression of the 1930s, when he wrestled with fundamental questions of the age: Could capitalism guarantee broad prosperity, or was it doomed to unremitting cycles of boom and bust? How could nations support those in need without choking off the dynamic energies of economic growth? Did liberal democracy have a future, or were ideals of classical liberalism—limited, representative government; individual freedom; and unrestricted trade—relics of the past? Most economists of his generation answered these questions by looking to Keynesian economics, which called for greater state involvement in economic affairs, primarily through the taxing and spending powers of the federal government. But from the start, Friedman worried these solutions were economically unsustainable and, worse, endangered individual liberty. This was of course a shibboleth of the reactionary conservatives who hated Franklin D. Roosevelt. In contrast, Friedman supported critical aspects of the New Deal, particularly its early response to the economic crisis. And throughout his life, he remained preoccupied by the problems of the 1930s and '40s, national and global. As it did for many American Jews, the Holocaust loomed large in Friedman's imagination. Characteristically, Friedman took this awareness in an unusual direction, seeing anti-Semitism as a ready lesson in the dangers of the state. Among his great triumphs as an economist was authoring, with the indispensable Anna Schwartz, a reinterpretation of the Great Depression that remains essential for scholarship on the downturn. At the same time, Friedman spent the bulk of his career working to erect an alternative to the political landscape carved by the Great Depression, the New Deal, and then World War II.

The decades after the war were a time of tremendous intellectual creativity for Friedman, as he set out a new policy framework centered on rules-based management of the monetary system and the free play of price and contract within all other markets. Recognizing that a larger government was here to stay, Friedman nonetheless sought to limit its scope and reach. In some cases he advocated outright repeal of established regulations, including rent control, price supports for agriculture, tariffs and import quotas, and controls on gas and oil production. In other areas of state involvement, Friedman often suggested that government function by dispersing financial resources directly to recipients, so that retirees, unemployed workers, or low-income families could bypass bureaucracy and buy what they needed in the market. Alternatively, he proposed that state enterprises like the U.S. Postal Service face private competition—a reform eventually implemented piecemeal across the 1970s and '80s that led to the rise of FedEx, DHL, and other overnight mail services. Overall, Friedman encouraged the state to structure and harness market forces rather than intervene directly in their operation. Again and again, he suggested that the price system—the free interaction of buyers and sellers—could produce better social outcomes than the decisions of politicians and regulators. Yet Friedman did not simply propose technical fixes to policy problems. He set his economic ideas within a broader philosophy of individual freedom that served as the moral grounding for his work. And he articulated a vision of the state that was starkly at odds with the one that emerged from the New Deal and the crisis of the 1930s.

Today, scholars describe this intellectual approach with the broad moniker of "neoliberalism," and have traced its influence across every continent. By the final decades of the twentieth century, Friedman's ideas helped a new political order emerge, as countries abandoned top-down economic planning in favor of market-based approaches. The disintegration of Bretton Woods and the overthrow of Chile's socialist government were early markers along the path. The political successes of Ronald Reagan and Margaret Thatcher were culminating events. In each case, the turn to markets had its own internal dynamics, powered by local and regional histories, political institutions, and resentments of class, caste, and religion. But in all of them were also traces of Friedman. Inevitably, he was somewhere in the mix, moonlighting as an adviser, beaming out from state TV, sitting down with the finance minister.[3]

Critically, Friedman's monetary economics accepted that the gold standard, abandoned during World War II, was not coming back. In many ways Friedman picked up where Keynes left off (due to his early death) in thinking through the risks and rewards of global fiat currency. Why did monetary systems sometimes break down catastrophically, as in the raging hyperinflation that preceded Hitler's rise? What about the opposite problem, when some sort of gravitational compression took over and shrank an economy from the inside out? Friedman had lived through that during the Great Depression, and would make explaining it his life's work. Perhaps even more important was the basic problem of keeping a modern monetary economy on a steady growth path. While Keynes himself considered money fundamental to these questions, many of his early American followers did not. As they looked increasingly to federal spending and regulation, Friedman was left nearly alone to focus on the role of money. The solution he proposed—a policy rule dictating a fixed rate of growth in the money supply—aspired to re-create the stability of the gold standard without its dangerous rigidities. Monetarism was compatible with Friedman's broader political economy, in that it suggested that many of the state interventions developed since the Depression were unjustified or unnecessary. At the same time, it was also a freestanding analysis of the necessary conditions for economic stability and growth. Friedman's monetarism has been revised, reformulated, and reinterpreted many times over, as monetary institutions and economic knowledge have evolved. Yet remarkably, it remains an essential starting point for understanding inflation and deflation.

Also like Keynes, Friedman was among the last economists shaped by the dying tradition of political economy, which blended economic, social, and ethical questions. His most bitter fights were with economists who fancied themselves practitioners of hard science, akin to being mathematicians or physicists. And his closest intellectual companions were economists working far from the disciplinary mainstream, like F. A. Hayek, who is most famous as a political philosopher; his lifelong friend George Stigler, a historian of economics; and his brother-in-law, Aaron Director, a professor of law. For nearly a quarter century—from 1946 until the early 1970s—Friedman counted himself an outsider to the main currents of economic thought. But as the basic assumptions of postwar economics were suddenly turned upside down by stagflation, the simultaneous arrival of high inflation and high unemployment, Friedman found a new audience for his views. In the last decades of his professional life, Friedman was no more a lonely voice speaking only to conservative audiences and fellow economists. He launched an extraordinary public career as a spokesman for a general rethinking of how nation-states and multinational organizations should—or should not—stimulate economic growth and manage economic calamity. As the author of numerous best-selling books, a columnist for the influential magazine *Newsweek*, and a television star, Friedman had tremendous reach.

Friedman's research on money, inflation, and currency regimes made him an indispensable thinker during the 1970s and '80s as the tectonic plates of economic regimes began to shift. The solutions that worked in 1945—Bretton Woods, social democracy, redistributive welfare states—were cracking apart.[4] All of these maladies had one obvious symptom: inflation. From Europe to the Middle East to South America, surging prices destabilized old international alliances, weakened political leaders, sharpened class divisions, and sent waves of discontent and uncertainty through business owners, workers, and shoppers alike. In retrospect, it was not just the old order dying but a new form of global capitalism being born. Inflation was the wrecking ball, coming to finish off social and political forms weakened by the upheavals of the 1960s, from the nuclear family to the union job to the factory pumping out goods made in the USA. The ironies were considerable. What Friedman had so long tried to prevent—more than a decade of consistently rising prices—ushered in a world closer to his ideal, where capital moved freely across borders, governments retrenched from social spending, and a culture of expressive individualism celebrated freedom above all else.

The reputation of any great thinker is never static, and Friedman is no exception. Raised in a household of Keynesian economists, the former Treasury secretary and Harvard president emeritus Larry Summers once recalled that Friedman was "a devil figure in my youth." Over time, though, Summers came "to have enormous respect for Friedman's views on a range of questions. That's a respect that is born of the power of his arguments as one considers them more and more deeply." I began my research in the aftermath of the 2008 financial crisis, when Friedman remained a formidable figure, a sort of skeleton key to historic events. After all, it was Friedman's academic research that the chair of the Federal Reserve invoked to justify the government's response, Friedman the champion of deregulation who appeared to others the ultimate source of the problem.[5]

Over the next years, Friedman's reputation dipped, in part because of the unconventional monetary policy that followed the recession. To many observers—including many economists inspired by Friedman—the extraordinary low interest rates of the aughts were a recipe for inflation. When none emerged, Friedman's ideas seemed irrelevant and his followers' prophecies fell flat. Then as I began writing this book, the other field of Friedman's influence—political conservatism—went through a profound transformation. The GOP establishment that had lionized Friedman, focused on low taxes, low regulation, and free trade, was challenged by Donald J. Trump. Scholars have yet to settle—and probably never will—whether Trump should be considered an outgrowth of the former Republican Party or a deviation from its essence. But undoubtedly a new set of ideas that were emerging on the right, focused on immigration restriction, industrial policy, and state support of traditional values, stood firmly opposed to the "dead consensus" Friedman once embodied. Amid resurgent socialism on the left and rising nationalism on the right, it seemed there was no place for Friedman's ideas anymore.[6]

Still, Friedman never left the conversation entirely, because taking sides on Friedman involves taking sides on the last fifty years of American life. Do you judge that free trade has been, on balance, good for the world, helping to lift billions out of poverty? Then you may well regard Friedman as a saint. If free trade appears, by contrast, to have been a conspiracy by capitalists of the global north against the downtrodden, disempowered worker, then Friedman appears close to an evil genius. Within the contours of American political debate, similar dynamics emerge. Are the thirty-odd years after Friedman's ideas became dominant "the Great Moderation," a long and welcome stretch of economic stability, free of the awful recessions that obliterate years of accumulated wealth overnight? Or are they a time of increasing inequality, socially devastating deindustrialization, irreversible environmental degradation, and rising deaths of despair? Did Friedman's low-tax, limited-government ideology, taken up in a bipartisan move to deregulate key industries and cope with a new inflationary landscape, loose the creative destruction of capitalism? Or did it hollow out state capacity, weakening Americans' ability to build critical infrastructure and fund basic science, while leaving the vulnerable to fend for themselves? Friedman alone cannot be credited or blamed for these deep structural changes, however they are understood. Nonetheless, his presence at so many turning points of the modern era is remarkable. Understanding the origins of Friedman's ideas, and how they intersected with the broader surrounding world, opens a path to answering these fundamental questions.

The return of inflation in 2021—increasingly understood as the result of a textbook Friedman-style "helicopter drop" of money—suggests the time is ripe for another rethinking of his legacy. Friedman's monetarism will not be resurrected whole cloth. But no more will concerns about the money supply be dismissed, or greeted by Fed officials with gentle condescension.[7] Paradoxically, the bipartisan assault on Friedman in recent years has opened the possibility of seeing his work anew. For example, one of the most fertile progressive policy experiments in recent times is universal basic income, an idea that traces its modern origins to a 1939 paper by Friedman. In his lifetime, Friedman's tight identification with conservatism muted the countervailing currents in his own thinking. Even conservative advocates of guaranteed-income-style policies seem unaware of Friedman's role in its history. As he increasingly came to symbolize a political movement, the nuance and complexity of his ideas was lost. At times, Friedman himself reduced his own ideas to slogans. At other points, the dynamics of professional economic debate were lost on outsiders. One goal of this book is to restore the fullness of Friedman's thought to his public image.

This book is the first full-length biography of Friedman based upon archival research. I weave together notes from his graduate classes, letters from lifelong collaborators and friends, rough drafts, political memos, and his extensive published works to show a mind in motion, at first reacting to the headlines of the day and then eventually shaping them. The story starts with Friedman's immigrant family in Rahway, New Jersey, follows his intellectual trajectory from an oddball misfit to the dominant force in economics, and finishes with his role in the global turn toward markets after the fall of Bretton Woods. For nearly a decade, I have immersed myself in his voluminous archive of more than two hundred paper-stuffed boxes, housed at Stanford University's Hoover Institution, where Friedman was a research fellow in the last decades of his life. As a faculty member in the history department at Stanford, I've benefited from near daily access to this material, as well as research support from the Hoover Institution and regular contact with Friedman's former colleagues and students. Many have been generous in explaining the fine points of his economics, but none have attempted to steer my research or conclusions. I approach Friedman as a scholar, intent on setting his ideas in context and making his achievements legible for a new generation, either friend or foe. As an intellectual historian, I strive to summarize and explain economic ideas, their transformation over time, and their broader social impact, meaning readers need no special background or expertise to follow the narrative. Many chapters focus on a relationship between Friedman and a central figure of his time—some of whose names are still familiar, like the British prime minister Margaret Thatcher, and some who have become less famous over time, like the Federal Reserve chairman Arthur Burns.

This book is also a partial biography of economics, the master discipline of the twentieth century. Growing out of the older tradition of political economy, modern economics employed graphs and equations to make human behavior in markets tractable and the terms of analysis uniform. Although Friedman was part of this change, he also stood apart from it. Many of his most important works were not technical papers but books that still repay reading and rereading. In an important sense Friedman remained a political economist, concerned with questions of governance, ethics, and justice. Nonetheless, he made his way as a professional economist, earning the field's highest laurels, including the Clark Medal, the Nobel Prize, and the presidency of the American Economic Association.

I focus particularly on two strains of economic thinking that Friedman embraced, revitalized, and popularized: Chicago price theory and monetarism. At the most basic level, Chicago price theory—named after its roots in the University of Chicago, where Friedman was educated and taught for decades—was simply microeconomics, the analysis of rational human choice under conditions of scarcity. It approximates what any economics student still encounters in college. But the "Chicago" version was different, for it refused to keep economic analysis within its traditional boundaries. Taking price theory out of the classroom, Friedman crafted a dizzying array of policies with a consistent theme: setting prices free. This idea underlay everything, from Friedman's support of school vouchers and his calls to abolish the draft to his insistence that governments stop controlling the price of their currencies. Despite its influence, Chicago price theory was for many decades a heterodox current in economics. Readers may be surprised to learn how vigorously Friedman resisted his discipline's turn to ever more sophisticated mathematics.

Within economics, Friedman was known primarily as a monetarist—the name he grudgingly accepted for his school of economics, centered on the quantity theory of money. At its most basic, the quantity theory was an equation that linked the price level to the amount of money in an economy. But Friedman expanded it into an entire heterodox school of economics, centered on the idea that money was a tidal force in economic life. Mocked for this seemingly obsessive focus on money, he was one of the few economists to see stagflation coming in the 1970s. As a result, monetarism birthed the modern study of inflation, with important legacies that persist today. Friedman's impact on the discipline came from leveraging the methodologies, approaches, and mediums that modern economics rejected. Burrowing deep into data, checking theory against measurement, and using history as a natural experiment, Friedman was fearless in his intellectual quest—never afraid to be wrong and, more important, never afraid to be unpopular.

There is an overlooked secret to Friedman's success that I am the first to highlight: a coterie of women economists critical to every stage in his career. Shy and retiring, Friedman's wife, Rose Director Friedman, did her best to stay a hidden figure—she burned the couple's correspondence and left no trace in his vast archive, which she helped organize and arrange. Nonetheless, I have sought to reconstruct her role in both Friedman's technical economics and his emergence as a public intellectual. Friedman's most important intellectual partner was Anna Jacobson Schwartz, a creative thinker and sophisticated researcher relegated to the role of worker bee by her male colleagues. Alone among his peers, Friedman grasped Schwartz's potential, and together they authored the landmark book *A Monetary History of the United States*—yet only Friedman was lauded in the Nobel Prize citation it garnered him. I illuminate this decades-long partnership, showing how Schwartz's love of history and narrative transformed a doorstop statistical study into a modern classic. And I rescue from anonymity an entire circle of women economists, regular visitors to the Friedmans' summer home, who in long midnight conversations hashed out a new set of ideas on consumption that helped restore Friedman's faltering reputation in economics.

Another wellspring of Friedman's power was the tight-knit male fraternity of Chicago economists. They ranged from Rose's brother, Aaron Director, another hidden figure, to the world-renowned Austrian economist F. A. Hayek, who connected Friedman to wealthy businessmen set on defeating the New Deal. There is also Friedman's mentor Henry

Simons. Mercurial and brilliant, Simons was at once an outspoken defender of free markets, an advocate of higher taxes, and a crusader for increased government regulation in key economic sectors. With his tragic suicide, this seemingly impossible combination faded as a force in Friedman's thinking.

Throughout the book I do my best to honestly address Friedman's blind spots and imperfections, among which must be counted his attitudes toward civil rights. His vocal opposition to the 1964 Civil Rights Act, the sweeping legislation that outlawed racial discrimination in hiring and public accommodations, casts a shadow over his legacy. While disagreeing profoundly with Friedman's stance, I have nonetheless tried to accurately depict how he came to this view, given his beliefs, life experiences, and social context.

But why do I call Friedman the last conservative? I settled on this title with some trepidation, as I am well aware that Friedman himself rejected the label. He preferred to call himself a liberal—meaning the classical sort, a believer in limited, representative government, free trade, and individual rights. He meant by this word the tradition of Adam Smith—not anarchism by any means, but a creed alert to the abuses of state power and convinced the domain of the market should be as wide as possible. Alas, in the United States it makes little sense to call Friedman a liberal, for that word has become inexorably associated with the New Deal order Friedman opposed throughout his life. In other countries, Friedman is widely known as a neoliberal, but the term has gained little purchase in the United States beyond limited circles of the educated elite. It seems unwise to use academic jargon as the primary way to describe a thinker who so successfully reached for a broader popular audience. What about "libertarian"? Friedman was similarly reluctant to embrace the term, but it well captures his interest in liberty and his celebration of individual freedom. Yet if considered a libertarian, Friedman would be a conservative one, for he remained stubbornly attached to the state management of money, unlike many other libertarians—especially in today's cryptocurrency era.

So we are back to that word "conservative," which I have become convinced fits Friedman in two critical ways. One is the tenor of his economic thought: Friedman built his career on the preservation of intellectual techniques, approaches, and ideas that others forsook. His was a creative conservatism, for he did not simply exhume ideas like the quantity theory of money but attempted to reframe and reinterpret them for current conditions. Similarly, as the techniques of institutional economics fell into disrepute at midcentury, Friedman and Schwartz relied on this tradition to develop a new interpretation of the Depression. If Friedman seems a bold, even revolutionary thinker, he often got there by looking backward and forward at the same time.

Friedman is a conservative in a second way—through his lifelong association with the self-avowedly conservative political movement. Just as "liberal" means something distinctive in the American political tradition, so too does "conservative." Like many scholars of American history, I have adopted a pragmatic use of the word "conservative," using it not to invoke a timeless intellectual orientation but in reference to a historically specific political movement that flourished after World War II and has dwindled only recently. Across the twentieth century, American conservatism was defined as a hybrid blend of libertarian economics, opposition to Communism, and defense of traditional values and hierarchies. Not coincidentally, the arc of *this* American conservatism follows the arc of Friedman's career, for he was one of its intellectual pillars. Determined to rescue American conservatism from its "fringe" elements, in his day Friedman leveraged his fame and academic success to redefine the center-right as a source of intellectual innovation rather than blind reaction.

And "the last" conservative? In all likelihood, conservatism will persist as a brand in American politics. But in the twenty-first century, the synthesis that Friedman represented—based in free market economics, individual liberty, and global cooperation—has cracked apart. Exactly where Friedman's ideas will settle remains unknown; some will fade from history, others will persist, perhaps taking a new form. Freed from the politics of his moment, Friedman becomes a resource for all those who are wrestling with the perennial questions of economic growth and state power, social welfare and individual liberty, the part and the whole. More than the story of one man's life, *Milton Friedman: The Last Conservative* is part elegy for a world gone by, part cautionary tale, and full testament to the power of ideas.

PART I

ORIGINS

1

FROM RAHWAY TO RUTGERS

> It is utterly inconceivable to me that graphs or mathematical formulae could facilitate the understanding of economic laws.
>
> —Friedrich Kleinwächter, 1871

"Have you ever thought what you are going to do when you get out of High School?" asked an editorial in Rahway High's *Scarlet and Black*. For the graduating class of 1927, a high school degree was worth $33,000 in lifetime earnings, the editorial explained. But real gold lay with higher education, worth at least three times more. "By going to college, you are more than tripling your chances for success in after life," exhorted the writer. Nor should money be a problem, for "in America, the land of opportunity[,] anything is possible."[1] Most seniors probably skipped over the column, not realizing it was a true scoop: the dawning of an intellectual sensibility that would come to define politics and economics in the twentieth century.

By the time Milton Friedman published this first effort at public persuasion, he was an established force in the small world of Rahway High School. Short of stature yet bursting with energy, he was a full year younger than his classmates and more than a head shorter than most. In a town ruled by Anglo-Protestants, he was among a handful of Jewish students at the school. None of this slowed him down. "Can you imagine . . . Milty Friedman not arguing?" ran a gossip item in the paper, while another ironic aside asked students to "imagine . . . Milton Friedman minding his own affairs."[2] The newspaper itself was one of his projects. He was on the founding editorial team and served as its editor in chief during his senior year. Along with his three older sisters, he dominated the top rungs of the academic rankings.

Milton's plunge into teenage society mirrored his parents' entry into Rahway more broadly. Sol and Sarah Friedman had moved to the New Jersey "commuter's paradise" just outside New York City in 1913, along with thirteen-month-old Milton and their daughters, Helen, Tillie, and Ruth.[3] When they arrived, the Friedmans were something like the tenth Jewish family in the entire town of scarcely ten thousand residents.[4] They set up shop on Main Street, arriving with enough capital to purchase a small building. Here they founded the Friedman Manufacturing Company, specializing in children's dresses. A few years later they shut down the factory and purchased a new building nearby, opening a dry goods store with living quarters above, unglamorously known as "Friedman."[5] Sarah minded the store. Sol was an arbitrageur who bought excess merchandise from manufacturers to resell at retail—a "jobber," in the day's parlance.

Graced with grand old maples, elms, and lindens, buoyed by a humming manufacturing sector, and boasting a coveted stop on the railway line into New York City, Rahway nonetheless had a dark side. One evening when Milton was twelve, a burning cross exploded only blocks from the Friedman home, one of three erected by the local Ku Klux Klan. The Klan owned a four-hundred-acre resort on the New Jersey coast and ran Alma White College in nearby Zarephath, which spewed forth venom at "the Hebrew." In town, Klan members gathered in robes but boldly removed their hoods, as if they had nothing to hide. It was part of a larger nativist reaction that shaped political life after World War I. Congress sharply curtailed immigration, while reform movements from Prohibition to women's suffrage fomented fear of foreigners. Xenophobia shaded into a Red Scare that came to Rahway when a member of New Jersey's Socialist Party was literally hosed off his soapbox by the town's mayor and three firemen.[6]

Throwing themselves into Rahway's small but growing Jewish community, Sol and Sarah created a protective cocoon around their children. Sol served as a trustee of the town's first synagogue, the vice president of the Rahway Hebrew Congregation, and the chairman of Rahway's Board of Education, while Sarah organized regular card parties for the Hebrew Women's Auxiliary. All four children received music lessons, and when Tillie graduated from high school, they threw a party with more than thirty guests.[7] Sol rebounded from a bankruptcy caused by a warehouse fire and opened an ice-cream parlor when he couldn't find a tenant for a new Rahway property. He drove a Model T Ford—a significant purchase at the time—and bought a piano for the living room.[8]

The prized only son of attentive and doting parents, Milton was an ebullient and self-assured princeling. He was a fixture at the local library, an ardent student at Hebrew school, and a willing scooper of ice cream in the family store. After he flew into the Ford's windshield in a minor accident, a scar lifted the corner of his upper right lip, adding to the impish cast of his features.[9]

Following his parents' cues, Milton developed an early attachment to Judaism. Family lore told of a young Milton coming across a dollar bill on the street one Saturday afternoon; rather than break the Sabbath injunction against handling money, he stood guard over his find until sundown.[10] Confronted by a non-kosher hot dog at a Boy Scout barbecue, Milton fled for home rather than cross his faith. He soon regrouped and convinced a local dentist to lead a troop for Jewish boys. But fierce as it had burned, Milton's piety would not last past his bar mitzvah. By the time of the ceremony—which he completed for the sake of filial obedience—he considered himself agnostic.[11]

Tragedy struck in November of his senior year. For years Sol had staved off recurrent chest pains by popping nitroglycerin pills. But on Halloween morning, the pain was bad enough that he went first to the doctor, then to the hospital. He died the next morning in his home; by the time the afternoon paper came out, his funeral was already under way. Milton's recorded memories of the event are curiously free of emotion. In retrospect, what stood out was not the loss, but the onerous requirement that he say Kaddish for the subsequent year, requiring daily bus trips to a neighboring town.[12]

Did Milton ponder his father's life on these solitary rides? At about the same age, Sol had started his journey across a thousand worlds in order to give his children a better start. Sometime in the 1880s, he left his home in the city of Beregszász and headed to Budapest, the heart of the Austro-Hungarian Empire. In this bustling center of European Jewry he cleaved to an elder half-brother named Friedman, and it was this surname he would give upon his 1892 arrival to the United States, when he was sixteen.[13] Milton never knew his original family name. His mother, Sarah Landau, followed a similar route, although she was only eleven when she disembarked in 1896. Immigration records list her origin as "Russia," but in fact she was from the same place as Sol Friedman. In Beregszász the Landau family had achieved some distinction; legend had it that whenever the town banker couldn't balance his books, he would call the patriarch, David Landau, to set matters straight.[14]

It was true that both Sol and Sarah Friedman made a living in the Jewish-dominated garment industry, but otherwise their path diverged from the prototypical urban immigrant experience. Although Milton later claimed his mother worked in a "sweatshop," any such backbreaking labor was at most a passing phase. Rather, her family operated a few rungs up the economic ladder, with one relative holding a lucrative position selling Singer sewing machines. After their marriage—likely fostered through hometown connections—Sol and Sarah briefly returned to Europe. Before the move to Rahway, they lived for a short time in East New York, a mixed immigrant neighborhood that was relatively prosperous, with clean streets, white picket fences, and large homes set among green hedges and lawns. Milton did not grow up in the world of the sweatshop, the tenement, the garment workers union, the socialist student group—those building blocks of the American Jewish community. Instead, he would live out the sort of small-town boyhood that was fast receding into myth as the nation became increasingly urban.[15]

Sol's death did not halt Milton's forward trajectory. Unlike for most of his classmates, there was no question that he would continue his schooling—and that his equally gifted sisters would not. As one family member recalled, "The girls went to work and the boy went to college." All three sisters had been honor students, in some cases outperforming Milton in their class rank. But he was the only one to develop a career plan. Given his love of math, one option stood out: he could become an actuary, running calculations for an insurance company or some other large firm. A plan to "succeed in the game of life" fell into place. In 1928 he graduated as Rahway High's valedictorian, winning $20 in gold for his academic accomplishments and a tuition scholarship to nearby Rutgers College.[16]

With two thousand students, divided between a men's college on the banks of the Raritan River and a women's college several miles away, Rutgers had yet to become a behemoth public mega-university. Many students commuted from home, as did most Jewish students, perhaps reflecting the university's long history as a bastion of anti-Semitism. Quotas on Jewish admissions were matched by open hostility toward those who came, including vandalization of a Jewish fraternity.[17] Nonetheless, Milton had fallen under the spell of the "college man" ideal and was determined to live on campus, even if he had to pay for room and board himself. He signed up for a dormitory in Winants Hall, moving in before the start of classes in September 1928.

At first there seemed no reason to deviate from his actuarial ambitions, and Friedman accordingly planned to major in mathematics. In his sophomore year, almost by accident, he took a two-semester introductory economics course. This first encounter with the field was not particularly memorable, in part because economics itself was in a quiescent period.[18]

Half a century earlier, economists had been at the center of fierce public debate and controversy, as leading figures allied themselves with socialism and an active labor movement. Indeed, it was radical scholars who organized the first professional society in 1885, the American Economic Association (AEA). Mostly Anglo-Protestants of middle-class background, they were deeply influenced by the Social Gospel, a form of liberal Christianity that sought to apply Christ's teachings to the problems of urban life and industrialization. Economists became an influential wing of the larger Progressive movement, a sprawling reform impulse taken up by muckraking journalists, crusading mayors, anti-vice campaigners, and good-governance advocates, among others. What united this group was a shared sense that industrial capitalism had failed. Recoiling from the belching factories and teeming tenements of the Gilded Age, Progressives concluded that unfettered capitalism was chaotic, wasteful, and divisive. Progressives turned to the government—local, state, and federal—to manage the inefficiencies and inequalities they saw in contemporary life.[19]

Whether inspired by socialism, Christianity, or the belief in the evolutionary and developmental nature of society known as historicism, Progressive economists believed economic knowledge should be informed by the pressing problems of the age. Economics itself would shift and change along with the social challenges it confronted. Laissez-faire, or minimal government interference in economic activity, might have been suitable for a bygone era. But as the United States became more urban and industrial, it should develop a new economic philosophy. Progressive economists envisioned themselves providing expert guidance to this emerging state.

In the opposing camp were the classical economists, who emphasized the enduring truths of human social behavior their science could uncover. Although the discipline might evolve, classical economists had a more fixed conception of economic knowledge. They continued the tradition of British political economy, with its defense of laissez-faire economics. This view was well represented by the Yale professor William Graham Sumner, who opposed tariffs, imperialism, and restrictions on the liberty of contract—such as the many Progressive initiatives to regulate hours and working conditions.[20]

The clash between Progressive and classical economics quickly became politicized. As labor disputes grew increasingly contentious during the 1880s, leading members of the AEA were caught in the crossfire, with several losing their university positions. Over time, even Progressives began to see that the tight identification between socialism and economics imperiled the field as a whole. Eventually, the influence of socialism in the AEA waned. Professional rather than political concerns came to dominate the group, bringing a measure of consensus to the discipline.[21]

At the same time a new ground of rapprochement emerged, which would also prove the bridge for Friedman—math. For much of its history, math had little place in economics. Rather, the origins of the field known as political economy lay in moral philosophy. American colleges first taught topics like capital, rent, and labor using books ranging from Adam Smith's *The Wealth of Nations* to Jane Marcet's popular textbook *Conversations on Political Economy*. The Christian socialists who founded the AEA were in this tradition. Traces of political economy still lingered when Friedman was at Rutgers, but the field had been transformed since the Gilded Age by two developments.

The first was the widespread practice of showing supply and demand on a graph. Today this seems the very heart of economics—indeed, in later life Friedman would use a rudimentary version on his personal stationery. But before the early years of the twentieth century, representing the push and pull of market bargaining in a two-dimensional space struck most economists as folly. One scholar found it "utterly inconceivable . . . that graphs or mathematical formulae could facilitate the understanding of economic laws." After all, *The Wealth of Nations* had no visuals. Smith illustrated basic concepts with words, like his famous description of a pin factory. It was another British economist who invented modern supply-and-demand diagrams—Alfred Marshall, anointed by his student John Maynard Keynes as "the founder of modern diagrammatic economics." Yet even Marshall stuck his diagrams into an appendix.[22] Nonetheless, he had opened the door to geometric reasoning.

A second way to quantify economic behavior emerged through the marginal revolution, a new current of thought emerging from Europe.[23] Marginal analysis offered a new take on the perennial problem of value. What determined a good's value in any given market? For

Milton and Rose D. Friedman
1750 Taylor Street
San Francisco, Ca., 94133

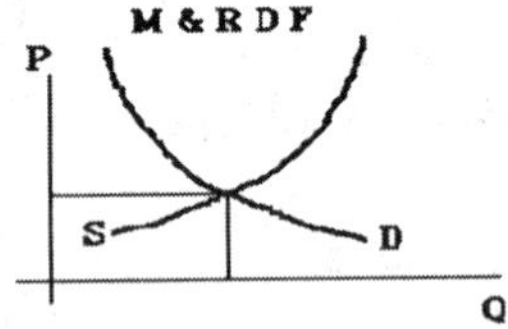

Later in life, Milton and Rose Friedman used a simple supply-and-demand graph on their personal stationery. (Milton Friedman Papers, Hoover Institution)

classical economists, following Smith, the cost of making that good was key. For Karl Marx, it was the labor embedded in the commodity. For marginalists, the essential idea was utility, or how much benefit the purchaser gained. Even more critical was marginal utility: the gain from consuming one more glass of beer or bushel of wheat. Utility was admittedly a slippery concept. It could not be directly observed or measured. The way to see it was through price. And price indicated the ultimate value of a good, affixing a number to the murky, unknowable depths of human desire.[24]

Like many scientific revolutions, marginalism emerged more or less simultaneously in the work of several scholars working independently in Austria, France, and England. Also like many scientific revolutions, in its aftermath it is difficult to grasp how unexpected the approach was at the time. The real breakthrough was conceptual—to sever a good's exchange value from what came before, be it labor or material inputs, and to focus on price. In turn, thinking of economic activity in terms of price opened up economics to pervasive quantification. Economists did not yet talk of "models," a word still understood to mean concrete, mechanical objects designed to illustrate concepts in physics. But in a major departure from previous practice, they were isolating selected factors from the real world—wages, interest, tariffs—to see how they worked in a controlled environment.[25]

Marginalism borrowed key concepts from physics, including the idea of equilibrium. In economics, equilibrium meant the point at which market forces of supply and demand balanced, all participants having reached a satisfactory level of utility. A related abstraction was "perfect competition," where prices were set exclusively by market forces of supply and demand. In perfect competition there was no ignorance, no mistakes, no delays—and no room for an individual seller to cut prices, as competitors would instantly respond. Perfect competition was a construct, akin to portraying gravity without friction. It turned out to be an unrealistic yet useful assumption that gave economists a common analytic framework and a powerful claim to scientific authority.

Marginal analysis carried within its wake not just new techniques but new assumptions that would upend the discipline, marking off political economy from economics and classical from neoclassical economics.[26] Although *Homo economicus* had lurked along the edges of classical economics, marginalism brought him to center stage. Who was *Homo economicus*? Above all he was calculating man, making decisions that maximized utility in any given transaction. This portrait was attacked as unrealistic from the start, and it was—as even marginalists admitted.[27] Nonetheless, stripping economic action down to rational, measurable, and predictable behavior was necessary to put it on a graph or in an equation.[28]

By the time Friedman first encountered the field in 1929, there was enough math in economics to attract an aspiring actuary. And the Gilded Age political disputes were long over, having yielded to an era of pluralism in method and approach. World War I had largely killed off the Progressive movement, but it had given its heirs, the second generation of historically minded economists, a new sense of mission. Service in the wartime bureaucracies crystallized these economists' sense of group identity and increased their prestige within the profession. Now calling themselves "institutional economists," they shed their political radicalism and focused increasingly on professional advancement. Some vestiges of Progressivism remained, particularly the key concept of "social control," which denoted the idea of scientific economic management. But with major Progressive goals met by the 1920s, ranging from antitrust laws to city charters to the federal Department of Labor, which gave "the voice of labor" a place in the presidential cabinet, institutionalist economists had become the establishment. They now pursued reform through academic research programs investigating law, labor, and business cycles.[29]

For their part, classical economists blended a laissez-faire approach to political economy with the new marginal analysis, leading one opponent to scorn them as "neoclassical economists"—a name that stuck.[30] Overall, they remained politically conservative and focused on unchanging fundamentals of economic life like supply and demand. If they had a counterpart in political life, it might be the Treasury secretary Andrew Mellon, who fought to repeal the estate tax, a linchpin of Progressive movement taxation. But it was hard to tell who was who; self-proclaimed institutionalists might dabble in marginal analysis, while neoclassical theorists proclaimed the need for greater "realism."

The Great Depression would undermine this hard-won consensus and thrust economics back into political strife. By the time Friedman was a junior at Rutgers, with two introductory econ classes under his belt, it was obvious the United States was in a severe crisis. Economic activity began to slow in 1929, with the Great Crash of October a first tocsin in the night. From there came the downward plunge: a drop in farm income of nearly 50 percent, a quarter of the workforce unemployed, and a wave of bank failures in 1933, the year after his college graduation. For Milton, the questions were starting to burn: "How to get out of the depression? How to reduce unemployment? What explained the paradox of great need on the one hand and the unused resources on the other?"[31] These were not merely the preoccupations of a bright undergraduate. They were the great questions of the age.

And they were questions that stumped economists, too. If any camp should have seen the downturn coming, it was the institutional economists, who paid careful attention to swings in economic activity. Compared to neoclassical economists, institutionalists were less inclined to see the best of all possible worlds, and more inclined to call out social problems. But none had anticipated the contraction, or gauged its severity accurately—and none had a remedy at hand.

Neoclassical economists did no better. They had a basic prescription for economic booms and busts: let wages and prices fall until activity restarted. But the scope, scale, and persistence of the downturn threw this remedy into question. Agricultural prices had plummeted, yet the crisis on American farms was worsening. "We will have a revolution in the countryside within twelve months," the normally staid American Farm Bureau warned Congress in early 1933.[32] Underlying it all was a conceptual problem. For all the discipline's growth, most economists focused on the level of the industry or the firm. Analyzing a slump in demand for shoes or cereal or children's dresses was one thing. Explaining why demand for everything fell all at once required habits of mind most economists simply did not possess.

If economics at Rutgers did not have answers to the Great Depression, it did have something even more important to a fatherless young man: the dashing Arthur Burns, a teacher to revere. Just twenty-seven years old, to his admiring student Burns appeared "a sophisticated man of the world—mature, almost elderly."[33] But in reality he was an idealized future version of Friedman himself. Like Friedman, Burns had been raised in a small New Jersey town by Jewish parents who had emigrated from Eastern Europe. Burns was ten when he arrived in the country and knew no English. But he rocketed through Columbia University, earning a bachelor's degree Phi Beta Kappa and a master's degree in the same year. Now he was teaching at Rutgers while working on his Ph.D.

Burns resolved the competing pressures of research and teaching with a move that was common, if pedagogically suspect: he had his students proofread a draft of his doctoral dissertation. Friedman and another student, registered for a course listed in the Rutgers catalog as Business Cycles, found themselves going over Burns's *Production Trends in the United States* "word for word, sentence by sentence." Friedman was thrilled. It was not so much the content of Burns's work as the form: "attention to detail, concern with scrupulous accuracy, checking of sources, and above all, openness to criticism." Burns was modeling the practice of scholarship for Friedman, in the process opening new vistas of possibility for his life. The bond between the two soon deepened beyond student and teacher, becoming more mentor and protégé. Friedman even came to see Burns as a "surrogate father."[34]

Despite their shared heritage, there were significant differences between the two. Burns had also worked his way through college, but along the way he crafted a convincing establishment persona. Between his tobacco and tweeds, he struck observers as being "of Scots origin" and "a native Ivy Leaguer," an impression fostered by dropping Burnseig, his family name, for Burns. Later, when he joined the government, Burns would appear as the quintessential New Dealer, with a "glassy stare through thick lenses, peering out from under a canopy of unruly hair parted in the middle, a large pipe with a curved stem."[35] In fact, Burns was a moderate Republican. Where Friedman would seek system, Burns was eclectic and pragmatic in his approach to economic problems. This flexibility, along with his polished air and commanding personality, would underwrite his meteoric career in the public sector. It also made him an ideal tour guide to the field of economics.

Burns's dissertation gave Friedman deep exposure to one of the most influential American approaches to economics: Wesley Mitchell's historical study of business cycles. Burns was Mitchell's favorite student at Columbia University, then a stronghold of institutional economics. Heir to the historicist approach of the first radical economists, as well as a muted version of their reform politics, Mitchell had mesmerized the field with his 1913 study *Business Cycles*. Burns described it as "one of the masterpieces in the world's economic literature."[36] Economists had long noticed that booms and busts seemed characteristic of market economies; indeed, the late nineteenth century had been littered with panics that threw millions out of work, destroyed banks and businesses alike, and disrupted national politics. Yet economists could offer little explanation, other than to assert that panics appeared mysteriously every ten years.[37]

Mitchell was the first to document, describe, and offer a theory of business cycles, in the process scoring a resounding victory for the empirical approach to economics. He began by emphasizing that the price system, a theoretical construct, lay atop a much more complex tangle of often irrational human instincts and habits, which he called the money economy. He drew attention away from the marginalist emphasis on consumer prices by highlighting the importance of wholesale costs and business expenses, both real and anticipated. Many different interlocking price systems, resting on an unstable base of human psychology, fed off one another in predictable ways: "A revival of activity develops into intense prosperity, by which this prosperity engenders a crisis, by which crisis turns into depression, and by which depression finally leads to such a revival of activity as that with which the cycle began."[38] Booms brought not only profit but also the stresses and strains that led to hard times; then the ensuing slump opened up new opportunities for business, turning the wheel yet again.

The previous crisis of World War I had been an important boost to Mitchell's approach. Drafted to help the government coordinate its war effort, he discovered that nobody was able "to put before the responsible authorities promptly the data they needed concerning men and commodities, ships and factories," as he told the American Statistical Association, of which he had just been elected president.[39] As a remedy, Mitchell helped found the National Bureau of Economic Research (NBER), a private organization that would bridge the worlds of academia, business, and government. The NBER would produce the facts and figures the government needed.

Despite his great faith in economics as a way to solve social problems, Mitchell insisted the NBER be scrupulously nonpartisan. He wanted to "democratize" economic data without re-creating the political controversy of earlier years. For a solid decade Mitchell remained one of the dominant voices in economics, with a strong presence at both Columbia and the NBER.

But it turned out that Mitchell was better at describing business cycles than at predicting, explaining, or fixing them. Given his expertise, Mitchell's lack of a convincing explanation for the depth and severity of the Great Depression—the business cycle to end all business cycles—was a significant failure. Just as World War I had made Mitchell's reputation, the Great Depression would unmake it.

Even as he immersed Friedman in institutionalism, Burns also introduced him to the profoundly different approach of the British neoclassical economist Alfred Marshall—he of the supply-and-demand diagrams. During Friedman's junior year, Burns taught a course focused on Marshall's *Principles of Economics*, first published in 1890. Although Friedman was not formally registered for the course, he attended the class anyway, as would become his practice in graduate school.[40] Reading Marshall with Burns was a turning point. *Principles of Economics* became for Friedman a book not to be simply read but to be savored, debated, and revisited over a lifetime.

Blending marginalism with the classical approach, *Principles of Economics* was an important stepping stone in the transition from political economy to economics. Marshall pioneered an ingenious synthesis between old and new, making two interrelated modifications to the doctrine of marginal utility. While accepting the importance of price, he emphasized the importance of time and the dynamics of supply.

Marshall proposed thinking in one of four blocks of time. The first would be a market period, where demand determines price because there is not sufficient time to alter supply. The short run, Marshall's second period, introduced a new wrinkle: by responding to demand, firms could increase supply, but only by spending more money. So prices might go up, set by the cost of supply, working in tandem with demand.

The third period, the long run, during which firms had time to develop new efficiencies, introduced a further complication. Now rising demand might trigger falling prices as businesses benefited from economies of scale and better organization.

The fourth period, secular time, was Marshall's nod to history itself. Secular time was generational time, which might see huge shifts in demographics, knowledge, or political organization, completely refiguring the dynamics of supply and demand. Marshall had found a way to integrate the glacial movements of the ages, the lurches and accelerations of the present, and the universalizing clarity of economic abstraction.

Here was the start of answers to the big questions Friedman had been pondering. Marshall was in all likelihood not his first introduction to basic concepts like utility, supply-and-demand curves, and marginal analysis. But he suggested that the concept of price, properly framed, could bring a heterogeneous range of human experience into one analytic frame. It was at the margin—where price trembled between one point and another—that economics shone its light into the depths of human motivation and action. Price was not a measure of motive, Marshall emphasized repeatedly, for no science could hope to measure "the ever changing and subtle forces of human nature." But it did allow the economist to indirectly gauge "the force" of motive.[41] And this measurement was what took economics from philosophy to science.

It was significant that a *book* opened the wonders of economics to Friedman. There would be other blockbuster economics books to come—but not many. By the time Friedman's professional career was well launched, papers in peer-reviewed journals drove the field. Books were at most a distraction, something a lightweight or gadfly economist might indulge in to raise his profile, or a vanity project produced by his students. But books remained central to Friedman's intellectual project. In this way he never completed the transition in motion around him, remaining at heart a political economist rather than an economist.

Balancing out these classroom discoveries was Friedman's hands-on experience in the local economy. In his first year, he found a job waiting tables, which came with a supposedly free lunch. Even then, he was enough of a budding economist to understand there was no such thing—the free lunch came instead of a higher wage. He spent his Saturdays working a second job at a local menswear store. This gave him an idea for a new enterprise. The following year, he teamed up with another Rutgers student to hawk the requisite green ties and white socks to freshmen. It was the kind of arbitrage his father had practiced, but the connection came from the other boy's father, who owned a department store in Rahway. Soon they moved on to used books, drawing the ire of the campus bookstore. Fortunately, the sock sales had been authorized by the dean, in a letter that could also be construed to cover books. During the summer, Friedman was equally entrepreneurial, starting a remedial summer school for Rahway High students, which was eventually taken over by a new assistant principal.[42]

All this activity primed Friedman for meeting the next economist who would become central to his life: the University of Chicago professor Frank Knight, the renowned theorist of entrepreneurship. The introduction came by way of Homer Jones, another Rutgers instructor whom Friedman admired. The bookish Jones lacked the presence of Burns. Enrolled in Jones's course on statistical methods, which promised to unite economics with his actuarial goals, Friedman quickly grasped that his teacher was "low man on the academic totem pole." Like Burns, he had yet to complete his doctorate. Apparently he had been assigned to teach statistics at the very last minute, meaning he barely knew more than his students. Understated and modest, Jones made no pretense of expertise. Precisely because Jones did not try to fake it, Friedman relished the experience, as teacher and student muddled through and learned together.[43]

The next year, Friedman enrolled in Jones's Principles of Insurance, which turned out to be a crash course in the ideas of Frank Knight. Here, Jones was in his element. He and Knight, his doctoral adviser, were extraordinarily close: "Disciple may not be too strong a word," writes one historian. Jones's wife, Alice Hanson, was also a Knight student and research assistant, and the two audited nearly every course taught by Knight at Chicago.[44] Knight's opus, *Risk, Uncertainty and Profit*, formed the basis of Jones's approach to insurance.

Knight's book picked up the foundational question of profit and refracted it through his own philosophical and skeptical temperament. He began by noting that under conditions of perfect competition, pure profit was theoretically impossible.[45] Perfect competition implied perfect knowledge, meaning prices would swiftly adjust to match producer costs and consumer utilities; any attempt to capture a surplus would be thwarted. For example, if every Rutgers student knew they could purchase socks and ties at a lower wholesale price, who would pay the retail markup?

Since profit obviously did exist in the real world, Knight used the concept to probe the gap between ideal and real. He concluded that economic theory was missing an adequate understanding of uncertainty, and that "profit is to be explained by uncertainty."[46] The willingness to act despite uncertainty was the value contributed by an entrepreneur. Milton and his friend had not really known if their venture would fly (although a captive consumer base suggested it would). Perhaps another store would have undercut their prices, or their selection might prove unpopular, or students could balk at their salesmanship. By proceeding anyway, they had created value and earned their profits.

Knight added a philosophical component to his economic theory by insisting on a distinction between risk and uncertainty. The key difference was that risk could be measured but uncertainty could not. Whereas risk could be translated into actuarial tables and hedged through insurance—here young Friedman must have brightened—uncertainty was something different, more akin to an existential condition. Uncertainty came into play in situations that were "entirely unique" yet apt to turn up in the course of business activity. True, businessmen could reflect on past experience to handle uncertainty, but they could only, at best, come up with an estimate. Thus profit "arises out of the inherent, absolute unpredictability of things, out of the sheer brute fact that the results of human activity cannot be anticipated and then only in so far as even a probability calculation in regard to them is impossible and meaningless." It was a worldview that joined turmoil and change to capitalist practice.[47]

Knight's real target in *Risk, Uncertainty and Profit* was socialism. It was not a strident apologia for capitalism—Knight scoffed at "the idea that because income is 'earned' it is 'deserved,'" and called for compulsory state social insurance to mitigate the impact of "luck." But at base the book was a defense of private property and a justification of the way market economies handled both risk and distribution. In a profession once led by starry-eyed reformers and still dominated by their institutionalist legacy, Knight claimed the role of skeptical naysayer, perfecting a cautionary cure-may-be-worse-than-the-disease logic. By the end of the book, uncertainty applied not simply to the idea of profit but to the very idea of making social change. It was appropriate for the entrepreneur to gamble his own resources, because he ultimately bore the responsibilities. But the reformer who did the same with society's funds faced no such sanction. "It is not too much to say that the very essence of free enterprise is the concentration of responsibility in its two aspects of making decisions and taking the consequences of decisions when put into effect," he claimed.[48] Socialist planners would have neither the incentive to excel nor basic accountability for their actions, he concluded.

Knight had first published these ideas in 1922, the year Rahway battled socialists, and Friedman encountered them a decade later, just as the Great Depression was revitalizing the American left and the idea of a managed economy. It was too early for Knight's acidic attacks on the New Deal, but nonetheless his politics did shine through Jones's yearlong course. Friedman's later description of Jones's views applied equally well to Knight: "He put major stress on individual freedom, was cynical and skeptical about attempts to interfere with the exercise of individual freedom in the name of social planning or collective values, yet he was by no means a nihilist." At the time, what impressed Friedman the most was how Jones used insurance as a window "into the more fundamental issues."[49] This, of course, was the core of Knight's approach. Uncertainty and risk were the hooks upon which he hung a larger defense of the market order. As Knight's stand-in, Jones passed along the same sensibility to his young student.

The idea of being an actuary had now faded considerably. In its place the idea of graduate study arose. Friedman was not quite ready to completely abandon math, however. He continued to collect honors in the field even though he had switched his major, winning a prize from the math department. He split the difference in his graduate applications, applying to a range of programs. By the time he graduated from Rutgers, he had two offers in hand for tuition scholarships, one in applied mathematics at Brown University, and one in economics from the University of Chicago. Jones, who had given him a glowing recommendation, pushed for Chicago.

Even more persuasive was the mood of the nation. By the spring of 1932, nearly a quarter of the workforce was unemployed, with bread lines springing up in major cities. The crisis had reached far beyond the working class and was now pulling down even educated Americans who had thought themselves immune from hard times. Touring Montana, one federal government investigator reported: "I saw old friends of mine—men I had been to school with—digging ditches and laying sewer pipe. They were wearing their regular business suits as they worked because they couldn't afford overalls and rubber boots."[50] In just a few months the nation would turn with relief to the charismatic figure of Franklin Delano Roosevelt. But for now, the current president, the Republican Herbert Hoover, inspired little confidence. It was clear, Friedman reflected later, that the "dominant problem of the times was economics." The field promised both intrinsic intellectual rewards and a direct connection "to the burning issues of the day."[51]

Nothing in the years from Rahway to Rutgers—save the loss of his father—had seriously challenged Friedman's characteristically sunny outlook on life. His had been an ever-upward trajectory from small town to national university, with little friction along the way. He had conquered Rutgers just as easily as he had Rahway High, graduating as his teachers' favorite with a clutch of prizes in hand. "In America, the land of opportunity[,] anything is possible," Friedman had editorialized in his high school newspaper. Four years later, the Depression had thrown up a profound challenge to this assumption. At Rutgers, he had found that economics might help him think through new questions. At Chicago, he would find more definitive answers.

2

THE CHICAGO PLAN

> If some malevolent genius had sought to aggravate the affliction of business and employment cycles, he could hardly have done better.
>
> —Henry Simons, 1933

She was impossible to miss, the only woman in a sea of first-year graduate students enrolled in Economics 301: Price and Distribution Theory. Friedman had better chances than most, due to a stroke of alphabetical luck that assigned him the seat next to Rose Director. But most students were simply in survival mode. At the front of the room strutted Professor Jacob Viner, "short and intense, like a bantam cock," as one student recalled. Along with the basics of price theory, Viner introduced the University of Chicago's brutal sink-or-swim ethos. Riffling through index cards printed with their names, he cold-called students during class, and was not kind when his victims struggled. "I am beyond my depth," gasped one after a few lame attempts at answering Viner's query. "Sir, you drown in shallow water," Viner gravely responded.[1] Once, in fury, he pelted a hapless student with chalk. This was not just a performance, to be softened later by avuncular advice. Viner was screening the new cohort, and after three whiffed answers, he kicked students out of his class—and effectively out of the department.

A few weeks in, Friedman spotted an opening. Viner, scribbling away at the blackboard, had incorrectly differentiated a function.

Friedman called out the mistake, a bold move in a class where the professor was rumored to fail a third of the students. Viner scoffed at the correction, although the mistake was obvious enough. Friedman pressed. Viner waved him off, carrying on as if nothing had happened. Only later, when all the others were gone, would he admit his mistake. But Rose knew. Despite Viner's effort to save face, her classmate had bested the professor. She invited Milton to join her for a lecture by the department's other titan, Professor Frank Knight, the theorist of entrepreneurship whose work Friedman had studied at Rutgers.[2]

It was only friendship at first, but from the start Rose was Milton's portal into a new world, defined not just by Chicago's rigorous courses but by a hidden curriculum in what it meant to be an economist.

Arriving in Chicago in the fall of 1932, Friedman followed the strategy that had seen him smoothly through Rutgers. He found another job waiting tables, this one complete with a free room and a free lunch—the only salary offered. But he had no income, and after a summer of unemployment in Rahway, no nest egg. Friedman secured a financial cushion thanks to a $300 loan from Helen, his telegraph-operator sister.

Although the Great Depression had yet to reach its awful nadir, the suffering in Chicago was palpable. "Everything around was closed down most of the time," remembered the economist Paul Samuelson, then a high school student living in Hyde Park. "Children and adults came daily to the door saying, 'We are starving, how about a potato?'"[3] On campus there was a distinct flavor of radicalism, according to a graduate student in political science: "There were strikes, sit-down strikes in plants not far from Chicago. And there were young Communists and socialists making lots of speeches on the campus. Serious people my age were discussing the collapse of the American economy we were living through and the future of the country."[4] Amid the presidential campaign, these debates and questions took on added urgency.

On the cusp of the election Milton and Rose attended Knight's lecture, intriguingly titled "The Case for Communism: From an Ex-Liberal." The lecture, which had attracted a large crowd, was Friedman's first real glimpse of Knight. "He was bald and had a closely clipped, bristling little gray mustache," remembered one student in attendance. "He wore silver-framed spectacles. His face was pink and round yet with nothing soft about it. He looked like a very intelligent little rodent, rather adorable to look at but well capable of giving one a nip which would not soon be forgotten."[5] One of the most renowned economists of his day, Knight was also a legend among Chicago students.

"The Case for Communism" was vintage Knight: ironic, sarcastic, despairing, polemical, and almost impossible to understand. Supposedly an endorsement of Communism, his lecture contained both a rhetorical conceit and a serious political argument. The conceit was that Knight had forsaken his belief in liberalism, or limited government, for Communism. "One of the best reasons for voting Communist is a belief in the principles of conservatism," Knight argued counterintuitively. This was because a strong Communist vote would stimulate an aristocratic or conservative reaction, which he thought "highly to be desired." Only a conservative party could truly govern, Knight averred, although the Communists might not do a bad job either, for they too understood "real government, exercising real 'control,' which 'of course' means the use of honest, self-respecting and respect-commanding force." Here he played with the idea that economic crisis necessitated a strong state, but he was not sincere.[6] It was an instrumental move, intended to force his radical audience to face the coercion lying behind their egalitarian ideals.

Shifting out of ironic mode into jeremiad, Knight declared that the nation—nay, the West—was at a political crossroads, for the dominant philosophy of liberalism "was bankrupt."[7] Knight was no more an "ex-liberal" than he was a Communist. He had been arguing the case against socialism and in favor of limited government for more than a decade. But now he was blackly pessimistic about liberalism's future prospects. The most pressing problem was "the cumulative tendency to greater inequality which is inherent in the system."[8] Once, perhaps, societies dominated by kings and popes had accepted such inequalities as part of the natural order. But in an egalitarian age of labor unions, socialism, and Communist revolution, it was no longer possible for limited government to survive; the only question was what would replace it.

Surveying the contemporary political scene, Knight claimed to see no alternative to Communism, which would at least usher in change of some kind. "Knight means well," commented a listener Rose believed to be a Communist student as they filed out of the auditorium. "But I am afraid we will have to shoot him along with the rest."[9]

Rose and Milton were too young to vote in the historic election that swept Roosevelt to power a few days later.[10] Nor have their responses to the campaign survived. Given their immigrant backgrounds and Hoover's dismal reputation, it would not be surprising if they rooted for Roosevelt.[11] Like every economist of the time, they were struggling to understand the forces still in play in the world around them. Yet as Knight seemed to dimly foresee, 1932 was one of those hinge years in history. Afterward would come a great scrambling, with the very categories of progressive and reactionary, conservative and liberal, altogether unmade and remade.

Intense, insular, and competitive, Chicago's economics department was among the nation's best, rivaled only by Harvard, Columbia, and Wisconsin.[12] Ten faculty members, along with a handful of instructors, presided over a graduate student body numbering slightly more than one hundred. Graduate student life revolved around the newly built Social Sciences Building, part of the university's main quadrangle. Course requirements were relatively unstructured, but grading was tough, professors were stern, and the academic calendar of three ten-week quarters left little opportunity for coasting, in the words of Samuelson. To most students, the department appeared "as a jungle red in tooth and claw," a place where only the strong survived.[13]

Neither Milton nor Rose was intimidated by the fearsome, even abusive, practices of the department. Friedman grasped that behind Viner's prickly exterior, the professor was having fun. Rose, too, was in on the game. She had an insider's view of the program thanks to her brother, Aaron, who was teaching while working on his Ph.D. Two years earlier she had arrived in Chicago as an undergraduate transfer student from Reed College, taking advantage of a tuition break linked to Aaron's position. He would be her guide and chaperone, Aaron promised their protective parents.

Rose was born in Charterisk, a small Russian village not far from Beregszász, the ancestral home of Sol and Sarah Friedman.[14] Her father, Sam Director, the proprietor of a grain mill, had carved out a precarious niche among a hostile gentile population. But when a careless farmer fell to his death in the mill's churning wheels, Director feared the communal wrath that might scapegoat a Jew. He fled to the United States in haste, leaving behind his four children and newly pregnant wife. Two years later he had accumulated enough money to pay their passage. His family joined him in Portland, Oregon, in 1913, the year Friedman's family moved to Rahway. Upon their arrival Sam met Esther Rachel—as the family then called her—for the first time. By then she had already forged a special, almost paternal bond with her eldest brother, Aaron, ten years her senior.

The Directors were at once more prosperous and less assimilated than the Friedmans. Starting off as a peddler, Sam quickly rose to owning a store. He installed his family in a series of different homes, each one better than the last, finally buying one with electric lights and later adding central heat. Sam picked up just enough English to run his affairs. Likewise his wife, Sarah (née Fish), never became fluent in English; Portland's Jewish community was large enough that she could live out her life in Yiddish.[15]

While this established Jewish presence had its benefits, it also meant an equally established tradition of anti-Semitism. The brunt of this discrimination fell on Aaron, who came of age amid peak nativism in the early 1920s. Excluded from everything from the debate team to social clubs, and faced with an unrelenting suspicion of being a Bolshevik,

"Red," or homosexual, Aaron banded together with a handful of other Jewish youths, including fellow immigrant Marcus Rothkowitz, later famous as the abstract impressionist painter Mark Rothko. Supported by a tolerant and well-connected teacher, the two friends were awarded scholarships to Yale.[16]

Provincial though she remained, Rose's mother made one critical break with tradition: she prized education for her daughters as well as for her sons. Each morning, Sarah baked the family's daily bread over a wood-fired stove, but forbade her daughters, Rose, Becky, and Anna, to learn the household arts. While the older children went to work, Sarah harbored higher hopes for Rose. At age five she enrolled her in classes at the nearby Neighborhood House, a settlement house run by members of Portland's established German Jewish community. Next came piano lessons and even Hebrew school, where Rose was the only girl. Hovering over her at every turn was Aaron. He walked her to grammar school every day and gave her a book of poetry when she finished, inscribed "May this be the first of many graduations." After high school, Rose enrolled as a commuter student at nearby Reed College.[17]

As a teenager, Rose thrived in Reed's permissive yet serious atmosphere. On the one hand, she assumed an immigrant's pragmatic approach to higher education: "I was going to college to get an education, to make life more interesting, but even more to prepare me to earn my living." Yet college also triggered a genuine intellectual revolution. Inspired by a course in ancient history, she shocked her father by arguing the Old Testament was "all fables." Sam was a devout man, who spent every Saturday at the synagogue and insisted that Sarah keep a kosher kitchen. But Rose detected a certain rote compliance on her mother's part, and herself dreaded the elaborate rituals of the high holy days. Reed crystallized these religious doubts and synthesized the contradictory elements in Rose's personality; she was at once a dutiful daughter and a free thinker, quietly studious yet unafraid to attack orthodoxy.[18]

At Chicago, the close connection between the two siblings continued. While their father was scandalized by Rose's incursions against religion, with Aaron she could talk freely about the big questions: "Was happiness the primary goal of life and what produced happiness? What was important in life?" Aaron introduced his sister to the department's luminaries and connected her to a few research jobs. By the time she earned a B.A., something important had shifted. A visit to immigration authorities revealed there was no Esther Director on file, only a Rose with the approximate right dates. Whatever the reason for the mistake, she chose to shed Esther, the name she had known all her life.[19]

Reborn as Rose Director, she set her sights on a Ph.D. in economics. This was an unusual decision for a woman of her era. The University of Chicago was more meritocratic than most institutions of higher learning. It was not wedded to reform, or to piety, or to forming the gentleman sons of commerce, but to the full-bore pursuit of ideas. A few years hence, the president would even abolish football, finding it distracted students from their studies. Women were admitted to the university on equal terms with men. But few carried on for graduate study, and even fewer chose the Department of Economics. During Rose's time, there were a handful of female graduate students—although apparently none in her entering class—and one female professor, the consumption expert Hazel Kyrk.[20] Rose was not interested in consumption economics, that unusual domain where being female was considered an asset, given its focus on households and shopping. Instead, she was interested in price theory, a foundational pillar of what would soon be called "Chicago economics."

At base, price theory was simply neoclassical economics, the fruit of the marginal revolution. In any given market, prices would gravitate toward equilibrium as buyers and sellers made decisions according to their respective marginal utilities. Later, these ideas would be expressed almost entirely in mathematical formulae, but as Viner's error showed, Chicago's star professors were not particularly skilled mathematicians. Instead, they continued to rely on verbal argument alongside equations.[21] Nor was price theory unique to Chicago. The same presentation of neoclassical ideas—with some local variation—could be found in many a university economics department, including at Harvard University.[22]

Nonetheless, there was something distinctive about Chicago price theory. Students often greeted it as revealed truth, describing their encounter as a conversion experience. There was for many a clear dividing line: before price theory and after. For Rose's brother, Aaron, it was a "windstorm" that "swept away the nebulous idealism and Socialist views" of his undergraduate years.[23] Viner was not the prime mover here; rather it was the ideas themselves that mattered. It may well have been price theory that transformed Esther into Rose, who would take Economics 301 multiple times. Religious metaphors proliferate: publishing an old price theory syllabus was "an act of piety," according to Gordon Tullock, who later pioneered public choice theory.[24] In an age where science had crowded out religion among the educated, price theory was something to believe in.

More than something to believe in—price theory was a way to think, an architecture of mind. It boasted the clarity and precision of mathematical concepts, but it was not math. Instead it was a method that pointed to patterns and causal chains, making the overwhelming complexity of economic and social life suddenly tractable. Markets and prices, Chicago professors emphasized, coordinated not just economic activity but the broader society itself. This expansive approach to price theory may explain its force and impact—particularly because Chicago did not blunt the approach by mixing in other alternatives, like institutional economics.

Price theory also came with a specific political economy, as Henry Simons made clear. Simons was an assistant professor who taught Economics 201, an undergraduate course. The "Simons syllabus"—at fifty-eight pages essentially a combined textbook and workbook—circulated widely among graduate students. Price theory concerned pricing "under a free enterprise economy—under a system characterized by private property, free contract, and free exchange," Simons explained in the syllabus.[25] By extension, economic planning was not necessary. As Knight wrote in his own textbook, "No one ever worked out a plan for such a system, or willed its existence . . . Yet in a fairly tolerable way, 'it works.'"[26] Society was abuzz and abloom with different and clashing activities, needs, and desires, yet somehow it all hung together with most people finding a way to get what they wanted.

Skepticism toward planning characterized Knight, Simons, and most economists who taught or practiced price theory. The neoclassical approach left plenty of room for robust government action in response to crisis. It was given that the state would establish laws, enforce liberty of contract, and provide necessary social relief. Nonetheless, neoclassical economics suggested market allocation was generally efficient and, as Knight stressed, preferable to the alternatives. By contrast, the rival school of institutional economists focused on the inequities and irrationalities of market dynamics. In order to overcome these basic flaws, planning was needed—expert intervention in the dynamics of supply and demand to ensure optimal production and fair pricing. It was certainly possible, in theory, to combine the neoclassical approach with planning. Students at Chicago, however, encountered price theory and planning as opposites.

At Chicago, the potency of price theory further reflected institutional forces. Student converts correctly grasped its importance to their future careers. The department required students to master the intricacies of price theory as the first step of graduate training—Economics 301 was one of the few required courses. Likewise, before advancing to dissertation research students had to pass an oral exam that measured their skill in applying price theory.[27] The message was unmistakable: this was the untouchable core of economics.

Friedman did not experience an abrupt conversion to price theory, even though he recognized Viner's course as "unquestionably the greatest intellectual experience of my life." What Viner had given him was fundamentally "a coherent set of tools," he explained later.[28] Over time, Friedman would come to use price theory as a frame of reference, a view on the world, and an all-purpose research methodology. He would embrace it as a unified field theory of economic behavior, a way to get beneath the chaotic stream of experience and divine the larger patterns dictating events. And he would be at the forefront of a movement that expanded price theory far beyond its origins in economic theory. But viewing price theory as a tool, he would not truly appreciate it until he started to build something.

All this skepticism of planning did not mean Chicago professors were indifferent to the Great Depression. To the contrary: the department was at the heart of several important efforts to find a solution to the crisis, including two landmark conferences featuring John Maynard Keynes and other prominent European scholars.[29] Chicago economists keenly felt "the burden of the fact of the 5,000,000 men walking the streets [unemployed] tonight because mistakes have been made," as one participant put it during a university-sponsored roundtable discussion.[30] Rose's and Milton's professors pointedly did not take the line of Treasury Secretary Andrew Mellon: "Liquidate labor, liquidate stocks, liquidate the farmers, liquidate real estate . . . Purge the rottenness out of the system."[31] Instead, in January 1932, eight months before Friedman arrived on campus, twenty-four economists—including all of Friedman's future professors—sent an urgent telegram to President Hoover. They urged sweeping federal action to combat the crisis, including spending on public works, unemployment insurance, forgiveness of international debts, and amending the Federal Reserve Act to bring more flexibility to monetary policy.[32] A few months later, the Chicago professors followed up with another memo to Congress calling for "generous Federal expenditures," including "large appropriations for public and semipublic improvements" as a method to check "severe depression and deflation" and spur recovery.[33] In the moment, these ideas had little impact. But they were evidence of the intellectual ferment stirred up by the crisis.

Price theory was not the main way Chicago professors understood the Great Depression, and it did not inspire their proposed solutions. Instead, they turned to the department's tradition of monetary economics and its cornerstone idea—the quantity theory of money. Though the quantity theory had a neoclassical pedigree, in the context of 1932 it pointed toward a vigorous role for the federal government in combating the Depression.

Rose and Milton encountered the quantity theory in a class taught by Lloyd Mints. Quiet and methodical, Mints lacked Viner's flair and charisma. Judging by the copious doodles with which Friedman festooned his class notes, he found the presentation less than riveting. But Mints referred students to Keynes's 1931 address to the Harris Foundation, tipping them off to the intense discussions happening outside the classroom walls.[34]

The quantity theory was both an economic truism and an important American contribution to neoclassical economics. Several centuries old in its most basic form, the quantity theory asserted that the overall level of prices was proportional to the amount of money circulating in an economy. Its basic assumptions undergirded the gold standard, the currency regime followed by the world's major trading nations. Because gold was scarce and difficult to procure, linking paper currency directly to gold was a natural check on the amount in circulation, and thus held prices steady. As a near universal standard of value, gold also made it easy to trade across national borders. Over the nineteenth century, the United States had slowly evolved toward a gold-backed currency, codifying the price of gold at $20.67 per ounce in 1900.[35] At the height of the gold standard regime in the 1920s, the Yale economist Irving Fisher described it with a simple equation that linked the money supply, velocity (how frequently money changed hands), price level, and total volume of transactions: MV = PT.*

At one level, the quantity theory was neoclassical economics in its finest hour, translating what Fisher called "the dance of the dollar" into a simplified and potent mathematical identity. Fisher emphasized the significance of elemental monetary forces—namely interest rates—that operated under the surface of seemingly unique historical events. But for all its abstraction, the quantity theory pointed to money and banks, the tangible institutions that made price manifest. The eccentric Fisher

* The equation was first rendered MV = PY, but today the Y is often replaced by T in order to denote all transactions.

was also one of the few neoclassical economists to dabble in Progressive politics, with enthusiasm for eugenics, vegetarianism, and index cards; he grew rich after inventing a filing system akin to the first Rolodex. Alas, he was equally enthusiastic about the stock market, plowing his cash into stocks and declaring they had reached "a permanently high plateau" just days before Black Monday. Neither his portfolio nor his reputation would recover.[36]

Mints continued to teach quantity theory as a basic paradigm, but he focused heavily on John Maynard Keynes's two-volume *Treatise on Money*, which attempted to link Fisher's equation to savings and investment. Appearing in 1930 just as the Great Depression was beginning, the *Treatise on Money* caught Keynes in an awkward transition between old and new ideas, "like someone who has been forcing his way through a confused jungle," as he admitted in the preface. Keynes emphasized the way demand for money could vary—in the terms of the quantity theory, velocity (V) could change. He placed particular emphasis on the problem of hoarding. This led him to a gentle push against traditional Victorian virtues: "For the engine which drives Enterprise is not Thrift, but Profit."[37] With the Depression under way, the problem of hoarding now stood out in sharp relief: banks would not loan, and depositors were stashing cash under mattresses.

The quantity theory of money thus offered a potential explanation for the Great Depression. Viewed through the lens of money, the Depression was first and foremost a deflation, rather than a matter of business cycles. If the banking system was the root of the problem, it could be reformed or reengineered. If money was to blame, then money itself could be reshaped. This was the route taken in Great Britain. In 1931, the Bank of England saved its teetering economy with a breathtaking decision: it went off gold. No more would the government redeem pound notes for a fixed quantity of the precious metal. It seemed an earthquake of almost cosmic proportions. During World War I, Britain had come off the standard. But to do it in peacetime was another event altogether. "Nobody told us we could do that!" exclaimed one politician in astonishment.[38] But now Britain's government had more latitude. Without the restrictions of gold redemption, it was easier to print more money and spend for relief. The Chicago telegrams urged the U.S. government to take a similarly fearless action.

In the winter, Friedman enrolled in Knight's Economics 302: History of Economic Thought. Where Viner introduced the details and applications of price theory, Knight cemented the paradigm by contrasting it to lesser alternatives.[39] Rather than historicizing economic thought, which might have suggested the provisional and tentative nature of economic knowledge, Knight used his course to defend neoclassical economics by presenting a Whiggish march from error to truth, dark to light. As he told students in Friedman's class, "our viewpoint in studying classical economics is to learn by their mistakes."[40] Knight might hedge with frequent reference to "relatively absolute absolutes," suggesting a pragmatist approach to truth.[41] And he could even allow that there might be "a different grammar or logic at different times."[42] But the bulk of his agenda lay in picking apart other approaches to economics and defending the neoclassical approach.

Knight also wove in his distinct political perspective. In class, he critiqued the institutionalist idea of "social control" for paternalistically assuming "that either the controlled have no pt of view or that their pt of view or welfare disregarded," as Friedman recorded in his notes.[43] But despite his vaunted individualism, much of his oeuvre was laced through with misanthropy. "Looking at the matter 'objectively,' one of the first serious suggestions for the improvement of the human race would be to have all their tongues removed at birth," he lashed in "The Case for Communism." Consensus through reasoned conversation was impossible; in fact the key to modern history was the "fundamental law of progressive intellectual degradation in all public discussion."[44] Ultimately, Knight's case for limited government was not an embrace of human freedom but a verdict on the alternative. He emphasized the nonrational and emotive sources of human behavior. These wellsprings of human irrationality, he believed, would shape governing institutions; better to let the market work it out through supply and demand. Undoubtedly

Knight saw these same dark forces operating in markets—but he seems to have judged that competition would serve as an effective check, just as factions were thought to balance one another in the constitutional order.

As his fall lecture revealed, Knight well knew the press of events threatened his cherished values of individualism and limited government. Roosevelt's election had brought no real resolution, instead plunging American politics into a state of suspended animation as the country awaited the new administration. As president-elect, Roosevelt avoided any action that would link him with Hoover's disastrous run, while the lame-duck president felt duty bound to hold off on any actions his successor did not approve.[45] In the meantime, the contours of crisis sharpened. It was now clear the economic slowdown was a global event, severe enough to upend the political order across continents. In Germany, Adolf Hitler was slowly rising to power, even as Benito Mussolini entered his second decade of fascist rule in Italy. An intermittent civil war continued to flare across China, while Japan's government grew increasingly militaristic. The turn toward "respect-commanding force" that Knight feared was well under way.

In the United States, what had begun as a business downturn and then snowballed into record unemployment was now entering a dangerous new phase. The malady had infected the banking system. The summer before Friedman started graduate school, nearly forty banks in the Chicago area had failed. Across the fall, the pace ticked up, and by early 1933 the rate of collapse had reached epidemic proportions. That year, more than four thousand American banks would collapse.[46]

Bank failures had long been a persistent feature of American life. Partially, this was because the dispersed banking sector was regulated by a patchwork of state laws, and consequently bank quality varied. Mainly, it was because fractional reserve banking was inherently unstable. Under the National Banking Act of 1863, Congress permitted national banks to loan up to 90 percent of their deposits. This also became standard practice among state and local banks. Holding a minimal reserve worked if money sluiced in and out on a regular basis. Indeed, fractional reserves levered small amounts of capital into something far bigger, underwriting economic growth.

Unfortunately, the mechanism also worked in reverse. Because banks actively loaned out the deposits they received, there was never enough cash on hand to satisfy all creditors at once. Trouble arose when more creditors than expected wanted their money back. If word got out a bank was in trouble, the demand for cash would escalate. By design, no bank could withstand this form of pressure on its own. And when a bank went under, all the cash held on its books—if not in its vaults—vanished. In ordinary times, a troubled bank could seek help from other banks. The occasional failed bank posed no threat, other than to those directly involved.

It was another story when multiple banks were in trouble at once. A bank run was a herd phenomenon, akin to a school of fish flowing suddenly in another direction, thousands moving as one. But being psychological in nature made the contagion no less serious. And in 1933 all the fish were swimming one way as fast as they could.

A bank run could break the whole financial system. During a run, one bank's insolvency quickly endangered others as panic spread. Moreover, people were most anxious about their money when times were tough and jobs were hard to come by. Henry Simons put it starkly: "If some malevolent genius had sought to aggravate the affliction of business and employment cycles, he could hardly have done better."[47] Just when a bank run was most dangerous, it was most likely.

Responding to this problem, in 1913 Congress had chartered the Federal Reserve System. A unique American institution modeled in part on the Bank of England, the Fed was a network of twelve regional banks topped by a presidentially appointed board. Politically independent yet part of the government, the Fed was intended to create a more elastic currency within the restrictions of the gold standard. When the system began to shake, the Fed would step in to stop the run.

The early Fed had several mechanisms at its disposal. One was newly created Federal Reserve notes, a sort of bank-to-bank currency that became an additional layer between bedrock gold and the swirl of dollars and cents that made up everyday commerce. The most important was the discount window, where a bank could borrow cash using its outstanding loans as collateral. During the postwar recession of

1920, the system had largely worked, with regional banks borrowing gold reserves from one another to prop up member banks that were under strain.[48]

Still, the Fed had significant limitations—among them that it only supported member banks. Vast swaths of the nation's most basic financial institutions lay beyond its reach. Further, it would not deign to support "speculative" loans—those intended to buy stocks. The Fed's focus on "real bills"—meaning commercial loans backed by tangible goods in production—was a significant liability in an era with a surging and unregulated stock market. Finally, the Fed's quintessentially American design, a unique blend of private and public interest, created significant coordination problems in the face of an unprecedented economic emergency.[49] If few economists appreciated the purgative powers of the downturn, the same could not be said of elite bankers. Cautious and conservative, few were willing to break ranks and press for action. Three years into the Great Depression, it was clear salvation would not come from the Fed. It would have to come from the White House.

Taking office in March 1933, Roosevelt began to move with lightning speed, embarking on a blizzard of legislation during his celebrated first hundred days. The day after his inauguration he declared a "bank holiday," closing all banks in the United States until further notice. Widely heralded as a success, this move broke the nationwide bank run and was a first step toward restoring general confidence in the economic system.

Galvanized by the bank holiday, Chicago's economists swung into action, drawing up the "Chicago plan" for banking reform. Written primarily by Simons, the six-page single-spaced typed memo provides a clear window into the thinking of Friedman's teachers at this critical moment.[50] It shows clearly that Chicago economists, despite their neoclassical orientation, carved out a large role for the federal government in meeting the emergency. Chicago's leading price theorists did not argue that the Depression was a necessary correction, or that economic activity would magically return to a desirable equilibrium. It was true they were not economic planners, but they had a plan.

Written ten days after the bank holiday began, the memo urged a significant expansion of federal power to meet the crisis. Broadly, it said that the federal government should attempt to increase the price level by around 15 percent. Specifically, it should take over the banking system, pass legislation breaking up the savings and lending functions of banks, and end the gold standard. It was a radical program of reform that would have profoundly changed the U.S. banking system.

All pieces of the proposed reforms were interwoven. The currency should be increased by issuance of new Federal Reserve notes, but additional liquidity would come from "federal guarantees of bank deposits."[51] This move alone would restore confidence in the banks and stop the destruction of money caused by each new bank failure. Yet the economists stressed the current banking system would have to go. After the currency had becalmed, the Federal Reserve would liquidate member banks and then establish a "new kind of institution": a "Deposit-Bank" for checking, with 100 percent reserve requirements. Another new institution, "The Lending Company," would loan for investment purposes. Also in the crosshairs was the gold standard. At the very least, the government should stop minting gold or silver coins upon demand; instead, individuals should only be able to exchange their gold for Federal Reserve notes, while imports and private exports of the metal were banned. It was, as the authors admitted, a "drastic and dangerous" set of proposals, but changes of similar scope "can hardly be avoided, except temporarily, in any event."[52]

Within days, Knight had succeeded in passing the memo to the secretary of agriculture, Henry Wallace, who pronounced it "awfully good" in a letter to Roosevelt.[53] The Chicago plan was among a chorus calling for similar reforms, rather than the essential voice. Nonetheless, it is striking how the memo anticipated major New Deal reforms that would reshape the financial sector, from deposit insurance to Roosevelt's decision to outlaw the ownership of gold. By June, its proposals to federally guarantee bank deposits and separate commercial and investment banking had become law through the Banking Act of 1933, also known as Glass-Steagall. An executive order confiscated private holdings of gold, and Congress followed up with legislation that established a quasi–gold standard. Dollars were still linked to gold but could no longer be redeemed upon demand.[54] One significant proposed reform, a 100 percent reserve requirement for bank deposits that would eliminate fractional reserve banking, remained undone. Colloquially known as "100 percent money," this idea would be touted in future iterations of the memo.

Monetary economics proved a vital counterpoint to price theory's emphasis on natural equilibrium. Quantity theory itself offered a rationale for state action to remedy the crisis. As Mints explained to his students, the state was fundamental to monetary development; indeed, he divided monetary history into three phases, the second being the "stage where state steps in." From there, monetary developments had passed on to "bank money," but the state remained important.[55] Through the eyes of price theory, it was possible to view an economic world governed primarily by supply and demand. The state was in the background, but not enmeshed in day-to-day market activity. Monetary theory, by contrast, centered a state authority that would regulate currency and the banking system. Therefore, in a downturn it was legitimate for state systems like the Federal Reserve to increase the money supply through lowering interest rates or buying government bonds.

It was also possible to effect monetary goals through direct government spending, later to be called fiscal policy. In today's parlance, the Chicago plan suggested "unconventional monetary policy"—taxing and spending instead of interest-rate manipulation.[56] Mints and Keynes had touched on this dynamic during the first Chicago meetings, when Mints had questioned Keynes's emphasis on lowering interest rates. "Won't public works bring about precisely the same results?" Mints asked Keynes, pointing out that public works could increase the rate of return for business firms and thereby raise overall investment. Keynes agreed, but worried that "unless you socialize the country to a degree that is unlikely, you will get to the end of the public works program . . . and you are no better off."[57] Mints, by contrast, appeared more optimistic about the political feasibility of direct government spending.

In these early years, it was still possible to favor government spending alongside monetary solutions: there were as of yet no hard and fast lines between different explanations for depression, and no corresponding policy divide.[58] Here was a world in which Keynes promoted a monetary solution to the Great Depression, while Mints of the University of Chicago favored a fiscal one!

But the question of what had caused the problem in the first place could only be temporarily suspended. The ancient clash between Progressive and classical economics was being revived around the question of the Great Depression. Was it a temporary maladjustment of the basic economic forces that, once reestablished, could be trusted to operate smoothly? Or was it a fundamental crisis of the capitalist system that called for far-reaching change? Against the backdrop of a national emergency, disciplinary debates were once again changing into political questions. And Friedman would end up in the front lines of both camps.

Despite the splendor of his first year at Chicago, Friedman found that there were clear inadequacies in his graduate training. He had chosen Chicago not for Viner or Knight but for the statistician Henry Schultz, his formal adviser. In the winter quarter he took Schultz's class Economics 311: Correlation and Curve Fitting, a welcome opportunity to combine his studies in economics with his interest in math.[59]

But before long Friedman had taken the other man's measure, and judged him the lesser intellect. He was probably right in his assessment—even generous posthumous tributes to Schultz emphasize his dogged work ethic over his native brilliance. "He may not have been a great mathematician, but he was certainly an accomplished one," as one colleague gently put it. But to Friedman, Schultz was simply slow. His first book had been on sugar, and now he had widened his ambit, barely, to encompass a handful of other commodities. Students were set to work measuring the elasticity of demand for wheat, potatoes, oats, barley, rye, and so forth, constructing demand curves based on price and consumption records. The crushing workload had only one redeeming feature—Rose was also in the class, and the two often worked late into the night, side by side in the statistics lab high atop the Social Sciences Building.[60]

In the spring, Friedman learned that Schultz would spend the coming year in Europe. The move would leave him without an adviser during his critical second year, and without a scholar who specialized in mathematical economics, where he hoped to make his mark. Accordingly, Schultz arranged for Friedman to spend the following year at Columbia University, where he would be guided by the renowned mathematician and economist Harold Hotelling. Making the deal all the sweeter, Columbia granted him a fellowship for the considerable sum of $1,500.[61]

For her part, Rose was beginning to feel the downside of Aaron's paternalism. She had pursued education in order to become independent, only to find herself dependent on her brother. Impressed by her work, the department prepared to offer her a fellowship for her second year of study, when Aaron intervened to say it was not necessary, for he could pay her tuition. Rose couldn't bring herself to tell Aaron she no longer wanted his help. Instead, as she planned her return to Portland for the summer, she toyed with the idea of dropping out and finding a job.[62]

At year's end, Milton, Rose, and a friend headed to the World's Fair. Hosted amid an unprecedented global recession, the fair lacked the triumphal tone of the famous 1892 exhibition that had established Chicago's reputation as the capital city of the Middle West. Still, the young people had much to celebrate: a successful year in school, an open future unfurling before them. Back on campus, after their companion had tactfully disappeared, Milton and Rose found themselves on a park bench, discussing what lay ahead. The moment had arrived; Milton would not see Rose for almost a year. He went in for a kiss, which Rose swiftly rebuffed. It was all in good humor, but a serious message had been sent. Rose would have plenty of time to think it over.[63]

3

THE ROOM SEVEN GANG

Economics is the one and all-inclusive science of conduct.

—Frank Knight, 1922

The department that Milton Friedman joined in September 1933 was about as far from Chicago as one could get, intellectually, politically, and socially. Columbia University hosted the nation's largest graduate program in economics, with more than three hundred students at peak enrollment, but had about the same number of tenured faculty as Chicago. Graduate students had the time—and money—to sample the sights and sounds of New York City, from Times Square to Broadway to the Empire State Building. Where Frank Knight had instructed his students to never use the word "control" when talking about economics, on the first day of class at Columbia, John Maurice Clark (the son of the AEA cofounder John Bates Clark) told students, "Economics has always aimed at control," adding that "19th c so called *laissez faire*, actually a different kind of control."[1] The department's two-semester Economic Theory Seminar was not a detailed exposition of one prized method—in fact, neoclassical price theory was deliberately not offered at Columbia.

Instead, the seminar exposed students to the cutting edge of economic debate over public policy, including a series of "seminar meetings on national economic planning," taught by Clark, Wesley Mitchell, and James Angell.[2] As a whole, the Columbia department was known for an approach to economics that placed planning front and center. At the time, while the general idea of "planning" covered a wide spectrum of ideas, all planners assumed "intervention—either through direct or indirect methods—was necessary for a well-functioning, dynamic economy," as one historian summarizes.[3] Planning thus represented a repudiation of the idea that markets would naturally find a socially acceptable equilibrium and was a significant departure from price theory. The seminar covered planning in action, showcasing the most significant proposals to attack the Depression, ranging from the creation of the National Recovery Administration to the La Follette Plan, a tax-reform bill that Clark had helped shape.

Students were also introduced to various theories of the Depression, from business cycles to the newly influential overproduction/underconsumption thesis. Promoted primarily by William T. Foster and Waddill Catchings, a pair of amateur economists, the theory held that an unbalanced economy had produced too many goods for cash-strapped workers to consume. The idea that unemployed workers simply could not afford to buy what they needed seemed broadly plausible to the public and key policy-makers.[4] It also offered an obvious solution: public-works spending to get these workers a salary, plus planning to balance out production and consumption. While historians now sometimes call the overproduction/underconsumption thesis a form of "proto-Keynesianism," this discussion owed little to Keynes himself, who had yet to publish his landmark book, *The General Theory of Employment, Interest, and Money.* There was no discussion of the quantity theory, or of a monetary explanation for the crash.

Casting about for an ally in this unfamiliar territory, Friedman soon found one in Moses Abramovitz, a second-year student who was housed, like Friedman, in a tiny cubicle at the top of Butler Library. "It's all right if I am in there alone, but if I get an idea, I have to move into the corridor," students joked. The tight quarters created tight bonds. Moe and Milton soon discovered a shared intellectual heritage: educated at Harvard, Abramovitz had been schooled in price theory at the knee of Jacob Viner's adviser, Frank Taussig. Both students were taken aback by the Columbia approach to economics, which differed considerably from their former training.[5]

As Abramovitz remembered, the Columbia predilection for planning had its roots in institutional economics. Columbia professors were not untutored in neoclassical economics, and might use it occasionally to explain simple matters, such as "why a grand piano cost more than a pair of shoes." But they were skeptical about "the theoretical assumptions that agents were foresighted, well-informed, and rational." If they had an economic theory, it was one about the inadequacies of theory. Abramovitz summarized the general outlook:

> They saw markets as characterized by various degrees of monopoly power . . . They tended to see the economy as a whole, not as tending to an equilibrium, but as generating long-term growth of productivity, income, and wealth . . . subject to recurrent fluctuations, loosely called "cyclical," in which advance was sometimes fast, sometimes slow, and sometimes negative.[6]

This was the latter-day version of Progressive-era historical economics, tinted by the marginal revolution but distinct from it. Eclectic and interdisciplinary, institutionalism took up questions of legal reform, corporate structure, and monopoly, relying on close observation and research rather than abstract theory. Institutionalism was more akin to the past of economics—political economy—than to its future as a quantitative discipline. Nonetheless, in the early years of the Depression it had a significant foothold beyond Columbia, including clusters at the University of Wisconsin, the Brookings Graduate School, Amherst College, and the National Bureau of Economic Research (NBER).

Friedman's reaction to this sudden immersion in a new school of thought is telling. Whereas Abramovitz was tortured by the conflict between price theory and institutionalism, Friedman shifted into evangelical mode. When faculty refused to approve a course on price theory, he convinced Abramovitz they should teach one themselves. The duo "organized a student-run seminar, worked out a list of topics, assigned students to prepare papers, and guided the presentation and discussion."[7] It was a significant undertaking for two second-year graduate students still completing their required coursework.

At the same time, Friedman thrived in Wesley Mitchell's two-semester class on business cycles, which echoed the Rutgers course he had taken with Arthur Burns. The class received a laborious exposition of the NBER technique: how to gather data, how far back to go, what to look for; differences between specific cycles and base cycles, and how to compare them; measuring business-cycle peaks and troughs; eliminating seasonal variations; relating expansions and contractions. Mitchell listed fourteen processes that the class would cover. On the general question of cyclical behavior, there were eight different aspects to ascertain, many with sub points. There was a signal amid the noise, but as he listened to the endless analysis of endless fluctuations, Abramovitz "could make nothing of it."[8] After a few weeks, he dropped Mitchell's class.

Friedman, it turned out, wasn't even listening for a signal. That Mitchell was challenging price theory wasn't clear to him, because Mitchell didn't have a straightforward competing theory of how business cycles worked. Where price theory simplified, Mitchell added layer upon layer of complexity. The picture of the economy that emerged—complex, interrelated, unstable, full of variation—was true to life but analytically unsatisfying. Abramovitz later saw that Mitchell's skepticism of neoclassical economics led to a broader principle: "Experience, not the logical implications of some generalized ideal, had to be our guide to life."[9] But to Friedman, institutionalism was something to be added to price theory, rather than a contender to supplant it.

Beyond institutionalism, the courses at Columbia promised immediate insight into the dramatic policy changes of the New Deal. While the faculty at Chicago churned out memos, former Columbia faculty like Rexford Tugwell, Raymond Moley, and Adolf Berle were now among the chief architects of the New Deal, helping implement their ideals of economic planning and social control. One of the most influential books of the time, Berle and Gardiner Means's *The Modern Corporation and Private Property*, described a "corporate revolution" in American capitalism that called for a "new form of economic organization of society." The world of Adam Smith no longer existed, argued the authors. Corporations had become so powerful, and their ownership so diffuse, that "the passive property right of today must yield before the larger interests of society." Along with the pop economics of Foster and Catchings, the academic arguments of Berle and Means suggested a greater role for the state in economic affairs, not just on an emergency basis but because of basic changes in the underlying system.[10] What this meant in practice was being worked out before the nation's eyes.

The showpiece legislation of the early New Deal, the National Industrial Recovery Act (NIRA), which established the National Recovery Administration (NRA), had been launched to great fanfare the summer before Friedman arrived at Columbia. In September, just as classes got under way, a historic parade filled the streets of New York with more than 250,000 marchers singing, "Join the good old N.R.A., Boys, and we will end this awful strife / Join it with the spirit that will give the Eagle life / Join it, folks, then push and pull, many millions strong / While we go marching to Prosperity." The propaganda campaign, directed by the same man who helped mobilize industry for World War I, was necessary because the federal government had little expertise or authority to impose wage, price, and production codes. Instead the NRA offered a controversial carrot: businesses that adopted the hastily drafted codes would not be subject to antitrust regulations. And they could advertise their cooperation by posting the famous NRA Blue Eagle, promising, "We Do Our Part."[11]

By November, it was clear that the NRA had satisfied nobody and aroused powerful opposition from across the political spectrum, including in the Senate. Businesses complained of burdensome regulations while labor reported widespread evasion of guidelines that set fair wages and working conditions. Both sides had justifiable complaints; hardware stores, for example, had to navigate nineteen separate codes because of their diverse inventory, while large industries like petroleum, steel, and automobiles were able to bend codes to their own interests, brushing aside workers' concerns. Perhaps the most effective argument was that the NRA sanctioned monopoly and punished the small producer, a theme carried to particular heights by the National Recovery Review Board, led by the celebrity attorney Clarence Darrow, which released an inflammatory report accusing the NRA of oppressing small business.[12]

In retrospect, the passage of the NIRA coincided with an important turning point in the Great Depression. In 1933, for the first time since the crash, industrial production, investment, and prices began to rise, and would continue on this upward trajectory for the next four years. Stabilizing the banking system had been critical, as had been slipping the golden fetters of metallic money. Just as important were Roosevelt's bold promises of action, which helped generate a new groundswell of confidence. Despite its failures, as a demonstration of the administration's commitment, the NRA surely played a role.[13] Yet little of this was evident at the time. Unemployment remained stubbornly high, and the Depression dragged on.

As the most obvious example of "planning" in action, the perceived failures of the NRA tainted economists associated with similar ideas.[14] This was not entirely fair, for the act was a patchy compromise between competing viewpoints within the administration, rather than a result of any coherent theory of recovery. But even if the NRA did not represent the type of coordinated, top-down planning that economists like Clark had called for, it did rest upon several assumptions widely shared at Columbia.

One was the belief that competition, rather than being the lifeblood of economic activity, was often wasteful and destructive. In this analysis, the rise of large corporations and concentrated economic power was inevitable, and rather than fight monopoly, government ought to channel it toward social purposes.[15] Folded within this conclusion was the assumption that economic principles might shift and change as societies developed, meaning that economics itself must also evolve. Finally, the NRA also grew out of belief in the overproduction/underconsumption thesis. Where Chicago professors argued that price was the sole mediator necessary to adjust supply and demand and allocate scarce resources, the NRA presumed that the government must help workers earn more.

Back at Chicago, the NRA hardened opinions against the New Deal. Over the summer Viner had taken a leave of absence to join the

Treasury Department, leaving Knight as the dominant force within the Chicago department. Schultz, Friedman's adviser, reported in a letter to Hotelling that "we do not think much of the so-called economists and statisticians who are connected with the NIRA administration. We have very good reason to believe they are economic ignoramuses, and that, well meaning as they are, their work is likely to lead to another crash." Schultz complained in particular about the NRA's suspension of antitrust laws and the "enthronement of monopolies."[16] Roosevelt had simultaneously launched other programs that were more in keeping with the earliest Chicago proposals: the Public Works Administration, intended to fund infrastructure projects, matched the calls from Chicago for relief spending to help inflate an economy stalled by the banking crisis. But the program got off to a slow start, leaving the NRA to symbolize the New Deal.

While Friedman remained intellectually oriented toward Chicago, as his price theory class shows, his political sympathies during this year remain unclear. Nor was the New Deal the only political backdrop that mattered. Although he had yet to declare himself Führer, Adolf Hitler's rapid rise in Germany was already a matter of some alarm. Abramovitz, who had recently traveled in Germany, provided eyewitness testimony of Nazis parading in the streets of Cologne and Heidelberg.[17] Still, it was possible to believe, as many of Abramovitz's German Jewish contacts did, that the enthusiasm for Hitler would soon burn itself out. Friedman appears to have been less sanguine. He struck up a friendship with the Austrian exile Fritz Machlup and the German visiting scholar Wilhelm Kromphardt, who both confirmed his worst fears about the Nazis.[18]

Although Columbia was known for its planners, the main attraction for Friedman was Hotelling. Despite being enthusiastically recruited from Stanford's math department, Hotelling felt like an outsider at Columbia. Later, he recalled that his economics was "so mathematical that no member of the distinguished economics faculty there could understand it."[19] It was true that Hotelling's work in mathematical economics lay at the far border of the discipline. A few suggestive articles and books attempting to bridge mathematics and economics had appeared, and in 1931 the Econometric Society, "an international society for the advancement of economic theory in its relation to statistics and mathematics," had been founded.[20] But most economics professors remained mathematically unsophisticated and uninterested in learning more.

The courses that Friedman took from Hotelling at Columbia mixed technical exposition, a deep conviction that mathematics could make economics into a truly scientific enterprise, and a contradictory modesty about human knowledge claims. In his Statistical Inference course Hotelling was sensitive to the impact bias and human error could have on statistical conclusions, and ginger about applications to the real world. "In matters dealing with external world [we] are concerned with degrees of belief," he emphasized in an early lecture.[21] In the second course that Friedman took, Mathematical Economics, Hotelling moved more sharply in the direction of framing economics as an objective science. The difference between economics and the natural sciences, he told his students, often pivoted around the idea of experimentation: economists did not experiment but scientists did. However, this was "not entirely true": it was possible to do experiments in economics, whereas physical sciences like astronomy or meteorology did not use experiments. Therefore, "better dividing line to be found in no. of relevant factors."[22] Friedman found him "an absolutely remarkable talented, original person" and even compared his teaching to Viner's price theory course.[23]

Nonetheless, Hotelling shared the general interventionist politics of his colleagues. Throughout the 1930s, his research probed the gap he saw between optimum social outcomes and market results. Hotelling was not necessarily a planner, nor did he support the NRA as it unfolded. Instead, he favored establishing state-run industries subsidized by taxation. These ideas did not particularly influence the classes Friedman took, which were technical and mathematical. Yet Hotelling's views, which could accurately be called market socialism, marked another difference between Columbia and Chicago.[24]

By the end of his second year in graduate school, Friedman had sampled a cornucopia of economic approaches. In addition to neoclassical price theory, the quantity theory of money, and institutional economics, he had received extensive training in mathematical economics. In many ways, the education he received from Hotelling was superior to that offered at Chicago, leaving him well positioned for the turn toward mathematics that would redefine postwar economics.[25] Intellectually, Columbia was a counterpoint to Chicago in almost every respect. Politically, Friedman had seen the broad range of positions an economist could take, encountering in Hotelling a mentor of unquestioned brilliance who favored market socialism. The choices before Friedman were clear; he was in an ideal position to chart his own path as a scholar.

In the fall of 1934, Friedman returned to a changed Chicago department, with Viner gone (he would return in the winter) and Knight ascendant. Knight's loose group of admirers had transformed into a solid block of "Swiss guards," forming a recognizable clique. There was George Stigler, a towering six-footer from the Pacific Northwest, and Allen Wallis, a Midwestern frat boy who had already done a year of graduate work at the University of Minnesota. A. G. Hart, who had been a student during Friedman's first year, was still around, teaching monetary economics and trying to sell the profession on the Chicago plan. On the fringes was the wunderkind Paul Samuelson, taking advantage of a Chicago program that let talented high school students enter the university on an accelerated track. Samuelson was pulled into the group's orbit after acing an introductory economics course taught by Aaron Director. Before long Samuelson turned up in Economics 301, where he reprised Friedman's show-stopping challenge to Viner at the blackboard. Word of his audacity trickled up to the older students, who welcomed him into the jam sessions of Room Seven, a dusty storeroom in the economics building that Wallis and Stigler had secured as their headquarters.[26]

Atop the Room Seven pyramid stood Henry Simons and Aaron Director. As assistant professors teaching undergraduates, Simons and Director inhabited a liminal space within the department. They were decidedly below the status of the feared full professors, but through their teaching positions they wielded greater intellectual authority than any graduate student. Yet neither man had tenure, or had even received his Ph.D. Caught in this molting phase, the young, single Simons acted more like a graduate student than a professor, spending long beery evenings at Jimmy's Woodlawn Taproom and living on campus in the Quadrangle Club. Director was his best friend and silent sidekick.

Never quite part of the group, but at the same time essential to it, was Rose Director. When Friedman arrived back in Hyde Park, a new electricity crackled between them. After a year spent entertaining parentally approved suitors in Portland, Rose was ready to take the plunge. Soon she and Friedman were a couple. Rose had received the same prestigious Social Science Research Council Fellowship as Milton, which would pay her a salary for working as Knight's research assistant. Her office was next to Knight's, where she divided her time between his research and her own. She planned to focus on capital theory, an area of live dispute between Knight and the Austrian economist F. A. Hayek, who at the time was teaching at the London School of Economics.[27] Although Rose rarely turned up at Jimmy's, her connections to her brother, Friedman, and Knight meant she was firmly ensconced in the world of Room Seven.

It was a universe that revolved primarily around Knight, remembered Wallis: "The dominant subject was always Frank Knight: what did he say and what did he mean? Did he make sense and was he right? What were the implications for this, that, or the other issue? Back again to, what did he mean?" A number of extracurricular projects spilled out of this fascination. Knight led a seminar on Max Weber, one of the few thinkers he did not scorn, which Friedman, Stigler, and Wallis attended irregularly before leaving it to a handful of sociology students.[28]

Friedman's participation in the group touched off an active search for an intellectual lineage. Perhaps from Rose, he procured a syllabus for Philosophy 212: Movements of Thought in the Nineteenth Century, a famous undergraduate course taught by the recently deceased George Herbert Meade. On the syllabus he marked numerous texts of interest. Next to a listing of required readings by John Stuart Mill, including *Utilitarianism* and *On Liberty*, Friedman added "50¢" and a one-word description: "individualistic." He made similar annotations on another syllabus, for Philosophy 327, with check marks that indicated either an interest in or familiarity with Plato's *Republic* and John Dewey's *Individualism Old and New.*[29]

Only a year earlier, Knight had declared that the old political ideas were bankrupt. Yet here was Friedman assigning himself key texts in this very tradition. In Mill, Friedman would have found a reformist vision of individualism as a force for positive social change, built upon a familiar Knightian assertion that individuals could best determine their own interests.[30] *On Liberty* defended individual sovereignty and worried about the dangers of government power, but it also emphasized human flourishing and the importance of protecting minorities. Along the way, Mill suggested that governments withdraw from "State education" and instead pay school fees directly, an idea that anticipated Friedman's later proposals for school vouchers.[31] It all added up to a shadow graduate degree, meted out not by exams and papers but through informal gatherings and debating sessions at local taverns or the homes of Director or Knight.

If Room Seven's attitude toward Knight "was basically hero worship," the flip side of this adulation was contempt for those judged not to measure up. As he worked closely with Schultz on his book manuscript, *The Theory and Measurement of Demand*, Friedman's confidence veered into arrogance. Particularly when contrasted with Hotelling, Schultz was a dullard. Nor did Friedman make any attempt to disguise his scorn. Coming to fetch Friedman for dinner, Wallis would hear his voice echoing down the halls of the Social Science Building, upbraiding his adviser: "But Mr. Schultz, don't you see?" A mild-mannered, unpretentious man, remembered as "modest almost to a fault," Schultz did not appear disturbed by this treatment, instead graciously accepting any clarifications Friedman offered.[32]

In part, Friedman's contempt stemmed from their work together, which led him to believe Schultz was of "limited intellectual capacity." Or as he put it to Wallis, "I think he is the god damndest, dumbest, bastard I have ever met." But he was also following a pattern established by Knight, whose disdain for Schultz was obvious. In front of new graduate students registering for classes, Knight asked Schultz to explain quadratic equations, feigning confusion even as his relentless questions made clear that Schultz "didn't know what he was talking about."[33] Schultz was in many respects a natural beta, awed by the powerful personalities of Knight and Friedman. But he also rightly perceived that Friedman could make important contributions to his research.

Seemingly effortlessly, Friedman produced an academic article bearing upon Schultz's project. Stigler recounted that after a two-day absence due to a cold, Friedman reappeared with an article critiquing the British economist Arthur Pigou's method for deriving demand curves from family-budget data. Encouraged by Schultz, Friedman sent the article first to Cambridge University's *Economic Journal*, where it was swiftly rejected by the editor, J. M. Keynes, who had shown the piece to Pigou himself. Friedman then placed the paper in Harvard's *Quarterly Journal of Economics*, where it was published a year later to Pigou's great displeasure.[34] The episode touched off a mini controversy adjudicated by an outside referee, who concluded Friedman had made "an advance." Nonetheless, the referee cautioned, Friedman had "overlooked" an important distinction between a mathematical constant and the quasi-constant that Pigou employed. Where Friedman called for precision, Pigou approximated. In an echo of Hotelling's fate at Columbia, Friedman and Pigou were literally speaking different languages.[35] Singular to Friedman—and foreshadowing his future career—was the bold attack upon a great name.

If Knight was the patriarch of Room Seven, Simons emerged as the heir apparent with *A Positive Program for Laissez Faire*, published in November 1934. The thirty-seven-page booklet, an outgrowth of the earlier Chicago plan, quickly rivaled the oracular Knight as a source text for the Room Seven gang. Samuelson found it "incomprehensible" that anyone would oppose Simons's ideas. The idea of 100 percent money, in particular, he thought would solve the terrible deflation of the Great Depression in one stroke. If banks couldn't lend money they didn't have, the money supply, the dollar, and the system itself would be stable.[36]

A Positive Program for Laissez Faire suggested something more: that policy innovation did not have to contradict a belief in price theory or limited government. In the pamphlet, Simons set his dramatic reform proposals within an orthodox price-theory framework. Where Knight had hidden behind sarcasm and irony, Simons strode in boldly with a declaration of allegiance to "traditional liberalism," which he claimed to be "the best escape from the moral confusion of current political and economic thought, and the best basis or rationale for a program of economic reconstruction."[37] Social control, Simons argued, should come through competition rather than planning.

Liberalism was for Simons not so much about limiting state power, as about preserving prices. Above all else, the government must protect "the heart of the contract"—by which Simons meant freely adjusting relative prices. All this was standard enough fare, the basic political economy of any Chicago price-theory course. But Simons then made a dramatic pivot, defining competition as the duty and responsibility of the state, and giving the government broad latitude in the service of keeping capitalism alive. His pamphlet described a broad scope of state powers that could be justified under this larger goal of preserving competition, everything from outlawing corporate cross-ownership to nationalizing railroads and utilities.[38]

Along the way, Simons developed a critical distinction between rules and administration or "discretionary management." Instead of planners he called for plans—"definite, intelligible, and inflexible" rules that would preserve and protect prices, which lay at the heart of not just "the contract" but of the economic system itself. This allowed him to attack the NRA—which he called "terrifying" in a footnote—while urging monetary reforms that would effectively outlaw banks. Even as he criticized "the naïve advocates of managed economy or national planning," he argued that a "positive program" of government action was necessary to preserve the price system. It was an important step in transforming price theory from an economic idea to a political program.[39]

To the contemporary eye, *A Positive Program for Laissez Faire* reads as a hopeless muddle of contradictory and almost nonsensical ideas, but it becomes more understandable when considered in context. Simons's attack on monopoly reads as a classic statement of American Progressivism. Yet it was articulated at the height of the NRA, widely perceived to be a government-sponsored monopoly, and thus represents a criticism of the New Deal. Similarly, Simons's defense of competition placed him within a distinctive anti-reform quadrant of the economics profession. Planners concluded that wasteful competition was one of the structural problems that had led to the Great Depression. Simons instead framed competition as an alternative to potentially dangerous state power, writing that competition "serves to protect the community as a whole and to give an essential flexibility to the economy."[40]

At the same time, Simons favored taxation, another intervention that reads as left-leaning. To him, however, taxation was a conservative method, a way to shape economic activity without intervening fundamentally in the price system. In fact, taxes were a sort of price; they could be analyzed economically, they could be anticipated, and they built on the same assumptions of rationality and utility maximization that undergirded price theory.[41] As he put it, taxes were the only method that would not "much [impair] the attractiveness of the economic game." Furthermore, they contrasted favorably with the other suggestions then on offer, including "widespread unionization, reduction of hours, and increase of wage rates *in a depression*." Significantly, Simons was writing before raising taxes emerged as a critical issue for the Roosevelt administration; partisan differences over taxation were temporarily muted.[42]

In the bleak days of the Depression, *A Positive Program for Laissez Faire* flared into the lives of Chicago's graduate students with special force. Denizens of Room Seven agreed with Knight's view that the New Deal, as it had unfolded over the past year, was deeply misguided. But with their own uncertain economic futures looming, Friedman and his peers were looking for something, anything, to end the Depression. Parting ways with the dark fatalism of Knight, Simons prophesied a bright future in which economic recovery would lead to social progress. He cast economists as the critical players, "custodians of the great liberal tradition out of which their discipline arose."[43] Moreover, Simons didn't have to be right in order to be influential; within the context of Chicago's disputatious student culture, he merely had to be, as Stigler and Wallis noted in a fawning letter to *The New York Times*, "brilliant and suggestive."[44] To his student audience, the contradictory nature of Simons's ideas was not a mark against them but a reason for their strong appeal. *A Positive Program for Laissez Faire* was proof that one could be both an orthodox economist and an innovative reformer.

The group found further inspiration in the work of Knight. As Knight's fiftieth birthday approached, Room Seven launched an ambitious project to publish his collected essays, resulting in a book titled *The Ethics of Competition*, which appeared in 1935. The Festschrift led his admirers deep into Knight's oeuvre, in the process answering some of the perpetual questions about what the great man meant. Friedman, Stigler, and Wallis sifted through Knight's voluminous writings; Simons chimed in with numerous suggestions, as did Viner when queried. Eventually the group settled on eleven articles, producing piles of detailed note cards in the process. Wallis recalled "long sessions composing, editing, and (most excruciatingly) punctuating," all driven by a powerful sense of mission.[45]

The volume opened with "Ethics and the Economic Interpretation," a 1922 article that caused particular excitement: "The reason we want to get out the book is to publish this article. It constitutes a complete justification for the publication; it will explain to the world why Chicagoans consider Knight The Great Economist," declared one of the group's note cards.[46]

What message from "The Great Economist" aroused such enthusiasm? Knight's capacious and wandering analysis contained an arresting idea about the discipline itself: "All ends and motives are economic in that they require the use of objective resources in their realization." Consequently, this opened a vastly expanded sphere to economic analysis. "Economics is the one and all-inclusive science of conduct," Knight wrote. Knight then sounded a critique, which his admirers seemed to have missed. Economics could explain human activity, but only on the most abstract level. For a deeper understanding of human behavior, Knight urged a turn to "biology, social psychology, and especially culture history." These other disciplines were vital to ethics, about which economics had little to say, Knight argued.[47]

Judging by their later work, Knight's students set aside his thoughts on ethics, instead taking his essay as a new and exciting extension of price theory. If economics was a universal "science of conduct," then its basic framework—supply and demand, marginal cost and return, equilibrium and competition—could be extended far beyond traditional economic "wants." It applied not only to trading activity in a market but to nearly any choice a person might make, from a spouse to a charitable donation to an interest in classical music. This was what later generations would call "economics imperialism," and it was not Knight's invention. But to his students, it might as well have been.[48]

This was the larger message Knight's acolytes wished to share with a waiting world: economics was a value-free science that could be used to analyze any form of human activity. It was a vision that offered his young followers the mantle of science, the rigor of truth, and the promise of unlimited territory to conquer.

Amid the Great Depression, Knight's vision was also a rebuttal to new currents in economics and policy. The students' introduction emphasized they had selected Knight essays "which have particular relevance to the problems faced by society to-day . . . a unifying thread may be found in the problem of social control and its various manifestations."[49] The Chicago professors' first response to the downturn, the Chicago plan, had largely been adopted in the banking and monetary reforms of Roosevelt's early months as president. The New Deal had then turned to "planning," elevating Columbia-style economics. Although the failings of the NRA would ultimately discredit planning, waiting in the wings were other approaches similarly critical of the neoclassical model.

Even before the ideas of Keynes became influential, a consensus was gathering that the neoclassical vision of prices determined in a free market was no longer meaningful in the contemporary American economy. From Britain came Joan Robinson's *Economics of Imperfect Competition*, published in 1933 nearly simultaneously with Edward Chamberlin's *Theory of Monopolistic Competition*. Although the two economists clashed bitterly, both were attempting to reorient economic theory away from neoclassical assumptions. The titles said it all. Rather than place perfect competition at the center of economic theory, Robinson argued the guiding assumption should be "imperfect competition"—limited information, markets distorted by powerful firms and coercive labor relationships, equilibrium reached despite inefficient production and workers fruitlessly seeking work. Similarly, Chamberlin contended that neoclassical theory had ignored the mix of competition and monopoly that pervaded most markets. In the work of both authors, the assumption of monopoly overshadowed the free operation of price.[50]

Relatedly, on the heels of *The Modern Corporation and Private Property*, the influential book he had coauthored with the FDR adviser Adolf Berle, the economist Gardiner Means refined his theory of administered prices. It might be still be true, Means admitted, that supply and demand determined prices in specific markets, such as those for agricultural goods. But most meaningful economic activity was controlled by large corporations, which set or "administered" prices internally.[51] Means took these ideas to a series of New Deal posts in the Department of Agriculture, the NRA, and the National Resources Committee.

The Progressive language of "social control" had passed. So too had the Progressive assumption that monopolies needed to be broken up and subject to competition. (Indeed it was Simons, the classical liberal, who most loudly called for this.) Assuming instead that monopolies were here to stay, economists proposed regulations and laws to make their activities more socially beneficial. If corporations now administered prices, government would administer competition. Economic theory would evolve to incorporate these new realities.

Knight interpreted all this as a portentous sign of further social decay, and a direct rebuke to his own ideas. No one appreciated his work, no one understood him, Knight complained bitterly to colleagues and to his students. Knight's admirers took up the charge. A group launched themselves against Chamberlin's *Theory of Monopolistic Competition*, meeting every Saturday morning to work through the text. *The Ethics of Competition* itself underscored how deeply Knight's students believed his ideas could be a viable alternative to the new line of economic thinking—if only they were widely appreciated.

At the moment, Friedman still expected he would be a mathematical economist of sorts, and had begun to plan a dissertation on commodity stocks. A synthesis of Mitchell, Schultz, and Hotelling, the thesis would combine annual prices with business cycle analysis, resulting in "an entirely new way to obtain statistical demand curves."[52] This was a technocratic side of the discipline that could be figured as almost entirely apolitical—although in practice, many pioneers like Hotelling thought their calculations could assist in the dawning age of state control. Nonetheless, even as he mapped out a data-driven dissertation, Friedman was gravitating toward philosophical individualism.

Editing *The Ethics of Competition* helped Friedman locate himself within the shifting tides of economic and political thought in the 1930s. The book's introduction made clear this was no exercise in arid scholasticism. Rather, the students had absorbed an ethos of politically engaged inquiry from Simons and Knight. They had arrayed themselves behind both an expansive vision of economic practice and a traditional commitment to limited government, free competition, and allocation through prices. It was a project both personal and political.

Along with the Festschrift, Friedman, Stigler, and Wallis hatched a plan to cheer Knight up with an elaborate party for his forty-ninth birthday. They reached out to his family for a biographical sketch, and drew up a guest list that included most of the department—except for the consumption expert Hazel Kyrk. Nationally known for her research, Kyrk was accorded little respect by the students, who joked that her Ph.D.

stood for "petticoat hanging down." It simply didn't occur to them to include her in what was shaping up as a stag dinner. Only Rose noticed that Kyrk was deeply hurt.[53]

Nor was Kyrk the only faculty member who had been wounded by Knight's group. It was not even the first dinner that had been planned to raise Knight's spirits! Indeed, Knight's moodiness was a sign of deeper trouble burbling under the surface. His congenital skepticism had by now shaded off into black depression. Increasingly, he trained his venom on another colleague, Paul Douglas.

Douglas, who had been at Chicago for more than a decade, was an important voice within the department and the discipline. He was primarily interested in labor, and had done some of the first statistical studies of wage rates in the United States. Yet Douglas was no mere gatherer of dry fact; working with a mathematician colleague, he had developed the Cobb-Douglas production function, a formula that made it possible to estimate the relative contributions of capital and labor to total output. Douglas regarded this work as confirmation of the marginal productivity theory of wages, and thus as a contribution to neoclassical economics.[54] Although Douglas did not teach price theory, he respected its insights and was cordial with his orthodox colleagues. He had helped draft the original Chicago banking memo and supported Simons's Chicago plan.[55]

At the same time, Douglas was a firm supporter of organized labor and an energetic advocate for a variety of reform causes. He had tackled a corrupt Chicago utility owner in a celebrated case that eventually earned him a Hearst newspaper column, and in 1927 had traveled to Russia as part of a trade-union delegation, meeting both Stalin and Trotsky. As the Depression unfolded, Douglas was in ever-greater demand, becoming a public intellectual of sorts. He advised candidate Roosevelt, swaying him to support unemployment insurance; consulted for the NRA (which he eventually came to oppose); and testified before Congress in favor of old-age pensions and unemployment insurance.[56]

From Douglas's perspective, none of this had any relationship to Knight. The men had once been extremely close; Douglas had helped recruit Knight to Chicago, and for years had considered him "one of my best friends."[57] Along with Schultz, he had planned the first Knight appreciation dinner, years earlier.

But now, Knight appeared to consider him a personal and professional enemy. Colleagues and graduate students began to recount insulting comments from Knight, the primary theme being that Douglas, like all reformers, sought fame and power. Once-warm relations turned frosty as Knight informed Douglas only egotists made public speeches, and Douglas shot back that Knight would do the same, if only he knew how.[58] Aaron Director, who had come to Chicago to work with Douglas, now moved decisively into Knight's corner, treating his former adviser as an embarrassment. Observing the massing of forces around Knight, Douglas rightly perceived the emergence of a hostile faction within the department.

Matters came to a head following a department meeting on Simons's and Director's futures at Chicago. The fate of both men had been much discussed over the past few years, as their lack of scholarship became ever more glaring and evidence piled up that both were poor teachers. The department had even voted several times against offering a permanent position to both men, but somehow they were still there, probably because no one else wanted their courses. But the lackluster teaching reviews could only be ignored for so long. In December, yet another vote was held, this one more decisive: Director and Simons were out. With the exception of Knight, everyone at the meeting had voted the same way.

But Knight singled out Douglas in a poisonous letter sent a few days later. "Your thirst for blood does not surprise me so very much," Knight informed Douglas, observing that it was only natural for a reformer to be ruthless. "I think you might pick on somebody nearer your own size," Knight continued, stating that Douglas was trying to "get" Director and Simons because of personal animus toward him. "They <u>are</u> friends of mine, in a somewhat special sense, and that if you succeed in getting their throats cut without the interests of our group and its work being rather clearly in evidence, as they are not now, I'm not going to make any pretense of liking it." He announced loftily, "I think you have been displaying an attitude of resentment toward me, for which there is no reason."[59] A remarkable document, the letter revealed Knight's comprehensive emotional and intellectual attachment to—even dependency upon—his two younger admirers.

Like the deft politician he would later become, Douglas took quick advantage of Knight's blunder, circulating the letter to every member of the department who had been at the meeting. Rightly offended by Knight's outlandish and insulting claims, Douglas also set down in painful detail how Simons and Director had fallen short. Director had failed to produce "research work of high quality" and was reportedly "becoming personally unpleasant in his classes and was not an effective teacher." To the distress of students, his course on labor economics had become a diatribe against unions. While Simons had done creditable "pamphleteering and propagandistic" work, this should not be the whole of an economist's output. And his teaching was toxic. Simons was apt to tell students that their questions were elementary, stupid, or both. Like Director, Simons radiated contempt from his very person: "Only those who thought precisely as he did could escape a sharp and scornful disapproval."[60] If Douglas hadn't been out for blood before, he certainly was now.

In the end, both Knight and Douglas got some of what they wanted. The vote to dismiss Director held; at the end of the academic year he would leave for a position at the Treasury Department. But Simons had friends in high places, among them the university's president, Robert Hutchins, who appreciated Simons's efforts at publicizing the Chicago plan on Capitol Hill. Simons had also caught the eye of Wilbur Katz, the dean of the law school, who was beginning to plan an ambitious new curriculum. After a brief reprieve in the economics department, Simons shifted to a new position, divided equally between the economics department and the law school.[61] Knight had succeeded in keeping Simons close, while Douglas had lanced Director.

Like mortals watching clashing gods in the sky above, Room Seven spun myths to comprehend. Following the lead of Knight, they interpreted the whole affair as a personal vendetta. Decades later, Rose could still not admit that her brother's dismissal might have been justified.[62] After close examination of the documents, Stigler concluded that Simons had not met the tenure bar, yet he still painted Knight in a sympathetic light. Professors "spent their days and their nights in company with one another," Stigler remembered. In such a closed, almost monastic community, "strong friendships and strong hostilities emerged," he rationalized.[63]

More than a textbook case of academic infighting, the Knight–Douglas controversy shows the 1930s Chicago school emerging across two dimensions, one methodological and one social—and both already advancing a counterpoint to the reigning ideas in Washington, D.C.[64] What distinguished the school methodologically was not the quantity theory, or even price theory, although it was true that at Chicago, these approaches took up the space other departments allocated to planning and eventually, Keynesianism. Rather, unique to Chicago was the application of price theory to social problems, an approach modeled by Simons and theorized by Knight. It would be years before this analytic move produced anything of consequence. But as Friedman's time at Columbia underscores, using price theory to think about policy and social problems remained a distinctive point of view in the 1930s.

Equally important was the Chicago social world, which ensured that price theory survived the upheavals of the Great Depression, even growing stronger during it. That price theory prospered through the 1930s was a matter of culture as much as of intellect. Some scholars have argued that there was no coherent Chicago school in these years, pointing to the diversity of the department's economics and politics.[65] But the links between Knight, Simons, and Director suggest otherwise. The three were so tight that an attack on one was perceived as an attack on all. This was the hidden curriculum of Chicago that Room Seven imbibed, the unspoken lessons on what it meant to be a colleague and an intellectual. Bound by ties personal and professional, the young acolytes absorbed the implicit messages that friendship and politics were interwoven, loyalty and belief inseparable.[66]

Room Seven was not just a break room, but rather the origin point of a conservative intelligentsia. From the Chicago classrooms came price theory and the quantity theory of money, two powerful frameworks for understanding the warp and woof of historical change. From Knight came a perception of siege, a sense of paradise lost and truth forgotten, leaving only a few lonely keepers of the flame. Clustered around a charismatic leader, held together by collectively forged norms and intellectual commitments, and animated by a sense of mission, Friedman's core group of friends merged the political, the social, and even the familial.

This dawning movement culture came at a moment when there was no organized, effective opposition to the emerging New Deal order. In the election of 1936 Roosevelt would win an overwhelming mandate, cracking up old political alliances and forging a new connection between urban and rural, North and South, that would define politics in America for decades to come. Few knew that the seed of a counter-establishment had already been planted.

PART II

NEW DEAL WASHINGTON

4

THE FISCAL REVOLUTION

> There is no significant study in the field of economics whose results are not likely to be used in public controversy.
>
> —Milton Friedman and Simon Kuznets, 1938

As the 1934–1935 academic year ended, there came a great scattering. Of the Room Seven gang only Henry Simons would remain in Hyde Park. Paul Samuelson was off to Harvard for a Ph.D. George Stigler had won the jackpot: a faculty position at Iowa State College, then considered a desirable post.[1] With Frank Knight going on leave, Rose decided to return to Portland. And Milton joined Aaron Director and Allen Wallis in making the pilgrimage to Washington, D.C., part of the great drift of educated young men into the nation's capital.

Like war, revolution, or plague, the economic cataclysm of the Great Depression created winners alongside the losers. The same forces that swept away family farms, vaporized life savings, and destroyed businesses large and small created a boom market for anyone with university training in economics. Indeed, with faculty positions scarce, working for the federal government became a common career path for graduate students in the 1930s. Akin to technicians and engineers, these fledgling economists were called to help the Roosevelt administration manage economic recovery. Soon they were doing more than that. As the New Deal wore on, economists became strategists and advisers to government at the highest rank. Centered in Washington, D.C., this surging demand washed away the last vestiges of gentlemanly political economy, leaving economics an ascendant discipline and favored handmaiden to power.

Friedman arrived in Washington amid a transition between what historians have retrospectively labeled the first and second New Deals. Roosevelt's first three years in office had been marked by the successful resolution of the banking crisis and the fiasco of the National Recovery Administration (NRA). In May, the Supreme Court had ruled key provisions of the NRA unconstitutional, while over the summer, a second wave of banking reform had culminated in the Banking Act of 1935.[2]

In the wake of these developments, the Roosevelt administration recalibrated its approach to economic recovery. With the political perils of restricting production now clear, New Deal agencies turned to the hopefully less-controversial task of stimulating consumption. Friedman was hired by the National Resources Committee, a new federal agency created to spearhead economic planning. He would be an associate economist on the Study of Consumer Purchases, a massive survey that would track the spending habits of 300,000 American families. His salary was funded by the Works Progress Administration, the same agency that paid workers to lay bricks and artists to paint murals. He was one of the new whiz kids tasked with ensuring the rigor and accuracy of government data.[3]

A year later Rose arrived, joining Milton for long Sunday brunches and walks among the blooming cherry trees. It was a pleasant interlude reminiscent of bygone times; Aaron Director was at the Treasury Department, Allen Wallis soon joined the study with Milton, and even Homer Jones was around, running research at the recently established Federal Deposit Insurance Corporation (FDIC), which had been created to insure bank deposits and avert a repeat of the banking crisis of 1931–1933. Rose interviewed at the FDIC with the economist Clark Warburton, who would later play a significant role in Friedman's monetary research. "She is unusually keen, and I was very favorably impressed with her abilities," Warburton noted in a weekly memorandum to his boss. Ultimately Rose joined the FDIC, assisting Jones. It was engaging work but had little to do with her planned dissertation on capital theory. Yet as she confessed to Jones in an unguarded moment, Rose expected to be married within the year. Looking ahead, she saw herself as Milton's wife and the mother of his children.[4]

But at the moment, Friedman was thinking about punch cards. The survey had gathered data on nearly a million families in fifty cities and rural regions, collecting further details on a subset of fifty thousand families. The survey was exhaustive, covering everything from how many yams a family ate per week, to money spent on "bathing suits, beach kimonos, riding habits, or other special sportswear." Did they receive income from selling poultry, livestock, "fruits, grapes, berries, nuts"? Were there roomers with board, boarders without room (only taking meals), tourists, or transients in the household? Had anyone died in the past year, and if so, how much did the funeral cost? Separate schedules focused on the habits of urban families, farm families, and town/village families. Now there were more than ten million punch cards to analyze, and the pressure was on to produce a timely report that could be used to craft policy.[5]

Ironically, Friedman was now toiling to assist the very economic planners his Chicago teachers had derided. The study's designers were a powerful group of institutional economists determined to continue planning despite the demise of the NRA. They hoped the study would "help design, justify, and implement economic policies that would raise mass purchasing power," one historian explains, describing the study as "the union of social science expertise . . . [and] leftist hopes for federal economic planning." Politics aside, the Study of Consumer Purchases was also a groundbreaking feat of statistical research that could only have occurred within the context of New Deal federal spending. Inadvertently, the Roosevelt administration had ushered in the first era of big data—all without the benefit of modern computers.[6]

Facing this deluge of punch cards, Friedman came up with a novel method of analysis, which he called "general rank correlation." The traditional technique, analysis of variance, assumed a normal distribution—a bell curve. But the survey's families had not fallen into the expected pattern. Friedman's method skirted this problem by instead ranking income and expenditure from lowest to highest for each family group, as defined by size and urban or rural location. From there, a statistician could ascertain the relationship of income to consumption, even in cases where the data did not follow a bell curve.[7] Bolstered by Allen Wallis and Dorothy Brady, an economist at the Department of Labor, Friedman began to promote his new method as the best way to grasp important features of the data. As the study bogged down under its own weight, Friedman's novel idea was routed to the National Resources Committee's Technical Committee and then on to a separate Hyper-Technical Subcommittee.[8]

Friedman's ideas found a better reception outside government. He presented the concept to the Econometric Society and published a related paper in the *Journal of the American Statistical Association*. Eventually, the technique now called "analysis of ranks" would be incorporated into the study's basic methodology, and even become a basic ingredient in statistical software, known as the "Friedman test," that is still used today. But it was most useful to Friedman as a ticket out of D.C.[9] As the paper made the rounds, he received a welcome offer from the National Bureau of Economic Research in New York.

Though the NBER was not a government agency, working there would still keep Friedman at the center of the evolving New Deal. The once hallowed NBER slumped after failing to predict the Depression. It was then revitalized by the pathbreaking work of Simon Kuznets. A Russian émigré who had been in the United States for less than a decade, Kuznets was the leading expert on national income, a relatively new concept that would become vital to the New Deal. Although economists had long measured output and prices in specific sectors or commodities—witness Henry Schultz's tome on sugar—only recently had they tried to combine numerous indexes into one aggregate figure of "national income." Kuznets's 1934 study, *National Income, 1929–1932*, became a minor sensation in D.C.[10] Funded by the Commerce Department, it would eventually shape policy at the highest levels. It was Kuznets who had scouted Friedman at a conference, but the

NBER was also home to Friedman's idol, Arthur Burns. Friedman didn't think twice about taking the job.

Nor was there much question that Rose would follow. Although she still planned to complete her Ph.D., she did not intend to become a professor. It wasn't simply a matter of dwindling ambition but realistic recognition of almost insurmountable obstacles ahead. Prestigious schools generally did not consider female job applicants, who were advised to focus on the relatively small number of women's colleges. It was worse for those married to other economists—or hoping to be. Most schools had nepotism rules, meaning the wives of faculty could not be hired in any paid position. Even at the relatively open-minded University of Chicago, the future Nobel Prize–winning physicist Maria Goeppert Mayer was a "voluntary" associate professor, receiving no salary. Institutional arrangements essentially forced a choice between career and family. While government work offered more opportunity, most of the female economists Rose knew were unmarried. She had little interest in becoming "a small, hard-working spinster," as *Time* characterized Milton's boss Hildegarde Kneeland, who had made a successful career for herself in D.C. And Milton made clear that two years of government work was more than enough. Rose began looking for another job, one that would take her to New York City.[11]

To escape the fate of a contract economist, crunching numbers for someone else's project, Friedman would need to finish a dissertation. In this era, almost no doctoral students received funding after they had finished classes. They completed a dissertation while working, or used family money to stay afloat. Relatedly, a dissertation was a formality that might be required for a faculty position, or might not. Allen Wallis, for example, never completed his degree but nonetheless was hired as an assistant professor at Stanford and then promoted to associate professor. Likewise, Friedman's teacher Lloyd Mints was also an associate professor with no more than a master's degree! But the same trend toward professionalization that brought Friedman to D.C. was making the doctoral degree newly essential. Ideally, working at the NBER could both pay the bills and advance his career.

Kuznets assigned Friedman to a project he had already begun, a study of income in five professions: medicine, dentistry, law, accounting, and engineering consulting. Upon his arrival Friedman took command and soon determined that this would be his doctoral dissertation. For financial reasons, he decided to pursue his degree through Columbia, not Chicago. He would be required to publish the final work, which his connection to the NBER would facilitate. Once upon a time, Friedman had planned a thesis on commodity prices, but this new project would study something far more touchy—the price of human labor.[12]

Linking the NBER's statistics with the economic theory he had learned at Chicago, Friedman turned the raw materials Kuznets had gathered into something very different. Combing through Kuznets's data with an eye to the big picture, he soon homed in on a differential between the incomes of dentists and doctors, believing they were, "of course, related professions requiring similar abilities and training."[13] Further, the data for these two professions was relatively straightforward, whereas various factors made the other samples less reliable.

What could account for the difference in income between doctors and dentists? Friedman began by correcting for the longer training period required of medicine and the consequently shorter professional life of doctors. Using an estimated interest rate for each year of forgone income, he calculated that doctors should earn about 17 percent more than dentists. Yet his figures demonstrated that the average income of doctors was 32 percent higher than the average income of dentists.

Then came the leap. Friedman argued that approximately half of the increased income was due to "restriction" in entry, or the difficulty in gaining admission to medical school and then passing boards. In other words, there was a medical cartel—the American Medical Association (AMA)—that artificially raised incomes. Given the "free working of the much abused law of supply and demand," doctors would only earn about 17 percent more than dentists.[14]

This conclusion seemed obviously wrong to Friedman's NBER

superiors. Wasn't it true that doctors were more skilled than dentists—particularly the specialists—and so commanded a higher wage? There were many ways to compute an average, and the metric Friedman had used, simply dividing the sum of all incomes by the number of practitioners, did not accurately capture the income variation within the profession. A more accurate measure would have been the median—or the midpoint of each income distribution.[15] Further, weren't medical boards vital to upholding professional standards and training? Where was the evidence that dentists would have liked to be doctors, or vice versa?

The first to express these concerns was the NBER director Frederick C. Mills, soon to be elected as president of the American Economic Association, who sat down with Friedman and then followed up with a detailed nine-page critique. Then came a letter from former Roosevelt adviser Winfield Riefler, now at the Institute for Advanced Study, objecting to publication of an early research summary. And finally the NBER director C. Reinhold Noyes circulated an ominous twenty-one-page memo to the entire board. "This has the making of an interesting and important investigation," Noyes announced. Then he attacked. "The authors appear to have allowed [economic theory] to blind them, to a large extent, to what their own results suggest," he declared.[16] Thus kicked off a dispute that would last for years.

Noyes's memo encapsulated the profound methodological, philosophical, and political differences between the NBER and Friedman. It was the same basic tension as between Columbia and Chicago, between institutionalism and neoclassical economics. Mills and Noyes were focused on the specific social reality before them. Friedman was soaring above in the realm of theory.

Neither Mills nor Noyes could swallow the contention that doctors and dentists were analogous: "The authors' supposition that medicine and dentistry are closely allied and call for the same qualifications, is so far from this ordinary observer's conclusions as to constitute a serious flaw in much of their reasoning," Noyes wrote. Yet that was far from the only problem. Noyes questioned their use of the arithmetic mean to measure inequality between professions, their estimate of return on investment, and their quotations from Adam Smith and Alfred Marshall, calling them not "an adequate basis for a statement of economic theory on this subject."[17] Attached to eight pages of discussion was another thirteen pages of line-by-line critique. With his dissertation at risk, Friedman took up the burden of responding, occasionally calling in reinforcements from Kuznets.

As it turned out, Friedman didn't care if his basic assumptions about doctors and dentists were unrealistic. To treat dentistry and medicine as interchangeable was to isolate the variable that interested him most: price, or the income that could be received from each profession. This meant, as he and Kuznets explained to Mills, that it only mattered that "a change in the relative attractiveness of the two professions . . . would cause some individuals to make a choice different from the one they would have made under the original conditions."[18] Although Friedman and Kuznets appeared to believe that dentistry and medicine were comparable in many respects, they also argued that the extent to which they were comparable was not particularly relevant. Here was the first whisper of Friedman's later famous theory of prediction.

Here too was the legacy of Simons and Knight. Friedman was doing exactly what they had taught. He had taken his basic framework and applied it not simply to economic dynamics within a profession but to the process of choosing a profession itself. It was taking Chicago price theory out of the classroom and applying it to the real world. Yet Mills profoundly doubted the choice of occupation was a purely economic calculation. Instead, he cited "qualitative differences in the abilities and temperaments suited to the two professions" and an individual's knowledge of "the earnings of men in the profession with whom they are in immediate contact."[19] Not only was the conflict a potential career killer, but it exposed a deep fissure in midcentury economics about the very basics of human nature.

It might have been different if Friedman had simply turned his back on institutionalism, forging ahead into statistics or mathematical economics. But like a termite burrowing from within, he took up institutionalist preoccupations and turned them to his own purposes. The AMA was exactly the sort of institution that his Columbia professors had underscored for its market-shaping powers. Yet Friedman did not approach it as an institutionalist might have, thinking about its broad social purpose or its vital function in the marketplace. Instead, he accused it of monopoly, measuring its function by price alone.

In truth, Friedman's suggestion that the AMA was a monopoly was not far-fetched. In 1938, the AMA was even sued by the Justice Department for restraint of trade when it tried to shut down the Group Health Association, an early effort at managed care. But as Noyes put it, accusing the AMA of monopoly was precisely the type of "hot poker" the NBER was designed to avoid; leave it to others to make politics out of its nonpartisan data.

Friedman rejected this argument. "There is no significant study in the field of economics whose results are not likely to be used in public controversy," he asserted to Mills. It was an unabashed embrace of the economist's new public role.[20]

At base, the dispute was more than a conflict about method: it was a conflict about the very definition of science. NBER researchers followed inductive reasoning, gathering facts before reaching any conclusions. Ideally, they farmed this last step out to others, leaving their hands clean of controversy. By contrast, Friedman led with theory—in this case, the theory that human behavior was profoundly shaped by price signals, that people wanted more of what was cheap and less of what was dear; or would prefer, ceteris paribus, a higher income to a lower one. But the ceteris paribus was to his critics a yawning gulf that one could not traverse with fancy footwork. It was in fact the nub of the problem. It seemed to Friedman's critics that he was not testing his theory with facts but using facts to confirm his theory.

Although NBER directors fingered price theory as the source of Friedman's errors, buried in a footnote was another profound motivation. As he was writing, the AMA passed a resolution urging a citizenship requirement for membership, and another requiring that foreign-born doctors complete a period of residency before being admitted to practice.[21] Against whom were these resolutions directed, and why now? Friedman concluded these new measures were intended to protect American doctors against competition from Jewish refugees fleeing Nazi Germany. Coming on the heels of Germany's Nuremberg

Laws, which stripped Jewish doctors of their licenses, and in the same year that Kristallnacht made Nazi brutality obvious, these stipulations seemed like rank discrimination. The AMA appeared as not just a cartel—but a bigoted cartel.[22] Sensitivity to prejudice added another layer to Friedman's conviction that the AMA unjustly propped up the incomes of doctors.

In the short run, Noyes's attack backfired by arousing sympathy for a besieged underling. Arthur Burns was a vocal supporter, as was Kuznets. But the accusations were serious enough that Wesley Mitchell himself intervened, spending a month combing over Friedman's data. What he found was disturbing: "M. had misused his data in several ways + reached an indefensible conclusion," he later recounted.[23] Happily, determined to be no Jacob Viner, Friedman quickly admitted the mistake. He and Kuznets went back to the drawing board to revise. They would make some adjustments on the margin, but their central argument remained.

Beyond the controversy, another aspect of Friedman's dissertation proved foundational. He had not originated the idea or generated the statistics, but he had turned them into something meaningful. Left alone to conceptualize and plan a dissertation, Milton might have floundered like Rose. Turned loose on a mess of data, he made it sing.

As this drama began to unfold, Rose was still in D.C. While she assumed they would be married soon, Milton apparently harbored some doubts. Around this time he poured out his heart to a mutual friend, Leo Rosten, while the two canoed on the Potomac. Rosten insisted he wise up and marry Rose without further delay. In all likelihood, Milton was probably worried about how to support a wife and children amid the uncertain economic climate. Rose had a good income for now but expected that, eventually, her "primary career would be as a mother; the economist would come second." The couple stayed in touch with daily letters, and Rose contented herself with occasional visits from Milton, who stayed on as a consultant to the study. But after a consulting trip to D.C. was canceled at the last minute, Rose took matters into her own hands. She booked a train ticket and a hotel room and headed north. By the time the weekend was over, it had been settled: five years after they first met in Viner's classroom, Rose and Milton were getting married.[24]

The wedding was a small affair, held at the Jewish Seminary in New York. Milton's mother and sisters attended, although Rose's distant family did not. Nonetheless, Rose insisted on a Jewish ceremony. This was no idle matter. The year before, Aaron had married a Christian woman. Shocked and betrayed, Sam and Sarah Director cut off all contact with the couple, a breach that would never heal.[25] Perhaps in response, Aaron and his new bride were spending the year in England, where he was working on a history of the Bank of England. He sent Rose a warm letter of congratulations, calling Milton "a fine person, whom I always liked. There is universal agreement on his very superior ability." Aaron added, "Tell him I shall not hold his very strong New Deal leanings—authoritarian to use an abusive term—against him."[26]

In the decades since, this offhand comment has become the foundation of a powerful origin story about Milton Friedman: that he was once a card-carrying liberal, who at a later, unknown point transformed into a libertarian.[27] It is true that Friedman cast his first vote for Roosevelt and took his first job on a New Deal project. Yet his actions must be understood within a broader context.

During this time, Friedman's political views were profoundly influenced by the unfolding tragedy in Europe. According to his own recollection, he cast his first vote for Roosevelt in 1936, while still working on the Study of Consumer Purchases.[28] It was at least a partial endorsement of the early New Deal. But the vote also reflected the enormous affection American Jews held for Roosevelt, who appointed prominent Jewish cabinet members, Supreme Court justices, and advisers. Further, opposition to Roosevelt was shot through with anti-Semitism. Roosevelt's political rivals muttered about "the Jew Deal" and hinted that the president himself might be Jewish.[29] Anti-Semitism took its most virulent form in Germany, but it was a pervasive American sentiment, too. In the mid-1930s there were many reasons to support FDR, beyond full sympathy for the New Deal.

A better way to understand Friedman's ideas during the second New Deal is to look at his teaching and private correspondence. Particularly when juxtaposed with new intellectual currents in economics, the depth of his allegiance to Chicago economics comes clear—as does the shallowness of any allegiance to the New Deal.

Shortly after Friedman's 1937 arrival in New York, a new approach to economics and policy-making came to prominence: the fiscal revolution, which would become a core legacy of New Deal liberalism.[30] Spending had always been part of the New Deal, but it had been ad hoc and eclectic. Pragmatic rather than principled, Roosevelt had experimented with multiple approaches to economic recovery, from plowing up crops to public works to the NRA's production guidelines. The fiscal revolution, by contrast, marked the arrival of a coherent theory about how the federal government could and should intervene to support economic life.

It began with an unprecedented event, the so-called Roosevelt recession of 1937. There had been several years of recovery, with strong annual growth and the slow reduction of unemployment to 14 percent—still alarmingly high, but an improvement over the worst years. Then suddenly, the economy plunged once again. Over the coming year, industrial production dropped by more than a third, manufacturing declined sharply, and unemployment spiked back to 20 percent. Standing alone, it was the third-worst contraction in the twentieth century. But it did not stand alone—it was a recession within a depression, a "double dip."

This was an unforeseen and frightening shock. The prevailing model of business cycles implied that once economic activity hit bottom, it would head back up. Falling costs would tempt new investment; unemployed workers would take new jobs. Eventually the economy would find a satisfactory equilibrium. There would be no unsold goods glutting warehouses, no idle factories awaiting orders, and no desperate men selling apples on the street. But what if a down cycle came, and stayed, as had happened over much of the past decade? What if economic recovery paused, and then reversed? Could equilibrium reset at a dreadfully low level? Was there even such thing as equilibrium?

The figures Kuznets had assembled offered some explanation, at least according to the presidential adviser Lauchlin Currie, a Harvard-trained economist. Poring over statistics, Currie discovered that in August, for the first time since 1931, the government's net contribution to national spending had fallen. This parsimony was intended to balance the budget, address Roosevelt's critics, and assuage the president's own vestigial discomfort with spending. But the result had been a reduction in aggregate national income, argued Currie. The recession now looked less mysterious, and a solution lay at hand: the government should boost national income through spending.[31]

Currie's argument received powerful reinforcement from the Harvard professor Alvin Hansen, a leading interpreter of John Maynard Keynes's recently published book, *The General Theory of Employment, Interest, and Money*, which appeared in 1936. The bookish son of a Dakota frontier family, Hansen was an established institutional economist, with a degree from the University of Wisconsin, when he first read *The General Theory*. He was not an early adopter. "The book under review is not a landmark in the sense that it lays a foundation for a 'new economics,'" Hansen informed readers of an economic journal. Soon he changed his mind. Taking up a new position at Harvard just as the double-dip recession unfolded, Hansen embraced Keynes's interpretation of the Great Depression.[32]

Keynes set forth a theoretical model that explained how an economy could stabilize far below expected levels. The key mechanism was the interest rate, previously seen by Keynes himself as a powerful method for stimulating economic activity. Now Keynes argued that in a depression, the interest rate could become powerless. Typically, economists assumed that a low interest rate would stimulate growth as businesses borrowed cheaply and expanded production or revamped old equipment.

But amid pervasive economic uncertainty, people would rather hold money than risk investment, Keynes hypothesized. Low interest rates could not break this psychology; all they did was diminish the distinction between cash and investments, and encourage investors to wait it out for a more profitable, high-interest-rate environment. Yet all the waiting meant this moment would never come.[33] It was a vicious cycle, reminiscent of the bank runs that had conjured economic ruin out of fear itself.

Keynes did not stop there. He laid out the policy implications: government spending must break the cycle. Relying on the concept of a "multiplier," he argued that a dollar spent was not simply a dollar spent, but would ramify throughout the economy as each individual passed a portion of this new income to another through consumption. Accordingly, government spending would "raise the income by more than the expenditure," as Hansen glossed the idea to Congress.[34]

Like Hansen at first, many established economists were unimpressed by Keynes's ideas. Knight published a twenty-five page review, concluding "with a feeling of keen disappointment." While recognizing that the book advanced "a new system of political economy," he doubted it was "much advance over more crudely 'monetary' weapons of thought." Viner was more appreciative, praising the book's "outstanding intellectual achievement," although he worried it would "have probably more persuasive power than it deserves." Yet even those who came to embrace Keynes's views were taken aback upon reading *The General Theory*, as Hansen's early review demonstrates.[35]

Part of the difficulty was that Keynes redefined economic terms to suit his purposes, as Currie himself groused: "All too often we find that familiar things are being described in unfamiliar language, that concepts cannot be given statistical meaning, and that precision and definiteness are being purchased at the expense of reality."[36] This new language was in fact one of Keynes's most lasting contributions. As one economist explains, "The basic feature of the new language is to look at economic processes in terms of the flow of incomes and expenditures, rather than in terms of relative prices or the stocks of money and other assets."[37] Thus a basic perspectival shift was necessary to follow the logic of Keynes's approach.

This shift in language signaled a transition to new ways of thinking about the economy as a whole—what later generations called macroeconomics. It wasn't as if macroeconomics didn't exist before Keynes. Indeed, monetary analysis was a systems-level approach, concerned with the whole over the part. But in the wake of Keynes's analysis, economists would begin talking less about money and more about budgetary aggregates—things like national income, national expenditure, total receipts. These were fundamental quantities of the federal budget, not the banking system. And they would tie these aggregates to broad metrics of economic performance, such as unemployment and growth in gross domestic product, making them objects of policy and research alike.

There was the further difficulty that *The General Theory* was in many ways an unfinished work, or what two contemporary observers call "a surface revolution with an undeveloped complex core."[38] Arresting, provocative, and politically relevant, *The General Theory* was nonetheless in desperate need of further explication and refinement.

These elements of the text made it irresistible to ambitious young economists. Hansen's soon to be famous Fiscal Policy Seminar filled with an eager crew of young Ph.D. candidates who were motivated to work through the implications of Keynes's theory. Among their number was the former Knight devotee Paul Samuelson, who quickly sloughed off the influence of his time at Chicago. Recalling the excitement of those years, Samuelson fell back on William Wordsworth, quoting the poet's reaction to the French Revolution: "Bliss was it in that dawn to be alive, / But to be young was very heaven."[39] It was Harvard's answer to Room Seven.

Meanwhile, Roosevelt had largely accepted Currie's explanation for the recession. No longer apologetic about deficits, or unsure that federal spending could help economic recovery, Roosevelt asked Congress for $3 billion worth of spending in April 1938. In a fireside chat radio address explaining his logic, Roosevelt announced that this spending was intended to raise national income, framing the new fiscal strategy as a "third round of ammunition" to join the established relief and credit programs. "It is up to us to create an economic upturn," the president declared.[40] This was the fiscal revolution in action. Economists using national income figures to determine specific levels of government spending—soon to be called aggregate demand management—was to become the prototypical New Deal approach and the signature policy idea of American liberalism.

Harvard economists played a significant role in legitimizing the fiscal revolution. More spending was not the only possible solution to the downturn. After all, deficit spending had been policy for five years; perhaps it had not worked, or perhaps deficits themselves were the problem, as traditional economic thought held. Indeed, the moniker "Roosevelt recession" was hung on the president by opponents who wanted to undermine the New Deal. Nor was the monetary explanation exhausted. In later years, Friedman and others would point to new reserve requirements for banks mandated by the Federal Reserve as a potential cause of the slump.[41]

In the moment, Hansen and Currie worked to establish a Keynesian interpretation of the Roosevelt recession—and the Great Depression—that supported increased federal spending. They held that a decline in federal spending had caused the recent recession, and only an increase in federal spending could end depression once and for all. In 1939 both testified before Congress in linked appearances that laid out the statistical and theoretical case for fiscal policy. "It appears doubtful that we can solve our problem of full employment by relying exclusively on private investment," Hansen told Congress. Instead, private investment "will have to be supplemented and, indeed, stimulated by public investment on a considerable scale." At first, Hansen defined public investment merely as durable projects. As his testimony wore on, he became more expansive, enthusing about "conservation and development of energy and natural resources . . . hospitalization, public health, pollution abatement, sewerage projects, public low-cost housing."[42] In some ways, he was echoing the Progressive movement of yesteryear. But Progressives had turned their energies equally on local and state governments, along with private efforts. Hansen offered a new vision not just of federal spending but of federal involvement in broad areas of American life.

Hansen tacked his own ideas about economic history onto his analysis of Keynes. He saw the United States "caught in the midst of powerful forces in the evolution of our economy which we but dimly understand." Previous economic growth had been driven by immigration, population growth, or breakthrough technologies like railroads. But now, Hansen worried, these motors of growth were spent, and government would have to replace them. In other venues, he would call this theory "secular stagnation," linking it to the closing of the frontier where he had been raised. The United States, he warned, faced a new economic era of "sick recoveries which die in their infancy and depressions which feed on themselves and leave a hard and seemingly immovable core of unemployment." To Congress, he stressed that "we are undergoing a fundamental change in the structure of our economic life."[43] Currie followed up with a memo to Roosevelt arguing that increased taxing and spending could move the United States to a stable, high-consumption economy. Together, these ideas became known as "Keynesianism"—in the United States at least, a current of thought both inspired by and at odds with Keynes himself.

This convergence between policy-makers and professors was significant. Keynes's ideas provided a theoretical rationale for continued New Deal spending. In turn, Keynesianism suggested a route to power for economists. Going far beyond the sort of technical work that Friedman had done, Keynes's ideas positioned economists as strategic policy experts, even arbiters of the government's role in society. By 1940, alumni of the Fiscal Policy Seminar found employment at the Commerce Department, the Federal Reserve, the National Resources Planning Board, and a newly created Fiscal Division within the Executive Office.[44]

In retrospect, *The General Theory* would set the intellectual agenda for Friedman's entire career, but when it appeared, he barely noticed. As Keynes's ideas were making landfall in American universities, Friedman offered a course through the Columbia University extension school that was a throwback to the early 1930s. Focused on individual demand curves, individual marginal utility, and individual economic decision-making, Friedman's course, Structure of Neo-classical Economics, made no mention of business cycles, national income, or current economic conditions. Drawing on the approach pioneered by Knight and Simons, it placed the question of "how free enterprise system solves economic problem" front and center.[45]

At the same time, Friedman did offer an implicit critique of the fiscal revolution, particularly Hansen's concept of secular stagnation. Picking up a theme from Knight, Friedman told his class, "Once wants are satisfied, new wants are going to be formed; the process of want formation is part of the basic drive."[46] There were two critical implications. First was that perpetual wanting would keep economies always in motion: "Impossibility of completely satisfying all wants. If the greatest want is the desire for new wants . . . the notion of satiety is silly." It was more than a philosophical point. Not only was it impossible for the economy to stagnate, but it would be impossible to design a government program that would adequately satisfy wants, which tended to continually increase.

Friedman drew out the second implication in another comment. "Attitude toward all policies will be affected by our ideas concerning wants," he argued.[47] In a letter to Arthur Burns, he was more direct. Reflecting on a road trip to visit Rose's family, he wrote, "The whole West, particularly California, and more particularly Southern California, gives you the feeling that the frontier is not yet gone and makes you feel like telling the stagnationites to come out and take a look."[48] Although he worked for the New Deal, Friedman was not a New Dealer. Nor was he a Keynesian. He thoroughly rejected the ideas that would most profoundly shape economics in the years ahead.

Instead, following in the footsteps of Henry Simons, he created an alternative approach to social welfare that relied not on the federal government but on the price system. An unpublished paper, "An Objective Standard of Living," triggered by conversations with the Swedish economist Gunnar Myrdal, attempted to address poverty without falling into dreaded planning or social control. Friedman met Myrdal, who would later become famous for *An American Dilemma*, his influential study of American race relations, in 1939 over a weekend gathering of economists in the New York countryside. Myrdal was a socialist who would go on to win the 1974 Nobel Prize in Economics (jointly awarded to F. A. Hayek, to their mutual dismay). This political difference led to lively discussions over a question both Friedman and Myrdal found pressing: how to guarantee a minimum income to the poorest Americans. Friedman then wrote up his ideas and shared them with Myrdal.

Drawing on his consumption research, Friedman proposed combining income data with measures of a nutritionally adequate diet, which could be measured with "objectivity or scientific value." Analysis could then determine at which income levels different families were able to acquire a nutritionally adequate diet, or "minimum standard of living." Friedman admitted there would be a "failure co-efficient," or families that did not purchase this diet despite adequate income, but this was the only solution he could fit with "a fundamental premise that in general the individual's choices are to be accepted."[49] Myrdal's assistant, Richard Sterner, was intrigued but not convinced. It was not really possible to define an "objective" standard of living, Sterner argued; even Friedman's assumption of individual choices "is, anyway, just a political one."[50] The correspondence then petered out. But that Myrdal and Friedman had met, however briefly, on the terrain of a guaranteed income was suggestive. Twenty-five years later, Friedman's minimum standard of living had become his famous negative income tax, lauded by both the left and the right. Today, it remains the taproot of discussions about universal basic income.[51]

A few years in Washington had not made Friedman into a New Dealer, nor had working for the NBER made him an institutionalist; rather, both experiences had helped him see how price theory could be applied outside the classroom. Theory held the key to cutting through endless facts. Likewise, the price system was a method for designing social interventions that were sustainable and economically sensible. Incubated within the challenges of applied government work and vociferous NBER debates over methodology, Friedman's emerging approach to economic problems combined neoclassical theory, attentiveness to institutions, and a philosophical commitment to what Alfred Marshall called "freedom of industry and enterprise."[52]

To outside observers, Friedman was not a price theorist, or a would-be public intellectual, but a cutting-edge statistician; at least this was how he appeared to Harold Groves, a University of Wisconsin economist who tendered Friedman his first long-awaited academic job offer in February 1940.[53]

On the one hand, this was a welcome development; on the other hand, neither Milton nor Rose really wanted to leave New York City. Although he was just an adjunct, Friedman truly loved teaching at Columbia. Rose had a good job as an assistant director at the federally funded NBER Corporate Bond Project, an early effort to evaluate private bond rating agencies that were increasingly important amid New Deal financial regulation. They lived well on their combined salaries. After work they came home to a spacious apartment in Manhattan Valley, a neighborhood adjacent to Central Park considered at the time an "upper class location," as Rose proudly remembered. Their building was relatively new, and their apartment large enough that Milton could take up a favored woodworking hobby in the living room, crafting a set of wooden furniture that would last for years. A maid cleaned and cooked dinner each day. The couple enjoyed an active social life, almost all of it with other economists. They lived just around the corner from Burns and his wife, Helen. Technically subordinate to Mitchell at the NBER, Burns was already establishing the formidable reputation that meant "where Arthur sits, there is the head of the table."[54] Friedman continued to idolize Burns, taking cues from him both personally and professionally. But even Burns did not have a university position, beyond his lecturing gig at Rutgers.

In part, this reflected endemic anti-Semitism in academia. The University of Chicago was unusual in that it boasted four economics faculty of Jewish descent and also enrolled a considerable number of Jewish students—up to a third of its undergraduates, by some estimates. Far more common were formal or informal quotas that limited the number of Jewish students on campus, alongside widespread discrimination in hiring. It was no coincidence that none of Friedman's friends who had received teaching positions were Jewish. Even after a spectacular graduate career at Harvard, Samuelson ended up at upstart MIT, a decidedly mediocre placement.[55] Against this backdrop, it made sense for Friedman to seriously consider the offer in Wisconsin, despite his attachment to New York.

Like the NBER, the University of Wisconsin was an institutionalist redoubt that had fallen upon hard times. Many New Deal–era innovations, from unemployment insurance to workers' compensation, had been designed and field-tested in Wisconsin by students of John R. Commons, the department's dominant force. Over time, Commons's rule had crowded out other approaches, and after his retirement the department went into a steep decline.[56] The man who wanted to hire Friedman, Harold Groves, had been at Wisconsin long enough to remember its glory days. He planned a comeback driven by statistics, a former area of strength that was now in abeyance. With his combination of government survey experience and published theoretical work, Friedman looked like the perfect candidate to restore Wisconsin's lost luster.

After some hesitation, Friedman agreed to a one-year appointment as a visiting professor, with the expectation that it would lead to something more permanent. He would teach business cycles and economic theory. Curiously, the department did not want him to teach either statistics or mathematical economics, the areas Groves had emphasized at first.

Arriving in Madison after a long cross-country road trip in the fall of 1940, Milton and Rose found trouble lying in wait. The department, as Groves had intimated, was divided into two distinct camps, and the Friedmans had already been arrayed on one side. Groves and his wife took the newcomers under their wing, and Selig Perlman, the only other Jewish man on the economics faculty, was welcoming. But as Friedman summarized when the year was over, "many members of the department made practically no attempts to become acquainted either with me personally or with the character of my work." Adding to the "tension and strain" was a palpable feeling of anti-Semitism.[57] Still home to generations of German immigrants and their descendants, Wisconsin was openly isolationist and even pro-German, whereas Friedman made no secret of his desire for intervening in the war in Europe. "Around here, I am a real warmonger," he reported to Arthur Burns.[58] Feeling distinctly out of step with his colleagues, Friedman took a page from Henry Simons's playbook and began fraternizing with the graduate students.

Rose's adjustment was no easier. "New Faculty Wives Added to U. Social Circle," trumpeted a headline in *The Capital Times*, which splashed Rose's picture on the front page of the society section shortly after their arrival.[59] Without a job for the first time in years, Rose was less than thrilled with the new domestic role she was expected to play. Upon moving into their new home on the outskirts of Madison, a neighbor "immediately came over and invited Rose to attend their weekly sewing circle!" Milton wrote to Burns. "As a concession to peace and harmony, Rose went," he continued, "and came home thoroughly imbued with the responsibilities of a housewife and with a fresh appreciation of the advantages of New York." Soon enough Rose discovered she was pregnant, making the whole arrangement more tolerable. But on balance, as Milton summarized, "our reactions to Wisconsin are very mixed."[60]

It turned out the feeling was mutual. After a bumpy first semester—with Rose enduring a difficult pregnancy and Milton receiving more contentious NBER communiqués about his unfinished dissertation—Friedman turned to administrata, writing up a memo on statistics at Wisconsin.

Produced as a favor for Groves, the memo briskly surveyed the "almost revolutionary" advances in the field. Any institution that moved quickly to teach these new methods would be richly rewarded, Friedman predicted, for business would soon be using statistics extensively. Even those teaching basic classes should know the latest methods. For color, he threw in a favorite saying of Harold Hotelling: "The task of leading the blind must not be turned over to the blind." His closing lines were equally blunt: "A student cannot secure training at the University of Wisconsin sufficient to qualify him to teach advanced statistics or to do independent work in the field of statistical methods. Even if he takes all the work offered he will be but indifferently qualified to do research involving the application of modern statistics."[61] For the most part, Friedman had made a decent impression as a smart and able colleague. But the memo, which circulated widely among the faculty, quickly overshadowed everything else.

Like a spark to tinder, the memo set aflame years of buried resentments, insecurities, and turf battles. The two professors who regularly taught statistics went to the barricades. Unlike Friedman, they had plenty of friends within the economics department and the university community; adding to the problem was Friedman's salary, which topped that of any other assistant professor.

By March, when the budget committee met to consider the question of his permanent appointment, no economists save Groves and Perlman were willing to support the motion. Surveying the situation, the dean detected something unsavory. After a meeting with one of Friedman's detractors, he declared, "This is not the Third Reich!"[62] He would hire Friedman anyway, the department be damned. Yet Friedman's enemies were not so easily cowed.

"Fireworks in U.W. Department as Instructor May Get $3500 Prof's Job," declared *The Capital Times* in a front-page article. Friedman went unnamed at first, but within days his anonymity was gone, and his antagonists had refined their narrative: "Opponents to Friedman's appointment to the assistant professorship cited his youth and lack of outstanding qualifications," wrote *The Daily Cardinal*.[63] The graduate students mounted a picket line in his defense, but Friedman's allies were finally ready to let him bow out. The university president even came up with an exit strategy. Friedman should write him citing his desire to assist in the "national emergency"; the president would respond with a letter lauding his outstanding performance at Wisconsin, setting the record straight.[64]

Why had Friedman let events reach this point? Some of it was loyalty to his supporters, who urged him to stay in the fight. Some of it was ego, as Friedman later admitted: "I was flattered that [the dean] should want to have me appointed to a tenured position."[65] And there was more than a little arrogance. "The people in the department are almost uniformly bad," he told Burns upon arrival, an opinion his colleagues no doubt detected.[66] And Chicago, too, had shaped his approach to the department. He had fallen almost immediately into a graduate student clique that was both fiercely loyal and powerless to defend him, and he had treated his colleagues with the same lack of respect he showed his doctoral adviser.

In later years, Friedman implied anti-Semitism had been his downfall. Doubtless this was an element. But Friedman's blind spots were considerable. It was not simply that he was lobbing grenades. It was that he did so unaware. He had given no thought to how his brash and snarky memo might be interpreted by others. Dismissive and negative, his analysis focused on the failings of his colleagues rather than touting what he had to offer. Nor had he considered the precariousness of his status. Friedman wasn't simply tripped up by his colleagues' jealousy and insecurity. He had profoundly misread the human dynamics of the situation.

It was in the end a critical learning experience. "The Wisconsin affair" was both the first of the factional fights into which Friedman would plunge, and the last he would lose. But for now, on top of rejection was humiliation, followed by anxiety about what might happen next.

Friedman dumped it all on Burns in a long, tortured letter. He was in some ways relieved. "Had it happened two months ago I would have regarded it as a very satisfactory termination of the affair," he told Burns. But coming near the end of the academic year, the whole thing looked fishy, and he had to quickly make plans. With Rose's pregnancy nearing term, he needed a good and stable job.[67]

One option was government work. Groves was headed to the Treasury Department for a year and wanted to bring Friedman along. Going to Washington "would be excellent face-saving; second, it would mean working on immediate problems of national defense and feeling as I do about our role in the war that is psychologically attractive," Friedman mused. True, he would rather be in New York. But returning so unexpectedly might lead "people at Columbia, Chicago, Washington and other universities" to conclude he had failed as a professor and was unsuited for academia. Working for the war effort did not have the same stigma, particularly with the cover story from Wisconsin's president, which had now been repeated in the newspapers.

In a sign of how much he valued teaching, Friedman ranked the possibility of resuming his Columbia extension course among the most attractive aspects of New York. Exhausted and overwhelmed, Friedman confessed: "I don't feel able at the moment to decide between the two alternatives and I very badly need your advice."[68] How important was it to salvage his reputation? Would the NBER welcome him back? What should he do next?

Eventually, Milton and Rose headed to Vermont, where the Burnses had a summer home near the tiny village of Ely. The area was popular with New York economists due to the proximity of the Dartmouth College library, just over the state border in Hanover, New Hampshire. Back in the familiar mix of Columbia professors, NBER colleagues, and old friends, Friedman continued to weigh his options. Ultimately he took a position at the Treasury Department, not with Groves but in connection with a separate tax study. Aaron Director was once again back at the Treasury Department and had just bought a rambling farmhouse in Maryland with plenty of room for Rose, Milton, and the baby. After delivering in New York City, the new family would head back to Washington, D.C.

Her labor began ordinarily enough, but the infant was breech, and Rose was petite. As the ordeal stretched on, Rose was all alone. It was the era when fathers were left to pace the hospital hallways until the doctor emerged with joyful news. But then Milton learned that behind those closed doors lay unbearable tragedy: their son had died.[69] Milton and Rose still had each other. But they had lost nearly everything else.

5

QUESTIONING KEYNES

Inflation is essentially a monetary phenomenon.

—Aaron Director, 1941

Almost worse than losing the baby was the howling loneliness that followed. Rose arrived at Aaron Director's remote Maryland farmhouse, once imagined as the bucolic playground of her firstborn, and dissolved into tears. There was a hasty change of plans; a new apartment was rented in bustling Dupont Circle, and Rose's friends pulled her quickly into their embrace. The stillbirth sent Rose briefly back into the working world, as she struggled to distract herself by assisting Dorothy Brady at the Bureau of Home Economics.

This unexpected move drew Rose and Milton into the lively women's world of consumption economics. The study of consumption grew out of household economics, the rare domain where being female was an asset rather than a liability, given women's presumed expertise in the domestic realm. With national income a defining concept for policy-makers, the flip sides of income—consumption and savings—were suddenly hot topics. But the transition was recent enough that researchers like Dorothy had not yet been edged out by male rivals. Despite her narrow job title—she was officially a "home economics specialist" in the USDA's Bureau of Human Nutrition and Home Economics—her research was anything but a backwater.[1]

More than a simple research project on savings and income, Rose's collaboration with Dorothy addressed a question foundational to the Keynesian revolution in economics. John Maynard Keynes argued there was a sort of "psychological law" that people would "increase their consumption as their income increases, but not by as much as the increase in their income."[2] This relationship between income and consumption, quickly dubbed "the consumption function" in the new mathematical language economists began to use for parsing Keynes, was assumed to be stable and predictable.[3]

What mattered was not just the equation but the assumptions that came with it. According to Keynes, when people earned more money, they didn't automatically spend it. Indeed, the richer they got, the greater the proportion of income they socked into savings. This was the great problem of hoarding, as Keynes saw it. It was also the problem of the Great Depression. Once investors were spooked, nothing could convince them to part with their pile. The economy would stall at equilibrium below full employment.

Alvin Hansen had built out his theory of secular stagnation from there. He argued that in mature economies, such as the United States in the 1930s, there weren't sufficient investment opportunities. The wealthy merely sat on their money. Therefore, instead of letting high earners accumulate useless savings, income should be taxed away and invested by the government. These ideas were also an implicit critique of inequality. Prior to Keynes, the savings of the rich could be seen as a necessary evil, since they funded new ventures and opportunities. But if savings no longer performed that function, they should be directly or indirectly redistributed. Lauchlin Currie made this point directly to President Roosevelt, calling for "higher-consumption and lower-saving," with programs to raise "the buying power of the poor."[4] People who needed money would spend it right away, boosting economic activity.

But what if it wasn't so simple? What if when people got richer, they didn't save more? Fresh data from the Study of Consumer Purchases and other nationwide budget studies painted a complicated picture. Farm families had different savings patterns than urban families; so too did residents of cities and villages. Adding to the problem was another blockbuster study by Simon Kuznets. He found that savings and consumption ratios were remarkably consistent over time, even as incomes rose. Contra Keynes, families that earned more continued to spend the same proportion of their income.

All this had immediate policy relevance. If the consumption function was unstable or unknowable, the basic logic of New Deal spending could also be questioned. If Keynes had been so confident about an economic relationship that wasn't holding up to empirical study—then what of his other ideas? The so-called Kuznets paradox was the first shadow of doubt falling across the emergent paradigm.[5] So while Dorothy and Rose were taking up a task Milton had abandoned several years back—making sense of the mounds of data generated by the Study of Consumer Purchases—they were doing so within a newly charged intellectual and political atmosphere.

Not prone to idle chitchat yet exquisitely aware of Rose's suffering, Dorothy redirected her attention to the joys of intellectual discovery. Dorothy's "excitement about a new idea and her exhilaration when it worked out were infectious," remembered a colleague from later years.[6] Both of them Westerners who had studied at Reed College, Dorothy and Rose fell into an easy partnership. Another woman occasionally orbited through the project, the Iowa State College professor Margaret Reid, who had earned her Ph.D. at Chicago under Hazel Kyrk.

Rose and Dorothy's research culminated in "Savings and the Income Distribution," a nineteen-page paper that marked a significant shift away from the social and cultural analyses characteristic of earlier consumption research. Across twenty-four community categories, ranging from New England Villages to Omaha, they found one key pattern: "Variations in the pattern of consumption and savings among groups of families at given income levels may be explained to a considerable degree by differences in the level and distribution of income."[7] What mattered to savings and spending, the authors explained, was not the *absolute* income a family received, but its *relative* income. For example, two families with an annual income of $3,000 could not be assumed to spend the same amount. However, two families that were both in the twentieth percentile of income, vis-à-vis their neighbors, were likely to spend similar proportions of their income. A quick prediction of spending based on income alone was not possible.

It wasn't even enough to know a family's relative income; the basic features of the community were important, too. In towns with fewer rich families, savings rates for all families were higher. The denser the population, the lower the savings, across all groups. Was it norms, traditions, or some other force that accounted for these regularities? The paper closed with an unobjectionable call for more data and analysis.

However modest the paper's overt claims, Dorothy and Rose had in fact challenged the emerging Keynesian synthesis, as the Harvard economist James Tobin understood. He recognized that their paper, along with the work of his colleague James Duesenberry, established a new "'relative income' hypothesis" that challenged the Keynesian "'absolute income' hypothesis." This new hypothesis was appealing, Tobin wrote, in light of Kuznets's findings: "It explains the relative constancy over the last 70 years of the percentage of national income saved. This invariance cannot be explained on the simple Keynesian theory that the saving ratio is a unique function of absolute real income."[8] In turn, the relative income hypothesis suggested that a quick and easy prediction of national income from family income was impossible. It was a strike against the edifice of policy and politics coming to rest upon Keynesian concepts of savings and consumption.

Years later, Friedman spelled out the ultimate implications. Dorothy and Rose's paper fed into a much larger body of research, the permanent income hypothesis, that "removes completely one of the pillars of the 'secular stagnation' thesis." It also had implications for the Keynesian proposition that there was "no automatic force in a monetary economy to assure the existence of a full-employment equilibrium."[9] On the surface, Dorothy and Rose had published a basic research report. Considered in the bigger picture, their conclusions spoke to the politically charged question of consumption.

Was the paper deliberately framed as an attack upon Keynes?[10] Both women were dedicated empiricists, and the problem in the data was compelling. At the same time, the solution they came up with dovetailed nicely with each woman's intellectual inclinations. The paper's emphasis on relative income reflected the traditional approach of consumption research that Dorothy knew well. Dorothy's long tenure in reformist D.C. agencies suggests that like most consumption economists, she was probably sympathetic to New Deal social spending. By contrast, although Rose has left little trace of her thinking in this period, she was among the most loyal of Frank Knight's students. His teachings would have primed her to be skeptical of both the New Deal and the Keynesian concepts that were newly popular among economists.

How much of the paper was Dorothy, how much was Rose—and how much was Milton? As one historian explains, what distinguished the paper was its "first attempt to provide a unifying hypothesis" to explain a widely noted anomaly.[11] This is what Rose's Chicago training would have emphasized: finding a general principle or relationship within the specific data, and moving quickly to the bigger picture of policy or procedure. Writing on her own, Dorothy was an able technician but not a groundbreaking scholar. Partnering with Rose, she made the most intellectually significant contribution of her career.[12] It is impossible to detect what role Milton played, although most certainly all three discussed the research project. At the very least, he had forged a durable connection to the female world of household economics and budget studies, a universe aspiring economics professors usually ignored. Eventually, these connections would become a secret weapon of sorts.

While Rose was probing the Keynesian consumption function, Milton was spending time before Congress as a representative of the Roosevelt administration. He was hired into the Division of Tax Research in the Treasury Department, the august bureaucracy charged with managing the nation's finances. Treasury did not make policy, exactly—Congress and the White House proposed legislation. But the Treasury Department collected taxes, paid the nation's bills, and managed both debt and currency. In the aftermath of the Great Depression, it had usurped responsibilities first delegated to the Federal Reserve System. Its secretary, a cabinet-level position, was appointed by the president. Accordingly, it had a voice in all major tax legislation, and an informal veto of sorts on policy. It mattered if the Treasury Department concluded that a plan was infeasible, impractical, or incompatible with existing practices. Yet across the New Deal, Treasury's primacy in economic matters had been challenged by the mushrooming bureaucracies set up to address the Depression. Although it was well stocked with economists, Treasury was a holdout against the Keynesian trend in Washington.

When Friedman joined, the department was dominated by Secretary Henry Morgenthau Jr., an idiosyncratic and powerful man with close ties to Roosevelt. A former gentleman farmer and college dropout, Morgenthau belonged to New York's wealthy German Jewish community. His father had served as the ambassador to the Ottoman Empire under Woodrow Wilson. A fiscal conservative, Morgenthau was among the key advisers who convinced the president to balance the budget in 1937. But three months after the Friedmans arrived in D.C., Japan attacked Pearl Harbor. Within days, the United States was at war with both Japan and its ally Nazi Germany.

With the outbreak of war, Morgenthau was now doing everything he could to increase deficit spending, including an energetic propaganda drive to sell war bonds. Like Friedman, he was motivated by a powerful urge to defeat Hitler. Fighting a war in Europe and Asia transformed the U.S. government. Over the course of World War II, total federal revenue would expand from $6.5 billion to $45 billion by 1944, with federal debt increasing from $50 billion to $260 billion.[13] Federal spending would eventually encompass nearly 40 percent of all economic activity in the country.

Despite this rapid expansion of government, the Treasury Department had two primary mandates that Friedman could wholeheartedly support: paying for the war and preventing inflation. Thus as he had anticipated to Burns, every tedious bureaucratic chore was in some sense a symbolic blow against the Nazis.[14]

For now, the unglamorous task at hand was getting a tax bill

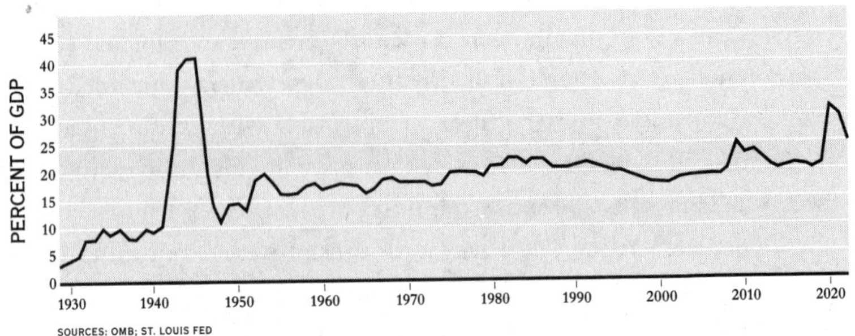

World War II led to a significant expansion in federal spending, and also in the number of Americans who paid taxes.

through Congress. Maneuvering against Keynesian adversaries in the Office of Price Administration (OPA), the Office of the Budget, the Federal Reserve, and a newly created Office of Economic Stabilization, Morgenthau was determined to stave off proposals for compulsory savings. Under this policy, popularized by Keynes's 1940 book *How to Pay for the War*, the government would increase its tax collections but hold a significant portion as savings, to be returned after the war.[15] Morgenthau favored instead voluntary bond drives, which would help inculcate patriotic spirit. Further, proposals for compulsory savings came with a regressive sales tax and confiscatory profits taxes. Morgenthau was eager to tax, but he favored a middle road: an expanded income tax on all but the poorest Americans, while leaving the profit motive intact.

At first, Friedman was but a foot soldier in this larger policy war, churning out memo after memo supporting the Treasury's positions. "The tax bill has kept us hopping night and day for a long time," Friedman reported to Burns, "and every time we get a little breather from that, the Sec'y seems to get excited and want his staff to do something super-duper rush."[16] Friedman defended Treasury taxation estimates against OPA criticisms, a battle that spilled into dueling papers presented at the Econometric Society's annual meeting.[17] Then came memos that pushed back against compulsory saving, showing it was less satisfactory than income taxation.[18]

Soon Morgenthau discovered that Friedman was a useful ally in Congress, where tightfisted senators resisted every new tax. Pearl Harbor had pushed the United States into war, but paying for it would not come easy. Morgenthau sent the glib and always confident Friedman to Congress several times representing the Treasury's view. Friedman critiqued the sales tax for "bearing most heavily on the persons who can least afford to pay." The income tax, he told Congress, was better because it "permits the cost of the war to be distributed explicitly in a socially desirable manner."[19] Here Friedman was not merely ventriloquizing Morgenthau's New Deal belief that taxation should advance equity. "In wartime, values change," he wrote in the *American Economic Review*, arguing that winning the war justified taxation that might limit "satisfaction of wants." Friedman's persuasive and polished appearances before Congress led to a new role: serving as Morgenthau's support man at important meetings. By Morgenthau's side he met Washington bigwigs, including Marriner Eccles, chair of the Federal Reserve, and Senator Robert Taft.

This up-close view of the secretary did not impress. "I repeatedly was amazed that anyone with such limitations could occupy so important a position," Friedman remembered in his memoir. Like his adviser Henry Schultz, the secretary seemed slow. Morgenthau spoke in platitudes and pressed his staff to use simple language—because he himself could not grasp the details, Friedman suspected. What he missed entirely was Morgenthau's skill—even strategic genius—on the larger battlefield of politics. A few years hence, it would be Morgenthau who spearheaded the international Bretton Woods Conference and then guided the subsequent agreements through Congress, ensuring the creation of a new international monetary system.[20]

In the short run, Morgenthau was focused on taxes—both to pay for the war and to prevent inflation. The run-up to war, and then its formal declaration, transformed the American economy. Long-dormant factories came back on line as government orders for armaments and matériel poured in. The draft slurped off a significant percentage of the unemployed, with the remaining labor force finding plentiful jobs. By 1943, unemployment had dwindled to less than 2 percent.[21] After suffering nearly a decade of punishing deflation, suddenly Washington was worried about inflation. Surging prices might dent the war effort and place the necessities of life outside the reach of the American consumer.

To the dismay of Friedman and his allies, the favored Washington solution was price controls, enforced through the newly created Office of Price Administration. In a memo written during the initial price controls debate, Aaron Director laid out the problems. Price controls would result in black markets, increase production costs, and lead to changes of grade and quality as "the vehicle for hidden price increases." Director preferred to let prices adjust freely as the economy transitioned toward war and producers sought the profits government sales would bring.[22] Ultimately, price controls would be ineffective, Director argued, because they struck at the symptom, not the cause.

"Inflation is essentially a monetary phenomenon," Director continued. With economic output constrained by the need for war matériel, yet government spending surging, too many dollars would be chasing too few goods, making for a general rise in prices. "Wartime demands of government are inflationary precisely because governments spend money which is additional to the expenditures of their citizens," Director wrote, but "the advocates of the price ceiling appear to be unaware of this underlying characteristic of inflationary movements." Following the quantity theory, Director preferred to check monetary expansion at the source.[23]

What kind of monetary policy would stop inflation? In a related article—one of the few he would publish in his lifetime—Director endorsed "a given criterion, such as a stable price level or fixed quantity of money."[24] Director did not appear interested in a return to the gold standard, the old method of preventing inflation. Rather, his memo recommended "some finance agency to formulate a definite policy for achieving price stability through monetary means."[25] This agency might tolerate price controls on selected war matériel, but it would focus on constraining private bank credit, controlling the money supply, and integrating its actions with tax policy.

Was this agency the Federal Reserve? Director didn't spell out his thinking, but he knew the Federal Reserve was powerless in its current configuration. New Deal banking reforms—the same ones that shored up the banking system more generally—had shifted significant responsibility for monetary policy to the Treasury Department, placing the Fed "in the backseat," as one historian characterizes this time. The pressure of war had further reduced the Fed's independence; even the Fed chairman considered himself a mere administrator of Treasury policy. Director's reference to a "finance agency" suggests he supported a proposal of Lloyd Mints, his former teacher in Chicago—creating a centralized "Monetary Agency" that would merge the decision-making powers of the Fed and the Treasury. For the moment, however, Director admitted "there seems to be little interest in methods of preventing monetary expansion in the first place." Even amid the ferment of wartime Washington, he apparently realized that a new administrative solution would not emerge anytime soon.[26]

Instead, he boosted the major policy alternative to price controls: wartime taxation, which he called "a step in the right direction."[27] In a related article, Director elaborated on taxation as a critical mechanism. He presented higher wartime taxation as essentially a form of monetary policy. It would lead to a "contraction of monetary demand by individuals whose income is curtailed," meaning they could not bid up prices. By contrast, the government would have new purchasing power. As prices in war industries remained steady or even increased, they would attract workers and investment, "the type of transfer which goes on, though on a smaller scale, as there is a shift in demand from one industry to another." Taxation had further advantages, according to Director. It would prevent excessive debt, which itself was inflationary. Unlike borrowing, wartime tax rates were short-term, and could be repealed or lowered when the war was over. Most important of all, taxation would prevent "authoritarian controls that might otherwise be imposed," he concluded.[28]

Friedman embraced Director's approach as his own. Indeed,

Director's 1941 explanation of inflation as a monetary phenomenon and his advocacy of "a given criterion," or policy rule, anticipated core ideas of Friedman's later monetarism. Friedman shared Director's opposition to price controls, and his belief that taxation offered a better alternative. In a letter to Burns, Friedman singled out Director's memo. "The only half-way decent analysis I have seen," Friedman told Burns, "was in a memorandum by a fellow in another division of the Treasury that I saw only because he was a personal friend of mine, and that I am fairly sure will never get outside his division." Otherwise, the "extremely important" work of analyzing the economics of price control was simply not being done. Friedman hoped that Burns, a well-placed economist working outside D.C., would engage in some "propagandizing" to help both the public and the profession grasp what was at stake in the choice between controls or "letting the price system do the job."[29] For now, the only ally he could find was his brother-in-law, toiling away in obscurity within the steadily growing administrative state.

Like Director, Friedman reconciled himself to using taxation to prevent inflation. If the best option—monetary means—was impractical at present, then taxes were immeasurably better than price controls. Unfortunately price controls were already in place. But if the Treasury Department could raise taxes, price controls could be limited.

The Treasury now began working on a new innovation, withholding taxes through payroll deductions. As it stood, taxpayers submitted income taxes on a quarterly basis. This was feasible when income taxes were limited to a small population of high earners and rates were relatively low. But to finance the war, the tax base would have to be expanded considerably, and rates would go up. Collecting taxes at source—directly from the employer, rather than the employee—was more efficient. It was also more politically advantageous, because the tax bite was less obvious. Finally, Treasury Department economists believed that withholding would more effectively fight inflation, removing funds before they circulated in the economy, pushing up prices.

Congress was skeptical. Withholding seemed like "a box of monkeys," as one member put it. How would it work, logistically? Could corporations pull it off? Would workers agree? Friedman was tasked with answering these questions. He visited Detroit to quiz the auto companies, studied withholding systems in Great Britain and Canada, and interviewed foreign experts. After this research, he authored several memos explaining how withholding could work in the United States.[30]

Ultimately, Congress approved a revenue bill that expanded the tax base and raised rates as the Treasury wanted—but it raised far less revenue than had been requested. Withholding, which remained controversial, would not pass until Friedman had left the department. In the final analysis, Friedman's work for the Treasury helped expand the taxpayer base more than tenfold, from a starting point of four million taxpayers in 1939 to an eventual forty-three million by the end of the war. As two experts summarized, the income tax had "changed its morning coat for overalls."[31] It was no longer a policy aimed at the rich, but one that touched many American workers.

Observing Friedman's energetic advocacy for taxation, historians have erroneously concluded that the 1940s represented a Keynesian phase in Friedman's life.[32] In part, this is because Keynes, and the economists who followed his analysis, regarded taxing and spending as the primary levers of economic policy. And in part, this misapprehension comes from Friedman himself. Reviewing his congressional testimony and publications derived from his Treasury work, Friedman confessed in his memoir, "I had completely forgotten how thoroughly Keynesian I then was!" He seems to have been most struck by the absence of monetary forces in his analysis of inflation. In his mind, not talking about money was equivalent to being a Keynesian. But there is almost no sense in which Friedman's views during this time can be meaningfully understood as Keynesian.[33]

First, Friedman's advocacy of taxation came as a federal employee of the Treasury Department, which set tax policy, and not as an independent intellectual. Even had he been expressing personal opinions, it is still clear that he judged taxation within the context of available policy options. Like Director, he understood that the realistic alternative to wartime taxation was not an unfettered free enterprise system paired with wise monetary management, but rather continuous monitoring of consumer and industry prices by a newly empowered government bureaucracy. As Friedman put it to Burns, while they waited for the tax bill to pass, "In the meantime we shall have price control and rationing and price rises." Taxation represented a less intrusive and more intrinsically conservative approach.[34]

From the perspective of his later economic views, it *is* striking that Friedman spoke openly of taxation as a method to control inflation. After all, he would become famous by arguing that inflation was always and everywhere a monetary phenomenon, and this concept of "monetarism" became a set piece opposing tax-based Keynesianism. But Friedman's private correspondence shows him embracing Director's monetary analysis of inflation.

Moreover, in his published work, Friedman made clear that his views on inflation in the 1940s were explicitly about wartime inflation. "In a war economy" are the very first words in *Taxing to Prevent Inflation*, the book he later coauthored, which was based on his wartime analysis. And as he argued while disputing an OPA economist, wartime policies had little general applicability: "The apparent usefulness of the resulting estimates for public policy during wartime have led many to suppose that a new technique has been developed for guiding public policy in peacetime . . . this is an illusion."[35] For Friedman, the years of World War II were no ordinary time.

Lumping Friedman with the Keynesians ignores the intellectual tradition from which he did draw guidance and inspiration—Chicago monetary economics.[36] As they had in the 1930s, Chicago professors continued to design policy solutions drawing upon the quantity theory of money. The work of Director and Mints shows it was entirely possible, within the administrative reality of the 1940s, to support taxation as a mechanism of monetary stability without accepting the Keynesian economic analysis. Contemporary economists well understood this. "It is as if Professor Mints had hibernated right through the Keynesian revolution," Abba Lerner wrote in response to a 1946 article by Mints—one that proposed taxation along with a new finance agency to direct monetary policy. To Lerner, who had imbibed Keynes's ideas directly from the source during a stint in Cambridge, the difference between Chicago and Keynes was obvious.[37]

Finally, there is ample historical evidence demonstrating that Friedman did not consider himself a Keynesian during the 1940s—and was not considered so by others. Even as he used fiscal tools to make wartime policy, in several short articles he explicitly set himself apart from Keynes's American followers. In a book review, he attacked "the Keynesian saving-investment theory which has had such vogue in recent years" as "unbelievably simple. Yet simply unbelievable." Another review dismissed the theory of monopolistic competition (an idea often used to justify the fiscal revolution) and defended Alfred Marshall and the "classical" economists.[38]

Likewise, Friedman had few—if any—associations with the Keynesians in Washington. By the early 1940s Keynesian economics had coalesced into a school of thought, a social identity, and a professional network, clustered around Alvin Hansen and Lauchlin Currie.[39] This identifiable group of economists accepted Keynes's analysis of the Great Depression, believed government spending was necessary to support full employment, and viewed his *General Theory of Employment, Interest, and Money* as a watershed moment in the history of economics. In the United States, acceptance of Hansen's secular stagnation thesis was another important marker. American Keynesians did not agree with the master on everything; for example, they favored price controls, which Keynes opposed. Nonetheless they were a distinct group, bound by their collective commitment to the new economic approach inspired by Keynes. Currie and Hansen were the great patrons, working to place simpatico young economists like John Kenneth Galbraith in the Office of Price Administration and Paul Samuelson at the National Resources Planning Board. Friedman was never part of this group. Indeed, these were the economists whose proposals he fought against while at Treasury. And his referent points remained Henry Simons and Director.

Like Director and Mints, Simons likewise embraced taxation without accepting the Keynesian analysis. In the years since his first book, *A Positive Program for Laissez Faire*, Simons had elevated taxation as the best way to blend his egalitarian sympathies and deep reverence for the price system. "Taxation is the proper means for mitigating inequality," Simons announced at the start of his second book, *Personal Income Taxation*, which launched him on another policy crusade.[40] Like Morgenthau, Simons believed income taxes were the best way to pay for the war, being both equitable and economically sound. Simons eagerly followed Friedman's work at Treasury. In a letter to Albert Hart, another Chicago grad working on tax policy, Simons noted that Friedman was "cooking up a tax scheme . . . which is exactly what you and I would pray for." After a two-week visit to D.C., during which he lodged with Director, Simons wrote again to Hart. "Couldn't you use Milton at your Hearings show, getting some congressmen to request his appearing as Treasury representative?" Simons asked.[41]

There is additional evidence—which previous historians have ignored—that further demonstrates the gap between Friedman, Keynes, and the New Deal: his teaching at Wisconsin during the 1940–1941 academic year. In his Wisconsin classes, Friedman revealed suspicions of government spending even more profound than his Chicago mentors'.[42] Whereas Knight, Viner, and Simons had thought spending on public works would have negligible economic effects—at least as compared to the problem of unemployment—Friedman told his class on business cycles that "public works had adverse effects on price structure . . . Hence no private investment. Also other business practices of the New Deal: NRA, SEC." He now even doubted the severity of the Great Depression, telling the class that consumption had remained steady throughout the 1930s (most likely a conclusion he reached from his work on the Study of Consumer Purchases).[43]

Friedman also concentrated fire on the emergent economic theory that powered the fiscal revolution. In his class, he turned to the 1937 downturn that had been so arresting for economists. Was it really true that the recovery had reversed direction because of a contraction in government spending? The statistics regarding this period were uncertain, he stated. "But we could argue that government intervention made for lack of recovery." Here Friedman foreshadowed a conclusion he would substantiate later in his career—that a 1937 change in reserve requirements had served to contract the money supply and trigger recession anew. It was a monetary, rather than a fiscal, interpretation of the Roosevelt recession.[44]

Friedman then began poking holes in the statistics Currie and Hansen touted. One could choose other series, besides government spending, and show them to have triggered recovery; and in any case, the important thing seemed to be the government's announcement that it would spend, not the actual spending; and finally one must look at all government activities, not a select few. The result was clear: "government spending argument not convincing."[45]

He closed the class with a sentiment that neatly encapsulated his philosophy of government: "Deficit spending is of course inevitable—for relief. And keep it as low as relief requirements make possible." It was a conclusion that represented the essence of Chicago teaching, carried forward across nearly ten years of the Depression with little modification. In an emergency, relief spending had its place. But economists should never assume that government spending was critical to the operation of a free market economy.[46]

As it turned out, getting a tax bill through Congress was easier than getting a neoclassical dissertation through the NBER. It was a quirk of Columbia's doctoral program that dissertations had to be published. At first, going through the NBER seemed a great advantage; since the bureau had commissioned Kuznets's study, there would be little additional cost.[47] But as a result, Friedman had to please not a small committee of scholars he knew well, but the larger NBER advisory board, laden with institutional economists. Even as wartime Washington vaulted Friedman far above his station, his doctorate remained out of reach. Years after the first internal attack, and countless revisions later, he still had not secured the necessary approval to publish.

Once again, Friedman brought his troubles to Burns, who made a helpful suggestion: bring in the big gun. Invoking Burns's authority, Kuznets wrote to Mitchell, asking him to remind the directors that he had already approved the manuscript for publication. Even Mitchell's sponsorship did not quell the opposition. Back came the manuscript for another round of revision.[48]

By then, Milton and Rose were on their way to New York City with a new baby in tow. Earlier in 1943, he had accepted a position as an associate director of the Statistical Research Group (SRG), one of the myriad quasi-academic projects that popped up in support of the war effort. Housed at Columbia University, the SRG brought together a top-flight group of statisticians to assist military decision-makers, including Friedman's former teacher Harold Hotelling and close friend George Stigler, and was presided over by yet another Chicago friend, Allen Wallis. Friedman delayed the job a few months so that Rose could give birth before they moved.

Their second pregnancy was as blessed as the first was cursed. Rose wound down her work with Dorothy Brady in favor of rest and relaxation. Taking no chances, they arranged for a cesarean delivery while still settled in D.C. After the peaceful arrival of daughter Janet, Milton set off to find an apartment for his new family, eventually choosing one across from Central Park.

The move ended the relatively egalitarian marriage the Friedmans had established. Beyond Janet, an infant with unending demands to fill the day, Milton and Rose could no longer talk about work. SRG projects were classified and security was high; Milton had to clear his desk and lock his papers up before leaving each day, and could have no dinnertime conversations with Rose about his latest intriguing idea. Instead, Rose tasked him with keeping the basic statistics of baby formula consumed and weight gained. Economics was never completely absent, given their social circle, now full of new mothers and absentee economist fathers. But if there was no specific decision point, it was also clear that Rose would pursue her dissertation no further. Before long she was pregnant again. By the end of the war she and Milton would also be the parents of a second child, David.

In the SRG, Milton found the wartime esprit de corps he had been seeking, minus the political infighting and stifling bureaucracy. Not counting the fleets of assistants and young women "computers," the group of principals was small, eighteen overall but typically around ten in residence at any one time, all recruited by the "old-boy network pure and unabashed," as Wallis later remembered. Shared intellectual interests, deep commitment to the war effort, and the feeling that their work truly mattered made the SRG an experience most remembered with pleasure. "I had not seen such concentrated cooperation before nor have I since," reminisced one statistician. The group was tasked with supporting all branches of the military, consulting on everything from the probability of anti-aircraft hits to the best angles for torpedo attacks on maneuvering warships.[49]

Once again, Friedman spun dross into gold, hitting upon a spectacular idea while pursuing federal research. At lunch one day, Wallis recounted a problem presented to the SRG by the navy. A routine practice—testing ordnance—had been transformed by the demands of a war fought on two fronts at opposite ends of the globe. The navy could no longer afford to follow traditional statistical methods, which called for detonating vast numbers of bombs to generate confident estimates of accuracy. Given the scope of the current conflict, the navy asked, was it possible to develop a more streamlined test? It was another problem of scale, a repeat of the challenge Friedman had confronted at the Study of Consumer Purchases. Almost immediately, he sketched the outlines of a "super colossal" test. He and Wallis attacked the problem with relish.[50]

Soon the two men came to a crossroads. The super-colossal test was deeply compelling on an intellectual level. Friedman believed "that the idea would prove a bigger one than either of us would hit on again in a lifetime." Wallis agreed, but felt he was out of his depth mathematically. Friedman felt more confident that given enough time, he could theoretically justify the test. But time was exactly what they didn't have. This wasn't a theoretical exercise; this could help turn the tide of war.[51]

After some soul-searching, Friedman and Wallis retailed the idea to the SRG's mathematicians. Their first target, Jack Wolfowitz, was scornful and dismissive. They went next to Abraham Wald, a Romanian-born mathematician who had joined the SRG after fleeing the Nazis in Vienna. Wolfowitz had already convinced Wald that the idea was bunk, but Hotelling was interested. He joined the meeting and translated Friedman's conception into a simple analogy: "If one is to toss a coin one hundred times to test its bias, and has established the criterion that a 60–40 division or worse will cast doubt on the coin, then there is no use continuing to 100 if earlier 60 heads or 60 tails will work."

In principle, it was possible to do exactly what the navy asked. Instead of testing a hundred rounds of ordnance, say, the SRG could develop an estimate that would allow for stopping at sixty. To Hotelling, it looked like Friedman was onto something important.[52]

Wald was skeptical. The next day, he felt a little more optimistic. A day later, he phoned to say, "Such tests do exist and are more powerful, and furthermore he could tell us how to make them. He came over the office and outlined his sequential probability ratio to us."[53] Friedman and Wallis had made the right choice to set their idea free. By the end of the war, sequential analysis proved so helpful that the army had it declassified early and Wald received expedited citizenship. Sequential analysis went on to become a key concept in postwar statistics. It proved particularly helpful in cases where testing an entire sample might be costly—as in military ordnance—or even dangerous, as in medical trials. If early results showed an experimental therapy to be saving lives, for example, it could immediately be extended to all patients without further testing. For example, had the famous handwashing experiments of the Viennese doctor Ignaz Semmelweis used sequential analysis, one scholar conjectured, more lives could have been saved. Although Friedman and Wallis had accepted the fact that they might never receive any credit, in his book Wald generously thanked both for their original formulation of the problem.[54]

With the coming of VE day, the SRG dissolved and Friedman was once again out of a job. This time, though, he was a Ph.D. economist. The NBER had finally published *Income from Independent Professional*

Practice with a highly unusual coda—a director's note by C. Reinhold Noyes, which critiqued the manuscript.[55] In the end, Friedman had simply worn the directors down. After all, he had far more to lose; the incentives for endless disputation were all on his side.

Reflecting back on the whole affair, Mitchell found his respect for Friedman shaken. In a long letter to Burns, he called Friedman "a problem that is painful indeed." Reviewing the controversy, he judged that Frederick C. Mills and Noyes had been right all along. Friedman had misread his data and botched the statistics. "The best thing about that sad affair was that M. frankly admitted his errors," Mitchell remembered. But that was small consolation. Although a tendency to selectively read data was a basic pitfall of research, "M. seems to be worse than usual in this respect." He would forever require careful watching, Mitchell warned Burns.[56]

Another problem, according to Mitchell, was Friedman's "lack of interest in and appreciation of nonrational factors that influence, + even at times dominate, economic behavior." Friedman admitted his argument was "most unrealistic." Under criticism, he had offered qualification after qualification. While these ultimately settled the doubts of enough directors, Mitchell thought they undermined the whole contribution of the research. The idea that costs might influence entry to professions was but "simple bits of truth" that did not need such complex expression.[57]

Burns had lauded Friedman as the best economist of his generation. Mitchell disagreed. "Whoever he may be, he has more insight into human nature than Milton has been blessed with," Mitchell wrote. It was not a question of Friedman's "acute mind"; it was a question of his character.[58]

Mitchell's damning critique scuttled any chance of a full-time position at the NBER. Luckily, with the close of war, Friedman faced a transformed landscape. As veterans streamed back into the United States, millions enrolled in college courtesy of the GI Bill, which provided generous tuition and housing benefits for returning service members. Almost overnight, American academia transformed into a mass-market business, making professors in high demand. And where once institutions had looked askance at Jewish faculty, or even used quotas to limit their presence, in the wake of Hitler those social barriers began to fall. Milton accepted a faculty position at the University of Minnesota, where Stigler had landed. And then a tantalizing tidbit came through the economics grapevine: the University of Chicago was hiring.

PART III

THE SECOND CHICAGO SCHOOL

6

CONQUERING COWLES

> The theory, the facts, the economic history are one whole; each illuminates the others and is illuminated by it.
>
> —Milton Friedman, 1946

It was a thick summer day when Milton bumped into Henry Simons on the street in Hyde Park. It should have been a joyful encounter. Milton had threaded the needle, beating out a formidable roster of rivals—including George Stigler and Paul Samuelson—for a coveted tenured post at the University of Chicago. Henry had been his man on the inside, feeding him details of faculty sentiment and departmental dynamics, guiding his every step. Now the two old friends would be neighbors and colleagues. Adding to the victory, due to Henry's tireless efforts Aaron Director had also received a Chicago offer, to run a new Institute of Political Economy. The stage was set for a reincarnation of Room Seven, a reprise of the glory days. Yet even the normally oblivious Milton could tell something was off. Henry rattled and rambled, and seemed "psychologically a very sick man," he recounted to Stigler. In their brief conversation, he even brought up the idea of suicide.[1]

Less than a week later, Simons was dead.

"U. of C. Professor Killed by Goof Pills," screamed the afternoon papers. His friends and colleagues quickly closed ranks, denying it was anything but an accidental overdose of sleeping pills. They had good reason to be so insistent. Simons had left behind a two-year-old daughter and a bereaved wife, both beneficiaries of an insurance policy that would be nullified by suicide. Only two days before his death, Simons had updated his will, and now the insurance company was investigating. "The fact is simply as bad as it possibly could be and there is no way of getting around it," Friedman wrote to Aaron Director in tones of dull despair. "Words won't help."[2]

Without Simons, returning to Chicago was not the homecoming Friedman had expected. He had lost his comrade-in-arms, the man he could count on for votes, schemes, and general bonhomie. The department was a changed place from his student days. Jacob Viner was gone to Princeton; Henry Schultz had died in a car accident. Paul Douglas had returned to the faculty after wartime service—as a volunteer, he saw combat in the Pacific—but was turning his attention toward a political career. In 1948, he was elected to the U.S. Senate as a Democrat. While Frank Knight was still a force, his retirement loomed. And there was an emergent center of power that threatened to redefine Chicago economics altogether: the Cowles Commission for Economic Research.

Cowles scholars represented a distinct tributary of mathematical economics with roots in continental Europe. Founded by a wealthy investor who wanted to develop a science of stock picking, the commission came to Chicago in 1939. It grew quickly, benefiting from the rapid outflow of scholarly talent from war-torn Europe. Many of its leaders were immigrants to the United States who had also crossed over from math, engineering, or physics. They imported into economics from these disciplines the concept of an "economic model": a mathematical representation of market activity.[3]

Friedman, too, used economic models—in some sense, any equation, graph, or even verbal statement was a model, stripping down reality to essential causal factors. By the strictest definition, supply-and-demand graphs were a model, as was any equation used to calculate marginal utility. But Cowles models, generally called structural models or econometric models, were a different beast. They intended to depict economic activity not just in one market but in multiple markets operating simultaneously. A Cowles model might string together fifty or more interdependent equations, to be solved by a computer working for more than a hundred hours. The end point of these models was "general equilibrium," the simultaneous balance point of intertwined markets, an attempt to capture the complexity of the economy itself.

Fundamental to Cowles's intellectual project was econometrics—the union of mathematics and statistics with economics. An econometric model took historical data, for example, interest rates or prices of a commodity, and then used probability theory to determine how the two factors interacted. The model could, theoretically, predict what would happen when variables changed. Theoretical criteria were used to judge the model. Were its predictions internally consistent? Did they fall within certain predetermined margins? Economists had long counted, of course. But there was a difference between employing statistical facts and using probabilistic reasoning to explain the relationship between economic variables. And there was yet another chasm between putting prices on a Cartesian plane and defining equilibrium

12 J. MARSCHAK I-1.2

can be affected only by variations in z_c. Best policy is the value $\hat{z}_c$ of z_c that gives ω its maximum value $\hat{\omega}$:

(1.17) $$\hat{\omega} = \max_{z_c} \omega_{\varphi^o}(z_c, z_u; \pi^o) = \omega_{\varphi^o}(\hat{z}_c, z_u; \pi^o).$$

By comparing the values of ω for varying z_c at fixed z_u, the best policy $\hat{z}_c$ can be determined for any given value of the uncontrollable variables z_u, provided the parameters π^o of the (observational) reduced form are known. But π^o can indeed be found from the observations X^o (section 1.2.2.2). The operation (1.13),

$$P_1 X^o = \pi^o,$$

depends on the model only and is called "predictive determination when structure is unchanged."[1] Operation P_1 provides, then, the parameters π^o, to be used for the choice of policy under unchanged structure.

Econometric models used by the Cowles Commission linked together dozens of equations. Friedman preferred a simpler approach. (cowles.yale.edu) with the pure math coming out of Paris and Vienna, like convex sets, game theory, and fixed-point theorems.[4] Cowles represented the larger transformation sweeping the field: political economy was dying, and modern economics was being born.

Politically, Cowles was stocked with leftists. The commission had studied better ways to implement price controls, concerned itself explicitly with discovering how "economic policy could improve the performance of the economy," and even boasted of having a genuine socialist politician, Oskar Lange (later to serve in Poland's Communist government).[5] For most, an economic model implied both a plan and a planner—and neither was problematic.

At first, Cowles scholars viewed Friedman as a real asset. Indeed, the commission's director, Jacob Marschak, played a key role in Friedman's hiring. In a letter to the university chancellor supporting his candidacy, Marschak called Friedman "extremely intelligent," singling out his "contributions to statistics proper" and his "remarkable" role in the development of sequential analysis. Marschak was aware that Friedman was "an obstinate partisan of the old tradition," but used this as an argument for hiring both him and Samuelson. Marschak enthused that with both men on board, Chicago would approach the heights of Cambridge, long driven by the rivalry between John Maynard Keynes and Arthur Pigou.[6]

The Knight faction knew just what to do with this post-partisan dream. When Stigler bombed his interview, Knight shifted his focus to Friedman. Above all else, Knight wanted to avoid hiring Samuelson, who in addition to being a Keynesian was perceived as "self-centered, haughty, or rude." Following Knight's lead were a number of professors, including Lloyd Mints, Hazel Kyrk, and Simons.[7]

In a critical department meeting, Knight took up Friedman's primary weakness—his limited number of publications—and turned it, judo-like, into a strength. Since Friedman was less well known than Samuelson, the Knight faction successfully argued, the department should invite him out first to be "looked over."[8] So even though Samuelson was ranked higher than Friedman by departmental vote, it was Friedman who came to campus first. He was not one to waste such an opportunity, sparkling before the department and the chancellor. Optimally positioned between the department's two centers of power, both less popular and less unpopular than Samuelson, it was Friedman who won the offer.[9]

As he advocated for Friedman, Marschak was missing a critical piece of information: Friedman was already changing his mind about mathematical economics.

Friedman's wartime work at the Statistical Research Group (SRG) both established his reputation as a quant and undermined his faith in the approach. One of his duties had been aiding the military in developing new metal alloys that could help planes fly faster, higher, and longer. To test a new alloy, turbine blades were placed in a red-hot furnace until they fractured. Friedman was tasked with analyzing test results and helping researchers improve their experiments.

Soon he wanted to contribute more directly. Friedman decided "it might be possible to summarize the test data from all the separate experiments by calculating a single equation."[10] Integrating stress, temperature, and other variables, this multiple regression might predict the strength of untested alloys. Even better, it could be used to design new alloys. Perhaps this was another potential breakthrough, akin to the super-colossal test.

To solve the equation, Friedman secured time on Harvard's Mark 1 computer, a huge IBM-manufactured conglomeration of wires, switches, counters, gears, control circuits, and punched paper tape that filled a gymnasium. The equation checked out: it matched all the data Friedman had collected from the field.

Now came a more fundamental test. Following his equation, Friedman designed two new alloys that he expected would exhibit unprecedented strength. He was even able to get a lab at MIT to create and test his new F-1 and F-2 alloys. The results were sobering: both failed within hours, a mediocre result. His extensive calculations had not mapped onto the physical world.

The episode left a deep mark on Friedman. And its lessons were readily transferable to economics. The simultaneous equations he had used for his alloys were the very same ones economists were beginning to use in constructing general equilibrium models. He had already been a policy-maker, without such complex tools. And ever after, when he thought about the predictive power of regression analysis, he would see F-1 and F-2, burning up amid the high temperatures they were designed to withstand.

Had Friedman's new colleagues been reading everything he published, they might have detected early warning signs. Even before SRG, some of these doubts were public. Reviewing a published volume that attempted to model the U.S. business cycle, Friedman doubted the fifty-equation "model" was anything more than a tautology. Because the author had not tested the model against data external to its construction, the multiple regression equations that had yielded impressive correlations "are simply tautological reformulations of *selected* economic data," Friedman wrote. To prove its mettle, he argued, the model would have to "agree with data other than those which they translate."[11] Friedman cited Wesley Mitchell on the perils of selective data, and suggested the NBER approach as an alternative. Interestingly, Keynes himself made similar criticisms while reviewing a related volume. Like Friedman, Keynes questioned whether statistical methods could be usefully applied to economics. Yet these doubts had little staying power, especially after Keynes's untimely death in 1946.[12]

By then, with his Chicago appointment in hand, Friedman had entirely lost patience with what he called "the taxonomic approach." In a blistering review of Lange's *Price Flexibility and Employment* that doubled as a "methodological sermon," Friedman laid out an extended critique of the Cowles approach. From his perspective, constructing econometric models was a narcissistic exercise that "provides formal models of imaginary worlds, not generalizations about the real world." The way Lange had structured his argument meant conclusions of the model were not "susceptible of empirical contradiction." This idea repeated his earlier review. But now Friedman provided example after example taken from Lange's text, and moved to the broader context of scientific methodology. The ultimate test of a theory, he argued, was "not conformity to the canons of formal logic but the ability to deduce facts that have not yet been observed, that are capable of being contradicted by observation, and that subsequent observation does not contradict." While mathematical economists hoped to make the discipline more scientific, Friedman argued they were doing the very opposite.[13]

By the time the review appeared, Lange had left Cowles, renounced his U.S. citizenship, and returned to Poland, where he would serve in the Communist government. Friedman's attack had been a real blow to his reputation, as even his admirers admitted. To Friedman's new colleagues at Cowles, it was a taste of things to come.[14]

Friedman's encounter with Cowles came amid a rapid convergence between academic economics and postwar statecraft. More than an idea, Keynesianism had become law. In the Employment Act of 1946, Congress explicitly declared it to be "the continuing policy and responsibility of the federal government . . . to promote maximum employment, production, and purchasing power."[15] It also set up two powerful institutions: the Council of Economic Advisers, to advise presidents, and the Joint Economic Committee, with members from both the Senate and the House of Representatives, to review and recommend policy. The federal government was now committed by statute and bureaucracy to Keynesian demand management. And economists had been given a permanent berth at its highest levels.

Keynesianism itself had been transformed, with Keynes's sprawling masterpiece boiled down to a simplified graph representing the relationship between interest rates, investment, output, and the demand for money: IS-LM. This was the basic supply-and-demand graph, blown up to fit the entire economy. The IS (investment-saving) curve showed how investment and thus the economy's output would increase as interest rates fell. Its slope was determined in part by the Keynesian multiplier. The LM (liquidity-money) curve showed demand for money, which went up with overall output, at the same time increasing the interest rate. The point where the two curves intersected was equilibrium—demand for real goods and money balanced at a specific GDP and interest rate. IS-LM was first proposed by the British econo-

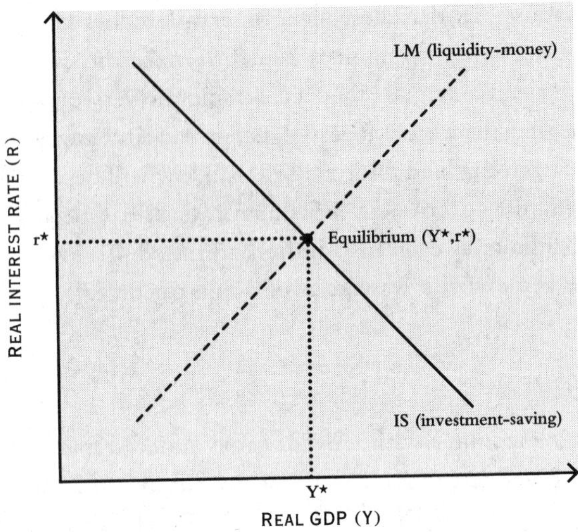

Keynes's *General Theory of Employment, Interest, and Money* (1936) contained no graphs, but soon IS-LM came to summarize American Keynesianism.

mist J. R. Hicks, who frankly called his analysis an "invented apparatus," a "simplification," and a "terribly rough and ready sort of affair."[16] He thought it should be used in classrooms as a basic introduction to key concepts, not in the crafting of policy.

But Alvin Hansen had no such qualms, embracing IS-LM as he became one of Keynes's most important American interpreters. Keenly attuned to the dynamics of American politics, Hansen understood how transforming Keynes into Keynesianism could set the fiscal revolution on a scientific footing. National income statistics had proved invaluable in the Depression-era fight against balanced budgets. Now that economists were tasked with supporting aggregate demand, how were they to defend their targets and proposals? IS-LM could be an objective measure supporting fiscal policy.

IS-LM put in visual form the essential promise of New Deal liberalism as it emerged from the war. The early New Deal interest in planning—Knight's dreaded social control—had become the fiscal revolution's emphasis on aggregate demand management.[17] In this new liberalism, the federal government would not plan or coordinate the workings of specific industries. Rather, it would seek to ensure that consumers spent enough money to keep the economy growing and jobs plentiful. IS-LM purported to show economists and policy-makers what would happen if government spending, interest rates, or taxation went up or down—in any imaginable combination. As such, it could be both a guide and a justification for policy.

Hansen's student Paul Samuelson made another critical intervention with *Foundations of Economic Analysis*, a pathbreaking book that translated basic economic concepts into the master language of mathematics. Equilibrium became a maximization problem, described in equations that could be manipulated to better understand relationships between variables and parameters. New hypotheses could be generated, and tested, out of the system itself. Drawing on thermodynamics, Samuelson argued a basic shared structure, discernible through mathematics, underlay a great variety of economic problems. In turn, these problems could be analyzed by tools hitherto unfamiliar to economists, such as dynamic analysis and differential, difference, or integral equations.[18] Together, IS-LM and Samuelson's mathematics led toward new, complex general equilibrium models like those being developed at Cowles.

While ostensibly geared to the needs of policy-makers, these models became increasingly technical, in turn changing the field of economics. The techniques Samuelson highlighted became basic requirements of graduate training; by the early 1960s nearly half of all economics journal articles employed some type of mathematical reasoning. In 1920, the high tide of institutional economics, none had.[19] Modeling was made far easier by the postwar growth in research computers. Soon behemoths like the Mark 1 would shrink down to room-size; eventually calculators were sold that could fit on a desktop, and then in a hand.

Although *Foundations of Economic Analysis* was primarily a technical work, Samuelson was known as a Keynesian. As a staff member at the wartime National Resources Planning Board, he coauthored a controversial pamphlet calling for postwar planning. He helped mathematically refine an idea burbling through Washington policy circles, the balanced-budget multiplier, showing that deficits when paired with taxation could be expansionary. When it came to individual decision-making—soon to be dubbed "microeconomics"—Samuelson had not wandered far from the price theory he had learned at Chicago, now expressed in advanced mathematics. Equilibrium remained a key concept, with supply equaling demand and markets continuing to clear.

But unlike his undergraduate professors, Samuelson let go of price theory in favor of Keynesian concepts when it came to thinking about aggregate demand and supply. Here markets might not clear unless the state stepped in. He called this the "neoclassical synthesis"—a blend of traditional price theory on the micro level and Keynesian analysis on the macro level. There was an inherent tension in this approach, to be sure. But what seemed important at the time was the synthesis, not the antithesis. After the war Samuelson returned to MIT, which rapidly became a center of Keynesian economics.[20]

Coming on the heels of the Great Depression, Samuelson's affinity for Keynesian-style demand management and his mathematical precocity cracked apart the discipline's long-standing intellectual and political alliances. The neoclassical synthesis continued the project of making economics more quantitative and theoretical, but newly welded this quest to the acceptance of government intervention that was once characteristic of the institutionalist school. In turn, universities stopped offering courses in business cycles, replacing them with macroeconomics. Institutionalists were pushed out of economics altogether.[21]

Samuelson was connected to Cowles through his first graduate student, Lawrence Klein, an important Keynesian figure in his own right. Klein came to Cowles to construct a comprehensive model of the U.S. economy. This was the holy grail of econometrics—and the very same project that had drawn Friedman's scorn, and Keynes's doubt. Nonetheless, the results of Klein's first efforts had been impressive. He was one of the few economists to predict, based on his work at Cowles, that the United States would not plunge back into a depression after the war. Unfortunately, Klein never published that prediction. Instead he made waves with another idea that better fit his Marxist politics: the

United States would suffer another "catastrophic depression" by the 1950s.[22] Klein's blooper came in *The Keynesian Revolution*, a book based on his dissertation, which helped popularize the term in academic and popular parlance.

During his time at Chicago, Klein was a member of the Communist Party. This was both a mark of the political gap between Friedman and Cowles and a sign that Klein inhabited the political fringe. It was long past the high tide of popularity for organized Communism in America; in the wake of the 1939 Nazi-Soviet pact, most intellectuals had deserted the party. Even the wartime alliance between Russia and the United States had not restored the party's good name. But Klein was a firm believer that "planning is superior to competition," as he put it in a letter to Samuelson.[23]

Klein and Friedman overlapped at Chicago for only one year, during which Friedman became a regular at the Cowles weekly seminar. At these meetings, new work by local or visiting scholars was presented for discussion and critique. Commonplace in academia today, the format was considered novel at the time. Sessions were intense, feeding off Chicago's singular atmosphere of intellectual combat.[24] At an early seminar, according to one witness, seemingly "on the spur of the moment," Friedman suggested that "a minimum test for the predictive efficacy of an econometric model is that it do better than a 'naïve model' which stated that the future would be like the past."[25] This was a profound challenge to the Cowles method. As he had argued in his review of Lange, Friedman was arguing that an economic model could not self-validate. Economists couldn't use statistical criteria to judge their models; they had to test them against the real world, against inputs not already incorporated in the model.

Intrigued, Cowles staffer Carl Christ enlisted Friedman's help testing one of Klein's models. Christ's Friedman-inspired test pitted Klein's predictions against those generated by a naïve, or simple, model positing past value plus a preselected variable. For example, a naïve model to determine next year's GDP might be based on current GDP plus the rate of change from the previous year. The result, as Christ delicately put it, indicated "that our econometric model is not yet the reliable predicting instrument which we would like it to be."[26] Friedman was vindicated, or so he thought. Christ and others were less sure a negative result meant the research was flawed. With a sufficiently large sample, Christ argued, an econometric model would do better than a naïve model. Cowles scholars would, however, go on to incorporate naïve testing into their validation process. Friedman had won an important battle, convincing the modelers to test findings against empirical data, and to adopt prediction as a measure of success.[27]

The following summer, Cowles burst out of its relative anonymity among economists with a broadside against institutionalism authored by Tjalling Koopmans, who was soon to succeed Marschak as the director of Cowles. Like many Cowles scholars, the Dutch-born Koopmans had originally trained as a physicist and mathematician in Europe before switching to economics. Thin, bearded, and serious in person—Rose found him "cold and authoritarian"—Koopmans poured his passion into an attack upon the NBER. "Measurement Without Theory" was ostensibly a review of Wesley Mitchell and Arthur Burns's *Measuring Business Cycles*. Its larger goal was to undermine the NBER approach to economics. In condescending tones, Koopmans characterized the rank empiricism of Burns and Mitchell as "the spirit of inquiry groping for guidance," accusing the authors of studying economic variables "as if they were the eruptions of a mysterious volcano whose boiling caldron can never be penetrated." The institutional economics of the NBER, Koopmans implied, was of the past; the future lay with his own mathematically driven approach.[28]

What Koopmans didn't say was that three years earlier, the NBER had pulled its financial support for a Cowles study of price controls. Moreover, the two groups were now rivals for the largesse of the Rockefeller Foundation, which rested atop the legendary Standard Oil fortune. As American academia expanded rapidly in the postwar era, tuition income was supplemented by government funds and private philanthropy. The Rockefeller Foundation was at the time a major funder of economic research, matched only by the Carnegie Foundation (and later supplanted by the Ford Foundation). Its early staff and presidents were Ph.D. economists who shared an interest in "social control," that Progressive byword. At the same time, the Rockefeller family was sensitive to accusations it was buying off critics with ill-gotten profits. Organizations like the NBER created the perfect buffer. This strategy only worked if the NBER was scrupulously nonpolitical—hence the tussle over Friedman's dissertation—and if the foundation itself did not pick favorites. Accordingly, Rockefeller had granted Cowles a small sum, although its staff shared Friedman's misgivings about its approach.[29]

Aimed at the jugular, Koopmans's article sought to delegitimize the NBER—and institutional economics—altogether. Although it was not the only reason institutional economics faded in the postwar years, to many readers Koopmans's article was a death blow to the ailing tradition. Friedman must have been sympathetic to part of this critique. After all, he had taken laborious notes on Mitchell's laborious lectures and battled the NBER over publication of his dissertation. Yet this methodological attack was also a personal attack on Burns, who had just taken over the directorship of the NBER from Mitchell.

Burns and Friedman remained extraordinarily close. When Burns shared details of staff discontent at the NBER, Friedman pledged his fealty in a gushing letter that praised a new mission statement as "masterly . . . beautifully organized, properly proportional, and entirely appropriate for the occasion." A few lines later, gossiping about job openings at Columbia, Friedman noted of his former professor: "I have never been one of Hotelling's men; but he's always thought well of me." The aside said much about Friedman's view of his profession and his relationship to Burns. In economics, well-placed senior scholars had "men": junior scholars, peers, and allies whose careers and scholarship they worked to advance. Friedman's encomiums left no doubt that he was one of Burns's men.[30]

A few months after the review appeared, Friedman agreed to present a paper to Cowles. Given the methodological, political, and personal differences simmering under the surface, the seminar must have come with a certain frisson. Nevertheless, this first presentation was an olive branch of sorts, for it highlighted the aspects of Friedman's intellectual profile that Cowles Commission members were likely to find most compelling.[31]

The paper was coauthored with James Savage, a colleague from the Chicago mathematics department, whom Friedman had come to know at the SRG. Although never lionized as part of Friedman's Chicago gang, Savage was one of the few people whom Friedman openly called "a genius" and their short-lived collaboration proved fertile for both.[32] Their paper, ultimately published as "The Utility Analysis of Choices Involving Risk," picked up on John von Neumann and Oskar Morgenstern's *Theory of Games and Economic Behavior*, a seminal text that would result in the new field of game theory.

Bringing this set of ideas into economics, Friedman and Savage attempted to explain two widespread economic behaviors: insurance, which minimized risk, and gambling, which exemplified it. It seemed contradictory that consumers would both pay to eliminate risk and pay to take on risk. To explain this paradox, the authors used von Neumann and Morgenstern's approach to decision-making. In game theory what mattered was how a decision-maker ranked relative choices against each other. Drawing on this idea, Friedman and Savage constructed a utility curve "of a special shape" that could bring "under the aegis of rational utility maximization much behavior that is ordinarily explained in other terms."[33] Previous theorists had understood risk as an encounter with the unknown. They had spliced risky behavior off into its own category, explaining risk in psychological rather than economic terms, as a product of ignorance rather than calculation. By contrast, Friedman and Savage argued that it was possible to understand risk as a form of utility maximization.

Cowles scholars would have understood the paper as an implicit rebuke of Frank Knight. After all, he had made his name with the idea of uncertainty, an existential category that encompassed unknowable events and unmeasurable possibilities. "The results of human activity cannot be anticipated," Knight had written in *Risk, Uncertainty and Profit*, "and then only in so far as even a probability calculation in regard to them is impossible and meaningless." Now here were Friedman and Savage with equations and diagrams claiming that even black swans could be incorporated into standard economic analysis. They never stated it so clearly, but as Friedman later asserted, "our thesis is there's no such thing as a distinction between risk and uncertainty."[34] Even as it broke with Knight's core concept, the paper made manifest Knight's less visible legacy to his students: his contention that economics was essentially the analysis of human wants. By setting aside the epistemic limits Knight always stressed, Friedman kicked open the door to economics as a universal science. Even gambling, the province of sin, impulse, and emotion, could be rationalized.

It was not unreasonable, however, for listeners to conclude Friedman was stepping away from Knight toward the new frontier of economics. Perhaps Friedman would become, like Samuelson, a builder of an alternate neoclassical synthesis, pairing price theory and econometrics but leaving out the Keynesian demand management. Published in 1948, Friedman and Savage's article was widely read and debated, enough so that they published a follow-up in 1952. This second article showed the pair deeply engaged with Marschak and Samuelson (who detected a mathematical error that Friedman and Savage readily acknowledged). In 1951 Friedman was awarded the John Bates Clark Medal, a new prize for the economist under forty years of age "judged to have made the most significant contribution to economic thought and knowledge."[35] Friedman was well positioned to ride the new mathematical wave to even greater renown. It was at this juncture, however, that he reversed course and headed to an isolated backwater: monetary economics.

It may seem strange to call money a backwater, given that all of economics concerns money in some basic sense. But in the years following World War II, as the Keynesian revolution became established in American universities, analysis of the role of money in the broader economy became less central, even peripheral. Economists started to view money as a mere "veil" that obscured the true causal forces at work. Reflecting on this era years later, Samuelson mused, "money got lost by economists." His work played an important part in this disciplinary amnesia. His best-selling textbook, which served for decades as the primary gateway into the field, spelled out deliberately just how little money mattered. "Today . . . we no longer hold out high hopes for effectively maintaining full employment and high production by means of Federal Reserve monetary policy," Samuelson wrote in the book's first edition.[36] In an early paper, he called the velocity of money, a key concept from the quantity theory, "irrelevant and misleading."[37] Economists looking to guide policy-makers should focus instead on fiscal policy—the appropriate level of government spending. Monetary economics—studying central banking, interest rates, the behavior of money—was simply not where the action was.

A 1948 American Economic Association publication noted the transformation. "The center of interest has in general shifted from the factors determining the quantity of money and its effect on the general level of prices," the report summarized, finding economists more interested in factors "determining the level of output and employment," such as the federal budget. Across thirteen chapters surveying the field, Keynes and Hicks (the inventor of IS-LM) were the two most cited economists. A recent 700-page textbook, the AEA reported, spent only 55 pages on money and the interest rate, compared to 205 pages on national income and employment.[38] Increasingly, economists assumed that money passively reflected other economic forces, having little independent role.

These changes reflected both intellectual currents and current events. The great driver was the dominant interpretation of the Great Depression, which held that "purely monetary devices . . . were found to be broadly ineffective, taken by themselves, in bringing about recovery," as the AEA report summarized. This was why Keynes's work had such impact—it at once explained the depth and severity of the Depression and offered a new solution, raising "output and employment" through government spending. Compounding the change was the Federal Reserve's newly restricted ambit. First reduced in its powers by New Deal banking reforms, the Fed had been further squashed by the needs of wartime finance. Becoming a handmaiden to the Treasury Department, the Fed had pledged to keep interest rates low so that war bonds could be more easily paid back. If the Fed could not manipulate interest rates in response to economic conditions, it was essentially powerless. "It seems quite likely that it will prove impossible to use [monetary] devices for the effective control of a future boom," concluded the AEA report. Thus there were ample reasons for economists to turn their focus away from money.[39]

So it was unexpected for a rising star to dive into a course on money and banking—but that was exactly what Friedman did in his first quarter at Chicago. He had no established expertise in monetary economics. The subject hadn't come up in the debates over his hiring, where he was envisioned by his future colleagues as a combination applied statistician / math wunderkind / theory head. True, Chicago had a tradition of monetary economics, but that garden was well tended by the unflashy Lloyd Mints. Nonetheless, it was clear that money held some allure for Friedman, because he readily agreed to teach both Money and Banking and Economic Theory in his first year, while resisting the suggestion that he offer a course in mathematical economics. Readying for his return to Chicago, Friedman sent Burns a long letter, telling him, "I'm terribly pleased about the money course. I think it will be real fun to give + that I will learn a lot."[40] As preparation, he recounted extensive reading in the money literature.

Friedman also revisited Alfred Marshall, the British economist whom Burns had introduced him to at Rutgers, finding inspiration anew. Almost as if he were writing in his own diary, Friedman mused to Burns: "It strikes me that there is a great need for a modern Marshall—(book as well as man). The beauty of Marshall is that the theory, the facts, the economic history are one whole; each illuminates the others and is illuminated by it."[41] At this critical inflection point in his career, on the cusp of returning to Chicago as a tenured professor, Friedman was beginning to visualize the kind of economist he wanted to become.

Burns was quick to grasp the potential congruity between his own interests and those of his protégé. Friedman's confessional letter showed a young scholar still in search of an identity, a dazzling yet malleable mind seeking direction. Burns had just taken over the helm of the NBER from Mitchell, and there was plenty of work to be done. Even better, Friedman was developing an independent interest in monetary economics, an area Mitchell had decreed critical just before his retirement.[42] No exact record of their conversation exists, but by early 1948 Burns had convinced Friedman to study the role of money in business cycles. Specifically, Burns set up a collaboration between Friedman and the woman who would be his cofounder of a new school of economics: Anna Jacobson Schwartz.

Like Rose Friedman, Schwartz was a brilliant woman destined to languish in the arid land of "all but dissertation." She was born three years after Milton Friedman, and her family was likewise part of the great migration of Jews out of eastern Europe and into New York City in the first decade of the twentieth century. Introspective and modest, Schwartz's unassuming demeanor masked an inner core of steel—which she would need as a working mother and professional economist.

Her intellect was more obvious. After she graduated summa cum laude from Barnard, a professor encouraged her to continue for the Ph.D. at Columbia, and invited her to join a study of British business cycles. After a brief stint in D.C.—also at the Study of Consumer Purchases, although she and Friedman did not overlap—she returned to New York. Over the next five years, Schwartz coauthored a monumental study, eventually published in two volumes as *The Growth and Fluctuation of the British Economy, 1790–1850*. Although the book was completed in 1941, it took nearly a decade to publish, due in part to wartime paper rationing. By then, she had married her sweetheart from Hebrew camp, Isaac Schwartz. While her husband began his career working for an import firm—eventually rising to controller—Schwartz took a research position at the NBER. She was assigned to the money section, which had no existing staff, and tasked with assembling a time series of U.S. currency and then banking deposits.[43]

It was here that Schwartz's career hit an unexpected roadblock: Arthur Burns. When she began the study of British business cycles, Schwartz believed a portion of it would eventually form the basis of her doctoral dissertation. But when the study was complete, Burns declared that a coauthored project was unacceptable as a Columbia dissertation.[44] Burns was now a force at Columbia; he had been hired as a tenured professor in 1945 and taken over Mitchell's famous course. No one was going to approve a dissertation on business cycles without his imprimatur. Of course, Burns had thrown his weight behind Friedman, whose coauthored NBER study served as his Columbia dissertation.

But he seemed to view Schwartz differently. Perhaps she hadn't done quite as much on the British study as Friedman had on *Incomes from Independent Professional Practice*; but perhaps she had. Perhaps she had even done more. One thing was certain—Schwartz had no powerful patron in her corner. In Friedman's parlance, she was nobody's "man." Her closest mentor and coauthor, a professor at Columbia's "women's annex," was outgunned. Her other coauthor, Walt Rostow, was bouncing around through temporary positions and government work. Eventually Rostow would achieve renown and serve as an adviser to Eisenhower, Kennedy, and Johnson, but he was of little help in the moment.[45]

It wasn't that Burns didn't respect Schwartz's intellect; he wouldn't have continued her NBER employment if he doubted her competency. Indeed, he may have blocked her dissertation precisely because he recognized her value to the NBER. Without a doctorate, Schwartz would be less likely to secure a teaching position. Most likely, Burns saw Schwartz the way most men in economics saw most women in economics: valuable as research assistants or even collaborators, but lacking the intellectual independence and drive to be considered true scholars in their own right.

As a result, where Friedman used Burns as a sounding board for his most private thoughts and longings, Schwartz viewed her boss as "a very arrogant man." Schwartz's loyalty to the NBER and its methods was lifelong, but she had little positive to say about its former director. "Nothing suited Arthur Burns better than cutting somebody down," she recalled.[46] Despite the power he held over her, Schwartz remained unbowed. When Schwartz began working full-time at the bureau she had two children, and Burns, also a father of two, instructed: "Now, don't have any more children, because you don't have time for anything else when you have children!" Schwartz went on to have two more children nonetheless. Although Schwartz always denied that there was "something extraordinary about my situation," citing the presence of other women at the NBER and Columbia, she was nonetheless operating in hostile territory.[47] What was her reaction, then, when Burns assigned Friedman to her project?

The two had actually met briefly years ago, when Milton and Rose turned up on Schwartz's doorstep to borrow a spare baby buggy. They were both on the edges of Columbia economics circles, and so it's likely Schwartz had some inkling of Friedman's capacity and character. She may have heard something about his conflict with the NBER directors over his dissertation. Professionally, she understood him to be "a statistician, and not particularly an up-and-coming economist." Furthermore, despite being assigned to her money project, "there really was no role for money in his analysis."[48] Nonetheless, Friedman was a Chicago professor, and close to Burns. In terms of her future prospects at the bureau, it could only be a good sign. That is, unless Friedman pushed her out or hogged all the glory.

Friedman struck the right notes in his first letter to Schwartz, writing in tones at once respectful, modest, and cooperative. "You doubtless know that I am going to undertake a study for the Bureau of monetary factors in cyclical fluctuations," he began. Rather than presenting their partnership as settled, he framed it as a possibility he hoped would come to pass, citing the benefits he might gain from her work. He was also careful to present himself, at this stage, as the junior partner, eager for her "suggestions about what I should be doing." Friedman closed with a brief discussion of a memorandum she had written about challenges in estimating bank deposits. "I feel some obligation to comment on it, and make suggestions on various points you raise; yet I really feel incompetent to do so." This wasn't just a function of his ignorance, though, because "at almost every point the internal evidence suggests that you have considered all the relevant factors." Overall, he was deeply impressed by the "evident care and attention to detail" in the memorandum. It was an auspicious beginning to a collaboration that would last for decades.[49]

It was also a relationship that resolved Friedman's search for an intellectual focus and identity. Within a year, he was describing the NBER project to his department chair as "the major research project I am working on." He and Rose rented a summer house in New Hampshire, conveniently near to both Burns and the all-important Dartmouth library. Here Friedman immersed himself in monetary history, working off a reading list provided by Schwartz.[50]

The contrast with the Cowles approach was striking. No Cowles economist would launch a major research project by spending several months reading history books. Rather, Cowles scholars worked collaboratively in weekly meetings to test, refine, and workshop the application of statistical and mathematical techniques to economic data. Equally striking were the similarities with his dissertation project. Once again, Friedman was joining an NBER research project that someone else had started. And once again, while ostensibly following the institutionalist method, Friedman was not working forward from facts, letting his theory emerge as he sifted data. Rather, he was starting with a theory that would be tested against facts.

By the end of his summertime reading, a key conclusion had emerged: "By and on the large the Federal Reserve system has probably been a destabilizing influence during its life and that we might very well have been better off if we had never had it," he summarized to his chair.[51] This perspective almost entirely reversed the conventional wisdom. Instead of the feckless Fed, unable to end the Depression, Friedman suggested it was a critical economic institution, potentially to blame for economic disaster. Where did this explosive idea come from?

Recent scholarship has emphasized the influence of Clark Warburton, an obscure FDIC economist who anticipated many arguments made by Friedman and Schwartz. For a decade starting in 1943, Warburton pumped out more than thirty articles, many benefiting from his access to government statistics and data. A consistent theme was the errors and mistakes of the Federal Reserve, and how they initiated business downswings. "The Federal Reserve System has been a failure," he pronounced in 1942. Warburton was undoubtedly an important interlocutor for Friedman, particularly once the money project was under way. It is possible, even likely, that Friedman also encountered his work in these early stages. Rose, at least, had a brush with Warburton when she interviewed at the FDIC. Maybe Friedman had come across one of his articles, or heard about his ideas from Homer Jones, who was also at the FDIC. Maybe Warburton was on the Schwartz syllabus (no copy survives). Or perhaps it was simply the cumulative impact of Schwartz's reading list, focused particularly on "volumes that give the reader a view of the banking system both before and after 1914," the first year of the Fed's operation, that led him to re-envision what might have been. Regardless, it would have been unusual for a student of monetary history to leave unexamined the role of the nation's central bank.[52]

There was also the Chicago tradition of monetary economics. Amid the Great Depression, Friedman's professors had thought boldly and fearlessly about the country's monetary institutions. Because of their grounding in the quantity theory of money, Chicago professors had used a monetary lens to think through the Great Depression. The Chicago plan had not directly attacked the Federal Reserve System but had recommended it immediately be taken over by the federal government. But skepticism of the Federal Reserve was essential to the idea of 100 percent money, the pet cause of Simons that would never come to pass. Fleshing out the idea, which would require banks to hold all of their deposits rather than loan against them, Simons scoffed, "Our much heralded achievements in control (witness the Federal Reserve System), being designed to yield greater 'elasticity' of credit, have served only to aggravate the underlying difficulty." He proposed no abolition of the Fed but envisioned it demoted to "a strictly administrative body," limited by "fixed rules of management."[53] More notably, even as he declined to sign on to the Chicago plan, Viner was an early critic of the Fed. While the Depression was unfolding, he had lambasted the Fed's "program of drift . . . rationalized by declarations of impotence."[54] Given Friedman's primordial exposure to these concepts, that a version of these ideas emerged from his reading is understandable.

Whatever the precise imprint, Chicago's monetary economics undoubtedly fortified Friedman's interest in the distinctly unfashionable topic of money. The presence of Schwartz on the NBER project was a giveaway. She had ended up there because no one else was interested in this seemingly dead-end topic. But Friedman was a contrarian, in part because he found inspiration in figures others had forgotten. An article he published in 1948, "A Monetary and Fiscal Framework for Stability," testified to the continued influence of his former professors, particularly Simons. A love letter of sorts to his lost friend, Friedman's framework article built upon a landmark Simons article from 1936, "Rules Versus Authorities in Monetary Policy." An extension of the Chicago plan, Simons's article made the case for "definite, stable, legislative rules of the game as to money," arguing this would create stability for borrowing and lending. The game metaphor—a favorite of Knight's—further suggested rules were important beyond the monetary sphere, and were vital for all economic activity.[55]

Picking up the cue, Friedman extended Simons's basic framework to encompass fiscal as well as monetary policy. He proposed four main reforms, two of which were straight-up Simons: 100 percent money, and use of the personal income tax as the main source of government revenue. The third reform also nested within a Simons framework of elevating rules over discretion: any transfer programs, like Social Security, should be "predetermined," with set rules and eligibility, thereby limiting discretionary action by policy-makers. Finally, Friedman stressed that most of the time, government spending on public services should reflect "the community's basic objectives," not broader economic conditions. "The program should not be changed in response to cyclical fluctuations in business activity," Friedman argued, directly contradicting the Keynesian idea of spending to support dips in economic activity. At the same time, Friedman stressed that by design the system would respond to booms and busts. "Absolute outlays, however, will vary automatically over the cycle," he noted.[56] Spending on unemployment payments would rise in recessions as people lost jobs, and tax receipts would fall as income declined—mechanisms today known as "automatic stabilizers." The idea was to avoid changes in policy driven by current events or grandstanding politicians. Setting up a plan, Friedman hoped, would usurp the planners.

Had they been adopted, Friedman's suggestions would have preempted the econometric models his colleagues were so assiduously building. Fiscal policy, in its essence, was designed to be discretionary. Economists were even beginning to believe the economy could be guided like a car on a freeway, with gentle pumping of the brakes or accelerator via fiscal policy. The nation's economic life was starting to appear like a chemical system, where one could mix in a dose of stimulus or change the ratio of elements by adding taxation and get a predictable reaction. Friedman's paper, by contrast, argued that the federal government should lay out an objective set of rules and then let the economy fluctuate within this basic framework.

Like the conviction the Federal Reserve had done more harm than good, rules were also a tenet of monetarism in embryonic form. So too were other ideas threaded throughout the paper, such as the idea of a policy lag. And where Keynesian interpretations minimized the link between the money supply and aggregate demand, Friedman's unstated assumption was of an important relationship between the two. He described "an increase in the stock of money" as a "fundamental corrective" to a hypothetical decline in demand, whereas Samuelson's textbook emphasized the opposite: that monetary policy had been helpless in the face of the Great Depression.[57] While the paper foreshadowed monetarism, it was distinct from the later school. In part, this was because it imagined a vastly different set of institutional arrangements than the ones monetarism would address: beyond 100 percent money, Friedman proposed abolition of the federal bond market![58] Nonetheless, Friedman had inherited important heterodox assumptions and ideas from his teachers, and these would shape the research he and Schwartz began.

Friedman's shift to money came alongside a noticeable cooling of relations with the Cowles Commission. In light of the naïve test, the tensions between Cowles and Friedman might have seemed productive, perhaps even welcome. In his 1949 annual report to the chair, Friedman proclaimed the "complete absence of any personal rancor or conflict" despite "diverse views, methodological preconceptions, and policy predilections" to be the outstanding feature of the Chicago department. "As a result we can discuss our differences amicably and with emphasis on the intellectual content of the differences," Friedman wrote. In the end, he continued, there would surely be a "reconciliation of views without dogmatic assumption of positions."[59] Written for public consumption by the department chair and university deans, this upbeat assessment falsified the dynamics on the ground.

In fact, by then Friedman was actively working to cut off Cowles's lifeblood. Asked by the Rockefeller Foundation to evaluate its work, Friedman doubted the commission was, at base, even part of economics. "The people listed are primarily mathematicians or statisticians rather than economists and have had no occasion to do careful scientific quantitative work on a limited segment of the economy," he wrote in a confidential letter. Koopmans, the commission's chair, was "able," he noted, but "came to economics relatively late from mathematics and statistics." Friedman had "no great confidence in his judgment about realistic economic problems."[60] Friedman's letter, which joined similar missives from Burns, was a significant threat to Cowles's funding.

Set against the long history of economic thought, Friedman and Cowles were part of an emerging neoclassical synthesis once held at bay by the powerful school of American institutionalism. In the postwar era the basic insights of marginal analysis were becoming the common language of economists, with utility maximization and general equilibrium models displacing the previous emphasis on institutions and social control. Friedman and Cowles were attempting to navigate the same transition: moving from the traditional economic focus on individual markets and behavior to an aggregate picture more suited to the emerging mass economy.

But the Cowles approach was to draw on mathematics to bridge this gap, while Friedman believed connections between the micro and the macro were best developed through fine-grained analysis of data collected in the field. Despite his allegiance to price theory, as a practicing economist Friedman was thoroughly empirical. On the Study of Consumer Purchases he had analyzed thousands of paper surveys, at the Treasury Department he interviewed businesses about the impact of tax withholding, and in writing his dissertation he gathered income figures for five professions. And while Friedman rejected the core propositions of institutional economics—namely its skepticism of economic theory—he retained its methods and even some of its intellectual orientation. He was beginning to see how monetary history could become a vehicle to analyze aggregate forces, connecting neoclassical insight with traditional institutionalist empiricism.

Because Friedman differed in approach from so many of his peers, he was forced to reflect on what he was doing—and ought to do—as an economist. In a celebrated essay, "The Methodology of Positive Economics," he tied together his various critiques of Cowles and offered a new standard for economic theory: prediction. What were economists trying to do, and how did they know if they had done it? Positive economics, Friedman contended, "is to be judged by the precision, scope, and conformity with experience of the predictions it yields."[61] The true test of a theory was not its internal structure, its consistency, or even its intuitive appeal; rather, theories must accurately predict. It was, in essence, another "methodological sermon" and a riposte to Koopmans's attack on the NBER.

But it was not a wholesale defense of the NBER's institutional approach. Just as he and Simon Kuznets had argued that it didn't really matter if dentists and doctors were comparable, Friedman considered the realism of a theory's assumptions beside the point. It wasn't possible, after all, to accurately capture the complexity of human decision-making or economic activity in a model; this was the failed quest of Cowles. Analytically, it wasn't important if a business owner actually tried to maximize profits. It was only important that collectively, businesses could be understood "as if" they were trying to do so. Friedman offered a billiards analogy borrowed from his work with Savage. It didn't matter if a pool shark was calculating precise angles in his mind as he moved to strike the cue ball. A scientist could nonetheless use geometry to understand why the ball went into the pocket or not.

Friedman was also comfortable with the idea that observation could never be truly neutral; the investigator had always a selection bias of some sort. The way out of the trap was a relentless focus on problem-solving. After observation came prediction, ensuring a theory did not rest on "purely formal or tautological analysis," as he put it in a thinly veiled reference to Cowles.[62] Sometimes taken as an effort to defend the abstract concept of *Homo economicus*, Friedman's methodological statement is better understood as part of his battle against Cowles. And it well summarized the productive tensions at the core of his thought. At once an empiricist and a theoretician, Friedman stressed research and set up experience—prediction—as the ultimate test. Yet simultaneously, he was unafraid to soar up and away into realms of abstraction where what mattered was the approximation, not the detail.

A 1951 conference organized by the NBER made public the growing tensions at Chicago. In discussion, Friedman returned to the naïve test. He was frustrated to find that Christ and others, while admitting the naïve test had shown significant flaws in the Cowles models, did not consider it grounds to shift their approach. Instead, they rationalized that even when a model failed the naïve test, it could still "predict consequences of alternative policy measures."[63] By contrast, in discussion Friedman essentially declared "that the whole econometric model-building enterprise had been shown to be worthless and congratulated the Cowles Commission on its self-immolation," according to an audience member.[64]

By now, the sparring between Friedman and Cowles was turning toxic. At seminar after seminar, Friedman pressed the same question: How were models chosen? If the commission wouldn't clarify its decisions, or publish information on models that hadn't worked, he would assume they were simply chosen based on the prejudice of the investigator. Repeated week in and week out, the criticism added up to the accusation that the Cowles inquiries were fundamentally corrupt. "But suppose the investigator is honest!" pleaded Koopmans in one exchange.[65]

Shaping the dynamic was Friedman's exceptional verbal acuity, which was impossible for the Dutch-born Koopmans and the Russian-born Marschak to match. In debate, Friedman was "tough and very fast and dangerous," remembered Franco Modigliani, who clashed with Friedman in an early seminar. Fragmentary notes from the meeting minutes capture the tenor of Friedman's intervention. "The statement that the situation envisioned by Modigliani is more 'typical' may therefore well be meaningless," Friedman told the group.[66] Even worse, these bruising words came from someone who understood intellectually what the Cowles economists were doing—unlike many economists at the time. "The more complex the regression, the more skeptical I am" was one of Friedman's favorite sayings. More than the self-professed "hair shirt" of Cowles, Friedman was a serious impediment to creating an atmosphere of shared purpose and mutual support in which new research might flourish.[67] And he was not just a symbolic threat.

In 1953, Koopmans and Marschak were shocked to learn their Rockefeller grant would not be renewed—and to receive, along with this news, a raft of extremely critical referee reports. Friedman had authored one of the reports, as Koopmans and Marschak surely knew. In a long letter back to the Rockefeller Foundation pleading their case, Koopmans defended their research approach against a hypothetical "adherent of the cruder method" who "chooses to live in a fool's paradise with regard to his notion of the accuracy with which he can estimate."[68] Although the protocols of the department were always elaborately courteous, with even close colleagues addressing each other as "Mr.," signs of tension were unmistakable. Marschak began offering an elective course, Modern Developments in Economic Theory, its title clearly aimed at Friedman's required course on price theory.

By some accounts, the loss of Rockefeller funding pushed Koopmans into a mental breakdown. Normally even-keeled and reserved, he now suffered outbursts of rage, at one point throwing a chair in anger. He confessed to colleagues that Friedman's relentless criticisms threatened his sanity. The following year, he took a leave of absence to attend a therapeutic music camp.[69] In the meantime, Friedman began to ramp up his new workshop, Money and Banking—now flush with Rockefeller funds. He was not even temped by the prospect of joining

Eisenhower's Council of Economic Advisers. Turning down a feeler from Burns, the chair of the council, Friedman explained he was too busy with the new workshop.[70]

Friedman also moved to shore up the critical beachhead of faculty appointments. Cowles could both appoint its own faculty and support joint appointments in economics. To offset the danger, Friedman began a perpetual drive to hire a friend, proposing in turn George Stigler, Arthur Burns, and Dorothy Brady.[71] Smacking as it did of personal fiefdom-building, these suggestions further inflamed the department atmosphere. Samuelson would eventually get his Chicago offer—and turn it down because he dreaded facing Friedman day in and day out. "It would polarize me, it would radicalize me," Samuelson feared.[72] Efforts to recruit Kenneth Arrow, now at Stanford, back to Cowles as its director faltered. So too did similar overtures to James Tobin at Yale. Neither wanted to head into the lion's den. The department chair swung behind Friedman's position, even suggesting that Cowles be dissolved into the university more broadly.[73] Soon Friedman was facing off against Koopmans and Marschak in nearly every departmental decision. He led a faction composed mainly of his former professors, including Knight and Mints. And acrimony had reached the heights of the Director-Simons tenure battle he had witnessed as a student.

Why was Friedman waging such a vicious guerrilla war against Cowles? At stake was nothing less than the University of Chicago's approach to the discipline. In a world as small as American economics, controlling a major university was no minor accomplishment. Further, dominating Chicago economics did not just mean shaping the flow of students, money, and ideas within the university. It was a potential platform for far wider impact. Harvard had launched the fiscal revolution; Wisconsin had pioneered Progressive reform; MIT was spreading mathematical techniques. Chicago had the potential to launch an equally influential new school.

Beyond monetary economics, Friedman wanted to elevate a distinctive approach he called "portioning" that hearkened to the years before general equilibrium models. Rather than try to capture the whole picture in one model—which Friedman doubted could be done, based in part on his failed alloy at the Statistical Research Group—instead the economist assembled an overarching theory from discrete pieces of economic activity. This portioning approach made economics a useful tool, "an engine for the discovery of concrete truth." By contrast, Cowles-style scholars prized "abstractness, generality, and mathematical elegance for its own sake," Friedman argued in the *Journal of Political Economy*.[74]

Considered in the abstract, this methodological allegiance did not necessarily have a political cast. But it acquired one when counterposed to general equilibrium modeling, which at the time carried an unmistakable Keynesian, pro-planning, even leftist tilt. In the context of midcentury America, a Cowles-style economics model rested on the assumption, as Klein put it to Samuelson, that planning was better than competition. A model "meant you could control the economy," believed young economists learning the technique.[75] By contrast, Friedman's preference for simple models matched his belief that the federal government should play a modest role in economic management. His battle against models thus became a political fight as much as an intellectual one.

Friedman's emerging framework was not anarchic or even anti-government. But he held to a circumscribed view of state action that was more common in the years before the New Deal and the Great Depression. Derived from neoclassical economics before the storm, his worldview intertwined the political and the economic.

To some, it was the high-water mark of Chicago economics. Friedman was not the only future Nobel laureate about the place; Koopmans and Arrow would both receive the prize decades later. To those who appreciated the Cowles approach, the commission was an exciting and dynamic environment, "a truly exceptional group of people," as Arrow recalled. He would publish his pathbreaking *Social Choice and Individual Values* in 1951 under the Cowles imprint. Likewise, another veteran remembered that the Chicago-Cowles combination was "unparalleled in the world . . . No one else even came close."[76] But Cowles nested uneasily alongside, and partially within, an economics department that had become openly hostile to its very existence.

Cowles blinked first. In the fall of 1954, the Cowles Commission and all its associated economists announced their departure for Yale. Friedman was gleeful in a letter to Burns: "You have doubtless heard rumors that the Cowles Commission is leaving the University of Chicago for what it hopes will be the more congenial + satisfactory corridors of Yale. I'm glad to be able to report that the rumors are entirely true + that both Marschak and Koopmans are going with the commission to Yale. Poor Yale."[77] Burns wrote back with congratulations, as if the departure of the Cowles Commission was yet another of Milton's laurels.

In fact, the departure of Cowles marked a major step in Friedman's ascent within the Chicago universe and his effort to reconfigure the world he had known as a graduate student. More than petty academic infighting, Cowles's retreat was a sign of Friedman's ability to shape the intellectual environment of a major university. Like Viner, he was introducing generations of students to the wonders of price theory. He had taken the senatorial courtesies of Knight to another level, proving himself the better tactician and street fighter. Now he had but to fill in the space Simons had created as a public intellectual and polemicist.

7

LAW AND ECONOMICS

> We became janissaries as a result of this experience.
>
> —Robert Bork, 1982

When Henry Simons died in 1946, Aaron Director was at a crossroads. After his first expulsion from the University of Chicago, he had spent years wandering through a series of quasi-academic positions. He never completed a dissertation, but in his peregrinations through Europe discovered a new mentor, the Austrian economist F. A. Hayek. It was Hayek who had schemed with Simons to create the new Institute of Political Economy, to be housed at Chicago and headed by Director. But in the raw aftermath of Simons's death, Director wasn't even sure he wanted the job. Hayek pushed the case. It was now "even more important than before that you should accept. It seems to me the only chance that the tradition which Henry Simons created will be kept alive and continued in Chicago," he argued.[1]

In the end, Friedman's support of the idea—and his presence in Chicago—was probably more critical. Alongside Hayek, he lobbied the administration on behalf of his brother-in-law. With the law school now missing its house economist, the university appointed Director an untenured professor of law, filling Simons's position. Undoubtedly, there was a personal draw as well. Director had been disowned by his parents when he married a gentile. Moving to Chicago would renew his lifelong bond with Rose. When the Friedmans purchased a run-down multifamily house near the university, they reserved the top floor for Director and his wife, Katherine. Now began the work Simons had hoped to make his own: the development of a political philosophy that could shape American ideas about the state, markets, and economics.

Friedman and his brother-in-law were a study in contrasts. Short and stocky, Friedman fizzed with energy. His emotions played rapidly across his elfin, expressive face, captured by an easy flow of words. Slim, passive, and withdrawn, Director cloaked his visage with a thick mustache, omnipresent pipe, and when possible a hat. Where Friedman was brash, even arrogant, Director was gentle. While Friedman was a quick draw, dominating the classroom like Jacob Viner before him, Director was patient. Puffing his pipe, he asked a few questions here and there. Simply phrased, the questions invariably struck at "the root of the matter" or "the core of the issue," students recalled.[2] Friedman's ideas spilled out in articles, pamphlets, letters to the editor, books, and memoranda. Director rarely put pen to paper. Witnessing Director's probing questions stop a seminar in its tracks, one law student hunted fruitlessly through the library card catalog for his publications. But it was by his students, not his writing, that Director would be known.

While Friedman held a tenured position in the economics department, Director had a far more precarious post: a five-year contract with the law school, underwritten by a private foundation—the William Volker Charities Fund. This was no Rockefeller Foundation, with a jaw-dropping endowment, professional staff, and international grants portfolio. Rather, the Volker Fund was built upon a successful Midwestern furniture business. While its founder was alive, it had mostly funded Kansas City charities. After his death in 1947, both the business and the Volker Fund were taken over by the patriarch's nephew, Harold Luhnow.

Luhnow was one of many Americans transfixed by *The Road to Serfdom*, Hayek's 1944 bestseller. Hayek had once been the standard-bearer of the Austrian school of economics, but his reputation had begun to slide during the Great Depression as he resisted government efforts to revive the sunken economy. Unlike his counterparts at the University of Chicago, Hayek did not call for immediate relief efforts and monetary reform. He viewed deflation as salutary, since it could break up wage and price rigidities—a position he later came to regret.[3] Instead, from his post at the London School of Economics, Hayek ruminated on connections between the rise of fascism in his homeland and the growing clamor for economic intervention in Great Britain.

Written amid the bombardment of London, *The Road to Serfdom* warned that socialism and economic planning would end in dictatorship, as illustrated by Nazi Germany. (Constrained by the wartime alliance with Russia, Hayek said little about the equally worrisome perils of Soviet Communism.) While it might appear planning had been successful in the United States and England, Hayek argued these were only the early stages. The national unity developed in war was bound to sunder in peace. And then, how would a nation agree on a plan? "An economic plan, to deserve the name, must have a unitary conception," Hayek argued. When disagreements arose, planners would turn to coercion. "A democracy which embarks on planning progressively relinquishes its powers," he warned.[4]

Hayek disagreed with the widespread idea that large industrial economies required planning. To the contrary, he argued it was only the hidden hand of the market—what he would later term spontaneous order—that could bring structure to an infinitely complex web of interdependent economic relationships. Along the lines of Frank Knight and Henry Simons, Hayek contended that the allocation in a mass society was best handled by the price system. Only prices could instantaneously respond to a multivalent onrush of human wants, desires, and constraints. Planners would always be one beat behind. Their plans would distort and disorient buyers and sellers.

At the same time, Hayek wanted to move beyond a "dogmatic laissez faire attitude" of "leaving things just as they are." Abandoning his former austerity, Hayek carved out a significant role for state action, although he tended to be vague about the particulars, referring to "an extensive system of social services" and "a comprehensive system of social insurance." Now open to some basic elements of the welfare state, Hayek also stressed how the state necessarily shaped what he later called "the competitive order." Even if a government didn't create economic plans, it powerfully shaped the social and legal climate. Without elaborating the details, Hayek called for a "systematic study of the forms of legal institutions which will make the competitive system work effectively." In a companion essay, he urged creation of "a new liberal program which appeals to the imagination."[5] This was akin to what Simons had called "a positive program for laissez faire" in the pamphlet that made his name.

Aaron Director passed Hayek's manuscript to the University of Chicago Press, helping secure its publication. Also important was praise from Knight and the unlikely figure of Jacob Marschak, the socialist director of the Cowles Commission, who judged Hayek's book would raise the level of discussion "between advocates and adversaries of free enterprise." None anticipated its wild success. Appearing as a comic in *Look* magazine and abridged in *Reader's Digest*—a magazine with an audience of nearly nine million readers—*The Road to Serfdom* became an overnight sensation in the United States. By the time Hayek arrived in New York in April 1945, he was an intellectual celebrity. Tweedy and reserved, Hayek was initially taken aback by his unexpected fame. Soon he relished speaking to overflow crowds across the nation, his Germanic accent no doubt underscoring his credibility even as it encumbered his pronunciation.[6]

The Road to Serfdom landed amid intense American debates about the fate of wartime planning. Not only had income taxation increased significantly during the war, but the federal government had developed an extensive apparatus to ration goods and control their prices. The Office of Price Administration had swelled to a force of 250,000 workers, both paid and voluntary, with field investigators empowered to monitor landlords and shopkeepers, while distributing ration stamps to shoppers.[7] From meat to rent, many of the daily prices Americans paid were set by the government. By the end of Hayek's first month on his book tour, however, the end of the war was in sight—both Roosevelt and Hitler were dead, and Nazi Germany was defeated. Even before Japan surrendered in August, the prospect of decontrol loomed. Weighty questions were at hand: How fast should wartime regulations be revoked? Should agencies like the Office of Price Administration be abolished, or retrofitted for peace? What about factories that were built to produce war goods—should these revert to private ownership, or be claimed by the state, as some suggested? Hayek's critique of planning spoke directly to these questions.

Even if wartime regulations were stripped away—as they were within a year—American employers still faced a transformed post–New Deal landscape in which federal law increasingly defined and shaped the employment they could offer. Working conditions and wages were now regulated through the Fair Labor Standards Act, and labor unions had received an enormous boost with the Wagner Act. Sharpening the issue was a wave of industrial strikes that broke out after war ended and continued for nearly a year. And in 1946, Winston Churchill described an "iron curtain" descending across Europe, with Soviet Communism emerging as a palpable totalitarian threat. Written during the war, *The Road to Serfdom* expressed a distrust of economic planning and worries about rising authoritarianism that remained relevant to the postwar era.

Hayek's critics were sure it was "big business" that was using the book to "spread distrust and fear of the New Deal." It was true that Hayek's book had been quickly repurposed for partisan gain, a move made easier by the popular adaptations that circulated more widely than his nuanced text. Most American readers encountered not Hayek's actual book but the comic strip or *Reader's Digest* abbreviated version—with important consequences for how his ideas were understood. Despite his disclaimers, many Americans read him as calling for a complete rollback of the New Deal and an unvarnished return to laissez-faire economics. It was also true that Hayek did have admirers who were executives of major corporations, including DuPont and General Motors. However, many of his most ardent fans were middling entrepreneurs and business owners who chafed at new federal controls—men like Luhnow of the Volker Fund.[8]

After Hayek spoke at the Detroit Economic Club, a friend introduced the two men. Wasting little time, Luhnow made a straightforward proposal: he wanted an American *Road to Serfdom*, a book with mass appeal designed specifically for a U.S. audience, and he was willing to pay for it.

Hearing that Hayek had the ear of a wealthy donor, Simons swung into action. Hayek and Simons had traded letters over the years, seeing in each other kindred spirits. Now they worked together on a new proposal. By May, shortly after meeting Luhnow, Hayek convinced him to broaden his horizons, suggesting a three-year "study of the conditions for an effective, competitive order in the United States."[9] Hayek could not run a multiyear study himself, he explained to Luhnow, but he could gather a group and oversee its work through regular visits to the United States. Eventually Luhnow pledged financial support to form an Institute of Political Economy, to be headquartered at Chicago and led by Director.[10]

In the aftermath of Simons's death, the proposal was refined into a slightly less ambitious Free Market Study, with Director still playing a starring role. Hollow though Chicago must have felt without Simons, Director dutifully proceeded with the project, an unsteady amalgamation of interests and motives that seemed uniquely ill-suited to his leadership. The primary deliverable was a book—to be authored by a man who had not even started, much less finished, a dissertation. Protracted negotiations had, however, given Director some room to maneuver. He had funding to hire researchers, and his only real supervisor was Hayek, who was an ocean away.

Moreover, Hayek needed Director too. Logical and principled in his economics, in his personal life Hayek was buffeted by strong emotions and irresolvable conflict. When a youthful infatuation with a distant cousin ended in her marriage to another man, he too married in haste. After decades of regret, Hayek determined to correct the mistake, planning to leave his first wife for his long-lost love. Divorce in this era was unusual, even scandalous. Hayek would need to make a clean break. And he would be obliged to support two families at once, something that he calculated could be done only with an American salary. Director was thus a critical ally as Hayek looked toward his next moves.[11]

If the Volker Fund was no Rockefeller Foundation, neither was the Free Market Study equivalent in scope, scale, or stature to the Cowles Commission—at least in the beginning. Whereas Cowles boasted a fearsome roster of established international talent alongside rising new stars, the Free Market Study was a small and eclectic group, composed of administrators and professors, including the chair of the economics department, the deans of the business school and law school, the law professor Edward Levi, and Frank Knight. Its main events, at first, were lunches at the university Quadrangle Club. In this group, it was Friedman and Director who drove the action. Although he would be honored with the presidency of the American Economic Association in 1950, Knight had his eye on retirement. Increasingly he turned his intellectual energies away from economics toward history and philosophy. And especially in the early months, when Director was still unmoored by the loss of Simons, it was Friedman who emerged as the most powerful influence.

When Director circulated a wandering outline of items the group might consider, Friedman responded with a detailed memo titled "A Program of Factual Research into Questions Basic to the Formulation of a Liberal Economic Policy." The memo advocated "careful, objective, and impartial research" but warned it could not be guided "in detail by the needs of the policy study" lest it turn "into hack work."[12] He was setting up the Free Market Study along the lines of an economics workshop, and moving to minimize the Volker Fund's influence.

Friedman had good reason to be suspicious of the Volker Fund. Only that past summer, he and George Stigler had tangled with another private funder, the Foundation for Economic Education. Before coming to Chicago, Friedman had spent the 1945–1946 academic year on the faculty at the University of Minnesota, where Stigler also taught.

Their conversations yielded a pamphlet that waded into the debate about removing wartime controls, *Roofs or Ceilings?*

The pamphlet took up Friedman's long-standing opposition to price controls, analyzing them through the lens of price theory. During the war, the Office of Price Administration regulated about 80 percent of the nation's housing stock. By the summer of 1946, industrial reconversion was well under way, with wage controls, allocations controls, and rationing all peeled back. Rent controls persisted, in part because of a housing shortage they were thought to assuage. Friedman and Stigler argued that price controls had actually triggered the current housing crisis: "The legal ceilings on rents are the reason there are so few places for rent." With rent control in place, there was no incentive for additional construction, and landlords were selling properties instead of renting at regulated low prices. Therefore, allowing housing prices to rise would ultimately create more housing stock. This was the kind of writing Friedman had urged Arthur Burns to take up a few years earlier: "propagandizing" to help the public understand the economics underlying policy debates. Friedman and Stigler hoped to publish in *Harper's Magazine* or *The New York Times*.[13]

Instead, they ended up with the Foundation for Economic Education. The brainchild of Leonard Read, formerly the head of the Los Angeles Chamber of Commerce, FEE was a new type of institution: a think tank dedicated to promoting free market ideas. Unlike the Volker Fund or the Rockefeller Foundation, FEE did not fund academic research and then step back. Its primary goal was to pump out pamphlets, leaflets, and abridged work suitable for a mass audience. Where the Volker Fund's capital grew out of a family business, FEE pooled donations from executives at large corporations like B. F. Goodrich, DuPont, General Motors, and Republic Steel. It also received funding directly from the Volker Fund, and Harold Luhnow sat on the board.[14]

FEE and the Volker Fund were part of a broader backlash against Keynesian economics, the same ideological tide that lifted Hayek to fame. Even as aggregate demand management was enshrined in the Employment Act of 1946, opponents of the New Deal order fought back. University-level economics was a critical front. In 1947 controversy erupted over an early Keynesian textbook after it was denounced by Rose Wilder Lane—a well-known magazine writer who was secretly ghosting her mother's famous *Little House on the Prairie* children's books. Lane was also editing the *Economic Council Review of Books* for the National Economic Council, yet another small private pro-business organization. The *Economic Council Review of Books* was an obscure publication, more like a pamphlet, and the NEC itself would soon fade to the anti-Semitic fringe. In the moment, however, Lane's vociferous critique circulated widely, igniting broader concerns about the state of economics. At MIT, Paul Samuelson faced a Visiting Committee that investigated his forthcoming textbook. Samuelson's *Economics: An Introductory Analysis* ultimately avoided controversy and became a staple of college economics courses.[15]

In retrospect, FEE and the Volker Fund have been recognized as important early manifestations of modern American conservatism.[16] Yet at the time, neither identified as a conservative organization. Indeed, the word "conservative" was somewhat of an orphan in political discussion immediately following World War II. "Among the most unpopular words in the American vocabulary," summarized one writer, while another called it "the Forbidden Faith." In 1948, even Senator Robert Taft, the storied legislator known as Mr. Republican, contended he was a liberal. In part, this was because conservatism was understood in philosophical or religious terms. If it had an economic component, it was not what critics derided as Manchester economics—full-throated support for laissez faire and free trade. Rather, observers presumed conservatives would support state intervention in the economy in order to create their preferred social order. The historian Arthur Schlesinger Jr. summed up the consensus: "Conservatism is not the private property of the National Association of Manufacturers. It is not a device for increasing the short-run security of business."[17]

Nonetheless, there were suggestive links between organized business opposition to the New Deal and the later emergence of political conservatism. Lane's critique of the Keynesian textbook, for example, was picked up by a young William F. Buckley Jr., who would in 1951 extend

Lane's ideas into a widely noted broadside against his alma mater, *God and Man at Yale.*[18] Later, Buckley founded *National Review*, the flagship magazine of postwar conservatism, and made Manchester economics a key component of conservatism as it evolved in the United States. Organizations like FEE preferred to identify themselves as advocates of "the freedom philosophy," as Read put it. And they were far from representative of the entire business community, as Read learned when potential donors expected FEE to support tariffs or lobby for special deals. When FEE opposed the Marshall Plan, which provided American aid to Europe, they found little corporate support. Nevertheless, FEE, the Volker Fund, and the larger community that surrounded them might usefully be called business conservatives, recognizing their funding sources and interest in restoring the pre–New Deal economic climate. Operating at one remove from politics, FEE and Volker focused intensely on spreading ideas, hoping to influence debate downstream.[19]

FEE had its stable of economists, although most were from a different era. A particular favorite was the irascible Austrian economist Ludwig von Mises, Hayek's mentor and star of the 1920s "socialist calculation debate." Looking to the enormous economic mobilization for World War I, European Marxists contended that even in peacetime, governments could successfully allocate goods and services, replacing prices altogether. Mises parried with an argument that calculation was impossible within a socialist system; fundamentally there would be no exchange, only transfers. The vogue for planning continued, but Mises had laid down a powerful rebuttal. FEE worked to set Mises up with a visiting professorship at New York University, and the Volker Fund agreed to pay his salary.[20] Another FEE favorite was Thomas Nixon Carver, a retired Harvard professor. Still, FEE wanted academic economists at the top of the "intellectual hierarchy," men on the rise, not relics from the past—men like Friedman and Stigler.[21]

Yet there was a considerable ideological gap between business opponents of the New Deal and their potential scholarly allies. Stigler jokingly called FEE "a Tory outfit."[22] Nonetheless, he and Friedman were shocked when FEE insisted on editing their pamphlet. Writing with a goal to "convince the open-minded, not those who already favor our position," Friedman and Stigler addressed the concern that removing controls would mean richer people got better housing. This was a problem, the authors noted, since they "would like even more equality than there is at present, not alone for housing but for all products."[23] The solution, however, was regulation of incomes through taxation, rather than controlling prices. With its egalitarian tone and advocacy for taxation over regulation, *Roofs or Ceilings?* was squarely in the tradition of *A Positive Program for Laissez Faire*, the Simons tract Friedman and Stigler had so admired as students.

But to FEE president Read and his deputy Orval Watts, equality and taxation had no place in the case for capitalism. Energetic and self-educated, Read had founded FEE specifically to avoid presenting "both sides" of current issues. From his vantage point, one side was already well represented in government and academia; FEE's mission was to present a clear alternative. While Watts held a Ph.D. from Harvard, where he had studied with Carver, he too had little patience for academic nuance. After a teaching career at Carleton College, paired with summer work educating business owners, Watts had moved to a full-time position with the Los Angeles Chamber of Commerce, and then joined Read at FEE. While not a full-blown eugenicist like his mentor Carver, Watts was openly antidemocratic, elitist, and given to social Darwinist–style logic.[24]

After considerable back and forth, Friedman and Stigler agreed to remove the taxation reference. But Friedman refused to delete the language about equality. "Sentence in question does not mention specific techniques for achieving equality," he stressed in a telegram to FEE. "I believe it is essential to make it clear wherein we are criticizing means and wherein ends." Talking about equality was not just a throwaway line. It had real consequences, he believed: "The failure of liberals to emphasize their objective seems to me one of chief reasons they are so often labeled reactionaries."[25] Here, Friedman was aligning himself with the larger project of Hayek and Simons to create a "new liberal program." Friedman and Stigler insisted the pamphlet include the reference to equality, or not be published at all.

But FEE could not spike the pamphlet because it had a contract with the National Association of Real Estate Boards. Rent control was not merely an economic puzzle for professors to clarify; it was a live political issue, linked to a larger attack on the New Deal. Caught in a bind, FEE published the pamphlet—adding without the authors' permission a querulous footnote accusing them of putting "equality above justice and liberty." A second condensed version created for the National Association of Real Estate Boards excised the offending paragraph on equality altogether. Half a million copies were printed for wide circulation.[26]

Friedman and Stigler had been played, and they were furious. Stigler erupted at Watts: "I must confess that I got sore as hell. I told him that it was intolerable to be pushed about by those punks in the National Real Estate Association [*sic*], that there was nothing but a little dubious fame in the printing for us and the complete loss of our reputations if we started suppressing our own views. He replied (1) that after all, the income tax is a crime, threatening savings and hence employment, (2) it's collectivistic to have more equality, and we have too much now, and (3) we could always write for equality—in some other place." In a later exchange of letters, Watts continued to attack "Robin Hood policy." After more heated back-and-forth, Friedman and Stigler agreed to let the matter drop. Writing to a colleague, Friedman admitted that "the foundation which published the pamphlet turned out to be a great deal worse than we had anticipated." In a letter to Burns, he wished it had never been published.[27]

In the wake of this episode, Friedman had ample reason to be wary about the Free Market Study. Did he know that Luhnow, who controlled the Volker Fund, also sat on FEE's board? Was he aware that Hayek had agreed to place Read on the Free Market Study oversight committee? Probably not—Hayek was the main contact point for the Volker Fund, so the specific arrangements may have remained obscure. And in his memoir, Friedman declared that after the pamphlet episode, "for some years we refused to have anything to do with the foundation or with Leonard Read." Either way, Friedman's comment that the study should avoid "hack work" no doubt reflected his experience with *Roofs or Ceilings?* As a result, he was determined that the Free Market Study should be above all a research enterprise.[28]

Friedman also genuinely wanted to work out just how far the logic of price could be extended. He recognized at least three great exceptions to market arrangements. Natural monopolies, like railroads or utilities, were cases in which it made economic sense to have one producer. Neighborhood effects—today called externalities—were times when the price of a commercial activity might not adequately capture the cost or benefit to "neighbors." The classic example was factory pollution blackening nearby air or water, but a park or green space that lifted the spirits of passersby could be a positive neighborhood effect. Then there was monopoly. It was always possible enterprises might collude in "a conspiracy against the public, or in some contrivance to raise prices," as Adam Smith famously observed. In these instances, Simons had advocated state intervention, calling for "outright dismantling of our gigantic corporations, and persistent prosecution of producers who organize, by whatever methods, for price maintenance or output limitation." For the most part, Friedman appeared to agree. But there must have been a fissure of doubt.[29]

As Friedman saw it, monopoly was a fundamental issue dividing Manchester or classical liberals from New Deal liberals:

> Many of those who believe monopoly, and hence state planning, inevitable would have their faith shaken if they were convinced that the supposed technical economies of gigantic enterprises are largely illusory. Similarly, our faith in the vigor of competition would be shaken if it were shown that, as is frequently claimed, monopoly has been growing by leaps and bounds and, even in the absence of direct governmental support, tends to drive competition out of field after field; while "their" faith in the inevitability of monopoly would be shaken if it were found that, government intervention aside, monopoly tends to disappear and competition to revive even where once dormant.[30]

Friedman's memo proposed to open an altogether new line of inquiry: Did monopoly really exist? Was it inevitable and durable, or did it tend "to disappear?" These were questions Simons hadn't even bothered to ask.

The assumption that monopoly was pervasive dated from the early Progressive era—the days of Standard Oil, muckrakers, and trust-busting. The Sherman Antitrust Act passed in 1890, and the Clayton Antitrust Act in 1914. This tradition had been given a boost during the New Deal. In some quarters, monopoly itself explained the downturn, the idea being that large producers made the economy rigid and unbalanced. Accordingly, some New Dealers, like Thurman Arnold, saw the fight against monopoly as essential. Yet other New Dealers, like Adolf Berle, believed monopoly was inevitable in advanced economies. They were even willing to highlight the upsides, like economic efficiency and stability—as long as monopolies were managed by planners.[31]

So Friedman was not quite right to frame monopoly as the basic cleavage between traditional and New Deal liberalism, given these disagreements. But it was true that monopoly occupied an important place in both American politics and economic theory. In 1941, the Temporary National Economic Committee, set up by Congress to investigate monopoly, published a widely noted report. "So great a proportion of all national savings and national wealth have fallen under the control of a few organized enterprises, that the opportunity of those individuals who will constitute the next generation will be completely foreclosed," the TNEC concluded. The committee's recommendations, such as expanding the Federal Trade Commission's powers and federal incorporation—state-managed companies—found little purchase. Yet its efforts to measure and define monopoly, including the publication of a 340-page study measuring concentration, provided fodder aplenty for economists. It was also widely believed that World War II had made the problem worse. By some estimates, 51 percent of wartime contracts had been awarded to thirty-three of the nation's largest companies.[32]

And at Chicago here was Warren Nutter, a Ph.D. student preparing to carry out the very sort of empirical study Friedman envisioned. Nutter was perhaps the last Chicago student to be "Simonized." A classmate remembered Nutter arriving at Chicago a socialist before enrolling in Simons's required economics course. At first, he regarded Simons "as a decidedly sinister figure." After weeks of silence, "he then began talking about economics from the essential position he held for the rest of his life."[33] Nutter was devastated by Simons's death. But he soon found new backers at the Free Market Study, becoming Friedman's first doctoral student.

In the spring of 1947, as his inaugural year teaching at Chicago wound down, Friedman took his first trip out of the country, on what Stigler called "a junket to Switzerland . . . to save liberalism"—the first meeting of the Mont Pelerin Society, Hayek's new international society of economists. The same discussions that led to Director's arrival at Chicago also yielded a Volker Fund pledge to support Hayek's nascent society. A Swiss businessman underwrote the remaining costs. Thus Hayek was able to offer his American participants an all-expenses-paid ten-day trip to Europe to discuss political and economic ideas. Although Friedman had two young children at home and was settling into a new job, this was not the kind of invitation he would decline.[34]

The tensions that marked *Roofs or Ceilings?* also defined the Mont Pelerin Society. Hayek was surprised when Luhnow objected to several names on his original invite list; although the specific names have been lost to history, Luhnow may well have meant Friedman and Stigler, given their recent clash with FEE. Whereas Hayek wanted to formulate a "new liberalism," Luhnow and his donors wanted to ensure that "real liberalism" was represented at the conference, especially if they were footing the cost of travel. Hayek mollified Luhnow not by removing names but by including several "observers" of his choice—among them Read and Watts of FEE.[35]

Thus Friedman crossed the Atlantic on the ocean liner RMS *Queen Elizabeth* with Director, Knight, Stigler, and Watts, his recent antagonist. There was no thaw with Watts, either during passage or at the meeting. But Friedman got on better with Henry Hazlitt, a *New York*

Times journalist who was a bit player in the pamphlet drama—he had passed *Roofs or Ceilings?* along to FEE after the *Times* declined. Hazlitt was a devotee of the classical gold standard, and whenever the seas calmed enough for conversation, he and Friedman carried on a running debate about money, gold, and the quantity theory.[36]

The group stopped briefly in London and Paris before arriving in the small lakeside town of Vevey, Switzerland. A funicular railway pulled them up to the mountaintop hamlet of Mont Pelerin. The conference was held in the belle époque Hotel du Parc, graced with a stunning chandelier in the lobby and views of Lake Geneva from the front terrace. Here they joined an eclectic group, including the British economist Lionel Robbins and the philosophers of science Karl Popper and Michael Polanyi. Hovering on the sidelines was Read, tasked with keeping tabs on any collectivist drift among the economists.

Simons didn't live to join the Mont Pelerin Society, but at that first meeting he was nonetheless a presence. Amid bridge, sightseeing, and back-to-back sessions about the problems of the world, Simons's friends rearticulated his view of classical liberalism. Knight used Simons's exact words when he called fractional reserve banking "diabolically designed" and argued for 100 percent money.[37] In a discussion of the group's agenda, Friedman argued that liberalism should be "dynamic and progressive. We want to make sure that our manifesto is concerned in the progress of man's welfare." Ventriloquizing Simons, Friedman continued: "We have to agree on the necessity for a positive approach."[38]

Similarly, Director began the meeting with an address that emphasized the "humanitarian tradition of liberalism," yet noted serious conflicts "between what liberals consider the social interests and the results of free enterprise." The problem the society needed to address was that "the liberal had no solution to offer derived from their fundamental philosophy."[39] Voiced by Director, Simons's ideas blended seamlessly into Hayek's desire for a new liberalism.

Friedman dilated on a specific example of an updated liberalism, touting the idea of "progressive negative taxation," an updated version of his 1939 proposal for guaranteed minimum income. He had now linked it explicitly to the tax system, as a sort of reverse withholding. Instead of removing taxes at the source, the government could pump money in at the source to those with low incomes.

In response to questions, Friedman offered several reasons why a minimum income was a liberal policy. "This would give an incentive to getting additional income," he argued. Here, Friedman seemed to be thinking of the traditional poor law, which removed benefits as income increased. By contrast, his approach provided a guaranteed minimum that could supplement any earned income. At the same time, Friedman stressed this approach would act as a "substitute, not as an addition, to present social policy," while noting that essential social services, such as "funds for orphans," would continue. This was important because cash grants would avoid the private-market impacts of public-sector job and relief programs. Finally, he suggested that individual income support would have positive macroeconomic consequences: "If you manage to have a liberal society with this flexibility, it would be very good from a cyclical point of view."[40] When wage earners fell beneath the basic-income line due to recession, they would find their income supplemented, stanching the deflationary spiral. In good times, the income supplement would be needed by far fewer people.

Throughout the meeting, Friedman insisted poverty was a critical issue for the group to tackle. Partially this was because other proposals to raise low incomes—like labor unions—had negative consequences for the competitive order. But he also insisted that poverty was a basic social reality liberals needed to address. "Even if we had completely free access to different employments, and to capital, there would still be the problem of poverty," he told the group. Amplifying his thoughts, Friedman asserted: "Men are not born equal . . . There are definitely people who cannot earn, in the marketplace, an income even that we could consider to be a minimum." But Friedman went on to discuss this vexing social problem in an engineering idiom, noting, "Other people have to pay for this help. Therefore we have progressive taxation. No democratic society is going to tolerate people starving to death, if there is food with which to feed them."[41] Was this a good thing or a bad thing? Friedman presented it as a basic social fact, drained of ethical content.

Not all meeting attendees agreed that classical liberalism even needed to be reformulated. "You're all socialists!" Mises stormed at one session, stalking out of the room.[42] Mises and his American admirers raised a ruckus any time the idea of monopoly—and state intervention to correct it—arose. Adherents of the Austrian school did not believe monopoly could persist in a truly competitive economy. State intervention was the cause of monopoly, by creating artificial barriers to entry, rather than its cure. "Why do people attack the monopoly, and not the patent law, the tariff, etc?" Mises asked. Summarizing Mises's thinking, Hazlitt argued, "The biggest problem of monopoly is of government created monopoly."[43] FEE representative Watts took a similar hard line, arguing that the "problem of [business] cycles has largely been caused by government," and criticizing unemployment relief, a policy supported by most other members.[44]

Similar tensions bubbled up over international affairs. When Watts claimed there was "growing dissatisfaction in America with American intervention in Europe," Friedman shot back quickly, "I don't think Watts's opinions are representative of the USA."[45] The jab revealed lingering animosity from the *Roofs or Ceilings?* episode. It also showcased the palpable divide between the pre-war outlook of Watts—isolationist in foreign affairs, darkly suspicious of any state action—and the more flexible and pragmatic liberalism Friedman hoped to promote.

Friedman called this "neo-liberalism" in a 1951 essay he published in a Norwegian magazine, edited by a Mont Pelerin contact. "We have a new faith to offer," Friedman wrote, answering Hayek's call for ideas that would stir the imagination. Echoing *The Road to Serfdom*, Friedman distinguished this new faith from laissez-faire, which he called "a negative philosophy." Where an earlier generation of liberals believed "the state could do only harm," new liberals "must explicitly recognize that there are important positive functions that must be performed by the state." What were these positive functions? Friedman was more specific than Hayek. He continued to believe preventing monopoly was important, lauding the Sherman Antitrust Act. There was a role for the state in providing monetary stability, he noted, an implicit argument against goldbugs like Hazlitt. And he assigned government a responsibility to relieve "acute misery and distress," noting, "Our world has become too complicated and intertwined, and we have become too sensitive, to leave this function entirely to private charity or local responsibility."[46] Although Friedman did not mention the Great Depression, he was pushing back against the ideas of men like the former president Herbert Hoover, who believed relief was the role of states and municipalities. Equally he was countering the Hayek of the early 1930s, who would leave the Depression to run its course. These were the demarcation lines between liberalism old and new.

Friedman had by now cast his lot definitively with the Republican Party, believing it to be the best supporter of his free market principles. Rose signed up to be a precinct worker in Hyde Park, which was notably short of Republicans. But it was not enough to find a location across the Republican-Democratic divide; the Friedmans had to find their place within the broader Republican universe itself.

The early 1950s was a fluid moment for the party, which had been out of the presidency since Herbert Hoover. There had been a brief rally in 1946, when Republican congressional candidates swept into the majority, based largely on their opposition to Harry Truman. But the Democratic president had regrouped with a famous upset of Thomas Dewey in the election of 1948, positioning himself as the heir and legatee of the New Deal.

In response, the Republicans faced a series of interlinked quandaries. Did they become the party of "me too," serving to ratify the New Deal order? Or did they continue to resist the emerging popular consensus that the federal government should, and could, underwrite economic prosperity?

In international affairs, while both parties vied to prove their anti-Communist bona fides, the Republicans also struggled with two powerful riptides. There was Joseph McCarthy's aggressive anti-Communism, which had proved an effective cudgel against Democrats but was clearly a weapon that could boomerang against Republicans. At the same time, the isolationist Old Right, which fought against the United States entering World War II, had yet to be fully displaced. Its elder statesmen were still alive, including President Hoover and Senator Robert Taft. These two seemingly contradictory impulses merged in an angry populism, typified by Robert McCormick's *Chicago Tribune*. In rhetoric tinted with anti-Semitism, McCormick and his far-right allies retailed a seductive story of American values sold out by a scheming internationalist elite.

Friedman thought highly of Taft. They had met while Friedman worked at the Treasury Department, and he appreciated Taft's quick mind and attention to detail. But Taft was an opponent of NATO, the military alliance that bound the United States and Western Europe; he publicly doubted the wisdom of executing German war criminals. His presidential ambitions had faltered twice before due to his uncompromising isolationism. In the postwar era, his isolationism would again be fatal. Friedman shared Taft's foreboding about the American state's new role in the economy, but not in the world. And this internationalist orientation would decisively shape his political outlook.

The Friedmans' commitment to American power was strengthened by time spent in Europe. In the fall of 1950, Friedman took several months' leave from Chicago to consult for the Marshall Plan, the U.S. government's omnibus aid package to war-torn Europe. For most of the time, the family lived in Parisian luxury, enjoying a rented home with servants, French schools for the children, and the chance to socialize with Mont Pelerin acquaintances.

But on a sightseeing trip to Frankfurt, they felt suddenly vulnerable. Upon seeing German police officers directing traffic, Rose remembered "the feeling of revulsion and fear was so great that we could not bring ourselves to stop for lunch until late in the afternoon when we reached an American military snack bar." Settling into a German hotel mainly patronized by American visitors did little to help. Rose reluctantly took the children to a nearby park, beset by "the nagging fear that they might suddenly disappear . . . there was always in my subconscious those terrible stories about what happened to Jewish children during the Nazi era." Likewise, Friedman confessed to Stigler: "I have seldom had so strong an emotional reaction as I did when we first drove into Germany." The couple was acutely aware that most Jewish families from their ancestral villages—in Rose's case, her birthplace—had not survived the war.[47]

Friedman's work for the Marshall Plan centered him in the new web of interlocking treaties and alliances that served to construct the postwar order. Prominent among these was Bretton Woods, the new currency union built atop the ruins of the classical gold standard. Bretton Woods placed the U.S. dollar at the center of global exchange. It also set up two multinational organizations: the World Bank, intended to support European economies damaged by war, and the International Monetary Fund, intended to stabilize currencies and prevent a repeat of the Great Depression. These were the international analogues of New Deal banking reform, and for the most part Friedman accepted them as necessary stops against another crisis. This was another mark of distinction between Friedman and FEE, which supported Hazlitt's unsuccessful crusade against the Marshall Plan.

Over time, Friedman would grow increasingly skeptical of foreign aid programs, particularly those that supported state-led economic development. In these years, however, the only sign of skepticism was his willingness to think beyond the current institutional arrangements. Continuing his effort to broadly apply price theory to policy questions, Friedman wondered what it would look like if prices, rather than institutions or officials, structured international trade. He wrote up a proposal for "floating" exchange rates—a system in which foreign currencies would trade in open markets, with their value set by markets rather than governments or international agreements. It was a wild idea at the time—but a regime that would emerge decades later after the decline of Bretton Woods.[48]

Friedman's support for a robust U.S. presence in Europe was widely held among moderate Republicans and helped motivate the 1952 candidacy of Dwight Eisenhower. Courted by both parties, the popular general was worried that a Taft presidency could undo the victories of World War II. He would eventually run as a Republican, enraging Taft's grassroots supporters.[49] Sharing Eisenhower's global outlook, and alert to dangerous currents on the American right, Friedman supported his candidacy.

In a remarkable exchange of letters with longtime friend Fritz Machlup, Friedman displayed a powerful, if tactical, partisan identity. After hearing that Machlup intended to vote for the Democrat Adlai Stevenson in the 1952 presidential election, Friedman was "shocked," given their shared commitment to free markets. After all, the Democrats favored "price control, rent control, wage control, etc."[50] But Machlup was motivated by opposition to McCarthy's zealous crusade against Communists, which was roiling universities across the nation as leftist professors lost jobs and worried administrators pushed loyalty oaths on faculty. An Austrian-born Jewish economist, Machlup saw in McCarthy the second coming of Nazism. He could not bring himself to vote for a presidential candidate who shared his party.

In response, Friedman argued that bad as McCarthy was, he would be better contained by a Republican administration. "Extremists are always far more potent when their party is out of power than when it is in power," he wrote, asking, "What is McCarthy going to talk about if E. is elected? Communists in the State Dep't or White House?"[51] In fact, Friedman had accidentally anticipated the direction of McCarthy's unhinged crusade; he would eventually accuse the Armed Forces of Communist sympathies. And as Friedman's scoffing reference suggested, this attack on an august American institution would prove to be McCarthy's downfall.

Friedman argued the greater danger was that an Eisenhower defeat would embolden McCarthyites and weaken moderate Republicanism: "They will be able to say that 4 times now the me-tooers + internationalist wing of the party has led them down to defeat." The triumph of this extreme wing of the party, which Friedman identified with both McCarthy and the *Chicago Tribune*, would be an "unmitigated disaster."[52] Friedman's opposition to McCarthy was sincere. At the same time, Friedman carefully set McCarthy in a global context when thinking about his own politics.

Friedman sternly rebuked Machlup's German analogy, using it to expand on the unique qualities of American political and intellectual life. "I believe that you are seeing ghosts under the table where there are none," he wrote. The key distinction was between German and American culture. "The democratic tradition here is deep and profound; it is really a part of our culture," Friedman wrote, even as he admitted, "McCarthy is not a new phenomenon." But if McCarthy was part of a line that included Palmer raids and Father Coughlin, it was also true that "again and again, the public at large has been taken in only so far and no farther. Let us keep a sense of perspective." Eisenhower was no Hindenburg, no puppet; he was "imbued with American ideals." These ideals, Friedman suggested, acted to constrain those in power. Yet they also served in some way as the substrate of political life: "You need not only a Hindenburg—Hitler—Von Papen; you also need a Hegel."[53] Here was a clue to how Friedman conceived his own purpose and mission as a thinker. Here also were traces of Hayek, who had written so urgently about the power of ideas. Even if Friedman did not think America was on the road to serfdom, he saw himself contributing to a powerful strand of American individualism that stood as a bulwark against tyranny, with profound political implications.

The emerging outlines of a worldview were coming into focus. Friedman did not want to be a reactionary—a word he associated with isolationism, anti-Semitism, and "hack work." He remained inspired by his former teachers Knight and Simons, even as he subjected their views to careful examination. He was experimenting with policies built atop the price system. And he was groping toward a new language of values that would complement his economic analysis.

In the meantime, Director took the Free Market Study in an unexpected direction. There had been no mention of teaching in the original discussions with the Volker Fund, but Director picked up Simons's courses in the law school. As an undergrad instructor, Director had been a flop. He had better luck playing off Edward Levi, who asked him to co-teach a course on antitrust law. Levi, who had been close to Simons, was a former special assistant to the New Deal trust-buster Thurman Arnold. In the Progressive tradition, Levi saw monopoly as pervasive and antitrust enforcement as key to market competition. Given how closely Director's early assumptions about the dangers of monopoly echoed Simons, Levi could not have imagined that by inviting Director into his classroom, he was unwittingly launching an intellectual revolution: law and economics.[54]

Before long, a recurrent clash of views unfolded. The first four days of the course were a solid rendition of established antitrust law, with Levi summarizing and synthesizing important cases using traditional legal reasoning. On Friday, Director took center stage, and the magic began. Director had been burrowing in the library stacks, and listening skeptically to Levi's ideas. From the perspective of Chicago price theory, existing antitrust law simply didn't make sense. One student remembered: "For one day each week Aaron Director would tell us that everything that Levi had told us the preceding four days was nonsense. He used economic analysis to show us that the legal analysis simply would not stand up." For some in the room, Director's teaching was nothing less than a revelation. Robert Bork recalled that a certain set of students "underwent what can only be called a religious conversion. It changed our view of the entire world . . . We became janissaries as a result of this experience."[55] Driven by the ongoing duel between Levi and Director, the classroom thrummed with excitement. After all these years, Director had bottled some of Knight's lightning.

There was another profound intellectual match unfolding before the students, unbeknownst to them: a struggle between Director and his deceased best friend, Simons. For all his fierce defense of the market, Simons had always reserved a large role for the state, going so far as to advocate nationalization of railroads and utilities. And he thought monopoly was rampant in the United States, threatening the small businesses, sole proprietors, and individual consumers who were the essence of American liberty. To preserve freedom itself—to help the people counteract the interests—antitrust law was essential.

But now, Director was systematically undermining not only the legal basis of antitrust law but the idea that monopoly itself fundamentally shaped economic life. Why was Director turning from Simons's views?

The essence of Director's approach was applying price theory to legal questions—just as Friedman applied price theory to political questions. A classroom discussion of predatory pricing, pre-Director, might revolve around established case law, findings, and remedies. But Director might ask, how was predatory pricing defined? As the law students began to respond, he would have another question: Was the firm selling or pricing below marginal cost? If the firm was pricing below marginal cost—that is, losing money on each item sold—how was that sustainable? Wouldn't it eventually need to raise prices again, thereby tempting rivals back into the market? Exposed to an objective measure and a specific test, lawyers found the concept of predatory pricing crumbling to dust.[56]

The publication of Nutter's dissertation, *The Extent of Enterprise Monopoly in the United States, 1899–1939*, added an empirical component to Director's readings in economic theory and legal doctrine.[57] The transformation of Nutter's thinking was among the most important consequences of Simons's death. Drawn to study monopoly by Simons's conviction that it was dominant, Nutter found his research did not "substantiate the claims about the extent and growth of monopoly advanced by the extreme proponents of the 'decline of competition' school." The dissertation he produced bore the mark of Friedman's statistical prowess; nearly half the book was charts and tables, measuring among other factors the concentration of output and share of national income generated by various industries. Nutter used this data to argue against economists who claimed concentration had increased during the twentieth century. He also tested the more theoretical proposition that "monopoly is automatically generated in a free market system," and concluded it was not. Joining a roiling debate over how to measure and define monopoly, Nutter's work was well received by other economists.[58]

Another likely influence on Director was Hayek, who shared the standard Austrian view that barring state intervention, monopolies would be undermined by the perpetual churn of capitalism.[59] In the years since Director had taken up his post at the law school, Hayek had embarked upon an international pilgrimage to secure a legal divorce. After exhausting other options he ended up in Arkansas, where he lived for several months to avail himself of the state's liberal divorce laws. Finally free, and with his new wife in tow, in 1950 he landed in an intellectual's paradise: the University of Chicago's Committee on Social Thought.

A relatively new interdisciplinary unit headed by the economic historian John Nef, the committee was becoming a refuge for economists fleeing the discipline's midcentury turn to math. Both Nef and Knight eventually migrated to the committee, where broad questions of social meaning were front and center. At the committee, Hayek found a congenial social world centered around Nef and his wife, Elinor, who drew on her inheritance and social circle to fund prominent visitors like the poet T. S. Eliot and the painter Marc Chagall.[60] Director had played a key role setting up Hayek's ten-year appointment, which came with minimal teaching duties and a generous salary underwritten by the Volker Fund.

Hayek repaid the favor by blocking and tackling for Director, who was making little progress on his planned book. Hayek admitted to Luhnow that he had "not actually seen any of Mr. Director's manuscript." Nonetheless, the two had "many long and highly interesting conversations," leaving Hayek with "no doubt that he is doing very interesting work and has made good progress on his book. I don't think you or I need regret the choice we made."[61] In fact, Director had done almost no writing—certainly not of the popular character that the fund anticipated. Without Hayek's unwavering support, he would most certainly have lost the grant that was paying his salary.

Assessing the situation on the ground, Hayek grasped the value of Director's teaching at the law school. When it came time to renew his funding, the idea of a book had dropped away. Instead, in 1952 the Volker Fund awarded Director a new, multiyear grant to be headquartered at the law school: the Antitrust Project.[62] Similar in approach to the Ford Foundation–funded Arbitration Project and Jury Project, also housed at the law school during this time, the Antitrust Project gave Director broad latitude to bring in outside scholars and support promising law students after their graduation. Interest in antitrust at other universities, including Harvard Law School, created new pathways for scholars using the approach. Around this time the Cowles Commission decamped for Yale. In its place the Antitrust Project grew up into a second shadow department flanking economics, this time on the right.

John McGee, a recent economics Ph.D. from Vanderbilt, described the process. First came a long lunch with Director and Friedman. Having passed muster, McGee came to Chicago set on studying monopolization. "I arrived on the scene confident that there was ever so much monopoly—malevolent—and that it could do almost anything you could imagine." Before long, Director had convinced him that firms were constrained by competitors and the imperative to make profit. "I had never looked at it that way at all," remembered McGee. "So economics was a constraint on a whole bag of imagined activities which when subjected to that constraint started evaporating."[63] The working group filled with scholars arguing that monopoly was less a problem of capitalism and more a problem of government. So long as the state did not erect barriers to entry, competition would undercut monopolistic practices.

Along with outposts of law and economics at Harvard and UCLA, the Antitrust Project helped reorient the basic approach of American antitrust law.[64] When Director began teaching, the dominant approach was a per se understanding of antitrust. That is, certain business practices were understood as intrinsically anticompetitive, ranging from tying, in which a customer had to purchase a second good to complete the sale, to exclusive dealing, where a distributor was contracted to sell from only one manufacturer. A judge had merely to determine that these business practices were being used, not to ascertain their effect. Antitrust Project scholars advocated for a higher, more complex standard: the rule of reason. Under this approach, the court would have to satisfy a more robust set of questions to prove that disputed business practices were restricting market entry or competition. Nutter's work had argued that monopoly was less prevalent than assumed. The Antitrust Project took a further step of redefining monopoly altogether.[65]

Both moves broke decisively with the legacy of Simons. "There must be explicit and unqualified repudiation of the so-called 'rule of reason,'" Simons argued in *A Positive Program for Laissez Faire.* Simons had been gone for nearly half a decade, and now his ideas were dying too.[66]

A key interlocutor for Friedman at this moment was his old friend George Stigler, then a professor at Columbia. Jocular and energetic, Stigler towered over Friedman—in jest, friends called them Mr. Micro and Mr. Macro. The two had been close since they overlapped for a year at Chicago as students—along with Director, Stigler had been part of the Room Seven gang that venerated Simons and Knight. Later, Friedman and Stigler spent a second year together at the wartime Statistical Research Group, and a third at the University of Minnesota as both launched academic careers. Afterward came regular letters back and forth, often bearing drafts of work in progress. Both had married their sweethearts from that pivotal Chicago year, started families around the same time, and together attended the first Mont Pelerin Society meeting. Inspired by Simons, they had made a joint debut as public intellectuals with *Roofs or Ceilings?*, the 1943 pamphlet opposing rent control. And now both men were grappling with Simons's legacy, sorting through what to keep and what to discard of their lost friend's lifework.

In a 1948 London lecture—given at the invitation of Hayek—Stigler picked up the question of equality. "More recently the desire for greater equality has grown strong," he told his audience. "Every policy is scrutinized for its effects on the distribution of income, and the results of this scrutiny weigh heavily in the final judgment of the desirability of the policy." Stigler didn't point out that he, too, had felt this imperative. After all, the entire clash with FEE had concerned Friedman and Stigler's ritualized invocation of equality as an important social goal. But now Stigler doubted equality could serve as an "ultimate goal." Why was equality important? Dipping into intellectual history, Stigler rejected what he called the utilitarian and the Keynesian justification. Instead he defended the classical economists, "from Smith to Marshall," who believed "greater equality of income was an objective, but it was one of the lesser objectives." Equality mattered for the classical economists, Stigler contended, because the desire for equality led to "independence, self-reliance, self-discipline" as men strove to increase their incomes.[67]

It was not a fully worked out thesis. Stigler claimed for equality what might be better understood as the desire for distinction. At critical points in his own argument, he inserted large chunks of text from the classical writers. But the lecture touched upon a fundamental tension: "The liberal goal is unattainable in the presence of great and permanent inequalities, and it is also unattainable in the presence of permanent equality." As Stigler saw it, if the "liberal goal" of maximum personal and economic freedom generated or emerged alongside vast social inequalities, it would fall to Communism, fascism, or social democracy. Yet some inequality, Stigler believed, was essential to freedom, as it allowed for different choices and outcomes. This was the paradox Knight had ruminated on during the 1930s, as capitalism seemed on the verge of collapse. It was akin to the Hungarian political scientist Karl Polanyi's "double movement," in which markets generated social problems that led to political movements hemming them in. And it was the problem Friedman hoped to resolve with his talk of "dynamic and progressive" new liberalism.[68]

Not surprisingly, Stigler's lecture hooked Friedman. "I've just read over for the second time, & thought over for the n'th," he wrote upon reading a copy, "and I know not what to say." Friedman seemed to agree with Stigler that equality was not a sufficient justification for policy or ethics. He too had moved away from Simons. Yet he wasn't sure Stigler's emphasis on "the improvement of the individual" was really "a way out of the dilemma which you quite properly say I & the other bastard descendants of the classical liberals are in." Stigler had approvingly cited Alfred Marshall, the great British economist. Yet Friedman was uneasy with Marshall's ideas about improving the human race, rightly detecting a eugenic tint. In a response to Stigler, he quoted a passage from Marshall's *Principles of Economics* that denigrated the Chinese. What Friedman seemed to want was a "touchstone" that was not "ambiguous." Friedman noted his unhappiness, both "with my own present or previous position, or with your solution. Yet I can't really say why."[69] Even as Friedman noted a change in his position, he retained vestigial loyalty to the Simons-style egalitarian rhetoric he and Stigler had once deployed.

At this critical moment Friedman mixed regularly with Hayek, whom he knew as Fritz. Hayek spent the entire decade of the 1950s at Chicago as he worked on his monumental book *The Constitution of Liberty*, which was eventually published in 1960. There are no letters between Friedman and Hayek recording their encounters as neighbors in a small academic enclave. Yet it is suggestive that Hayekian phrases and ideas, from "new liberalism" to "competitive order," recurred through Friedman's writing. In his course on price theory, Friedman assigned Hayek's short essay "The Use of Knowledge in Society," an unusual choice for an economics class in that era.[70] Friedman was far from a blind follower; when a motion was raised to grant Hayek a courtesy appointment in economics—generally an honorific with no real power—he was not a supporter. Hayek's Austrian economics was not empirical enough for Friedman. Nonetheless, Hayek was undeniably a powerful thinker, widely read with a capacious frame of reference. And the two were in regular contact; Friedman dropped in on Hayek's social theory seminars, and the two had overlapping social circles. Like Knight long ago, Hayek helped reorient Friedman away from a narrow focus on economics.

The shifts in Friedman's thinking emerged clearly in 1956, during a series of summer lectures at Wabash College, a small men's college in Indiana. Eventually these lectures would form the seedbed of *Capitalism and Freedom*, his later book aimed at a general readership. At the time, they were one of several invitation-only summer conferences sponsored by the Volker Fund. Accordingly, Friedman confronted a mixed audience. Some were Volker Fund regulars, the "reactionaries" Friedman had long opposed. Also in attendance were the academic children and grandchildren of Knight, ranging from Stigler to Nutter to public choice founder James Buchanan, who would later win a Nobel Prize. Catering to neither group, Friedman blazed a trail down the center, using Chicago price theory to carve out a unique social and political framework.

Like Director, Friedman had turned decisively away from Simons's views on monopoly. "With reluctance," Friedman explained, he concluded that "private monopoly may be the least of evils." Private monopoly was likely to be eliminated, he contended, whereas government agencies like the Interstate Commerce Commission could live forever. Similarly, while Friedman did not reject taxation altogether, he worried about its impact on incentives and investment. And where Simons suggested taxation as a remedy for inequality, Friedman identified "the extension and widening of educational opportunities" as more critical.[71]

Friedman also rebutted the Depression-era fears of Simons and Knight that capitalism generated dangerous inequality. To the contrary, he argued that capitalism would do a decent job of leveling, even if that was not its purpose or justification. Western European countries and the United States had less inequality than "a status society like India or a backward country like Egypt," he argued. Similarly, "economic progress achieved in the capitalist societies has by and large meant a drastic diminution of inequality."[72] Living in a booming postwar economy that brought Americans to new heights of consumption, Friedman shifted away from Knight's guarded embrace of capitalism.

Friedman's belief that capitalism reduced inequality was widely held by economists—because it appeared clearly in the available income data. In 1953, Simon Kuznets had released yet another blockbuster statistical study, drawing on tax data going back to 1913. He found that in the past forty years, income inequality had fallen significantly. Kuznets linked this finding to the broader process of economic growth, arguing that after a first surge in inequality, industrial societies drew those with low incomes into better-paying work. Over time, developed capitalist societies became more equal, not less. Friedman knew Kuznets well from their earlier collaboration, of course. But Kuznets was far from a minor figure in economics. In 1955 he was elected president of the American Economic Association, to which he gave a major address explaining his findings, the so-called Kuznets curve. He was a sort of anti-Piketty of his day, depicting capitalism as an engine of equality. In light of this evidence, it was not surprising that Friedman abandoned Knight's dark ruminations about "the cumulative tendency to greater inequality which is inherent in the system."[73]

Across these changes, Friedman held fast to Simons's conviction that "old-fashioned liberalism" could be more than blind reaction, that price theory could inform a positive program. Returning to the negative income tax proposal he debuted at the Mont Pelerin Society, Friedman expanded upon its basic logic. A negative income tax replaced government programs targeted at the poor—and their attendant bureaucracies—with a simple cash grant. The same could be done in other cases, such as "price supports, minimum wage laws, tariffs, and the like." If farmers or workers needed more money, instead of regulating businesses and commodities markets, the government could disburse funds directly. Ideally, Friedman imagined, governments could address social problems without creating cumbersome administrative structures. The basic principle was that "as far as possible, the program should, while operating through the market, not distort the market or impede its functioning."[74] Here was a way to incorporate Director's "humanitarian sentiments" while respecting Simons's "heart of the contract." And here was the beginning of an alternative policy paradigm to social democracy and New Deal liberalism.

At the same time, Friedman continued his maneuvering against the hard-line views of FEE and the Volker Fund. Many curious byways in the lectures were directed against Friedman's right flank, from his explanation of flaws in the gold standard to his argument against property-based voting restrictions (both pet causes of men like Hazlitt who were in attendance). He repeated his commitments to free trade and international engagement. And he made clear his was not an anarchist philosophy, or even one of laissez-faire. Even pure capitalism "implicitly depends on state action . . . property rights are matters of law and social convention and there is no way to avoid state action in defining and enforcing them," he reminded his listeners.[75]

Finally, Friedman returned to the themes of Stigler's lecture. Like the classical economists, he didn't want to place equality at the center of his thought. Yet neither did he want to embrace inequality—what he called the "capitalist ethic," or "payment according to product." This would be taking laissez-faire as an ethical principle—market outcomes justified as fair, no matter what. Here he was probably thinking of Watts, with his extreme aversion to equality. Or perhaps he was thinking of the early Hayek, who could not find a reason to intervene during the Depression. Friedman knew unequal incomes were not simply the deserved result of unequal effort; there were "initial differences of endowment, both of human capacities and of property." Yet at the same time, he remained concerned that mitigating inequality, for example through progressive taxation, could be "a clear case of coercion." Contemplating the capitalist ethic, Friedman was stuck: "The more I have thought about it, the more difficult I have found it to justify either accepting or rejecting this ethic."[76] This was the same quandary Stigler's lecture had raised. The liberal had to find some way to balance equality and inequality.

But now, Friedman solved his dilemma by stepping sideways. Capitalism did not contain its own complete ethic but must be justified by "some other principle such as freedom," Friedman argued. It was a resolution that seemed to solve many problems at once. It marked him apart from the reactionaries he had battled since the days of *Roofs and Ceilings?*, the men like Watts who thought inequality was a positive good. Freedom would also differentiate him from Keynesian economists and New Deal liberals, serving as a safeguard against an expansive state. And if freedom was the first principle, equality no longer lay at the center of politics. In Stigler's framing, it would once again become a proximate, rather than an ultimate goal. And if Friedman had stepped away from equality, he had retained yet another echo of Simons, who wrote about "the religion of freedom" in letters to Hayek.[77]

In retrospect, it appears a simple, even simplistic resolution. Was "freedom" really a better, less "ambiguous" touchstone than "equality"? Yet it is notable—remarkable even—that in his London lecture Stigler never used the word! Never did Stigler invoke even "liberty." Within their ideological, professional, and social context, Friedman was doing something distinctive, something that owed much to Hayek but was rendered in an American accent.

Freedom fit the temper of the times. In an age riven with totalitarian systems of control, freedom was becoming a watchword of political and economic life. At once capacious and specific, freedom meshed disparate value systems into a recognizable American parlance. A few years hence, the *National Review* editor Frank Meyer would bring peace to warring conservative factions by arguing economic and personal freedom were "fundamentally in accord" with a belief in "the conservative view of man's nature and destiny." Freedom was the touchstone, Meyer argued, the ideal that worked on both a philosophical and a practical level. It was a discovery Friedman had already made.[78]

Friedman's "new faith" had now taken definitive form and shape through the Wabash lectures. While scholarly accounts emphasize the importance of the Mont Pelerin Society to Friedman's development, he did not regularly attend the transatlantic meeting during this time. He was, however, a consistent presence at the seminars, conferences, and meetings hosted by the Volker Fund. Through the Free Market Study and the Antitrust Project, he and Director developed an expansive vision of what the price system could do. In the Wabash lectures, Friedman experimented with new modes of expression, moving away from his academic emphasis on efficiency to articulate the moral and philosophical case for freedom.

Friedman's synthesis did much to smooth relations between Chicago, FEE, and the Volker Fund. Monopoly and taxation, the main grounds of difference, simply did not occupy the place in Friedman's thought they had in Simons's. In 1950 Watts left FEE—possibly because of his relentless attacks on Mises, FEE's house economist, for his "failure to denounce democracy."[79] In his place, the more genial Read handled scholarly outreach. In 1957, a year after the Wabash lectures, Friedman and Read were stranded together for hours in the Paris airport, en route from a Mont Pelerin Society meeting. Back home again, the men exchanged warm letters. "It was the first time we really had an opportunity to see a little of one another as people, instead of economists or executives," Friedman reflected, while Read promised to cook a bouillabaisse for Friedman and Stigler.[80] The three men who had once argued so bitterly now counted themselves friends.

Simultaneously, there was an ingathering that strengthened the bonds and power of Room Seven alumni. Allen Wallis had been at Chicago all along, returning in the same year as Friedman to a professorship at the business school, eventually serving as dean. He was a fixture in Friedman's world, helping him strategize against the Cowles Commission and serving as the treasurer of the Mont Pelerin Society. Just a few months after the Read-Friedman reconciliation, Wallis helped recruit Stigler to the university as the first Walgreen Foundation Professor. Funded in the 1930s by drugstore magnate Charles Walgreen, who was upset by the radical doctrines his niece had imbibed at Chicago, the position was intended to support the study of "American institutions," and was subject to a donor's veto. The foundation languished, in part because all efforts to appoint faculty in the early 1950s faltered. None could satisfy the new gatekeeper, a trusted family counselor: Leonard Read.[81]

Wallis gambled he could get a candidate through Read. If the university would give the business school the chair, he would fill it. Wallis's first choice, a publishing executive and college president, declined the position. Then an associate dean attended the Wabash conferences, where his gaze shifted to Stigler. Only three years earlier, the economics department had tried unsuccessfully to recruit Stigler. Now the business school had a much better offer: nearly a million dollars of Walgreen funds, and double his Columbia salary.[82] Stigler returned to Chicago in 1958, teaching at the business school until his retirement.

By then, Friedman had long since displaced Knight at the center of his friends' intellectual universe. When the visiting scholar Ronald Coase arrived to defend his celebrated article "The Problem of Social Cost," it was Friedman who "did most of the talking and most of the thinking," as Stigler described it. Coase's theorem, as the group understood it, addressed a case similar to monopoly: externalities or neighborhood effects, those instances where pollution, noise, or other side effects of economic activity were not captured in the market price, or impacted third parties.[83]

Making moves similar to Friedman, Coase argued that these costs could in fact be priced and then traded. The key was a stable legal framework supporting private property. In an ideal environment of no transaction costs—which Coase admitted was impossible—regulation would not be required at all. In the existing world, the theorem suggested much economic activity that was regulated could instead be handled by courts or markets. Bargaining was key. For example, in an actual case reported in the news, a noisy chemical plant offered its neighbors chocolate as recompense. In another case, the Vittel water company bargained with nearby farmers to reduce nitrogen runoff that was damaging its mineral spring. Gathered at Director's house, a group of twenty economists went from skepticism to acceptance of Coase's ideas—led every step of the way by Friedman. "What an exhilarating event!" declared Stigler, who witnessed the evening. Coase's ideas became influential in tort law and were incorporated into environmental economics, among other fields. In the mid-1960s, after Director's retirement, Coase would take up his faculty position and become the editor of *The Journal of Law and Economics*.[84]

The journal itself was another Volker Fund project, launched in 1958. It transformed Director into a patron of the highest rank, one who could offer publication opportunities, research fellowships, and targeted financial support to scholars. From its lowly beginnings in faculty club lunches, the Free Market Study had grown into a major node in the law and economics network, which stretched across multiple universities into the federal government and judiciary. Not only had Friedman scared off the Cowles Commission, but he had helped nurture an academic movement that would prove equally influential. No one had seen it coming, but there was now a distinctive Chicago school in law as well as economics.

Stigler's arrival opened up a third front in the business school. Appointed jointly to the Department of Economics, Stigler quickly got with the program on monopoly. Under the influence of Director's "luminous mind," he stopped testifying as an expert witness in antitrust lawsuits, accepting that "monopoly power is of no value in explaining many phenomena which have efficiency explanations." Stigler used funds from the Walgreen Foundation to support a new Workshop in Industrial Organization, a home for research that sought to apply price theory "to the causes and effects of public regulation." Workshop studies yielded a collective insight about politics that could have come from Knight: "No matter how disinterested the goal of public policy, the policy is bent to help politically influential groups at the cost of the less influential." A skilled institution-builder, Stigler eventually founded the Center for the Study of the Economy and the State at the university.[85]

Related efforts were under way at the University of Virginia, led by the former Knight students James Buchanan and Warren Nutter. Where Stigler suggested that state regulation of economic activity was itself an economic activity, susceptible to analysis by the basic tools of supply and demand, the emerging Virginia school turned this lens on political actors. Politicians were motivated by the same purposive and self-interested behavior found in any marketplace; they competed for votes instead of customer dollars. It was an audacious return to the expansive perspective of political economy, and a successful incursion into the new disciplinary terrain of political science. Stigler hoped that before long, "economic logic may pervade the study of all branches of human behavior."[86] In some ways, Knight's students had turned their back on economics just as he had, refusing the econometric turn. In another way, they had proved far more effective conduits of neoclassical economics than the modelers and mathematicians. Here, in pieces, was what Luhnow had wanted: a *Road to Serfdom* customized to American problems and institutions.

Yet the work of Stigler and his allies did not so much amplify Hayek's work as complement it. Whereas Hayek's most memorable critique of planning was political—it would lead to dictatorship—Stigler's group offered an economic analysis. Efforts to regulate prices and market entry were not so much morally naïve as inefficient. Hayek's dark forebodings had been resonant amid wartime catastrophe. By contrast, his Chicago colleagues were fluent in the new language of politics: prices and efficiency. As policy-makers became ever more reliant on economists to structure aggregate demand, the economic way of thinking permeated government decision-making. Effective opposition necessarily employed the same terminology.

Chicago law and economics and Stigler's workshop fed into larger intellectual currents, what one scholar terms a shift from industries to markets.[87] Under approaches inherited from the New Deal, industries with social importance could justifiably be regulated, and many were. Railroads, trucking, airlines, natural gas, electricity, and telecommunications—all were subject to industry-specific regulations, including set prices and state licenses restricting entry. When policy-makers thought about industries, they thought in terms of firms, workers, interests, rights. Shifting the lens to markets meant these concepts dropped out and were replaced by different ideas and ideals—most notably efficiency. In turn, efficiency encouraged cost-benefit analysis as the most relevant measure of policy success. This conceptual shift undercut the rationale for regulation. It also opened new opportunities for Chicago-trained economists and lawyers. In much of Washington, policy was about prices: how to get them higher, or keep them down, or manipulate them for greater social good. By contrast, at Chicago and its offshoots, price *was* the policy—allowing the price to be freely set by market forces was itself the social good. Within the appropriate legal framework, price competition could regulate monopoly, reduce corruption, ensure freedom. It was an alternative approach well positioned to move from fringe to mainstream.

More than twenty years after Friedman first came to Hyde Park as a young man, Room Seven had regenerated itself. To a remarkable degree, the students who had bonded in the Frank Knight "affinity group" were together once again: Friedman, Wallis, Stigler, Aaron Director, the former Rose Director. Sprawling evenings of discussion and debate had moved from the neighborhood pub to faculty homes or the Quadrangle Club. Although reluctant to call themselves conservatives, the group cohered around a shared opposition to both Keynesian economics and New Deal liberalism. Where great East Coast universities like Harvard, MIT, and Yale fed a steady stream of economists into government positions and policy work, Chicago alone cultivated a different set of intellectuals, set upon constraining the constraints government put on market forces.

8

HIDDEN FIGURES

> He couldn't have done it without her.
>
> —Michael Bordo, 2018

In late June 1950, the Communist government of North Korea invaded its southern neighbor, turning the Cold War hot. Within days, the capital city of Seoul had fallen. Detecting the hidden hand of the Soviet Union, President Harry Truman committed U.S. forces in support of a U.N. resolution to roll back the Communist advance. Although never formally declared a war, the police action on the Korean peninsula would last for three years and ultimately cost more than a million lives, including more than thirty-five thousand Americans. Korea was the first major test of containment—the guiding foreign policy idea that called for hemming in Communist advances across the globe. When war broke out, the administration hastily adopted NSC-68, a secret strategy for military buildup that had been languishing in bureaucratic purgatory. And with a new bulge in defense spending on the horizon, prices began to shoot up in anticipation of shortages and rearmament. By year's end, they were rising at a rate of 8 percent. Inflation was again a live political issue—as were price controls. Under the Defense Production Act, a landmark bill pushed through Congress to meet the crisis, Truman authorized a general wage and price freeze in January 1951.

Chagrined by the return of price controls, Aaron Director spent some of his Volker Fund money on an ambitious conference, "Defense, Controls, and Inflation," held in April 1951, at White Sulphur Springs, West Virginia. The participants were genuinely diverse in outlook; the conference mixed Volker Fund regulars like Friedman, Director, F. A. Hayek, and Ludwig von Mises with high-level union officials, members of Congress, the star Keynesian economist Alvin Hansen, and even the director of the new wartime Office of Price Stabilization. In their unrelenting opposition to price controls, Friedman, Director, and their colleague Lloyd Mints represented a decidedly minority position. Director summarized the case: "Inflation can be prevented at its source by preventing an increase in the supply of money." Even conference attendees who were skeptical of price controls found these ideas unreasonable; as a former governor of the Federal Reserve argued, the Chicago view "vastly overstates the role of monetary policy." In the early 1950s, at the high tide of faith in fiscal policy and just after the centralized mobilization for World War II, controlling inflation by monetary measures alone was not just heretical; it was almost nonsensical.[1]

In many ways the conference represented the ultimate Chicago ideal, featuring vigorous debate and a genuine clash of views—but it also left a palpable impression of Friedman as an outsider, even a kook. His former professor Jacob Viner arrived having heard "rumors about a 'Chicago school' which was engaged in *organized* battle for laissez-faire and 'quantity theory of money' and against 'imperfect competition' theorizing and 'Keynesianism.'" The conference made clear the rumors were true; Viner found it "rigidly structured" and was shocked to learn "the financing of the conference, as I found out later, was ideologically loaded."[2] And it was not just Viner. When Director circulated a summary of the conference—drafted with generous input from Friedman—it generated so much opposition that the published version bristled with querulous footnotes calling it "deficient," "shows substantial bias," and "neglects a number of critical points."[3] Any goodwill the conference had generated was undone by the perception its published proceedings were being slanted to support the Chicago view. The battle against the Cowles Commission, which peaked a few years later, further eroded Friedman's scholarly reputation. A collective picture of Friedman was emerging: a retrograde thinker at best, a political hack at worst.

But Friedman had a secret weapon. Or rather, secret weapons. Already an outlier to the discipline's mainstream views on money and inflation, he took advantage of another vast blind spot in economics: male chauvinism. He would rebuild his intellectual reputation by harnessing the intellectual firepower of four overlooked women: Anna Schwartz, Rose Friedman, Dorothy Brady, and Margaret Reid.

At the start of their working relationship in 1948, Anna Schwartz had been the teacher, Friedman the student. She wrote the syllabus that Friedman used to get oriented. And she posed the hard questions about what, exactly, he hoped to accomplish. Friedman wanted a statistical "series of government obligations held by individuals, business firms, and all banks," but from Schwartz's vantage point deep within the data, this didn't make sense. She pelted Friedman with questions. Why consider bank reserves, which, lacking purchasing power, were akin to gold in Fort Knox? What about postal savings deposits? Life insurance policies? She also posed broader queries about the role of banks, his concept of wealth, and his depiction of falling prices.[4] Even as Friedman sought to establish himself as research director, Schwartz was making clear she would be no meek assistant.

Friedman responded warmly. Her comments were "exactly the kind of questions that should be raised and that I would have overlooked because of not recognizing the actual difficulties of getting the figures together." To clarify his goals and ambitions, he enclosed a copy of his 1948 monetary-framework article. "I now see the point of the series you have in mind," Schwartz wrote back.[5]

By the end of the summer, Friedman had read much of Schwartz's list and the two had settled on a strategy. They would begin with a series of time deposits (savings accounts with dates of maturity, similar to certificates of deposit) held by residents of selected U.S. states.[6] These would form the building blocks for a larger measure of historical trends in the money supply. The point of measuring money in all its various forms was to create a baseline narrative—not just of individual states but of the United States. At this point, the scope and scale of the project remained unclear. Certainly, neither expected it would take fifteen years to publish their results.

The first years of Friedman and Schwartz's collaboration were marked by confusion and frustration. Although it made sense to use individual states as units of analysis, each state gathered banking data differently. Some calculated month to month, others midmonth to midmonth. It was hard to know where to begin, where to end, and how to compare across categories. Making progress required intense intellectual labor, both to stay with the details and to make big-picture decisions about what mattered and why.

In a typical letter from this period, Friedman confessed after looking at data from three states, "I have been finding it very difficult to reach a conclusion about the right thing to do." With little confidence in his ultimate decision, Friedman invited Schwartz to nullify his plan if she had different ideas. Similarly, even after a trip to Washington, D.C., to scrounge additional data, Schwartz noted that "the final date for our series seems nebulous." In another letter, Schwartz described a "perfect fury" of work to develop vault cash figures, which required combing through both original sources and abstracts of reports from national banks, nonnational banks, and county banks.[7]

Another difficulty was synchronizing the minds of two scholars—one buried in data, the other only glancingly on the topic when time allowed. Friedman tried to see Schwartz whenever he came to New York, but that was at most a few times a year. Phone calls were too expensive. Instead, they exchanged long, dense letters that needed careful reading and rereading. Assumptions needed to be stated, restated, adjusted; misreadings required corrections and clarification. Sometimes Friedman lost the plot entirely. In the middle of their third summer working together, he wrote: "I am greatly confused about what is being done by whom + why. Could you send me a systematic list of the steps that remain, in as much detail as possible, with an indication of status?"[8]

Working nearly exclusively on the money project, Schwartz grasped the granularity of the data in a way Friedman never could. It fell to Schwartz to run "downtown to use the machines" when her babysitter showed up, negotiate with NBER staff on which of the young female "computers" would perform necessary calculations, and report back to Friedman on data that couldn't be found or conclusions that made no sense.[9]

Why gather all this data? Simply put, Friedman was looking to validate hypotheses that had bubbled up from Schwartz's syllabus, and from his long immersion in the Chicago monetary tradition. In many ways, the project was analogous to the Free Market Study on monopoly. Once again, the ideas of Henry Simons would be the basic foundations upon which Friedman built. And just as Friedman used Warren Nutter's dissertation to test the proposition that monopoly was inevitable, he wanted to use Schwartz's data to understand the role of money in business cycles. With enough data at hand, history itself could become a sort of "controlled experiment," as Friedman later explained.[10]

One of the project's first publications demonstrated this approach. In a 1952 *American Economic Review* article, Friedman compared price changes and monetary changes during the Civil War, World War I, and World War II. In these episodes, the rise in prices was similar but "other crucial features varied, offering the opportunity to test alternative hypotheses designed to explain price changes." Notably, there were no price controls during the Civil War. Friedman set up the data to test the quantity theory against "income-expenditure theory," his term for Keynesian economics. Which one better explained inflation? "Our conclusions favor the proponents of monetary policy," Friedman summarized. "If you want to control prices and incomes, they say in about as clear tones as empirical evidence ever speaks, control the stock of money." The paper offered new evidence to support the connections Friedman saw between changes in the quantity of money and the price level.[11] It also underscored how the past could open new vistas on the present.

There was another reason to turn to history: it provided a clearer lens on the power of the Federal Reserve, the nation's central banking system. As the Volker Fund conference made clear, most economists thought monetary policy alone could not manage inflation. In part, these views stemmed from the Keynesian interpretation of the Great Depression. But they also reflected the contemporary situation, for the Fed had been structurally neutered for almost a decade by the demands of wartime finance. World War II had been funded significantly by debt, making the interest rate—the cost to the federal government of repayment—an essential affair of state. As payer of the nation's bills, the Treasury desired a "stable pattern of rates" that kept costs predictable. Yet it was the Federal Reserve, a quasi-independent, quasi-public institution, that exerted influence over interest rates. For nine years the Fed bowed to Treasury, making no moves that would raise interest rates, and duly purchasing notes and bills that failed to sell. Thus when economists argued that money and monetary policy were ancillary to the real factors driving the economy, they were right. But all that was about to change.[12]

In 1951 came a new dispensation: the fabled Treasury-Fed Accord. It began with the Korean War inflation. Even though price controls were in place, the Fed was also tasked with price stability under its charter and the Employment Act of 1946. But it could not slow down the overall rise in prices without a rise in interest rates, which the Treasury vigorously resisted. For the first six months, the agencies muddled through a series of working compromises that attempted to hem in inflation. But when Truman took Treasury's side and browbeat the governors in person, open conflict broke out.[13] After a high-level huddle, representatives of the warring bureaucracies emerged with a peace treaty: the Treasury-Fed Accord.

Cautious in its language, the accord did not appear to be a revolutionary agreement. It set the Federal Reserve free from Treasury imperatives, allowing it to focus on preventing general price rises. At the same time, the Fed agreed to continue supporting Treasury policy. Nonetheless, the accord fundamentally rebalanced power between the agencies. And it transformed the object of Friedman and Schwartz's research from a passive adjunct of the Treasury into a consequential Washington player.

Leading the Fed into this new era was William McChesney Martin, who became the chairman of the Federal Reserve in mid-1951. His father had helped draft the original Federal Reserve Act, and soon Martin showed similar loyalties. While paying lingering respects to Treasury wishes, Martin buttressed the Fed's new independence with a major renovation.[14] Among his most important changes was to strengthen the Federal Open Market Committee (FOMC), a regular meeting of directors that made operating decisions. The Fed had several ways to influence the economy through the banking system. Not every U.S. bank was a member of the Federal Reserve System, but generally the biggest and most influential banks in any given region were, and the Fed could tell these banks what to do. Specifically, it could mandate the level of reserves a member bank could hold. Or it could adjust the discount rate—how much it charged a bank that wanted to borrow directly from the Fed. But most of the time, banks did not want to come to the discount window, for it suggested they couldn't borrow elsewhere. And it would be unsettling to change reserve requirements too often. This left open market operations, and the FOMC, as the main initiator of policy.

Although they were called "open market operations," in reality the Fed mainly traded with a captive market composed of "primary dealers"—the nation's biggest investment banks. These dealers agreed to regularly participate in Fed auctions; in return they could mark up securities to their customers. The system for determining primary dealers shifted over time, but by 1960 the eligibility criteria had been formalized, and financial firms needed to apply for the position. In this era, under the "bills only" doctrine, the FOMC confined itself to trading in short-term Treasury bills, mostly leaving untouched longer-term Treasury issues.[15]

At each meeting, FOMC members considered basically three options: buy, sell, or hold the course. If the FOMC decided to buy more securities, it would be expanding the money supply. Imagine an individual receiving dollars for a T-bill—they now have more to spend. On the system level, this meant the Fed increased member bank reserves and took T-bills in return. The banks now had more money to loan. When Friedman talked about the Fed "printing money," this is what he meant. Buying securities could also be called cheap money, loosening policy, or lowering rates. When money was plentiful, its price—the interest rate—tumbled.

By contrast, if the FOMC decided to sell the securities it held, the Fed would be slurping money out of the economy, squirreling it away in the vaults. This was called "tightening money" or raising rates. Banks would have fewer funds available to lend and hence would raise the price of borrowing. In turn, the proliferation of available bonds meant only high returns would attract buyers. Across the economy, interest rates would rise. Because the market for short-term government securities was so vast, its prices influenced all types of bonds and credit. Open market operations were thus an indirect means to influence interest rates in general.

Open market operations also had a fairly immediate impact on the federal funds rate, or the interest rate Federal Reserve member banks charged each other. Despite its name, this was not a rate the FOMC directly controlled. Rather, it reflected banking activity as a whole. Each night enormous quantities of money sloshed back and forth across the banking system as checks cleared, deposits were made, and loans were finalized. Banks borrowed from each other to meet immediate obligations, planning to settle when other pending transactions wrapped up. This dance of the dollar was at once essential to the basic functioning of the financial system and a powerful point of intervention into the economy. Changes in the prices of these foundational loans, which were highly sensitive to FOMC actions, rippled out almost immediately to business and consumer lending. And just as government securities influenced all other bonds, so too did the rates charged by Federal Reserve member banks percolate out to all banks in the country. Thus the decision-makers of the Federal Reserve stood at one remove from the nation's banks, working indirect levers that nonetheless had powerful and predictable consequences.

To a degree nearly unimaginable today, the Fed's actions in the

1950s were shrouded in secrecy. Attendance at FOMC meetings and its topics of discussion were not publicly available. The delphic Record of Policy Actions generated by each meeting came out only once—in a batch at the end of the year.[16] To spot patterns and larger meaning in this sparse information required an expert eye. Most market participants gleaned what was happening by the actions of the New York Fed trading desk, which was charged with making bids or offers. Economic data released by the Fed was spotty and difficult to parse—especially historic data. A modern-day Friedman and Schwartz would spend most of their research time in Fed databases; the real-life Friedman and Schwartz had to construct their own. Even within the banking fraternity, the Fed was an insider's world.

After the accord set interest rates free, they duly began to drift upward. Although from a later vantage point the rate increases were minuscule—about half a point across all maturities—interest rates had not shifted so much in decades.[17] The change immediately attracted the ire of Wright Patman, a populist Democrat from Texas who would serve in Congress for nearly half a century. Patman hated banks and "money power." During the Great Depression he even tried to impeach Treasury Secretary Andrew Mellon for "high crimes and misdemeanors" (Mellon was rescued by a timely appointment to the British ambassadorship). Now Patman was alarmed at the rise in interest rates, which he considered "avoidable, if not conspiratorial." High interest rates benefited banks at the expense of farmers, wage earners, and everyday people. Patman doubted the wisdom of the accord altogether. In his mind, what the Fed needed was more control and accountability, not less.[18]

Patman had an unlikely ally in this cause—Senator Paul Douglas, the former Chicago economics professor who had clashed so bitterly with Knight over the tenure cases of Aaron Director and Henry Simons. In the years since, Douglas had signed up to fight in World War II and then ran for Congress, eventually rising to become a liberal lion of the Senate. Douglas was a Democrat. Yet he was not a Keynesian: he accorded monetary policy a central role in economic health, and had been an original signatory to the Chicago plan hatched during the Great Depression. He played a critical role in helping to hammer out the Treasury-Fed Accord. But now, Douglas became concerned the Fed was *too* independent from Congress. When Patman launched congressional hearings in 1952, Douglas invited Friedman to testify.[19]

Friedman did not disappoint. "I would like to see the Federal Reserve System in its present form abolished," he told Congress, generating sensational headlines. What Friedman wanted instead, he explained, was "a 100-percent reserve deposit banking system in which there was no monetary authority possessing discretionary powers over the quantity of money."[20] Six years after Simons's death, Friedman still believed in his Chicago plan. Friedman submitted into the record not only the plan for 100 percent money but Simons's proposal for dividing the lending and savings functions of banks, creating new institutions to invest and warehouse money.

Friedman's critique of the Fed did not line up exactly with the views of Patman or Douglas. Both men wanted the Fed to end its bills-only policy and focus on controlling long-term interest rates. Friedman cared more about ending price controls than lowering interest rates. Nor were Patman and Douglas always in agreement; after all, Douglas had helped design the accord that Patman opposed. Nonetheless, both men recognized that Friedman's economic indictment of the Fed bolstered their political critique, adding intellectual gravity to their concerns. And all three men shared a basic belief that monetary policy was essential to the nation's economic life. In the coming years, Friedman would become a favorite witness in the Douglas-Patman crusade against the Fed, returning to testify multiple times.

While members of Congress respectfully pressed Friedman on his testimony, Paul Samuelson was scathing. Taking the stand after Friedman, Samuelson mocked the quantity theory as "almost completely fallacious." Samuelson gibed at Friedman's "mystical view," "sophomore fallacies," and "vague generality," calling the quantity of money "a fabricated concept." (Friedman probably would have agreed with this last point, without considering it a fatal flaw; indeed he and Schwartz had been busy fabricating for years.)

Samuelson continued on to attack Friedman's basic methodology and approach; clearly he was familiar with his recent paper on wartime inflation. "Sometime in the 1920s," Samuelson explained, sitting only a short distance from his target in the House of Representatives, "it became fashionable to decide that you could chop off the chain at a given place, and could add together what you call M, the amount of money, and M', what you arbitrarily call the amount of adjusted demand deposits, and then suddenly this particular time series, out of all the time series, in the Federal Reserve chart book is given an especial potency in explaining events—especially in explaining them retroactively."[21] Samuelson's scoffing reprised the Cowles Commission attacks on the NBER. To the mathematically inclined Samuelson, painstakingly assembling figures from history to derive economic theory appeared a waste of time.

The most important voice on monetary policy, however, was not Friedman or Samuelson, but Chairman Martin. Establishment to his core, the Yale graduate Martin had a gift for making monetary policy intelligible while preserving maximum flexibility for his operations. He told Congress it was the Fed's job to "lean against the wind" of inflation or deflation. In another memorable speech, he characterized the Fed as a "chaperone who has ordered the punch bowl removed just when the party was really warming up."[22] Senator Douglas and Congressman Patman had little patience for these nostrums, particularly when interest rates spiked. Like Friedman, they doubted the wisdom of giving one man so much discretion to chart policy.

In the short term, little came of the 1952 Patman hearings. Eisenhower took office soon after and made balanced budgets a priority, reducing the burden on monetary policy. Price controls were lifted early in 1953. The system under Martin remained wedded to bills only, allowing the Fed to declaim responsibility for long-term rates. Martin was a creature of money markets, focused primarily on short-term shifts; indeed, one of his edicts barred forecasting. Secretive and aloof in an era when government institutions were generally trusted, the Fed could get by without formalizing its thinking or spelling out its guiding assumptions. Like Patman and Douglas, Friedman was a voice baying from the outside.

Even as Friedman's scholarship was mocked before Congress by other economists like Samuelson, his authority was unquestioned within the Gothic quadrangles of Chicago. Partially, this was because the Department of Economics was a remarkably stable institution. The chair who hired Friedman, T. W. Schultz (no relation to Henry Schultz, his doctoral adviser), went on to serve a twenty-year term. The director of graduate studies was in office for thirty years. Further, the department was unusually inbred. Chicago faculty liked to hire Chicago graduates. "Our department is too homogenous in several ways," worried the faculty authors of a 1957 internal committee report. It was not for want of trying, the memo continued: "First, we more or less agree that we ought to diversify by seeking a socialist, or an institutionalist, or something of the sort. Then we consider names of economists who might qualify, and one by one we reject them on the grounds that they are not really good economists. The discussion ends when someone says, 'There's really nobody good in that category.'" Friedman's response to the memo perfectly encapsulated this dynamic. Near a passage that identified history of economic thought as an area of interest, he scribbled one word: "Stigler."[23]

The real key to Friedman's influence, however, was his pole position teaching two required courses: Price Theory, and Money and Banking. Eventually, he alternated teaching Price Theory with two former students, Gary Becker and Arnold Harberger, but after Mints's retirement he established a monopoly on Money and Banking.[24] These were graduate classes—indeed, there were scarcely any undergraduates to be found in the department; they were educated almost entirely by a dedicated college within the university. By definition, every student Friedman encountered was hoping to become a professional economist. To get there, they had to pass both Friedman's classes and linked comprehensive exams. Along the way, they would endure an extended hazing process, as a widely discussed student memo made clear. The memo's tips and suggestions offered an alarming glimpse of daily departmental life. "Treat the student not like a dog," it recommended, admitting, "This is a hard one to handle." Still, it was important to realize that "students do not like to be insulted," the memo asserted.[25]

Friedman was a significant part of the problem. He had inherited Viner's Price Theory course as well as his intimidating classroom manner. A visiting reporter captured his aura: "Gray eyed, broad shouldered, bull necked and bald, he looks more like a football tackle than a brilliant professor of economics."[26] Lecturing from the front of the room where he sketched out diagrams and equations on a blackboard, "his thinking was fast and he could react to statements by others almost immediately," remembered a student. "One or two wishing to show off were easily put down and taught a lesson."[27] Twenty minutes into his first Price Theory class, Becker leapt to answer a question. Friedman dispatched him curtly: "That is no answer, for you are only restating the question in other words." Cheeks burning, Becker slumped in his seat. But soon he decided it was "magic" to be Friedman's student. Off to class, Becker radiated excitement. "Are you going out on a date with a beautiful woman?" wondered a classmate. "No, I'm going to a class in economics," Becker responded. As it had for generations of students, price theory became the highlight of his life at Chicago. Even scathing feedback from Friedman on a first dissertation chapter—"the grammar is faulty, the sentences illogical, the statements incomplete"—proved little deterrent.[28]

Becker recognized, however, that his reaction was unusual; in fact, most of the brightest students seemed to avoid Friedman. "They could not take the heat," Becker realized. "They could not handle psychologically his sharp and blunt criticisms, and his quick insights. In essence, they feared being overwhelmed intellectually."[29] James Buchanan, perhaps the last student Frank Knight converted to Chicago price theory, confirmed the impression: Friedman's "dominating intellectual brilliance," he found, relegated the student "to the role of fourth-best imitation."[30] Buchanan kept his distance. Revelry at an annual department party captures the general impression. "Of laissez-faire I am the champ, / Outstanding member of the liberal camp," graduate students sang of Friedman in a lengthy parody of the Gilbert and Sullivan operetta *H.M.S. Pinafore*. The verse concluded with a subtle jab: "If you want to climb the academic tree, / Stick close to your texts and never disagree / And you all may be professors at the U. of C."[31]

After the mid-1950s, a new system of graduate training emerged: Students who made it through exams could escape to a specialized workshop. A distinctive feature of the department soon taken up across Chicago and other leading universities, workshops were really advanced graduate classes, or seminars as they are often called today. Students had to be enrolled in a workshop while writing a dissertation and received academic credit for participating. They might stay in the workshop for several years, as new members arrived and others graduated.[32]

Friedman's version diverged from the general departmental approach. Rather than being a closed community, Money and Banking was open to bystanders and visiting scholars. Unlike other workshop leaders, Friedman did not allow the featured scholar to present. Instead, he led a discussion through the paper, page by page. The overall gist of the workshop was simple, according to one participant: "prove it." In this hothouse environment student research grew into papers, and then dissertations. For Friedman, the workshop became an essential forum to test, refine, and expand his ideas about money, while forming a school of rising scholars steeped in his approach to the subject.[33]

Friedman saw a direct link between his research, his students, and what he called "an aberrant tradition" of Chicago monetary economics, focused on the quantity theory of money. In a 1956 volume, he celebrated the "subtle and relevant version" of quantity theory developed at Chicago in the Depression era by Simons, Mints, Knight, and Viner. This version of the quantity theory, Friedman argued, was "a flexible and sensitive tool for interpreting movements in aggregate economic activity and for developing relevant policy prescriptions." Here, he was no doubt referring to the 1933 Chicago plan, the department's response to the Great Depression.[34]

Friedman called Chicago monetary economics an "oral tradition," but in fact his colleague Mints's 1950 book, *Monetary Policy for a Competitive Economy*, was a recent installment. Sidelined for more than a decade by a troubled marriage—and work on his monumental *History of Banking Theory*—Mints was a signatory to the original Chicago plan. He was firmly ensconced in the faculty and student group around Knight. In his bachelor days, he had a standing invitation to Sunday dinner at Knight's house, where he would often find Aaron or Rose Director, too. Mints had been drafted into teaching at Chicago while still a doctoral student; as a result he never received his Ph.D., and never rose beyond the rank of associate professor. Nonetheless he was widely recognized as part of a distinctive Chicago school; the leading Keynesian Alvin Hansen even criticized "the Mints-Simons program," while another scholar referred to Mints as "a leading member of the Chicago radical school." Until Mints's retirement in 1953, he and Friedman traded off the teaching of monetary economics, and thanked each other regularly in their published work.[35]

Friedman's mention of an oral tradition might have been a nod to Director, who retained a keen interest in money from his perch at the law school. In the early years, Director occasionally ran the money workshop when Friedman was out of town. Although Director did not publish on money—or much else—his teaching and speeches continued to emphasize the quantity theory approach. In his own 1956 lecture at Wabash College, Director assumed the royal "we" to describe Chicago thinking on money. "On the basis of the little evidence that now exists," Director recounted, "we are inclined [to believe] that the primary source of instability . . . has been changes in the quantity of money." Accordingly, he continued, "we have been gradually departing from . . . the emphasis on 100 percent reserves." Director framed this shift in terms of new evidence, indirectly referencing Schwartz. While noting the ideas were not yet "well established," he emphasized "this is an empirical, not theoretical, question." The "aberrant" Chicago tradition was very much alive—and evolving.[36]

In tandem with the workshop and Schwartz's findings, Friedman, Director, and Mints set the 1930s Chicago approach on firm empirical footing and modified it significantly.[37] Some innovations reflected changed circumstance. Where Simons had emphasized both monetary and fiscal factors like taxation as ways to influence the money supply, in the wake of the accord, open market operations looked powerful enough on their own. Some were matters of emphasis: 100 percent money remained desirable, but all three economists acknowledged this change was less necessary after New Deal financial reforms, like the FDIC. And some were empirical, growing out of Schwartz's research, which made it possible to verify or discard previous hypotheses.

An important new theme was the Federal Reserve's role as chief villain in the Great Depression. The Chicago plan had not exactly been enthusiastic about the Fed, but Simons had emphasized the inherent instability of fractional reserve banking—hence 100 percent money. As Director's speech noted, however, the revised Chicago tradition looked instead to changes in the quantity of money as a driver of economic cycles. Therefore, after the Fed's 1914 founding, all roads led to its door. Where the 1930s Chicago tradition worried about the instability of capitalism itself, the 1950s approach had narrowed the problem to one key institution. In turn, this matched the more positive perspective on capitalism that Friedman had expressed at Wabash.

Closely linked to these transformations was a different understanding of velocity, the measure of how often money changed hands. Velocity was the V in the quantity equation: MV = PT. It was the driver of economic expansions—as money moved faster and faster through the economy—and contractions, if it stagnated in bank accounts or under mattresses. The instability of velocity was critical to the Keynesian diagnosis of depression and its remedy. If velocity was unstable and private enterprise erratic, it was the federal government alone that could be counted upon. Yet now, Mints began to argue that velocity was stable, considered over time. In general, people held and spent a consistent amount of money. Considered in Alfred Marshall's terms, even if velocity appeared to fluctuate wildly in the market period or short run, stepping back to the long run and secular time revealed a relatively stable trend. This was important because if velocity unto itself was stable, yet behaved unpredictably, the cause would lie elsewhere—in the money supply. This idea now became Friedman's theme.

The stability of velocity and the depredations of the Fed had both been suggested by the FDIC economist Clark Warburton, who was in contact with both Mints and Friedman during this period. In 1951, as the money project was developing, Friedman and Warburton exchanged long letters. Awkward and stiff in person, Warburton came alive in his acerbic written criticisms of Friedman. Another man might have made an alliance with Friedman, grasping their mutual interests. Instead, Warburton pronounced Friedman's 1948 monetary and fiscal framework, presented in the *American Economic Review*, "so complicated and delicately balanced in terms of plans and controls that it could only be achieved by a totalitarian government." These were fighting words, and Friedman was offended. "Simply nonsense," he returned, "an irresponsible statement. There is nothing complicated or delicately balanced about my scheme." Over time, however, Friedman would come to agree with Warburton. Moving away from his 1948 fiscal approach, Friedman embraced the simplicity of open market operations acting on the money supply. In the moment, however, he was not ready to yield ground.[38]

Not surprisingly, Warburton's extended critique of Friedman was rejected by the *Journal of Political Economy*, Chicago's influential house journal. Instead, two massive articles appeared in *The Journal of Finance*. They turned out to be a last hurrah of sorts; shortly thereafter, Warburton's superiors at the FDIC, perhaps goaded by an affronted Fed, forbade him to publish further on the topic. Thus by 1953, with Mints retired and Warburton muzzled, Friedman was positioned to emerge as the leading proponent of a revised quantity theory.[39]

History was a critical buttress of the emerging school, as demonstrated by four essays developed in the workshop and published as *Studies in the Quantity Theory of Money* in 1956. While the quantity of money was not the only force influencing prices, Friedman wrote in the introduction, looking to history provided a unique window into its importance. His student Eugene Lerner, for example, found that a reduction in the stock of money in the Confederacy during the Civil War "had a more significant influence on prices" than "invading Union armies, the impending military defeat, the reduction in foreign trade, the disorganized government, and the low morale of the Confederate army." Episodes of hyperinflation were also fruitful, as Phillip Cagan wrote: "Astronomical increases in prices and money dwarf the changes in real income and other real factors . . . monetary factors can be studied, therefore, in what almost amounts to isolation from the real sector of the economy."[40] Together, the historical analysis added up to a clear conclusion: printing money created inflation.

Indeed, armed with conclusions from the workshop, Friedman was ready to propose a basic theory of inflation: as the quantity of money increased, prices rose; as it fell, so too did prices. "This uniformity is, I suspect, of the same order as many of the uniformities that form the basis of the physical sciences," Friedman wrote in the opening essay. Once again, history was a critical proving ground. "There is perhaps no other empirical relation in economics that has been observed to recur so uniformly under so wide a variety of circumstances as the relation between substantial changes over short periods in the stock of money and in prices," Friedman wrote; "the one is invariably linked with the other and is in the same direction."[41] Here was the dream of finding an economic law akin to gravity or the conservation of energy.

Reviews of the volume were generally respectful, although most noted the embryonic nature of the work. At best, the volume succeeded in "roughing out some of the boundaries of an approach to the problem," a reviewer noted. "But one should not demand the millennium from a single set of exploratory studies," summarized another review, in the *Journal of the American Statistical Association*. "This volume is one of the most important contributions to monetary theory to be made in many years."[42] As of yet, Friedman had propounded no alternative narrative of the Great Depression to match Keynes. Nor was the term "monetarism" yet applied to his views.[43] But *Studies in the Quantity Theory of Money* showed him working, paper by paper, to erect a counter-theory.

Few students in the workshop knew much about Schwartz. "I viewed her as a research assistant in the background," one student recollected. "I thought she put the data and history together but Friedman was the brains behind the operation." Only years later did the fullness of her role dawn upon him: "He couldn't have done it without her."[44] Far more than a computer, Schwartz shaped the project's direction and Friedman's own thinking.

Most significantly, Schwartz convinced Friedman to expand the project into a nearly hundred-year monetary history of the United States. In 1954, with the Chicago workshop just taking off, she sent her first tentative outline of the project to Friedman. "I don't even know at this point whether you envisage our final report as more than a collection of estimates," she noted, before continuing, "I shall be highly disappointed if you will decide in favor of a restricted data report with no attempt to tackle the basic economic issues, the importance of which is the only justification for our time expenditure on the estimates."[45] The title of the outline was "money supply in the United States, 1907–1953." Friedman agreed they should do "substantive analysis of the figures," but wanted only to "skim the cream," warning against a long, drawn-out project.[46]

But Schwartz had a love and feel for history that Friedman did not share. She confessed in early days to having "stole some time" from compiling bank vault cash figures to dig further into Confederate finance. At first, Friedman brushed off her interests, passing Civil War material she had gathered on to a student.[47] Schwartz kept at it, writing up a narrative stretching from the end of the Civil War in 1865 to the resumption of gold payments for paper currency in 1879, which she sent to another Friedman student, Phillip Cagan.[48] A few months later Friedman requested permission to share the piece with the workshop students, calling it particularly valuable for modeling "careful and intensive use of detailed empirical evidence."[49] He now agreed to lengthen the chronology of their study. Schwartz's paper would become the building block of chapter two in the final book.

As the writing began, Friedman began to understand some of Schwartz's desire for scope and scale. After scolding her for a long draft, Friedman wrote again a few days later to say "my face is red. Having started out with the objective of greatly reducing the size of your chapter 2, I herewith submit the first section, which is, unless I am mistaken, rather longer than your draft!"[50] The agony of data gathering and analysis behind them, the two scholars began working in earnest on the body of their book.

In 1958, with the full draft almost in hand, Schwartz wrote Friedman with a plaintive tale. "All these years I have maintained the fiction that I am a graduate student at Columbia and occupied a cubicle in the library. Today I had a call . . . to notify me that unless I registered a dissertation subject under a sponsor, the department would no longer record me the status of a graduate student."[51] At stake was not so much the library cubicle but the reminder that she remained without that essential marker of scholarly status, the Ph.D.

The phone call rekindled in Schwartz a desire to hold the doctorate. She asked Friedman about the possibility of offering as her dissertation part two of their manuscript, plus some separate analysis she would write up for that purpose. Friedman thought the idea absurd. Why not just offer the whole manuscript, with emphasis on part two? That was, after all, what he had done for his dissertation, also published as a coauthored book, he told Schwartz. "It seems to me too bad that you didn't follow this procedure with respect to the British volume that you did with Rostow and Gayer," Friedman added.[52] Of course, this was the very solution Schwartz had attempted years before. She told Friedman nothing of Arthur Burns's successful effort to block her degree.

Even with Friedman on her side, Schwartz got nowhere. It was not just Burns who objected; other gatekeepers included NBER directors who served as Columbia faculty. After a few months of stonewalling, Friedman resolved to take "the bit in my teeth" and write directly to the recalcitrant faculty members. Their attitude was "deplorable," he told Schwartz, interpreting their resistance as a bureaucratic impulse to "set up hurdles rather than perform an educational function."[53] Another six months ticked by. Schwartz was still being passed from director to director, with each declaiming the authority to make a decision. A letter from one she found "menacing," with the requirement that she pass an hour-long inquisition about her work. "If I can't discuss the ideas in this manuscript for one hour or so, on the one hand, I'd say I don't deserve the degree," she reflected to Friedman. "On the other hand," she wrote, "if this is not going to be a friendly hearing, I probably won't think straight, much less express myself well."[54] Schwartz sensed her colleagues were setting her up to fail.

As his Columbia peers sidelined Schwartz, Friedman was reaping rewards from his long-standing relationships with several other unsung female economists. In 1957 he published a field-changing book that largely restored his reputation, *A Theory of the Consumption Function*. No longer could he be easily dismissed by stars like Samuelson, or derided for clinging to the bygone obsessions of Chicago. Instead of focusing on the supposedly irrelevant quantity theory of money, this book took up questions of consumption that lay at the very heart of contemporary economics and politics. While it was lauded by economists of all political bents, Friedman nonetheless regarded the book as fundamentally challenging "a cornerstone" of Keynes's "theoretical structure in the general theory." As with his monetary economics, research on the consumption function yielded a relatively stable and robust capitalism.

Only Friedman's name would go on the title page. But the book and its central ideas emerged from years of conversations between Rose, Milton, Dorothy Brady, and Margaret Reid.[55]

The story begins in 1948, when Milton intercepted a paper on food expenditures that Brady had sent to Rose. Friedman found the paper "enormously intriguing" but doubted Brady's results could support the hypothesis. In follow-up correspondence, the two debated different ways to approach the data.[56] Brady agreed that her paper was incomplete, offering a sentiment that eerily prefigured Friedman's 1953 essay on methodology: "Fundamentally, the only real test of a theory is in reasonably accurate prediction and this experiment did not lead to a 'formula' that could be used for prediction."[57] Was Brady the first to make this claim, more than five years before Friedman's essay appeared in print? Or was she merely repeating back to Friedman a truism from their ongoing conversations? Whatever the case, the reference revealed how much the two old friends inhabited the same intellectual universe.

Brady also introduced another figure, the economist Margaret Reid, to Friedman's world. Quiet, reserved, and married to her work, Reid had earned a Ph.D. in economics from Chicago in 1931, just before Milton arrived; as an undergrad Rose may have known her. Among the few women of her era who successfully pursued an academic career, Reid was also a keen social observer. Her meticulous diary was filled with detailed impressions—psychological profiles, really—of almost everyone she encountered. During a temporary wartime position in Washington, D.C., she met Brady—"unusually intelligent, clear thinker, high standard of workmanship, marked social conscience, able, systematic, thorough, sensitive to people, sense of humor," Reid judged in her diary. In other words, Brady looked like the perfect collaborator. After securing a faculty position at the University of Illinois at war's end, Reid recruited Brady to help with a mountain of farm consumption data she had accumulated over years.[58]

Brady arrived bearing a reference from Friedman: the chapter in his dissertation with Kuznets that distinguished between one-time "windfall" or transitory income, and more regular "permanent" income.[59] Reid's farmers were beset by an extreme version of the dynamic Friedman and Kuznets had detected in doctors and dentists. Vagaries of weather, prices, and the need for new equipment could make farm consumption swing wildly from year to year. Although Reid was studying consumption, not income, Friedman and Kuznets's distinctions were still helpful.[60]

Brady also invited Reid to "the Hideaway," the Friedmans' new summer home in New Hampshire. It was a modest cabin surrounded by a thick grove of trees, located close to the Connecticut River, in an area that was by now becoming an economists' colony. After purchasing the Hideaway in 1949, the family spent every summer there. Near the house—but not too near—was an artists' studio, with a large glass window looking out to the woods and perfect light. Friedman considered it "a nearly ideal place" to work.[61] Splendid isolation was important, but so too was a steady stream of economist friends. As the children drifted off to sleep in a balcony above the firelit living room, they heard below the steady hum of adult voices. Brady was a regular visitor, often arriving with a female friend. No announcements were made, but over time the children came to understand this was her partner.[62]

When both Brady and Reid visited, the evenings became an impromptu seminar on consumption research. Often they were joined by Ruth Mack, a neighbor and an NBER staffer who had worked with Milton on his long-ago wartime taxation publications. At the crux of their conversation was the Keynesian consumption function. This was the mathematical relationship at the heart of the Keynesian revolution, which showed the relationship between money earned and money spent. Many of the predictions economists were making—and many of the econometric models now being designed—hinged on the consumption function. It enabled policy-makers to forecast how increased spending, or lower taxes, would impact household buying choices and thus the overall health of the economy. As Alvin Hansen put it: "It has been my conviction for many years that the great contribution of the General Theory was the clear and specific formulation of the consumption function."[63] Yet while Hansen considered the consumption function "clear and specific," empirical data did not reveal a coherent picture. The consumption function might predict a certain level of spending, given income, but when economists tracked what families spent, real-world figures did not match. The data refused to cooperate. Actual family budgets and spending might match a given consumption function—or they might not.

Accordingly, almost a decade earlier, Rose and Dorothy had been among the first economists to suggest that consumption did not have a clear and specific relationship to income, but rather varied with family location, family size, and, most critically, how much money a family made in comparison to its neighbors. This idea was now called the "relative income hypothesis." Other economists, notably James Tobin, had suggested an alternate explanation that seemed to redeem the original Keynesian idea. Tobin's "wealth-income hypothesis" added wealth, rather than just income, to help explain consumption. Yet now, as Brady and Reid dived deep into mounds of consumption data accumulated by New Deal agencies, neither explanation really seemed to fit.

Over the summers, yet another hypothesis began to evolve. During late evenings at the Hideaway, the group added Friedman and Kuznets's concept of permanent income to Brady and Reid's consumption data and began to think through the implications. What if spending was not the result of income, per se, but of "permanent" income? What if consumers—like Reid's farmers—based their spending and savings on a forecasted average of income over several years, or even their lifetimes? As the conversations progressed, the scholars became convinced that their permanent income hypothesis, as Friedman claimed in the finished work, was an idea that was "potentially more fruitful and is in some measure more general" than the alternatives.[64]

Simultaneously, Reid and Brady were under consideration for jobs at the University of Chicago. Hazel Kyrk, who had advised Reid's dissertation, was on the cusp of retirement. While there was no rule her replacement need be a woman, both department tradition and the nature of the appointment—joint with Home Economics—opened a rare opportunity. In March 1951, Reid and Brady sent a long memo on consumption research to the department's head, T. W. Schultz. (Reid's diary entry on Schultz, whom she had known for years, suggested a receptive target: "meditative, considerative, genial.") Landing amid Friedman's maneuvering against the Cowles Commission, and no doubt written at his urging, the memo suggested consumption as a new focus for the Chicago department. Along the way, it boldly defended and celebrated the unsung work of consumption researchers.[65]

Consumption had moved to "the forefront of economic discussion" due to the Keynesian revolution, the memo noted. Yet economists had ignored a century-old tradition of empirical work. "The early efforts to discover the consumption function through the use of family data were carried on almost as if nothing had previously been done in this field," Brady and Reid declared tartly, leaving unspoken that women had done most of the prior research. For decades, consumption researchers like Kyrk had built an entire field of economics atop the apparent minutiae of new school shoes, what sorts of furniture families bought, and how they spent money for fun. Because it ignored the field's pioneering scholarship, the new work "has been spotty and much of it shoddy,"

Brady and Reid declared. They went on to propose a program in consumption research, centered at a university.[66]

The department took up the hiring question in May. With Friedman operating behind the scenes, department chair Schultz led discussion. The retirement of Kyrk, Schultz noted, opened up the possibility of "undertaking to put resources into the field of consumption research." The department should even consider "a full scale workshop directed by a team consisting of Miss Reid and Mrs. Brady."[67] For now, though, they had funding for one joint appointment. In a second meeting, Schultz pressed for a detailed resolution stating that the department would hire Reid "as the first move in the establishment of the research enterprise, with the hope that Miss Reid soon could be joined by Mrs. Dorothy Brady." The motion to hire Reid passed unanimously, but the department proved unwilling to enlarge its informal half-woman quota.[68] Any future moves would depend on outside funding and the department's willingness to offer Reid a workshop similar to those run by her colleagues.

As these deliberations unfolded, Friedman decided to write up "a rough statement" of the ideas he called "our tentative hypothesis."[69] He sent a copy to Brady, Schultz, and Reid. He also rewrote the proposal Brady and Reid had already submitted to the Chicago department and forwarded a copy to Schultz. In another letter to Brady, Friedman referenced "the consumption hypothesis we have so far arrived at."[70] Brady wrote back encouraging Friedman to develop it into a journal article. "I believe that you included all of the logic as I remember your oral summary late one night a month ago," she noted.[71] With Reid now heading to Chicago and leaving the University of Illinois, Brady returned to her government job. Friedman continued to lobby for hiring Brady at Chicago, even suggesting her as a potential director of the Cowles Commission.[72]

Reid's involvement in the permanent income hypothesis was common knowledge. She was closely involved in discussions around possibly hiring Tobin, and discussed consumption with him at length during an interview. (The idea fizzled when Cowles instead joined Tobin at Yale.) Her presentation of a related paper at the 1953 American Economic Association (AEA) meeting drew the attention of a Cowles

Commission postdoc. He wanted to "translate my hypothesis into algebra," she told Friedman.[73] Reid also shared her extended take with Franco Modigliani, her AEA co-panelist. Twenty years later he cited the never-published paper, along with the "path-breaking" article by Rose and Brady, in his Nobel Prize address. Modigliani called Reid's paper a "highly imaginative analysis" that made a "fundamental contribution" to his life-cycle analysis of savings.[74]

Nevertheless, it was Friedman who ultimately took ownership, turning it from "our tentative hypothesis" into "my hypothesis."[75] After Reid was hired, the ideas languished until the summer of 1953, when Friedman went on a tear. "I have been meaning to write to you all summer, for you have been much in my thoughts," he told Reid. "I finally got around to writing up the theory of consumption, and naturally drew much on your paper." The result was "a beast" and "a mammoth" of a manuscript, running to 140 handwritten pages. It had turned out better than he dared even hope, for much of the evidence conformed to the hypothesis. "I am beginning to believe we really have something," he reported excitedly.[76] His second letter, sent ten days later, slipped between "my paper" and "our approach," as he referred to the completed paper, which Brady was having typed up. Friedman then departed to Oxford for a year abroad, leaving the hypothesis to be tended by Reid and Brady.

While Friedman was away, a thunderstorm descended on Brady. She was suspended from her government job in early 1954 due to a loyalty investigation. Perhaps the McCarthyite dragnet had caught up Dorothy because of her ex-husband, a known political radical. Although they were long divorced, decades-old associations with suspected Communists could still end careers.[77] Or was she a victim of the lavender scare, with a suspected same-sex relationship deemed a security risk? Regardless, the community of women economists drew together around her. Unable to work until her case was resolved, Brady was stressed and haggard. "She looked dreadful," Schwartz reported to Friedman, passing on Brady's thanks for a letter he had written on her behalf.[78] A month later, Brady's case was closed and she was able to resume work. But she remained "whipped" by the experience, as

Schwartz saw it.[79] She returned reluctantly to her former job at the Bureau of Labor Statistics.

Arriving back in the United States the following summer, Friedman alerted Tobin to his new idea and asked for criticism.[80] He made no mention of his collaborators when corresponding with Tobin, a curious omission, given Reid's recent AEA paper and the fact that Tobin had publicly commented on Brady and Rose's now obscure paper, the very first iteration of the hypothesis. By August 1954, as Friedman prepared the manuscript for submission, it had definitively become, in the words of the NBER director Solomon Fabricant, "your manuscript."[81] In a sad irony, the NBER hired Rose to check the footnotes on the finished work. When Friedman debuted the completed manuscript to the field at a Princeton conference, Brady, Reid, and Rose had faded away entirely. The experts at the conference may have known about Brady and Rose's original paper, or Reid's research. But their remarks addressed Friedman and offered him credit and blame for a hypothesis they found at once "splendid and stimulating" yet not entirely convincing.[82]

In the book, Friedman credited Reid with both testing the theory and then pressing him to write it up "so that she could refer to it in a paper presenting her conclusions."[83] Why had Reid not taken this next step herself? She may have believed that she lacked the technical training and knowledge to do the hypothesis justice. This had not, however, been an obstacle in their conversations. Perhaps she understood that her work would go farther, faster if it rested upon a theory developed by a well-known male economist. Did Friedman unfairly claim singular credit for *A Theory of the Consumption Function*? In the book's introduction, he went so far as to call it "a joint product of the group," humbly claiming "my hand held the pen."[84] But there is no evidence that he seriously attempted to publish the book as a coauthored work, even though much of his early work was jointly authored.[85]

Although Brady received no formal credit for her work on the consumption hypothesis, it did pay tangible rewards in her career. Shortly after the disastrous loyalty investigation, in 1955 she took a visiting professorship at Chicago, supported no doubt by both Friedman and

Reid. From this position she secured a permanent, tenured position at the Wharton School, University of Pennsylvania. Had Friedman pushed for her hiring there, as he had at Chicago? Brady's papers do not survive, making it hard to know for sure. But doubtless a year at Chicago burnished her résumé as an economist. At Wharton, Brady's interests began to shift toward economic history, where she drew on her statistical studies to depict economic life and relative prices in the nineteenth century. By the time of her death in 1977, she was a beloved figure to former colleagues and students.[86]

Unlike his work in monetary theory, *A Theory of the Consumption Function* helped restore Friedman's flagging reputation in economics. Despite its political tint, the book addressed critical issues in the mainstream of the field, meaning economists need not share Friedman's policy preferences to recognize the contribution. Even Tobin, who loved to spar with Friedman, laid down a favorable verdict: "Research on the consumer behavior will be different in the future than it has been in the past as a result of this work. The kinds of phenomena that will have to be investigated in any future study have been changed as a result of this work."[87] It was the ultimate academic compliment. And even if they didn't know it, Friedman had forced the field to contend with the woman's world of consumption economics.

Friedman saw *A Theory of the Consumption Function* as a direct blow against the Keynesian consensus. Accepting the permanent income hypothesis, he claimed, "removes completely one of the pillars of the 'secular stagnation' thesis." A key part of New Deal thinking, secular stagnation held that higher incomes meant higher savings—and lower growth, because capital would not be invested but would lie idle. One solution was taxing high incomes. Yet replacing the Keynesian consumption function with the permanent income theory suggested higher income did not necessarily lead to higher savings, as believers in secular stagnation feared. Further, permanent income "destroys the case for one proposed remedy" to secular stagnation, Friedman argued. Reducing inequality, Keynesians believed, would by definition reduce savings and stimulate the economy. Taxes on high incomes would provide funds for the government to spend. Some of this money would end up in the pockets of those with lower incomes, who would then spend it, raising consumption. The permanent income hypothesis, however, showed that reducing inequality "is neutral with respect to the savings ratio."[88] In short, secular stagnation did not exist; and even if it did exist, it could not be solved by standard solutions. *A Theory of the Consumption Function* was not simply offering a new way to read consumption data. It was weakening the fundamental assumptions that had guided policy since the New Deal.

This was not merely Friedmanism grafted onto the text—surviving letters show that Brady, at least, shared his interest in critically assessing Keynesian economics. She may have been a key interlocutor shifting Friedman toward the view, expressed in his Wabash lectures, that inequality in capitalist societies actually declined, rather than increased. Even before the Kuznets curve became widely known, Brady had been immersed in consumption and income data. In an undated letter, she referred to an apparently ongoing conversation they were having about the gap between this data and the current political discussion. "The incredible inequality of income (Hansen's adjective) may not be the explosive variable to watch," Dorothy wrote, citing an article from the *Encyclopedia of Social Science.* Rather, the important factor was "the convergence of that measure among great groups in the population." She went on to hypothesize that maybe the concern was really with "equality as status, the equality of income being almost, if not actually, achieved." Full discussion would have to wait until they met again, Brady noted.[89]

This skepticism of Keynesian analysis made *A Theory of the Consumption Function* a work both of technical economics and of a piece with Friedman's larger political philosophy. With permanent income incorporated into economic analysis, Friedman argued, the upshot was "an inherently cyclically more stable system."[90] Business cycles came and went—as did relief programs—but people decided to save or spend based on their long-term expectations of permanent income. Taken together with his studies in money, the book created a new composite picture of the economy. What appeared as shifts in income and consumption smoothed out over the long run. In turn, this went to the crux of the matter: How much government intervention was necessary for capitalism to function?

Friedman's professional collaborations did not mean the Friedmans' marriage was egalitarian. A staged press photograph captured the dynamic: Milton in his basement woodworking shop, Janet and Rose looking on in admiration. Although the household was Rose's domain, even there she played a supporting role. "When I married Milton I lost half my conversations," she liked to joke, "and when David came along I lost the other half." Presented as jest, the humor nonetheless captured a palpable family dynamic. Dictionaries and encyclopedias came out at family dinners, where debate was perpetual. David was a senior in high school before he realized "there were forms of conversation other than argument." While debates usually persisted across dinners, the family relied upon a numerical code to establish clear victories: a declaration of 2 stood for "you are right, I was wrong."[91]

This intense family culture settled differently on the children. Accelerated repeatedly in school, David ended up younger than most of his classmates. His parents functioned as his peer group, and he thrived on matching wits with his argumentative father. But the family could not insulate Janet from the social tax of being a "very smart girl" in 1950s America. To her dismay, unlike David she was never invited into Aaron Director's woodworking shop for a building project. Instead, she was shunted off to learn weaving with his wife, an accomplished artisan. Summers in New Hampshire brought new freedom. Milton urged Janet on through grueling hikes and took her regularly to a neighbor's farm. While A grades in school were expected from both children and brought little comment, "When I could ride a horse . . . were they impressed!" Janet remembered. Rather than arguing with her father, Janet engaged in subterranean battles with her mother, who liked to keep tabs on all aspects of her children's lives.[92]

As David saw it, "The conservative-libertarian split ran right down our dinner table." While the couple was in sync politically, they had very different personalities. Rose loved the opera and symphony, but when she invited Milton along, he brought a book to read during the performance. "Why would I spend my time going to museums?" he asked Schwartz when she enthused about Paris. From college majors to engagement proposals, Rose did not hesitate to offer her opinions. By contrast, Milton was a conveniently hands-off parent. When a visiting teenage cousin requested a drink at cocktail hour, he handed her a stiff one. One Halloween he instituted a completely laissez-faire policy on candy consumption, under the theory the children would eventually become sated. Regulation followed when the theory proved false. When a stipend to the children at an amusement park turned out to be unexpectedly lavish, Rose and Milton endured hours of games and rides rather than retract the payment.[93]

While never hidden, the family's Jewish identity was firmly cultural, rather than religious. Their roots were communicated through family—primarily Rose's family. Aaron Director was a constant presence in their home, often arriving with a small trinket for the children. Jewish holidays were spent with Rose's relatives in the Chicago area, and trips to Portland might last days or weeks. By contrast, the annual stopover in Rahway on the way to New Hampshire was brief. Milton's relatives felt the distance. A holiday card featuring a Christmas tree set off a mini-scandal among his extended family, perhaps reflecting a larger sense of abandonment.[94] In addition to the verboten Christmas tree, there was a regular Christmas letter to friends and family. Janet also spent several years attending a Unitarian Sunday school. This ecumenical experiment ended when the school put on a play about Jesus; in his "only Judaic action," as Janet put it, Milton withdrew her immediately. "He just wasn't aware of the fact they were still going to believe in Jesus," she remembered. But when David revealed in grade school he was an atheist, his father counted himself in agreement.[95]

Although Rose complained about Chicago winters and doing the taxes even when they could afford an accountant, there was never any serious reconsideration of their traditional domestic arrangement. Underlying this allocation of roles and responsibilities was a genuine affection between Rose and Milton, built upon their long history and the yin and yang of their contrasting temperaments, one quiet and reserved, the other effervescent and extroverted. After two years in a rundown starter home, the couple upgraded to "the best house in the area," a remodeled Victorian in the Kenwood neighborhood, within walking distance of the university.[96] The renowned Laboratory School was also nearby, as were most of their closest faculty friends, including Aaron.

This idyll was shattered one fall evening in 1955 when Milton was in India, consulting for a U.S. agency, the International Cooperation Administration. An intruder climbed in a lower window of the family home and raped Rose at gunpoint, while the children slept nearby.[97] Rose's screams eventually awakened a neighbor and scared off the assailant, who was never apprehended. Roused from sleep by the terrible news, the family's circle reacted immediately. A relative spirited away the children while Rose, dazed and traumatized, sheltered at Aaron and Katherine's nearby home. Without waiting to be asked, Dorothy arrived on the first plane she could catch to Chicago, as did Rose's sister.

Milton was then thousands of miles away in New Delhi. At first, he saw no reason to change his plans, which called for an additional two months abroad. With communication limited to cables—and given the mores of the time—it was hard to convey what exactly had happened. Here Arthur Burns stepped up. Using his considerable powers of persuasion and his sway as a surrogate father figure, Burns worked the lines until Friedman agreed to drop everything and come home. In the aftermath, Rose wanted to move out of Hyde Park to a nearby suburb. But Milton refused to leave his comfortable berth near the university. Eventually they would relocate to a doorman building on the shores of Lake Michigan.

In retrospect, the economic history of the 1950s appears placid, marked by stodgy corporations, peaceful labor relations, rising standards of living, and low inflation. President Eisenhower, a Republican, favored balanced budgets, but just as he accepted New Deal programs like

Social Security, so too did he embrace countercyclical spending. During two recessions in 1953–1954 and 1957–1958 he let the budget run into the red, assuming the shortfall would be recovered when good times returned. Yet American political culture was still marked by the traumas of the 1930s, meaning even these relatively mild downturns brought fear and recrimination. They were particularly troubling to Wright Patman, who worried about rising unemployment, which reached more than 7 percent in 1957.

By then, Patman had ascended to new heights: he was now chairman of the Joint Economic Committee (JEC). Established by the Employment Act of 1946, the committee combined a roster of senators and representatives from both parties, tasked with responding to the president's annual economic report and monitoring the state of the economy more generally. Now Patman, always suspicious of banks, suspected the Fed had something to do with the recent downturn. Under his guidance, the JEC launched a full-scale investigation into the Fed that brought Friedman back into the center of debate, with two separate appearances before Congress, in May and October 1959. By then, he and Schwartz had a working draft of their manuscript and Friedman had considerably refined his analysis. He was ready to debut updated Chicago monetary economics for a new era.

Appearing before Congress, Friedman focused his energies with newfound discipline on a central idea: regulating the growth of the money supply with a predetermined rule. "This can best be done by assigning the monetary authorities the task of keeping the stock of money growing at a regular and steady rate, month in and month out," he explained, ballparking 4 percent as an ideal annual rate.[98] The general idea of a monetary rule was a long-standing one in Friedman's thinking. But rarely had he stated it so clearly, and never before had he made it the centerpiece of his argument. *A Program for Monetary Stability*, a short book published the following year, made clear that Friedman had not abandoned his interest in 100 percent money and associated structural reforms.[99] Rather, he had learned that telling Congress the entire banking system needed to be redesigned from the ground up was not a productive approach. Instead, his easy-to-grasp monetary growth rule would become the signature policy idea of monetarism.

Friedman supported the rule with two other critical concepts: the importance of expectations and policy lags. "Expectations of inflation have become more and more widespread, and partly for that reason, interest rates have risen," Friedman explained, prefiguring his later arguments about inflation.[100] He also explained the twelve-to-eighteen-month lag historically between a monetary action and its impact, using the idea to criticize William McChesney Martin. "The real problem is to lean against a wind that has not started blowing yet," he told Congress. "Neither you nor I nor somebody else really knows how to lean today against next year's wind."[101] Instead of trying to do the impossible, Friedman recommended the Fed target a fixed rate of money growth and hold to it through fair weather and foul.

Even as he pounded away at the money growth rule, Friedman struggled to articulate the central paradox of monetary policy. It was at once neutral and active, weak and powerful. If mismanaged, money could crater the entire economic system. But managed right, it simply faded into the background. It could make things worse but could not make them better. Pressed by Senator Prescott Bush about the recent recession, Friedman attempted to clarify. "I think the stock of money is extraordinarily important in its effect, but what is important about it is the instability in its behavior."[102] It was this instability that a rule would prevent, Friedman believed. The specific rule was not the point—rather, the point was to have a rule that was transparent, known, and simple.

In the end, the paradox of monetary policy linked Friedman's empirical economics to the broader philosophy he had solidified across the 1950s. The role of Simons remained critical. Friedman had fully adopted Simons's argument for rules over discretion in monetary policy, expressed in Simons's landmark 1936 article.[103] At the same time, he had modified Simons's particular recommendation for price level stabilization through the Treasury Department. Changes in the Fed since the 1930s, along with Schwartz's historical research, convinced Friedman and Director that the quantity of money was a better target. As

Director stressed: "The late Professor Simons's original emphasis was primarily on the rule of stable rules than on the character of the rules themselves."[104] Once again, Friedman and Director had rearranged the content of Simons's ideas, retaining the form. Monetary rules were also a concrete example of positive liberalism, for they captured Hayek's stress on the "competitive order" and rule of law. With a monetary rule, the state used its monopoly in the field of money to create legible rules of the game for all.

Hayek stood in uneasy relationship to Chicago monetary economics. "He had one good idea and always stressed it," remembered Mints of Hayek—without specifying what that idea was! Could it have been Hayek's emphasis on the competitive order? On the importance of a stable legal framework? Hayek accorded money a central role in the business cycle, but was skeptical about the monetary growth rule. While Friedman believed the money supply must expand to accommodate economic growth itself, Hayek viewed this increase as inflation, pure and simple. Nor was he really sure it would work; at the Wabash lecture, he wondered to Director what would happen if prices surged 10 to 12 percent under a monetary growth rule. Director batted away the question, suggesting it was a familiar objection: "Our position—these things will not happen in such a system." Director stressed again this was an empirical question, not a matter of theory.[105]

Despite Hayek's doubts about the idea, Friedman's emerging monetarism encapsulated the Mont Pelerin Society's call for a new liberalism. Two of monetarism's central claims—inflation was "always and everywhere a monetary phenomenon," and the way to manage it was with a monetary growth rule—relied upon government control of money in one form or another. Here was the state, playing an active role to ensure economic prosperity and social stability. But not *too* active a role, for monetarism nested with a specific political economy that prioritized private economic activity. A monetary rule "would be no panacea," Friedman reflected in his opening statement to Congress. "The springs of economic progress are to be found elsewhere; in the qualities of the people, their inventiveness, thrift, and responsibility, in public policies that give a free field for private initiative and promote competition and free trade at home and abroad."[106] He had now connected the dots between Keynes and Knight, linked together Simons and Volker.

With *Studies in the Quantity Theory of Money* and *A Theory of the Consumption Function*, Friedman completed the first stage of his theoretical attack on Keynesianism. He had begun with the battle against the Cowles Commission and the rehabilitation of Alfred Marshall. His 1953 essay on the importance of prediction to science had established a standard for judgment. Next he had added bulk and heft to his positive program with a rearticulation of the quantity theory, backed by an echelon of workshop scholars. And then he had taken the battle to the Keynesians' home turf, offering a powerful intervention into consumption economics. It was a stunning output for any economist, and one that earned him new respect beyond Chicago.

Even so, this prodigious body of theoretical and applied economics did not quite add up to the "new faith" Friedman had promised as the decade dawned. To articulate that new faith, he would need not just models, data, and paradigms, but a story. In a pattern that was now among his defining characteristics as an intellectual, Friedman would find that story through his work with Schwartz, and that language in his partnership with Rose.

PART IV

CONSCIENCE OF A CONSERVATIVE

9

POLITICAL ECONOMIST

This is one of the most important books of our time.

—*The American Historical Review*, 1964

Seldom in American history do new decades announce themselves so obviously as the 1960s, when an auspiciously timed presidential election created a visual contrast that was impossible to ignore. Offered a choice between the glowering vice president Richard Nixon or the dashing young senator John F. Kennedy, the nation appeared to have struck out symbolically for the new. Kennedy himself enthusiastically fostered this impression. "The world is changing. The old era is ending. The old ways will not do," he declared in his nomination speech, announcing a "New Frontier" in American life.[1]

In truth, the 1960 election was closer than anyone cared to admit; Kennedy had barely bested Nixon. Republicans, too, had their own version of Camelot, "the tall, bronzed, lean-jawed, silver-haired" senator Barry Goldwater, in the words of *Time*. With Nixon's loss, media favorite Goldwater was well positioned for a presidential run four years hence. And in all the excitement over Kennedy's victory, it was easy to miss another distinctive trend of the decade: the quickening of American conservatism.

The vineyard in which Friedman had been toiling for years was bearing new fruit. There was the group Young Americans for Freedom, founded under graceful Connecticut elms on the family estate of William F. Buckley Jr. Chapters of the Intercollegiate Society of Individualists were popping up on college campuses, including at the University of Chicago. And membership was surging at the conspiratorial John Birch Society. Looking across this new landscape, Friedman saw at least three types of conservatives: libertarians, traditional conservatives, and "crackpot conservatives of the radical right fringe."[2] Friedman considered himself to have little in common with the latter group. But escaping the fringe would not be easy.

Friedman had long wanted to "distinguish positive, liberal, conservatism from reaction," as he told a group of Chicago undergraduates.[3] In the 1940s, fighting "reaction" meant joining Mont Pelerin Society efforts to craft a "new liberalism." In the 1950s, it meant distinguishing the Republican Party from Joseph McCarthy. In the 1960s, Birchers were the problem.

Named after an American missionary killed by Chinese Communists, the John Birch Society was founded in 1958 to eradicate Communism, wherever it could be found. Fighting Communism was not a fringe idea. It was, in fact, the stated foreign policy of the United States. Americans were constantly being reminded of the Soviet menace. There were nuclear-bomb drills for schoolchildren, sensational televised hearings exposing Soviet spies in government, and dire warnings of Russian military might. During the campaign, Kennedy had harped on a "missile gap" that supposedly left Americans dangerously exposed. Driven by fear, citizens flocked to myriad grassroots crusades, flushing out suspected Communists in their local schools, patronizing patriotic bookstores, or plugging into a flourishing network of anti-Communist schools and study groups.

Birchers went one step further. Mimicking the enemy, they organized into secret cells. Following the lead of their eccentric founder, the candy magnate Robert Welch, Birchers argued the United States was honeycombed with Communists, up to and including President

Eisenhower. Welch's allies also voiced a nasty note of anti-Semitism. Essentially, Birchers continued the conspiratorial tradition of the pre-war Old Right, minus the isolationism. Once exposed by the media, Birchers became synonymous, in many minds, with conservatism.

Friedman strove to correct this impression. In a debate before the national Chamber of Commerce, Friedman crossed swords with the Pennsylvania senator Joseph Clark. Faced with Friedman's rapier wit, Clark spluttered that Friedman would make "a fine candidate for the next president of the John Birch Society."[4] After the audience loudly booed Clark, Friedman seized the opportunity to differentiate himself. Accusing Clark of "guilt by association," Friedman attacked the society as "fundamentally wrong."[5]

Clark's conflation of the two was a mistake. But it pointed to a larger truth. If the Birchers were out of the mainstream, so too were Friedman's economic views.

In part, this was because the mainstream was rapidly shifting. Eisenhower's presidency had been marked by a traditional concern with budget deficits and inflation. It had also been marked by years of slow growth, low inflation, and two recessions. By the time Kennedy took office, unemployment stood at 6.6 percent. The slowdowns did not approach Great Depression levels, but they gave candidate Kennedy a handy slogan—he would "get the country moving again."

Once elected, Kennedy relied on a powerhouse gang of Keynesian economists to execute this pledge. His Council of Economic Advisers (CEA) was led by Walter Heller, a pragmatic Midwesterner and the last institutional economist to reach such heights. (As a student at the University of Wisconsin, Heller led a picket line protesting Friedman's firing.) The president devoured Heller's pithy memos, which also served as economics tutorials. The other major player on the council was the Yale professor James Tobin. Bookish and quiet, a self-professed "ivory tower economist," Tobin took a leave of absence from the Cowles Commission at Yale to join the CEA. Hovering in the background was Paul Samuelson, who turned down an official position due to the six children in his household, but nonetheless remained a force in the council's thinking. Guided by these advisers, only weeks after taking office Kennedy launched a series of spending programs intended to stimulate aggregate demand. Federal money would build new post offices; accelerate construction on schools, highways, and public housing; increase farm price supports; and establish a new food stamps program.[6]

Kennedy's "new economics"—as the press quickly dubbed it—was marked by an optimistic belief the fetters of the past could be slipped. According to Tobin, a major novelty of the new approach was "the conviction that business cycles were not inevitable, that government policy could and should keep the economy close to a path of steady real growth at a constant target rate of unemployment."[7] It was a stark contrast with Eisenhower's CEA, helmed by the business-cycles expert Arthur Burns. Nor did the Kennedy CEA stay in the background, cultivating a private relationship with the president, as had Burns's council. Instead, the trio transformed the 1962 Economic Report of the President—an annual statement to Congress required by law—into a landmark document that set out their thinking.

Getting the country moving again, according to the report, required departing from the past decade's orthodoxy. Along with the business cycle, the traditional fear of deficits would need to be set aside. Among the many who assumed balanced budgets were sacrosanct was President Kennedy. But the professors were making headway with their new pupil. About a year into his term, Kennedy evinced a shift in his thinking. The fear of deficits was an "old and automatic cliché," he argued in a commencement speech. "Obviously deficits are sometimes dangerous," Kennedy admitted, but this was not always true. Similarly, debt could be positive: "Borrowing can lead to over-extension and collapse. But it can also lead to expansion and strength."[8] This was an apt summary of the CEA's Keynesianism.

More important, the new economics was not simply a retread of the New Deal. Some types of fiscal stimulus were similar to those offered by Roosevelt, including new post offices, roads, and other construction projects. But in general, the CEA steered away from new public works in favor of policies that adjusted economic incentives or relative prices. For example, Kennedy's first recovery program lowered federal mortgage rates and bolstered loans to farmers and small businesses. And deficits were not simply about spending; they also made tax reductions possible. Kennedy's advisers favored quick-acting, temporary cuts that could help the government "time its fiscal transactions to offset and to dampen fluctuations in the private economy." Keynesian demand management sought to blend New Deal relief spending with structural policies that would actually grow the economy's potential.[9]

In place of the balanced budget, the CEA proposed a "full employment budget" in which budget deficits were an essential growth strategy. Unlike previous councils, Kennedy's CEA was willing to make specific numerical forecasts. For the first time, the CEA defined "full employment" as 4 percent unemployment. This was not a measure of labor force participation but of the number of people currently seeking work. It wouldn't be realistic to shoot for zero unemployment. Not everyone who wanted a job could find one, at least not right away; there would be inefficiencies, churn, and cyclical shifts in the labor market. Kennedy's CEA called 4 percent unemployment "a modest goal."[10]

Another key concept was "potential" gross national product, or GNP (the equivalent figure today is GDP, gross domestic product). The idea of GNP, which combined all of the country's output into one number, grew out of Simon Kuznets's national income figures. "Potential" GNP was another conceptual innovation, the idea being that economists could calculate what output *should* be, if better conditions obtained. And the gap between the GNP the country did have and what it should have would guide the sizing and timing of any stimulus. It was the economic version of Kennedy's missile gap.

The CEA's thinking on inflation was influenced by the Phillips curve, an economic concept popularized in 1960 by Samuelson and Robert Solow, his MIT colleague and a senior staffer at the CEA. The curve was rather abstract compared to its namesake's other invention, a full-scale hydraulic model of the British economy consisting of tubes and tanks filled with colored water. The MONIAC, as it became known, was so impressive it immediately earned William Phillips, an enterprising New Zealand economist, a teaching position at the London School of Economics. In 1958, Phillips plotted out his namesake curve based on decades of British data. He found a statistical relationship between unemployment and inflation, with higher inflation associated with lower unemployment.[11]

Plotting their own American version of the curve, Samuelson and Solow found the same result. It seemed that lower unemployment could, in some respect, be achieved by accepting higher inflation. While the formalized Phillips curve was new to economists, it matched existing folk wisdom. As Tobin noted in later reflections, "a more ambitious employment target would be considered irresponsibly inflationary by many influential critics at home and abroad. Their opposition might cripple an expansionary policy." Therefore, "with an eye on the Phillips curve," the CEA chose 4 percent as the definition of full employment. In the recent past, this rate of unemployment had coincidentally matched an inflation rate of 4 percent. Thus an unemployment target, as Tobin suggested, was in some sense also an inflation target. While it was admittedly unclear if the relationship would hold, at the very least it offered political cover.[12]

Was it coincidence that this ersatz inflation target matched Friedman's 4 percent monetary growth rule? Friedman may well have been one of those "influential critics" Tobin feared, given his repeat appearances before Congress. Regardless, the CEA did not see the same relationship between the money supply and inflation as Friedman. Like most economists at the time, they believed the money supply reacted to other forces in the economy. "As the economy advances toward full employment, it will need more liquidity," the 1962 report argued. Eventually, at full employment, the money supply would need to grow at an annual rate of 7 or even 8 percent, the report suggested, far higher than Friedman's recommendation.[13] This posed no inflationary risks, the council believed, for they pinned inflation on aggregate demand, not monetary conditions.

The key to preventing inflation was getting the GNP gap right. "Demand-pull" was the reigning theory of inflation, the idea being that aggregate demand could, potentially, get out ahead of the economy's productive capacity. Analogous to wartime, a flood of government stimulus money might find limited outlets in existing enterprises and factories, sending prices higher. In some ways, demand-pull layered easily atop a monetary interpretation of inflation. It was a fiscal version of "too much money chasing too few goods." But too much demand was not linked directly to monetary stimulus, as in Friedman's theory. Alternatively, inflation could be "cost-push," triggered by increasing prices (cost) of raw materials and higher wages (push). Regardless, the main forces at work were not monetary. They could be fiscal, in terms of the federal budget, or institutional, like powerful labor unions, or even random events, such as commodity shortages.

No matter the cause, if inflation did break out, the CEA offered a remedy: voluntary wage and price guideposts. These were linked, once again, to overall GNP. "The general guide," according to the 1962 report, was "the rate of increase in wage rates (including fringe benefits) in each industry be equal to the trend rate of overall productivity increase." If it looked like inflation was breaking out in any area of the economy, the guideposts would kick in, ensuring companies and labor unions kept wages and prices in bounds. How were these guideposts to be enforced? Through moral suasion, in which "an informed public . . . can help to create an atmosphere in which the parties to such decisions will exercise their powers responsibly."[14] It was a thin policy that reflected the CEA's relaxed attitude toward inflation, and economists' overall confidence in the predictive power of their models. The CEA was not alone in imagining that policy-makers could readily discern what was happening in the economy, time their actions accordingly, and expect a desired result. The widely used term "fine-tuning" summed up this aspect of the new economics.

Friedman doubted almost every element of this new synthesis. "Don't take full employment too seriously," he told an audience in Peoria. "We can have full employment without prosperity, such as they have in prison or in the Army."[15] Even before Kennedy took office, Friedman feared full employment was impossible to attain without inflation. As the *Chicago Tribune* reported, "the major source of inflationary pressure is a government's acceptance of responsibility for full employment, Dr. Friedman believes."[16] Friedman had never put much trust in large-scale macroeconomic models. He disliked them as economics, and even less as policy. He also had an entirely different take on inflation, as his book with Anna Schwartz would soon make clear.

Friedman was not an unreconstructed defender of laissez-faire. He agreed that budget deficits did not inevitably lead to inflation. He even accepted the general "climate of opinion" the CEA lauded, in which "the Government has been expected to assume, and has assumed, greater responsibility for economic stabilization."[17] But stabilization was not the same as managing, guiding, and improving the economy—fine-tuning through active fiscal policy. It was not so much a philosophical difference as an epistemological one. Friedman simply did not believe policy-makers could accurately grasp what was happening in the economy, respond in a timely fashion, and correctly anticipate the outcome. Instead, his countervailing vision focused on stable monetary growth as the government's chief responsibility toward economic life. Beyond that, allocation and exchange should be governed by prices, pulsing through the economy as signals of countless faceless exchanges. Prices couldn't play favorites. Prices couldn't be lobbied. Government had to set up basic rules and institutions to let the price system operate, but then it should simply get out of the way.

Friedman's alarm about the John Birch Society was shared by another man who looked, from a distance, like the very sort of reactionary conservative he had long opposed: William F. Buckley Jr., the editor of *National Review.* Filthy rich, painfully pretentious, and a pious Catholic, Buckley was also witty, congenial, and deeply libertarian. His notorious 1951 debut book, *God and Man at Yale,* attacked his alma mater for atheism and Keynesianism, which Buckley seemed to regard as equally grave sins. Further, alone among the many inheritances from his businessman father, Buckley rebuked anti-Semitism. This was no small move for a man whose life's ambition was to become a force on the American right. The pre-war Old Right, which took isolationism as its cause, contained a substantial measure of anti-Semites. By contrast, Buckley's fierce anti-Communism led him to advocate for broad American power overseas. And he sought out Jewish writers and editors as he worked to launch his new magazine. Friedman was the perfect embodiment of the conservatism Buckley sought to create: educated, articulate, credentialed. By contrast, the John Birch Society represented everything he was trying to overcome.

Friedman did not warm to the young upstart right away. After all, when Buckley founded *National Review* in 1955, Friedman had already spent nearly a decade working for the cause. Along with Aaron Director and George Stigler, he scolded Buckley when *National Review* published a critical note about the Mont Pelerin Society.[18]

Relations thawed as Buckley mounted a public campaign against the John Birch Society, publishing disapproving editorials in 1961 and 1962. For all their kookiness, the Birchers were popular, strong, and organized. Buckley had to tread carefully. Further, he would need—as Stigler would have put it—a rival theory to displace the Birchers' lunacy. Friedman soon appeared helpful in this cause. Buckley solicited (unsuccessfully) a paper on foreign aid for *National Review*, and in turn Friedman congratulated his recent sallies against Welch.[19]

The struggle against Welch marked a new and critical phase in the evolution of conservatism from intellectual pet project to coming political force. In earlier days, Friedman had gone up against the likes of Ludwig von Mises on an isolated European mountaintop. Now the battle to define conservatism played out on a much larger landscape, and the stakes were far higher.

Among the key prizes was the Sunbelt sensation Barry Goldwater. If Buckley was the man who crafted a new variant of conservatism, Goldwater could—possibly—sell it to the masses.

Ruggedly handsome and often photographed with a rifle and horse, the charismatic Goldwater seemed like the mythical American cowboy come to life. Elected to the Senate from Arizona the same year Dwight Eisenhower became president, Goldwater had achieved a national reputation through televised Senate hearings investigating corruption in labor unions. When he won reelection in the face of an AFL-CIO campaign against him, *The Saturday Evening Post* anointed him "the glittering Mr. Goldwater."[20]

Goldwater's hostility to labor also earned him the devotion of an earnest cadre of conservative businessmen and political organizers who dreamed he might one day be president. They convinced Goldwater to publish a political manifesto, *The Conscience of a Conservative*, that became a publishing sensation in 1960. "Conservatism, we are told, is out-of-date. The charge is preposterous and we ought boldly to say so," Goldwater blared in the opening pages.[21] A modest printing of ten thousand copies sold out; a second printing of the same size was ordered a month later; and then the next month an additional fifty thousand copies flooded the marketplace. Astoundingly, it was not just the usual suspects—low-tax businessmen—drawn to Goldwater's banner. His book sold briskly on college campuses and achieved a cult following among "young fogies"—what the newspapers sometimes called college-age Republicans. More than a politician, Goldwater was "the favorite son of a state of mind," as *Fortune* put it.[22]

The Conscience of a Conservative put to rest backroom battles about what conservatism in America was, and dinner-party debates over whether it even existed. The book articulated a fusionist conservatism that drew together the three strands Friedman had identified—libertarians, traditional conservatives, and ardent cold warriors (what Friedman called the radical right fringe). "The conservative has learned that the economic and spiritual aspects of man's nature are inextricably intertwined," asserted Goldwater. "He cannot be economically free, or even economically efficient, if he is enslaved politically; conversely, man's political freedom is illusory if he is dependent for his economic needs on the State."[23] Programmatically, this meant repudiation of the New Deal, an embrace of states' rights, and keen attention to "the Soviet menace." It was no coincidence that this blended conservatism overlapped with the program of *National Review*, for Buckley's brother-in-law L. Brent Bozell had written the text.

Goldwater, it turned out, was a reluctant warrior for the cause. The backers of *The Conscience of a Conservative* hoped it would push Goldwater into presidential politics. But in the 1960 primary season, he instead fell into line behind Nixon.

Goldwater was also wobbly on Birchers. He well knew that many of his most fervent supporters were members of the society. He also knew they were a significant political liability. Goldwater split the difference, refusing to publicly disavow the society while privately criticizing Welch.[24]

Even so, Goldwater appeared as a potential ally to Friedman. Shortly after Kennedy's victory, Friedman wrote to Goldwater as "a fellow believer in a free society based on free enterprise, and as a professional economist." Friedman was concerned about a recent statement Goldwater had made to *The Wall Street Journal* favoring exchange restrictions, or limitation on the number of dollars tourists could take out of the United States. This was a scheme intended to address the gold drain that threatened Bretton Woods. Such a policy was "the first step toward full exchange control," Friedman warned, "one of the few really modern devices invented to enable the state to control its citizens." Friedman went on to urge the senator to support floating exchange rates, enclosing a paper he had written on the topic. Further, he offered to set up a meeting between Goldwater and a group of Chicago economists, at any date that would be convenient.[25] In the short run, the overture went nowhere; Goldwater dismissed Friedman with a perfunctory response. But the letter reflected an epochal shift in Friedman's life.

In their 1962 Christmas card, posted from Jerusalem, Milton and Rose noted a phase transition in their household. Janet was at Bryn Mawr, and David at Harvard. "Unencumbered by children, small or large, for the first time in nineteen years, Rose has been making hay," the couple wrote. She was now free to travel, and even indulge in "some more serious activity like organizing the material for one of Milton's books."[26] In a later recollection, Rose was more frank; finally, she "felt like a free person."[27]

She began with Milton's notoriously messy office. His desk was legendary. It was covered in teetering stacks of paper and books, looming over the professor's tiny frame. In a department skit, students satirized the scene. Hearing a knock upon his office door, the dramatized Friedman responded "just a minute," then dumped a huge box of papers over his desk.[28] Rose ventured into this domain determined to bring order to chaos.

Her larger goal was redemption of sorts. Although ostensibly helping her husband, Rose was also focused on her brother. Unfinished business was by now Aaron's specialty. He'd never managed to complete a Ph.D., although he had earned tenure at the law school. Nor had he written anything for the Volker Fund, even though he had been hired specifically to author the American equivalent of F. A. Hayek's *The Road to Serfdom.*

Over time, it dawned on the funders that Friedman was a better bet. His lectures from Wabash College held special appeal. Delivered by an established scholar and blending first principles, economics, and specific policy advice, they were exactly what the Volker Fund had in mind. The foundation leadership began to exert "friendly pressure" on him to make the lectures into a book.[29]

Behind the "friendly pressure" lay a considerable measure of guilt. The Volker Fund had provided much and asked little in return. But there was also the darker memory of Henry Simons. His tragic death had brought Director to Chicago. And in trying to make up for Simons's loss, Director had accepted a task for which he was spectacularly ill-suited. Turning Milton's lectures into a book, then, promised to expunge several layers of obligation. Rose would use her freedom to discharge her brother's debt.

It was not a straightforward task of simply publishing the lectures. In the past decade, Friedman had spoken to countless student and business groups. Sometimes he spoke from typed text, but other times he used handwritten notes, scratched out in nearly illegible cursive. Many talks were delivered multiple times.

Rose set to work repurposing bits and pieces of the lectures, pulling out the best examples and most convincing arguments. Also in the mix were published articles, and bits and bobs from his research with Schwartz, which Rose whittled down or glossed for the general reader. By Milton's account, she "pieced together the scraps of the various lectures, coalesced different versions, translated lectures into something more closely approaching with written English."[30] Out of this primal stew came a trim 202-page book, composed of two philosophical chapters followed by ten more on specific policy issues. Rose's name was on the title page, but not the cover.

Rose had done more than get the manuscript over the finish line. She had found an Archimedean point between shifting generations at Chicago, bridging the considerable gaps between Frank Knight and Milton Friedman, Henry Simons and Aaron Director. After all, she had been at Chicago even longer than Milton. Skillfully she drew in the insights of the department's rising star, Gary Becker, Friedman's top graduate student. And then she pushed into new territory, using economic principles and logic to address contemporary political problems. In the process, she became an unsung architect of postwar conservatism.

Published in 1962 during the high tide of the New Frontier, *Capitalism and Freedom* seemed perversely opposed to the zeitgeist. The book began with a frank assault on 1960s idealism. The first sentence disapprovingly cited Kennedy's famous inaugural plea to collective service: "Ask not what your country can do for you—ask what you can do for your country." According to the Friedmans, this paternalistic sentiment was not "worthy of the ideals of free men in a free society." Rather than serve their country, readers ought to safeguard freedom, "a rare and delicate plant."[31] If freedom was the first principle, the second and third principles concerned the state: government must be both limited and dispersed.

What would limited government look like? Although *Capitalism and Freedom* mostly dwelled in abstractions, occasionally flashes of a startling alternate world came through. Rose and Milton argued one possible justification for state action was "neighborhood effects"—circumstances under which strictly voluntary exchange was impossible or too costly. For example, how could anyone determine who benefited from a neighborhood park, surrounded by residents and passersby? "The entrances to a national park like Yellowstone, on the other hand, are few," continued the Friedmans. It would be easy to set up tolls at the entrance. "If the public wants this kind of an activity enough to pay for it, private enterprise will have every incentive to provide such parks," they concluded. Similar logic extended to the post office, public housing, toll roads, and even Social Security. Each of these could be more efficiently handled by private enterprise, the Friedmans proposed, enumerating a list of fourteen "activities currently undertaken by government in the U.S." that could not be justified by their principles. "This list is far from comprehensive," the authors noted.[32]

It was no coincidence that almost everything on the Friedmans' list had its counterpart on the Kennedy agenda. "The renewal of cities, the reconstruction of transportation facilities, the improvement of education at all levels, the provision of new facilities for the arts, the expansion of medical care facilities, the conservation and expansion of our national parks and forests," were all unfilled needs waiting for public expenditure, enthused the 1962 *Economic Report of the President.*[33] Many had also found their place in Kennedy's first round of stimulus spending. The Friedmans' call to meet these needs through the private sector instead—akin to what later generations would call privatization—was both the ultimate logic of price theory and a contrarian rejection of the status quo.

Capitalism and Freedom stuck it to the Man years before doing so became trendy. Expecting "the usual espousal of big government and the welfare state that all intelligent people—especially intelligent economists—are known to support," an audience at Haverford College jolted awake when Friedman laid down theses from the book. "The speaker attacked almost every institution dear to the modern liberal, among them socialized medicine, public housing, foreign aid, large government agencies and farm price supports," reported the student newspaper. Campus liberals rallied to counterattack, only to be overwhelmed "by a bevy of facts and quick retorts."[34] The Friedmans rejected the idealism of Kennedy liberalism. At the same time, their provocative, anti-establishment proposals foreshadowed another rising mood of the decade.

But was anyone paying attention? Goldwater's *The Conscience of a Conservative* had been headline news. Coming scarcely two years later, *Capitalism and Freedom* surfaced many of the same themes, ingeniously linking them to policy and fresh economic research. Yet the book suffered what a later defender called "the brushoff by important book review media," equivalent to an intellectual "blacklisting."[35] After publication, it effectively disappeared without a trace. Part of the problem was that Friedman, too, vanished. He and Rose spent most of the following year abroad. There would be no high-profile book tour, no major media interviews. Indeed, the book could scarcely be found, Friedman informed the hapless University of Chicago Press in a series of querulous letters criticizing their sales efforts.[36]

Unexpectedly, it was another joint production that would provide the rocket fuel for Friedman's public reputation and career. After more than a decade of research, he and Schwartz were ready to publish their monumental study of money. Clocking in at 860 pages, bedecked with footnotes, tables, and several graphs so large they folded out of the text like a children's pop-up book, *A Monetary History of the United States, 1867–1960*, was an unlikely launching pad for fame and fortune. But appearing as Goldwater began his presidential campaign, it became just that.

From an insider's perspective, the book was old news. "The presentation supports what we know to be his general position," concluded *The Journal of American History*, while a reviewer in *The Journal of Finance* wrote that "it adds little fuel to the long-lived controversy over the exact role of money . . . it is not likely to change anyone's mind."[37] It was true that Friedman's views on money were well known within the economics profession, thanks to the money and banking workshop and *Studies in the Quantity Theory of Money.* In follow-up writings like *A Program for Monetary Stability* he had continued to refine his emerging paradigm.[38]

But this work paled in comparison to the force and impact of *A Monetary History of the United States.* What had begun as a favor to Arthur Burns had become a book that would turn the conventional wisdom of academic economists, policy-makers, and politicians alike upside down. *The American Historical Review* put it simply: "This is one of the most important books of our time."[39] Friedman and Schwartz presented voluminous data on nearly a century of U.S. history; but beyond piling up facts, they also advanced a theory of how money worked in the economy.

How did money affect business cycles? Friedman and Schwartz had an answer they considered definitive: money mattered. It was the hidden force behind the ups and downs, the breadlines and the bubbles. Friedman knew the book would make an impact. He knew it was the best work he had ever done, or would ever do. He knew that for all his deviationist politics, for all the force of Keynesian assumption, for all the habitual scorn heaped upon the quantity theory of money, their book would have to be answered. It would compel conversation.

The book's centerpiece was its stunning analysis of the Great Depression. Friedman and Schwartz's data showed a precipitous 33 percent decline in the quantity of money during what they called "the great contraction." They convincingly argued that this lack of money transformed an unremarkable dip in the business cycle into a crisis of global proportions. Here was a provocative new explanation for a disaster that continued to cast its shadow across the century. But threaded through the economic argument was another thesis. In 1914, the United States had created a central bank system designed expressly to stabilize the economy. As the lender of last resort, the Federal Reserve Board could have opened the spigots and flooded the economy with cash. Why did it fail to do so?

The answer lay not in economic theory but in personality. *A Monetary History of the United States* dwelled with the intensity of a psychologist upon the differences between the New York bankers George L.

Harrison and Benjamin Strong Jr., men depicted as holding the power to redirect history itself. The absent hero was Strong, who died just before the crash. Examining Strong's earlier career, Friedman and Schwartz argued that he would have reacted to the liquidity crisis with "strenuous and appropriate measures to head it off." Beyond financial acumen, Strong had "the personal force to make his own views prevail, and also the courage to act upon them." By contrast, his successor, Harrison, was a cautious bureaucrat who "placed great value on conciliating opposing points of view and achieving harmony."[40] Unwilling to dominate others or push his views, Harrison acquiesced to a policy of masterly inactivity. The Fed stood by as money drained from the banking system and the economy collapsed. What appeared to be a failure of markets was in fact a failure of men.

Presented as Greek drama with a tragic hero and epic catastrophe, *A Monetary History of the United States* had broad appeal to political pundits and the chattering class. Here was history as decision-makers and their courtiers imagined it to be: brimming with critical moments, tough calls, and choices that could resound into millions of lives. "A masterful work . . . which deserves to be read and reread," summarized *The Washington Post* in a laudatory review.[41]

Schwartz deserved much of the credit for the book's success, particularly its reverberation beyond academic economics. Left to his own devices, Friedman would have created a compendium of charts and graphs. It was Schwartz who dove into Confederate money, anchoring the narrative in the Civil War era. And it was Schwartz who dug into the archives and pulled out the compelling human stories that brought the book to life.

Yet still she got no respect. As their book neared publication, the campaign to keep her from becoming Dr. Schwartz reached absurd heights. The newest wrinkle, she reported, was that because her "dissertation" was now in bound galleys, she could not incorporate feedback from her committee members, and therefore could not qualify for a degree.[42] It was ludicrous enough to break through Friedman's naivete. Finally, he grasped that she was up against something more insidious than academic bureaucracy.

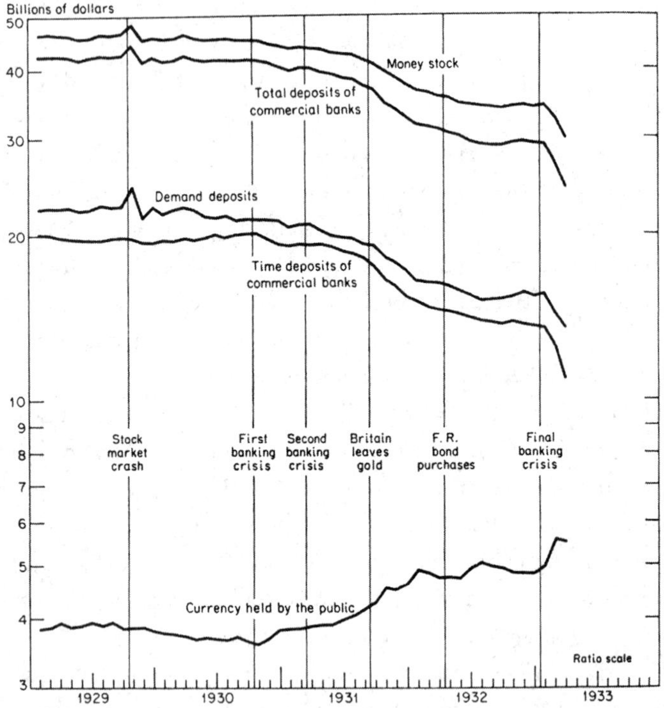

ABOVE AND OPPOSITE: Friedman and Schwartz documented a 33 percent decline in the money stock across the Depression years 1929–1933. (*A Monetary History of the United States*, Princeton University Press, 1963, 302–303)

Friedman had reached the mountaintop. To his credit, he wanted Schwartz there, too. He roared as much in a phone call to the chair of Columbia's economics department, which was trying to hire him away from Chicago. A sharp letter followed. "The one thing I am clear about is that by any standards whatsoever she has demonstrated her qualifications for the PhD degree, that her getting a degree at this stage has no great advantage for her and will honor Columbia more than it will help her," Friedman wrote.[43] Schwartz finally had what apparently every woman in economics needed: a powerful male patron. Within

Prices, Personal Income, and Industrial Production, Monthly, 1929–March 1933

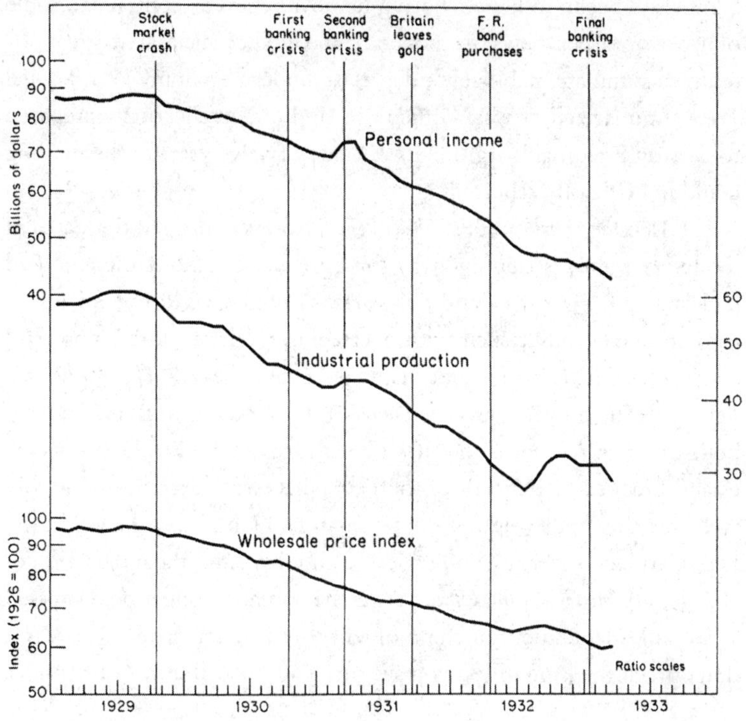

a year, she had her doctorate, too. Now Columbia as well as Chicago could claim some connection to a book that would resound into economic thinking and global monetary policy.

A Monetary History of the United States would not convert all its readers to the quantity theory, but it would permanently alter thinking about the Great Depression. The terrible years of the 1930s—still a living memory to many policy-makers—now appeared not as a natural disaster but as preventable human error. Even economists who resisted Friedman's larger policy analyses, such as James Tobin, largely accepted

Friedman and Schwartz's account of the Great Depression.[44] In turn, this led to a reassessment of money's role in the economy overall. Paul Samuelson began to hedge, noting he now believed "contrary to some of my own earlier views . . . monetary and credit policies have great potency to stimulate, stabilize, or depress a modern economy." As *Business Week* summarized, it was "difficult to find one intellectually prepared to destroy Friedman's arguments." A book twelve years in the making could not be easily rebutted.[45]

A Monetary History of the United States forever changed the status of monetary policy, stripping away the bureaucratic anonymity the Fed had enjoyed. Friedman and Schwartz painted a vivid portrait of an error-prone agency tasked with overseeing monetary forces powerful enough to cause enormous social and political upheaval. *The Washington Post* made the book's relevance clear: "It is unsparing in its criticism of both the men and ideas that have been identified with the monetary establishment . . . Officials of the Federal Reserve System will hardly welcome this stout volume."[46] Friedman had long banged away at the Fed in articles, speeches, and expert testimony. After the publication of *A Monetary History of the United States*, he could no longer be dismissed as a crank ideologue. For the moment, the Fed was speechless. "You don't fire at the king unless you are sure you can kill him," one insider remarked.[47]

The book captured the attention of Goldwater, who was emerging as a serious contender for the GOP presidential nomination. "I have just finished the advance manuscript of your coming book and I want you to know that I think it is superb," he raved in a personal letter. He particularly appreciated the book's academic pedigree yet accessible format. "Professors sometimes have the habit of writing only for other professors," Goldwater noted, "but your book is written in a way that the man on the street will understand and get your message."[48] Grasping the importance of the book to the conservative cause, he promised to plug it in his syndicated column.

Why was Goldwater so taken with *A Monetary History of the United States*? As *Business Week* explained, focusing on money undermined the Keynesian case for spending. "If Friedman is right in thinking that the

U.S. can avoid serious recessions through monetary policy alone," the magazine noted, "the strongest and most appealing argument for giving government a big role tumbles to the ground."[49] Indeed, this was exactly how Friedman himself saw the book. More than an economic theory, it was a vindication of capitalism itself. *A Monetary History of the United States* was "a documented refutation of the view that the deficiencies of free enterprise are responsible for economic instability," he chastised *The Wall Street Journal* after it published a tepid review. Friedman was livid that the *Journal*, of all places, had missed his achievement.[50]

Soon after the book was published, Friedman and Goldwater finally met in person. The occasion was a salon at the Washington home of William J. Baroody Sr., the head of the American Enterprise Institute. One of the nation's oldest think tanks, the AEI sought to educate lawmakers about the merits of free enterprise with pamphlets and legislative analyses. Friedman had been on its Economic Advisory Board for years, regularly traveling to Washington for daylong meetings that included dinner, socializing, and debating research proposals. Similar in purpose to the Chicago Free Market Study, the AEI operated on a much larger and more public scale. As Baroody's network and reputation grew, he was able to connect his stable of favored academics with national politicians like Goldwater.

The Friedman-Goldwater meeting was widely noted in the press, triggering a steady stream of articles linking the two men. *Newsweek* claimed that the "short, baldish economist" might "do for Barry Goldwater what Galbraith once did for John F. Kennedy."[51] *The Daily Northwestern* identified him as "economic consultant to Barry Goldwater," while the *Chicago Tribune* struggled to understand exactly what this meant. "Last fall they had a long talk in Washington, and since then Friedman has sent reports and memoranda for Goldwater's use in speeches and position papers," reported the *Tribune*.[52]

Friedman also drew the renewed attention of Fed nemesis Wright Patman, the populist Democrat from Texas. Over his forty-seven-year congressional career, Patman sampled many economic schools of thought, from sound money to Keynesianism to monetarism. The through line was a profound distrust of the Federal Reserve, a symbol of corrupt money power. "He wanted people to know that their economic well-being hinged on their access to banks and on the wisdom of monetary policy," remembered a staffer. "He wanted them to know that monetary policy was decided in secret by persons who, by virtue of the Fed's freedom from normal governmental appropriations and audit processes, and their long tenures, were de jure unaccountable for their decisions, and often erred grievously." Patman found in Friedman's writings the perfect cudgel with which to beat the Fed.[53]

As Goldwater's campaign was surging, Patman launched yet another round of hearings into the Federal Reserve, quizzing officials about changes in the money stock while probing the system's credit policies, finances, and overall structure. Friedman testified in a lengthy session, expounding on Federal Reserve history and advocating for a money growth rule. Once upon a time, it might have been possible to fend Patman off as an ill-informed "rural populist." But now Friedman's views had begun to permeate widely in the monetary field. An outside expert retained by the Board of Governors "adopts very much the same position" as Friedman, *The Washington Post* noted.[54]

Patman had also staffed up for this latest crusade, hiring Allan Meltzer and Karl Brunner, soon to emerge as a monetarist duo second only to Friedman and Schwartz. Neither man was Friedman's student, but their research unfolded in his shadow. The Swiss-born Brunner had a life-changing encounter with Friedman when he passed through Chicago in 1950. Meltzer was Brunner's student at UCLA. Once on the left—he even served as a delegate for the Progressive Party presidential candidate Henry Wallace—Meltzer later filled in for Friedman at Chicago when he took leave. After producing four jointly authored reports for Patman, Brunner and Meltzer kept collaborating, regularly publishing together for the rest of their careers. Meltzer taught at Carnegie Mellon for almost six decades, authoring more than a hundred papers and a monumental multivolume history of the Federal Reserve. Brunner established monetarism as an international presence through posts at American and European universities. Although they often criticized Friedman, in a larger sense Brunner and Meltzer became the vanguard carrying his ideas forward.[55]

During their staff work for Patman, Brunner and Meltzer uncovered oddities aplenty that strengthened their conviction the Fed needed massive changes. Pressed on his decision-making process, William McChesney Martin responded: "Well monetary policy is like a river. And you have to keep the river within the banks. You don't want to get over the banks, but you don't want to get too low either." Other Fed officials offered a nearly identical answer, the economists found to their chagrin. The Fed eschewed formal frameworks and numerical targets, operating instead by nebulous ideas of "tone and feel." The Federal Open Market Committee (FOMC) used "feel" to discuss market professionals' state of mind, and "tone" to denote the Fed's position in the market. All this metaphor gave the New York trading desk, which implemented FOMC directives, broad discretion. Unlike Friedman and Schwartz, Brunner and Meltzer emphasized weaknesses in the Fed's intellectual framework rather than failures of leadership. Nonetheless, they came to share Friedman's belief that rules were better than discretion. And their detailed reports were powerful fodder for Patman and other Fed critics.[56]

What if Goldwater became president? What if he appointed Friedman chair of the Council of Economic Advisers, as the *Chicago Tribune* speculated? Would he even replace Martin, the current Fed chair, with Friedman? Establishment opinion closed ranks in a lengthy *Business Week* puff piece. Ostensibly a news story about the Fed's "remodel," the article was in fact an extended argument against Friedman. The article portrayed the Fed as a flexible, open-minded institution, "willing to listen" to the views of Friedman, but not convinced that "any one man—has all the answers." The article concluded: "Judgment may be improved, but it cannot be replaced by an automatic increase in the money stock."[57] Friedman's sudden rise, it was clear, had unnerved the lords of finance.

For all his enthusiasm over *A Monetary History of the United States*, it was hard to tell just what Goldwater might do as president. His disorganized campaign, *The Washington Post* found, hadn't formally approached many of the men it identified as the candidate's advisers, including Friedman. "They form at least the shadow of a developing Goldwater 'brain trust,'" the newspaper ventured.[58] Goldwater was handicapped by his preferences for Arizona insiders whom he could trust, but who had no experience running national campaigns.

Seeking insight into Goldwater, reporters began closely following Friedman, in turn discovering the cornucopia of proposals buried in *Capitalism and Freedom*. The once obscure text now appeared like the Rosetta stone, able to clarify Goldwater's ideas and agenda.[59] Floating exchange rates, Friedman's favored international monetary reform, was the subject of a long article in *The Christian Science Monitor*. Reporting on Friedman's appearance before the Joint Economic Committee on the same topic, *The Washington Post* enthused, "No other American economist of the first rank can match Friedman's forensic skills and persuasive powers." Journalists were discovering that Friedman made good copy; as Representative Henry S. Reuss blurted out after hearing his testimony, "You thrill me as nobody has since Teddy Roosevelt."[60]

In assessing Goldwater, Friedman could make some basic comparisons to other name-brand politicians he had known. There was Senator Robert Taft, a.k.a. Mr. Republican, whom he briefed while employed at Treasury. In the 1950s, Friedman had a long one-on-one session with Vice President Nixon, set up by Chicago buddy Allen Wallis, then serving as a special assistant to Eisenhower. And in countless congressional appearances, Friedman had watched the gladiatorial maneuverings over politics and policy. When he looked at Goldwater, Friedman liked what he saw: a man of firm principles who was willing to be unpopular in their defense, but who also responded to reasoned argument. In short, Friedman saw in Goldwater many of the qualities he prized in himself. What he did not see was Goldwater the politician, a man fundamentally oriented to the accumulation and maintenance of political power.

When factions grew up wanting to run him for the presidency, Goldwater had protested too much before acquiescing to an electoral strategy built not upon free market principles but upon appeal to Southern segregationists. This development was in many ways unpredictable. Prior to the Civil Rights Movement, Goldwater was known, in the day's parlance, as a "racial liberal": a white person willing to cross racial barriers and work for interracial cooperation. He had desegregated the family store in Phoenix, helped finance a lawsuit against school segregation, and hired an African American female lawyer as his chief legislative aide in the Senate. In 1957 and 1960 he voted for civil rights bills that increased the federal government's power to investigate voting rights violations. These were signs of his principled belief in racial equality, one that grew in part from his own Jewish background.

Yet Goldwater was not just a principled man; he was a pragmatic and strategic politician who saw the Democratic Party's hold on the Solid South was slipping as the party became increasingly identified with civil rights. In the years after Kennedy's election, Goldwater let himself emerge as the figurehead of a Republican faction that sought to shift the party's power base away from the Northeast—including its still significant Black Republican vote—to the South, rich with potential white Republican voters.

At first, it appeared a quixotic strategy. The Eastern establishment and the Republican Party were nearly synonymous; how could they be challenged? By contrast, in most Southern states the party existed only on paper, due to its role in post–Civil War Reconstruction. But careful watchers noted Goldwater's undeniable appeal below the Mason-Dixon Line. Whenever Goldwater gave a speech lambasting the federal government, he minted Southern GOP volunteers and enthusiasts, ready to build something new. Goldwater supporters began to form a party within the party, organizing through informal networks and key organizations like the Young Republicans. As the pace of civil rights campaigning and white backlash picked up in 1963—the year of Bull Connor's fire hoses and police dogs—the potency of Goldwater's strategy became apparent. Kennedy's advisers began to worry that Goldwater could ride white backlash into the White House.

Libertarian ideas about limited government were newly freighted with racial meaning. Friedman himself had experienced this transformation. A decade earlier, he had proposed a voucher system that would enable parents to purchase "approved educational services" instead of sending their children to public school. When he had written the essay in 1953, it had seemed a quintessentially academic exercise: float a radical idea and hope it went somewhere. If there was any relevant political context, it was the success of the GI Bill, essentially a voucher system for World War II veterans.[61]

But a year later came *Brown v. Board of Education*, the landmark Supreme Court ruling that outlawed state-enforced segregation in education. In their effort to subvert the court ruling and maintain Jim Crow, Southern legislators seized upon the idea of school vouchers. Within a few months of the Supreme Court ruling, it was clear that tuition grants would be an essential part of the South's resistance to integrated schools.[62]

At first, Friedman was concerned that his idea had been hijacked by political opportunists. But thinking it over, he eventually concluded that vouchers were now even more important as a "third alternative."[63] In *Capitalism and Freedom*, he and Rose argued that vouchers were "the appropriate solution that permits the avoidance of both evils . . . enforced segregation or enforced integration." In their telling, vouchers would underwrite a diverse universe of schools, "some all white, some all Negro, some mixed."[64] By then, multiple Southern states had passed legislation—and in some cases amended state constitutions—so that vouchers could be provided to parents who did not wish their children to attend integrated schools. Over time, Southern proposals for vouchers had taken up the language of educational reform in order to mask segregationist intent. Driven in part by lawsuits, this move also reflected the influence of Friedman's essay.[65]

Friedman made only feeble efforts to disassociate his ideas from their new champions. True, he stated his opposition to Jim Crow laws. He averred his abhorrence for racism. But still he struggled and faltered to offer any critique of segregated schools. The best he could do was to call them a "bad solution." And his final resolution was tortured, unclear, and almost apologetic: "If one must choose between the evils of enforced segregation or enforced integration, I myself would find it impossible not to choose integration."[66] Friedman distinguished himself from the segregationist position—but only by the slimmest possible margin.

Friedman's hesitant endorsement of integration was not necessarily predictable. After all, he and Rose chose to enroll Janet and David in the progressive Laboratory School, which began admitting African American students in 1942, far ahead of other private schools in the area. He was willing to mentor and cheerlead the rare African American doctoral student who ended up at Chicago, most notably Thomas Sowell.[67] Although his denunciation of racial prejudice sounds hollow today, not all of Friedman's contemporaries were willing to openly state personal opposition to discrimination. Indeed, early in his career Buckley defended segregation as the prerogative of the "advanced race." In 1965, Stigler argued the "basic problem of the Negro in America . . . is that on average he lacks a desire to improve himself." In this social context, it is notable that Friedman avoided sweeping generalizations based on race or ethnicity and asserted "color of skin is an irrelevant characteristic."[68] Why then didn't he denounce the segregationist use of vouchers?

An example from his personal life is illustrative. While the children were still living at home, Friedman became exercised over the policies of the University Colony Club, an exclusive children's social group that drew heavily from the Laboratory School. The precipitating incident was most likely David's exclusion from the group, which his vigilant parents read as anti-Semitism. Friedman sent university administrators a long letter arguing the club was discriminatory. He included a statistical analysis comparing the religious and racial composition of the club's membership with the Laboratory School, along with a list of university members and excerpts from Illinois state law on fraternities and sororities. He suggested the university sever ties with the organization or expel Laboratory School students who did not drop their affiliation.[69]

At the same time, however, he noted it was fully within the club's right to discriminate: "I do not question the right of individuals to be anti-negro or antisemitic and to choose their friends and associates and even schools for their children, accordingly."[70] The problem was a clash between the university's educational mission, its reputation for tolerance, and the practices of the club. Even with his son in the crosshairs, Friedman would not abandon his principles.

Friedman's position on integration mattered. The Goldwater movement had stirred up the long-running clash between moderate and conservative Republicans. Once this divide had spun around the axes of class and education: the country clubbers vs. the McCarthyites. In that era, Friedman was a moderate, scornful of conspiracy and devoted to debate and dialogue. But now the axis had shifted. In the era of civil rights, moderate Republicans defined themselves as civil rights supporters. "How can you be against civil rights in the year 1964?" wondered Pennsylvania's Republican governor, William Scranton. And it was more than a posture; with Congress still dominated by segregationist Southern Democrats, it took Republican votes to move civil rights legislation forward. Moderate Republicans like George Romney, Nelson Rockefeller, and John Lindsay favored business-friendly, market-oriented solutions to discrimination and poverty. But even as they worked to put a Republican tint on legislation, they argued that civil rights was a cause above partisanship; it was a matter of basic American principles.[71]

Goldwater's entire campaign rejected that premise. And so too did Friedman, whose celebration of individual freedom would not find common cause with the Civil Rights Movement, but was arrayed against it.

In the background of the Friedmans' reckoning with race were two important influences. First was the research of Gary Becker, Friedman's graduate advisee. After his first scattershot effort drew Friedman's wrath, Becker persisted with a dissertation that would end up influencing his adviser profoundly. Becker tackled a topic—the economics of discrimination—that was fundamentally altered by the emergence of the Civil Rights Movement. Begun in the early 1950s, his dissertation was an effort to see if racial discrimination, a seemingly irrational behavior, could be analyzed using price theory. Here, he was mining a rich seam exposed by his Chicago forebears. A generation ago, Knight had pointed out that economics was the basic science of human action; its tools could conceivably explain anything. Earlier in his career, Friedman had toyed with this idea by analyzing gambling. But it was Becker who would take this capacious approach to economics the furthest. And then the rapidly changing political environment would transform his ideas from an intellectual experiment to a politically charged analysis of prejudice.

Becker's influence was palpable in *Capitalism and Freedom*. From Becker, the Friedmans imported the idea that discrimination was essentially a product. "The man who exercises discrimination pays a price for doing so. He is, as it were, 'buying' what he regards as a 'product,'" they wrote, summarizing Becker's basic analysis in *The Economics of Discrimination*. The Friedmans' double entendre suggested it was a mistake to value "irrelevant characteristics," such as race, which would put a businessman or entrepreneur "at a disadvantage," as they traded away efficiency in order to discriminate. Nonetheless, transmuting racial prejudice into "taste" profoundly diminished its significance, even as it opened new analytic avenues. In an economics dissertation, discrimination as taste was perhaps an interesting trick: if discrimination was a product, it could be priced, modeled, and theorized.[72]

Outside the confines of professional economics, however, such logic took on a different flavor. "It is hard to see that discrimination can have any meaning other than a 'taste' of others that one does not share," wrote the Friedmans. "Is there any difference in principle between the taste that leads a householder to prefer an attractive servant to an ugly one and the taste that leads another to prefer a Negro to a white or a white to a Negro, except that we sympathize and agree with the one taste and may not with the other?" Emmett Till, his mutilated face displayed in an open casket; churches smoldering from KKK bombs; angry mobs and the National Guard: evidence abounded that Becker's taste analysis did not adequately capture the social conventions of the segregated South. Nonetheless, the Friedmans argued on behalf of an imaginary store owner forced to hire an African American clerk, explaining it as "the tastes of the community" that if outlawed would "appreciably" harm the store owner.[73] Even against a backdrop of racial violence, the sympathies of *Capitalism and Freedom* lay firmly with anyone who might be required by law to alter their racial preferences.

It was also relevant that both the Friedmans and Becker were of Jewish descent. On the one hand, being a member of a religious minority created a measure of personal sympathy for those facing prejudice. In Milton's case, however, Judaism also powerfully influenced his belief in the beneficence of markets and the dangers of state intervention. He was convinced that capitalism had played an essential part in freeing Jews from systematic social prejudice. Economic regulations and laws restricting trade, in Friedman's perspective, were often little more than disguised efforts to keep Jews in their place. It was not simply a historical case of czarist Russia dictating what professions were open to Jews. Friedman saw the same dynamic in modern America, arguing in his dissertation that in the 1930s the American Medical Association used licensure requirements to deliberately exclude refugee Jewish doctors.[74]

And Friedman saw civil rights efforts through a similar lens. Addressing the Fair Employment Practices Committee, the forerunner of modern employment law, the Friedmans drew an astonishing parallel to "the Hitler Nuremberg laws and the laws in the southern states imposing special disabilities upon Negroes," calling them "examples of laws similar in principle to FEPC."[75] As they read the situation, regulations requiring neutrality in hiring with regard to race—as did the FEPC—were similar to laws targeting specific racial or ethnic groups, as did Jim Crow and Nazi policies.

It was not that Friedman doubted the existence of prejudice. It was rather his own success, and that of other Jewish economists like Becker and Burns, convinced him that ethnic prejudice was no true barrier to accomplishment. From his perspective, Jews had not needed the federal government to break down quotas and stamp out anti-Semitism—although in another sense, the war against Hitler had been a global crusade for Jewish civil rights. Nonetheless, the postwar dip in anti-Semitism that Friedman lived through suggested prejudice need not be a permanent feature of American life.[76] He would not see the legacy of forced African diaspora, marked by systemic violence, dispossession, and slavery. His reference point rather would be the immigrant experience of the Jews, a people who had long faced discrimination, but also carried the boons of freedom, literacy, capital, and kin.

Growing out of this complex personal and intellectual matrix, the Friedmans' opinions were nonetheless an apologia for racism. By the time of *Capitalism and Freedom* the stakes were clear. A new footnote clarified that any "minimum requirements" for schools did not include the issue of segregation.[77] Vouchers, in other words, were suitable for use whatever the racial composition of the schools they supported. Again, the Friedmans stressed their own lack of prejudice by noting vouchers might improve educational prospects for African American students in the South and in cities like Chicago. But they would support their proposals on their philosophical merits, not on political outcomes.

Goldwater made a similar trade-off. What really energized him were the *Atlas Shrugged*–toting conservative radicals on campus, whose political concerns revolved not around integrated schools but rather Soviet power and the threat of Communism. But Goldwater was not above riling up a Southern audience with a rousing defense of states' rights, "hunting where the ducks are," in his own memorable phrase.[78]

Over time, Goldwater grew increasingly comfortable with his dualistic appeal, with the mixture of stars and bars and American flags that appeared at rallies even in places like California.[79] He could plainly see that his supporters drank from two springs: a globalized fear of government, fed by the Cold War and conservative ideology; and a more specific reaction to civil rights and racial integration. The first spring, which brought zealous conservative organizers aboard, would deliver him the Republican nomination. The second was his only hope to win a presidential election—although it might cost him one, too.

This devil's bargain was made plain when Goldwater voted against the 1964 Civil Rights Act. This wide-ranging bill would decisively place the federal government on the side of African Americans being denied fundamental rights. The act would breathe life into the moribund post–Civil War amendments that nearly a century before had guaranteed citizenship and equal protection of the laws to the formerly enslaved and their descendants. Drawing on the interstate commerce clause, the act forbade discrimination in "public accommodations," in one stroke outlawing segregated restaurants, movie theaters, hotels, drinking fountains—the entire elaborate system of Jim Crow law and custom that had created two tiers of citizenship. Massive resistance in the South made clear that racism would not simply fade away; push had come to shove.

Goldwater, and Friedman alongside him, viewed the proposed law with suspicion. It would have been relatively easy for Friedman to avoid commenting on the topic. Instead, as the campaign progressed, Friedman became increasingly vocal. In an appearance before Harvard students, Friedman launched into a long diatribe against the Civil Rights Act. "The majority in this country are prejudiced and it is naïve—no, it's undemocratic,—to suppose you're going to get people to vote against themselves," he argued.[80] In an interview with the *Chicago Tribune*, he veered off topic to explain and defend Goldwater's position. "Sen. Goldwater believes improvement in the lot of the Negro depends primarily on freedom of economic opportunity and on changing attitudes on the part of individuals," he explained, presenting Goldwater's views as equivalent to his. "He believes that laws by the federal government cannot effectively improve the Negro's position, but can only undermine the basic right of individuals to be free from government interference," Friedman continued.[81]

The reality of Goldwater's engagement with race was rather more complex. His efforts on behalf of integration in his personal life had been genuine. Now, he agonized over the Civil Rights Act. He understood that voting against the bill would be viewed as a racist act, pure and simple. Still he did not believe the law was constitutional. His closest legal advisers—Robert Bork and William Rehnquist—told him as much. If he had asked Friedman's advice, he would have received the same message. The vote came in June, just two weeks after Goldwater had won the California primary and locked up the Republican nomination. Ultimately, it was not a political calculus that determined his vote. Talking about states' rights in the South brought little risk. Voting on a civil rights bill with the nation's eyes upon him was different.

Goldwater knew he might lose as many moderate voters as those he gained by linking himself to massive resistance. "If my vote is misconstrued, let it be, and let me suffer its consequences," he announced on the Senate floor.[82]

In truth, Goldwater's fate had been sealed seven months earlier, in November 1963, by the murder of President Kennedy. The assassination, widely misattributed to a radical right-winger, cast a pall over Goldwater's once quirky conservatism. After years of positive press celebrating his maverick views, unusual hobbies, and penchant for daredevil recreation, Goldwater was suddenly portrayed as a dangerous extremist. And the loss of Kennedy also brought a new opponent: the unscrupulous Lyndon Johnson. Accidentally elevated to the presidency, the former vice president was determined to win election in his own right.

The first Southern president since Reconstruction, Johnson understood that Goldwater's tortured views on race were widely shared. By 1963, early support for the Civil Rights Movement among white voters was beginning to erode.[83] Even as he pushed the Civil Rights Act through Congress, Johnson judged it would cost the Democratic Party its longtime base in the Southern states. And if the broader electorate came to view Goldwater as a fair-minded individual who urged only caution and fidelity to the Constitution when it came to civil rights, it might be Johnson who seemed the dangerous radical. Goldwater's weakness, Johnson's team determined, was not race. It was rather his enthusiastic embrace of the Cold War—up to and including nuclear weapons.[84]

The Johnson campaign sought to vilify Goldwater, and by extension the conservative insurgency sweeping the GOP. There was plenty of tinder at hand. Goldwater's casual quips about nuclear weapons reappeared in sinister campaign ads urging voters to choose the more "responsible" candidate. The most notorious ad, featuring a tiny girl plucking daisy petals until obliterated by a nuclear blast, was so inflammatory it only ran once. The message nonetheless had gotten through: Goldwater was a warmonger who should never be trusted with the presidency.

Many leading Republicans were no less horrified by Goldwater.

Party mandarins rightly understood his candidacy as a play to push them out and build a new conservative party.[85] Top-tier Republicans who treasured the party of Lincoln blanched to see Goldwater's intransigence on civil rights. Dedicated internationalists feared careless rhetoric might touch off a war. Major institutions of the Republican establishment, like the *New York Herald Tribune*, began defecting from the candidate. Countering these forces was a groundswell of conservative Goldwater loyalists who had been planning and plotting for years. It was too late now for the establishment to turn them back.

After securing his party's nomination in a tumultuous July convention, Goldwater convened a first—and only—meeting with his economic advisers. Meeting in "a blue carpeted parlor of Washington's International Inn," Goldwater gathered a small group of economists, including Friedman and his former student Warren Nutter.[86] What unified these men, *Newsweek* explained, was their deviation from "the economic orthodoxy [of] the past 20 years: the acceptance . . . of the crucial role the federal government plays in keeping the economy on an even keel." It was likely this orthodoxy would persist, even if Goldwater won the presidency. But his economists "would set a new Washington tone," *Newsweek* noted.[87]

Meanwhile, across town, LBJ convened a meeting of all the economists who had ever served on a presidential Council of Economic Advisers. This unprecedented gathering of luminaries overshadowed Goldwater's ragtag group. LBJ's show sent an unmistakable message: the smart money was on him.[88]

By then, even the Friedmans could detect that Goldwater was in trouble. Trooping over to a neighbor's house in New Hampshire to watch the news coverage of his campaign kickoff on TV, the Friedmans realized that Goldwater appeared "a racist and extremist," even to their friendly eyes.[89]

Determined to stanch the wound, Friedman depicted Goldwater as a mild-mannered conservative in a lengthy essay for *The New York Times Magazine*. Goldwater's philosophy, according to Friedman, was about "freedom and opportunity." Government was not bad, but it must be strictly limited. Although his article "The Goldwater View of

Economics" hewed closely to his own views, Friedman was careful to cloak the radical outcomes he otherwise enjoyed flaunting. "His means are various but always conservative, in the position that they emphasize gradualness, order, and dependability, the limitations of our present knowledge and the need to learn from experience," Friedman wrote reassuringly.[90]

But there was only so much Friedman could do. The idea of President Barry Goldwater had always been more an activist's fever dream than a realistic proposition. In the end, Johnson would win the landslide he had so coveted, laying the groundwork for the Great Society, his ambitious expansion of the federal government, as well as escalation in Vietnam. Tellingly, the only states that broke for Goldwater, besides Arizona, were the Deep South states of the former Confederacy: Louisiana, Mississippi, Alabama, Georgia, and South Carolina. The map made the dynamic clear. Goldwater—and Friedman too—might be a true believer in limited government for its own sake. But many voters saw him as a champion of racial segregation.

Goldwater's stunning loss seemed to vindicate the general climate of opinion. Conservatives were kooks and crazies; the Republican Party capitulated to conservatism at its own peril. "He has wrecked his party for a long time to come and is not even likely to control the wreckage," summarized *The New York Times*.[91] "The election had finished the Goldwater school of political reaction," added *Commentary* in a retrospective analysis.[92] Clearly, the future lay with moderate Republicanism, with standard-bearers in the mold of Eisenhower or Rockefeller.

Yet Goldwater's loss is now understood as a victory of sorts. Conservatism as an intellectual and political movement did not slink off into the shadows. Rather, in defeat it became more unified and self-aware. "It was something more than just finding ideological soulmates," a historian of the campaign explains. "It was learning how to *act* . . . it was something beyond the week, the year, the campaign, even the decade: it was a cause."[93] Perhaps even more critically, the magnitude of Goldwater's defeat made the liberal establishment appear more powerful than it actually was. With overconfidence came overreach.

The 1964 election was a more straightforward triumph for Friedman. In just a few months, he had emerged as a force in the critical domains of academic economics, conservative opinion, and Republican national politics. Riding the coattails of *A Monetary History of the United States*, his and Rose's overlooked *Capitalism and Freedom* had emerged as a source text for the "New Conservatism."

Friedman would now become emblematic of "new currents" on the right, a reliable source for ideas, opinions, and juicy quotes. Journalists could look to him, instead of the John Birch Society. In turn, he could redefine conservatism as a thinking man's creed, grounded in rigorous economics and oriented to an increasingly global future. His views, "at the same time conservative and beyond the pale of the conventional wisdom," as *The Washington Post* summarized, would at last circulate far beyond the confines of Hyde Park.[94]

But amid this forward momentum was a hidden loss. In teaming up with Goldwater and vigorously defending his position on civil rights, Friedman had solidified an alliance between libertarian economics and reactionary populism.

1. Milton Friedman in 1917 as a boy in Rahway, New Jersey, pictured with his family. Back row, from left: parents Sarah and Sol, sister Tillie. Front row, from left: Helen, Milton, Ruth.

2. A young Rose—then known as Esther Director—poses for a formal portrait in Portland, Oregon, in 1918.

3. Social Sciences Research Building, University of Chicago. The economics department in the 1930s was "a jungle red in tooth and claw," according to the economist Paul Samuelson, a former student.

4. Brilliant, eccentric, and difficult, Frank Knight mesmerized the graduate students who clustered in Room Seven, parsing his every word.

5. Soon to be married, Rose and Milton visited the blooming cherry trees near the Washington Monument in 1937. Despite their growing opposition to Keynesian economics and the fiscal revolution, they both worked on New Deal projects.

6. Mercurial and intense, Henry Simons was an outspoken defender of free markets, an advocate of higher taxes, and a crusader for increased government regulation in key economic sectors. With his tragic suicide in 1946, this seemingly impossible combination, along with Simons's deeply felt commitment to social equality, faded as a force in Friedman's thinking.

7. Friedman joined his longtime friend George Stigler and his brother-in-law Aaron Director at the 1947 founding meeting of F. A. Hayek's Mont Pelerin Society in Switzerland. It was his first trip abroad.

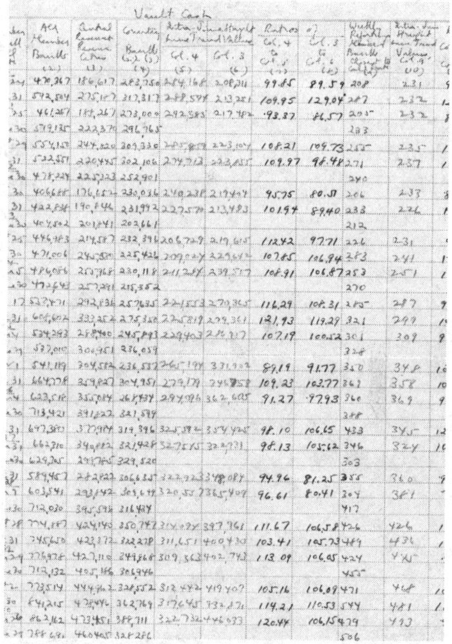

8. Although Columbia University refused for years to grant her a Ph.D., Anna Schwartz had already coauthored a monumental study of the British economy when she met Friedman. Their collaboration would be a decisive influence on his career.

9. Lacking basic historical data on money and banks that today's economists take for granted, Schwartz worked for more than a decade to painstakingly assemble a unique historical database of the money supply, later known as "monetary aggregates." These figures became the empirical bedrock of Friedman's monetarism.

10. A major influence on Friedman's thought, the Austrian economist F. A. Hayek organized and secured funding for the influential Free Market Study project at the University of Chicago. Hayek spent the 1950s on the faculty at Chicago, with an appointment to the Committee on Social Thought.

11. The only tenured woman in Chicago's economics department, Margaret Reid was among a group of women economists who with Friedman developed the permanent income hypothesis.

12. Lifelong friends Friedman and Stigler were known around campus as Mr. Macro and Mr. Micro—an ironic pun on their differing heights and economic focuses. When he returned to Chicago in 1958, Stigler created yet another "Chicago school," centered in the business school.

13. Friedman was known as one of Chicago's most effective—and intimidating—teachers.

14. Friedman's first brush with fame came when he advised Barry Goldwater's unsuccessful 1964 presidential campaign. Although Goldwater lost the election, he helped define twentieth-century conservatism for decades after.

15. Friedman struck up a lifelong friendship with William F. Buckley Jr., founder of the flagship conservative magazine *National Review*, when Buckley attempted to purge the "crackpot" John Birch Society. Buckley saw Friedman as the embodiment of the modern conservatism he hoped to create: educated, articulate, credentialed. Here, Buckley laughs as he holds up a piece of hate mail.

16. By the late 1960s, Friedman had become a household name, due to the rising influence of monetarism and his public profile as an adviser to Republican politicians.

17. Friedman's decades-long friendship with Arthur Burns fractured during Burns's term as chairman of the Federal Reserve, an institution Friedman had long criticized.

18. Friedman reached the height of his influence during the Nixon administration, due to his close relationship with Secretary of the Treasury George Shultz. Together, both men shaped the new global financial system that emerged after the collapse of Bretton Woods in 1973.

19. Amid 1970s stagflation, the unexpected combination of high inflation and high unemployment, Friedman's ideas became broadly influential, even as he spent more time away from Chicago at his Vermont retreat, Capitaf (named for his bestselling book *Capitalism and Freedom*).

20. Milton and Rose enjoy a dance at the Nobel Ball. Friedman's 1976 Nobel Prize in Economics marked the pinnacle of his storied career.

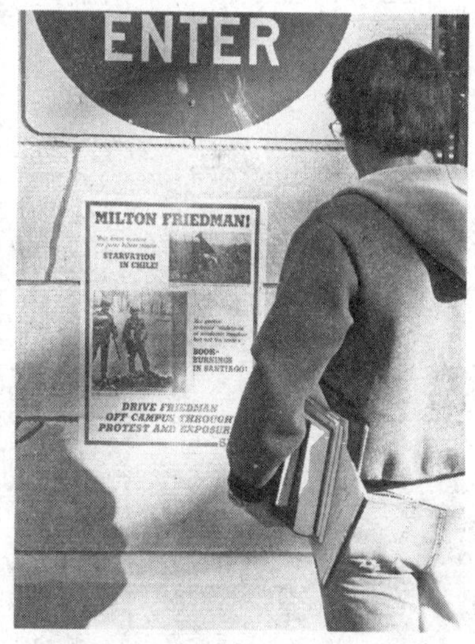

21. Friedman became an increasingly controversial figure during the 1970s, as critics linked him to Augusto Pinochet, the authoritarian leader of Chile. Friedman regularly faced protests at his public appearances and on the Chicago campus.

22. Friedman had a prickly relationship with the legendary Federal Reserve chairman Paul Volcker, who tamed inflation by strategically deploying Friedman's ideas about the money supply.

23. By the 1980s, Anna Schwartz was finally recognized by her fellow economists for her pathbreaking contributions. She was a key figure on the influential Shadow Open Market Committee and an inspiration to a new generation of rising female scholars.

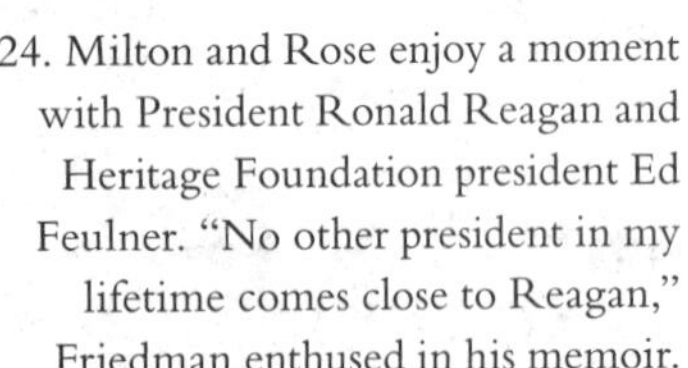

24. Milton and Rose enjoy a moment with President Ronald Reagan and Heritage Foundation president Ed Feulner. "No other president in my lifetime comes close to Reagan," Friedman enthused in his memoir.

25. After three visits to China in the 1980s, Friedman argued that the country's turn toward capitalism would bring democracy. By the end of his life, he was less optimistic.

10

THE PHILLIPS CURVE

> Everything reminds Milton of the money supply. Well everything reminds me of sex, but I keep it out of the paper.
>
> —Robert Solow, 1966

Barry Goldwater might have been gone, but Milton Friedman was here to stay. *Newsweek* was the first to place its bets, offering Friedman a regular column alternating with Paul Samuelson. "If you had to summarize the right in one word, Milton is your word," declared an unnamed economist to *The National Observer.* Former Kennedy intimate John Kenneth Galbraith was more caustic. Friedman was nothing more than a "romantic artist," he sniffed, with an enormous "capacity for brilliant irrelevance."[1] This assessment was wide of the mark—about as far off as the assumption that conservatism had died as a political force.

Goldwater's defeat set Friedman free. No longer linked to a controversial politician, his policy proposals became more relevant, not less. Liberated from the hothouse of partisan politics and amplified by the *Newsweek* megaphone, his ideas could now be taken on their merits. From the negative income tax to abolishing the draft, seemingly daft proposals from *Capitalism and Freedom* now became the object of mainstream politics. Friedman's interest in an idea could even serve a legitimating function. Simply put, Friedman had cachet.

In part this cachet reflected a general scrambling of left and right that seemed characteristic of the times. "In the course of the 1960s, the left adopted almost wholesale the arguments of the right," observed Daniel Patrick Moynihan, a domestic policy adviser to all three of the decade's presidents. "This was not a rude act of usurpation, but rather a symmetrical, almost elegant, process of transfer." Exaggerating for effect—but not to the point of inaccuracy—Moynihan remembered that by decade's end, "an advanced student at an elite eastern college could be depended on to avow many of the more striking views of the Liberty League and its equivalents in the hate-Roosevelt era; for example that the growth of federal power was the greatest threat to democracy, that foreign entanglements were the work of demented plutocrats, that government snooping (by the Social Security Administration or the United States Continental Army Command) was destroying freedom, that the largest number of functions should be entrusted to the smallest jurisdictions, and so across the spectrum of this viewpoint."[2] Driven primarily by the expanding war in Vietnam, this new current on the left took up individualistic and anti-statist themes that were once the province of the right.

Another part of this convergence was the rise of the economics profession. The new economics appeared a success on its own terms; growth had picked up across the Kennedy years. By 1965, GNP had increased for five straight years. Unemployment was down to 4.9 percent, and would soon drop below the 4 percent goal of full employment. As James Tobin reflected, "economists were riding the crest of a wave of enthusiasm and self-confidence. They seemed, after all, to have some tools of analysis and policy other people didn't have, and their policy seemed to be working."[3] With institutional economics a vanquished force, most economists accepted the tenets of the neoclassical revolution: individuals making rational choices subject to the incentives created by supply and demand. Approaching policy with an economic lens cut across established political lines, which were often the creation of brokered coalitions, habit, or historical precedent. Economic analysis was at once disruptive, since it failed to honor these accidental accretions, and familiar, since it spoke a market language resonant with business-friendly political culture.[4]

Amid this ideological confluence, Friedman continued his dour rumblings and warnings. Ignoring the positive trends in basic indicators of economic health, from inflation to unemployment to GDP, he argued fiscal demand management was misguided, warned Bretton Woods was about to collapse, predicted imminent inflation, and castigated the Federal Reserve's basic approach. Friedman's quixotic quest—and the media attention it generated—infuriated many of his peers. Friedman, it seemed, was bent on fixing economic theories and institutions that were not broken.

The first of Friedman's ideas to be co-opted by the liberal establishment was his negative income tax proposal advanced in *Capitalism and Freedom.* With Friedman's favored candidate safely in political exile, rival James Tobin stepped forward to claim the concept as his own in the liberal organ *Daedalus.* "The idea has sometimes been called a negative income tax," Tobin delicately explained, without mentioning Friedman.[5] Framing it as a civil rights proposal that would particularly aid racial minorities, Tobin explained the mechanism: "The proposal is that the Treasury pay any family who falls below a certain income a fraction of the shortfall." Tobin surely knew that Friedman had been an early advocate of this idea, as did the *Chicago Tribune.* "Wonders never cease in Washington," the paper remarked sarcastically, noting how Friedman's idea was being enthusiastically embraced by his ideological opposites.[6]

The idea of setting some sort of income floor under the poorest Americans had long been part of Friedman's thinking. In fact, the very first policy proposal he ever crafted was for a guaranteed income in 1939, at the tail end of the Depression. The idea had bubbled up in conversations between Friedman and the Swedish socialist Gunnar Myrdal, later famous for *An American Dilemma: The Negro Problem and Modern Democracy.* In the late 1930s, both men were part of a broad universe of scholars orbiting around Columbia's economics department. A long weekend conversation about poverty yielded "a plan for guaranteeing a minimum income to all," as Friedman titled a follow-up paper.[7]

The never-published paper was a revealing window into Friedman's early thinking about poverty. In one version, he began with a biblical allusion—"the poor are always with us"—before asserting that "poverty is reprehensible no matter whom it hits. It should be attacked by general measures." The advantage of a guaranteed income, he argued, was its very generality. Programs aimed at specific groups both "involved detailed intervention into economic activity" and "leave large groups unaided."[8] In an extended version, Friedman drew on his background at the Study of Consumer Purchases to argue that breakthroughs in consumption economics and nutrition made it possible, for the first time ever, to arrive at an "objective method of determining a 'minimum standard of living.'"[9] The minimum income could be pegged to the nutritional needs of a family and therefore calculated scientifically.

Aside from touting it at Mont Pelerin, Friedman didn't do much with the idea for decades. Instead, George Stigler picked it up and in 1946 advocated a tax with "negative rates" in the pages of the *American Economic Review*.[10] Either Stigler's formulation or his own immersion in tax policy at the Treasury Department shifted Friedman's approach to the issue. By the time of *Capitalism and Freedom*, the idea appeared as a negative income tax—or NIT. As Friedman framed it, the NIT "would fit directly into our current income tax system and could be administered along with it."[11] He laid out a few scenarios in which existing welfare programs could be repurposed into cash grants to the poorest 10 percent, 20 percent, or even 30 percent of Americans.

By the mid-1960s, the time was ripe for a new policy addressing poverty, of whatever vintage. After winning the presidency in his own right, Lyndon Johnson announced a sweeping program of domestic programs, the Great Society. Central to this effort was an "unconditional war on poverty." That was just the beginning. In his first State of the Union address, Johnson staked out numerous goals, including health care for elders, a tax cut, and new homes, schools, libraries, and hospitals. All this, Johnson assured his audience in January 1965, can be "done by this summer, and it can be done without any increase in spending."[12] Johnson intended to match the legislative heights of Franklin Roosevelt's hundred days—without a crisis at his back.

Not only did Johnson's ambitions surpass those of Kennedy, but so too did his optimistic belief that federal programs could solve intractable social problems. Part of this was Johnson's own utopian tendencies. And part of it was the economy's strength. Even a sober commentator like Walter Lippmann—whose earlier skepticism about the New Deal had helped inspire the Mont Pelerin Society—imagined that "we are escaping from the immemorial human predicament of the haves and the have-nots."[13] If the business cycle had been defeated, what next? The United States, it seemed, could afford to dream big. The hunt was on for new ways to spend.

Soon proposals for some form of guaranteed income were circulating through the newly created Office of Economic Opportunity (OEO), a policy lab run by Kennedy's brother-in-law Sargent Shriver. In June 1966, the White House Conference on Civil Rights recommended "explicit acceptance of the government's responsibility for guaranteeing a minimum income to all Americans."[14] The language was telling, for the report's concrete recommendations were job guarantees and higher welfare payments, now reframed in the trending language of a guaranteed income. Meanwhile, the OEO released a series of positive reports on the idea.

Enthusiasm for the NIT reflected shifting dynamics in American liberalism.[15] Kennedy's new economics was growth liberalism, which argued a rising tide would lift all boats. During the Johnson administration, growth liberalism was challenged by new buzzwords: structural unemployment. Books like Michael Harrington's *The Other America* led to a "rediscovery" of poverty amid plenty. Harrington portrayed the poor as a nation apart, marked by a distinctive culture. Growth might flow around, rather than through, these isolated communities. Then there was automation. During and after World War II, factories began to swap out manpower for machines, setting in motion a process of deindustrialization that had already hollowed out once proud industrial cities like Detroit. Now it was looking like these jobs might never come back. Another profound concern was civil rights. During the New Deal, poverty was imagined largely in terms of white rural communities. By the time of Johnson's presidency, poverty was increasingly linked to African American communities, and to racial discrimination in hiring and education. These concerns added up to a growing conviction the American economy was fundamentally unable to meet the goal of full employment.[16]

The NIT appeared to straddle this divide between growth liberalism and structural understandings of poverty. Its greatest advocates were economists, who appreciated its efficiency and the potential stimulus effect of cash. But it could also be advertised as a civil rights idea—despite the fact that leaders of major civil rights organizations favored structural remedies, such as a higher minimum wage, public works programs, or antidiscrimination legislation. Many observers also believed that if automation had fundamentally changed the labor market, a cash grant might help. "Because of the onslaught of automation, class boundaries are becoming more rigid," summarized a Cornell student in an essay on poverty that jumped off from Friedman's proposal. "Without a diploma or at least some technical training there is little hope or opportunity."[17] Whatever the concern, be it lack of purchasing power, a flawed labor market, or the onslaught of technology, cash grants seemed to strike at the heart of the problem with clarity and directness. The very simplicity of a cash transfer disguised the policy's tendency to be all things to all policy-makers.

Amid this ferment, Friedman's version of the negative income tax received particular attention. The very oddity of a known conservative promoting poverty reduction attracted comment, much to Friedman's annoyance. "Friedman asked that it never be said that it was 'ironic' that a conservative like himself should want to help the poor," noted one newspaper. The irony reflected a truth: as Moynihan remembered, the Republicans "had almost no thinkers, almost no writers, almost no reputation for a sophisticated or even compassionate view of social policy." Friedman aside, anti-poverty policy was the near-exclusive province of the Democratic Party.[18]

And the NIT did create unusual coalitions. "If the Chamber of Commerce of the United States had undertaken to investigate flying saucers Washington couldn't have been more surprised," observed *The Christian Science Monitor* upon the occasion of a widely publicized 1966 symposium on the negative income tax.[19] The Chamber of Commerce brought together a panel of opponents and supporters, including Friedman, to debate the idea. Among the challenges was getting the media to stop treating the whole affair as a joke. "Three Economists Are Advocates of Paying Men for Doing Nothing," headlined a Los Angeles newspaper, explaining that "while Adam Smith and Horatio Alger revolved in their graves, a distinguished panel considered the matter with the utmost seriousness."[20] Beyond the man bites dog appeal, Friedman's presence in the debate helped reassure journalists that this novel idea might have legs.

Friedman's proposal was in fact a revolutionary departure in American social policy.[21] Discussion of the poor was historically laden with judgment. Whether the funds came from private or public sources, it seemed vital to distinguish between the deserving and the undeserving. By contrast, Friedman's monetary understanding of poverty took the poor as fundamentally similar to the rest of the country—except for their lack of purchasing power.

What made Friedman's NIT so ideologically unique was its fundamental grounding in economic theory. True, celebrations of the free market and ritualized distrust of government had long been important to American conservatives—part of the folk vernacular, or "Main Street" conservatism, as *The Washington Post* called it. But these had been intuitions or instincts or reactions, unformalized and rarely, the *Post* noted, "expressed as a complete system."[22] By contrast, Chicago price theory translated these normative beliefs into a coherent logical system with efficiency at its core. Importantly, price theory lacked the more obvious moral content of conservatism—the judging, censure, and condemnation. Indeed, when introducing the idea in *Capitalism and Freedom*, Friedman called the NIT an "arrangement that recommends itself on purely mechanical grounds." And he emphasized that the NIT, unlike other remedies such as a minimum wage, did not "distort the market or impede its functioning."[23] Rather, the NIT intended to bolster low-income Americans' participation in market exchange.

At the same time, Friedman's NIT did have veiled moral content—a dedication to individual freedom, that "delicate flower" which

Capitalism and Freedom praised in its opening pages. At a basic level, as Friedman openly noted, the NIT let the market be, honoring one of his core principles. But in his public discussion of the idea, he developed another idea latent in *Capitalism and Freedom.* At the Chamber of Commerce symposium, Friedman argued that the present system involved an "'intolerable degree of paternalism," transforming social workers into "police officers and spies."[24] By contrast, the mechanistic NIT would leave the poor with their dignity and privacy intact. This was not mere window dressing; *Capitalism and Freedom* was suffused with a general horror of anyone telling anyone else what to do. But in typical conservative rhetoric it was businessmen, not welfare recipients, who felt the brunt of federal force. Friedman loved to flip the script by pointing out plenty of businesses took "welfare" from the federal government but were not judged. Why couldn't poor individuals do the same?

Friedman did admit that a cash grant could impact incentives. Potentially, it could turn recipients into "a gaggle of lazy bums," as *The Washington Post* mused.[25] But he also noted an income subsidy might make work more attractive: "An extra dollar earned always means more money available for expenditure."[26] The suggestion that a cash grant might have a salutary effect upon the recipient—perhaps even strengthening rather than sapping the work ethic—represented another striking departure in American discussions of poverty.[27] On some level, Friedman recognized the durability of old attitudes. In public forums, he made an important modification to the proposal: capping the grant at 50 percent of a specified income level.[28] The recipients would get not a free ride but a subsidized one.

Even this modified position sparked incredulity. The Foundation for Economic Education favorite Henry Hazlitt, who had lost his *Newsweek* berth to Friedman, reacted "with scorn" during the Chamber of Commerce debate. The money would be "thrown away on liquor or the races," argued Hazlitt, calling a negative income tax "morally indefensible."[29] Recipients of relief, Hazlitt contended, should lose the right to vote. Friedman had a quick retort at the ready: were this standard adopted, he declared, "there is not a person in this room who would have the right to vote."[30] After all, he continued, businessmen were known to feed at the federal trough.

Another notable dissenter was Rose Friedman. In a rare show of independence, having dutifully presented the NIT in *Capitalism and Freedom*, Rose published an alternate take in a slim pamphlet issued by the American Enterprise Institute. Most of the pamphlet contested the technical definition of poverty, responding directly to a Johnson administration report. Rose disagreed with the method used to calculate the poverty line, and argued that at most 10 percent of the nation was poor, in contrast to the administration's figure of 20 percent.

Beyond the technical dispute, Rose voiced a different attitude toward poverty than her husband. Milton invariably explained poverty as a function of government action, portraying low-wage workers as victims of constricted opportunity caused by regulation.[31] By contrast, Rose wondered why poverty should be a "major public issue," noting rising incomes, consumption, and economic growth since the end of the 1930s. The cause was "probably changing public attitudes about individual and social responsibility for men's actions and their consequences," Rose wrote. By the standards of history, she noted, "there is negligible poverty in the United States today." Under it all lay a racial subtext that occasionally broke the surface. Large families were an "important cause of poverty," Rose reminded her readers, and nonwhite families were on average larger families.[32] The link between poverty and race was unremarkable for its moment, but Rose's rhetoric stands out for its utter lack of empathy. Not once did she invoke poor children, struggling mothers, or industrious fathers out of work. These were the kind of sour sentiments journalists expected conservatives to voice on the issue of poverty.

Pedantic and hard to follow, Rose's pamphlet was coy about its most radical implications, which would have significantly reduced government support of the poor. By contrast, Milton's NIT wore its radicalism openly, promising to sweep away the old apparatus of state support and replace it all with a price mechanism. True, in the first blush of excitement over a new idea, this aspect of Friedman's NIT was often overlooked. Johnson staffers generally presented the NIT as an add-on to current or even expanded government programs. By contrast, Friedman hoped it would ultimately shrink the size of government. He never hid this aspect of his proposal. Nor did he emphasize his profound differences with liberals, preferring instead to keep the conversation going. Over time, this gap between left and right would prove fatal.

For all the press, the NIT never became a centerpiece of Johnson's anti-poverty program. First out of the gate were "services" programs in the model of New Deal liberalism, like Head Start and Community Action. Further innovation was foreclosed by Democratic losses in the 1966 congressional elections, and by Johnson's declining popularity. Driven by the optimistic hopes of the administration's early months, the NIT fell into temporary neglect as the political mood changed.

Back at Chicago, Friedman didn't let fame go to his head. He still schlumped around in ill-fitting suits, "a short Jewish guy who talked too fast," as one student put it; his office remained a disaster zone. His children were surprised when they realized, courtesy of classmates, that their father was famous—more famous than the average Chicago professor, that is.[33] With a column appearing every few weeks in *Newsweek*, Friedman was becoming a celebrity economist. Much as she had with *Capitalism and Freedom*, Rose made herself essential to the production of Milton's *Newsweek* column. She and David had been the big advocates of the opportunity, convincing Milton to accept after several days of nonstop argument. Next, instead of ghostwriting from drafts, Rose playacted the uninformed everyperson with her husband. With a tape recorder whirring, she would ask him questions, "and she kept pushing him to say it better, find a different way to explain it." A session might last a few hours, after which Rose transcribed the recording and then crafted it into a column.[34] Rose's questions elicited colorful metaphors and made his written word sparkle with the verbal wordplay Friedman relished.

There were some changes to daily life; Friedman traveled more, and his teaching style had evolved. Over the years, survivors had merged their price theory notes into a samizdat document that circulated through the graduate student underground, much as Henry Simons's famous syllabus had done in the 1930s. Eventually Friedman caught on, elevating the makeshift textbook into an official part of the course and publishing a semi-polished version as *Price Theory: A Provisional Text*. Now the class felt more like the money workshop, with Friedman going through the book page by page and asking if there were any questions.[35]

The mood in the department had also curdled a bit, thanks to a new recruit, the Canadian Harry Johnson. His hiring in 1959 had actually been Friedman's idea, for the two had met in Britain years earlier, during Friedman's visiting stint at Cambridge.[36] Johnson was a scholar of international trade. As Britain slowly liberated its central bank from political constraints—a move akin to the 1951 Treasury-Fed Accord—Johnson turned his eye to money. Here his interests began to intersect with a new international emphasis in Friedman's thought.

Friedman was becoming increasingly pessimistic about Bretton Woods. Interviewed about *A Monetary History of the United States*, Friedman fretted about the possibility of a "collapse of the present world currency system comparable to what happened in 1931 when Britain went off gold."[37] Friedman was right to worry about the long-term stability of the international financial system. As Europe's war-torn economies recovered and foreign corporations sold ever more goods to Americans, they accumulated dollars. One natural outlet for these profits would have been U.S. stocks or bonds, but foreign investment was tightly regulated and controlled. Instead, these firms carried these dollars back to their own central banks, trading them in for their own currency. Now the dollars went to European banks, who under Bretton Woods could request gold from the U.S. Treasury in exchange for dollars. Over time, the United States began running low on gold. No one knew what the endgame looked like, but the "balance of payments" problem, as it was termed, could not go on indefinitely.

Friedman had a solution at hand: set the financial system free, ending capital controls and state-mandated exchange rates. Under Bretton

Woods, international currencies were exchangeable one for the other according to fixed exchange rates. Central banks coordinated to keep these rates viable. Instead, Friedman favored floating exchange rates; currencies would be valued against each other according to worldwide demand. The idea fit perfectly with his larger framework. Currencies, like any product, should have their prices set by the market. "Use the free market to determine what the value of various currencies are," he explained to the *New York Herald Tribune*. End the gold exchange standard and let currencies "float."[38]

As the United States faced recurring balance of payments issues across the 1960s, floating exchange rates, once a radical idea, attracted increased attention. But it was not simply an economic problem. Designed in the aftermath of World War II, Bretton Woods was equally a political institution, intended to stabilize western Europe through economic integration. Thus, setting exchange rates free might have unforeseen ramifications. According to *The Washington Post*, members of Congress feared that switching to a floating rate "might well destroy the international organizations which are essential to the preservation of political alliances." At the same time, the newspaper surmised that as the difficulties facing Bretton Woods multiplied, "an antagonist will be troubled by the gnawing suspicion that [Friedman] may be right."[39] Friedman was far from the only person worried by this problem; indeed, policy patches to address the issue were made repeatedly over the 1960s. But he was one of the few willing to openly speak the unspeakable: the system was not built to last.[40]

Friedman's new colleague Johnson supported floating exchange rates, although he doubted their political viability. He was also a student of banking history, called before Parliament when it considered changes to the Bank of England procedures. Johnson even wanted to create a Friedman-Schwartz-style money supply series for the United Kingdom (a project ultimately stymied by lack of funds). Later in life, he would develop what he called a "neo-quantity theory approach."[41] Johnson rightly appeared to Friedman as a scholar whose research would profoundly complement his own. At the same time, as a creature of the commonwealth and a recognized man of the left, Johnson was Keynesian enough to count as bringing intellectual diversity to Chicago.

What Johnson ultimately brought, however, was a tangle of psychological conflicts revolving around Friedman. Pudgy and disheveled, sporting alternatively a five-o'clock shadow or a beard, Johnson was a prodigious drinker. It was said he boarded transatlantic flights with an unopened bottle of duty-free scotch, emerging at the end with a new academic paper and an empty bottle. No matter how far in his cups, however, he could always carry an argument about economics. Johnson was widely known to economists in Britain, Canada, the United States, and even farther afield, thanks to his love of travel. As part of his appointment at Chicago, Johnson became the editor of the *Journal of Political Economy*, a position that leveraged his encyclopedic command of the literature and his peregrinations on the international conference circuit.

Johnson was also a brawler. Shortly before he joined the Chicago faculty, he and Friedman tangled over an injudicious footnote that accused another economist, a Friedman ally, of producing "propaganda." It was a first hint of more trouble to come.[42]

It did not take Johnson long to discover that mocking Friedman made any boozy evening more convivial. "I have heard it said that Chicago is the only department in the country where a Ph.D. is a joint degree in economics and theology," Johnson joked in a cocktail-hour address to the graduate Political Economy Club, "but this is an unfair exaggeration." Nonetheless, he asserted, it was true the department treated marginal productivity "as a manifestation of divine justice." With Friedman listening, Johnson described department workshops as akin to "Buffalo Bill's Wild West Show," complete with Buffalo Bill charging "out to the rescue with pistols blazing, long golden hair streaming in the breeze, followed by his cowboys." In case the audience hadn't connected the dots yet, Johnson praised the Chicago tradition of "empirical work on hypothesis testing," lamenting only that it was "restricted to a narrow range of problems, and to be dominated by the objective of proving either that the price system is efficient or that the government is not."[43] This was rough stuff, even in the harsh culture of Chicago. Johnson had his partisans; given Friedman's dominance, there was a countercurrent of resistance and resentment that he effectively tapped. But after this calamitous evening, much of the department shunned Johnson.

Making the situation worse, the two men occupied adjacent offices, large suites separated by a hallway. After scarcely a year in Chicago, Johnson began searching for another job. By 1966 he had accepted an unusual appointment split between Chicago and the London School of Economics, spending the fall and winter quarter abroad and the rest of the year in Chicago. As Friedman also regularly spent time away from campus in New Hampshire or Vermont, there were fewer opportunities to clash.

While Johnson's attacks were exceptionally acerbic, they reflected a larger struggle over Friedman's place in the economics profession. Outside of Chicago, he had long been the butt of jokes; in Harvard seminars, mere mentions of Friedman's name brought laughter to the room.[44] By the mid-1960s, however, the titters were fading as Friedman's rivals began to seriously engage with his work. The bulk and heft of *A Monetary History of the United States* had drawn grudging admiration from even his most consistent detractors. Still, few economists prized the quantity theory as Friedman did.

The mainstream of economics remained Keynesian, in the American sense. Less orthodox followers of Keynes than pioneers of the new economics, liberal economists James Tobin, Robert Solow, Paul Samuelson, and Franco Modigliani bestrode the discipline. The Keynesian consensus stretched from Washington to the major universities; after serving in the White House, Tobin and Solow returned to respective posts at Yale and MIT, where they churned out cohort after cohort of like-minded graduate students. Samuelson's textbook dominated introductory economics courses, and his column alternated with Friedman's in *Newsweek*, giving him a similar triangle of influence in academic, policy, and public discussion. Far from monolithic, the Keynesians had their own disagreements and rivalries. But compared to Friedman, their mathematics were more sophisticated and their politics more liberal. Their models, elaborate descendants of the original IS-LM, were sets of linear equations linking consumption, employment, interest rates, and other economic factors, resulting in quantitative predictions about policy impacts. Like the work of the Cowles Commission scholars, these models came with a built-in assumption of federal economic management.

To a remarkable degree, the "Big Four" who arrayed themselves against Friedman had much in common with one another, and with their antagonist. Samuelson, Solow, Tobin, and Modigliani were all men of Jewish descent, profoundly shaped by the Great Depression and World War II. Most were just a few years younger than Friedman—but that could be a crucial few years. The gap placed Samuelson at Chicago as an undergraduate, meaning his early exposure to Frank Knight wore off. As a graduate student at Harvard, Samuelson intersected with the undergraduate Tobin, a brilliant Midwesterner brought East by a new scholarship program. Immortalized in *The Caine Mutiny* (written by a classmate) as "a mandarin-like midshipman named Tobit, with a domed forehead, measured quiet speech, and a mind like a sponge," Tobin was too young for the fiscal seminar, but not too young to read *The General Theory of Employment, Interest, and Money* in a sophomore tutorial. Arriving on campus from a home stocked with *The Nation* and other little magazines, Tobin found Keynesian economics merged easily with his liberal politics.[45]

As the leading Keynesian expert on money, it was Tobin who went up against Friedman most frequently, and Tobin who felt most deeply the anguish of confrontation. He mourned the days of the early 1960s, when "from outside, the economics profession appeared quite unified, as befits a guild of technicians and pragmatists."[46] The Kennedy vision of economists as value-free problem-solvers had been Tobin's theme. The rise of Friedman to prominence would be Tobin's loss. Yet to outside observers, their conflict was the engine driving the field forward; economics evolved, it seemed, in six-month cycles of Friedman and Tobin reading and rebutting each other's most recent paper.[47] It was even almost true, as Stigler liked to joke, "the people at MIT and

Harvard didn't know what they were going to work on until Milton made a speech."[48]

To all these men, Friedman was a shadow self, sharing so much sociologically and so little intellectually and politically. Trying to debate Friedman could do more harm than good. Defending the CEA's wage and price guidelines at a conference, Solow mocked Friedman's focus on history as arid scholasticism, wondering why these "extreme cases" were "at all relevant to the problem that economic policy faces right now." Then he made an unadvised crack: "Everything reminds Milton of the money supply. Well everything reminds me of sex, but I keep it out of the paper." To Solow's chagrin, this gibe became famous—almost as famous as his long-run economic growth model.[49]

It was particularly galling that Friedman would not recognize the successes of the new economics. The surging economy, he made clear, was a function of one thing, and one thing only: the increased money supply. Speaking before Congress, Friedman noted the connection between money supply and economic growth "is particularly close and impressive in the current expansion." Monetary policy had ended the 1960 recession, caused a brief slowdown, and then powered "an acceleration in economic activity and a rapid growth in income despite the absence of the tax cut that had been advertised as a *sine qua non* of continued recovery." Most economists did not agree that monetary policy over the past few years had been expansionary. They looked at interest rates, and seeing they remained stable, also believed monetary policy to be stable.[50]

By contrast, Friedman preferred direct measures of the money supply, akin to the ones he and Schwartz had painstakingly constructed. These direct measures—soon to be called "monetary aggregates"—told a different story than interest rates. But they were not yet widely used as a gauge of policy, or even widely known, given the Fed's mystery. In 1960 the *Federal Reserve Bulletin* published M1, the first modern aggregate, which measured the sum of all currency, checking accounts, and savings deposits at member banks. In all likelihood the decision to release an official M1 reflected the growing influence of Friedman's approach, even before publication of *A Monetary History of the United States.* M1 would thenceforth become a regular feature of the Fed's bimonthly statistical release. Subject to revision, reporting changes, seasonal adjustments, and other updates, these early M1 figures were not well suited for long-run economic research. Friedman and Schwartz remained unique for their immersion in a world of monetary aggregates they had built.

It wasn't that Friedman ignored interest rates altogether. He considered them an important indicator, but not a straightforward one: "Interest rates are largely determined by a wide range of forces of which the quantity of money is only one," he told Congress.[51] Looking at the money supply told a story of steady expansion, which matched overall economic growth.

Around the time of *A Monetary History of the United States*, Friedman unleashed another arrow. The book was suffused with NBER neutrality, arguing its most political points indirectly. In his regular academic work, he could be more free. In a project that grew out of the money workshop, Friedman decided to test a key question: Which was more relevant to macroeconomic performance, the Keynesian multiplier or the money supply? Friedman's chosen time frame was 1897 to 1958. But in a very real sense, he was testing the new economics.

Working with David Meiselman, a graduate student, Friedman devised a simple test of monetary expansion versus "autonomous expenditure" (a proxy for Keynesian demand management). Which had a greater impact upon consumption, and hence economic growth? "The results are strikingly one-sided," Friedman and Meiselman reported: monetary policy was far more impactful on national consumption.[52] This was a narrative derived from *A Monetary History of the United States*, but it was also a model aimed at other economists. It was not in the Cowles style but was rather a "reduced form" or "single equation" model, scarcely more complicated than the quantity theory of money, MV = PT. This new equation contained the V (velocity) and M (money supply—based on Friedman and Schwartz's historical research), but it added in consumption, autonomous expenditures, and a Keynesian multiplier. When the variables were manipulated to test their relationship, money was more important than autonomous expenditure.

It was not a completely anti-Keynesian result. In fact, Friedman and Meiselman excluded the years of the Great Depression from their analysis, conceding that the multiplier worked in some circumstances. This move fit with Friedman's support for significant portions of the New Deal, and his rejection of Austrian economics–style austerity. Keynes was right, the authors noted, to argue that the government must prop up demand in a crisis. Unfortunately, the profession had extended this finding to ordinary time and "been led to discard the general case for a very special one."[53] In so doing, they had cast aside what really mattered—money.

Friedman then situated the paper at the center of a "striking division" within economics. "One view is that the quantity of money matters little; the other, that it is a key factor in understanding, and even more, controlling economic change," he wrote. Much of the profession had converted from one view to the other "on the basis of essentially no evidence," Friedman continued. But now that the tests were in, it was obvious "the simple version of the income expenditure theory . . . is almost completely useless as a description of stable empirical relationships, as judged by six decades of experience in the United States," he concluded. Lest he be accused of attacking a straw man, Friedman dropped a footnote to Samuelson's textbook and Alvin Hansen's *Business Cycles and National Income*.[54]

The paper further critiqued the new economics by suggesting that recent economic growth had been misattributed to spending, rather than easy money. As Walter Heller, the CEA chair who was being widely celebrated as the architect of economic growth, wrote bitterly, "Apparently, we were just playing fiscal tiddlywinks in Washington."[55] After various drafts circulated around the money workshop, Friedman took the paper on the road, inflaming an audience at MIT, home of Samuelson, Solow, and Modigliani. Rising to the bait, Friedman's doubters began reworking the tests with their own data and categories, creating a new parlor game for economists. Critiques, revisions, and rejoinders flew back and forth between Friedman and the growing circle of scholars who had seen the paper. By the time it was finally published in 1963—the same year as *A Monetary History of the United States*—a small literature was forming around Friedman and Meiselman.

First of the Big Four into battle was Modigliani. Cosmopolitan and intense, the Italian-born Modigliani "once ran into a cement wall trying to get the ball," his tennis partner Samuelson remembered. Modigliani fled his native Italy for Paris as Mussolini rose to power. He ended up in the United States as a protégé of Jacob Marschak, eventually following him to the Cowles Commission before settling in at MIT.[56] Modigliani had a long-standing interest in money; one of his goals was to bring financial and monetary factors more fully into Keynesian models.

Teaming up with the University of Pennsylvania professor Albert Ando, Modigliani attacked Friedman in the epic "Battle of the Radio Stations," a debate named for the participants' initials (FM/AM: Friedman-Meiselman/Ando-Modigliani), that consumed nearly a hundred pages of the *American Economic Review* in 1965. Although there were two other economists also in the fray, the real action centered around AM's critique and FM's vigorous counterattack. Conceding the validity of Friedman's result, Ando and Modigliani nonetheless argued against its significance. Mimicking Friedman's combative tone, AM declared "their elaborate battery of tests essentially worthless." The problems were multifold, ranging from "serious misrepresentations of the Keynesian theory" to the historical time period used to a variety of statistical errors.[57]

AM's overarching critique of the paper—that FM had created a rigged game favoring their interpretation—turned out to be a powerful engine for driving controversy and, by extension, spreading Friedman's ideas. Hoping to see for themselves, economists began replicating Friedman's methodology. Now numerous economists were using the very sort of reduced-form models that had been displaced in favor of more elaborate structural models. And in refuting Friedman's claim for the superiority of money, AM were drawn into articulating numerous claims about money's significance. "There is absolutely no justification for treating autonomous expenditure and money supply as mutually exclusive stabilization devices," blasted AM, leveling a critique at

Friedman that also hit the Keynesianism characteristic of *The Economic Report of the President, January 1962*. AM even closed with a call that economists "buckle down to the unended and unending labor of . . . charting the complex and still ill-understood channels through which money and the tools of monetary policy affect economic activity."[58] A more powerful endorsement of the money workshop's agenda was hard to imagine.

Who won the Battle of the Radio Stations? In large part, the answer depended on an economists' perspective. If one accepted the validity of Friedman and Meiselman's approach, they remained on top. If one constructed an alternative measure, the importance of money could diminish and that of fiscal policy increase. However, it would then be clear that the model had been constructed with a purpose—the same accusation leveled against the original authors. In the end, the paper successfully created a debate around what had previously been a truism—the potency and importance of fiscal demand management.[59]

With its strong language and sweeping claims, the Friedman-Meiselman paper conjured the very divide it identified; Friedman was not so much responding to a great schism in economics as creating one. When the paper was written, "students of economic affairs" were not neatly divided between Keynesians and monetary economists, as the paper had it. Rather, it was the broadly Keynesian consensus against Friedman and his renegade workshop, "a small abrasive counterrevolutionary cell," as Meiselman put it.[60] The debate's prominence in the *American Economic Review* and the combatants' status made the conflict evident to all economists, no matter how far they were situated from the great heights of the profession. By the time it was all over, the debate had generated twenty-six papers. The term "monetarism" began catching on as Friedman's views spread beyond those who knew him personally. Soon it would denote an entire school of thought, becoming a rampart for any scholar who was restive with the disciplinary status quo. Along with *A Monetary History of the United States*, the paper helped Friedman set the larger agenda of the profession, which did begin to meaningfully polarize around his work. A pronouncement by Friedman created its own weather pattern in the profession, setting off a storm of claims and counterclaims.

In 1967 Friedman became president of the American Economic Association, voted into office by his peers. The position was largely ceremonial, but it did come with one important privilege and duty: delivering a presidential address at the annual meeting, a well-attended pilgrimage traditionally scheduled between Christmas and New Year's Day. Settling into the auditorium, the audience of several thousand economists would have expected nothing less than a war dance, and Friedman did not disappoint. He offered at once a provocative theoretical exposition of macroeconomics, a policy prescription, and a prediction.[61]

The policy guidance was familiar: monetary authorities should "avoid sharp swings in policy" and focus on "steady monetary growth." The Federal Reserve should concentrate on a magnitude it could directly control; otherwise, it would "be like a space vehicle that has taken a fix on the wrong star."[62] This meant ignoring interest rates and focusing on the quantity of money. It mattered less what rate of growth was chosen, Friedman reminded his audience, than that the Fed publicly commit to a target and follow through.

The theory was audacious, although it would not have been unfamiliar to those closely following his work. Facing an auditorium packed with professional economists, Friedman took up a familiar conundrum: the vexing trade-off between inflation and unemployment. Stable prices and maximum employment were the two overarching policy mandates of the postwar era, enshrined in the Employment Act of 1946. The goal of policy was to tack gracefully between the mandates, keeping the rise in prices if not perfectly stable, at least to a minimal annual rise of, say 1 to 2 percent and keeping employment "full," meaning in the CEA's terms around 4 percent unemployment. Yet it was far from agreed that "these goals are mutually compatible," as Friedman noted in his opening lines.[63]

Indeed, the influential cost-push paradigm of inflation suggested there was an inherent trade-off. Low unemployment would raise the overall price level, it was believed, as labor unions bid up wages. Therefore, inflation was a sign of a booming economy, widespread economic growth, and a tight labor market. Of course, too much inflation was bad—witness the German hyperinflation that followed World War I and laid the groundwork for the rise of the Nazis. But a little inflation was like a little wine; it gave everyone a nice buzz, with no headache the next morning. The new economics had not set aside all concerns with inflation. But the price level had been remarkably stable since the end of the Korean War, while recessions had spiked unemployment above 4 percent. Both recent history and cost-push theory suggested inflation was the lesser evil. Letting inflation rise in order to gain a reduction in unemployment might even be a wise policy.

Friedman warned that this widely accepted idea was illusory. Inflation had costs, while its benefits were oversold. Critically, he argued that inflation had its own momentum—an idea soon known as the "accelerationist thesis." Once it got going, stopping inflation would be difficult and painful.

Further, there was no scientific reason that inflation and unemployment couldn't rise together—creating "stagflation," as a British politician had recently mourned. Indeed, Britain's economy showed perplexing symptoms: rising prices atop a sluggish economy. In an earlier *Newsweek* column, Friedman pointed out a similar situation in the United States during the 1957–1958 recession.[64] The facts were out there—but without a corresponding theory, they had yet to penetrate the economics profession. Now Friedman offered that theory.

The scenario went as follows. Imagine an economy with stable prices but with higher unemployment rates than are preferred by the powers that be. Responding, perhaps, to political pressure, the central bank lowers reserve requirements or buys lots of bonds, sending a mild flush of cash through the system. In turn, business activity picks up, including hiring; unemployment declines. "This much is pretty standard doctrine," Friedman summarized, although he was setting up a far from uncontroversial monetary description of inflation.[65]

But before long, as overall demand increases, selling prices—consumer prices—begin to rise. It is easier to swap out stickers on a shelf than change the prices of basic economic inputs. So when workers take their paychecks to the store, they find everything is more expensive. Their *nominal* wages—the numbers on the pay stub—may have risen. But *real* wages—in terms of purchasing power—have not. Indeed, they may even have declined. The workers' play is clear: ask for more money.

But now, the generally rising price level will have caught up to employers. They can no longer offer workers a nominal wage increase; they must offer a real wage increase. Some will be able to do this, and some will not. Further, with rising prices now clear to everyone, employers begin to shed increasingly expensive labor. Unemployment returns to the previously unacceptable level.

This sounded, so far, something like the cost-push or wage-price theory of inflation. Prices were driven ever upward by an unholy bargain between workers and employers.

But that was the agitation of waves on the surface; Friedman went to the tidal currents below, focusing on the shifts in money that set off the reaction and even worsened it. In Friedman's worst-case scenario, the monetary authorities react to unemployment and sluggish growth with another dose of monetary expansion, setting off the cycle once again. It was true, Friedman noted, that a rising rate of inflation "may reduce unemployment." But eventually, the music would stop, and the gains would be lost. "There is always a temporary trade-off between inflation and unemployment; there is no permanent trade-off," he summarized.[66]

In place of a trade-off, Friedman offered a new concept: the "natural" rate of unemployment. This was the level of employment that would prevail with the economy in equilibrium. Seemingly reminiscent of social Darwinism, "natural unemployment" was exactly the type of language to send an American liberal into paroxysms. As if he anticipated such a reaction, Friedman clarified that his use of the word was technical, intended to "separate the real forces from the monetary forces." (Later, economists would replace it with the inelegant but sterile acronym NAIRU—the Non-Accelerating Inflation Rate of Unemployment, coined by none other than Modigliani of AM fame.) Natural unemployment was not "immutable and unchangeable . . . many of the market characteristics that determine its level are man-made and policy-made," Friedman asserted. Nonetheless, if the natural rate of unemployment could vary with the composition of the workforce and other broad, non-cyclical trends, it was not something that could be manipulated by a short-term policy. If unemployment were artificially forced down by monetary expansion, inflation would result. "The true springs of economic growth," Friedman concluded, were "those basic forces of enterprise, ingenuity, invention, hard work, and thrift."[67] Private economic activity, not government stimulus, remained paramount.

In a final gamble, Friedman made a prophecy. First, he laid out a basic timeline for the dynamic he had described. "The initial effects of a higher and unanticipated rate of inflation last for something like two to five years," he argued, and then the effect was reversed. Here is where the unlovely combination of high unemployment and high inflation would occur. Eventually, the economy would recover, but "full adjustment to the new rate of inflation takes about as long for unemployment as for interest rates, say, a couple of decades." Then he got specific. At the end of 1966, Friedman argued, the Fed had made one of its "drastic and erratic changes of direction," expanding the money supply "at a more rapid pace than can long be maintained without appreciable inflation."[68] The math was simple. If Friedman was right, by 1972 the beneficial effects of this expansion would have expired, and unemployment would surge. It would then take up to twenty years for the economy to stabilize and recover the good times.

In front of the most well-informed and critical audience possible, Friedman had challenged widely held assumptions about inflation, proposed a rival theory, spelled out the unpopular political implications, and then made a series of predictions about the future. It was the academic equivalent of a high dive.

Had Friedman pulled it off, or had he belly flopped? The arguments began at once, with his address dominating conference chitchat afterward. The audience rightly understood Friedman had launched a public attack on Keynesian economics that could not be ignored. Although Friedman was explicitly arguing that monetary policy could not lower unemployment in any meaningful, sustained way, he was also saying the same about fiscal policy. One prominent clue was his reference to "the celebrated Phillips curve," which had guided the Kennedy CEA's conception of full employment. Friedman argued that the Phillips curve "contains a basic defect—the failure to distinguish between *nominal* wages and *real* wages."[69] This was perhaps understandable because the curve was scarcely a decade old. The American version, in particular, had been conceptualized after a decade of unusually stable prices.

In their famous 1960 paper, Samuelson and Solow qualified their arguments and highlighted numerous unknowns. But in publishing graphs of an American Phillips curve, they did much to enshrine the concept in economic thinking. And by labeling their curve "a menu of choice between different degrees of unemployment and price stability," they unwittingly promoted the simplistic idea that policy-makers could easily choose various points along the curve to reach a desired outcome. Further, with the optimism characteristic of the new economics, Samuelson and Solow set aside fears about inflation. There was a good chance a wage-price spiral, should it emerge, would be harmless. "It may be that creeping inflation leads only to creeping inflation," the authors wrote, in a sentiment that Friedman would directly challenge with his accelerationist thesis.[70]

Almost immediately, other economists put his arguments to the test. In one of those coincidences that have marked scientific discovery across the ages, the economist Edmund Phelps—ironically a Cowles Commission alum—almost simultaneously published the same argument Friedman had made. Phelps's more mathematical approach powerfully complemented Friedman's address; subsequently, the ideas became known as Friedman-Phelps.[71] By the end of January, New York University held a conference on inflation at which Friedman's ideas took center stage; the "accelerationist" controversy was well under way. Conveniently, measures of unemployment and inflation were plentiful, public, and relatively easy to interpret, unlike historical data on the money supply. Friedman's theories could be assessed using any number of familiar approaches. He was back in the center of economic debate.[72]

The most fruitful arguments revolved around Friedman's stress on anticipation. In his address, much like Alfred Marshall might have done, Friedman had explained the power of anticipated inflation in plain English. The effort of workers, consumers, and businesses to stay ahead of rising prices was, ironically, a key driver of inflation itself. It was this element that meant "inflation has a momentum of its own; it cannot be turned off like a water tap," as he put it to *Newsweek* readers.[73] This psychological dynamic was not unknown to economists; in fact, Samuelson and Solow had used it to explain why inflation didn't really matter. They optimistically hypothesized that if everyone expected inflation, "schoolteachers, pensioners, and others" would "devise institutions to protect their real incomes from erosion by higher prices." But expectations did not play a significant causal role in the contemporary theory of inflation until Friedman placed new emphasis upon them.[74]

Even as the clash of professors unfolded, beyond the ivory tower lay a world of central bankers and policy-makers keenly attuned to Friedman's ideas. In keeping with the intrinsic paradox of monetary theory, his address had at once stressed the impotence of monetary policy and elevated the power of central banks. You couldn't juice the economy with money, Friedman was arguing, but you could powerfully throw it off course. He had restated the central insight of the quantity theory: "Every major inflation has been produced by monetary expansion."[75] For those directly responsible for the wealth of nations, the idea was intriguing in its simplicity and power. As academic papers, formulas, and graphs rained down, this compelling formula remained far from a settled truth.

In retrospect, 1965 had been another one of those hinge years. It was a triumphant time for Lyndon Johnson, who pushed through the Voting Rights Act, one of the most consequential pieces of legislation in

American history. Interposing the federal government between disenfranchised citizens and state governments, the act empowered the Justice Department to oversee elections in selected states. It also gave an enormous moral and legal boost to voter registration efforts. The larger work of the Civil Rights Movement was just beginning. But with the passage of a second major federal law, it had reached the end of its classic phase. The sober suits and ties of churchgoing elders would soon give way to the defiant Afros and raised fists of a younger generation.

Passage of the Voting Rights Act altered dynamics across the political landscape. On the left, it coincided with a growing movement toward racial separatism in leading civil rights organizations, meaning that white student activists increasingly turned their attention to the Vietnam War. On the right, passage of the act deflated the most overt segregationist arguments and appeals.[76] Resistance to integration and racial equality continued, but took new forms. Two legislative battles in a row had been lost; and it proved difficult to argue against voting rights. Friedman made no comment on the law.

On the surface, 1965 was another year of strong economic growth, with the new economics enjoying peak prestige. The War on Poverty, Johnson's signature domestic initiative, was the brainchild of Heller, the chair of the CEA under both Kennedy and Johnson. Unbeknownst to Heller, even as Johnson embraced an expansive vision that hearkened back to the New Deal, he had another priority that would cost billions: staving off defeat in Vietnam. The Korean War had been over for nearly a decade, having ended where it began, with the country divided in two. But the United States was still supporting a government beleaguered by a Communist insurgency in nearby Vietnam, and Johnson hungered for a clear-cut victory. In 1964 he had secured from Congress the Gulf of Tonkin Resolution, ultimately giving him a free hand in Vietnam. It was another of those 1960s ironies. As Moynihan summarized, "All the worst things liberals had intimated might occur were conservatives elected, did occur almost the moment the conservatives were defeated," including "a demented military adventure in Asia."[77]

Part of what made the new economics work, it turned out, was that very convergence between left and right that Moynihan had identified. In 1964 Johnson ushered through Congress a comprehensive tax cut, first introduced by Kennedy, that drastically lowered tax rates across the board. Individual income tax rates tumbled, particularly in the highest brackets, where they fell from 90 percent to 71 percent. Corporate income tax was also reduced. The CEA was ambivalent about the legislation; Tobin stepped down at that juncture, in part to register frustration with the policy. While the CEA had convinced Kennedy that a tax cut could stimulate the economy, they wanted a temporary cut, well suited to fine-tuning. Instead, permanent marginal tax cuts won the day. The CEA feared that an irreversible tax cut would hamper future economic growth, preventing new spending that might be needed to stimulate demand.

The CEA was right, but not for the reasons it expected. There had always been a bit of artistic leeway in the federal budget, no matter who was making the projections, but the figures Johnson fed to his CEA were unimaginably wrong. In 1965, the CEA expected the defense budget might rise by $2 billion or even $5 billion—instead it went up by $12 billion. A year later the cost of the war had already reached $20 billion—nearly double the original estimates of the entire conflict. Over at the Defense Department, staffers were expected to budget as if the war would end in 1967. It was deception, pure and simple, driven by Johnson's fear that he would have to choose between guns and butter. "Lovingly caressing their cheerful economic indicators," recounts one historian, the economists at the CEA "were oblivious to the gathering storm." It was one thing to support a tax cut amid peace and prosperity. It was another thing entirely to cut taxes on the eve of a major military expenditure. By the time the economists clued in and began pressing for new taxes, it was too late to plug the gaping budgetary hole.[78]

It was harder to temporarily disguise the social costs of the war, specifically the draft, which soon became a volatile political issue. When Johnson assumed office, draft call-ups were minimal and congressional reauthorization pro forma. In 1962, the year *Capitalism and Freedom* appeared, 82,060 Americans were drafted, the lowest number since the years immediately after World War II. As Johnson committed ground troops to the conflict in Vietnam, the numbers began to tick upward. In 1965 the number of inductees passed 200,000 and then climbed in a year to nearly 400,000.[79] Even those who escaped the draft were now awakened to a system that plucked some from peaceful lives and plunged them into the machinery of war. The most vociferous protests came not from those shipping out but from college students insulated from the conflict by educational deferments.

Events began to move at warp speed, with the war accelerating decades of social change into years and even months. Sit-ins, be-ins, and flower children were regulars in the news. LSD menaced the youth. College campuses convulsed with activism and protest. Vietnam powered a broad critique of U.S. power. In this analysis, the war was yet another example of capitalist imperialism that had divided the world into rich and poor. It also highlighted domestic racism. As the Black Panther Huey Newton declared, "In America, black people are treated very much like the Vietnamese people, or any other colonized people."[80] The conflict turbocharged the New Left on campuses, re-creating political and social divisions that had faded during the prosperous 1950s.

While some professors were shocked to the right by campus activism, Friedman worked assiduously to convert the protesters' anti-war demands into a viable policy solution: the volunteer military.[81] In *Capitalism and Freedom*, Milton and Rose called a volunteer military the "appropriate free market arrangement," criticizing the draft as inequitable, arbitrary, and inefficient.[82] Most Americans rightly understood the campus protests and street marches as an anti-war movement, but there was another strain of protest that was not so much anti-war, as anti-draft. It was entirely possible to oppose the draft while dismissing Marxist theories of imperialism. It was even possible, following the lead of Ayn Rand, to denounce the draft, the war, *and* the hippies. These fault lines cracked apart Young Americans for Freedom, the premier conservative youth organization, which was soon roiled by divides over the war. Many student conservatives saw Vietnam as essential to the fight against Communism. Young libertarians, by contrast, saw the draft as sheer coercion and joined in the mass protests without buying the case against capitalism.[83]

Friedman had a direct personal connection to the campus anti-draft movement through his son, David. Precocious, verbally gifted, and congenitally argumentative, David entered Harvard at age sixteen. Although he showed an early interest in economics, Rose and Milton pushed him instead toward physics. It would be better for David to flourish outside his father's long shadow, they believed. Milton was more accepting of David's politics, even when he emerged as a leading anarcho-capitalist with his first book, *The Machinery of Freedom.*[84] When he enrolled at the University of Chicago for a Ph.D. in physics, David joined a cluster around the *New Individualist Review,* a magazine started by several of F. A. Hayek's students. In 1962, after his ten-year grant from the Volker Fund expired, Hayek returned to Europe. In his place, Friedman became the main faculty supporter of the magazine, even publishing excerpts from *Capitalism and Freedom* in its pages.

While the University of Chicago saw its share of anti-war protests, it also became a major source of intellectual arguments against the draft. Friedman was not the only faculty voice in support of a volunteer army, but he was one of the most prominent. In 1966, the university hosted a major conference on the draft that drew an eclectic group of academics and policy-makers, including luminaries like Margaret Mead, Ted Kennedy, and the young Illinois congressman Donald Rumsfeld. At the conference, Friedman studiously avoided commenting on the war itself, making only a mild chest thump about the need for "a large military force and a strong one."[85] Instead, he swung his support behind the economic analysis of a Chicago Ph.D. graduate, Walter Oi.[86]

Nearly blind, and with a compelling personal story—he had spent part of his childhood living in a horse stall during the wartime internment of Japanese Americans—Oi mesmerized the conference with a virtuoso display of Chicago price theory, applied to the military budget. During a brief stint at the Pentagon, Oi had come up with something explosive: an annual cost estimate for the volunteer military of around $5 billion, far below the figure of $18 billion the brass liked to use to shut down discussion. Rather than focus on the seen costs of supporting soldiers, Oi focused on the unseen cost of drafting them.

"The real economic cost of maintaining a defense establishment is partially concealed," he argued.[87] In Oi's analysis, conscription was a tax—consisting of the lost wages and disrupted careers of young men. If these costs were factored in, then conscription was underpriced, narrowing the cost gap between a voluntary military and the draft. It was yet another example of how applying economics to policy changed the political game.

The Chicago conference was a turning point in U.S. military history, leading to a fundamental reconfiguration of the nation's armed forces. While the idea of a volunteer military had occasionally surfaced into political debate, often touted by conservatives—Robert Taft and William F. Buckley had both noted their support—it had stalled in the realm of the impractical. As one conference participant judged, it was "politically naïve in the extreme."[88] But the conference did much to undermine this view. Oi's estimates broke the problem down into manageable pieces, and Friedman's support helped turn the tide.

The most important convert turned out to be Richard Nixon. Mulling a return to political life from his perch as a high-priced New York lawyer, Nixon gathered a small group of advisers in 1966 to think through the possibilities. Among them was Martin Anderson, a Columbia Business School professor. Anderson was connected to the student libertarian movement through his friendship with Rand. Objectivists were a small but vocal part of the anti-draft movement, and Anderson had imbibed Rand's ethical case against conscription. In a campaign memo to Nixon, however, he knew better than to quote *Atlas Shrugged*, instead blending his objectivist sympathies with Oi's figures and the idea of an implicit tax. Nixon grasped immediately that eliminating the draft was good politics; it would cut down on student unrest and differentiate him from the Johnson administration. Nixon made headlines when he announced his support for an all-volunteer military. Once in office, he would appoint Friedman and other scholars from the 1966 conference to the Gates Commission. By 1973, the draft was no more.[89]

How important were Friedman's ideas to this momentous policy shift? Certainly, his writings were extremely influential among student libertarians.[90] In another sense, however, the draft debates showed the limits of Friedman's framework. The move to a volunteer military came to be seen, in retrospect, as the triumph of a "market paradigm."[91] But this analysis mistakes justification for cause. Not even Friedman advocated the change because it would set capitalism free. Instead, concerns about justice, coercion, and politics were jumbled together. Oi's estimates moved these contrasting motivations onto safe territory: lowering taxes and helping economic growth.

In this context, Friedman had two roles to play. First was name-brand support of Oi's counterintuitive calculations. Not only was Friedman the head of the American Economic Association; he had a national platform through *Newsweek* and plenty of experience pushing ideas into the political system. Second, his advocacy severed the link between opposing the war and opposing the draft. Amazingly, Friedman avoided voicing an actual opinion on the war! Many anti-draft organizers did the same, hoping to keep their coalition both broad and focused. Friedman's reputation, affect, rhetoric, and reputation all combined to powerfully legitimate the idea of a volunteer military. With his suits, thick glasses, and upbeat, genial delivery, Friedman changed abolishing the draft from a pet cause of longhairs to a reform that Republican professors embraced. He pushed the idea in articles for *Newsweek* and *The New York Times Magazine*, lent his name to the Council for a Volunteer Military, and testified before Congress. This activity helped establish ending the draft as a Republican issue; several GOP members of Congress even published a book called *How to End the Draft*.[92] Prying apart the anti-war and anti-draft components of the issue gave a politician like Nixon room to glide through.

In the end, it was not ideas but politics that drove the shift. The draft was a unique issue that bound military and executive decision-making tightly into American families. The late 1960s were also a unique political moment. The war in Vietnam was widely regarded as a project of the Democratic Party—started under Kennedy, escalated under Johnson. The partisan cast of the war gave Nixon maneuvering room to disown conscription. And so too did Nixon's reputation as an ardent cold warrior. Just as only Nixon could go to China, only Nixon could end the draft.

By any measure, the 1968 presidential campaign was extraordinary. In March, facing the unthinkable prospect that he might lose his own party's presidential nomination—a humiliating first for a sitting president with another term to go—Johnson withdrew from the race. During the scramble that followed, Robert Kennedy emerged as the favorite, only to be felled by an assassin's bullet after sweeping the California primary. Deprived of a favorite son, the Democratic Party descended into open warfare between moderates and radicals, culminating in a raucous late-summer convention that anointed Johnson's vice president, Hubert Humphrey, as their candidate. Beyond the unpopular war, continued social upheaval was a major liability for the Democratic Party. In April, Martin Luther King Jr. was gunned down in Memphis, sparking riots in multiple cities. Protests against the war, assassinations of national leaders, widespread news coverage of crime and disorder—all suggested a nation spinning out of control.

This tableau of unrest was the perfect backdrop for the Republican Party stalwart Nixon. His disciplined campaign presented the candidate as a wise elder statesman, well versed in foreign policy and a familiar, safe hand on the tiller amid domestic storms. Nixon faced not just Humphrey but a second challenge: the Independent Party candidacy of Alabama's governor, George Wallace.[93] "Segregation now, segregation tomorrow, segregation forever!" Wallace thundered upon taking office as governor in 1963, instantly achieving notoriety. There was little chance that Wallace would win the election outright. But in a three-way race he could be a spoiler, especially if he locked up the entire South, throwing the election into the Democratic-dominated House of Representatives.

In response to the pincer threat of Humphrey on his left and Wallace on his right, Nixon strove to blaze a wide path down the center.[94]

Writing off the segregationist vote to Wallace, Nixon concentrated on "New South" states like Florida, Tennessee, and North Carolina, where he stressed traditional Republican themes of limited government, economic growth, and racial moderation. He also strove to pick off Humphrey voters who were disillusioned with Democratic governance. Among his most resonant themes was "law and order"—at once a genuine response to social disarray and a message that resonated with white racial anxieties.[95] These appeals were not always effective; Texas, for example, would stick with Humphrey. But in keeping with the general policy drift of the times, Nixon wanted to offer something to everyone, to blur rather than sharpen partisan divisions that might cost him votes.

Friedman had several direct personal connections to Nixon. Arthur Burns played a critical role on the campaign, tapping men Friedman knew and trusted, such as fellow Chicago professor George Shultz, to offer policy advice. Friedman agreed to be one of a large group—150 people—who served on various task forces laying out a potential agenda for the Nixon administration.

That didn't mean he liked Nixon very much. Friedman had met the vice president during the Eisenhower years and noted his sharp intellect. As a campaign consultant, however, he saw a different side of the man. At a long session with advisers, Nixon was focused and serious, even professorial. Later that same day a new Nixon emerged for a press barbecue, "hail-fellow-well-met, arms waving, emotional, the farthest thing from the intellectual you might have taken him for earlier in the day," Friedman recounted sardonically in his memoir.[96] Unlike Goldwater, it was impossible to ignore Nixon the politician, impossible to understand him as a man of principle.

Still, once the returns were in, there was cause for optimism and relief. Johnson's dead weight had dragged down Humphrey, and Wallace had carried off a good chunk of the formerly Democratic Solid South. Even though the popular vote was less than 1 percent apart, Nixon had won 56 percent of the electoral college. After the Goldwater debacle, the Republican Party appeared to have grown up, choosing a candidate who could fly on "two wings"—moderate and conservative.

Yet there were good reasons that President Johnson had not contested the election. The Great Society and the war in Vietnam were an economic booby trap waiting for the new administration. Already the signs of economic strain were visible. Prices were heading upward, propelled by monetary ease and a flood of new defense contracts. In 1966, the Consumer Price Index, a widely watched indicator, nearly doubled from the previous year, hitting 3 percent. It was "the early stages" of a serious inflationary episode, Friedman warned. "Monetary rise has been accelerated, and the price rise has accelerated even more rapidly as anticipations of inflation have become widespread," he told an audience in Chicago.[97] Inflation had followed the major wars of the century. Americans rightfully anticipated that Vietnam would be no exception. The next year inflation would briefly slow as the Fed pushed up interest rates; then it would edge up past 4 percent, the biggest change since 1951.

Friedman was keying into a significant expansion in the money supply, driven by Fed policy. To finance the war, the Treasury Department had been vigorously selling bonds. And although it was nominally independent, under master conciliator William McChesney Martin the Fed had been helping Treasury by expanding bank reserves in order to hold interest rates on an "even keel," so that low-returning T-bills were competitive. A low-interest man in the populist vein of Wright Patman, Johnson applauded the move and pressured Martin any time he tried to raise rates.[98]

From the top down, inflation had its benefits. For one, it was considered a by-product of lower unemployment, a major political goal. More cynically, it would boost revenue as taxpayers were bumped into higher brackets. Favoring debtors over creditors, historically inflation was thought to help the little guy. Across the nineteenth century, farmers had battled East Coast bankers for a more expansionary policy that would lighten their burden of debt. In this case, though, the biggest debtor was the federal government.

Previous wars had been financed with high taxes—yet the CEA had barely finished celebrating an across-the-board tax cut. Guideposts were no help, as unions and corporations negotiated guideline-busting wage increases and prices surged. Johnson's economists were now desperate for a tax hike, but a temporary surcharge in 1968 made little impact.[99] Knowing it was temporary, most taxpayers did not alter their spending patterns. In turn, this unexpected natural experiment became powerful evidence for the permanent income hypothesis developed by Friedman, Margaret Reid, Dorothy Brady, and Rose Friedman. As the economic situation deteriorated, Friedman's predictions seemed increasingly right.

By then, Friedman was no longer alone in his pessimism about the economy. Members of Johnson's CEA were well aware they had a runaway horse on their hands, even calling the economy "schizophrenic" and "unhinged."[100] With Nixon heading to the White House, it would be left to longtime Friedman allies like Arthur Burns to clean up the mess.

PART V

THE GREAT INFLATION

11

THE INFLATIONARY FED

> Never in my wildest dreams did I believe that the central bank virus was so potent that it could corrupt even you in so short a time.
>
> —Milton Friedman, 1970

In 1969, a year into Nixon's presidency, *Time* posed the question of the moment: "Will there be a recession?" On the cover, a stylized image of Milton Friedman loomed, amid jagged lines of red and green and a gridded background, all suggesting a chart of economic growth or decline. Inside, the magazine pinpointed a mood of rising economic anxiety and pessimism, linking it directly to "the bearish warnings of one economist who was once ignored and ridiculed, but whose views have lately had an important influence on Government policy." The article explained that Friedman had mounted a half-successful challenge to Keynes, resulting in economists who were "Friedmanly, some Friedmanian, some Friedmanesque, some Friedmanic and some Friedmaniacs." His ideas were spreading fast; there was even a Friedman fan club at Harvard.[1]

It was not true, as the article claimed, that Friedman believed the money supply to be "the most important and fastest-acting of the economic regulators at the Government's disposal." Indeed, the lag between monetary policy and economic performance—and the impossibility of policy-makers correctly anticipating the size of that lag—was a persistent theme in Friedman's work. But the article correctly gauged inflation as Richard Nixon's "No. 1 domestic problem" and noted the political dangers of "Nixon's inflation." What *Time* did not foresee was how inflation was becoming not just a national but an international crisis. Nor did the magazine anticipate how profoundly the rising tide of prices would vindicate Friedman's ideas about the potency of monetary policy.[2]

For all his reservations about Nixon, the years of his presidency swept Friedman to the highest levels of global power. Debates that had first taken shape in Chicago's Quadrangle Club now echoed across the West Wing. Arguments that once unfolded before roaring fires in the New Hampshire countryside now played out across the pages of *Newsweek* and *The New York Times*. And the ideas that had once branded Friedman a "pixie or a pest" (as *Time* put it) came to reshape the global financial system. Inflation emerged as an entwined economic, political, and social problem. It made tangible the risks and rewards of capitalist economies, and became the ultimate test of economic institutions and ideas. Suddenly, money mattered. Friedman's expertise on the topic would have commanded attention, no matter what. But with close allies in the White House, he vaulted from commentator to player.

Nixon's electoral victory revived the flagging career of Arthur Burns. After years of struggle, he had lost his leadership post at the NBER, and the profession had turned decisively away from the doggedly empirical study of business cycles that was his métier. But in his prime, Burns had made an important friend. Immersed in the mystical signals of intuitive economics, such as the thickness of cigar smoke in GM salesrooms, Burns warned presidential contender Richard Nixon that a recession was coming, and that it would cost him the 1960 election. Nixon, who never forgot a slight, never forgot this dismayingly accurate forecast either. As he revived his political ambitions nearly a decade later, Nixon drew Burns into his campaign.

Still remembering Burns's political perspicacity, Nixon intended to appoint him chairman of the Federal Reserve Board. But the first year would be a waiting game, as the longtime chair William McChesney Martin refused to relinquish power. Until then, Burns enjoyed an undefined role as economic counselor to the president, alongside the self-identified "Friedmanesque" Paul McCracken, the official chair of the Council of Economic Advisers.

In the interregnum, Burns maneuvered himself into a position of considerable influence. He didn't quite make it into the White House, but set up with a staff in the nearby Executive Office Building. Taking a cue from Nixon, Burns interpreted his role as counselor to the president generously. Basking in the sun and presidential attention during an Easter weekend in Key Biscayne, Florida, Burns made an unsettling discovery: the president was about to propose thoroughgoing welfare reform. Specifically, as Burns noted in an alarmist memo, Nixon had endorsed "a specific application of the negative income tax, as formulated by Milton Friedman." Burns had seen the first version of the Family Assistance Plan.[3]

It was true Nixon's proposal owed much to Friedman—but it was also touted by another man, Daniel Patrick Moynihan. Rumpled and professorial, favoring cable-knit sweaters over a suit and tie, Moynihan came with a long history of government service and almost as long a history of controversy. A former cabinet-level appointee in the Kennedy and Johnson administrations, he had inflamed liberal opinion with a 1965 report on African American family breakdown that was widely read as blaming the victim.[4] Moynihan retreated from the heat to a position at Harvard. A few years later, while still remaining a Democrat, he agreed to join Nixon's administration, chairing the Urban Affairs Council. He knew all about Friedman's negative income tax (NIT), which he called "a spanking good idea, with much of the clarity and symmetry of the economic vision of the time."[5] Although Moynihan did not have a direct hand in the original proposal, he quickly became a supporter.

Nixon's Family Assistance Plan (FAP), the eventual name of the shifting proposals that incorporated the NIT, sought to address the so-called welfare mess.[6] Over the 1960s, caseloads in the nation's signature welfare program, Aid to Families with Dependent Children (AFDC), had exploded. Influential governors and mayors, whose budgets bore the brunt, were begging for fiscal relief. The original FAP would have federalized much welfare and established more uniform nationwide benefit levels. Its most revolutionary idea, however, was to extend eligibility to working families, not just the unemployed. Nixon hoped to defuse the idea that federal programs only benefited poor African Americans at the expense of white taxpayers. Crucially, benefits would come as cash (or government checks), with the amount linked to income. As Burns perceived, the FAP essentially re-created Friedman's 1939 goal to guarantee "a minimum standard of living," now translated into the modern welfare state.

In his private diary, Burns vowed to quickly end the "mad adventure" of a guaranteed income, which he called "reminiscent of the social dreaming and histrionics of FDR."[7] In a long memo, Burns's staffer Martin Anderson offered a history of British poor laws, alleging they had destroyed those they intended to help: "Their productive capacity was drained, their independence destroyed, their self-respect shattered."[8] Then Burns countered with his own proposal, calling for expanding AFDC, requiring welfare recipients to work, and establishing a vast network of government run day-care centers. It was a proposal antithetical to the views of Friedman on every dimension, from its punitive approach to its call for a vast new federal program.

The original NIT vision soon received reinforcements from Secretary of Labor George Shultz, a confidant of Friedman's since their time together on the Chicago faculty. Shultz and Moynihan crafted a compromise plan that added work incentives to the FAP. Where Burns wielded the stick, Shultz offered a carrot. In the existing system, earned income reduced benefit levels. To Shultz this was perverse; no wonder once on welfare, people stayed there. Under the revised FAP, income was partially sheltered from taxes and benefit reductions. Following Friedman, Shultz hoped to make work pay.[9] Burns counterattacked with a doomsday memo warning the plan would endanger "the moral fiber of America" and trap "self-reliant working people in a state of dependency."[10] Eventually the administration proposed legislation that mushed together elements favored by Shultz, Moynihan, and Burns.

Amid the sausage-making, Friedman himself lost enthusiasm. Having no idea of Burns's role, he saw the final FAP proposal as old-fashioned logrolling. Food stamps had been added in to satisfy "the well-fed farm bloc," he fumed in *Newsweek*. Worse of all, when food stamps and state supplements were combined with the FAP, "many families would be better off to earn less than to earn more," Friedman argued. This was the problem Shultz had tried to solve; given variations in state programs, he had not succeeded in all cases, as Friedman demonstrated with a simple chart.[11]

Ultimately, the FAP made it through the House of Representatives, before stalling in the Senate. There were multiple reasons for its failure. As a creature of both the left and the right, the FAP ended up politically homeless, with no clear champions and opponents from both sides. Built into the policy was a contradiction: The FAP criticized the existing welfare system even as it proposed to expand it. Finally, the active opposition of Burns was devastating. His objections reduced Nixon's willingness to flaunt the program's innovations, meaning it emerged into public view as yet another flawed welfare program.[12] Burns's energetic presence in the poverty debate also established a recurring divide of the Nixon years: Friedman on one side, his oldest friend on the other.

Around the same time, Friedman's ideas were also the center of discussion at the venerable Brookings Institution. Almost as old as the Federal Reserve, Brookings was the nation's first think tank, devoted to fact-based study of policy issues. Founded in the Progressive era, Brookings never lost its tilt toward social reform, emerging as a pillar of the liberal order by the 1960s. As LBJ told an audience at the institution's fiftieth anniversary gala, "If you did not exist we would have to ask someone to create you." Still, Brookings prided itself on maintaining academic rigor and objectivity above all else. Once upon a time, it had even granted Ph.D.s. In 1970, the institution launched the *Brookings Papers on Economic Activity*, a new publication series based on biannual conferences in which established and emerging economists tackled critical policy issues. The *Papers* kicked off with an extended debate on the Phillips curve.[13]

In the beginning, it was not clear that Friedman's 1967 lecture, which had challenged the Phillips curve, would survive the scrutiny. After all, this was the home of the "Brookings model," a vast econometric system of over 150 equations that generated quarterly macroeconomic predictions. Descended from the early Cowles Commission models and designed in collaboration with IBM, the Brookings model enshrined the sort of mathematical simulation Friedman had long decried.

And this approach was still dominant in economics, as demonstrated by a *Journal of Political Economy* exchange between Friedman and five of his most prominent critics. Robert Gordon, the editor of the publication, convinced Friedman to step away from his preferred mode of analysis and write up a general mathematical model of money and aggregate demand. In an inverse of the Battle of the Radio Stations, Friedman had been lured into hostile territory. Even his students and allies harshly judged the result; Friedman himself appeared shocked by the critiques.[14] Other attacks were piling up, including a marquee article in *The Quarterly Journal of Economics* by James Tobin, "Money and Income: Post Hoc Ergo Prompter Hoc?" He translated the argument for readers of *The Washington Post*: "The fact that the rate of change of money stock leads [turning points in business activity] . . . proves nothing whatsoever about causation." Robert Solow, who along with Paul Samuelson had popularized the Phillips curve, took a whack at Friedman's lecture in a symposium on inflation.[15]

As the Brookings series began, Friedman's critique of the Phillips curve appeared undoubtedly fertile—hence the upwelling of papers and conferences—but not necessarily right. As one economist summarized it, Friedman and co-discoverer Edmund Phelps had made "a very coherent and sensible theoretical argument that, for one reason or another, the data did not support."[16] The first three papers in the series reflected this assessment. They were authored by the methodical Gordon—the same scholar who had convinced Friedman to translate monetarism into models for the *Journal of Political Economy*. Dogged and fearless, Gordon was also a junior faculty member at Chicago, well aware of the risks in challenging Friedman (in fact, he would shortly be denied tenure there). He set to work modeling Friedman's theory with recent economic data. In his first paper, Gordon noted a worrisome and dramatic rise in inflation, but argued this was not proof of the "accelerationist" thesis attributed to Friedman.[17]

Other economists were reaching different conclusions, most notably Harry Johnson. At a 1971 conference in Amsterdam, Johnson observed that the Phillips curve had "broken down completely in the face of the inflationary facts of the past two years or so." He went on to call the general monetarist position "the only alternative consistent with the facts (as distinct from the myths) of historical experience."[18] Johnson had not become a pure monetarist. But he embraced Friedman and Schwartz's interpretation of the Great Depression and the larger argument that the real economy was stable, subject primarily to monetary disturbances that could be managed by monetary policy.

This was unmistakably a major development. Although he was Friedman's part-time colleague, Johnson was emphatically not part of his "Chicago school." Just a year earlier, he devoted his 1970 Ely Lecture—an important honorific in the field—to an attack on Friedman. Charging Friedman with "scholarly chicanery," Johnson alleged he had rewritten history to support his monetarist counterrevolution. Given his obvious dislike of Friedman, it was news indeed that Johnson had moved clearly away from Keynesianism toward monetarism.[19] And given Johnson's visibility beyond the United States, it was a significant gain for monetarism.

A similar transformation occurred at Brookings, driven by the galloping inflation of the early 1970s. Since 1966, the price level had risen at a fairly steady clip. By 1968, it had reached 4.3 percent as measured by the Consumer Price Index, and in the year Nixon took office, inflation reached 5.4 percent. If the Phillips curve held, unemployment should have dropped; yet in 1970 it suddenly jumped to 5.8 percent.[20]

Friedman's timing was "impeccable and even uncanny," Gordon remembered.[21] As he continued to feed quarterly data into his econometric models, the changing events in the U.S. economy dissolved the Phillips curve. Friedman had explained the dynamic in his speech to the American Economic Association: "There is always a temporary tradeoff between inflation and unemployment; there is no permanent tradeoff."[22] The stable relationship observed in the 1960s was simply too short a time period to see the dynamics at work.

By 1972, Gordon had a new model showing "any attempt to reduce the rate of unemployment below its natural rate causes inflation to increase." And then inflation would accelerate, potentially reaching "the Brazilian range" of nearly 15 percent. Earlier models that relied on pre-1968 data were simply "obsolete," Gordon pronounced.[23] Presented not just to academics but to a D.C. audience—including future policy-makers like Alan Greenspan—these were arresting conclusions.

In the end, the Phillips curve did not disappear, but it changed. The original curve had assumed "money illusion"—that individuals failed to notice their money was worth less due to inflation. The new curve was "expectations augmented"—not only was money illusion set aside but the assumption that people expected a certain amount of inflation was built in.

Attacks on the Phillips curve ultimately killed off the new economics. The curve had been "a lynchpin of the large-scale macroeconometric models which were the focus of research activity in the 1960s," Gordon remembered.[24] But inflation had been their "Achilles' heel."[25] The natural rate of unemployment assumed new prominence in economic thinking. Policy-makers could not, it turned out, order up their preferred combination of joblessness and rising prices, as they would steak and potatoes. Instead they would have to operate within the constraints of the natural rate.

Critically, Friedman's "accelerationist" thesis was now confirmed. Over time, inflation had not held steady but had surged upward. Expectations helped explain this. If workers, consumers, investors, and business owners all expected inflation to rise, they would try to get out in front by charging more, demanding higher wages, or accepting a high interest rate—assuming it was headed even higher. All this would create a pernicious updraft, igniting more inflation. The new economics had not feared inflation. Friedman's economics taught a different lesson—one ultimately supported not by academic papers alone but by the onrush of events.

When Burns was finally appointed chair of the Fed in January 1970, Friedman had reason to rejoice. It was a joy to see an old friend rise again and cap his career with such a laurel. Also, Burns had deep exposure to Friedman's views on monetary policy, and an almost Godlike ability to put them into action.

The basic structure of the Fed had not changed much from the institution Friedman and Schwartz had so deeply scrutinized. "The Fed" was not one central bank but a network of twelve regional banking systems. Atop this national network was the Federal Reserve Board, consisting of seven presidential appointees serving staggered fourteen-year terms. The real action, however, took place at the larger Federal Open Market Committee. Voting members of the FOMC included all members of the board, the president of the New York Fed, and a rotating set of regional Fed presidents. Even if they were not voting, all Fed presidents attended meetings and had their say. If the board was set up to encourage long-term decision-making that transcended the political cycle, the FOMC fostered short-termism by design. During the 1970s, the FOMC met as often as every three weeks, a hangover from the "fine-tuning" approach to economic policy.

Under the pressure of Wright Patman's relentless congressional hearings, the Fed had inched toward transparency. In 1967, attendance at the FOMC and its topics of discussion were finally made public. The inscrutable Record of Policy Actions generated by each meeting, previously released only in one annual batch, now came out after ninety days, accompanied by new Minutes of Action. The Fed also committed to releasing more detailed official minutes and memoranda—after a five-year lag.[26]

Power in this complex system was the chair's for the taking, if he could avoid political snares. The former Fed president Martin called the Federal Reserve "independent within the government," a maddeningly opaque charge that left much to interpretation. Martin's interpretation was that consensus helped maintain independence, and he followed this philosophy to a fault. Martin hated a divided board, and he hated to go against the president or Congress.[27]

Burns seemed destined to be a defining force at the Fed. If past history was to be a guide, his four-year term might be repeatedly renewed, giving him unusual power. Already, Burns was a Washington veteran. To a degree Martin would have considered unseemly, Burns was close to Nixon and a fixture in the White House. It was also important that Burns was fluent in economics, the language of policy. Friedman certainly believed Burns was uniquely poised to tackle inflation. And the media widely interpreted Burns's appointment as a victory for Friedman. With Burns at the helm, "the Fed will never again be quite so casual about whether or not 'money matters,'" wrote *The New York Times Magazine* in a lengthy profile of Friedman.[28]

The first signs of Burns's tenure were positive, from Friedman's perspective. To his delight, Burns seemed to be shifting the Fed toward emphasizing the quantity of money. This meant paying attention to monetary aggregates, which were a broad measure of available money, usually totaled at month's end from legally mandated bank reports. Aggregates made it possible to see if the amount of money in an economy was rising, falling, or staying the same. In 1960 the Fed began tracking a monetary aggregate called M1, composed of currency in circulation and bank deposits easily convertible to cash (such as checking accounts). Under Burns, the Fed announced it would report another aggregate, called M2, which added savings deposits to M1.[29] Friedman was pleased; M2 was the aggregate he and Schwartz preferred. "All reports that I hear concur about the excellent changes that you have been producing at the Fed," he wrote his mentor a few months into Burns's tenure. "I'm not surprised but I am delighted."[30] Although Burns had not announced that he was a monetarist, the new focus on aggregates implied sympathy for the approach. Friedman anticipated a golden era of Fed policy driven by science and research.

But then came a shock. Opening the newspaper one May evening, Friedman saw unbelievable headlines: "Wage Guide Urged by Burns in Break with Nixon Policy," announced *The New York Times*, while *The Wall Street Journal* had "Burns Backs Use of Wage-Price Program of Some Sort to Bolster Inflation Fight." All the major newspapers carried the story. In a speech at Hot Springs, Virginia, before a "glittering group of foreign central bankers, Government officials and private bankers from at home and abroad," convened for the American Bankers Association annual conference, Burns had come out in favor of "incomes policy." It would need to be short-term, Burns stressed, but "provided it stopped well short of direct wage and price controls," an incomes policy "might speed us through this transitional period of cost-push inflation." Despite the furor his remarks created, Burns declined to elaborate. It was not even a real recommendation, he noted, just a possibility to which "we shouldn't close our minds," he repeated twice for emphasis.[31]

Incomes policy had been in the air—but it was a Democratic Party idea. Generally, "incomes policy" referred to a range of regulations on wages and prices that stopped short of actual controls. It could encompass everything from "jawboning"—presidential rhetoric and coordinated social pressure—to voluntary guidelines like the New Deal's National Recovery Administration. The modern version was "guideposts," which Kennedy's Council of Economic Advisers (CEA) had popularized in 1962. The guideposts had done nothing to stop the outbreak of inflation at the end of Johnson's term. But they remained a favorite Democratic policy to address "Nixon's inflation." Some wanted to go farther; the Democratic-led Congress even passed legislation authorizing the president to impose wage and price controls.

Far more than a policy disagreement, for Friedman the speech was a profound rupture in his emotional universe. Later that evening, after hours of tossing and turning, Friedman arose from his bed and poured out his anguish. The "incomes policy speech" had left him sleepless, "saddened, dismayed, + depressed," he wrote to Burns in a passionate letter. "Though I know this is not fair or right or generous—the word that keeps coming to mind is 'betrayed.'" How could Burns—who had repeated again and again his stance against wage and price controls—make such a reversal?[32]

The letter tacked between incredulity and loss. "Never in my wildest dreams did I believe that the central bank virus was so potent that it could corrupt even you in so short a time," Friedman mourned. Maybe there was a case to be made for incomes policy, but he simply could not imagine what it was. "Incomes policy, in any shape + form, is bad economics + the entering wedge for still worse economics," he wrote. It would obscure the real progress recently made in slowing inflation. Incomes policy would get the credit that belonged to monetary restraint. And, Friedman continued, the proposal "verges, in my mind, on the dishonest in spreading lies to the public." It was simply not true that inflation was "produced by unions"—rather it was produced "only in Washington," by misguided policy.[33] Even Burns himself had said as much, in the past. Although Friedman called only the policy dishonest, the implications extended to Burns's character.

Stepping back, for a moment Friedman grasped that his letter was "melodramatic rather than cold and logical." But his missives to Burns had always resembled diary entries; never before had he dissembled or masked his feelings. It was obvious to all who knew him that Friedman loved being the smartest guy in the room. It was also clear he loved to smash idols. Pigou, Keynes, Samuelson—his whole life, names others worshipped were his targets. But underneath all this, imperceptibly running through the years, was a contrapuntal desire for a wise man, a counselor, a superior, someone to admire and esteem. Burns, arriving in the fatherless Friedman's life just as he considered his professional future, had played this role for decades. "Arthur, there remains no one whom I so admire + feel so close to—Rose only excepted—and so hate to hurt," Friedman told him in his closing lines.[34]

As a fellow Jewish man with immigrant roots who had risen fast and far, Burns was in some ways a natural father figure, but in other ways he never quite fit the role. Friedman's closest relationships were always with those who shared his fundamental orientation to economics and politics. True, he retained cordial relationships with his opponents. But friendship, as it developed in his life, was rarely about the simple joy of companionship. From his student days in Chicago to his marriage with Rose, Friedman had always blended ideological, professional, and personal ties. Burns's speech, with its reference to cost-push inflation, revealed a truth that was perhaps the most painful of all: Burns did not accept Friedman's theory of inflation.

The evidence had always been there. In 1946, Burns had even signed a letter to *The New York Times* in favor of extending the Office of Price Administration. And most tellingly of all, Burns offered no comments on *A Monetary History of the United States*, making vague excuses about a conflict of interest.[35] Through it all, Friedman had somehow managed to evade the obvious. Burns was an institutional economist and a moderate Republican, but he was not a Friedmanite or even Friedmanesque. The two men were poles apart on the most important economic issue of the time.

Soon after, Friedman realized to his horror that their differences would be the subject of wide public discussion. Two days after the first letter, and before Burns had responded, Friedman attached a lengthy postscript. At two recent talks in New York City—one to the Jewish United Fund and the other to a financial and investment group—audience members had asked, unprompted, for his views on Burns's speech. Friedman had anticipated he would have to stop praising Burns. But he had not yet processed that he would need to criticize him openly. Now he warned Burns, "I shall have to attack [the speech] publicly—as I was forced to last night—which I hate to do. Yet if Mr. Martin had made that comment, I would have blasted him + I must do the same in my next *Newsweek* column."[36] A few days later, he sent a draft of the column, which argued that an incomes policy is "likely to do immense harm."[37] A personal note repeated hopes they could meet soon in D.C. or Ely, Vermont, for the upcoming holiday weekend.

When the two finally connected over the phone, more than a week after Friedman's first midnight letter, Burns was cold. In fact, he didn't want to talk to anyone over the holiday, he told Friedman. "You were clearly politely saying that you did not want to talk to me," Friedman reflected in a second late-night scrawl. "I was so taken aback + so slow in comprehending what you were really saying that I fear I lapsed into incoherence." Their awkward conversation showed Friedman that "my earlier letter was a major blunder."[38] No less than Friedman, Burns must have felt betrayal, too. Here he was at the pinnacle of his career, under the white-hot lights of national fame—and his most trusted admirer and friend had only criticism to offer.

Disoriented, Friedman attempted to restore their former dynamic. "I had no intention of wrecking a friendship of near-40 years standing," he vowed, moving into abject apology. "The harm to me is clearly greater than to you," he stressed, as if Burns could slough him off at will. "Attribute the depth of my feeling to the depth of my regard for you," he pleaded. The groveling helped. But there had been a fundamental shift. Even Friedman's apologetic letter had a hidden barb; many others had similar reactions to the speech, he explained, but only he had been "foolishly impulsive" enough to tell Burns directly.[39]

In fact, it was fairly obvious that Burns had stepped in it. Thus far Nixon's chosen policy to combat inflation was gradualism. The name came from a comment by the CEA's chair, Paul McCracken, who told the press that stopping inflation "will have to be done easily. It will have to be done gradually."[40] Gradualism was inverted new economics. Instead of pursuing low unemployment and tolerating a little inflation along the way, gradualists pursued lower inflation and hoped unemployment would be tolerable. The alternative was a sharp crackdown. Friedman supported gradualism because it fit with his overarching goal for consistent, constrained money growth. Like the CEA, Friedman understood that a full frontal assault on inflation would create as many problems as it solved. It would cause a sharp recession, which was bad enough. And the resultant political fallout would lead the policy to be abandoned, he feared, potentially restarting the inflationary cycle.

Burns's sudden conversion to incomes policy threatened to undo all the careful work of the administration's first year. Newspaper reports widely noted that Burns had a reputation for opposing incomes policy, and speculated on the shift. *The Wall Street Journal* relied on Burns himself to argue against the policy, filling an editorial with his own past critiques of wage and price guidelines.[41] *The New York Times* marveled at his brinkmanship. From administration reports immediately contradicting the speech, it was clear he had gone rogue. "Having failed to make an impression on the White House," the newspaper explained, Burns had gone public. And this meant, the *Times* continued, he believed the economy was in deep peril. Good times were not right around the corner, as the administration proclaimed. Friedman reported a similar reaction from Wall Street executives: "My God, are things really that bad!" he paraphrased. "That [Arthur Burns] is led to reverse himself completely! Inflation must be really out of hand."[42] In the battle against inflation, perception was critical. Burns had just given inflationary expectations a huge boost.

Nixon was furious. He'd already been tiring of Burns's pipe puffing and his soporific lectures on economics. "Freeze" him out, he directed his lieutenant H. R. Haldeman.[43] Coming at this moment, the letters from Friedman were a considerable blow.

New patterns emerged in the aftermath. As Friedman reverted to technical letters about monetary policy, Burns interposed his staff between them, assigning others to respond in lengthy memos that Friedman found "defensive." It all sounded familiar, as if Friedman was still writing letters to Martin's Fed.[44] In turn, Friedman hit upon a new tactic: the cc. Where his letters had once gone only to Burns, now they were invariably copied to two other members of the administration: CEA chair McCracken and Shultz. If he couldn't influence Burns, perhaps these men could.

Everyone knew how Friedman venerated Burns. Few were aware of the growing bond between him and Shultz. Though born only a few miles away and eight years later than Friedman, Shultz was shaped by vastly different circumstances. His comfortable Protestant family sent him to boarding school and Princeton. Rather than the Great Depression, service in the U.S. Marines was the defining event of his youth. After the war, he pursued a doctorate in economics at MIT and was then hired on as a professor. At MIT, he had his first encounter with Friedman, watching in awe as he went up against Samuelson: "The evening consisted of a back and forth between the two of them, and one of them could say one word and the other one would know where they're going and say another word, and it was back and forth, and you got an evening where you came away saying, I just watched two of the most brilliant people I ever heard of talk." MIT left Shultz with a good understanding of the Samuelson approach to economic modeling. As he summarized, "Think of the economy as just a big computer, it's a big feedback mechanism. Prices and wages and quantities are put in and they interact and outcomes arrive . . . that's the way the economy works." But as an industrial economist—focused on labor markets—his education was also leavened by professors who were trained in psychology and economics, direct observation of labor negotiations, community studies, and even time spent living on a TVA demonstration farm in Tennessee.[45] In 1955, Shultz joined the Council of Economic Advisers under Burns. Afterward he returned to his professorial post at MIT.

A move to the University of Chicago in 1957 drew Shultz into Friedman's orbit. He joined the business school as a professor of industrial relations. Appointed dean a few years later, he moved into an office next to George Stigler, and the friendship with Friedman took off from there. Shultz had always been curious about Friedman's ideas, perhaps because they were verboten at MIT. While not a combatant in the wars over methodology, he had quietly moved away from Samuelson's mathematical approach to economic modeling. At Chicago, he thrived in the university's "intense intellectual turmoil," joining an overlapping group of scholars in the law school, economics department, and business school who were all interested in labor. The son of a man who taught finance at the New York Stock Exchange, Shultz had never been a radical, and now he imbibed a strong dose of Chicago price theory that reinforced his basic market orientation.

If Friedman's ideas were increasingly important to Shultz, there were nonetheless profound differences between the two. Where Friedman stood out immediately in any group, Shultz had a light touch and a willingness to move in and out of focus as circumstances dictated. *Newsweek* called him, sneeringly, "the greyest of the grey" in Nixon's administration.[46] What Shultz lacked in charisma he made up in empathy and a shrewd understanding of power. A pure intellectual, Friedman had never wanted anything other than an academic career. By contrast, Shultz had accumulated a variety of professional experiences in the military, as a university dean and labor arbitrator, and on government commissions. This background shaped his opinion of economics and policy. He was a solid Republican and a believer in free enterprise, but lacked Friedman's utopian cast. While Friedman insisted an unfettered price system would over time dissolve racial prejudice, Shultz advocated a different approach, derived from his time negotiating contracts in the segregated South. At the Chicago business school, he worked deliberately to increase enrollments of African American students and would go on to support federal affirmative action.[47] In short, Shultz was a generalist and a pragmatist. Or as Friedman summed it up: "George is a man of principle, not an ideologue like I am."[48] The joke obscured the one shared trait that bonded the men above all: a willingness to be unpopular in the pursuit of principle.

Nixon's election marked the start of Shultz's meteoric rise. Burns selected him to advise the candidate, and in 1969 came a plum offer: secretary of labor. A year later—just after Friedman sent Burns his tormented letters—Shultz was appointed as the first director of the newly created Office of Management and Budget. Nixon intended the OMB to assert executive power over the sprawling federal bureaucracy, and Shultz's appointment was a mark of his reputation for getting things done. In effect, Shultz had been designated chief budgetary officer of the U.S. government, with power to influence the spending decisions of all cabinet agencies. In a sign of his growing influence within the administration, he was given an office in the White House close to the president.

Friedman now shifted his attention to Shultz. As the manager of the budget, Shultz was concerned with inflation, insofar as it contributed to the general economic climate. But Friedman wrote to Shultz as if he were the chair of the Federal Reserve, sending him a continuous stream of updates on the money supply, all cc'd to Burns.

From Friedman's perspective, it was hard to say what was worse: Burns's fondness for incomes policy or his monetary policy, which looked increasingly reckless. In an October 1970 letter to Shultz, cc'd to Burns and McCracken, he offered a stark warning: The annual rate of growth in M1 (6 percent) and M2 (9 percent) "are higher levels than can be maintained indefinitely without a resumption of inflation."[49] Why was monetary growth so high? Friedman was writing a month before the midterm elections. In all likelihood, Burns was remembering the election of 1960, which had cost Nixon the presidency. Both Burns and Nixon believed that without a recession, Nixon would have won. The way to prevent a Republican shellacking now was by keeping money loose.

It wasn't that Burns single-handedly controlled the money supply. But he operated successfully within the FOMC's norm of unanimity. Every three weeks, the FOMC had to decide whether to buy more bonds—"printing" money—or to sell more bonds, "tightening" money. During Burns's term these regular meetings felt "like a graduate seminar," remembered one participant: Burns was the professor, and the committee members were his students. At each meeting the FOMC considered three scenarios or policy projections laid out in the Bluebook, named for its light blue cover. The Bluebook was composed by the Fed's professional staff in the Division of Research and Statistics, Ph.D. economists who had access to the latest legally mandated bank reports and figures. Derived from this data, scenarios A, B, and C suggested differing future paths for monetary aggregates, bank reserves, and interest rates. These scenarios would be achieved indirectly, through open market operations (sales or purchases of bonds).

Ostensibly, the board debated each scenario and then voted to choose one, which would be sent to the New York desk for execution. In practice, Burns always maneuvered the board to scenario B, seemingly the moderate consensus position. Yet scenario B was no technocratic projection, but a set of numbers Burns had forcefully negotiated beforehand with his staff. "It was all orchestrated," remembered one researcher bitterly, while another called the whole exercise "a sham."[50]

Easy money proved little help to Republicans in the 1970 election. Democrats held on to the Senate and increased their majority in the House of Representatives. In light of the election results, pressure began to mount within the White House to do something: incomes policy to cut down inflation, or goose the money supply to stimulate more growth. Shultz brought Friedman by the White House to reassure the president that the present economic policy was sound.[51] Though he encouraged the president to stick with gradualism, Friedman was worried. True, everyone was now talking about monetary aggregates. But Burns and Nixon focused primarily on M1, cash and checking accounts. The really dangerous growth, Friedman insisted, was coming in M2, which included savings deposits. Indeed, M2 had been growing at the astronomical rate of 10 percent across the past year; hence the increasingly urgent tone of his letters. In February 1971 he offered a less than reassuring conclusion: "It is too early to panic."[52] Friedman's message was consistent. Money growth was too high; the Fed was playing with fire.

As the figures revealed increasingly rapid money growth, Friedman lost his cool and started badgering Burns again. "I am appalled at the recent extremely rapid growth of all the monetary aggregates," he wrote in March 1971, tempering the letter with a postscript about the career prospects of Burns's son Joe. A long memo critiqued the Fed's operating procedures and suggested changes, perhaps to be developed in a Chicago workshop. Burns pushed back: "We are dealing here with a very short-term matter, and you must not exaggerate its implications for the future."[53] Even as economists at Brookings were confirming Friedman's accelerationist thesis, Burns saw inflation as a transitory threat. Nor did he see a real connection between monetary policy and inflation.

Instead, Burns began to argue that inflation should be tamed with wage and price controls—incomes policy having proven, as Friedman predicted, the "entering wedge for still worse economic policies." In June, Burns wrote to the president recommending a wage and price review board to be followed by "a six-month wage and price freeze." These extraordinary measures were necessary, he explained, because "the structure of the economy has changed profoundly." Economic models based on the 1940s or 1950s no longer applied, he argued, in an implicit reference to Friedman. And the Fed itself had nothing more to offer: "Monetary policy, I feel, has done its job fully."[54]

Mapping out the other side of the debate, Shultz counseled patience. The prescription for economic policy, Shultz argued, was "steady as you go." In a speech quoting Friedman, he argued that the Nixon administration was on course for low inflation, reduced unemployment, and steady economic expansion. But as Shultz would learn, "An economist's lag is a politician's nightmare."[55] Gradualism was turning out to be too gradual.

Even as Nixon portrayed himself as a free market stalwart, he had already begun to backslide. By midsummer 1971, he was determined to change course on economic policy.

To shake things up, Nixon turned to his charismatic new secretary of the Treasury, the Texas Democrat John Connally, most famous for having been shot by the same bullets that felled JFK in Dallas. Connally was the administration's new voice of economic policy, Nixon announced: "No more of this crap." One voice, one man, one policy.[56] At first, it seemed Connally had bought gradualism more time. The administration was on track, he boomed at a July press conference. There would be no wage and price controls, no wage-price board, no tax cuts, and no new spending. But Connally had been brought in to disrupt, and disrupt he would.

The package Connally devised—the inadvertently Soviet-sounding New Economic Plan—blended favored elements of both the Republican and Democratic parties. The NEP included tax cuts plus a wage and price freeze, similar to what Burns had suggested. Aware that such a drastic reversal might spook the international markets, Connally tacked on another provision: the United States would stop exchanging dollars for gold. In the parlance of the day, "the gold window" would be slammed shut.

Turbulence in international markets forced a quick adoption of the New Economic Plan. As inflation picked up, foreign firms selling to the U.S. market earned ever more dollars. These profits were more useful in a firm's home currency. So firms then approached their own central banks to make a currency exchange. But these central banks were bound by Bretton Woods parities, meaning they would be forced to print more of their own currency to meet the dollar onslaught—effectively importing inflation. Investing in the United States was one solution, but the U.S. markets were highly regulated for foreign investors. Instead, foreign central banks accepted all those dollars and requested the United States turn them into gold.

The steady stream of gold heading overseas became an atmospheric river. By early August, according to the Treasury undersecretary Paul Volcker, the United States was on "the brink of a market panic that willy-nilly would force us off gold."[57] Each morning when he arrived at work, Volcker found yet another request for gold crossing his desk. How long would foreign governments be willing to stick with the falling dollar? As cracks in the foundation spread, what if speculators began to dump dollars? The conditions for a bank run of global proportions were falling into place.

Nixon convened an emergency meeting of his top advisers, bundling them off to the presidential retreat of Camp David. Gradualism went down without much of a struggle. Despite the administration's public stance against controls, it was imagined that a temporary freeze would not be too hypocritical.

The real debate came over gold, and the real debater was Burns. Valiantly, he defended the importance of gold and the international system it underpinned. When Connally made a loaded statement against money changers—playing to Nixon's deep anti-Semitism—the Jewish Burns bravely forged onward. "May I speak up for the 'money changers'?" he asked, reminding the president that "central bankers are important to you."[58] Nixon listened, but was unconvinced. In the end, Burns vowed to support the president anyhow. He had gotten much of what he wanted. Worse than closing the gold window would be opening an irreparable breach between the president and the Federal Reserve.

Although it marked a breathtaking reversal in policy—only six weeks earlier, Connally had vowed the administration would not do any of the things it was now doing—the wage and price freeze proved incredibly popular. The "image of action" Nixon strove to project was in fact exactly what the nation craved. By far, the most popular part of the package was the freeze. Ordinary Americans cheered the break from rising prices. Business leaders were sure Nixon had reset the nation's mood, at once boosting confidence and defeating inflationary expectations. Labor leaders were among the few vocal dissenters. As the only interest group benefiting directly from inflation—in the form of generous wage hikes in contract after contract—labor unions rightly understood they had been targeted. But in Nixon's political calculus, a policy so popular could afford to create a few new enemies.

Friedman came out swinging against the freeze. "The result is likely to be more inflationary pressure, not less," he argued in *Newsweek*. The president would find he "has a tiger by the tail. Reluctant as he was to grasp it, he will find it hard to let go."[59] Once again, Friedman was right. By November, the sixty-day freeze had been extended.

Nixon worried about Friedman's move into open antagonism. Shultz was tasked to mollify Friedman, and invited him to the White House for a personal meeting with the president. "Don't blame George," Nixon told him. In Friedman's memory, he offered a zinger in response: "I don't blame George, Mr. President, I blame you."[60] No one pointed out there was at least one other man to blame: Arthur Burns.

Despite his opposition to domestic price controls, Friedman saw opportunity beyond the nation's borders. Before the inauguration, Friedman warned Nixon that "the balance of payments will be a running sore requiring action and capable of erupting into a crisis at any time." He explained his solution—a regime of floating exchange rates, where currencies traded freely without the constraints of Bretton Woods. Nixon ignored the memo. Now that the crisis had erupted, Friedman tried again.[61] Setting up a back channel to Shultz, Friedman worked to shape a fluid environment. After meeting with foreign central bank officials, he reported to Shultz: "They still have not faced up to the fact this is a new ball game."[62] Most countries eventually converged on a so-called dirty float: their exchange rates against the dollar could now fluctuate, but within a centrally determined range. The situation was tantalizingly close to a floating exchange rate regime.

Once again, Friedman found himself working at cross-purposes to Burns. Recognizing the links between currency and geopolitics, Burns began cultivating Henry Kissinger, who had been sidelined in the original discussions. Like Nixon, the national security advisor considered trade and economic questions "low diplomacy." In the vacuum, Connally had convinced the president to use these very issues to reassert American power on the global stage. Now Kissinger was paying attention. The NEP was cowboy diplomacy: swaggering, rough around the edges, willing to move fast and break things. Kissinger and Burns placed a much higher value on international relationships and traditional diplomacy. As the situation dragged on into the fall, Kissinger and Burns pushed Nixon to negotiate a settlement that reinstated the basic contours of what had been.

In the other corner was Shultz, who wanted to give Bretton Woods one last shove, letting floating exchange rates emerge in its place. He leaned on Friedman for support, setting up a meeting with him and Connally. In a follow-up letter, Friedman was strategic in his advice. Rather than pushing floating exchange rates—which had half evolved, anyway—he urged the secretary to hold firm, calling the post-NEP international monetary system "almost ideal for us." He further invoked Connally's sense of nationalism. It was critical that the United States "refuse to submit our domestic policies to control by foreign officials," he wrote, adding, "do not let the Eastern liberal press . . . mislead you on this score."[63]

In the short run, it was Kissinger and Burns who prevailed, helped by a stock market slowdown attributed to the international impasse. Historic summits with China and Russia were on the horizon; Nixon needed to arrive as the leader of a unified Western alliance. At the Smithsonian Institution in Washington, a new regime was hammered out. The United States would devalue the dollar while keeping the gold window closed. Fixed exchange rates negotiated from the top down remained. But setting a new, lower price for the dollar would reduce the inflationary pressure on other countries.

Friedman viewed these developments with dismay, calling them "defeat snatched from the jaws of victory."[64] In his view, the changes in exchange markets since August were excellent: "Flexibility has replaced rigidity. We do not need and should not seek specific commitments from other countries about exchange rates."[65] With new top-down exchange rates in place, the old system had been brought back to life, it seemed.

But in the long run, Bretton Woods was dead.[66] One of its fundamental pillars—gold convertibility—had been toppled. While the Smithsonian accords framed this as temporary, the United States would never again agree to convert foreign currencies into gold. The second major pillar of the system, fixed exchange rates, had been resurrected. But the interim had shown that currencies could indeed float one against the other. In his original paper, Friedman had argued that floating exchange rates did not mean instability and disorder. In fact, he argued the opposite. Rigid exchange rates could not accommodate change; only a crisis could break through. This "urge for certainty" was "itself a major source of insecurity by promoting measures that reduce the adaptability of our economic systems." The ultimate outcome, he argued, would be "a system of reasonably stable exchange rates."[67] Friedman, along with others, had been right in the first analysis: the old order was unsustainable. In the brief months after the ending of gold convertibility, some evidence had accumulated showing his second analysis might be right, too.

During the fall of 1971, Nixon's attention shifted increasingly toward the presidential election of 1972. There were many reasons to be optimistic. Price controls—now administered by a full-blown Pay Board and Price Commission—had put a lid on inflation. During the next critical election year, the Consumer Price Index (CPI), a widely accepted measure of inflation, would average a respectable 3.27 percent. Nixon's policy of "Vietnamization" had begun to drain urgency from the anti-war movement and made credible his claims that peace was in sight. There had not been a major urban riot since 1969.

Despite the odds, Nixon was paranoid. Out of the paranoia came a mixed bag of dirty tricks meant to ensure his reelection, including the fateful burglary at the Watergate complex.

Nixon's paranoia also led to monomania about the money supply, a sign of vestigial trauma from his 1960 loss. Burns shared Nixon's sensitivity to tight money in an election year. But the drastic changes of the New Economic Plan—particularly the closing of the gold window—had unexpected implications for monetary policy.

Coming into the NEP, interest rates were relatively high. The Fed still followed Martin's dictum of leaning against the wind, so for much of 1971 policy had been expansive, in order to lower interest rates. But the NEP changed the game. First, foreign buyers rushed to U.S. Treasurys amid uncertainty. This pushed interest rates lower because buyers wanted security, not a high return. Second, Nixon's dramatic announcement created uncertainty about how the NEP would work. Business borrowers adopted a "wait and see" mentality, slowing loan activity and further depressing rates. All the Fed could see, however, was that interest rates were now sinking too low. The FOMC had overshot the mark, its members believed. Like a sailboat drifting off course, they had to change direction to get where they wanted to go. In order to raise interest rates, they had to make money scarce. A letter Friedman sent to Shultz in November 1971 recorded the result. Monetary growth had slowed sharply after the August NEP. For most of the year, M2 had grown at an annual rate of 16.2 percent. From late August through October, it had fallen to 3.1 percent. Growth in M1 had turned negative. Burns's policy now looked reckless in the other direction.

While Friedman was no fan of expansionary policy, neither did he approve of sudden tightening. The whole point of a monetary rule was stable and steady monetary growth that faded away into background noise, leaving businesses, workers, and consumers free to transact without worrying about radical price changes. With the sudden fall in available money, however, the stage was set for a recession when the contraction took hold, he warned Shultz. This was the central lesson Friedman had learned from the Great Depression: deprive the economy of money too quickly, and disaster would result. Friedman followed up with a letter to Shultz summarizing their discussion. "I feel like an unimaginative dullard to say the same thing over and over again, yet I repeat what I have said all along," Friedman wrote. Ignore interest rates, focus on aggregates, and stick to 4 to 5 percent money growth.[68]

Shultz took this warning to Nixon, who immediately understood its gravity. The next day, Burns recorded alarming news in his diary. If economic conditions worsened, "the White House staff has formulated a plan to blame the Fed . . . The argument will be that Fed failed to permit a sufficiently rapid rate of growth of the money supply." Nixon followed up with a stern letter instructing him to expand the money supply. And then came the very same sentiments from Friedman, leaving little doubt of his role in the campaign.[69]

Ironically, Burns needed little urging to loosen money—he already had a plan in place. Timing was everything. While Burns had not accepted many of Friedman's ideas, he and the FOMC understood that lags were part of monetary policy. It took time for FOMC decisions to percolate through the economy. While Friedman was worried about a future recession, Burns felt confident he could head it off with a dose of expansion. The trick would be to time that expansion with the political cycle. With an eye on the upcoming 1972 election, Burns told the FOMC in October 1971 that he didn't want to act too soon. If the Fed was too expansive now, it might have to change course and raise interest rates in 1972, which "could result in serious difficulties," the minutes recorded. There was little further discussion, as the FOMC caught his drift.[70]

Meanwhile, Friedman was growing almost hysterical. "What in God's name is happening?" he blasted Burns in a December letter, cc'ing Shultz. The most recent figures showed money was still tight. True, he had worried about "the danger of overheating . . . but the danger provided no excuse for going to the other extreme and putting the economy in the deep freeze." Friedman repeated his fear of recession. Like Burns, he wanted to see Nixon reelected; he even referenced the fateful 1960 slowdown. His letter also raised another worry—"a swing back to the other extreme of an inflationary rate of monetary growth." At some point, Friedman anticipated, the Fed would switch course and make another of its "wild swings."[71] In less than a month, his prediction would come true.

Heading into 1972, Burns was finally ready to chart a course for monetary ease. In January, he rescheduled the FOMC meeting to create more runway for monetary policy. In February, he proposed that M2 grow at 12 percent each quarter. Not all members of the FOMC were comfortable with this path; debates about policy in this critical period were "one of the most protracted there had even been," one board member recalled. As chairman, Burns successfully fended off minority voices worried about excessive monetary expansion.[72]

It helped that most of the board—all men with backgrounds in finance and business—were Democratic appointees familiar with the logic of the new economics. The thinking went as follows. Unemployment was now higher than 4 percent, the magic number denoting full employment. Therefore, many FOMC members believed there was "slack" in the economy—a gap between actual and potential GNP. In turn, this meant there was plenty of room for economic expansion without inflation. Like the Kennedy CEA, members of the FOMC believed price controls would effectively handle any inflationary outbreak. And for the time being, they did, depriving the FOMC of critical feedback. The FOMC experienced the upside of expanding the money supply, pushing off the downside until after the election.[73]

In retrospect, it is easy to draw a link between Nixon's political anxieties and the surge in monetary growth that unfolded across 1972. But if there were no election, and no pressure campaign, would Burns have conducted monetary policy differently? Given the overall pattern of his eight-year tenure, presidential pressure cannot be the root explanation of his monetary policy, or of the Great Inflation it abetted.

Burns's approach to inflation was flawed. Critically, he did not distinguish between changes in relative prices and systemic inflation—a rise in the general price level. That allowed him to believe that inflation could be cordoned off into specific parts of the economy and tamed with price controls. This was a surprising conclusion for a student of business cycles to reach. It was even more surprising given his reputation as an inflation fighter. But Burns was not a monetarist, or a macroeconomist, or a price theorist; he was not even really a follower of the new economics, although sometimes he sounded like it. Rather, Burns was an institutionalist. In his mind, it was reasonable that policies and approaches from another time—even those he had once followed—should adjust with the path of history. Because he believed the fundamentals of the economy had changed, Burns had confidence that wage and price controls would control inflation. As he announced to Nixon's cabinet in 1972, "Without a lower wage guideline next year . . . inflation cannot be brought under control."[74] There was nothing else the Fed could do—for good or for ill.

Here was where shutting out Friedman did the most damage. Friedman was among a small handful of economists who rightly understood the Fed's awesome powers and the dangers of inflation. Burns had at his fingertips an independent expert who would not trim, sugarcoat, or prevaricate to please the boss. It was not that Friedman was right all the time. Yet his overall big-picture impressions were dead-on. Friedman had amassed impressive evidence showing that monetary policy was relevant to inflation. The prideful Burns pushed these efforts away. Even as it was gaining credibility among economists, Burns conspicuously resisted Friedman's accelerationist thesis—the idea that inflation tended to get worse over time. Not only did he reject the idea; he never even paused to consider the possibility it could be true. His time horizon remained stubbornly short.

As it turned out, the machinations from money to Watergate were largely superfluous to the election of 1972. Simply put, the Democratic

Party had not recovered from the Johnson years. The fall of LBJ had empowered activists in the party, who moved to disenfranchise the working-class machines that had once made and broken candidates. Now in the thrall of the "new politics," Democrats nominated George McGovern, an anti-war senator beloved by the new grassroots.[75] Easily stereotyped as a liberal supporter of "amnesty, abortion, and acid," the peacenik McGovern was little threat to Nixon's dream of a broad majority. Just as Republican elders had hung back from Barry Goldwater, so too did the Democratic Party leaders view McGovern with unease. A few high-profile names even converted into "Democrats for Nixon."

In the end, McGovern carried only the District of Columbia and one state—Massachusetts. Within a few years, this would be a claim to fame, yielding the popular bumper sticker "Don't Blame Me." But for now, a new Nixon had emerged. Even before the election, Nixon could taste victory. As Burns recorded in his diary, Nixon appeared "relaxed, seems to have more confidence in himself . . . A man who feels that he finally has not only position in the world, but great power as well."[76]

By then, Shultz had been vaulted onto a much larger playing field: Nixon named him secretary of the Treasury after Connally departed. The position came with senior positions in the multinational organizations that governed international finance. Friedman's closest administration confidant would be a governor of the International Monetary Fund, which administered the wheezing Bretton Woods system, and a high-ranking official at the World Bank and the Inter-American Development Bank. He was now the longest-serving member of the so-called Troika—an interagency group drawn from the OMB, the CEA, and Treasury—that shaped U.S. economic policy. More important, he still held Nixon's confidence. The president insisted Shultz keep his offices in the White House to underscore his closeness to the chief.

The first order of business was Bretton Woods. The Smithsonian Agreement had solved the immediate impasse, but it did not inspire confidence. "I hope it lasts three months," Volcker had prayed aloud at its signing. Volcker knew, as did most at Treasury, that it was a tenuous and unstable arrangement. Nonetheless, he had a fealty to the system that defied logic or analysis. Bretton Woods was "a way of life," Volcker remembered, and he was not prepared to see it go.[77]

The stable dollar, the fixed gold price: these were the emblems of peace, prosperity, and American leadership. For Europeans, they stood between order and chaos, staving off another world war. For Americans, they symbolized national prestige and responsibility. "Certainly, the idea that a devaluation of the dollar might be needed or that we might initiate a change in the gold price was not a respectable matter for discussion in the halls of the Treasury," recollected Volcker, who had been there for more than a decade.[78] When Shultz pressed Connally for floating exchange rates, Volcker rebuffed his efforts. The Treasury had a plan, Shultz was told, and the plan was secret.

Once he became the boss, Shultz divined the truth: there was no plan.[79] The idea was to muddle through. Shultz turned to Friedman. The two men were already simpatico, believing floating exchange rates ought to rest at the center of international exchange.

This was the ultimate extension of Chicago price theory. Without government regulation, the price of money itself was subject to supply and demand. Nations themselves would become like producers of goods, forced to compete in an international market, compelled to offer political stability, desirable products, and attractive opportunities for capital investment. However appealing this idea was to Shultz and Friedman, they realized few were ready to follow their logic. Volcker described Shultz's earlier suggestion of floating exchange rates as a "bombshell." According to him, it would "plainly not be negotiable, could only further poison the atmosphere, and was not in any event desirable."[80] Volcker's response was a basic failure of the imagination, clothed in the inheritance of history.

Shultz and Friedman's idea incorporated this basic failure of imagination, while moving toward their ultimate goal. "I talked over it a lot with Milton, and in our discussions, we came up with a basic idea,"

Shultz remembered. "People liked what were called par values," in which the relative values of currencies were officially designated, much as they had been under the original Bretton Woods agreement. But now, Friedman and Shultz proposed, these par values would be linked to the reserves a country held, and would automatically change as the reserves changed. Essentially, "we concocted a floating-rate system in the clothing of a par-value system," Shultz concluded.[81] It was like countless discussions over economics and policy Friedman had conducted with his friends. But this time, the conclusion went not into an academic paper but into a speech Shultz delivered before the annual World Bank and IMF meeting.

If gold was the bang, floating rates were the whimper. Although it was not immediately adopted, Shultz and Friedman's proposal proved an essential step toward legitimating the idea of floating exchange rates. Indeed, Shultz had maneuvered so tactfully that Volcker believed the plan was his own doing, with Friedman providing only "some useful rhetorical flourishes."[82] (In fact, Volcker had guided most of the staff work, but remained unaware of Friedman's coordination with Shultz.) At the same time, Volcker and other Bretton Woods loyalists dimly suspected they had been deceived. "Some cynically concluded the whole proposal might be a complicated smoke screen," Volcker recounted. The proposal threw down a challenge: Could "really meaningful elements of exchange rate flexibility be introduced into a par value system without that system's shaking apart sooner or later"?[83] Friedman and Shultz believed the answer was no. But having lost the intellectual debate, due in large part to the emotional sway of Bretton Woods, they set up a real-world test of the concept.

By that time, events were in the saddle. Another shock came in the fall of 1973. Upset about the United States' support for Israel in the Yom Kippur War, the major oil-producing countries—organized in the OPEC cartel—engineered both a steep price rise in oil and an embargo against the United States. The U.S. pullback from Bretton Woods had effectively removed price control on gold. Now the prices of gold, oil, and dollars all began to gyrate. By the end of 1974, the

European nations had realized there was little possibility of restoring "a highly structured system," in Volcker's words.[84] They formally withdrew from negotiations to restore Bretton Woods.

It helped that Shultz had little incentive to renew the discussion. The dirty float and the period of "muddle through" had done much to help central bankers and finance ministers imagine a world beyond fixed rates. The world had not fallen apart, after all. The most important result was perhaps the most predictable. The dollar remained dominant.[85] Even without gold, even given the problems in its economy, the power of the United States made it a par value unto itself. In time, the IMF would formalize the new order with a revision to Article 4 of its charter. Where the original Bretton Woods Agreement called for a "system of stable exchange rates," the revised wording committed nations to a "stable system of exchange rates."[86]

Considered narrowly, the 1978 agreement simply codified reality, and as such was not a revolution. But the end of Bretton Woods surely was. As Volcker knew, Bretton Woods was something larger than paper. It had undergirded a certain way of looking at the world, one in which the United States valued alliances and codependency more than independence. If Friedman was right to see that tearing down the system would presage an era of greater interconnectedness through trade, he missed the diplomatic work that the agreements were doing. Further, Bretton Woods connected to a larger political economy in which the federal government accepted responsibility for full employment, supported welfare programs ranging from medical care to retirement insurance, and mediated between big business and big labor.[87] As the United States turned, so did the rest of the world.

Shultz's tenure at Treasury marked the high-water mark of Friedman's influence. In many ways, Shultz became Friedman's "instrument of policy," as a longtime student and friend summarized.[88] Together, the two were a formidable team, each compensating for the other's weaknesses. Friedman was the seer, giving Shultz a measure of his clairvoyance. Shultz was the doer, keeping the confidence of the president, fading to gray even as he pulled the puppet strings. Throughout the Nixon administration, Friedman had been learning important lessons. One was to frame policy in terms of election results, while still staying focused on the long run. The single most important lesson, however, was to find the right messenger.

Despite their long association, Friedman was powerless against Burns's rudderless monetary policy. The two men traded dueling velocity figures across 1973, even as Burns maintained the economy was now doing fine. Manifestly, it was not. The year of Nixon's reelection had been the calm before the storm, with price controls holding down inflation to a reasonable 3.2 percent. After controls were relaxed postelection, inflation roared back, surging to 6.1 percent during 1973. Interest rates were also high, with the benchmark ten-year Treasury note reaching 8.16 percent, even as unemployment remained uncomfortably high at 4.9 percent.[89] All the elements Friedman had predicted in 1967 were now in place. "Stagflation," that unpleasant combination of high unemployment and high inflation, was no longer a controversial theory but a lived reality. And Friedman's once absurd insistence that interest rates were not the key to inflation was making increasing sense. Conventional wisdom held that high interest rates would slow down the economy. But the economic indicators that were supposed to balance one another out—unemployment, inflation, and interest rates—were instead all moving together to new heights.

Friedman had an explanation for the interest-rate puzzle that would become widely accepted. It went back to the same distinction between *nominal* and *real* that he highlighted in his presidential address. "Is an interest rate of 10 percent high?" he asked *Newsweek* readers in 1976.[90] It was a trick question. That might be the nominal rate—announced at the bank, in the newspapers, by the Treasury Department. If prices were stable, 10 percent was indeed high. But if inflation was running at 9 percent, the *real* interest was low—scarcely 1 percent. This had huge implications for Fed policy. The Fed looked at nominal interest rates, and thought money was tight. But across the 1970s real interest rates were low, a sign of monetary ease. This difference between real

The 1970s appearance of stagflation—high unemployment and high inflation at the same time—was powerful support for Friedman's ideas.

and nominal fed into another critical distinction from the presidential address, one that went back to Alfred Marshall. In the short run, a high interest rate might dampen economic activity and slow inflation. But over the long run, causality reversed. To be meaningful, interest rates had to be higher than inflation. Over time, if inflation was rising, so too would interest rates.

The reputation of Burns was beginning to slide. As Patman entered the final years of his half-century-long political career—he would die in 1976—a new group of Fed critics emerged, the Shadow Open Market Committee (SOMC). Founded in 1973 by Anna Schwartz, Allan Meltzer, and other leading monetarists, the group was modeled on the British political system, where the opposition party staffed a shadow cabinet to criticize the government. In this case, the SOMC paralleled the real FOMC, bringing together a group of twelve economists for regular meetings and then releasing a public statement. The SOMC produced steady criticism of Burns's "poorly conceived" policy, announcing after its first meeting "the failure to control inflation was not inevitable." The SOMC was widely covered in the press and became a formidable training ground for policy-makers. Eventually, its members would end up at the OMB, the White House, and even the Fed.[91]

The group rescued Schwartz from her relative anonymity. She hardly ever missed a meeting and served on the small committee that drafted each group statement, insisting the group state its positions "clearly and forcefully." Seeing her in action, Meltzer was wowed. She was "as skilled in her use of language as in her economic analysis," he remembered.[92] As Schwartz's profile rose, she began to collaborate with other economists, often Friedman students. Monetarism was now more than Friedman and Schwartz: a distinct school had emerged that took their work as a launching point. Brunner and Meltzer were out in force, working to translate monetarism into a model non-monetarists could appreciate. New publication series, conferences, and academic journals were started, including the *Journal of Monetary Economics* and the *Journal of Money, Credit and Banking*. The Fed, with its insulated appointees serving fourteen-year terms, remained impervious.

It was more than a matter of understanding inflation. Economists were beginning to accept that in the long run—which might be shorter than anyone wished—it was not possible to push down unemployment without accelerating inflation. They could clearly see that high inflation, high unemployment, and high interest rates could coexist. Maybe Friedman was right that monetary aggregates were the key. He had been right to argue guideposts and controls would not work. Yet even if Friedman were right about everything—there still seemed to be no painless way to rein in inflation. The SOMC warned darkly: "There is no way to end inflation without cost." The nation was caught in an inflation trap. Monetary contraction of any kind implied a deliberate and protracted economic slowdown. Growth was the watchword of Washington. Who would deliberately cause a recession?[93]

In midsummer, Friedman received a pointed letter from a reader he did not know. "You used to flagellate the Federal Reserve for its misdeeds. And you had good reason," remembered the reader. "But the reasons you have had since 1969 have been far more compelling. And yet for the most part you seem to have remained silent and diplomatic."[94] The letter prompted a reckoning of sorts. "Mea culpa," Friedman pleaded in response, explaining, "Arthur Burns is a revered former teacher of mine, one of my closest personal friends for forty years, and also a man for whose character and ability I have tremendous admiration."[95] He had offered some critiques of the Fed recently, Friedman noted. Nonetheless Friedman agreed the Fed was basically inflationary. He would say as much in his next *Newsweek* column.

Almost as if he could see it coming, Burns granted *The New York Times* an interview defending his approach. The article noted a steady drumbeat of criticism against the Fed: "It has been possible in the last three or four months for an outsider to make something of a joke of the Federal Reserve." Every month, the newspaper recounted, the FOMC would declare that monetary growth should be slow, "and then the numbers would come in. Growth of money and credit had, in fact, been very fast." In the interview, Burns passed the buck. Private supply and demand, including a global commodities boom, were at fault. He closed with a direct jab at Friedman. Whether money grew at 4.5 percent or 6.1 percent, "the difference would have been negligible."[96] The very same day, Friedman posted to Burns a draft of his latest column, titled "The Inflationary Fed."

Written for the lay reader, in the column Friedman stuck to basic facts. Since January 1970, M1 had averaged 7 percent, in contrast to the low inflation years of 1948 to 1966, which saw average M1 growth of 2.3 percent. While Burns said all the right things, leading economists to expect a new period of restraint, "our hopes have been shattered." What could explain the shift? "I must confess that I am baffled," Friedman concluded.[97]

When Burns responded with a defensive letter, Friedman set down a longer, more technical response. Given an expected lag of eighteen months in monetary policy, he warned Burns that "we have so far only experienced the initial effects of the past 2½ years of rapid monetary growth, that regardless of near-term monetary policy, regardless of controls, regardless of whether we have slowdown, mini recession, or recession in 1974, the prospect is for at least 1½ to 2 years of inflationary pressure at about 5 percent to 7 percent rate for CPI." Expecting anything else, Friedman continued, was "wishful thinking."[98]

Among the last substantive letters that Friedman would send to Burns, this one revealed that his patience was running out. Friedman recognized that correcting inflation might cause more unemployment, but if a change of course was not politically feasible, then the nation would simply have to accept high inflation as a norm—and prepare for still higher inflation in the future. He offered a stinging defense of his approach:

> This may be "crude quantity theory," but I know the objections raised thereto, the other factors emphasized, and believe—rightly or wrongly—that no qualifications introduced by sophisticated quantity theorists or by crude or sophisticated Keynesians alter the broad outlines of this analysis. I am also quite aware that correlation is not causation, + devoted my contribution to 1964 annual report of the NBER entirely to that question in re. money and business.

The letter closed on an ominous note. He was writing not for a reply but because he felt impelled to share "my strong feeling that the severity of the inflation problem that we face is greatly underestimated." The following year, inflation in the United States clocked in at 11 percent.[99]

By then, both Shultz and Nixon were gone. When the president reimposed wage controls, Shultz stepped down. He would leave office in March 1974, four months before Nixon resigned amid the Watergate scandal. Vice President Gerald Ford took up the presidency and continued the ineffectual fight against rising prices, most famously in his Whip Inflation Now program of voluntary restraint. But now the Great Inflation was well under way and would not be so easily stopped.

Over time, Friedman's verdict on Burns's culpability became widely accepted. The early 1970s were threaded with economic turmoil and change, from Bretton Woods to the oil shocks. Underlying it all was an expansive monetary policy, guided by Burns. "Monetary policy lost its anchor," summarizes one economist. Other industrialized nations, from Germany to Japan, weathered the same macroeconomic storms with stable prices.[100] Before Watergate closed over his head, Nixon renominated Burns to a second term chairing the Federal Reserve Board. He would serve until 1978.

Friedman had always venerated Burns, continuing to treat him with deference even as his career transformed them into equals. In turn, Burns perpetually regarded Friedman as some sort of overgrown undergraduate; a welcome contributor to research, but certainly not someone with meaningful ideas that might alter his own. He may even have perversely resisted his former student's advice, just to keep the hierarchy intact.

During the Ford administration, Friedman's letters to Burns trickled to a halt. Inflation remained stubbornly high, hovering at almost 9 percent in 1975 before surging again to 11 percent and then, in 1980, reaching an unprecedented 13.5 percent. Burns would go down in history as the man on the watch during the Great Inflation, with prices during his tenure climbing an average of 7 percent annually.[101] What was there left to say, except "I told you so"?

12

SIX DAYS IN SANTIAGO

> By locking up productive resources within our tight economic borders, the country remains dependent on the growth rate of its small domestic markets.
>
> —El Ladrillo, 1973

It was a moment with all the pomp and circumstance the Royal Court of Sweden could summon: a stage ringed with pink roses and row upon row of white-tie-clad dignitaries, a gleaming orchestra blaring trumpet voluntary, the honorees seated in a semicircle steps from the boyish king and his new queen, glittering in a tiara and yellow gown. Silence fell as Milton Friedman stood, light on his feet, buoyant as the announcer intoned, "I now turn to you . . ." A sharp whistle cut over his next words. At first it seemed a mistake. Then, insistently, the whistle sounded again, twice more. A hoarse shout broke across the room: "Friedman go home!"

All eyes swung to a young man in the upper seats, now struggling with his neighbors. As a police officer closed in, he shouted out again, arms waving. Friedman's upper lip twitched once, almost imperceptibly. Then an icy mask settled over his face as he watched the interloper, a leftist university student, disrupt this pinnacle moment of his life.

The minutes dragged into hours, it seemed, as the flailing activist was pulled from his seat, one last cry of "Vive Chile!" echoing across the shocked room before the announcer regained command. "I am so sorry for this incident," he said stiffly. "It could have been worse." At this Friedman's trademark grin broke across his face, as welcome as the sun on a cloudy day, and the room exhaled in a grateful laugh.[1]

Unprecedented as the disturbance had been, it had not been impossible to predict. Friedman's selection as the winner of the 1976 Nobel Prize in Economics had been immediately denounced in an open letter to *The New York Times*. Outside the ceremony, five thousand protesters swarmed the streets of Stockholm, hoisting signs that read "Friedman-murderer" and "No to Friedman."[2] At issue was Friedman's connection to the murderous regime of Augusto Pinochet in Chile. A year ago, Friedman had paid his first visit to the country. During his six-day stay, he met with government officials, including Pinochet. In the context of his widening fame—which the Nobel Prize dramatically increased—this brief meeting transformed him into a global emblem of the twentieth century's central political conflict: the struggle between socialism and capitalism, top-down economic planning and free markets.

Smasher of idols no more, Friedman himself was now the target.

"We are all monetarists," announced Franco Modigliani in his 1976 presidential address to the American Economic Association, "if by monetarism is meant assigning to the stock of money a major role in determining output and prices." It was a stunning admission. Modigliani and Friedman had long been on opposite sides of economic debate. Modigliani had designed a large econometric model for the Federal Reserve, the institution Friedman unceasingly attacked. The two had fought the legendary Battle of the Radio Stations, dueling over the relative impact of fiscal and monetary policy. MIT, home to both Modigliani and Paul Samuelson, had defined itself against the Chicago school for much of the postwar era.[3]

Coming exactly ten years after Friedman's speech, which included his famous attack on the Phillips curve, Modigliani's address was not a complete surrender. Even as he detailed how "the Monetarists' criticisms of early, simple-minded Keynesianism has proved in considerable measure correct," Modigliani noted the importance of oligopolistic pricing, questioned Friedman's historic measures of monetary stability, and asserted that Keynesian analyses were still relevant in the medium and short term. Most important, Modigliani stressed that stabilization policies could not be abandoned or replaced with a rule. Modigliani did have a long-standing interest in money; Friedman even considered some of his early work proto-monetarism. Nonetheless, it was a major retreat. Along with Robert Solow, James Tobin, and Samuelson, Modigliani had embodied Keynesianism for decades.[4]

Even as Modigliani totted up the wins and losses, the battlefield was transforming. "The old division between monetarists and Keynesians is no longer relevant," Robert Hall wrote in a widely read 1976 workshop paper. From an emerging scholar's vantage point, Modigliani's certification narrative was old news. As Hall noted, "What used to be the standard monetarist view is now middle-of-the-road, and is widely represented, for example, in Cambridge, Massachusetts."[5] Instead, Hall divided the field into "saltwater" and "freshwater" economists. By saltwater, Hall mainly meant universities on the East Coast, the old stomping grounds of the new economics. Freshwater was not just Chicago but also included Minnesota and Carnegie Mellon. And freshwater was not really about Friedman—it denoted a new Chicago school: rational expectations theory. Sometimes cast as "a special and extreme case of monetarism," or even the "third Chicago school," rational expectations was most closely associated with Robert Lucas, who joined the Chicago faculty in 1974, just three years before Friedman's retirement.[6]

The new school jumped off Friedman's insistence that expectations were a critical driver of inflation. Lucas clarified a key piece of Friedman's story in his presidential address: the part where a storekeeper confronts a sudden influx of buyers willing to pay higher prices. The storekeeper hires new help, Lucas argued, only if this new demand is unexpected and misunderstood as a fundamental change in the business. If the storekeeper knew it was just inflation at work, retail prices might go up. But there would be no additional hiring, as the shopkeeper anticipated everything else would also cost more.

This was all the process of academic discovery working as it should; Friedman had opened a door, and younger scholars were walking through it. In important ways, rational expectations vindicated Friedman. Early papers by Lucas and Thomas Sargent, another key leader in the field, provided theoretical validation for the natural rate and accelerationist hypotheses. Both economists were also inspired by Friedman's book *A Theory of the Consumption Function*, which applied expectations of future income to explain consumer behavior.[7]

But in other ways rational expectations abandoned key tenets of monetarism. Friedman claimed money was fundamentally neutral, in that it alone could not generate real or sustained economic activity. Lucas and his followers extended neutrality further. In the same paper where he claimed "it is widely agreed that monetary policy should follow a rule," Sargent advanced what was later called the "policy ineffectiveness proposition."[8] If the Federal Reserve fell into the habit of surging money to combat recessions, eventually people would catch on, and they would no longer respond with more hiring and spending. "People do read the newspapers," Sargent stated in *Newsweek*, which reported on "the newest theory of inflation."[9] Rational expectations was adding up to the claim that even monetary policy didn't matter. As Hall noted: "An important element of fresh-water doctrine is the proposition that monetary policy has no real effect."[10] This idea went beyond the paradox of monetary policy that Friedman had often noted, and came close to recapitulating the older view of a passive monetary veil. It threatened to defang monetary policy altogether.

Fiscal policy was subject to the same challenge, according to the new school. Government stimulus worked by widening the gap between business profits and costs—especially labor. Wage rates stayed constant while business owners enjoyed increased sales and prices. But what if workers expected this change, and bargained for higher wages as soon as stimulus policies were announced? The policy channel would no longer work. In short, viewed through a rational expectations lens, demand management was a fool's errand. Of course, outside of exceptional times like the Great Depression, Friedman had never wanted activist policy, fiscal or monetary. Both he and Lucas agreed on the need for stable monetary rules—one reason Lucas was sometimes mistaken for a monetarist. But Lucas and Friedman opposed discretionary monetary policy for different reasons. Friedman thought policymakers would make bad decisions; rational expectations taught that their decisions were irrelevant.[11]

Rational expectations was at once testimony to Friedman's influence and a reorientation of economics away from his favored approach. Lucas created general equilibrium models—of the Cowles Commission style that Friedman had once decried—that incorporated the idea of expectations. The real goal of rational expectations was to reformulate Samuelson's neoclassical synthesis. There had always been a troublesome disjuncture between price theory, applied to individual decision-making, and Keynesian demand management, applied to the macroeconomy. The Lucas models bridged this gap by rigorously applying utility functions, budget constraints, and other tools of price theory to macro behavior, like inflation. The Lucas models also included monetary policy rules. A model with expectations had to bring together unpredictable movements with regular and predictable patterns of behavior—in essence, a rule. But monetary rules were not needed for philosophical or political reasons about the role of government; they were needed to make the model work.

Lucas was not shy about the implications of his work. "Keynesianism economics is dead," he told a Chicago audience. The paradigm had failed; the only remaining task was to "sort through the wreckage," Lucas and Sargent wrote in a 1979 Fed publication.[12] This was hyperbole—sort of. Just as Friedman had once set the weather in economics, Lucas-style rational expectations models and approaches rapidly became dominant. Even skeptics of the approach found themselves using the methodology. By the mid-1970s, papers using any other approach looked dated.

Friedman was ambivalent about the new school. As his colleague Arnold Harberger summarized: "He liked it, and he didn't like it." According to Gary Becker, Friedman opposed the new literature at first, but ended up "making an accommodation with it."[13] Friedman could see rational expectations was the rising trend in economics, perceived the ways it validated some of his most treasured ideas, and supported

Lucas's hiring at Chicago. Yet he criticized the more extreme versions of the theory, worrying that "there is a tendency to carry them much too far and convert them into fads."[14] Expectations might adjust to policy, Friedman argued, but they did so slowly. Whether he chose to view rational expectations as vindication or a challenge, its arrival marked a change of seasons in economics. New men and new ideas were now defining the cutting edge.

At the same time, Friedman's intellectual energies were shifting to a wider canvas. He and Rose left Chicago often, visiting five countries in 1969 and four in 1970, along with numerous stops across the United States. The couple upgraded from "the Hideaway" to "Capitaf," a stunning new custom-built home on 110 acres in the Vermont woods. Inspired by the Freedom School, a libertarian retreat in Colorado that the Friedmans had visited, Capitaf was a hexagon, twenty-two feet on each side, centered on "a massive Vermont slate fireplace rising to a cathedral ceiling of huge beams," as a realtor's description enthused. Wide windows opened to a spectacular view across the hills, while a summer wing added living space for guests. "It is beautiful here in all months," continued the house description, "white birches are etched against green pine and spruce in summer; and oaks, maples, aspens and beech flame in the autumn."[15] Starting in 1971, the Friedmans began spending June to December in this paradise.

As he spent more time away from Chicago, Friedman began detaching himself from professional debates. In 1970 he had been willing to write up a monetarist model in a professional journal, an effort published in book form as *Milton Friedman's Monetary Framework: A Debate with His Critics*.[16] But the drubbing he took had not been pleasant. Ultimately, Friedman concluded, "it was really a waste, I think, trying to reconcile the Keynesian thinking with the monetarist thinking."[17] The pugilist of the Battle of the Radio Stations was now content to let others, like Anna Schwartz, Karl Brunner, and Allan Meltzer, carry monetarism forward. Friedman would continue to publish articles, review essays, and even another book with Schwartz. He turned up at roundtables and conferences on his work. But he was drawing on research from previous decades rather than generating new material, and none of these publications would impact the field like his earlier work. Increasingly he granted interviews, gave lectures, wrote op-eds, and offered comments on others' research.

A series of health scares hastened the turn from academic economics. Like Sol Friedman so many decades ago, Friedman began suffering from chest pains, the telltale signs of a heart attack. Unlike Sol, his son had access to life-changing medical care. In 1972 he underwent bypass surgery—then a fairly novel procedure—at the Mayo Clinic, convalescing for several months in California. The following year Rose underwent a mastectomy. The procedures were remarkably successful, ushering in decades of good health and ensuring the couple could enjoy new milestones, including a first grandchild. By the time they had recovered, rational expectations was reshaping economics, and inflation was reshaping politics.[18]

When Friedman and Schwartz began their research into money in the late 1940s, inflation had been a quintessentially academic subject. The devastating consequences of Germany's World War I–era hyperinflation were widely acknowledged, and the United States had faced a surge in prices after the war. But throughout the Eisenhower and Kennedy administrations, the relatively steady price level had faded into the background as a political and economic consideration. This was one of the reasons Friedman and Schwartz had the field of money largely to themselves. Yet by 1974 inflation was a pressing problem in the United States and a scourge around the world. Beyond the professors was a whole world of policy-makers increasingly interested in Friedman's thoughts on money, inflation, and currency regimes. Rather than battle the field in highly technical papers and tense seminars, Friedman could take his inflation cure right to where it was needed.

Friedman's 1975 trip to Chile perfectly embodied the new dynamics of his career. Earlier in his professional life, trips abroad had basically been work in a different place. He had spent significant time in-country and embedded in local institutions—universities or government agencies—often going as part of U.S. government foreign-aid efforts. In Germany, he had proposed changes to the Marshall Plan during a stay of several months. In India, he had worked with the Ministry of Finance. As a visiting professor at Cambridge University, he had held tutorials and thrown himself into faculty life. By contrast, Chile was a six-day stint, organized by a former student and underwritten by a private Chilean foundation.[19]

Milton and Rose landed in Santiago at a critical moment in the country's history: two years into the military dictatorship of General Augusto Pinochet. In 1970, the world took note when Chilean elections yielded a new coalition of six leftist political parties, the Popular Unity, headed by Salvador Allende. "Marxist Threat in the Americas," blared *Time*, placing a pink-and-red image of the new president on the cover.[20] Allende lasted only three years. In 1973 he was ousted by Pinochet in a coup notorious for its brutality. Leftist students at the University of Chile were gunned down on campus; corpses bobbed in the Mapocho River as it wended through the capital city. After two years, the dictatorship had accomplished little. True, inflation was down from its peak of 600 percent during the Allende years. Yet with prices still rising more than 300 percent a year, it seemed clear something needed to change. A new group of economists, the Chicago Boys, convinced Pinochet to give their ideas a try. In turn, they called in Friedman for reinforcement.

The Friedmans' visit was just the latest installment in a long-standing relationship between the University of Chicago and Chile's economics profession. In 1953 a serendipitous encounter in Santiago between the Chicago department chair T. W. Schultz and a U.S. official yielded a proposal for regular academic exchange between the two countries. The idea stalled at the University of Chile, a university with close links to leftist political parties. Across town, however, the Pontifical Catholic University of Chile was stocked with the sons of businessmen languishing in gentlemanly mediocrity. University officials embraced the chance to build closer connections with the United

States. The eventual U.S. government–funded contract drew students from both universities, and committed the Catholic University to hiring at least four professors of economics from the cohort.[21]

Why was the U.S. government so interested in Chilean economics? Like other developing nations, Chile had emerged from World War II with an economic orthodoxy known as import substitution industrialization (ISI). According to this widely embraced set of ideas, governments should nurture domestic industries as a substitute for imports. Government-led industrialization, it was believed, would foster more broadly shared prosperity, potentially transforming peasants, subsistence-level farmers, and casual laborers into well-paid, productive industrial workers. ISI was particularly attractive in nations like Chile that depended heavily on the export of one key commodity—in Chile's case, copper. Prices of global commodities could fluctuate wildly, leading to feast or famine. By contrast, import substitution sought to create a more balanced economy in which a nation produced a range of needed goods. In times of low copper prices, so the thinking went, Chileans would not need to purchase foreign cars, appliances, or manufactured goods—they would have produced their own domestically.[22]

A descendant of centuries-old mercantilism and protectionist policies, ISI acquired a political cast in the Cold War era. Across Latin America, promoters of ISI promised a continental renaissance outside the shadow of American or European power. From the perspective of Washington, D.C., ISI could skate uncomfortably close to socialism. In practice, ISI meant high tariff barriers, government support for selected industries, and capital controls, meaning critical economic decisions were made by elected officials and government agencies, rather than the private sector.[23] Corruption, cronyism, and Communism alike might flourish in this atmosphere. With concerns about leftist drift in the hemisphere deepening across the 1950s, U.S. policy-makers took an increasing interest in the political valence of economic ideas.

The Chicago-Chile program was dominated by Arnold Harberger, an expert in international trade who was not a particularly close ally of Friedman's in the department. Harberger was part of a hard-drinking crew that included Harry Johnson, Friedman's bitter enemy. He was a regular at the Chileans' raucous Saturday-night parties, eventually marrying a woman he met there. His workshop on public finance became a refuge of sorts for graduate students who could not tolerate Friedman's domineering style. Earlier in his career, he had been part of the Cowles Commission.[24]

Nonetheless, Harberger's economics was inflected by Chicago price theory and Friedman's teaching specifically. As a graduate student at Chicago, Harberger had not undergone any sort of conversion experience. He found the Chicago teaching to largely replicate the basics of supply and demand he had already learned at Johns Hopkins, calling it "the same goddamn stuff again." At the same time, Friedman's performance in the classroom did leave a mark. Harberger took Price Theory during Friedman's golden age as a teacher, when he worked the room without notes, spinning out long explanations and firing off rapid questions. "It becomes part of your blood, so to speak, by the time he's finished with you," Harberger recalled. His doctoral work focused on the demand for imports in the United States, and he was highly sought after in the booming postwar academic job market. Eventually, Harberger would hold dual appointments at Chicago and UCLA, while also working for the IMF and the U.S. government.[25]

Harberger's views on Chile derived from his professional training and his experience in the country. Arriving in Chile in the early 1950s, he found the country full of promise but rife with inefficiencies caused by government policy. The Ricardian theory of comparative advantage—countries should specialize in goods they could best produce, and trade for the rest—seemed obviously true when he compared Chilean markets to the consumer bounty of the United States. As a result of import tariffs, automobiles were scarce and overpriced. Cars offered for sale in Chile "would have been chopped up and sold like old iron" in the United States, he wrote to his colleagues. His old clunker of a Ford was selling for a five-times markup. Phones were so difficult to obtain that Chileans joked that "a person does not buy a house, but a phone with a house built around it." Price controls in agriculture had benefited farmers in nearby Argentina, who with their huge farms could afford to sell at low prices, but they had eviscerated Chile's own farming sector.[26]

Harberger determined to teach his Chilean students "good economics," by which he meant the basic tenets of competition, free pricing, and free trade. He knew many Chilean business owners believed ISI was needed; there was "a widespread idea that customs protection is necessary—that without protection, local industries . . . would die." But Harberger taught his students this fear of deindustrialization was "completely false." If tariffs were removed and the "fictitiously low exchange rate" allowed to rise, some industries would decline but others would take their place, increasing the country's production overall by a third or more.[27] Increased production would raise the standard of living for all Chileans. The combination of scientific teaching and social betterment proved intoxicating to the Chileans who came to Chicago. Forming tight bonds akin to Friedman's Room Seven doctoral crew, they threw themselves into academic competition and pooled resources to survive on slim stipends.

While Chicago professors noted with distaste the Chilean tradition of direct links between universities and political parties, it proved impossible to depoliticize economics altogether. Not only was the dominant Chilean approach to economics and statecraft—ISI—understood by Chicago economists to be fundamentally misguided, but ISI had woven close connections between industries and the state. Any effort to change policy would raise the ire of protected firms and their politically connected beneficiaries. In this context, promoting "good economics" was inherently a political project. Indeed, when they returned to Chile, the Chicago students formed a recognizable bloc in business and political associations, and at Catholic University. This tight network—more like an extended family—soon became known by friend and foe alike as the Chicago Boys. By 1970, the year Allende won election, close to a hundred Chilean students had received economics training at Chicago.[28]

Although Allende was a Marxist, intellectually speaking, he was determined to effect "irreversible reform" working within the established democratic institutions of Chile. But his electoral mandate for change was slim.[29] He had barely bested a business-friendly, status quo candidate; the vote totals of the second- and third-place finishers far eclipsed his own. Likewise, the Chilean Congress was controlled by opposition parties. It was not an auspicious ground for radical reform.

Heralding the "Chilean road to socialism," the Allende government nonetheless launched an ambitious campaign of economic and social change, instituting widespread nationalization, breaking up large landholdings, and imposing price controls on more than three thousand goods. Although it bore some resemblance to ISI, Allende's plan went far beyond state encouragement of industrialization. Rather than set up new industries or fund government firms, the Allende government seized private businesses in operation. No sector was immune. Eventually, the state controlled more than 70 percent of enterprises in the mining, utilities, transportation, communications, and financial industries. More than half the country's agricultural land was redistributed. And the changes came remarkably fast. A year in, bragged a treasury official, "the nationalization of the banking system is practically complete. The state now controls . . . 90% of all credit." The government also laid plans to nationalize entirely the pivotal copper industry, including the holdings of two large U.S. firms.[30]

At first, Allende's program brought increased economic growth and new benefits to the poor; unemployment dropped in half. But in the second year of his presidency, Chile began the populist cycle away from euphoria toward doom.[31] There were external challenges, to be sure: worldwide copper prices plunged just as foreign investment dried up, scared off by the government's nationalization program. Yet many of Allende's problems were self-inflicted. Expropriated businesses were expected to yield expropriated profits. Instead, as talent fled overseas and inexperienced state managers struggled in their place, the rapidly expanding "social property area" became a significant liability. To subsidize these new state enterprises and pay for expanded social services, the government cranked up the money printer, more than doubling the money in circulation. Surging inflation reached a peak of 600 percent by the third year of Allende's presidency. The rise in prices, combined with widespread shortages of food and basic goods, alienated middle-class voters and energized Allende's opponents.[32] The streets of Santiago shook with protest marches both for and against the government.

Compounding these internal problems were external enemies. Despite his dedication to détente with the USSR, Richard Nixon quickly reverted to classic Cold War mode when confronted with socialism in Chile.[33] The country was often touted as the crown jewel of the Alliance for Progress, an American-led effort to support Latin American development and political moderation. What if Allende now portended a Red tide rising over the region? Such was the hope of Fidel Castro, who provided security for the new president and toured the country on a twenty-three-day state visit. Once considered irrelevant, Chile became the object of intense focus for the U.S. national security apparatus. In the immediate aftermath of the election, the idea of sponsoring a coup was even bruited about. Critical to these discussions was Friedman's former student Warren Nutter, whose study of monopoly had helped shift Chicago thinking in the 1950s. A fierce anti-Communist and Soviet expert, Nutter spent three years serving as the assistant secretary of defense for International Security Affairs, overlapping the start of Allende's term. Friedman had no awareness of these confidential deliberations, which ended in an abstract plan of "promoting a coup environment." Nutter left the government soon afterward. The CIA launched an extended program of covert operations intended to destabilize Allende's government, all the while professing friendship in public.[34]

In September, Pinochet and his henchmen moved efficiently and brutally to seize power. Tanks rolled into Santiago and planes strafed the Presidential Palace, where Allende made one last defiant speech before taking his own life. Although the U.S. government had not been involved in Pinochet's specific plot—in contrast to the intelligence services of neighboring Brazil, already ruled by a military dictatorship—it now offered support as the general consolidated power.[35] The junta recessed Congress, banned political parties, and postponed all further elections. As if recognizing the durability of Chile's democratic traditions, Pinochet was determined to snuff out opposition. Suspected leftists and Popular Unity loyalists were herded into the Santiago stadium, which had been converted into a prison camp. In the countryside, members of the opposition were shot or simply disappeared. The terror persisted throughout Pinochet's seventeen-year regime. In the end, an estimated 3,065 people had been killed by the state, and more than 38,000 Chileans were tortured, imprisoned, or abused. An estimated 200,000 Chileans were forcibly exiled.[36]

For all his resolve to wrest power from the left, Pinochet had few plans for governance. Steeped in ISI, the military showed little inclination to reverse many Allende policies. The regime ended up following its own version of "gradualism," hoping to slowly return to the pre-Allende years. While some state corporations were reprivatized, in others military officials were swapped for the commissars who had administered prices and devised production targets. Money continued to pour out of the central bank, keeping inflation at a shocking 369 percent, as measured at the end of 1974.[37] Here was the moment the Chicago Boys had been waiting for. Several were already serving in minor government positions. Now they began a coordinated push for an economic policy overhaul.

Key to their arguments was El Ladrillo—the Brick—a hefty compendium of policies and proposals crafted by a group of Harberger's students. Started as campaign planning for one of Allende's political rivals, the Brick eventually developed into a sort of shadow economic policy.

More than a departure from ISI, the Brick was its mirror image, not merely repudiating ISI but flipping it entirely. Fundamental to ISI had been the goal of diversifying industrial production, but the Brick's authors concluded that diversification prevented "the advantages of specialization in a few lines of production and, therefore, hinders a broader opening up to foreign trade." Isolated from world markets, Chile was also isolated from technological advances, leading to overall stagnation and low growth: "By locking up productive resources within our tight economic borders, the country remains dependent on the growth rate of its small domestic markets."[38] Expanding on Harberger's decades-old observation, the Brick argued the low price of food had hampered Chilean agriculture, creating a new and dangerous dependency. Price controls and tariffs should be removed. The report contended that reversing ISI would unleash Chile's economic potential, and this broad growth would particularly benefit those mired in extreme poverty. Were the plan to succeed, the Brick's authors recognized that their ideas would fundamentally transform Chilean society.

How would this transformational change happen? The authors ducked the question, noting that "this report assumes a radical change in the current situation and is conceived in terms of the existence of a national conciliation government, which is respected for its objectivity and impartiality and whose authority is therefore generally accepted." It was not a matter of the state withering away, for the Brick rejected "the erroneous conclusion that the state should totally withdraw from the economic sphere." Instead, it gave the state "responsibility to oversee the whole economic system, to set global targets, to design the institutional framework, to establish planning and control mechanisms, to develop the necessary infrastructure, to perform activities where the social benefit is greater than the private return, and so on."[39] Here the report blended early Chicago with the Chilean heritage of an active state.

Was the Brick inherently authoritarian? Later critics would claim the document was both motivation and justification for the coup. It was true that some members of the Chilean navy circulated the Brick as the coup unfolded. Yet it was far from a blueprint for Pinochet's rule. Nor was the coup initiated in order to implement ideas in the Brick. Germinated in American universities, the economics of the Brick lacked an indigenous pedigree.[40] While the Chicago Boys came to seem all-powerful, upon returning from Chicago they were brushed aside by local entrepreneurs and businessmen, seemingly their natural constituency. Likewise military leaders inclined to corporatist, top-down solutions, and the Brick's ideas made little sense to men steeped in the long history of ISI.

It took another year of economic decline to rouse interest in the Brick's claim of "a consistent, integrated formula for how to achieve a decentralized economy that will maximize the efficient utilization of the country's resources."[41] In 1974, Pinochet appointed a new finance minister, Jorge Cauas, signaling the start of a larger shift. A former minister in the Christian Democratic government, Cauas was not actually a Chicago Boy—his training was from Columbia University. Nor had he helped author the Brick. Nonetheless, he now threw his weight behind the Chicago network. A new plan emerged. Instead of trying to go slowly back to the time before Allende, the government would push forward to a new future, guided by the Brick.

With their star on the rise, the Chicago Boys turned to their former teachers. The need for legitimation was profound. Pinochet had become a global pariah, condemned by leaders from the United Nations to exiled Argentinean ruler Juan Perón. It meant something for American-trained economists to join his administration, and it meant something for famous names like Milton Friedman to visit the country. Indeed, Friedman's visit was part of a larger internal campaign to fortify the turn from gradualism. A private foundation linked to the Chicago Boys agreed to sponsor a visit by Friedman, Harberger, and a third Chicago-trained economist from Brazil. One of the main organizers was the banker Rolf Luders, the only Chilean student who wrote a dissertation under Friedman.[42]

Friedman's six-day trip was an extraordinary immersion into the highest levels of Chilean politics and society. Immediately upon arrival, after dropping Rose and his luggage at the local Sheraton, he was whisked off to "a planning session of some ministry" stocked with "our people"—Chicago economics Ph.D.s. The Chicago Boys ran Friedman through the basics of the Chilean economy, including 9 to 10 percent unemployment and raging inflation, and gave an overview of various policies that had been pursued since the junta took power. Next came a session with deputies from the Banco Central de Chile, covering the government budget, the monetary and banking system, monetary aggregates, and the capital markets. Now Friedman had his primary diagnosis: "This is an absolutely clear case of an inflation financed by money created to pay for a government fiscal deficit," he wrote in his ex post reflections.[43] The day concluded with a stag dinner at a private club, hosted by one of the country's largest financial holding companies.

The next five days kept up the pace. There were meetings with the national chamber of commerce, large landowners, and agricultural groups; interviews with the leading newspaper and TV station; talks at three universities; sessions with the minister of economy; a trip to a coastal resort town; and lunch at the central bank. Some of these were social events, but most gave Friedman access to unique information about the economy and government. He questioned business owners about how they managed inflation, observed reprivatized farms in operation, and was given the latest figures on money, banking, agricultural production, unemployment, and trade. By the time it was over, Friedman had met the American and French ambassadors, several of the country's wealthiest men, and numerous generals—including Pinochet himself.

Friedman took his ideas about inflation right to the top. Along with Harberger and Luders, he spent about forty-five minutes with the president. Speaking through a translator, Friedman laid out the case for fighting inflation with a "shock treatment"—a drastic change in economic policy. This could seem a curious position for the former voice of gradualism. But in the United States, Friedman had fretted to Arthur Burns when growth in M1 reached 6 percent. In Chile, growth of M1 during Allende's first year was 119 percent.[44] Under the junta, it was still extremely high. As he summarized in a follow-up letter to Pinochet, "For Chile, where inflation is raging at 10 to 20 per cent a month, I believe gradualism is not feasible. It would involve so painful an operation over so long a period that I fear the patient would not survive." Instead, Friedman supported a "shock program [that] could end inflation in months."[45] The main elements were sharp reductions in government spending and a credible commitment to stop printing money. Friedman also specified that relief measures should be included in any reform package.

Across the barrier of language, Friedman detected that Pinochet was "sympathetically attracted to the idea of a shock treatment but was clearly distressed at the possible temporary unemployment that might be caused." Indeed, this was not the first Pinochet had heard of a shock treatment. But just like Nixon, the general worried that the cost of defeating inflation might be too high. This was the primary reaction Friedman encountered in Chile, and the importance of pushing through the pain would become his primary message to Chileans. The transition would be hard, Friedman averred, but as he told a Chilean magazine, "This is like cutting a dog's tail. You cut it all at once or suffering is prolonged." About a month later, the government announced a National Recovery Program that broadly followed Friedman's outline.[46]

How important was Friedman's visit to shaping economic policy in Chile? As it turns out, the decision to shift away from gradualism had already been taken by the time he arrived.[47] Friedman's visit was less a catalyst than a demonstration of how much sway the Chicago Boys had already established. Nor did his visit with Pinochet contain much of substance; he offered the kind of basic advice that could have been gleaned from reading his *Newsweek* columns. It is possible the personal audience with a foreign luminary did influence Pinochet, or shore up his decision to empower the Chicago Boys.

But what really mattered were Friedman's nonstop meetings with the military and political elite. To brace the government for what was to come, the Chicago Boys had flown in a ringer. In a meeting with nearly seven hundred military officials—neatly arrayed in a strict hierarchy from generals and admirals to lieutenants—Friedman fielded questions about recession and unemployment. The same concerns came up in a repeat session with hundreds of government appointees, and in a smaller session with the junta's military advisory committee. In nearly all these meetings with the Chilean deep state, Friedman met the worry that curbing inflation would spike unemployment and immiserate the poor. Left unsaid was the possibility that if Pinochet could not improve on Allende, his presidency too might end.

It was up to Friedman to counter these fears, to set the idea of shock treatment in context, to reassure his audiences that on the other side lay a more prosperous and stable Chile. Along the way, he took shots at the other misconceptions he found, ranging from "belief that somehow there was something wrong with speculation" to "the problems of Chile were to be blamed on foreign developments such as the low price of copper."[48] He continued this campaign in his interviews and public talks, telling *El Mercurio*, "Chilean problems are made in Chile."[49] Friedman did not design Chile's fight against inflation. But he did explain and defend it.

Friedman spent less time reflecting on Chile's politics, although the military presence was inescapable. "It is not that the soldiers are so numerous; there are probably no more of them than there are policemen," Friedman mused after the visit. "But they are clearly soldiers and not policemen, each one having a small machine gun slung over his body and looking as if he were ready to use it on the slightest of provocations." Nonetheless, Friedman registered little judgment of Pinochet, comparing his office setup to the White House and noting: "It is very hard to get much of an idea of the character of the man." He appeared to separate Pinochet almost entirely from the crimes of the regime, noting that torture was "more or less standard procedure of intelligence agencies in Chile and other South American countries for decades. That does not excuse it or justify it, but does help to explain its persistence."[50] While Friedman's notes on economic conditions bristled with his usual irreverence, when turning to political matters they became dispassionate, even anthropological in tone.

At a small dinner hosted by the first secretary of the French embassy, Friedman came face-to-face with two regime critics. One was a wealthy businessman, originally a junta supporter, who had swung against Pinochet from the right. The other was a Lutheran bishop whose church was riven over his active work for human rights. Attaching himself to Friedman, the bishop recited figures on the numbers of Chileans detained, arrested, and tortured. When he began to boast of leading peasants to expropriate land, Friedman argued back that this was "a contribution to violence since it led to the destruction of a free society." Friedman realized afterward that the dinner had been his only meeting not stocked with government officials. Everyone there, including the two ambassadors, "tended to be highly critical of the junta for what they regarded as a cavalier disregard of human rights and of the rights of the poorest people among the Chileans."[51] This was surely no accident. The dinner's host must have imagined that if he were given an accurate image of life in Chile, the famous libertarian Friedman would condemn Pinochet. But this one dinner could not counterbalance the remainder of the week, which layered a thick crust of policy briefings and statistics over the violence at the core, leaving Friedman ill-equipped to understand the reaction his visit would trigger.

Literal-minded to a fault, Friedman failed to appreciate the optics of meeting with Pinochet, who was widely viewed as a U.S. stooge. To Chilean exiles in particular, it appeared that the U.S. government had installed a vicious dictator, and then sent over its most famous economist to consolidate his hold on power. To Friedman, visiting Chile was no worse than visiting the Soviet Union or Communist Yugoslavia, two countries he had toured. But the origins of those regimes lay in the distant past, whereas less than two years had passed since the Chilean military's brutal takeover. Friedman also showed little interest in U.S. involvement in the country's politics. There had been a steady drip of front-page stories about CIA involvement in Chile, part of a series that triggered the famous Church Committee, a wide-ranging congressional inquiry into covert activities.[52] Although these investigations—which included a specific report on U.S. activities in Chile—were just beginning during Friedman's visit, they were widely publicized.

Afterward, Friedman framed himself as a critic of the regime. He touted his decision to decline two honorary degrees, lest they be interpreted as an endorsement of the government. While existing transcripts and media coverage contain no evidence he spoke out against Pinochet's infringements on personal freedom, such as the outlawing of political parties and the closure of Chile's Congress, these sorts of remarks may have been stricken from the censored press. According to at least one witness, Friedman did tell Pinochet that liberalizing the economy "would lead to political freedom."[53] And he did deliver at least one seemingly provocative talk, "The Fragility of Freedom."

Addressing the topic of freedom to an audience living under military dictatorship implied a certain boldness and risk. Most likely,

Friedman did begin by baldly stating Chile was not free.[54] But in the bulk of his address, Friedman attacked not the current authoritarianism in Chile but the prelude to Pinochet. "The government incessantly spread its influence giving rise eventually to the Allende regime that threatened to bring about totalitarian rule of the left," he lectured the Chileans. He then launched into an extended disquisition on political versus economic freedom. Most people did not realize, Friedman explained, that "the economic market is a freer, more democratic market than the political marketplace." This was because political choices—votes—were binary, yes or no. By definition, many would be disenfranchised. In an economic market, however, individual choice could flourish and innumerable needs and wants be satisfied. It was an argument that left the audience astonished, Friedman remembered proudly in his memoir.[55]

But this was not the United States in the 1960s, fat and flush and satisfied, ready to startle awake as Friedman stuck a finger in the eye of complacent liberalism. Pinochet's Chile was not the time and place to assert that what felt like freedom was actually the road to serfdom, with the unspoken implication Chileans were now freer than they knew. It was the mid-1970s, with concerns about human rights moving front and center in the global conversation. Realists like Henry Kissinger, now the secretary of state, were being challenged by a new moral code that took a government's treatment of its citizens as the ultimate test of legitimacy. Friedman did not explicitly align himself with Pinochet. But neither did he decry the awful powers wielded by a militarized state.[56]

There are several ways to understand Friedman's silences on Chile. One is to recognize his commitment to engagement rather than isolation. Like a diplomat who argues for ongoing dialogue with rogue regimes, Friedman genuinely believed that connecting Pinochet's government to outsiders was the best strategy for change. This approach was not without merit. But it was unfashionable in the dawning era of human rights, defined by sanctions, boycotts, and divestment; increasingly, activists found power in purity. Friedman may also have felt constrained by personal relationships with his hosts, and his desire to support their agenda. Coming out swinging against Pinochet would have been at the least ungracious and at the most a serious impediment to the advancement of policies he supported. Given his genuine belief that stabilizing the economy would benefit all Chileans, he may have judged that remaining silent would be the greatest good. Finally, it is possible Friedman simply did not care about the violence of the regime. Never did he argue that the violence was defensible or that Chile's left brought persecution on themselves. He just remained focused on the omelet rather than the eggs.

Friedman's presence in Chile was probably enough to transform him into a symbol, no matter what he said or did. In truth, he played almost no role in policy design. The imprint of the Chicago school in Chile was palpable. But important roles were also played by economists trained at other American universities, who converged on the same rejection of Allende's program.[57] The development economist Paul Rosenstein-Rodan, a self-identified "center left man" who called himself "violently opposed to Friedman's theories and policies," nonetheless told a UN official "under the catastrophic economic earthquake circumstances, the economic policy is necessary." Rosenstein-Rodan had worked for the pre-Allende Chilean government and knew the country well. Later he wrote of Allende's monetary policy: "Any undergraduate economics student would have known better."[58] In 1981 Chile would introduce more classic Friedman-style reforms, like school vouchers and a private pension system. But the primary action in 1975 was economic stabilization and the fight against inflation, where Friedman's views were not exceptional. Moreover, while the Chicago Boys had certainly imbibed Friedman's ideas while at Chicago, it was Harberger who was the lifeblood of the program.

But it was far easier to say Friedman's trip had been the cause, rather than rehearse the long history of academic exchange between the United States and Chile, or talk about techniques for fighting inflation. And it was far more convenient to focus on Friedman—widely known through his popular media appearances—than the obscure Harberger. If Friedman was the cause, then Friedman could be blamed. The issue could be frozen, personalized, polarized.

In the aftermath of Friedman's visit, Chile's political diaspora mobilized to make the ebullient economist the face of Pinochet. Exiles from Chile were politically savvy, often well educated, and able to build connections with existing leftist parties in Europe. The role of Andre Gunder Frank, a renegade Friedman doctoral student, was a case in point. After a checkered career at Chicago, made nearly untenable by his open Marxism, Frank ended up in Chile. He joined the Allende administration, fleeing when the junta took over. From exile in Europe, he concentrated his wrath on Friedman and Harberger, accusing them of "economic genocide" in a series of open letters and a book.[59] An even more hysterical indictment came from the Austrian econometrician Gerhard Tintner, who imagined Friedman to display a framed and signed picture of Pinochet over his desk. In a letter copied to seventeen other academics and printed in the student-run *Chicago Maroon*, Tintner offered to send Friedman a replacement with Hitler's image instead.[60] Major media like *The New York Times* and *The Washington Post* made similar linkages, minus the vitriol, attributing Pinochet's economic policy to Friedman's guidance. An enormous amount of plain old misinformation circulated, with some sources claiming Friedman regularly visited Chile to dispense advice.[61]

The charges reached a crescendo in an August 1976 essay authored by Orlando Letelier, Allende's foreign minister, which was published in the American magazine *The Nation*. The Chicago Boys were "deeply involved in the preparation of the coup," Letelier asserted, and it was "obviously Friedman and company" who had prepared the recent shift in economic policy. Letelier's essay throbbed with moral outrage—understandably so, as he had been imprisoned by Pinochet's regime and even dangled from a helicopter over open seas. Now in forced exile in the United States, Letelier was incensed that Friedman should write about economic freedom and then prescribe "shock treatment" for Chile. In the context of a deeply unequal society, he argued, the cost of fighting inflation and trimming government spending was too steep, leading to "a picture of hunger and deprivation never before seen in Chile." Arguing from both "an economic and a moral point of view," Letelier contended that Friedman's policies were a disaster for Chile.[62]

More than impugning Friedman, Letelier made a direct link between free market economics and authoritarian government. It was not possible, Letelier argued, to separate economic policy from politics. Rather, "Repression for the majorities and 'economic freedom' for small privileged groups are in Chile two sides of the same coin." The revival of capitalism under an authoritarian regime was not just a coincidence, or the baleful mingling of the good and the bad. There was an "inner harmony" between the two sides of the regime. The shift away from ISI and the economic approach of Allende was not intended to foster development or growth, Letelier argued. From his perspective, the economics of the counterrevolution had one broad purpose: "to secure the economic and political power of a small dominant class by effecting a massive transfer of wealth from the lower and middle classes to a select group of monopolists and financial speculators." Concentration of wealth was not an accident or a marginal outcome but "the base for a social project."[63] In this telling, the approach of Friedman and Harberger had nothing to offer everyday Chileans except pain and suffering.

Looking at the same country, Friedman and Letelier saw two different places. According to Letelier, the fallen Allende had nearly realized a just society, only to be undermined by selfishness and greed: "For the first time in history a society attempted to build socialism by peaceful means. During Allende's time in office, there was a marked improvement in the conditions of employment, health, housing, land tenure and education of the masses. And as this occurred, the privileged domestic groups and the dominant foreign interests perceived themselves to be seriously threatened." Letelier argued that the economic breakdown of Allende's last years was caused by an organized program of sabotage, not by the failings of government.[64]

By contrast, Friedman depicted Allende's social programs as fundamentally unsustainable. To explain the country's plight, he offered some unpleasant fiscal arithmetic:

> As time passes, the number of people on whom the state is trying to bestow benefits becomes larger and larger, while the number from whom it can extract taxes does not grow, with the result that a situation arises in which half the people are trying to extract funds

> from the other half. Because Chile is a poor country, the breaking point came as a result of government spending about 40 per cent of the national income. At that point the amount that could in fact be extracted in taxes was about 30 per cent of the national income, so the balance had to be financed by printing money and Chile entered into a violent inflation.

As it turned out, even these numbers underestimated the problem. Friedman argued government deficit spending was around 10 percent of GDP—the gap between spending 40 percent of national income and recouping only 30 percent through taxes. But later analyses showed that Allende's deficit spending reached 30 percent of GDP at the end, three times more than Friedman anticipated. Friedman argued it was inflation, along with the social and economic chaos it unleashed, that led to the dictatorship. Chilean welfare spending was not only unsustainable but immoral, he continued, with "extortion and coercion at its very centre, because in order to do good the welfare state must use force to take people's money away from them." Here was another reason why Friedman, not Harberger, became a target for popular outrage. Calm and even-keeled, Harberger spoke and wrote in the language of a government commission. Friedman instead took up the tones of a preacher, doling out moral condemnation along with technical detail. Yet this moral condemnation seemed one-sided, as it was directed primarily at Allende, not Pinochet.[65]

The debate might have quietly simmered for years, a predictable exchange of views in predictable venues from predictable partisans, were it not for the bomb that exploded in Washington, D.C., on September 21, 1976. Planted by Pinochet's secret police, it blew apart the car carrying Letelier and his American-born assistant, killing both. It was a first strike in Operation Condor, the notorious campaign of state-sponsored terrorism Pinochet coordinated.[66] The assassination of a high-ranking political refugee on U.S. soil brought immediate condemnation and widespread media coverage. Letelier's death was reported all over the world. His *Nation* essay, published only weeks before, became a martyr's last testament.

And then three weeks later came the announcement of Friedman's Nobel Prize. The news was a gut punch to Pinochet's victims. Although Friedman had nothing to do with Letelier's death, the timing was atrocious. With Friedman mistakenly understood as a Pinochet intimate, it seemed as if the dictator himself had been honored. At the very least, the bien-pensant of the world had shrugged off his crimes. In truth, the committee had tried to be scrupulously evenhanded in its administration of the economics prize. An arriviste to the pantheon of greats—the first was awarded in 1969, decades after the original prizes in peace, literature, medicine, chemistry, and physics—in its early years the economics medal alternated between European and American, planner and market advocate. Sometimes the committee split the difference, as when both F. A. Hayek and Gunnar Myrdal were honored in 1974. Yet this time, the bankers failed miserably to appreciate the unfortunate symbolism of their choice.

But Pinochet's opponents knew they had been handed an opportunity. In the opinion centers of the Western world, Friedman was far more relatable and recognizable than the iron-faced Pinochet. The very incongruity of joining the general and the professor was good copy. Further, Friedman's ideas were influential within conservative parties of many nations. So if Friedman and Pinochet were linked, then there was a new weapon with which to fight conservatism, even in liberal democracies that were a far cry from Chile. The Nobel made Friedman central to what *The New York Times* called "unquestionably a worldwide Marxist campaign to blacken the junta and exalt the chaotic Allende regime."[67] A luncheon at the American Enterprise Institute meeting to honor his prize generated a protest inside the convention hall, where the Union for Radical Political Economics passed out a pamphlet called "The Economics of Milton Friedman and the Chilean Junta."[68] The Spartacus Youth League dogged his campus visits and other public events. He and Rose were ushered into events through side doors and kitchens, as if they were under Secret Service protection.

Why did Friedman's short trip to Chile generate such sustained protest? In part, it was the result of a highly motivated and organized network, a sort of pre-Twitter mob of the global left, seizing upon a celebrity to gain greater visibility. But underlying the protest was a profound philosophical and political question, perhaps the central problem of the age.

Allende powered the dream that socialism in the poorest countries did not need a violent revolution to succeed. It was possible, his supporters believed, to radically redistribute private property, economic power, and political power within the bounds of a constitutional, democratic system. Socialism did not require a Stalin, a Mao, a Pol Pot. But if the *vía Chilena* was impassable—the dream must die. As Rosenstein-Rodan summarized, the fall of Allende "has been taken as proof that socialism and democracy are incompatible, that only a dictatorship can impose socialism."[69] Blaming nefarious outsiders let the dream live. Even better, blaming Friedman might redeem the bloodstained legacy of Marxism. Empirically, the death toll of Pinochet's dictatorship was incommensurate with the millions killed in Stalinist-style Communist regimes. It was an Orwellian mind trick of sorts, impugning capitalism for the very sins that were so deeply embedded in the Communist project.[70] And finally, stigmatizing capitalism as authoritarian foreclosed any need to think seriously about how Friedman's ideas might actually work in practice—or how actually existing socialism might not.

Friedman was used to being unpopular, but this was a new level entirely. He had tumbled out of the decorous debates of American politics into the raw wounds of the twentieth century. This was not fiscal policy versus monetarism, debated on a televised roundtable; this was Fascism versus Communism, fought on the streets with bombs and blood and bullets. He had been pulled back to the horrors of the 1930s that had first shaped his libertarian instincts. But since then, his reference points had shifted to accommodate the placid postwar world. Now they would need to shift again.

At first, Friedman reacted with irritation. His go-to response was to demand why he had not been criticized for travel to other unfree nations, like the USSR or Yugoslavia. His next line of defense, taken up briefly, minimized the repression of Pinochet. In an argument that drew on Hayek's distinction between totalitarianism and authoritarianism, he wrote to Tintner that in contrast to Allende's Communist totalitarianism, "There is at least one thing to be said for the military junta—there is more chance of a return to a democratic society." Citing the experience of Greece, Friedman argued that military dictatorship lacked the "totalitarian philosophy" and thus allowed a private sphere of life.[71] Over time, this made a return of freedom possible.

Only rarely did Friedman reveal the toll of the personal attacks. In San Francisco, he told the Commonwealth Club, "It is not a pleasant thing to face a mob of protestors when you go into a building, to be hissed at, to see unfriendly signs." Friedman characterized this as "liberal McCarthyism."[72] In the question-and-answer session, his daughter was amazed to see him near tears at the mention of a recent gossip column referring to him as "Herr Professor."[73]

From Friedman's perspective, the influence of his ideas in Chile should have been celebrated, not condemned. As predicted, Chile had entered a sharp recession once the National Recovery Program began. This economic contraction was the expected price of reducing inflation. In Chile, it was all the more painful given the preexisting level of poverty and the swollen public sector. Allende's supporters had briefly enjoyed artificially inflated wages and benefits through government jobs.[74] Now cast out into the free price system, few could recoup the loss. Yet over time, inflation declined considerably, although it still remained high at 84 percent in 1977. The economy also began to grow at a fast clip of 10 percent in the late 1970s.

Still, it was not clear this was pure Friedmanism at work.[75] Friedman, after all, did not have a monopoly on the idea of fiscal and monetary restraint. Moreover, the inflation-fighting mechanism Chile used was not Friedman's favored focus on the money supply but exchange rates. Setting aside Friedman's belief in floating exchange rates, Chile's economic advisers pegged the peso to the dollar.[76] It was not simply the left that benefited from blurring the truth about Friedman's connection to Chile. Even as the Chicago Boys basked in his reputation, they charted their own course away from the master.

Friedman never shifted from his belief that engaging rather than isolating Pinochet had been the right decision. Still, over time, the protests made an impact. Believing Friedman could influence Pinochet, human rights groups convinced him to send several letters on behalf of regime prisoners. In these petitions, Friedman began to make a stronger connection between economic and political freedom, calling them "indivisible" in a letter to Pinochet.[77] For most of his career, Friedman had been at pains to emphasize that economic freedom was essential to political freedom; indeed, it was freedom itself. This was largely because he believed American liberals ignored or denigrated economic freedom. But now he understood that exclusively emphasizing economic freedom could be read as accepting political repression. Friedman started to recalibrate his public statements to clarify there was no acceptable trade-off between the two.

Watching other conservatives react to Chile may have sharpened his thinking. Hayek, for example, visited Chile in 1977 and 1981. Here he wandered close to an endorsement of the regime, telling an interviewer, "I personally prefer a liberal dictator to a democratic government lacking liberalism." Hayek's skepticism about unlimited democracy was well established in his political writings but took on a darker tone when publicly proclaimed from inside a repressive state. He followed up with several ill-considered defenses of Pinochet in major European newspapers.[78]

Hayek's remarks augured a broader split on the right that spilled into view during the 1981 Mont Pelerin Society meeting, held in the Chilean resort town of Viña del Mar.[79] Bringing the conference to Chile seemed to outsiders an unabashed celebration of Pinochet. This was something Friedman himself feared. He convinced the organizers to disinvite the powerful minister and Chicago Boy Sergio de Castro to avoid linking the meeting to the regime.[80] In the end, the conference was marked by vigorous debate on the connection between capitalism and authoritarianism. The issue was far from academic. Only a year earlier, the government had pushed through a new constitution that set up a future democratic presidential plebiscite. This was, potentially, Hayek's transitional dictatorship in action. But much would depend upon the next eight years and the willingness of both the military and Chile's political elites to accept change. Against this backdrop, the ideas circulating in the Mont Pelerin Society had real consequences.

Most disturbing to Friedman was the possibility that some on the right were beginning to accept the left's argument that dictatorships were fundamental to capitalism. He was horrified when the meeting's first speaker declared, "After forty years of socialist recklessness only one road remained open to us—'Friedmanism'—always provided we had a government strong and courageous enough to establish it."[81] In remarks that were reported in the nation's press, Friedman took the floor next and declared, as one newspaper paraphrased, "The belief that only a strong government can generate a social market economy or markets open to the world was dangerous to assert." According to the paper, Friedman argued that "it was also possible to generate a free market economic policy in a democratic political regime."[82] Friedman had never believed in a simplistic equation between economic and political freedom. Capitalist countries were not always free. But it was one thing to note a historical fact, and another entirely to argue there was a necessary connection between capitalism and coercion.

Back in the United States, he wrote a *Newsweek* column that summarized the shift in his thinking. There was a new "proposition" he needed to stress, Friedman wrote. There was still a difference between economic and political freedom. And economic freedom was still vital. But injecting a Marshallian notion of time, he now argued that political freedom "is a necessary condition for the long-term maintenance of economic freedom."[83] Here still lived a sliver of Hayek's liberal dictator, at least in the short term. But before, Friedman had always made economic freedom the base, political freedom the superstructure. Now, after watching his ideas blown up on the world stage, he had reversed the equation.

13

MONEY MATTERS

The battle has now begun.

—Margaret Thatcher, 1979

In 1977 Rose and Milton Friedman left Chicago behind and settled in California, where Milton accepted a position as a senior research fellow at the Hoover Institution, part of Stanford University. For decades after he lost the presidency to Roosevelt in 1932, the indefatigable Herbert Hoover had dedicated his energies to Stanford, his alma mater, and the global fight against Communism. His namesake institution soon emerged as a critical terrain of struggle. Originally founded as a library and archive, the institution picked up a new mission in 1959: to "constantly and dynamically point the road to peace, to personal freedom, and to the safeguards of the American system," in the words of a statement written by Hoover. He added another brief that would inflame faculty opinion: "The purpose of this institution must be, by its research and publications, to demonstrate the evils of the doctrines of Karl Marx."[1] After weathering the resultant controversy, including an attempted hostile takeover by the Stanford faculty, in 1964 Hoover installed his handpicked successor, the American Enterprise Institute economist Glenn Campbell.

Campbell staged a raid on Chicago, recruiting Aaron Director as one of his first new hires. Ten years older than Rose and Milton,

Director had hit the age of mandatory retirement. At Hoover, he continued his life of quiet influence. The Stanford law professor Richard Posner told of a fateful encounter: "I noticed the name Aaron Director on the door of an office . . . I thought that since I was going to do antitrust I would meet this fellow." Not long afterward, Posner emerged as the single most important scholar in law and economics, yet another of Director's conquests.[2]

Did Campbell suspect Director's presence might eventually lure his distinguished brother-in-law? It took a while to work out the details—Friedman was not offered an appointment in economics, as he had apparently hoped to receive. Given his age and the increasingly mathematical drift of the field, this was perhaps understandable. More surprising was that he joined Hoover not as a senior fellow, the title commensurate with his stature, but as a senior research fellow, one step below. This position, however, did not require formal university approval, a daunting process amid the organized Chilean campaign against Friedman. Appointment as a research fellow needed only the approval of Campbell, who lauded Friedman as "one Hoover scholar who never needed introduction, no matter where in the world." In a fitting symmetry, shortly after Friedman's appointment the institution received an unexpected gift—the $7 million balance of the Volker Fund.[3] The capital and the scholars transformed the Hoover Institution from a regional manuscript depository to an organization with national reach. By 1981, *The Washington Post* was calling Hoover "the prestigious, conservative think tank currently in fashion."[4]

Several times a week Friedman tooled down to Stanford from his San Francisco high-rise apartment, driving a car with the custom vanity plates MV=PY, the quantity theory of money's fundamental equation. It turned out that California license plates didn't allow an equal sign, so Friedman created one with strategically placed pieces of black tape. Every so often, an eagle-eyed state trooper would notice the illegal modification and ticket Friedman. And then the tape would go back on the license plate for the next trip along the California coast.[5]

One of the joys of retirement was travel, often designed to take advantage of Milton's burgeoning international network. In 1978 he and Rose were dinner guests at the London home of Ralph Harris, the head of the Institute of Economic Affairs. Founded in 1955 and akin to a British version of the Volker Fund, the IEA was playing the long game of intellectual change. Inspired by F. A. Hayek and explicitly modeled on the socialist Fabian Society, the IEA sought to reverse the political trend in England by promoting conservative ideas and thinkers. Over the course of the 1970s, the IEA published at least seven pamphlets by Friedman—some original and some reissues of classics like *Roofs or Ceilings?* Dinner on this occasion featured a last-minute guest, swapped in when another canceled: Margaret Thatcher.

By this time, Thatcher had reached political heights unknown for a woman in the modern world, and was destined to climb higher still. She was a longtime Member of Parliament and the elected leader of the Conservative Party (colloquially called Tories). Should the party triumph in the coming year's election, she would become prime minister. Most distinctively, she was not the wife, daughter, or relative of a politically powerful man. She was instead a daughter of middle England, raised above a grocery store and educated in local schools. Shaped primarily by this bourgeois background and her Methodist religion, Thatcher had an instinctive dislike of labor unions, inflation, and what she called "dependency" on government.

As she ascended the ladder of Tory politics, Thatcher sought to crystallize her beliefs by reading the conservative intellectuals of her day, including Friedman.[6] Soon she emerged as leader of a faction within the Conservative Party, the "monetarists." In some ways a parallel movement to the Goldwater insurgency within the Republican Party, the monetarists sought to change the direction of their party, making it more ideologically distinct from its main rival, the Labour Party. Monetarism was a misnomer, in the sense that Friedman was not the primary inspiration for Thatcher or the movement that came to take her name.[7] At the same time, there was a fundamental connection between Friedman and the political revolution dawning in the United Kingdom.

Inflation would drive Thatcher's career, much as it had driven Friedman's academic renown. In the late 1960s and the 1970s, Britain suffered a remarkably parallel course of events to the United States. First came persistently rising prices, caused in part by the ripple effect of LBJ's "guns and butter," but also by the United Kingdom's desperate "dash for growth." Hoping to cure the "British disease" of slow growth, low investment, and declining productivity, both parties pursued expansionary spending and tax cuts.[8] Monetary policy was the cart following the fiscal horse, with little awareness of what lay ahead. At the same time, Britain's powerful trade unions, which dwarfed American labor power, regularly pushed through stupendous pay increases, with annual wage increases of 25 percent or even 37 percent.[9] As inflation became a political issue, the Conservative Party pinned these economic troubles on the Labour Party, pulling off a political upset in the 1970 election.

Then came the infamous U-turn. Just as Richard Nixon would denounce incomes policy and price supports, then do an unashamed volte-face, so did the Tories. In the aftermath of crippling strikes by miners and dockers unions, the Conservative prime minister, Edward Heath, announced an immediate sixty-day wage and price freeze, to be followed by three stages of further controls. Although the move was intended to placate the miners, they struck again anyway, in a fearsome industrial act that forced the country to a three-day workweek amid mass blackouts. In the course of his four-year term, Heath declared five states of emergency, all linked to strikes that imperiled basic services such as garbage collection, electricity, and heat. In 1974, Labour triumphed in national elections, rendering the Conservatives a minority party once again.[10]

In part, these matching American and British trajectories reflected political systems overwhelmed by global economic trends, from oil shocks to the crumbling of Bretton Woods. But they also reflected the similar structure—and vulnerability—of the welfare states in both countries. In contrast to the other advanced industrial democracies of the world, the Anglo-American welfare state was funded by income taxes on the wealthy, not the middle class. Relations between business and government were deliberately adversarial, rather than following a corporatist model of negotiated cooperation.[11]

Inflation profoundly disrupted these relationships. It distorted the tax base, suddenly subjecting pensioners and midlevel wage earners to new tax rates as their nominal incomes soared. And it amplified preexisting suspicion between business and labor. This dynamic was particularly punishing in Britain. In an era when inflation was widely blamed on unions, the Labour Party came with built-in political liability. Yet solutions to this new price crunch remained unclear. President Nixon and Prime Minister Heath both reached for incomes policy because they feared their only other options were unemployment and recession.

Into the breach came Friedman's ideas, which helped strengthen and deepen the political currents already in flow. His focus on money recast and rejuvenated an older tradition within the Conservative Party that had fallen into abeyance. While British monetarism would never be identical to Friedman's economics, his stature within the profession played a critical role in bolstering the new ideas driving Thatcher's faction. Important converts came from the financial press, as editors came to see monetarism as increasingly relevant and plausible.[12]

A leading writer for the *Financial Times*—once an adviser to Labour governments—identified Friedman's attack on the Phillips curve in his 1967 presidential address as a catalyst. The basic message of the speech, "that conventional full-employment policies are futile and that an arbitrarily chosen unemployment target is likely to lead not merely to inflation but to accelerating inflation," transformed him from "a fashionable growth man to that of an IEA sympathizer."[13] In British universities, where monetarism had established a handful of redoubts in the 1960s, attitudes began to shift. Once, monetarism had been "an unfortunate but embarrassing affliction which people were usually too polite to mention," as one university professor remembered. Now it began to attract adherents.[14]

To a degree remarkable for an American economist, Friedman became a critical reference point—and favored term of insult—within the British political universe.[15] According to a high-ranking Labour politician, Thatcherism was nothing but the "half-understood, half-baked theories of that Jewish leprechaun Milton Friedman."[16] *The Guardian* denounced him as "a prize political fool" and "that cantankerous bigot."[17] Once the controversy over his Nobel broke out, leftists hastened to link Thatcher to Friedman, hoping to discredit conservatives.

Friedman further inflamed the situation through a series of broadsides directed against social democracy in the United Kingdom. Adopting a new role as prophet of doom, in 1976 he predicted to a British magazine that "odds are at least 50–50 that, within the next 5 years, British freedom and democracy will have been destroyed."[18] He embraced the Chilean connection, arguing that both countries had embarked upon an unsustainable path of ever increasing welfare spending and nationalization that would end in disaster. None of this was far from what Brits themselves were saying; indeed a sense of foreboding pervaded the country as inflation surged over 20 percent and crippling strikes continued. Inflation combined with the dislocations of Bretton Woods to destabilize the British pound; in 1976, the country accepted a humiliating loan from the IMF. Then came the Winter of Discontent, where more than two thousand strikes erupted across the nation.

This was the era of economic, social, and political crisis when Friedman and Thatcher met. As leader of the opposition, Thatcher was well positioned to take advantage of Labour's stumbles amid the growing chaos. Critical segments of elite opinion, from the dailies to the financial markets, were giving British monetarism a second look. The stage was set for the Thatcher revolution.

Friedman's assessment of the Iron Lady was wide of the mark. "She's a very attractive and interesting lady," he wrote with a touch of condescension after the dinner. "Whether she really has the capacities Britain so badly needs at this time, I must confess, it seems to me still a very open question but we shall I hope have some proof of that in the not too distant future."[19] He spent most of dinner arguing Britain should remove all exchange controls—the same reform he had pressed on Barry Goldwater and also Richard Nixon. Unsuccessfully, Friedman sought to convince Thatcher that renewed confidence in Britain's economic path would more than offset any currency decline.[20] Like the other politicians who had encountered this argument, Thatcher reacted with caution.

Still, she valued her connection to Friedman. When she was elected prime minister less than a year after their dinner, Friedman sent a congratulatory telegram. In response, Thatcher cabled: "The battle has now begun. We must win." She added the handwritten postscript "by implementing the things in which we believe."[21] The time to show her stuff had come.

As Thatcher's premiership began, her advisers sought to use Friedman to their advantage. In early 1980, the Friedmans were bound for Britain to tape part of their upcoming TV series, *Free to Choose*. He would have an audience with Thatcher, and her staff prepared with an extensive memo. "You may wish to reassure Prof. Friedman about the seriousness and commitment with which the government are approaching their task," the memo instructed. "Though he is well aware as anyone of the inevitable pains and costs involved in pursuing tight monetary policies, he may have been a little discouraged by recent newspaper reports or impressions drawn from his TV discussions."[22] A personal audience with the prime minister ought to shore up his support, the memo's authors hoped.

Friedman's visit came during a critical time for Thatcher. She was locked in a silent battle with "wets" in the cabinet—Conservatives left over from Heath's government who preferred a cautious, conciliatory approach. Their attitudes went against Thatcher's instinctive desire for sweeping change, but the wets could not simply be brushed aside—yet. Thatcher hoped to convince Friedman that she was no compromiser but a true believer, simply moving step by step. As she wrote in a follow-up note to their meeting, "I know so many of the things you stand for I stand for, too."[23] She also knew that currying favor with Friedman would help her larger goal of building connections between the conservative parties of Britain and the United States.

The meeting did not succeed, however, in causing Friedman to hold his fire. In June he made headlines by denouncing the Conservative Party's Green Paper on monetary control. "I could hardly believe my eyes," he told the Commons Select Committee in written testimony. "Only a Rip Van Winkle, who had not read any of the flood of literature during the past decade and more on the money supply process, could have written it." Instead of talking about money, the Green Paper asserted that fiscal policy and interest rates would be used to control inflation. Surveying the British scene, Friedman concluded the government was riding "several horses at once by simultaneously trying to control monetary aggregates, interest rates, and foreign exchange rates—in the process introducing excessive variability into all three."[24] Friedman prescribed his typical medicine: slow and steady growth in the money supply, ignoring other indicators such as interest rates.[25]

Nearly identical to the advice he offered in the United States, Friedman's recommendations overlooked a significant difference between the two countries: who controlled interest rates. Technically, American interest rates were set by financial markets, although Fed actions were a powerful influence. It was plausible, if deceptive, for the Federal Reserve to disclaim responsibility for interest rates, as indeed it had done when threatened by Wright Patman.[26] But in Britain, interest rates were set directly by a committee inside Her Majesty's Treasury. There was no tradition of central bank independence. The Bank of England was owned by Treasury, which was managed by the ruling party. Interest rates were unavoidably political. Ignoring them altogether would be impossible.

Thatcher's team scrambled to make the best of his "unhelpful advice." A memo prepping Thatcher for a meeting with British economists noted that "Prof. Friedman's evidence deserves special attention because of his eminence, because much of it has been reprinted in *The Observer*, because he is known to be a supporter of the government strategy, and because his evidence is (in some passages but not others) quite outspokenly critical of aspects of current policy." Nonetheless, argued the memo, "As a whole there is more in it to help than to harm our presentation," drawing Thatcher's attention to his overall "firm support for our economic strategy as the only means of curing inflation."[27] Thatcher's team rightly understood that Friedman could be a powerful symbol of intellectual legitimacy, useful for burnishing the government's reputation. At the same time, they did not want to shackle policy too tightly to Friedman.

Indeed, multiple variants of monetarism circulated through Thatcher's first government. Monetary policy was not only a compromise between 10 Downing Street, the Bank of England, and Her Majesty's Treasury, but a blend of at least three different monetarist approaches.[28] The genuine monetarists were akin to Friedman, believing inflation was always and everywhere a monetary phenomenon. Accordingly, they wanted to act on the "monetary base." Equivalent to open market operations in the United States, operating on the monetary base in the United Kingdom implied a basic shift in perspective. Instead of responding to the needs of the banking system, serving as "lender of first resort," under monetary base control the Bank of England would sell or buy a predetermined amount of Treasury and commercial bills. The bank would focus on its own balance sheet, and nothing else. Thatcher was sympathetic to this argument, keeping it alive despite opposition in her government.

Other influential ministers converged on so-called pragmatic monetarism, concluding that operating on the base might be effective but was ultimately impractical. While the Bank of England was not independent by statute, neither did it lack opinions or influence. Monetary base control represented a dramatic change in operating procedures that the bank staunchly resisted. Nigel Lawson, later to serve as Chancellor of the Exchequer, wrote that he was "personally attracted to the idea" of monetary base control, but believed it would never work "given the Bank's profound antipathy."[29] A third grouping was the political monetarists, who did not really believe controlling money would work. Political monetarists might acquiesce on the surface to a policy targeting aggregates, but their real goal was to curb demand for money through fiscal probity and interest rates.

Friedman did not know the contours of the policy struggle, but he could sense the outcome. "It is essential to distinguish lip service from a change in policy," he told the House of Commons.[30] Although the government had announced monetary growth targets—as had the previous Labour government—this was not by his reckoning true monetarism. His blunt comments struck an uncomfortable truth. Rather than following a coherent doctrine, British monetarism was a mix of ideas, with an equally mixed outcome.

There was one devilish problem: Which monetary aggregate to target? Friedman favored controlling the aggregate closest to M2 in the United States, called the base or M0 in Britain. M0 consisted of cash held by the public plus money banks had in the till or deposited at the Bank of England. Against Friedman's advice, however, the government committed to reducing M3, a broader measure of money that included short-term deposits, foreign currency, and public-sector deposits.[31] Critically, M3 incorporated government spending, so it was not strictly speaking a monetary aggregate but a combined monetary and fiscal measure. After so much fanfare about fighting monetary growth, the outcome was farcical. M3 shot up by 20 percent, where growth in M0 dropped almost to zero. In some ways, this was predictable. Because M3 included government spending, it was countercyclical, getting larger as the economy got worse. Whatever the announced policy, it was clear that a sharp contraction in M0 was undesirable.

Massive shifts in the wrong aggregate threatened to undo government policy altogether. The British economy was already weak, and a monetary contraction, even if accidental, would make it worse. "Though we were trying to do Friedman, we were actually doing Hayek," moaned one adviser, using Friedman as a shorthand for the gradualist approach to inflation.[32] By contrast, Hayek had been arguing in the British press for a decisive shock treatment. Thatcher's advisers had brushed away this idea as politically infeasible. But now it appeared they might have accidentally triggered a much deeper and steeper recession than expected. Simple on paper, monetarism was diabolical in practice.

Even so, the public linkage between Thatcher and Friedman solidified during an uproar over the 1981 budget. As unemployment surged, Thatcher refused countercyclical policies, sending out a budget that cut spending and raised taxes. The budget aroused immediate condemnation from a large group of British economists, who rightly perceived it as "a climax in the Keynesian/monetarist debate."[33] For decades, governments had spent in bad times—and good. It had led to debt, inflation, and slow growth.

To reverse the trend, Thatcher was trying what many deemed impossible: an expansionary fiscal contraction. Instead of spending more as the economy slowed, she would spend less, believing that the ultimate driver of the problem was too much spending. In terms of the budget, she was crafting pro-cyclical, rather than countercyclical strategy. Eventually, the thinking went, this would produce a private sector–led expansion. To Britain's economists, such a nonsensical strategy could only be the work of Friedman, a cunning "charlatan" who had mesmerized the prime minister.[34] But it more accurately reflected Thatcher's capacious philosophy of monetarism, in which private enterprise was the only true wellspring of economic growth.

The spending cuts diverted attention from another critical part of the package: the government's subtle lowering of interest rates. Money watchers knew the truth. Despite the accidental growth in the target aggregate M3, money—as denoted by M0—was too tight. Indeed, M3 had proved meaningless, yet the government was now publicly tied to it. Announcing and holding to a monetary target was the Thatcherites' "Ark of the new Covenant," a banker remembered sardonically, "differentiating their whole approach from that of every other government since the last war."[35] Friedman had hoped that policy rules would create transparency and bind politicians to their promises. He hadn't realized it also would bind them to their mistakes. As a Conservative Party internal group dryly concluded, "The publication of precise monetary targets has made political life more difficult than would otherwise have been the case."[36] Without anyone admitting it, interest rate policy was responding to the meaningful aggregate, M0, not the announced M3. Always more flexible than her reputation, Thatcher was in fact turning.

Simultaneously, Thatcher continued to maintain her public connection with Friedman. Heading to Prime Minister's Questions, she brushed up on Friedman's critique of the Phillips curve. And in a speech to a conservative gathering, she invoked Friedman to set her policy goals within a broader framework of liberty. "I constantly say that to get inflation down is not enough . . . you must keep incentive and motivation in society, otherwise you will not have the positive element to get expansion going."[37] Remarks like these fostered the impression that Thatcher relied on Friedman for advice and inspiration. It was no wonder that Radio New Zealand greeted Thatcher with this question: "Are you a Milton Friedman disciple?"[38]

It was an ironic twist. Friedman's breakthrough on inflation had been tied to the idea of expectations. Prices weren't just neutral information signals. They were tangled up in hopes and fears about what might happen next. If shopkeepers assumed their wholesale costs would tick ever upward, they would jack up prices on the shelves to keep their margins intact. If workers believed the price of milk and meat would soon be out of reach, they would risk a strike to get a higher wage. Shoppers would rush to buy staples before they cost too much. And if a politician arrived upon the scene claiming to fix all this, the merchant, the worker, and the shopper would shrug it off as just more theater.

But if that same politician announced herself to be a devotee of the market extremist Milton Friedman, who had cracked the code on inflation—then perhaps that shopkeeper would pause at current prices and see what happened. The union leader facing down that same politician might feint with a large wage proposal, then settle for less. The housewife might decide to buy only what her family needed for that week, rather than stockpile. Slowly, the air would begin to leak out of the balloon. So Thatcher's government might embrace Friedman wholeheartedly, yet leave out the most important parts.

In the end, it was not Friedman's specific recommendations for monetary base control that broke the inflationary fever. Rather, it was Thatcher's broader political revolution, of which bastardized monetarism was an essential element. Flying Friedman's flag helped Thatcher telegraph her determination to break with the past and set a new course for economic policy. Like Friedman, she embraced a limited role for government that was a significant departure from decades of Keynesian economics, state-run industries, and welfare spending. Friedman had won the war but lost the battle.

Whereas Friedman reacted coolly to his first encounter with Thatcher, he had a very different reaction to her American counterpart, Ronald Reagan. The two first met in 1967, when Reagan was the governor of California and Friedman was teaching for a quarter at UCLA. "We had a pleasant meeting and I was very favorably impressed," Friedman remembered.[39] It was an auspicious beginning. A few years later, Friedman's relationship with Reagan flourished in connection with a newly potent policy issue: limiting state government spending.

Before California's famous Proposition 13—a bellwether ballot measure capping property taxes that was quickly imitated in more than a dozen states—there was Proposition 1. In 1973 Reagan's staff approached Friedman with an idea for a constitutional amendment that would limit annual state spending. Friedman agreed to advise the governor's task force, and then took to the skies with Reagan on a statewide publicity blitz. Flying from press conference to press conference across the Golden State, the governor "talked freely about both his life and his views," Friedman remembered. Reagan was a Friedman admirer, having drifted to the right just as Friedman emerged as a new voice of conservatism in the early 1960s. Friedman's presence on the campaign trail gave an imprimatur of economic expertise to the ballot proposal (which would nonetheless be defeated). At the end of the day, when asked if he would support Reagan for president, Friedman offered a resounding yes.[40]

Friedman was an early adopter of a man and a movement that would mature politically across the 1970s. The idea of restricting government's ability to tax and spend had a long history on the fringes of American politics, but inflation gave this quixotic campaign new life.[41] Working on the state level, conservative activists began advancing a plethora of measures designed to limit state spending. Some initiatives focused on the outflow, setting spending at a fixed percentage of a state's revenue.

Others tried to roll back or freeze current tax collections. At first, spending limitations appeared in state legislatures. But they quickly became most common as ballot measures that would either amend state constitutions or enact legislation through popular vote. Similarly, while the movement began with political elites, it gained popular traction with inflation. As the price level rose, households were pushed into higher tax brackets, even as their dollars purchased less. Supporters argued that reining in spending would both lower taxes and help dent inflation.

Friedman was happy to lend his name to the cause, and the time was right. After George Shultz's departure, he had fewer allies in the White House. The nomination of Alan Greenspan to chair the Council of Economic Advisers was one bright spot. The two had struck up a friendship during the Nixon campaign, with Friedman becoming an avid subscriber to Greenspan's proprietary economic forecasts. Greenspan stayed on after Nixon resigned in 1974, serving in the same role for Nixon's replacement, Gerald Ford. But even before Ford lost the 1976 election to the Democrat Jimmy Carter, there had been a great reshuffling in Washington. In came the "Watergate babies"—ninety-three new members of Congress, most of them Democrats elected in November 1974 on a great wave of popular anger at corrupt politicians like Nixon. Out into the political wilderness went forty-nine Republican officeholders along with countless staffers and sympathizers, wondering if their party would ever recover from Watergate.[42]

Undeterred, Friedman was one of many who focused anew on state policy. He spoke on state spending limits at the first meeting of the new American Legislative Exchange Council (ALEC), a group designed to share conservative state-level policy ideas. When Tennessee held a constitutional convention, he picked up the phone to lobby delegates. The new constitution would be the first to enshrine a spending limit.[43] At the moment his Nobel Prize was announced, Friedman was in Detroit campaigning for a spending limitation ballot measure. "As we parked the car at the Press Club, we noticed reporters and photographers waiting outside," recounted his companions for the day, two anti-tax activists. "They ran up to us in the parking lot and started snapping photos of Professor Friedman."[44] Quickly the group realized it was not Proposal C but Friedman's prize that had caused all the excitement.

The tax-limitation movement matched Friedman's increasing pessimism about government. Early in his career Friedman and his allies, like Aaron Director, had taken pains to clarify they were not fundamentally anti-government. But after watching both the Democrat Lyndon Johnson and the Republican Richard Nixon expand the scope and scale of federal action, Friedman was beginning to sound more like the anti-government right he had once rejected. "Our basic long-term need is to stop the explosive growth in government spending," he wrote in 1975. "I am persuaded that the only effective way to do this is by cutting taxes—at any time for any excuse in any way."[45] The fundamental dynamic of government was growth, he now believed. Politicians could not be trusted to turn away from the political boondoggle of new programs and new spending. Tax limitation, he believed, "was our only hope" to rein in government.[46] Friedman had not adopted the position that deficits didn't matter. But he was headed in that direction.

The change in Friedman's views was driven, in part, by public choice theory. By 1980, he and Rose were identifying this "fresh approach to political science that has come mainly from economists" as the main evolution in their ideas since *Capitalism and Freedom*.[47] Public choice had many tributaries, emerging at the University of Rochester and Virginia Polytechnical Institute and from scholars with no Chicago training, but one important source was Frank Knight, Friedman's long-ago Chicago idol.[48]

Among Knight's last students was James Buchanan, who translated Knight's acidulous views into a theory of political action, arguing politicians and voters were driven by self-interest just as in the marketplace. "Persons do not readily become economic eunuchs as they shift from market to political participation," Buchanan wrote. "Those who respond predictably to ordinary incentives in the marketplace do not fail to respond at all when they act as citizens."[49] Although it seemed a simple insight, applying the assumptions of self-interest and maximizing behavior to the political realm yielded a range of analytic fruits.

Politicians were "political entrepreneurs," creating new markets for votes with new programs; industries and special interests trying to influence policy were "rent-seeking," hoping to stifle competition, gain advantage, and pass the costs to someone else.[50]

Public choice scholars also developed constitutional models that continued the Chicago legacy of rules over discretion. The original pioneer of this approach was Henry Simons, who focused on monetary policy. Over time, Simons's approach had been generalized into a focus on what Knight called "the rules of the game," rather than the game itself. Another complementary approach was the work of F. A. Hayek. In the 1960s, both Buchanan and Hayek had proposed constitutional structures intended to support markets and constrain the state, ranging from the requirement of supermajorities to redefining the role of legislative bodies.[51]

The tax-limitation movement drew on similar logic, hoping to embed spending limits in state constitutions where they would form the substrate of all future politics. As Friedman put it, rather than focus on individual politicians or political parties, "We shall do far better to seek a change in our effective political constitution that will narrowly limit the power of those whom we elect and thereby alter the incentives of both politicians and voters." Some amendments also included Buchanan's recommendations for a supermajority vote—three-fourths of a legislature—to implement tax hikes. No wonder Friedman found public choice appealing. It was yet another variant of the Chicago school emphasis on price theory and policy rules.[52]

There was another force animating Friedman's appreciation of public choice theory: a newfound fear of redistribution. It was now almost half a century since he had attended the first Mont Pelerin Society meeting, where liberals fretted about central planning. "We thought the major threat to freedom was the extension of wartime programs of central governmental control of production and the organization of resources," Friedman reflected. But central planning had fallen of its own weight, Friedman concluded. And now "this decade's battle cry of socialism is a call for greater *transfers*."[53] The threat had shifted from top-down commissars to redistribution. Instead of socializing the means of production, Friedman argued, the left now wanted to socialize the results.

Friedman was aware this new threat presented a public relations challenge. He quoted Simon Newcomb, a nineteenth-century political economist who spoke in the Darwinist idiom of his day. According to Newcomb, "The greater the number of degraded classes who are allowed to produce offspring, which are allowed to grow to maturity, the more rapidly will these classes increase." Even as he repeated this argument, Friedman admitted, "That's a statement which nobody today would have the nerve to present in that naked, unashamed way."[54] He then endorsed Newcomb's point that charity created a "demand" for poor people.

Although Friedman did not embrace Newcomb's loaded language of fitness and degradation, focusing on the dangers of redistribution jeopardized the careful egalitarianism he had displayed in his earlier writings. In the 1960s, Friedman's writing on poverty had been notable for treating the poor with scrupulous neutrality. Amid incendiary debates about the Black family, Friedman stuck to a technocratic understanding of poverty defined by measures of income or wealth. But it was hard to challenge redistribution without attacking those who benefited. Friedman solved the problem by concentrating his fire on bureaucracies that depended upon the poor, the "new class" of "social reformers who have gone into government service to do good and have ended up doing very well."[55] Continuing with the public choice perspective, Friedman viewed the self-interest of bureaucrats as paramount.

Inflation and tax limitation offered a better way to discuss the problems of a growing state. Even as he promoted monetarism to stabilize prices, Friedman knew that inflation brought opportunity. "Nothing offers either more hope or more danger than the inflation we have been experiencing," he told an audience at the University of Rochester. "It offers danger because, if the inflation is not contained, it will destroy society as we know it. But it offers hope because it is the most effective force promoting a revolt by the public against the continued expansion in the scope of government," he argued.[56] Indeed, over time, tax-limitation activists were finding success as they refined their proposals to address the problem of inflation. New proposals focused less on limiting spending and more on limiting taxes.

For many Americans, the hardest bite of inflation came with property taxes. In many localities, home valuations were adjusted each year and soon soared far beyond salaries. It was one thing to pay 1 percent annual tax on a home you could afford to buy. It was another to pay the same rate on a house that was appreciating at an annual rate of 10 percent or more. More than half of all American households owned a home, which served combined needs of shelter, nest egg, and retirement plan. Home ownership was far more than a private matter; home-building was a key economic sector, and all the goodies that made a house a home powered the consumer economy. Recognizing the potency of property taxes, longtime balanced budget activists dusted off California's Proposition 1 and rewrote it as Proposition 13, which froze assessments and capped any increase at 2 percent annually, until the home was sold.[57] When Proposition 13 passed in 1978, it made national headlines.

Quickly imitated in a dozen other states, Proposition 13 also had a counterpart on the national level: the Kemp-Roth tax cut. Named after its two congressional sponsors, the proposal was linked most closely to its media-savvy junior sponsor, the telegenic Jack Kemp. A former professional football player for the Buffalo Bills, Kemp now represented the team's declining upstate New York district. Once a powerhouse of the steel industry, Buffalo was rapidly losing jobs and factories. Deindustrialization was a long-term trend, driven by declining productivity and competition from nonunionized "mini-mills."[58] But like so much of economic life, the turn from capital-intensive industry was accelerated by inflation.

If property taxes destroyed household balance sheets, depreciation was the bane of corporate finance. Companies offset large expenditures with tax breaks based on anticipated depreciation, or the decline of an item's value over its lifetime. For example, the cost of a factory upgrade expected to last ten years could translate into a decade's worth of reduced taxes. But in a legislative quirk reflecting the postwar era's heretofore stable prices, depreciation was based on the original cost of equipment. In an inflationary environment, there could be a shocking price difference between the original cost and the current price tag. It made sense for corporations to defer upgrades, expansion, or even maintenance.[59] Reduced business spending translated into job loss. During the early 1970s, when Kemp was first elected to Congress, his district suffered 11 to 14 percent unemployment.[60]

In search of a solution, Kemp stumbled upon supply-side economics. As its name suggested, this new current in economic policy was a riposte to the Keynesian emphasis on stimulating the "demand side" of the economy. Supply-siders put the fiscal revolution in reverse: tax cuts would stimulate private spending. This would lift the overall level of economic activity, in the end creating greater tax receipts. Supporters also argued tax-rate cuts would cure inflation without a painful recession, by boosting production to match the money in circulation.

Critically, supply-siders focused on marginal tax rates—the tax paid on each additional increment of income. Americans did not pay the same rate on all their income. Rather, as their income passed certain thresholds, the tax rate on that additional income went up. At the time, the highest rate of 70 percent was paid on earnings over $100,000. Supply-siders believed these high rates fundamentally damaged incentives to economic risk-taking and hard work. Lowering rates would foster investment and stir the "animal spirits" that powered economic life. Their opponents saw lower rates as simply a giveaway to the rich.

In its purest form—tax cuts will pay for themselves—supply-side was a new synthesis. Its leading publicist was Jude Wanniski of *The Wall Street Journal*, and its leading theoreticians were two renegade Chicago economists, Robert Mundell and Arthur Laffer. The two overlapped briefly with Friedman in his last years as a professor, but he wasn't close to either. Mundell was a specialist in international monetary economics, pumping out sober academic works that would eventually earn him a Nobel. Laffer flitted through Chicago on the way to the Nixon administration, where he worked with George Shultz at the Office of Management and Budget. He immortalized the supply-side idea in the Laffer curve, graphing tax rates against tax revenue.

The curve dramatized the power of incentives. At one end of the curve, there were no taxes and no revenue. More important was the other end of the curve—100 percent taxes, which also showed no revenue, because nobody works for free. The trick was finding the place where lower tax rates actually boosted revenue, as the government took a smaller slice of a larger pie. Laffer took to scribbling the simplified diagram on napkins, most famously at a dinner with Donald Rumsfeld and Dick Cheney. The complete supply-side package also included a return to the gold standard. While not as outlandish as it would appear today—after all, the gold window had been closed for less than a decade—the idea was far outside the economics mainstream. Even within the world of conservative think tanks, supply-side economics was the province of upstarts and outsiders.[61]

In its basic outlines, however, supply-side had a much longer history, including the 1964 Kennedy tax cut. Although the Kennedy tax cut had lowered rates, it had hardly simplified the system; there were still twenty-five separate individual income tax rates. With inflation on the rise, Americans were rapidly ascending into the higher brackets. As *The Washington Post* observed a few years later, "Taxes devised for the rich are now beginning to hit the entire middle class."[62] It was unclear if supply-side would actually help with inflation. But it would certainly help with the consequences of inflation by cutting back overgrown tax bills.

Kemp became an evangelist for supply-side. He had long supported tax cuts, which were an essential tool of Republican policy-making. President Ford had touted tax breaks as a way out of recession. And in 1975 Friedman's negative income tax was reborn as the Earned Income Tax Credit, a rebate for low-income Americans. Intended as a temporary measure to address inflation, by 1978 it had become permanent.[63]

Still, Kemp-Roth marked a significant departure in tax policy. Instead of aiming for the largest overall tax cut, the bill targeted the highest marginal rates, which were thought to damage incentives the most. Moreover, Kemp-Roth abandoned an even more venerable Republican tradition—balanced budgets. "I don't worship at the shrine of the balanced budget," Kemp told *Fortune*.[64]

Friedman was immediately critical. "I think it is misleading to suppose that you're going to be able to reduce taxes and increase spending—that is a contradiction in terms," he told the conservative *Santa Ana Register* in 1979. "There are no doubt some kinds of taxes in which the rates have such great disincentive effect that by reducing those rates you would increase total receipts," he continued. "But I do not believe that is true for the tax system as a whole and consequently I believe it is very misleading to argue that you can simultaneously spend more and tax less."[65] Nonetheless, Friedman counted himself a supporter of Kemp-Roth. Although he did not believe the bill would magically pay for itself, he reasoned that it would inhibit spending by cutting overall revenue. The bill made it through Congress before withering under threat of presidential veto. Yet even Carter was not immune to the tax-cutting fever; he signed off on a significant reduction in the capital gains tax.

Gearing up for another run at the presidency in 1980, Reagan's advisers were alert to the possibilities revealed by Proposition 13 and Kemp-Roth. Tax cuts were easy to explain and relatively straightforward to deliver; they were certainly more achievable than solving intractable social problems or ending years of inflation. But tax cuts were Kemp's issue, and the blow-dried, sporty Kemp looked like a plausible challenger to the aging Reagan. The campaign solved that problem with a straightforward buyout: Kemp-Roth would become the centerpiece of Reagan's economic agenda, to the benefit of both men. At the same time, rumors began to circulate that the handsome Kemp, who was said to favor weekend retreats with male staffers, was homosexual. In the end, Kemp never mounted his own presidential bid.[66]

Reagan's reinvention as the candidate of the tax cut led him to a new rhetoric of possibility rather than blame. Campaigning for governor of California in the late 1960s, Reagan blasted rioters and campus protesters, claiming he would "clean up the mess at Berkeley." Once in office, he followed through by sending helicopters and the National Guard to fight the so-called Battle for People's Park. He had been traditional in economics, hewing to balanced-budget orthodoxy. To keep the state in the black, he had raised taxes—twice.

With Kemp-Roth in his back pocket, Reagan could shift the conversation to the brighter days ahead. He stopped dwelling on welfare queens and instead began "preaching economic hope through tax cuts," two journalists observed. This was seen as a promising strategy for the party as a whole. "Every negative you could put on the Republican Party had been done because of Vietnam, civil rights, Nixon, Watergate," reflected the Republican National chairman in 1977.[67] Not only had Nixon's resignation—and Ford's pardon—delivered the White House to the Democrat Jimmy Carter. The post-Watergate blowout had reduced Republicans to thirty-seven seats in the Senate and delivered a two-thirds Democratic supermajority in the House. The party had no place to go but up.

Reagan's focus on economics got a boost from *Free to Choose*, Rose and Milton's blockbuster television show. This was Friedman's major post-Chicago project, and at first he wasn't interested. It was Rose who grasped the power of television to spread her husband's ideas, and Rose who convinced him to do it—just as she had with his *Newsweek* column.

Once again, her instincts were right. *Free to Choose* proved a major platform for Friedman's views, dovetailing with the emergent anti-government, tax-cutting sentiment the Reagan campaign was built on. In the nine months leading up to the presidential election, *Free to Choose* aired on nearly 75 percent of the nation's PBS television channels. Each of the ten episodes attracted an estimated three million viewers, while a companion volume was the best-selling nonfiction book of 1980.[68]

Free to Choose crystallized all the free-floating anti-government sentiment of the era, showcasing inefficient bureaucrats, runaway federal spending, and harried, harassed ordinary citizens struggling against red tape and regulation. It repackaged the fatigue and letdown of the Carter years into a coherent ideology about the dangers of too much government. Across ten hour-long installments, divided into a solo feature and then a staged debate between Friedman and opponents,

Free to Choose offered one overarching thesis: the fifty years since the New Deal were a dangerous departure from first principles. This theme recurred as Friedman wandered the streets of Hong Kong, interviewed public-housing residents in Britain, and shook his head at the foolishness of consumer product safety testing.

At a moment when social democracy seemed to have run its course, the idea of a fifty-year wrong turn had resonance. It was not that viewers of *Free to Choose* wanted to roll back the entire legacy of the New Deal, including Social Security, the SEC, the FDIC, and modern employment law. But in talking about the past, Friedman was really gesturing toward the future. It appeared that New Deal liberalism could no longer deliver economic stability and prosperity; but before it had come depression and ruin. Friedman reached back instead to a glorified vision of the nineteenth century, touchstone and exemplar of all that free market capitalism could deliver. Reflecting on the Gilded Age, he celebrated the hardy independence of immigrants like his mother. "There were few government programs to turn to and nobody expected them. But also, there were few rules and regulations. There were no licenses, no permits, no red tape to restrict them. They found in fact, a free market, and most of them thrived on it."[69] Friedman's message was that it was possible—even American—to live this way again.

And the Depression? Leaving behind the subtlety of his academic work, Friedman declared: "Far from being a failure of free market capitalism, the depression was a failure of government."[70] He went on to summarize the argument of *A Monetary History of the United States.* Once, the Federal Reserve, the state manager of money, had symbolized Friedman's interest in breaking with the intellectual tradition of laissez-faire. Now he used the central bank as a stand-in for government incompetence and overreach.

Keeping just outside the camera frame, Rose was omnipresent. As Milton remembered, Rose "participated in every planning session and every editing session; she was on every shoot and involved in every discussion about the content of my statements to the camera."[71] Before the camera started running, Rose warmed up the star. Although there was no formal script for the series—Milton preferred speaking from memory guided only by sketchy notes—some practice was required. Heads together at the side of the set, Milton would toss out lines and ideas that Rose would shoot down or approve. Credited as an associate producer, Rose was far more, serving as a manager, agent, director, and entourage. Like Anna Schwartz, Rose authored a powerful narrative that itself shaped political history.

Reagan's election reversed the fortunes of the Republican Party. He defeated Carter by nearly ten points in the popular vote, while the GOP recaptured the Senate. There had not been this many Republican senators since the days of Herbert Hoover. Democrats still held the House, but as *CQ Almanac* noted, "Several pillars of Democratic liberalism went down to defeat," including powerful committee chairs and the 1972 presidential nominee, George McGovern. Incoming Republicans were both more conservative and younger, the paper observed, giving "conservatives the ability to control or substantially influence national policy in the executive and legislative branches of government."[72] The ghost of Richard Nixon had been banished.

Beyond his embrace of free market economics, Reagan had brought critical new constituencies into the party. Some were working-class white voters of the urban North, the so-called Reagan Democrats. Inflation, taxes, and humiliating foreign policy setbacks like the Iranian hostage crisis had swung their loyalties to Reagan and his promises of national rebirth. Even more significant was the arrival of politically energized evangelical Christians. The nation's fastest-growing religious denominations were evangelical, and many had cast their first-ever votes for Carter, a born-again Christian. But when Carter disappointed them by taking liberal positions, particularly on feminism and gay rights, evangelicals sought a new political leader. Reagan was the first presidential candidate to openly court the evangelical vote. His victory helped shatter the Democratic Party's once powerful grip on the Southern electorate, establishing new political dynamics that would shape the decades ahead.[73]

Friedman was by now the most famous economist in the world. Even his one plausible rival for the title, John Kenneth Galbraith, admitted as much; at the end of the 1970s, Galbraith wrote, "the age of

John Maynard Keynes gave way to the age of Milton Friedman." When Friedman appeared at the San Francisco Fed for a conference or presentation, which he did frequently during his California years, "he sucked the air out of the room," observed a junior staffer. "He did not even need to assert himself; everyone just focused on him." Fame masked an agonizing paradox lying in wait. Monetarism's new repute was born of desperation. More than a decade of inflation had destroyed its competitors in the academic and political realms. But inflation had also profoundly changed the conditions under which monetarism would operate. Slowly, painfully, Friedman would learn that monetarism was built on data from a world that no longer existed: the regulated and regimented postwar era, the land the New Deal built and inflation swept away.[74]

14

THE VOLCKER SHOCK

> It is illusory to expect central banks to put an end to the inflation that now afflicts the industrial democracies.
>
> —Arthur Burns, 1979

Ronald Reagan's triumph offered Milton Friedman a reprise of the influence he had enjoyed under Richard Nixon. The conduit this time was the longtime Reagan aide Martin Anderson, a onetime Columbia Business School professor with a knack for appearing at critical junctures in Friedman's life. Anderson made his name with *The Federal Bulldozer*, an attack on urban renewal during its height of fashion in the Johnson years. Along with his wife, Annelise, an influential official at the Office of Management and Budget—the two would soon be anointed "Reagan's Ranking Couple" by *The Washington Post*—Anderson had traveled from Ayn Rand's collective through the Nixon campaign and into the White House. It was Anderson who had worked closely with Arthur Burns to scuttle the negative income tax, and Anderson who helped Nixon end the draft. Since 1971 he had been a senior fellow at the Hoover Institution, where he and Friedman became close. Anderson joined Reagan's presidential campaign in 1979 and went on to play a key role coordinating policy in the White House.

Anderson's brainchild was PEPAB—the President's Economic Policy Advisory Board. The group was chaired by George Shultz, then a business executive but soon to be appointed secretary of state. Formulated as an independent group of outside experts, PEPAB aroused suspicion and bureaucratic jealousy within the administration, but was treasured by Reagan. The board met at the White House six times during Reagan's first year, "strongly reinforcing his long-held views on economic policy," according to Anderson. The president took particular delight in Friedman's presence. "His eyes sparkled with delight every time he engaged in a dialogue with him," Anderson remembered, judging Friedman among the most influential of the PEPAB group.[1]

A month after the election, Friedman sent Anderson a memo titled "The Importance of the Fed." Drawing on his observations of Britain, Friedman warned that if the money supply were not reduced, it would accelerate inflation, "a repetition of what the Bank of England did to Margaret Thatcher." And if the administration did not act quickly to address inflation, the "inevitable recession" would be blamed on Reagan, not on Carter. Better to get it over with now, so that a recovery could be well under way by the next election. The challenge, he noted, was "how to exercise leverage on the Fed." Thinking it over, Friedman concluded the "only possibility I can see is a straight talk with Volcker about the problem."[2] Here Friedman referred to the relatively new chairman of the Federal Reserve, in office for just over a year.

Paul Volcker knew Friedman from his time at Treasury, and he was not a fan. The two men were opposites in temperament, approach, and even physical appearance, with Volcker as strikingly tall as Friedman was short. While Volcker appeared every inch the Republican banker, he was actually a Democrat. Where Friedman prized "straight talk," Volcker cultivated mystique, shielding his face in clouds of cigar smoke when testifying before Congress. Volcker was an insider's insider, reminiscent of "a breed of eastern money men who have run US economic and financial policy since Alexander Hamilton and the founding of the Republic," as an admiring biographer summarized.[3] He came to the post with a formidable résumé, including positions at the Treasury Department and the New York Federal Reserve, and a sterling reputation among financial markets and European bankers.

There had been one other Fed chair after Burns, the corporate executive George Miller. An outsider to the Fed, Miller made little headway against inflation and even less against the Federal Open Market Committee (FOMC), which went into open revolt when he tried to ban smoking during meetings. After serving a little more than a year, Miller was moved to secretary of the Treasury amid Carter's disastrous cabinet shake-up. Intended to telegraph bold resolve and new thinking, the simultaneous resignation of six cabinet members at the request of Carter instead made him appear disorganized and shambolic. Volcker's appointment—in retrospect among the most important decisions Carter would make—was a by-product of this turbulent period.

When Volcker assumed office in August 1979, it was not quite as bad as Britain's Winter of Discontent, but close. The consumer price index soon leaped past 11 percent, a spike driven by a second oil shock. Caused by political turmoil in Iran, the drop in oil imports made gasoline either unaffordable or unobtainable. Frustrated truckers blocked highways in protest; filling stations saw fights and even murders. Compounding the problem was an elaborate series of regulations that dictated where retailers could purchase oil and regulated the price according to when and where it had been drilled. Under normal market conditions, supply and demand flowed through these long-standing channels. Amid the oil shock, the carefully calibrated structure created bottlenecks and backups.[4]

Across the nation, inflation was colliding with an economic compact set up in the distant era of the New Deal and refined in the equally distant land of Eisenhower's America. The problem of the Depression had been deflation, not inflation. And the world of the 1950s revolved around stodgy institutions designed for stability, including the large corporation, the national political party jury-rigged around mutually incompatible interests—like Southern segregationists and African American voters—and the clunky system of international gold exchange and currency ratios. None of them would pass unchanged through the crucible of inflation.

High prices, persistent now for nearly a decade, were rewriting the social compact of postwar America. As one scholar summarizes it: "The American consumer economy was based on the mortgage-financed suburban single-family home. Every element of that agreement—the price of housing, the availability and price of the credit that gave access to the housing, and the price of the gasoline that allowed workers to travel to those suburbs and brought low-cost goods all over the country—came undone by inflation."[5] This was what Friedman meant when he said inflation could "destroy society as we know it." And these were the entwined social, economic, and political problems Volcker would face as chairman of the Federal Reserve.

To Friedman, Volcker's long years of government service under multiple administrations, both Republican and Democrat, were not a sign of statesmanship but a worrying dedication to bureaucracy. In turn, Volcker knew Friedman as a perpetual irritant. A fast believer in Bretton Woods, Volcker had struggled to minimize Friedman's influence as the system came unstuck. After shuttling around the globe to help financial markets and ministers navigate economic turmoil, he saw Friedman's faith in liberated markets as dangerously simple. Nonetheless, Volcker had followed the rise of monetarism from his vantage point at the New York Fed. "Monetary aggregate targets are a useful—even a necessary—gauge of appropriate monetary policy action in bringing inflation under control," he wrote in 1977.[6] Volcker was not a true believer, but he was well informed about Friedman's ideas.

And like the Thatcherites, Volcker was not above practicing a little ersatz monetarism. Friedman's high-profile column at *Newsweek* made his commentary on the Fed and the economy impossible to ignore. Monetarism had adherents not just among economists but among the New York finance crowd and other market makers. When Friedman gave a talk at Oppenheimer Holdings in 1968, the bank hired him on the spot, retaining him as a consultant for sixteen years. On his way to an appearance on the TV show *Wall $treet Week with Louis Rukeyser*, Friedman was flagged down by another guest, the investment analyst Mary Farrell. Claiming that she had no ride, Farrell asked to join Friedman in his town car from the train station. "I count this personal time with one of the leading economic thinkers of the twentieth century as a true honor," Farrell recounted, calling Friedman one of the "best minds in finance." Likewise, Charles Fahy, the author of *The Streetwise Investor,* justified his stock-picking system by citing a brief conversation with Friedman, casting him as an unimpeachable authority on all things financial.[7] Now this very reputation made monetarism useful to an establishment figure needing an unambiguous signal of policy change.

Without invoking Friedman explicitly—he had after all been appointed by Carter—in the fall of 1979 Volcker announced a dramatic shift in policy. "We will talk about growth in the aggregates as the fundamental objective of the economy," he told the press at an unusual weekend press conference. In a break with tradition, Volcker himself handled most of the questions. He shared news of an unscheduled FOMC meeting held earlier that day. The FOMC had decided to focus policy on bank reserves, a move Friedman had long recommended. "Constraining the growth of the money supply through the reserve mechanism, we think we can get firmer control over the growth in money supply in a shorter period of time," Volcker explained. The implications would have been clear to financial traders, Volcker's key audience. Reserves—the money held by banks, at the ready should depositors want it—were a key ingredient of monetary aggregates. Using reserves as the measure of policy meant the Fed was newly focused on the quantity of money. The Fed had gone monetarist.[8]

Looking back, Volcker had a pithy explanation for the change: "We would control the quantity of money (the money supply) rather than the price of money (the interest rate)." This could seem circuitous logic to anyone who understood supply and demand; after all, the price of most goods was essentially related to its supply, whether it was plentiful or scarce. What difference did it make if the Fed focused on the price or the supply of money?[9]

For one thing, Volcker's announcement conveyed a substantive operating change at the Fed. To know if policy was on track—if the FOMC should buy, sell, or hold the course—Volcker's Fed would pore over the latest monetary aggregates. While the Fed had watched aggregates for years, and even announced targets when Congress required it, never before had the money supply served as the essential "thermostat," determining whether the economy should be heated or cooled.

Relatedly, the announcement downgraded interest rates as a policy instrument. Although it was not then widely understood by the general public—and still is not today—the Fed has never directly controlled general interest rates. Sometimes the press talked about the Fed "setting" the federal funds rate—the benchmark rate banks charge each other for overnight loans. Although it sounded like an official figure, the name was just a holdover from the 1920s, when Fed banks were among the few that could manage overnight transactions, courtesy of their newfangled telegraphic network. So while in the United Kingdom the Chancellor of the Exchequer (and later the Bank of England) could announce an official bank rate, the Fed had more limited powers. True, it could set the discount rate for banks that wanted to borrow money directly, and it could raise or lower reserve requirements. Typically these tools were used sparingly given their limited reach, although Volcker's Fed used both to fight inflation. The most powerful mechanism, however, was the federal funds rate. And the FOMC could only act indirectly on that rate through its sales and purchases of bonds. Traditionally, the Fed targeted a narrow range of allowable interest rates it hoped to reach through these sales. And when the Fed "leaned against the wind," it was usually leaning against interest rates.

But now, Volcker noted, interest rates would no longer be the focus of monetary policy. Although the Fed would still maintain a target range, it would be far broader than in the past. "We at the Federal Reserve will take less interest, if you will, in the daily fluctuations of that very short-term rate," Volcker explained to journalists. There would not be the same "official chaperonage" of the federal funds rate, nor would the Fed "shepherd the market so closely from day to day." Instead, "there will be substantial freedom in the market." The Fed's actions would be guided by aggregates, not interest rates. Accordingly, the federal funds rate might "fluctuate over a wider range than has been the practice in recent years." It was not hard to read between the lines.

High interest rates would no longer provoke an immediate reaction from the Fed—unless they were accompanied by an unwanted change in monetary aggregates. The guardrails were off.[10]

Why was the Fed moving away from interest rates? In part, the change reflected Friedman's influence. The Fed ought to "renounce its love affair with controlling interest rates," he instructed Volcker in *Newsweek*.[11] Friedman had long argued that interest rates were a crude and indirect way of regulating economic activity. He labored to explain that contrary to conventional wisdom, high interest rates did not necessarily mean low inflation or restrained economic growth. Indeed, they could mean the opposite: that inflationary expectations were so entrenched borrowers were willing to take credit at a high price because they thought it would go even higher.

When Friedman made these arguments in the 1950s and 1960s, they seemed either utterly wrong, or irrelevant. But the 1970s showed that high inflation and high interest rates could coexist. They also highlighted the importance of another Friedman theme: the difference between nominal interest rates—the stated figure that appeared on contracts and the like—and real interest rates, or the true cost of borrowing. Amid stable prices, this point could be dismissed as a distinction without a difference. It became relevant amid high inflation. For example, a 9 percent nominal interest rate, when prices were rising 7 percent, really only returned 2 percent. As a result, the Fed could think it was raising interest rates more than it actually was.

While the difference between real and nominal seems commonsensical today, it was not incorporated into Fed thinking until the late 1970s. Volcker's turn from interest rates marked his awareness that in an inflationary environment, interest rates could lose both their predictive power and their ability to slow down economic activity. "The significance of a particular level of interest rates is more difficult to interpret during a period of accelerating inflation," he explained in a speech to the press.[12] If Friedman was also right about aggregates, making them the focus of Fed policy would offer better insight into what was really happening in the economy while yielding a more powerful, direct, and consistent mechanism of control.

The new policy was also meant to capture the public's attention, again reflecting Friedman's insights. Expectations had been critical to his "accelerationist" thesis—that inflation took on a life of its own once buyers and sellers decided it was here to stay. This idea, which had been fully incorporated into the academic understanding of inflation, matched Volcker's understanding of how Fed actions were interpreted. Talk was not enough—Burns had talked and talked about fighting inflation, making himself a laughingstock by the end of his term as prices relentlessly rose. Indeed, the very day Volcker finalized his new approach, Burns had just delivered a widely noted lecture, "The Anguish of Central Banking." Addressing an audience gathered for the Annual Meetings of the International Monetary Fund, Burns concluded: "It is illusory to expect central banks to put an end to the inflation that now afflicts the industrial democracies." No central banker, Burns was sure, would risk the necessary "difficult adjustments."[13] Volcker announcing a new focus on aggregates signaled a break with the Burns era. It clearly communicated that the Fed was getting serious about inflation. "People don't need an advanced degree in economics to understand that inflation has something to do with too much money," Volcker reflected years later.[14]

It was also a play to borrow Friedman's reputational capital. Although Volcker called his approach "practical monetarism," he always kept Friedman at arm's length. Like most central bankers, he considered Friedman's concept of a fixed monetary growth rule too mechanistic and abstract. And he was well aware that Friedman had long advocated ending central bank independence, by subsuming the Fed under Treasury or making it more accountable to Congress. Nor did he appear to like Friedman personally. But Volcker recognized that Friedman's dictum, "Inflation is always and everywhere a monetary phenomenon," had wide currency. "The simplicity of that thesis helped provide a basis for presenting a new approach to the American public," Volker summarized in his memoir. Moreover, he understood that a public declaration of monetarism would impose discipline on the FOMC. As Thatcher's team had discovered, once a monetarist policy was announced, backing away from it became increasingly difficult.[15]

Beyond strategy, Volcker was also embracing a central part of Friedman's economic message—that there was no long-run trade-off between inflation and unemployment. In the short run, it might appear possible to lower unemployment by letting inflation increase. Over time, though, both would move together; high inflation would choke off growth and raise unemployment, while low inflation would create the conditions for sustainable economic expansion, including hiring. Hence, the central bank ought to prioritize fighting inflation over maintaining full employment. "My basic philosophy is over time we have no choice but to deal with the inflationary situation because over time inflation and the unemployment go together," he told the National Press Club, aptly summarizing Friedman's American Economic Association presidential address. It wasn't Friedman's thinking alone, of course, but "the lesson of the 1970s," as Volcker put it. By law, the Fed had a "dual mandate," tasked with keeping an eye on both critical indicators. In practice, the Fed typically tried to avoid high unemployment, even at the cost of inflation. Volcker was warning he would not do the same.[16]

Friedman was not about to give up his lifelong role as Fed critic, even with an inflation hawk at the helm talking about money supply. As Volcker took office, the two exchanged courteous letters.[17] When Volcker announced the shift to aggregates, Friedman was cautiously optimistic. "Has the Fed finally gotten [the monetarist] message? The Fed's release sounds like it," he told his *Newsweek* readers. But he had heard this kind of talk before. "I hope that this time will be different—but remain skeptical until performance matches pronouncements."[18] He did not have long to wait.

It was one thing for the Fed to announce a policy of controlling monetary aggregates. It was another to actually control them. Just as the spotlight moved onto the aggregate M1—a broad measure of money supply that included circulating currency and checking account deposits—it went berserk. In the first months of 1980, M1 plunged nearly

15 percent. This turned out to be the unexpected by-product of credit controls, an inflation-fighting policy pushed by Carter. Americans had responded to Carter's call to pay off their credit cards with zeal, draining money from their checking accounts. The Fed had opposed Carter's program before agreeing to publicly support it, and the drop in money it caused had little to do with Volcker's new policy.

But now the Fed was responsible for M1, through thick or thin. The FOMC didn't know exactly what had happened—it would take time to grasp the impact of the credit controls—but it did know M1 had to come up. Frantically, the New York desk bought as many bonds as it could. The result was another jag in the money supply that Friedman so hated. "What Fed inflation fight?" he scoffed in *Newsweek* at year's end.[19] Volcker looked like yet another Fed chair saying one thing and doing another.

Carter was no happier. As Volcker had suggested they might, when no longer constrained by Fed policy, interest rates did indeed fluctuate. First they went down, just like M1. Then they shot up. Weeks before the election the federal funds rate was heading past 12 percent, and by year's end the daily rate hit 22 percent. Another Fed chair would have changed course, fast, in the face of such high rates before a presidential election. But Volcker feared further retreat would only make the inflation problem worse. After the election, Carter was sure Fed meddling had cost him the presidency.

Watching from the sidelines, Arthur Burns was growing increasingly alarmed. Only weeks after Reagan's election he turned up in Volcker's office, agitated and almost paranoid. He told his successor that Friedman was on the warpath. It wasn't just jokes about the Fed being replaced by a computer. Friedman had helped author an internal planning document that questioned the Fed's independence. Burns had beaten the group back to vague invocations of accountability. But the real danger was the esteem President-elect Reagan held for Friedman. "You know how persuasive he can be," Burns reminded Volcker. Growing red in the face, Burns boomed out a warning: "Do not forget that for as long as you are in this office!"[20] Lacking a personal connection to Friedman, Volcker would never find his criticisms so disturbing.

But he picked up the hint and began talking about a gradual reduction in the money supply. Yet as Reagan's first year in office unfolded, the money supply continued to zigzag.

In the summer of 1981, Washington's attention shifted to the traditional field of economic policy-making—the federal budget. A veteran of the California campaign to limit state taxes, Reagan was ready to implement similar ideas on the national level. Following his campaign pledge, he sent in a budget with considerable tax reductions. The Economic Recovery Tax Act, or ERTA, came in two main buckets: changes to business depreciation schedules, and significant across-the-board tax cuts for individuals, Kemp-Roth style. The version that eventually passed dropped marginal tax rates as low as 11 percent, with the highest rate reduced from 70 to 50 percent.

It was in some ways a reprise of the Kennedy tax cut, with a crucial difference: whereas JFK had proposed a tax cut to stimulate a placid economy, Reagan was proposing the same medicine for an economy clearly in trouble, riven with inflation, persistent high unemployment, and record-setting interest rates. Instead of fighting the basic premise, Democrats jumped in with a smaller tax cut of their own. An intense bidding war was on, as lobbyists sought bespoke exemptions, playing each party against the other.

The fiscal revolution had been turned upside down. For decades—since the New Deal—Democrats had pushed deficit spending as a necessary part of economic growth. In response, Republicans had settled into the role of fiscal watchdogs. Countercyclical deficits, intended to stabilize the business cycle on the downside, were permissible. Nonetheless, most Republican officeholders believed budget deficits were inherently inflationary. They assumed the Fed would hold interest rates low to make government debt attractive, as had happened in the Johnson years, leading to inflation. Or government borrowing would "crowd out" private investment, bidding up the cost of capital and everything else. The track record of the last decade seemed further evidence of the point. First came the excess spending, then inflation, then stagnation. The standard Republican approach was spending cuts, then tax cuts.

Now Reagan had inverted the formula. In addition to the tax cuts, he wanted increased military spending. How would it all hold together? Supply-side economics promised a spurt of growth as lower taxes spurred ingenuity and hard work. Yet many traditional Republican constituencies—including big business—were immediately skeptical. A former leader of the Business Roundtable called the tax cut "political rhetoric," created by men who were not "economists or students of the economy . . . it ought to be discarded now." Reagan's own vice president, George H. W. Bush, mocked the approach as "voo-doo economics" while campaigning against Reagan for the nomination. Bush was now in the fold as Reagan's VP, but the clash continued between supply-side economics and the traditional balanced-budget wing of the GOP.[21]

Friedman emerged to cheerlead the new GOP approach to deficit spending. He hastened to assure his readers that tax cuts would not contribute to inflation. More important, he argued, "a cut in taxes will mean a cut in government spending. And there is no other way to get a cut in spending." He continued to downplay the threat of deficits. "The deficit is definitely inflationary only if it is financed by creating new money," he argued. "But the deficit need not be so financed."[22] Moreover, he noted, deficits could restrain future spending. They could act as a sort of informal constitutional amendment limiting state activity.

Friedman's views on deficits were in transition, mirroring broader shifts in the Republican Party. In 1978, he warned that the original Kemp-Roth promised "a free lunch for everyone."[23] Still, he had been willing to support the bill for its other benefits. Now, while minimizing the potential harm of deficits, Friedman assumed that Reagan's administration would be characterized by fiscal restraint. In *Newsweek* he touted the tax cut, but linked it explicitly to "a lower ceiling on total expenditures." Laying out his timetable for "steady growth, low inflation," he likewise noted, "I assume that federal spending is reduced gradually."[24] As the budget battle began, he continued to argue that

Reagan would "achieve a balanced budget" by reducing government spending even as he cut taxes.[25] Friedman was making two arguments at once. First, budget deficits would not cause inflation. Second, they would not get out of hand because of spending cuts.

In the end, the bill that Reagan got through Congress was able to satisfy both the supply-siders and the balanced-budget wing of the party—just barely. It was not quite the chicanery of LBJ, but Reagan's budget director, David Stockman, was certainly creative. An important innovation was what Stockman called "the magic asterisk"—denoting future savings "to be identified."[26] The idea that tax cuts would pay for themselves did not carry the day. Instead, the administration relied on a mix of arguments about fighting inflation, restoring incentives, and reaping the benefits of monetary policy.[27] Supportive last-minute forecasts from the well-regarded, nonpartisan Congressional Budget Office also helped. Perhaps the most effective argument was the most basic: Economic policy was broken, so why not try something new? "The President wanted it, and nothing else had worked," one lawmaker explained to *The New York Times*.[28] Or as *The Washington Post* summarized: "The most important point about supply-side theory is that after incentives are changed, the future can no longer be projected as a continuation of the past."[29] ERTA passed in August.

Among the observers unconvinced by supply-side logic was Volcker. He had not been won over by the new idea that tax cuts would pay for themselves. Nor had he let go of the idea that budget deficits were inflationary. Even more important, he believed the financial markets had not let go of this idea. High interest rates reflected bond traders' basic assessment that inflation would continue unabated, as it had during the last three presidential administrations. This meant the administration and the Fed were pulling in different directions. The Fed was "the only game in town," as one member of the FOMC told Volcker.[30] It was true Volcker thought there was no painless way out of inflation. Yet the prospect of ballooning deficits became another major driver of the Fed's austerity: Volcker felt obliged to counterbalance the administration.

During 1981, there were plenty of reasons to reconsider the Fed's

AFTER THE REVENUE ACT OF 1964		AFTER THE ECONOMIC RECOVERY TAX ACT OF 1981		AFTER THE TAX REFORM ACT OF 1986	
RATE	INCOME BRACKET	RATE	INCOME BRACKET	RATE	INCOME BRACKET
14%	$0 to $500	0%	$0 to $2,300	15%	$0 to $17,850
15%	$500 to $1,000	11%	$2,300 to $3,400	28%	Over $17,850
16%	$1,000 to $1,500	13%	$3,400 to $4,400		
17%	$1,500 to $2,000	15%	$4,400 to $8,500		
19%	$2,000 to $4,000	17%	$8,500 to $10,800		
22%	$4,000 to $6,000	19%	$10,800 to $12,900		
25%	$6,000 to $8,000	21%	$12,900 to $15,000		
28%	$8,000 to $10,000	24%	$15,000 to $18,200		
32%	$10,000 to $12,000	28%	$18,200 to $23,500		
36%	$12,000 to $14,000	32%	$23,500 to $28,800		
39%	$14,000 to $16,000	36%	$28,800 to $34,100		
42%	$16,000 to $18,000	40%	$34,100 to $41,500		
45%	$18,000 to $20,000	45%	$41,500 to $55,300		
48%	$20,000 to $22,000	50%	Over $55,300		
50%	$22,000 to $26,000				
53%	$26,000 to $32,000				
55%	$32,000 to $38,000				
58%	$38,000 to $44,000				
60%	$44,000 to $50,000				
62%	$50,000 to $60,000				
64%	$60,000 to $70,000				
66%	$70,000 to $80,000				
68%	$80,000 to $90,000				
69%	$90,000 to $100,000				
70%	Over $100,000				

Inflation pushed wage earners into ever higher tax brackets, creating a political constituency for tax cuts that significantly reduced both marginal rates and the overall number of tax brackets.

new policy. While the Fed was aiming for stable and constrained monetary growth, the aggregates refused to cooperate. "We are back to square one," Friedman announced, citing a 12 percent rate of growth in M2 for the first four months of the year. This was far from the announced target of 6 to 9 percent annual rate of growth.[31] It looked like a repeat of the 1980 credit controls debacle, in reverse. The Fed had loosened too much; now it would have to tighten. Actually, the Fed still wanted to keep money tight and had lost none of its inflation-fighting nerve. But it was finding it increasingly hard to control, or even measure, the quantity of money. Just in time for their star turn, monetary aggregates had become unstable.

The cause was financial deregulation passed in the waning days of the Carter administration. It sounded bland and technocratic, but the Depository Institutions Deregulation and Monetary Control Act of 1980 represented a sweeping change in the financial system, driven by inflation and corresponding high interest rates. Prior to the legislation, checking accounts could not earn interest. This was one of many strictures that made sense, or didn't matter, in an environment of stable prices. But when the cost of everything was rising nearly 7 percent annually, as happened during the 1970s, money in checking accounts was losing a corresponding amount of value. Traditional banks began to lose business to new products like mutual funds, which had less regulation. But these new products were generally available only to those with considerable balances. Thus the new law had an equalizing thrust; now banks could entice the small saver to keep their money—in a checking account that for the first time paid interest.

This new reality collided with aggregates built for a regulated world. Definitions of M1, for example, assumed that money in checking accounts was rapidly circulating through the economy. But now it made sense to take money out of savings accounts and park it in checking, where it could both earn interest and be used for everyday transactions. So checking accounts now held large pools of inactive money, meaning the increase in M1 had lost much of its significance.[32] This was the opposite of what Congress had intended. In fact, the 1980 law had been billed as increasing "monetary control"—because it required all banks, not just members of the Federal Reserve System, to hold specified levels of reserves. While this did give the Fed more power over the banking system, the rest of the law cut in the other direction. Aggregates had long been a meaningful measure of economic activity. But now a surge or fall in money was nearly impossible to interpret. The Fed had not been caught unaware by this change, and tried to adjust accordingly. But the picture remained fundamentally cloudy: a rise in M1 could be a sign of monetary ease, or it could be a by-product of changing consumer behavior. The aggregates could not be controlled, or even predicted.

Interest rates were on an equally wild ride, driven by the same deregulatory dynamics. When Volcker announced the shift to monetary aggregates in 1979, many interest rates were capped by Regulation Q, a New Deal–era banking regulation. But across the 1970s, as market interest rates rose above the legal ceiling, Regulation Q became deeply unpopular. Large banks could play in international markets or trade commercial paper not subject to the cap. Or they could design new consumer products to evade the regulation. But these were for the wealthy—customers with $100,000 or more. Consumer advocates like Ralph Nader cried foul, arguing that regular Americans were losing access to credit as money flowed into less-regulated channels. Nonprofit and community banks, which could not compete with the larger firms, also complained as they began losing deposits. Soon a coordinated consumer-interest lobbying campaign against Regulation Q was under way.

Congress axed Regulation Q in the Depository Institutions Deregulation and Monetary Control Act of 1980, the same financial deregulation law that had destabilized M1. The limits on bank interest rates—5.25 percent at the time—would be phased out. Thus the two major checks on interest rates throughout the postwar era—Fed policy and Regulation Q—were gone.[33] And with inflation firmly entrenched, there was a natural dynamic pushing interest rates up. Anyone looking to lend money wanted a return higher than the rate of inflation, otherwise they could end up being paid back less than they had loaned. In 1981 the daily federal funds rate surged back to the stratospheric height of 22 percent. It was a shocking figure; 5 percent was considered a high interest rate for most of the postwar era.[34] And the federal funds rate immediately spilled over into the cost of all other credit, such as home loans, car loans, and business loans.

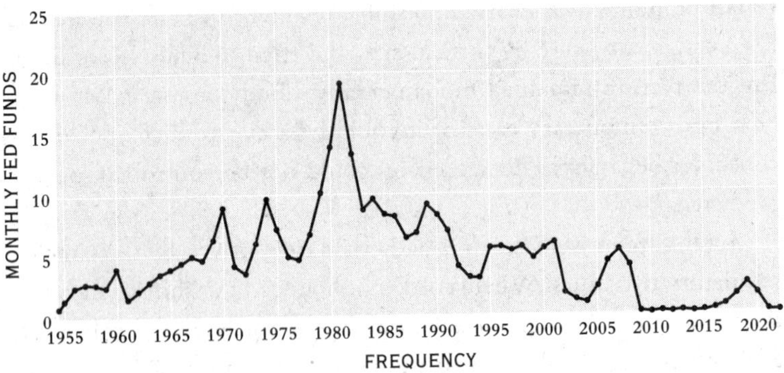

For much of the postwar era, interest rates remained under 5 percent, meaning the nearly 20 percent average interest rates under Volcker were truly shocking.

In the second half of 1981, the dark powers of interest rates, long dormant, returned. For years, economic activity had persisted despite high interest rates, as borrowers and lenders sought to get ahead of inflation. But rates near 20 percent were too much to bear. Finally, real interest rates had gotten far enough ahead of inflation to bite. The cost of credit moved beyond reach for most Americans, and with it the big-ticket items of consumerism—houses and cars. The contraction rippled through the wider economy. Unemployment ticked up to around 8 percent and looked to be heading even higher.

At the end of the year, one promising number emerged: the CPI for 1981 was down to 10 percent. It was still a shockingly high figure, but the trend was in the right direction. The report convinced Volcker that the monetarist medicine was beginning to work. Typically, when faced with an economic slowdown and rising unemployment, the Fed would set to work lowering interest rates and expanding money. It was part of the fine-tuning approach to macroeconomic management—read the latest indicators, adjust policy accordingly. But Volcker believed that easing up now would just reignite inflation. "Any slackening of our commitment to see the effort through could only jeopardize prospects for full success," he told a skeptical convention of home builders in January 1982.[35] At least for the time being, Volcker was following the monetary rule he had announced: focus on aggregates, ignore interest rates.

By then, unemployment was heading toward 10 percent, the highest rate since the Great Depression. In home building and auto manufacturing, unemployment reached 1930s levels of nearly 25 percent. Appearing before Congress, Volcker refused to change course. "The need for disciplined financial policies to carry through the anti-inflation effort is not lessened by the current recession," he told the Joint Economic Committee in January. The market continued to drive interest rates higher, which meant traders still expected inflation to return. In February, the FOMC even raised the target band for interest rates, indicating a tolerance range of 12 to 16 percent.[36] It was the opposite of Fed tradition: Volcker's Fed was leaning into the wind, not against it. "It would be shortsighted for the Federal Reserve to abandon a strong sense of discipline in monetary policy in an attempt to bring down interest rates," Volcker told Congress.[37] Like nothing else, the Fed's refusal to change direction telegraphed how dramatically its priorities had changed. The country was heading into a second year of severe recession. But unlike past economic downturns, this one did not seem like the predictable turn of the business cycle, or even an unpredictable natural calamity, akin to war or hurricane. This recession had a name and a face: the press dubbed it "the Volcker shock."[38]

Not only had the Fed lost its traditional anonymity; it was becoming famous, even infamous. Volcker was right that people connected money with inflation. They also connected the Fed with unemployment. Irate home builders mailed the Fed chunks of lumber, while out-of-business auto dealers sent car keys. Gone were the sober talks to sober audiences of bankers; Volcker now confronted hostile activists at his speeches and protesters outside the Fed's marbled headquarters. With reluctance, he accepted a security detail.[39] Increasingly the Federal Reserve appeared to many Americans as it had to Wright Patman: secretive, powerful, utterly lacking in accountability. Each passing day demonstrated Friedman's argument about the importance of money and the powers of the Fed. Monetary policy had moved to the center of the nation's economic, political, and social life.

Friedman's reaction to Volcker was mixed. Like Volcker, he could see a break in the clouds, even in the early months of 1982. "Average

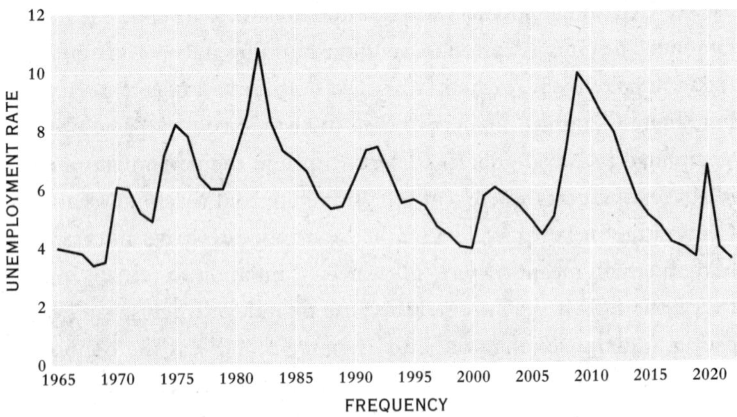

The Volcker shock precipitated a steep recession, but it was short.

money growth over the past two years has been fairly good—decidedly lower than earlier. That is why inflation is declining," he told readers of *Newsweek*. But this positive trend masked continued swings in the money supply that "put the economy through a dismaying roller coaster." Friedman was also keenly aware that the Fed's monetarist revolution was incomplete.

The Fed was watching aggregates, but it had yet to make other technical changes Friedman considered essential. Among the most important of these was ending lagged reporting of reserves—the Fed's practice of using reserve figures from the previous fourteen days to measure money. These delayed figures significantly reduced the Fed's ability to control aggregates and introduced excessive variability into all its data, Friedman and other monetarists argued repeatedly.[40] Friedman wanted the Fed to use instead only the most contemporaneous figures available. Further, he wanted the Fed to ignore interest rates altogether—specifically, to stop publishing a target federal funds rate, even a loose one. Without these changes, Friedman sensed, the Fed was undermining monetarism even as it pushed inflation down.

But in the broader picture, Friedman's ideas provided powerful support for Volcker's mission. At the start of Reagan's presidency, Friedman had warned a recession was coming; he had even counseled it should come sooner, rather than later. And Friedman was Reagan's favorite economist. "Though it was not generally known," observed one journalist, "Reagan was the first modern president who could fairly be labelled a monetarist." Reagan had absorbed Friedman's teaching that inflation was always and everywhere a monetary phenomenon. His advisers grew accustomed to worried talk about "zooming" the money supply. To carry the point, Reagan used his hands to draw in the air a historical graph of the U.S. money supply—probably derived from *A Monetary History*'s pullout charts.[41] Reagan accepted recession as the cost of ending a decade of inflation. There would be no organized pressure campaign against Volcker. "The policies of the past have failed," Reagan summarized in his annual Economic Report of the President, delivered to Congress in early 1982. Later that year, with midterm elections on the horizon, Reagan devised a slogan that summarized his state of mind: "Stay the course."[42]

Still, the recession had its own political force. By the summer of 1982, Congress was beginning to panic. Inflation was coming down quickly, which overall was good news. But Reagan's budget had assumed high inflation would bring in high tax receipts, at least for a few years. As falling incomes and prices systematically lowered taxes on many Americans, the predicted fiscal deficit grew even larger. Primordial Republican instincts kicked in, with Senator Bob Dole leading a balanced-budget drive in Congress. Many of the tax cuts were reversed; they had not even lasted a year. Critically, the marginal tax rates for individuals were retained, but the corporate tax breaks were rescinded. Friedman was dismayed. The legislation was "a monstrosity that should not be passed," he opined. "Bad monetary policy does not alter the need to lower tax rates rather than to raise them."[43]

Even as inflation continued to dwindle, monetarism's stock was sinking. On the one hand, inflation was clearly on the run. More quickly than Volcker had dared to hope, in 1982 the consumer price index continued to fall, month after month. On the other hand, it wasn't clear that targeting aggregates had made the difference. Redefining and adjusting the aggregates, as the Fed did several times, brought no clarity. Inflation, hiring, lending, housing starts—everything but M1 was headed down. The relationship between aggregates and economic activity that Friedman and Anna Schwartz had so painstakingly documented was gone.

Friedman had explanations for all this—mainly that the Fed was doing it wrong. He considered, and dismissed as "mostly rationalization," the argument that deregulation had fundamentally distorted the aggregates. "The Fed knows how to produce more stable monetary growth," Friedman insisted. But it resisted the "bureaucratic disruptions" required, including abolishing lagged reserve reporting and the interest rate target. Unless it made the necessary changes, progress against inflation would be only temporary. The "Yo-Yo Economy" of the 1970s would return.[44]

Unsurprisingly, the Fed drew different conclusions. In a March speech, the chair of the Boston Federal Reserve laid out the case in plain language: "The one thing we are well positioned to control through bank reserves, M-1, is no longer a meaningful target for monetary policy."[45] And the recession was starting to spread. High interest rates reset the calculation on debt, for borrowers not just in the United States but also in other countries. Several U.S. banks were in trouble, and so was the government of Mexico. In the meantime, the summer tax hike had soothed the worst of Volcker's budget worries.

After subtly shifting away from the aggregates for a few months, in October 1982 Volcker announced a formal change. With inflation tamed at 5 percent, the Fed would return its attention to interest rates. The monetarist era was over.

Friedman did not hesitate to announce Volcker's monetarist experiment was a failure—not even monetarism, in fact—but his powers of perception had dimmed. As Volcker shifted away from aggregates, inflation continued to fall. Unemployment came down and economic activity restarted, just in time to reward Reagan for the 1984 election. But to hear Friedman tell it, the United States was still on the precipice.

"Continued monetary growth at anything like recent rates would mean an upsurge in inflation in 1984 or 1985 at the very latest," he wrote in 1983.[46] Noting the decline in inflation—which he grudgingly credited to the Fed—he was sure this was only temporary. "We shall be fortunate indeed if we escape either a return to double-digit inflation rates or renewed recession in 1984."[47] But Volcker had licked inflation. His term marked a phase transition. Afterward, inflation would fade into the background as an economic concern, much as any monetarist would have dreamed. And not just in the United States: with the exception of gravely mismanaged economies, it would be licked everywhere—for at least forty years.[48]

Once again, events in the United Kingdom mirrored those in the United States. The dire predictions about Thatcher's 1981 budget had come true: unemployment surged, and growth slowed. But the other predictions came true, too. For most of the 1980s, inflation stayed around 5 percent, a manageable rate, especially compared to its previous height. Thanks to a stable currency and sweeping deregulation, London emerged as a global leader in financial services, even as British manufacturing continued its historic decline. Growth resumed, although unemployment remained stubbornly high. Akin to the Volcker shock in the United States, the 1981 budget was a watershed in Britain's transition to a new economic era.

In Britain, as in the United States, monetary targets had proved extraordinarily difficult to implement. Similar deregulation in the banking sector destabilized aggregates, making them nearly useless as instruments of prediction or control. And switching between aggregates made things worse. Chancellor Nigel Lawson, the closest analogue to Volcker in Britain, soon discovered that London financiers were "inclined to believe that any departure from the original rules was politically expedient and therefore economically unsound."[49] Lacking credibility, monetary policy was powerless against rumor and speculation. Lawson eventually gravitated toward exchange rates, which provided powerful feedback between government policy and capital markets. It wasn't in the theory, but it worked.

A decade later, Volcker summarized the mixed record. Rampant inflation underscored the importance of "the classic indirect means of monetary control—that is, control over bank reserves and the monetary base," he recounted to a packed audience of central bankers. Then he continued, "At the same time, the new market situation and the inflationary environment meant that the restrictive effect of any particular level of the money supply and of interest rates became increasingly difficult to judge."[50] Whereas Friedman presented monetarism as a natural science, Volcker experienced it as an art.

Had Volcker cynically used monetarism for its PR value? Volcker's critics—including Friedman—later argued that aggregates were a veil, a sort of feint that allowed Volcker to push up interest rates while distracting everyone with the money supply.[51] In retrospect, amid the challenges of M1 and Friedman's many failed predictions, it was easy to forget monetarism's former magnetism. Certainly Volcker paid more attention to interest rates than monetarists advised. And from the start, the Fed accepted that short-term rates might rise with monetarist policy. At the same time, Volcker believed long-term rates would decline rapidly as inflationary expectations were dashed.

But the inflation fight was full of surprises. Transcripts of FOMC meetings, released years after the Volcker shock, show a reactive Fed navigating unexpected surges in money, unanticipated spikes in interest rates, and unpredictable politics. In line with Friedman's teaching, the Fed believed monetary aggregates could be easily controlled and would have consistent effects upon the real economy.[52] Instead they found the opposite: aggregates were hard to measure, harder to manipulate, and an unreliable anchor amid rapid regulatory change.

In the end it was a question of perspective. From thirty thousand feet up, it was impossible to miss how monetarism had transformed not just the academic study of money but the practices of central banking and the politics of inflation. As Lawson summarized, he had learned from Friedman and Schwartz that "excesses in monetary policy—whether in the direction of an extension or a contraction in the supply of money—will cause a greater or lesser degree of economic collapse and large-scale unemployment." From this flowed the central responsibility of governments to maintain a stable currency.

Lawson also imbibed a more subtle lesson: although Friedman was known for contending that "money matters," in another sense he argued that money didn't matter at all. Monetary policy couldn't, as Lawson noted, "have a sustained and predictable expansionary impact on real things such as output and employment."[53] It could make things worse, but not really make them better. Like Thatcher, Lawson embraced Friedman's overall vision of government and society, becoming a key architect of Britain's privatization. It was this zoomed-out view that Friedman later adopted, crediting Reagan with beating inflation.

But when it came to his own legacy, Friedman was back again in the granularity of the peer-reviewed paper or the seminar room. Here the most dangerous enemy was not the opponent but the student who misunderstood and popularized the doctrine—a man like Volcker who did as he wished with Friedman's ideas.

PART VI

THE AGE OF MONETARISM

15

TWO LUCKY PEOPLE

> Only with heavy dependence on market pricing mechanisms can there be realized quasi-efficient and quasi-progressive organization of societies involving humans as Darwinian history has bequeathed them.
>
> —Paul Samuelson, 1995

If the 1980s really were the Age of Friedman, it did not always feel like it to Milton Friedman. Looking back at his extraordinary career, Friedman's pride mingled with disappointment. It was infuriating to see monetarism all over the news, even as he considered Paul Volcker's policies "antimonetarist." Attending the 1984 Mont Pelerin Society meeting, Friedman vented some of these frustrations to a friendly crowd. He proposed an alternative title for his talk, "How to Give Monetarism a Bad Name."[1]

Friedman bemoaned monetarism's "bad name," but the capacious understanding of his ideas that circulated in the 1980s pointed to a larger truth. If aggregates were no longer the target of monetary policy, nonetheless the other basics of monetarism had been adopted into conventional wisdom: money matters, central banks can control inflation, rules and frameworks were better than fine-tuning.

More than an academic theory, monetarism denoted an entire political economy. "Monetarism, in short, turned out to be a bulldozer that could raze a building but could not erect one," writes a critical historian.[2] Yet this is not true. What grew out of monetarism's wake was a world that approximated many of Friedman's dreams. Capital flowed freely across national borders. Politicians focused on getting taxes down. The hot new idea in education was vouchers. The armed forces recruited rather than conscripted. Antitrust policy was transformed by Chicago Ph.D.s. Politicians looked to the Fed, rather than the federal budget, to create economic growth. Government did not shrink in overall terms, but its rate of growth slowed and then stabilized, no mean feat. Friedman made history, it might be said, but not under the conditions of his choosing.

Life after the Volcker shock settled into a pattern of grandchildren, foreign travel, press interviews, and keynote speeches. Milton and Rose divided their time between San Francisco, Stanford, and a second home in Sea Ranch, a planned community up the Northern California coast. A ski trip to Utah with William F. Buckley Jr. became a new annual tradition. Friedman's longtime secretary, Gloria Valentine, had come west with the Friedmans and kept his office at the Hoover Institution whirring along as he fielded a steady stream of correspondence and sifted through his papers.

In 1982 Friedman and Anna Schwartz topped off their decades of research with another tome, *Monetary Trends in the United States and the United Kingdom*, but the monetarist moment had passed. Respectful but restrained, most reviews skipped lightly over the book and instead reflected appreciatively on their past work.[3]

Nonetheless, Schwartz's reputation among economists was now well established. In addition to her constant presence on the Shadow Open Market Committee, she became a legend in NBER circles. For thirty years after her retirement from the NBER she went into the office every day anyhow, up to age ninety-four. She attended presentations and conferences, reading each paper closely. "When Anna spoke, everyone listened," remembered Christina Romer, who was watching closely as one of the few other women in the room. Calling her the

"Iron Lady of Economics," Romer learned from Schwartz that "it was okay for a woman economist to be tough."[4] Michael Bordo, a Friedman student who wrote more than thirty papers with Schwartz, summarized the experience: "She was very sparing in her praise. Her judgements ranged from 'it was flawed' to 'it doesn't make sense' to . . . 'it is a contribution.'"[5] Professional honors finally came her way, including being named a Distinguished Fellow of the AEA and a Fellow of the American Academy of Arts and Sciences. The woman who had once struggled for a doctorate now had nine honorary degrees in recognition of her work. In 1981 she was appointed the executive director of the U.S. Gold Commission, a congressional body charged with examining the role of gold in the U.S. monetary system. Ultimately the commission supported a proposal for limited nonlegal tender coinage of gold.[6]

Friedman's major collaborator was now Rose. "My husband never wrote anything without my reading it over and talking about it," she told an interviewer in Singapore. "Now you can't tell who wrote what, the style is the same throughout the books. I always tell people we work as one; we are one."[7] A book based on the TV show *Free to Choose*, bearing both authors' names, became an instant bestseller, unlike the sleeper hit *Capitalism and Freedom*. But like its predecessor, *Free to Choose* served as a guide to the conservative worldview, encapsulating much of the logic now shaping economic policy in Ronald Reagan's administration. Rose and Milton began working on a joint memoir, *Two Lucky People*, a book that nearly approached *A Monetary History of the United States* in length. It would prove almost as influential in shaping how Friedman was remembered.

As Rose gained a measure of fame in her own right, occasional discordant notes emerged. "I do all the monetary dirty work," she complained to an interviewer, explaining she paid the bills and did the taxes. "It's a game for him but not for me," Rose concluded.[8] In most interviews, she staunchly defended their traditional division of labor, denying any regrets. "I'm not a competitive person, or I would have ordered my life differently," went the claim.[9] Still, at times there was a burn. Whenever she was introduced as Dr. Friedman, Rose confessed to another interviewer, "I feel upset inside when that happens. It's hard to come out and say at the time, 'I'm sorry, but I'm not a doctor,' but I don't want to fly under false colors." In 1986, that problem was solved when Pepperdine University awarded her an honorary doctorate. A picture of a glowing Rose, surrounded by family at the commencement ceremony, was included in *Two Lucky People*, just after snapshots of Milton in Stockholm.[10]

Occasionally Friedman wrote an article or letter to the editor—*The Wall Street Journal* was a favorite—but mostly he counted on journalists to come to him. Sometimes he wrote a paper drawing on recent monetary data, but his days of active research were over. No longer did his every pronouncement shake the field. Eventually he would publish a final book, *Money Mischief*, drawing heavily on his past work. As elder statesman of a political movement that was now in the flush of power, Friedman was a draw at conservative confabs from *National Review* cruises to Hoover Institution retreats.

Yet Friedman was not only a symbol and figurehead to American conservatives; he became a touchstone of the vast transformation in economic and political ideas that had shaped the twentieth century. The Friedmans traveled to China three times between 1980 and 1993, where they witnessed the slow unfolding of market-oriented reform.

By now, Friedman understood how the game worked. Invited to a widely publicized session with the general secretary of the Communist Party, Friedman took this to be a sign the secretary "was in deep trouble." Facing criticism within the party for ending price controls, Zhao Ziyang hoped hobnobbing with a foreign dignitary would shore up his position. As in Chile and the United Kingdom, connecting with Friedman became a way to explain and defend market reforms. After their visit, Friedman judged Zhao had "a real understanding of what it means to free the market." Indeed, Friedman had become an aspirational figure among the region's emerging capitalists. Visiting the Hong Kong home of an admirer, Friedman was astonished to see his own signature transformed into a mosaic that stretched across the living-room wall.[11]

In the United Kingdom, Margaret Thatcher's revolution ricocheted from monetarism to privatization, another idea Friedman had promoted in the hazy days of the early 1960s. While *Capitalism and*

Freedom had argued that key assets of the U.S. government should be in private hands, from the post office to the national parks, it was in Thatcher's Britain that these ideas were most fully implemented. In part, this was because the British state had far more assets to privatize: when Thatcher came to power, key industries from railroads to steel to coal mines were in state hands.

Like monetarism, privatization was an idea that had kicked around the Conservative Party for years. Its adaptation in Britain was piecemeal, in the beginning; Thatcher's government originally offered shares of British Telecom to stanch a budget deficit. It was not even the first to do so, for in the 1970s Labour had sold shares in British Petroleum to meet its own fiscal shortfall. But once Thatcher saw the political benefits of privatization, she embraced it wholeheartedly. British Aerospace, British Ports, British Airways, and nearly fifty others offered shares to the public and became private companies. Corporations that had once drawn subsidies from the Treasury now returned revenue, helping lower the country's debt burden. Thatcher's Britain came closest to Friedman's ideal of a state that shrank itself.[12]

In the United States, the steep recession of 1981–1982 transformed into a swift and sustained recovery. "The Seven Fat Years," one booster proclaimed, but in fact the post-Volcker economic expansion lasted nearly twenty-five years, except for a brief slowdown in 1990–1991. During most of this time, inflation remained well under 5 percent, with unemployment hovering between 5 and 7.5 percent. This stability masked the uneven returns to financialization and globalization, which accrued most to workers with advanced degrees and existing wealth. Whether measured by wages, wealth, or income, inequality was on the rise.[13] Like deregulation, this was a trend that predated Reagan but accelerated during his presidency. Even so, without the devastating reversals of recession or depression, it was an unprecedented spell of prosperity. The age-old dream of taming the business cycle appeared at hand.

Stability also masked the continued shift from manufacturing to finance, a long-term trend accelerated by stagflation and the Volcker shock. Lured by high interest rates and new opportunities, even venerable

American corporations shifted away from workaday production toward new financial strategies. The CEO of U.S. Steel announced that it "was no longer in the business of making steel." Instead, it was "in the business of making profits."[14] The architects of corporate financial strategies came from business schools or universities, not the factory floor. Bonds between executive and worker were weakening, making it easier than ever to close down plants.

Eventually interest rates returned to moderate levels, but taking their place was another new mechanism of deindustrialization: a strong dollar. As U.S. currency stabilized, its value increased relative to other currencies. Steel and everything else made in America would be more expensive. U.S. manufacturers that had resisted the financial turn now found their goods uncompetitively priced in world markets. Thus the economy of the 1980s bifurcated. Employment in manufacturing continued its steady decline, even as real estate, high tech, insurance, and finance boomed.

In this new "Deal Decade," innovation came as often in financial structure as in consumer products, with the hostile takeover emerging as a new trend. Corporate raiders descended on unwitting corporations, using public markets to wrest control from owners and management. Amid these economic changes, shareholder value became a new cultural touch point, propelled by increasing public ownership of stock, breathless media coverage of mergers and acquisitions, and brash capitalists trumpeting, in the immortal words of Ivan Boesky, "Greed is healthy."[15]

These attitudes gave new life to a long-lost Friedman essay from *The New York Times Magazine*. Published in 1970 amid a wave of social activism aimed at business, Friedman's article offered a traditional defense of corporate profit-making, regurgitated from *Capitalism and Freedom*. What distinguished the essay was not Friedman's position—that corporations existed to make profits was hardly contestable—but his unwillingness to grant even rhetorical ground to social concerns. "There is one and only one social responsibility of business—to use its resources and engage in activities designed to increase its profits so long as it stays within the rules of the game," Friedman argued. A corporate executive only had "direct responsibility to his employers." To divert resources to other goals would be unethical, "spending someone else's money for a general social interest." In the 1980s, amid a booming stock market that was increasingly accessible to small investors, Friedman's emphasis on shareholders took on new meaning. It appeared to be a powerful philosophy that was converting executives and reordering business life.[16]

The real force making shareholder value so important to corporate America was less obvious, although it too bore a connection to Friedman: law and economics. The movement that Aaron Director and Friedman had done so much to catalyze made a profound impact on antitrust law. The Reagan Justice Department adopted the movement's focus on prices and markets, loosening restrictions on corporate ownership. The mergers-and-acquisitions boom took off from there. Nearly 30 percent of companies listed in the Fortune 500 had been acquired by the end of the 1980s. Most of these were "friendly" mergers, but hostile takeovers loomed as a perpetual threat. In turn, this powered a new focus on stock prices. Only with a high valuation could corporate leaders fend off or prevent a hostile takeover; shareholder primacy was a survival strategy for a new economic era.[17]

As stagflation faded into memory, Americans seemed smitten with their newfound prosperity. The press looked with wonderment upon an economy pumping out personal computers and the Walkman, a stock market surging to new heights, and a sound dollar. Paul Volcker was idolized like a rock star. "America's Money Master," proclaimed *Newsweek* in 1986, calling him "the man who made money mean something again" and "the godfather" of the economy.[18]

Leaving behind edgy loners or rebels, pop culture began to rotate around clean-cut strivers and capitalists. On TV, the Young Republican Alex Keaton became the surprise fan favorite in *Family Ties*; in an early episode, he loses his virginity after taking a date to a Milton Friedman lecture. Adam Smith ties, a staple of Friedman's wardrobe, popped up all over Washington, D.C. In the 1960s, the nation had been swept by "cohorts of young college graduates who were summoned to fight poverty, fix up Latin America, educate Africa, revive Appalachia, integrate Alabama," as Daniel Patrick Moynihan, now a senator from New York, remembered.[19] In the 1980s, there was the opposite trend: the yuppie.

Yuppies were college graduates—young urban professionals—who flocked to cities like New York, drawn to Wall Street and related financial and legal firms. By the end of the 1980s, nearly a third of graduates from the nation's most elite universities became investment bankers. Clustered in urban centers, they formed a recognizable "newly discovered class," as one historian summarizes, "who earned high salaries, coveted loft apartments, trained for marathons, owned Cuisinarts, and supped on sushi and chardonnay."[20] Yuppies flowed into segments of the New York finance world that had taken Friedman and Volcker as heroes. Yet having grown up in the aftermath of the 1960s social movements, many reacted strongly against the GOP's new religious conservatism. Many became reliable Democratic donors, and their embrace of meritocracy, innovation, and technology would profoundly influence the Democratic Party.

Even before the yuppies, market thinking had begun to reshape the Democratic establishment. Although Reagan would be remembered as the ultimate champion of limited government, it was Democrats like Ted Kennedy who began the push for deregulation in critical sectors during Jimmy Carter's presidency. Responding to both inflationary pressures and consumer activists like Ralph Nader, Carter appointees approved deregulation of the airline, railroad, and trucking industries. It was the closest the United States came to privatization, and as airline fares and shipping rates tumbled, it was judged a success.[21]

Even Paul Samuelson, an exemplar of the Kennedy new economics, had ceded major ground to Friedman's outlook. Still, he could not quite bear to say it. "Only with heavy dependence on market pricing mechanisms can there be realized quasi-efficient and quasi-progressive organization of societies involving humans as Darwinian history has bequeathed them," Samuelson affirmed, attributing the argument to F. A. Hayek.[22]

Likewise, the Democratic Party scrambled to find a new set of economic messages that could resonate in a Reaganite political culture.

A rump movement of "Atari Democrats" sought to reinvent growth economics for a globalized era. Some favored full-blown industrial policy to support key industries—or more aptly, postindustrial policy that sought to nurture the entrepreneurial ethos. Others wanted to direct government investments toward education and research rather than social programs. Embracing the federal government, this loose group of "neoliberals"—as they sometimes labeled themselves—nonetheless sought to make the state more efficient and responsive to markets.[23] After the 1984 election, another current arose in the Democratic Leadership Council. Less yuppie and more Southern, the DLC crafted business-friendly policies while toying with values themes that were more typical of Republicans. These efforts would make little headway until 1992 and the election of a Democratic president, Bill Clinton, who drew on both groups to articulate a "third way" between "do-nothing" and "big" government.[24]

Although there was every reason for celebration, casting his gaze over the 1980s Friedman was chastened. He admitted he had been wrong to forecast a renewal of inflation—and even admitted he didn't understand why. He told a journalist: "I was wrong, absolutely wrong. And I have no good explanation as to why I was wrong."[25] Alongside this confession, Friedman created a new narrative crediting Reagan with defeating inflation. In this reading, Reagan's major contribution was negative: he did not pressure the Fed to change course throughout the 1982 recession.

Volcker's replacement in 1987 with Alan Greenspan offered some relief. Dour and methodical—Ayn Rand nicknamed him "the undertaker"—Greenspan had none of Friedman's sizzle. Nonetheless the two men were longtime friends and correspondents. When Greenspan chaired President Ford's Council of Economic Advisers, he made use of Friedman's inflation analyses. As Greenspan's profile rose, Friedman peppered him with a steady stream of comments, corrections, and requests, occasionally sounding like a professor corralling a wayward grad student. In turn, Greenspan encouraged Friedman to keep writing to him "if you think I'm off on the wrong track." It was never far from either's mind that Greenspan might end up running the Fed someday.

"Delighted to have kept a friend, but sorry to have lost a Chairman," Friedman wrote when Reagan reappointed Volcker in 1983.[26]

Nor did Greenspan abandon Friedman when he finally took the helm. Near the start of his tenure chairing the Fed, he visited Rose and Milton for several days in "Paradise," the seaside home on the Northern California coast that had replaced Capitaf. It was the type of relationship Friedman once expected to have with Greenspan's mentor—Arthur Burns. Where Burns had been curt, dismissive, and wounded in the face of Friedman's constant commentary, Greenspan was curious and responsive. When Friedman started fiddling with M2 figures and sent Greenspan his findings, he learned that the Fed staff had already embarked on much the same project. Greenspan facilitated a back and forth between his staff and Friedman, injecting comments of his own. When Friedman complained a student's paper critiquing "Too Big to Fail"—a prescient 1991 analysis of moral hazard in the banking sector—was being suppressed by the Richmond Fed, Greenspan saw that it was published. Upon Friedman's request he asked the Treasury undersecretary Larry Summers to share internal data with Anna Schwartz.[27]

This comity did not mean Greenspan agreed with Friedman on the details of policy or even the Fed's role. Like Burns, Greenspan was eclectic in his approach to economics. While he kept an eye on aggregates, his real focus was the traditional federal funds rate, which influenced interest rates across the economy. Greenspan's monetary policy blended objectivist first principles with his long immersion in business forecasting—the dry statistics of sheet-rolled metal, factory inventories, and retail sales. He explicitly rejected the idea of monetary rules, defending the importance of discretion. Like every other Fed chair, he treasured the institution's independence. As Friedman acknowledged, "This is a longstanding disagreement between us." Yet there was no doubt Greenspan deeply admired Friedman. He liked to joke that the diminutive economist had "the world's biggest brain per square inch of body."[28]

More seriously, when the stock market quavered in 1987, just a few months into Greenspan's term, he followed the Friedman-Schwartz playbook. The Fed issued a strong statement affirming "its readiness to serve as a source of liquidity to support the economic and financial system." Buoyed by Fed support, the stock market recovered and no recession emerged. Over time, Friedman became increasingly impressed with Greenspan. "As you know, I have long advocated abolishing the Fed," he told *The Chicago Maroon.* "If it must exist, however, I can think of no one I would rather have running it than Alan Greenspan."[29] In turn, while Greenspan never embraced monetarism, he framed his approach as deriving generally from Friedman's work.[30]

The fall of the Berlin Wall in 1989 and subsequent collapse of the USSR two years later kicked capitalist triumphalism into overdrive. Not only had unfettered markets apparently solved the problems of the United States; they had vanquished the nation's long-standing rival and brought the Cold War to a peaceful end. The crumbling of Soviet Communism seemed proof of Thatcher's once contentious claim—there is no alternative. In an essay that encapsulated the zeitgeist, the political theorist Francis Fukuyama proclaimed "the End of History." What he really meant was the long rivalry between Communism and capitalism was over; there had been a "total exhaustion of viable systemic alternatives to Western liberalism." But his grandiose framing captured the sense that irrevocable change was under way.[31]

In the former Soviet bloc, new democratic political leaders looked to Friedman as a symbol of the future. After the Velvet Revolution, the Czech leader Václav Klaus emerged with a deliberately Friedmanite statement: "I want to reestablish markets, but markets without objectives." To make sure reporters got the point, he wore a tie from the Chicago business school.[32] In Mongolia, the new finance minister planned a statue of Friedman overlooking the capital of Ulan Bator—a counterpoint to the existing statue of Lenin.[33]

The 1990s came closest to the Age of Friedman, for during that decade a new intellectual and political unanimity about markets emerged—one that spanned the globe but was often called the Washington consensus. The name came from a list of ten policies enumerated by the economist John Williamson, ranging from free trade to privatization to deregulation. "The policies that Washington urges on the rest of the world may be summarized as prudent macroeconomic policies, outward orientation, and free-market capitalism," Williamson summarized. He went on to muse, "A striking fact about the list of policies on which Washington does have a collective view is that they all stem from classical mainstream economic theory."[34] Williamson created his list with an eye on Latin America, where many nations reeled from successive debt crises and hyperinflations.

But the essay landed just as the USSR crumbled and a broader disenchantment with socialism arose. Thus the Washington consensus spread rapidly beyond the western hemisphere into Asia and Europe. "At the beginning of the decade an inordinate number of countries in different continents, each with a different development experience and with wildly varying economic structures and political systems, embarked on experiments with market reforms, all guided by their also wildly varying interpretations of the Washington Consensus," summarized the editor of *Foreign Policy*. The Washington consensus became, as Williamson reflected later, "an ideology for a world that was pining for something to replace the god of socialism that had just failed."[35] In the post–World War II years, states from Britain to Iran nationalized companies in hopes of shared prosperity; now in the final years of the century they did the opposite, selling off state firms, removing capital controls, lowering tariffs, and cutting budgets.

While there was no one intellectual source of the Washington consensus—the consensus itself was debatable—in many ways the concept epitomized Friedman's economics. At the most basic level, the Washington consensus inverted import substitution industrialization (ISI), the protectionist, state-oriented school of economics that had been dominant since the 1950s in many developing nations. As one commentator noted, "It may now seem obvious, for example, that large public deficits and loose monetary policies fuel inflation. However, for a long time, in many developing countries, especially in Latin America, South Asia, and Africa these ideas were dismissed as a rather myopic form of 'monetarism.'"[36] Critically, the Washington consensus gave monetary policy pride of place. Balanced budgets and responsible fiscal policy were important. But none of it would work without an independent central bank dedicated to price stability. Without independence, a central bank might inflate the currency to satisfy populist politicians. Internal price stability would also help the country's exchange rate, whether the country floated or pegged to another currency.

If the Washington consensus was the repudiation of ISI, it was also Chile's El Ladrillo blown up to world scale. Decades earlier under the guidance of the Chicago Boys, Chile had moved away from ISI and liberalized its markets, if not its politics. After taming inflation, the free market reformers moved on to set up a voucher system in education and a private pension system. As in the United Kingdom, privatization went farther, faster than it ever did in the United States. In 1980, a popular referendum approved a new constitution and set up a future plebiscite on Augusto Pinochet. Chile did not yet conform to Friedman's cherished formula of entwined economic and political freedom, but the road ahead had opened. In 1988, the plebiscite dealt Pinochet a solid defeat; a year later a new president from the Social Democratic Party won the election. In the meantime, Chile's economic performance had outshone its neighbors. The country clocked successive years of economic growth, reduced poverty, and reduced inequality. Now shorn of its dictator, Chile emerged as a model nation.

Characteristically, Friedman had a contrarian take on the Washington consensus. Ironically, the turn toward markets gave new life to the classic institutions of the postwar managed economy, namely the World Bank and the International Monetary Fund (IMF). No longer working to stabilize a gold-backed currency, the two international organizations offered loans to emerging economies—typically conditional upon implementing some version of the Washington consensus. This was a primary mechanism by which the consensus spread, the carrot that lured nations into making change. But to Friedman, their continued existence was a textbook case of bureaucratic overreach. Now that

Bretton Woods was dead, so too should its administrative apparatus be killed off.

In the wake of currency crises in Mexico and Asia, Friedman and George Shultz emerged with double-barreled interviews calling for the end of the IMF. "Let the IMF be abolished," Friedman told *Forbes.* "Distribute the assets to each country and let the markets take care of the fallout." For both men, the main problem was moral hazard. Foreign capital had poured into developing economies. But just as quickly it had flooded out, leaving destruction behind. "By encouraging people to speculate with other people's money, the IMF has been a destabilizing factor in East Asia," Friedman summarized. It was not the conditions of structural adjustment. Rather, the IMF sheltered "private financial institutions from the consequences of unwise investments."[37] In Friedman's eyes, as long as the IMF continued to exist, liberalization would be incomplete. It was in some sense the worst of both worlds: changed rules and frameworks had opened to capitalist activity, but the institutions of state management remained, distorting incentives and weakening the private sector.[38]

Within the political mainstream, there was little appetite for the argument. But in an echo of the topsy-turvy 1960s, a radical left antiglobalization movement would soon emerge to make a similar argument, albeit from different premises.

The Washington consensus also shaped life within the United States, promoting free trade in a series of landmark agreements. In 1993 President Clinton signed the North American Free Trade Agreement, significantly lowering trade barriers between the United States, Canada, and Mexico. Once upon a time, labor leaders and Democratic Party politicians would have howled about the threat to U.S. workers from cheap labor in the south. But as history ended, the most public campaign against NAFTA was launched by a political maverick, the independent presidential candidate Ross Perot.

The ultimate expression of the free trade faith came in 2001, when the United States accepted China's entry into the World Trade Organization. The WTO itself was a new organization, born from the postwar General Agreement on Tariffs and Trade (GATT). Reflecting the rapid pace of innovation in technology, media, and medicine, the WTO encompassed trade in services and protected intellectual property rights. Friedman cheered China's inclusion in this new regime, believing capitalism would spread democracy. "The same thing will happen in China that happened in Chile. Political freedom will ultimately break out of its shackles," he told an interviewer.[39] How could he think otherwise, amid the sweet vindication of a democratic Chile?

Nor was Friedman an outlier. Free trade commanded wide support across the political spectrum. As the Democrat Rahm Emanuel argued, "Not one worker gets better pay, a better education, or cleaner water by denying the citizens of emerging markets the access to the power of the American economy or the values of our political system." It was also true, Emanuel added, that "neither party can be nationally competitive absent a credible international agenda."[40] With the Cold War over, extending U.S. soft power through trade became diplomatic policy, with the IMF, World Bank, and WTO the main theaters of action. The 1980s "New Democrat" debates about industrial policy dissolved into a bipartisan embrace of free trade.

Domestic deregulation also took on a life of its own, now moving into the financial sector. Even a scandal in the savings-and-loan industry—more fallout from Regulation Q—did little to stem the tide. More pillars of the New Deal order rotted at the foundation and then toppled. As the tempo of bank mergers and acquisitions increased, laws like the 1933 Banking Act—otherwise known as Glass-Steagall—appeared to be fusty and inconvenient relics. In particular, Glass-Steagall had built a firewall between banks that made speculative investments and those that took deposits and made conventional loans. Other ancient rules prohibited banks from operating in more than one state, limiting their size. Traditional banks were bound by traditional regulation. But what about nontraditional banks?

Just as 1970s banks had innovated around Regulation Q, a new "shadow banking" sector emerged. In the 1980s, banks began circumventing interstate regulations through holding companies; eventually in 1994 a federal law repealed the restriction, opening the door to national chains. Now well practiced in the black arts, these bigger banks began spinning out new entities with dubious legal underpinnings. Of the banking system but not in it, these new "financial entities" used traditional bank capital for forbidden speculation. Like a Mafia don sending his daughter to a cotillion, the banks began to push for their ex post legitimation. Lobbied by boldface names, Congress repealed key provisions of Glass-Steagall in 1999. Because most of its restrictions had already been rendered moot, the move was less a watershed than a sign that the times had changed.

Reaching a crescendo, the late-century mood spun out a new narrative. Capitalism had stumbled once, decades back. It had been reconstructed, but the rebuilders had been too cautious, too conservative. They had traded off growth and innovation for stability and stasis. After an object lesson taught by 1970s stagflation, policy-makers and voters alike had recovered the importance of profits, risk-taking, and incentives. These vital ingredients of prosperity came with their own internal checks and balances; the real danger was the dead hand of government choking off wealth. The fall of the Soviet Union showed this was a universal pattern.

This metanarrative had a large measure of truth. But it was defined not just by what was included but by what was left out. Bureaucracies might be sclerotic, regulation stifling, politicians dangerously self-interested. But what would capitalism look like without this drag? Increasingly, there were few voices who could still remember. The 1970s had displaced the 1930s as the point of reference for a political culture hurtling into a limitless future.

Watching globalization in practice, Friedman evinced some uneasiness. As an adviser to the Fraser Institute in Canada, he spearheaded the creation of its *Economic Freedom of the World Report*, one of a variety of indexes crafted by nonprofits. By the time of the sixth report, published in 2002, his ideas were changing. "Privatize, privatize, privatize" had been his mantra after the Berlin Wall fell, he told an audience at the institute. "But, I was wrong. That wasn't enough." Sounding a Hayekian note, Friedman asserted that "rule of law" was vital, in fact "probably more basic than privatization." It was a return to the ideas of the early Mont Pelerin Society; markets and freedom had to be constructed and supported by the state, not simply conjured into existence.[41]

Increasingly, Friedman observed that capitalism and freedom did not always go together—although he believed they should. He hoped that China's economic liberalization would bring political freedom. But the experience of Hong Kong and Singapore, he told the Fraser Institute, convinced him there were really three kinds of freedom at stake: "economic freedom; social or civil freedom; and political freedom." Unfortunately, it appeared that political freedom could be sacrificed without endangering the other two. That is, citizens could enjoy private property rights along with freedom of expression and assembly, even as they had no choice of political ruler. But Friedman maintained that ultimately political freedom needed economic freedom in order to maintain "some independent source of authority" beyond the state.[42]

Friedman was by then approaching his nineties, gamely tapping out e-mails even as he limited his travel, gave up skiing, and weathered health crises. Many of the things he had pressed for throughout his professional life had come to pass. Globally, capital was freer than ever and privatization was on the march. Economic orthodoxy in the United States had shifted away from Keynesian demand management to a focus on Federal Reserve policy as a stabilizer and individual entrepreneurship as a driver. Still, Friedman did little gloating. "The economy will keep on growing slowly, and sooner or later we'll have another recession. No economy has been able to avoid all recessions," he told *The Wall Street Journal*.[43]

In fact, Friedman was surprised by what economists would call the Great Moderation—the quarter century of price stability and economic expansion that stretched from the Volcker shock to the 2007–2008 financial crisis. Ten years in, the economist John Taylor found Friedman restive and unresolved, printing out graphs of M1, M2, and velocity from his perch amid the San Francisco skyline. The charts showed the breakdown of once clear relationships; the money supply and GDP diverged in 1982, around the same time that the velocity of M1 and M2 fell off a stable trend line. Friedman had no good explanation for what he was seeing.

Speaking of the Fed, he wondered to Taylor, "They haven't learned anything they didn't know before. There's no additional knowledge. Literally, I'm baffled."[44] The encounter was poignant, given that Taylor himself was evidence of Friedman's impact. A Stanford professor and senior fellow at the Hoover Institution, Taylor positioned himself explicitly in the lineage of Henry Simons and Friedman.[45] His namesake Taylor rule, which dictated the appropriate interest rate as linked to macroeconomic indicators, was a reborn monetary-growth rule that soon became a widespread heuristic in monetary policy. Although monetarism did not become the new orthodoxy, central bankers had learned much from Friedman.

Three pillars of post-Volcker central bank practice descended from Friedman's body of work: rules, responsibilities, and transparency. With crucial modifications, Friedman's relentless calls for a monetary growth rule left a mark. Rather than rely on charismatic leaders or punch-bowl metaphors, central banks across the world shifted to quantitative goals. These weren't rules but rather frameworks: openly stated goals for monetary policy, along with identification of specific tools or policies to be used. Ideally, frameworks captured the best of both rules and discretion.

Among the most successful frameworks used was inflation targeting, which evolved from earlier monetary targets. A pledge to maintain stable prices integrated the accountability Friedman sought while preserving the freedom of action policy-makers needed.[46] Policy-makers' convergence on 2 percent as a reasonable inflation target also matched Friedman's emphases. It was about as close to zero as Friedman thought reasonable, given a growing economy. It also acknowledged what the new economics had not—that inflation rates much higher might accelerate into dangerous territory.

It was also now clear that central banks held awesome responsibilities, for good and for ill. Battles over the budget became political theater, while the real center of economic policy-making shifted to central bank appointments and press conferences. Always a tight fraternity with connections to multiple centers of financial and political power, central bankers developed a more coherent professional ethos and culture. Their ideas and actions were shaped increasingly by economic research, shared experience, and agreement on principles of independence and price stability. There would be fewer idiosyncratic chieftains like Arthur Burns or William McChesney Martin, blithely reliant on personal intuition and able to silence naysayers with the force of personality.

Finally, as expectations became the new common sense of inflation management, Friedman's dream of predictable and stable monetary policy transformed into a new commitment to transparency. Fedspeak did not disappear; parsing the chair's words remained an obligatory rite of passage for financial journalists. But in 1994, the Federal Open Market Committee started announcing its policy decisions, cutting off the ritualized guessing game that followed each meeting. In 2000, it began offering general assessments of the macroeconomy, offering a hint of where policy might be heading in the near future. Slowly, surely, the temple was yielding its secrets. Derived from Friedman's emphasis on expectations, these moves reflected the consensus that inflation was both a monetary and a psychological phenomenon. Knowing what the Fed was doing and thinking tamped down speculative swings. Transparency built upon Volcker's hard-earned credibility even as it rendered his monetary discipline obsolete.

If the Great Moderation was not Friedman's accomplishment, it was nonetheless a significant part of his legacy. The 1987 crash was one of several macro shocks that surged through the global economic system without triggering a depression or runaway inflation, in large part because the Fed embraced its responsibilities and communicated its intentions. Friedman had every right to rejoice at the tangible impact of his research.

Within universities, the picture was more complicated. Newly ascendant monetary theories started with monetarism's Achilles' heel—financial innovation—and concluded with its nemesis, the interest rate. "There is every reason to expect further innovations," wrote the economist Michael Woodford, "due to improvements in information processing and to increased creativity in the evasion of the remaining regulatory constraints." Believing aggregates were forever destabilized, Woodford theorized monetary policy without money. It was possible, he argued, to manage inflation without reference to "the money supply or to a money demand relation." The key mechanism was the interest rate, Woodford elaborated in his influential book *Interest and Prices: Foundations of a Theory of Monetary Policy.*[47]

Rational expectations continued to influence the field. Over time, Robert Lucas modulated the more extreme versions of money neutrality, confining them to the long run and asserting a relationship between inflation and monetary growth.[48] But another Lucas-inspired offshoot, real business cycle theory, similarly minimized the role of money. "Before real business cycle theory," complained one critic, "almost all macroeconomists seemed to agree on one conclusion: money matters." But in real business cycle theory, despite the object lesson of the Volcker shock, banking was treated no differently than any other sector. Banks had outputs and productivity, and no particularly unique role in the economy. There was no inherent business cycle, only external shocks that threw otherwise stable economies into disarray.[49]

Rational expectations also fed into the efficient markets hypothesis, developed by the University of Chicago business school professor Eugene Fama. At its most basic, the hypothesis argued that financial markets incorporated all available information into prices. For the finance world, the implications were immense. If markets were efficient, the best investment strategy was essentially passive—index funds that tracked the market, rather than qualitative research into business prospects. Fama's work helped birth quantitative finance, which in turn broke down long-standing barriers between financial and academic economics.[50]

Friedman watched Fama's emergence with skepticism. When Fama wrote a paper on banking, Friedman told him "you are treading on old ground," referencing his 1960 book *A Program for Monetary Stability.* Fama was unimpressed. "Contrary to your footnote, I do claim that there is nothing 'inherently unstable' about a regulated deposit system," Fama wrote in a potshot at Friedman's fondness for 100 percent money.

"Indeed, this is probably the main point of my paper," he added.[51] Simons's malevolent genius had been exorcised. Increasingly Chicago economics was defined by confidence about the wisdom of market participants and the stability of the economic world they created.

These new currents—which one critic dubbed "utopian economics"—were the university version of post–Cold War triumphalism. And they existed in ambivalent relationship to Friedman. On the one hand, he looked sourly at their elaborate mathematics and fantastic assumptions of economic stability. "Those interpretations are inconsistent with an enormous amount of empirical evidence," Friedman told Fama after reading a paper on real business cycle theory. On the other hand, Friedman himself had provided a powerful defense—indeed the only real defense—of the idea that assumptions in economics need not be realistic. "Did you ever read Friedman's essay on Positive Economics?" came the inevitable question to any dissent.[52]

In the end, monetary theory reconstructed itself around the Lucas critique. Even as Woodford acknowledged the historic contribution of monetarism, his defense of interest rates owed far more to rational expectations. Over time, it was expectations alone that seemed to matter. By the turn of the century, Woodford was arguing that in a liquidity trap, the central bank should act "with a view to signaling the nature of its policy commitments, and not for the purpose of creating some sort of 'direct' effects."[53] Volcker's Germanic quest for credibility had evolved into a dance of the seven veils, with the Fed by turns reassuring and mystifying the private sector. From the solidity of Friedman's quantity theory, monetary policy had become utterly postmodern: detached from money itself, performative to its core.

In a signal irony, Friedman's ideas found a home in what its practitioners called the new Keynesian economics. "At research seminars, people do not take Keynesian theorizing seriously any more—audience starts to whisper, giggles to one another," Lucas claimed.[54] This may have been true in Chicago, but beyond the Great Lakes economists were busy with a new synthesis. The new Keynesian economists had not escaped the imprint of rational expectations. They built their models Lucas-style, adding in rigidities to modify the assumption of frictionless rationality. Yet they kept the large space for money carved out by monetarism.[55]

Some were even ready to celebrate Friedman. "The influence of monetarism on how we all think about macroeconomics today has been deep, pervasive, and subtle," argued the Berkeley professor Bradford DeLong, identifying four different "varieties or subspecies" of monetarism.[56] According to DeLong, professional economists had adopted major tenets of Classic Monetarism, from the Non-Accelerating Inflation Rate of Unemployment to policy rules to the potency of monetary policy.

This synthesis had been obscured by Political Monetarism, which DeLong characterized as the simplistic belief that "everything that went wrong in the macroeconomy had a single, simple cause: the central bank had failed to make the money supply grow at the appropriate rate." Political Monetarism "crashed and burned in the 1980s," just as large elements of Classic Monetarism "were achieving their intellectual hegemony." In the aftermath, there was a re-sorting. Economists who shared Friedman's skepticism about government action clustered around the rational expectations approach. A remnant of sympathizers continued the monetarist tradition. Most significantly, Friedman's ideas about money quietly lived on under the new Keynesian flag. This was sometimes difficult to see, as monetarism in its heyday had such strong partisan connotations. Although the Volcker shock had discredited monetary aggregates as a guide to Fed operations, it had validated Friedman's stance on the potency of monetary policy.

DeLong also noted a second paradox. When it came to the banking system, Friedman in his classic phase called for more regulation, not less; the elimination of fractional reserve banking, tighter congressional control of the Fed. Perhaps, DeLong mused, had these reforms been passed, M1 and M2 would have mapped onto the real economy, and velocity would have remained stable.

Friedman appeared to take little comfort from the new Keynesian embrace of his ideas. "I thought we killed any real reliance on the Phillips curve years ago, but clearly I was mistaken," he complained to Greenspan after seeing news coverage of his congressional testimony.

"It is alive and well, and enables people who don't understand anything to talk as if they do."[57] The post-Volcker Phillips curve, however, was different from the one Friedman had attacked. Precisely because the long-run Phillips curve did not work, the short-run trade-off was critical. If policy-makers were too enthusiastic in their pursuit of low unemployment, they might risk stagflation and recession.

Eventually Friedman settled on a resolution that brought some satisfaction. Looking at the United States, he rediscovered the correlation between M2 and inflation. It had taken some time to adjust to the personal computer and modem, but by the end of the 1980s Friedman had approximated the money workshop in his own residence. He shared the findings first with Greenspan, explaining he had "been trying to understand that apparent breakdown during the 1970s and 1980s in the timing relations between money and inflation." After much frustration, returning to basics with "more elementary tools" had yielded a finding: "The close relation is alive and well, apparently completely recovered from its breakdown during the earlier '80s." Greenspan agreed that "the long-run relationship between M2 and prices seems quite strong," but pointed out the short and intermediate run "are considerably more complex." This was the crux of the matter. Friedman the scholar had the luxury of the long run; Greenspan the policy-maker did not.[58]

Nonetheless, Friedman had recovered the faith. Interviewed by two economists at the American Economic Association's annual meeting, he recounted his analysis that "from about 1985 on the earlier demand function with M2 is re-established, but not with M1 or the base; they are very unstable." He also came to adopt a broader perspective on his work, stepping away from the keen disappointment of the Volcker era. "If you eliminate the perturbations and you look at the general direction over the period from 1980 to 1995 in every country in the world aggregate, monetary growth has come way down and with it has come inflation," he summarized. "So I think that the experiment in all of the countries of the world has been enormously confirmatory of the proposition that inflation is a monetary phenomenon," he concluded.[59]

Still, Friedman knew that monetarism had been gravely wounded. Greenspan took to citing the M2 correlations in his speeches. But over

Friedman's objections, in 1988 he reverted the Fed back to lagged reporting of reserves. In 1984 the Fed had finally embraced contemporaneous reserve reporting—this was the fundamental reform Volcker had left undone, and one of the reasons Friedman believed his effort to achieve stable money growth had failed. Now Greenspan was reversing that victory. The move, Friedman wrote to Greenspan, "essentially forecloses the System from operating in other ways than through interest rates." Without contemporaneous reporting, it would be impossible to get a firm grip on the money supply. In 2003, Friedman made a stark admission to the *Financial Times*: "The use of quantity of money as a target has not been a success. I'm not sure I would as of today push it as hard as I once did." Friedman was still a quantity theorist, still a monetarist. But the brash thinker once defined by certainty and confidence now voiced a note of humility.[60]

While Friedman never relinquished his belief in monetarism, the passage of time gave him a new appreciation of the "ubiquitous and often unanticipated effects of what seem like trivial changes in monetary institutions," as he wrote in his final book, *Money Mischief.* Addressing a popular audience, Friedman dwelled on an uncertain future. "A world monetary system has emerged that has no historical precedent," he wrote, referring to the rise of paper money unbacked by gold or a similar commodity, so-called fiat money. "The ultimate consequences of this development are shrouded in uncertainty," Friedman continued. A robust scientific literature elaborated various elements of monetary reform but had largely ignored an "alarmist and hard-money" popular belief that fiat currency would be inevitably destroyed by inflation. Friedman was no goldbug. But the popular fear of inflation was not misplaced, he argued. After all, he wrote, "We must find a nominal anchor to replace the physical limit." Could monetary policy be that anchor? Friedman was unwilling to give a final answer.[61]

Friedman's other disappointment was political. He recognized that Reagan's two terms had provided unprecedented scope for his philosophical and policy preferences. "No other president in my lifetime comes close to Reagan in adherence to clearly specified principles dedicated to promoting and maintaining a free society," Friedman enthused in his memoir. By his last years of life, with the USSR gone and China and India opening up, he noted with satisfaction that "the world as a whole has more or less embraced freedom." Old-fashioned socialism—state ownership—had virtually disappeared, leaving only "government extraction of income from the haves and giving it to the have-nots." Nonetheless, the metric Friedman cared about most was the size of the U.S. government, and here the record was mixed. He and Rose believed they had won the battle of ideas, but "judging by practice, we have been, despite some advances, mostly on the losing side." The size of the U.S. government had stabilized since 1980, he admitted. But flat growth was not what the Friedmans wanted. They had hoped for a decisive turn to smaller government, something akin to the Thatcher pullback.[62]

What bothered Friedman in the closing years of his life were taxes. "Federal taxes are at an all time high," he complained to *The Wall Street Journal* in 1999. "The average taxpayer is currently forking over roughly 40 percent of his or her income to federal, state, and local governments compared with less than 30 percent in 1945." His ideal, Friedman revealed, was closer to 10 or 15 percent, corresponding to the pre-Depression state.[63] Friedman rued the presidency of George H. W. Bush, calling his selection by Reagan "the worst decision not only of his life but of his presidency." Facing unprecedented budget deficits, Bush had raised taxes. Friedman was unimpressed by this show of fiscal responsibility, which continued into the next administration, dismissing it all as "the sorry Bush-Clinton period."[64]

Nor was he concerned about the other bogeyman of the 1990s, the burgeoning federal debt. This was the legacy of Reagan's "Big Budget Bang"—eight years of repeated budget deficits, born of reduced taxes and increased defense spending.[65] Fear of this outcome had motivated Volcker to hold the course on tight money, deepening the Volcker shock. But neither Volcker nor anyone else predicted what happened next.

Starting in the 1980s, high interest rates drew in a flood of foreign capital, now free to choose its path in a post–Bretton Woods world.

First came buyers from Japan, then China, all hungry for U.S. Treasurys. Even when interest rates went down, foreign capital stayed. Although he hadn't seen it coming, Friedman grasped the mechanism: "What is most attractive about the U.S. to people and countries with wealth is that it can provide security, insurance really, against political instability. Nobody is afraid that the money they place in the U.S. is at risk of expropriation or of in some other way being taken away."[66] This was not the world Friedman had anticipated when he campaigned against Bretton Woods, but it was one that he accepted.

There was one troubling indicator: the extraordinarily low interest rate. Around the year 2000, long-term interest rates plummeted to around 2 percent, which he considered "a very, very low real rate of return." Friedman's monetarism had critiqued the interest rate as the default instrument of policy. But he still considered it an important indicator. Once again, his reading cut against the grain. "The low interest rate . . . is being taken as clearly a good sign," he worried to a journalist, "whereas I think it's fundamentally an indication of something wrong." If there wasn't strong demand for capital, growth and innovation would slow.[67]

There was another unpredictable dynamic at work: if foreigners were willing to hold U.S. debt indefinitely and under almost any conditions, the political penalty for deficits would vanish. The balanced-budget wing of the Republican Party withered away, leaving only Friedman's relentless drive to cut taxes "under any circumstances, in any way, in any form, whatsoever . . . on any pretext, because that's the only way to keep down government spending." No doubt, some politicians shared Friedman's philosophical goal, but for those trying to win elections, there was another calculus: tax cuts gave Republicans a goodie to counter Democratic spending.[68] The result was a "two Santa Clauses" model of politics, where one party promised higher spending and the other countered with tax cuts.[69] This was not the scenario Friedman had envisioned, but it was one he was willing to defend.

When the United States unexpectedly swung into a budget surplus during the Clinton years, Friedman was unmoved. Hearing that his old antagonist Robert Solow opposed rebating the surplus to taxpayers,

Friedman jousted back: "Enable the American people to do what the American people want to do, not what Bob Solow thinks they ought to do."[70] Friedman had converged on a final position: cut taxes and shrink the government, no matter what. It was a position that became increasingly central to the Republican Party, as groups like Americans for Tax Reform successfully made tax-cutting a political priority.

Federal spending also influenced Friedman's views on immigration. First among globalists, he had long supported the free movement of people and capital across borders. But as immigration to the United States from Mexico surged during the 1980s, his views began to shift. It was not that Friedman disliked immigration, to which he paid the ultimate compliment—it was "good for freedom." It was that he believed a welfare state would draw the wrong kind of immigrants, those looking for benefits and unwilling to work. Friedman accommodated the tension with an unusual resolution. "Now, that Mexican immigration, over the border, is a good thing. It's a good thing for the illegal immigrants," he told an audience at Stanford. "It's a good thing for the United States. It's a good thing for the citizens of the country. But, it's only good so long as it's illegal."[71] It was one last provocation, directed at both the left and the right.

In the closing years of their sixty-eight-year marriage, Milton and Rose finally disagreed, profoundly and irreconcilably, about the 2003 war in Iraq. "We should not have gone into Iraq," Milton flatly told anyone who asked. But Rose was a supporter, believing aggression against "the monster" Saddam Hussein was justified. The war complicated Friedman's verdict on George W. Bush. A certain alignment was clear: Bush even awarded Friedman the Presidential Medal of Freedom. Bush was a tax-cutter, and wanted to privatize Social Security. But "war is an enemy of freedom," Friedman told Fox News. And further, "This administration is showing very little spending restraint," he admitted to *The Wall Street Journal*.[72]

Here, Friedman's lament prefigured a mood that would become ever more pronounced on the political right. Conservatives kept winning elections, yet the government continued to grow. Across the 1990s, new voices of conservatism, like the radio star Rush Limbaugh, would emerge with a new answer: it was a corrupt elite that won office, then broke all its promises.[73] The idea reinvigorated the traditional split between insurgent grassroots and party establishment that had churned since the days of Barry Goldwater. By now, Friedman was too much the establishment himself to pick up the theme with any vigor.

Yet it was there anyhow, in his favored explanation for the Clinton-era surplus: divided government. In this reading, government growth slowed only if one party controlled the presidency, the other Congress. The resultant gridlock would grind spending to a halt. Buried inside was subtle recognition of an important shift—it was not the Democrats alone who had blown up the budget.

A final area of concern that remained was education. Coming from a modest background, Friedman had found in Rahway's public schools a springboard to the commanding heights of intellectual achievement. Increasingly, though, this path seemed closed off to future Friedmans. Global surveys revealed U.S. students slipping farther behind other countries in math, reading, and basic academic skills. For a believer in meritocracy, uneven schooling in the early years was the ultimate injustice.

Friedman folded this social concern into his long-standing support of privatization and his belief in competition. "We've had such an increase in inequality because a quarter of American kids don't finish high school!" he told an interviewer. "In the current world, with the skills needed, those dropouts are condemned to being members of the underclass. In my view, this is a fault of the American school system, which is a government monopoly."[74] Since his 1953 essay on vouchers, a successful educational-reform movement had emerged, promoting both school vouchers and hybrid solutions like charter schools. In retirement Friedman became an active presence in this network, advising, strategizing, and encouraging a web of correspondents. While at first he had envisioned vouchers creating a mixed ecosystem with competing public, private, and charter schools, increasingly he came to believe the public system should be supplanted altogether. In 1996, Milton and Rose created a private foundation, now known as EdChoice, dedicated to supporting school choice in its many variations. It was Simons who had first taught Milton and Rose to worry about inequality, making the foundation one last echo of early Chicago across the years.

Friedman remained lucid to the last months of his life. A visiting reporter from *The Wall Street Journal* found the couple at Stanford, bickering gently about Iraq, Rose wrapped in a mink coat in preparation for an evening event on the Quad. Both remained active in the affairs of the Friedman Foundation for Educational Choice. Just weeks from the end, a board member found him "curious, cheerful, combative, and resolute," ready as ever to talk economics.

After Friedman's death in November 2006, tributes poured in from around the world. "One of the greatest economists of all time," wrote Britain's left-leaning *Guardian* newspaper. "Free market believers lost a hero," mourned *Forbes*. "On a par with giants like John Maynard Keynes and Paul Samuelson," opined *The New York Times*. "Universally regarded as one of the most influential economic thinkers of the 20th century," wrote Australia's *The Age*.[75] Friedman had outlived most of his closest friends and collaborators, including Henry Simons, George Stigler, Arthur Burns, and Aaron Director. Of the original Chicago Room Seven, only Rose was left.

Instead of these men, when the University of Chicago convened a memorial service in early 2007, there came another column of six dark suits to the Rockefeller Memorial Chapel. Each represented a facet of Friedman's storied career. The university's president testified to Friedman's lifelong association with Chicago. There was heavyset Arnold Harberger, the leader of the Chicago Boys, stepping carefully to the chancel, cane in hand. Slim and serious, Gary Becker was the Friedman advisee who came nearest to his professional stature. Václav Klaus, the president of the Czech Republic, offered a memory of his youthful pilgrimage by Greyhound bus to the campus where Friedman taught. The director of the Fraser Institute symbolized Friedman's long-standing links to private philanthropy. And the head of the Chicago Mercantile

Exchange, now trading currency along with hog futures, represented his connection to finance.[76]

As one, the eulogies painted a portrait of brilliance—and innocence. A letter read aloud from Greenspan lauded Friedman's "utter disregard for status." Harberger, who had known Milton almost as long as Rose, summarized his character: "no frills, no pettiness, no fear." Never once, Harberger said admiringly, had he seen Milton resort to a personal attack, insinuation, or innuendo. Instead, it was "as if an iron will kept driving him to talk about the merits of the case, and only the merits of the case, all of the time." Becker, a longtime veteran of the Chicago workshop tradition, admitted that Friedman was prone to attack. But it was always in the service of improving others' ideas. Never would he "soften his view to curry favor." Ever the optimist, animated by a "missionary zeal to convert the heathen," Friedman took his case for markets and freedom to whomever would listen.

As the only serving head of state in attendance—President Bush sent a letter—Klaus testified to the power of this message across space and time. "For us, who lived in the communist world, Milton Friedman was the greatest champion of freedom, of limited, unobtrusive government, and of free markets," Klaus explained. "Because of him I became a true believer in the unrestricted market economy." Although *Capitalism and Freedom* was verboten, even behind the iron curtain Klaus could get his hands on the *American Economic Review*, where he derived the larger message of Friedman's work. "Already then, my heart was fully on his side," he told the audience.

Underscoring the point, Leo Melamed described his efforts to bring currency trading to the Chicago Mercantile Exchange. Decades before, on the run from the Holocaust, his father had delivered an impromptu seminar on floating exchange rates. Waving aloft two currencies, Polish zloty and Lithuanian litas, he told his son "government's official rate doesn't mean a thing." Money was measured by what it would buy in the market.

When Melamed tried to realize this vision amid the collapsing Bretton Woods order, he found the "idea of a futures market in currency . . . was sheer heresy, akin to suggesting monotheism to a pagan."

Luckily Melamed knew a famous pagan. With a feasibility study from Friedman in hand, doors began to open. In meetings with government officials, bank presidents, corporate treasurers, brokers, "each and every time his name made the difference." Emblematic was the reaction of George Shultz, the secretary of the Treasury when Melamed started his efforts: "If it's good enough for Milton, its good enough for me." The International Monetary Market ushered in "the modern era of financial derivatives," with its futures exchange judged among the most important financial innovations of the time.

Harberger too struck a global theme. After fifty years working in the developing world, he appreciated with special force the Friedmans' latter-day emphasis on education. "True opportunity for one's children is a wonderful glue to hold a society together," Harberger reflected. He offered a summary of Friedman's truth: "Market economy, genuine opportunity, and advancement based on merit in a competitive setting, these elements reinforce each other. Together, they give us the best prescription for the future of a free economy in a free society." With Friedman's passing, these ideas had lost their best champion.

EPILOGUE: HELICOPTER DROP

> Milton Friedman isn't running the show anymore!
>
> —Joe Biden, 2020

For an economist who lived only six years into the twenty-first century, Milton Friedman's ideas displayed enormous staying power in its turbulent opening decades. During the 2007–2008 great financial crisis, policy-makers and observers alike evaluated the situation against the backdrop of Friedman and Schwartz. The lesson of *A Monetary History of the United States* was clear: the Fed must have, as the Federal Reserve's chairman, Ben Bernanke, put it, "the courage to act." A student of the Great Depression drawn into the topic by Friedman and Schwartz, Bernanke retained a keen awareness of the Fed's role and responsibility. Only a few years earlier, at a conference celebrating Friedman's ninetieth birthday, Bernanke famously paid homage to the pair: "Regarding the Great Depression. You're right, we did it. We're very sorry. But thanks to you, we won't do it again."[1] This connection between the Fed and economic depression—burned into public consciousness by Friedman and Schwartz's pathbreaking book—would be the essential starting point for navigating the crisis.

We'll never know how Friedman would have reacted to the unprecedented policies initiated by Bernanke's Fed. Schwartz, for one, was highly critical, accusing the Fed of "fighting the last war." She was particularly harsh on Treasury's decision to rescue insolvent banks.

"Firms that made wrong decisions should fail," she argued.[2] Would Friedman have agreed? Or would he have responded as he did to the Great Depression and World War II—with the recognition that extraordinary times could justify robust federal action? Regardless, we do know that Friedman and Schwartz provided one of the basic frameworks for averting a second Great Depression.

The years after the financial crisis, however, represented a forgetting. New monetary policies emerged that seemed a decisive break with the past. The Fed took interest rates down to the previously hypothetical "zero lower bound"—approaching zero percent. And it introduced quantitative easing, or QE, which went far beyond conventional manipulation of the federal funds rate through Federal Open Market Committee (FOMC) bond purchases. To support weak financial markets, the Fed slurped up a vast array of assets, from dodgy mortgage-backed securities to commercial paper to auto, student, and credit card loans. Conceived in an emergency, both policies would persist for more than a decade.[3] The interest rate remained well below pre-crisis levels, while QE went through four phases, much like Nixon's supposedly six-week price controls.

Inspired in part by Friedman and Schwartz's opus, this unconventional monetary policy seemed, over time, to threaten the very meaning of their life's work. Friedman had ultimately concluded that specific aggregates aside, the global low inflation of the post-Volcker years was attributable to monetary restraint. Accordingly, with the Fed so expansionary, wasn't inflation sure to follow? And if the low interest rates of the aughts had been a concern, wouldn't the zero lower bound overheat the economy? Yet as the Fed continued its unprecedented purchases, the price level remained steady. Some of Friedman's followers emerged with warnings. In a 2010 "Open Letter to Ben Bernanke," a host of Republican economists argued that "the planned asset purchases risk currency debasement and inflation." Similarly, in 2013 Allan Meltzer foretold "America cannot escape inflation forever," calling the Fed's policies "Quantitative Quicksand." These critiques made little dent, largely because inflation did not emerge, staying near the Fed's 2 percent target. These failed predictions of inflation were a repeat of Friedman's early 1980s flail, and they exerted a similar downward pull on his reputation. "What happened to the monetary aggregates?" Schwartz plaintively asked a friend near the end of her life in 2012.[4]

There were other explanations, less obvious to the public eye, that were compatible with monetarism. What if QE didn't balloon the money supply that mattered? Some unrepentant monetarists pursued this argument. Amid the crisis, they pointed out, in 2008 the Fed introduced a new tool, the galactic-sounding IORB (interest on reserve balances). For the first time, the Fed would pay banks interest on their reserves. IORB was an administered rate, meaning the Fed set it directly. As a consequence, the Fed had new leverage on the federal funds rate; any gap between the two would be quickly arbitraged away by banks, driving convergence of the rates.

IORB was another idea originally proposed by Friedman—and in another posthumous paradox, it was one that from a distance served to undermine monetarism's standing. Not only was the Fed paying interest on reserves, but it had raised capital and liquidity requirements to prevent any more disastrous risk-taking.[5] All this meant that while QE appeared expansionary, little of the new Fed-created money circulated outside bank vaults. Watching monetarists noted that M2, Friedman's favorite indicator, was holding steady at around 6.5 percent annual growth.

By then, the aggregates had been reconstructed, with findings that both confirmed and modified essential parts of Friedman's approach. The most important departures were around the velocity of money, which Friedman had insisted was generally stable. Yet in crises—perhaps the most important moments of all—velocity was erratic. And as Volcker had found in the 1980s, it could also be unpredictable amid regulatory and political change. Nonetheless, error correction frameworks made it possible to distinguish between short-term fluctuations and long-term trends. From there, a clear finding emerged: while the monetary base and M1 did not correlate with broader economic activity, over time M2 did. Now conceptualized as "broad money," the aggregate had expanded beyond currency, coins, and checking and savings accounts to incorporate innovations like money market funds and small-time deposits like CDs. "Divisia" aggregates, a new and complex measure of money, showed similar trends.[6]

From the monetarist perspective, then, it was little mystery that QE had not caused inflation. Not only was M2 steady, its velocity was low, meaning new money was not moving rapidly through the economy. As Meltzer noted, "Banks circulated only 2 percent of QE2's contribution, leaving the rest idle." The figures were similar for all four rounds of QE. The situation could not continue indefinitely, Meltzer warned: "The reserves that the Fed—and almost all other major central banks—are building will eventually be used." It was simply another monetary lag.[7]

Yet the lag opened space to imagine that Friedman had been decisively refuted. If inflation wasn't a monetary phenomenon, what else could it be? Ideas of cost-push inflation gained currency once again. Without strong labor unions, it was argued, there was no upward pressure on wages. So too did China's endless pool of low-wage workers and flood of cheap goods hold down wages and prices.[8] On the left, a new school of modern monetary theory (MMT) became influential. Calling for a fundamental overhaul of fiscal and monetary institutions, MMT argued government spending could be funded by printing new money. MMT didn't ignore inflation altogether but saw it as a fiscal issue, easily reined in by taxation or avoided altogether by carefully matching spending to the economy's true capacity.[9] It was an unconstrained vision that would surely have drawn Friedman's ire. Ignoring the bill, he might have said, is not the same thing as a free lunch.

Even more significant were shifts at the Federal Reserve. In 2020 the Fed revised its strategic statement. Instead of a 2 percent inflation target, it announced a goal of 2 percent average inflation. This subtle change had important ramifications. Previous policy had been symmetric, meaning the Fed responded to inflation above or below the target. Now the Fed announced an "asymmetric" policy: it would tolerate inflation higher than 2 percent in order to reach its average goal. What was the time frame over which the Fed would measure inflation? This remained unclear in the brief strategic document, which focused on the broad outlines of policy, eschewing numerical specificity. Through other seemingly minor shifts in wording, the Fed also communicated a greater concern with unemployment over inflation, a tilt in the dual mandate reminiscent of the new economics. Also like the new economics, it represented a break with Friedman's views: "a more discretionary and less predictable or systematic approach to monetary policymaking," in the words of two critics.[10]

The coronavirus pandemic and its aftermath brought Friedman's ideas once again back to center stage. Faced with an unprecedented economic shock, the Fed went straight for the zero bound. Replicating and even surpassing its responses to the 2008 crisis, it rolled out programs familiar and new: purchases of Treasurys and mortgage-backed securities, liquidity swap lines offering dollars to European and Asian markets, and support for payroll, mutual funds, corporate bonds, small and medium businesses, even municipalities. QE went into yet another phase of vast open-market purchases; at its height, the Fed bought a million dollars of bonds each second. Within weeks, these extraordinary measures would calm markets, including the pivotal market for U.S. Treasurys.[11]

Yet it was not Friedman and Schwartz's masterwork that inspired this response but rather another obscure Friedman concept: the helicopter drop. "Let us suppose now that one day a helicopter flies over [a] community and drops an additional $1000 in bills from the sky, which is, of course, hastily collected by members of the community," Friedman wrote in a 1969 essay. If everyone understood the helicopter only came once, Friedman argued, most of this money would be spent fairly quickly. People already held the money they wanted, and the cash from above would not change the fundamentals of economic life. The example was artificial and abstract, a thought experiment intended to demonstrate the importance of money demand. But it was also evocative, and its Zen-like simplicity captured Bernanke's attention.[12] Maybe it could inform monetary policy at the zero bound, where the traditional tool of interest rates was powerless. As a newbie to the FOMC, years before he became chair, in 2002 Bernanke speculated on the possibilities in a widely noted speech. Faced with deflation, the government could cut taxes, and to pay for it, instead of buying bonds the Federal Reserve could simply credit Treasury's account. It was a straight-up expansion of the money supply, and it would cause inflation; but sometimes inflation was needed. The benefit of helicopter money was that it added to the money supply without adding debt. And it had nothing to do with interest rates, which were tapped out. Bernanke considered all of this a reasonable riff on Friedman; but Fed watchers mocked him with the nickname "Helicopter Ben."[13]

The threat of corona collapse renewed the idea. "Coronavirus: The Moment for Helicopter Money," declared the *Financial Times*. While sometimes used as a catchall for spending, in 2020 helicopter money had at least two meanings. Economists tended to use it like Bernanke, referring to unconventional financing of stimulus programs. But the name also encompassed the new Fed programs that lent directly to small businesses, large corporations, and nonprofits—entities that never before experienced Fed largesse firsthand. In popular usage, helicopter money came to mean almost any coronavirus relief spending, whether monetary (from the Fed) or fiscal (direct from Treasury). Together, both pointed to a third overarching meaning, which was that "conventional taboos in economic policy thinking are swiftly being swept away," as the *Financial Times* summarized.[14] In the United States, Republican lawmakers sounded like Friedman as they argued coronavirus relief should come as cash payments, rather than traditional benefits in kind. "Surge cash to low and middle-income Americans," declared a press release from the Arkansas senator Tom Cotton as the virus emerged. By December, the Missouri senator Josh Hawley was even ready to partner with the socialist Vermont senator Bernie Sanders in pushing for another round of cash relief.[15] In the end, the basic idea of spending vast sums to help Americans through the crisis found support across the political aisle. It was a rare moment of unity, soon drowned out by the mask and vaccine wars.

There was only one problem: helicopter money, after all, was inflationary. Indeed, Bernanke had originally envisioned it as a solution to some hypothetical future deflation. Friedman well understood this. In 1997 he proposed a helicopter drop of sorts for Japan's stalled economy, grumbling to *Forbes*, "They should be printing more money." Coronavirus threatened to create not a stalled economy but a contracting one—the ideal moment for inflationary stimulus.[16]

The challenge was knowing when that moment had passed. And increasingly during 2021, evidence began to mount that neither the federal government nor the Federal Reserve had got the timing right. After four rounds of stimulus under Donald Trump, in March 2021 the Biden administration added one last shot with the American Rescue Plan, sending up to $1,400 to qualifying individuals.

In the meantime, after years of quiescence, M2 was on the move. Before the pandemic, it was growing at about 7 percent annually. That figure shot up to 25 percent across 2020 and into the following year. Accordingly, followers of Friedman's work predicted inflation was soon to arrive. In July 2021, the Johns Hopkins economist Steve Hanke made the case in *The Wall Street Journal*: "Plug numbers into the model and solve for M, and money supply (M2) should be growing at around 6 percent a year for the Fed to hit its inflation target of 2 percent. With M2 growing at nearly four times the 'ideal' rate since March 2020, inflation is baked into the cake."[17] At first, these claims were ridiculed. "When you and I studied economics a million years ago," the Federal Reserve's chair, Jerome Powell, patiently explained to a member of Congress, "M2 and monetary aggregates generally seemed to have a relationship to economic growth. Right now, I would say the growth of M2, which is quite substantial, does not really have important implications for the economic outlook . . . that classic relationship between monetary aggregates and economic growth and the size of the economy, it just no longer holds."[18] Even when inflation began to emerge, it was explained as a temporary bulge in a blocked supply chain, or fallout from global turmoil. A high-profile group of economists and officials, soon known as "team transitory," batted away its significance. Yet inflation steadily rose to heights not seen since the 1970s. By the summer of 2022, financial leaders from Treasury Secretary Janet Yellen to Powell—the inspiration for team transitory—had identified inflation, then running around 8 percent, as a major economic problem. "I was wrong," Yellen told the media. In the fall, the Fed began to roll

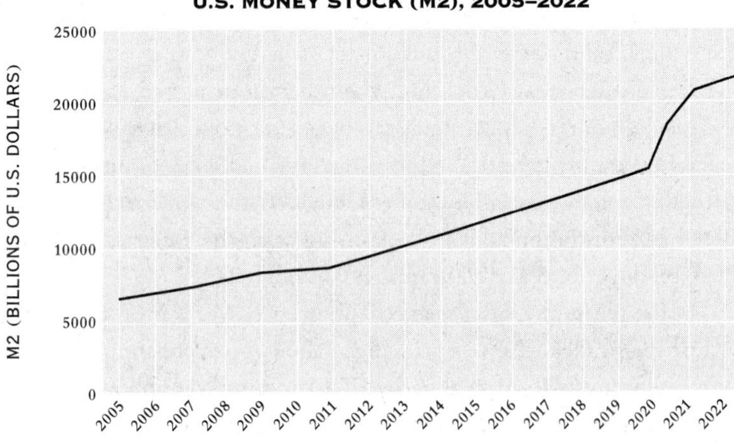

During the coronavirus pandemic, Friedman's admirers pointed with alarm to the rapid rise in M2, the monetary aggregate Friedman considered most important.

out interest rate increases. Powell began bringing up Paul Volcker in his speeches.[19]

However one understood inflation, it was no longer possible to dismiss the monetary interpretation. It was not that monetarism returned in its strong form. Even economists worried about M2 acknowledged the impact of geopolitical uncertainty, from sluggish supply chains to war to energy shocks (although they also pointed out that prior to the war in Ukraine, U.S. inflation far exceeded that of other nations). Other economists emphasized the extraordinarily tight labor market, a product of the pandemic-induced Great Resignation.[20] All those factors inhibited economic growth and production. Yet even accounting for too few goods, there was still the other half of the equation: too much money. "The simple fact is that M2—one broad measure of the money supply—went up about 40 percent between February 2020 and February 2022," wrote the economist Tyler Cowen in *The Washington Post*. "In the quantity theory approach, that would be reason to expect additional inflation, and of course that is exactly what happened . . . this is consistent with one of the longest-standing truths of economic history, from the inflationary episodes of ancient Rome to the French Revolution to Weimar Germany." Cowen noted the flaws in Friedman's monetarism. Yet his article signaled a new appreciation for Friedman's truth: "Inflation is always and everywhere a monetary phenomenon."[21]

And if few people were talking—*yet*—about aggregates as the foundation of monetary policy, they were talking about the Taylor rule, a descendant of Friedman's work. A modification of Friedman's call for fixed monetary growth, the Taylor rule (or rules, since there are several versions) is an interest rate target derived from various economic indicators, including the rate of inflation. Its lineage goes all the way back to Henry Simons's Depression-era article "Rules Versus Authorities in Monetary Policy." The basic idea is that a transparent, openly stated monetary policy "rule" can avoid the worst human errors, including the temptation to repeatedly change course. While Friedman opposed the use of interest rates as the main instrument of monetary policy, the Taylor rule, first published in 1993, pragmatically recognized their dominant role.

Like monetarism, the Taylor rule was a casualty of the zero bound era, despite an impressive record in the years prior. Economists like Berkeley's Barry Eichengreen noticed the Fed had basically followed the Taylor rule until 2002, when interest rates headed down to nearly three percentage points below the guidance and stayed there. Along with many others, Eichengreen suggested this deviation from the Taylor rule had touched off the great financial crisis boom-and-bust that followed a few years later.[22] Thus, looking back across the long run, there was some evidence the Taylor rule could lead to stable monetary growth, Friedman's lifelong wish. Moreover, John Taylor himself was an active critic of QE and the Fed's response to pandemic-era inflation. However configured, the Taylor rule suggested a far higher interest rate target than the Fed had ever publicly stated. In the summer of 2022 the Fed quietly restored a section on policy rules to its annual *Monetary Policy Report*, highlighting the Taylor rule.[23]

The path of inflation in the United States remains uncertain and may not be known for years. Beyond the uncertainties of an interconnected and interdependent globe, it will depend tremendously on the actions of the Federal Reserve. Will there be a repeat of the Burns era, in which the Fed is buffeted by a mix of political pressures and ignorance? Or has the Fed already emerged from 1970s easy money and begun charting a path toward the 1980s, including a second Volcker shock? One clue lies in the Fed's veiled invocation of the Taylor rule, which by some accounts points to a federal funds rate of 7.6 percent.[24] The buried reference, noticed immediately by Fed watchers, is perhaps the contemporary equivalent of Volcker talking about aggregates, the opening shot in a larger war.

In another sign of Friedman's relevance, into the twenty-first century he remained a favorite target of political attacks, a notable accomplishment for a dead economist. "When did Milton Friedman die and become king?" Joe Biden asked sarcastically in 2019, using Friedman as a symbol of everything he was not. When Biden became president, a chorus of voices emerged to accuse Friedman of intellectual and moral bankruptcy. He "aided and abetted segregationists in his quest to privatize school education," one historian told readers of an economics blog. To a journalist, Friedman's ideas were "a legacy of ruin" worth a 2021 cover story in *The New Republic.* The director of the Hewlett Foundation, a patron of these writers, concurred: Friedman's ideas had "reshaped the entire world," and not for the better. Jeffrey Sachs declared, "Almost nothing remains of his intellectual legacy," an interesting claim from an economist who helped the USSR privatize its state holdings and tamed hyperinflation in Bolivia, which he understood through the "1956 classic definition" advanced by Friedman's Chicago money workshop. According to an all-star cast writing in *The New York Times,* Friedman's 1971 essay on corporate social responsibility had liberated corporations to trample workers, ignore communities, and bend the knee to shareholders.[25]

The intensity of these attacks obscured a startling reality: This argument about Friedman is as much an intramural dispute on the left as a blow against the right. The coordinated fusillade betrays an anxiety of influence, implicitly acknowledging how fundamental Friedman's style of economic analysis and his skepticism about government regulation have become to liberals as well as conservatives. One sign of a political order, notes the historian Gary Gerstle, "is the ability of the ideologically dominant party to bend the opposition party to its will." By Gerstle's reckoning, Friedman-inspired neoliberalism became truly powerful only when it captured the Democratic Party in the 1990s.[26]

Nor is this influence a vestige of the past. There are echoes of Friedman in supply-side liberalism, a new intellectual movement that stresses how regulation has hamstrung not private economic activity but the public sector, including the capacity to build needed housing and infrastructure. One of the most vaunted progressive policy experiments in recent years is universal basic income, a lineal descendant of Friedman's negative income tax. In both examples, his ideas are creatively used to cut through a policy impasse. But for many on the left even these dilutions of Friedman remain untouchable, because while progressive in one register, in another they block a return to robust social democratic–style policies. So to attack Friedman is to undermine the liberal market consensus, to demarcate a line between Larry Summers and modern monetary theory, carbon taxes and banning carbon-intensive industries, charter schools and teachers' unions, a Fed focused on inflation and unemployment and one focused on green energy.[27]

The progressive or liberal case against Friedman is often made in terms of inequality. "He did not care a whit about fairness in the economy or the accumulation of wealth and power by the few over the many," charged one critic after his death.[28] Such an egregious misreading ignores the vast energy Friedman poured into the negative income tax, his opposition to licensure requirements that blocked small players in favor of established entrants, his ceaseless push to abolish the military draft, his pointed arguments about regulatory capture. It is true that Friedman was never an egalitarian. Yet concern about inequality was a fairly consistent theme in his thinking, if not his public persona. At the height of his fame he spoke less about inequality than at the outset of his career. In part, this reflected the success of the negative income tax (NIT), which was his favored solution to poverty and inequality. In 1975 his basic concept was incorporated into the Earned Income Tax Credit. Widely judged one of the nation's most successful anti-poverty measures, the ETIC would be expanded several times—and it also underlies more recent programs like the Biden administration's temporary Child Tax Credit. With the NIT at least partially implemented, Friedman no longer spoke about inequality of income but shifted his focus to education.

Believing the public school system was a failed government monopoly that did not effectively educate children, Friedman considered privatization an essential remedy against inequality. "There is no respect in which inhabitants of a low-income neighborhood are so disadvantaged as in the kind of schooling they can get for their children," he argued. Friedman linked educational reform specifically to globalization, which he called a "second industrial revolution" that had created "a sharp widening in the differential between the wages of highly skilled and low-skilled labor in the United States." Friedman concluded education was "the only major force in sight" that could offset this growing social stratification. Agree or disagree with this analysis, it is simply not the case that Friedman ignored inequality as a social problem. It is far more generative to engage Friedman's proposed solutions than to imagine them away.[29]

In his waning years, Friedman grappled once again with capitalism as an engine of inequality. This was after all what both Frank Knight and Henry Simons feared as they surveyed the awful landscape of the 1930s, and in his early years Friedman shared this sensibility. Over time he shifted away from this concern, even asserting a link between market exchange and greater equality. This reflected the reality he saw around him, and the income and consumption statistics he pored over, as most of his working life spanned the so-called Great Compression, the roughly thirty years after World War II when incomes converged in the United States. Looking to the broader world, like his onetime Chicago colleague Deirdre Nansen McCloskey, he pointed unfailingly to the "Great Enrichment"—the astonishing rise in living standards across the second half of the twentieth century.[30] "The only cases in which the masses have escaped from the kind of grinding poverty . . . are where they have had capitalism and largely free trade," he lectured talk-show host Phil Donahue in 1979. "If you want to know where the masses are worse off, worst off, it's exactly in the kinds of societies that depart from that," he argued, likely thinking of Latin America and the Soviet bloc. Yet by 1995, Friedman recognized there were new dynamics at play. The twin revolutions of liberalized international trade and communications technology "promise a major increase in world output," he wrote in *The Washington Post*, "but they also threaten advanced countries with serious social conflict arising from a widening gap between the incomes of the highly skilled (cognitive elite) and the unskilled." Although he continued to support free trade, Friedman recognized globalization came with serious risks and drawbacks. And he was not willing to let inequality "proceed unchecked," hence his focus on the educational system.[31]

What about inequality of caste, based on race, ethnicity, or gender? As an economist, Friedman tended to see numbers, and as an individualist, he saw people rather than groups. Apart from his thinking about regulatory capture or political competition, he spent little time reflecting on intergroup relations. As a result, his concept of freedom was woefully thin. Most glaring is his failure to understand state-sponsored segregation in the South as a violation of African Americans' freedom. This was no minor oversight, given how civil rights became the fulcrum on which the identities of both major political parties turned. Imagine the forces of moderate Republicanism buttressed by Friedman's intellect! In the geopolitical realm, Friedman developed a more complex understanding of freedom, mulling over its various attenuated forms. Yet he never revisited his position on civil rights. And in 1998, he improbably claimed that men now faced gender discrimination within academic economics.[32] While his celebration of freedom resonated for many readers during the Cold War, it was studded with grievous omissions.

On the right, the place of Friedman remains unclear. No longer does he define the cutting edge; no longer are his ideas subversive, fresh, edgy. Beyond the youthful socialist boom, evinced in the rebirth of Democratic Socialists of America and the Bernie Sanders campaign, the great financial crisis triggered a generational shift away from capitalism that was not confined to the left. "Even my business school students have doubts about capitalism," reported an economist. By 2021, these sentiments had opened new opportunities for a conservative critique of the market. "Instead of exporting 'economic freedom,' we exported our industrial strength, and the result has been an economic, social, and geopolitical disaster," the Florida senator Marco Rubio declared to a new think tank, American Compass. Rubio was attempting to put a soft edge on Trump's ranting about bad deals, but his opposition to the "flawed bipartisan consensus" was no less intense. Indeed, skepticism about free trade—and immigration—had become a potent brew on the right, even stronger than the establishment conservatism Friedman once represented. It mingled with resurgent nationalism and gathered strength from the uneven post-2008 recovery. All this augured a conservative movement distinct from the one Friedman did so much to shape.[33]

On the other hand, the right's new nationalism flowed through familiar channels. In February 2021, the Republican senator Mitt Romney proposed the Family Security Act, a monthly cash benefit for families with children. Following Friedman's logic almost completely, the policy was advertised as "a new national commitment to American families by modernizing and streamlining antiquated federal policies into a monthly cash benefit." Framed in terms of family values, the bill updated the Family Assistance Plan's failed attempt to erase divisions between the working and nonworking poor. "Equal treatment for both working and stay-at-home parents," affirmed Romney's website, suggesting the wholesome image of a mom and kids. Friedman's ideal benefit was linked to income alone, taking no account of an individual's family status. Yet Romney's proposal, which limited cash benefits to parents with children under eighteen, more accurately reflected the possibilities of American political culture.[34] Should it eventually become law, it will be yet another mark of Friedman's long-lasting influence.

How then shall we remember Friedman? Which Friedman will it be—the economist, the political figurehead, the philosopher of freedom? And what to make of the symmetry between his economics, which often uncovered the smooth working of market dynamics, and his fierce small-government partisanship? Friedman wanted a political world of maximum individual choice, and an economic system where individuals were likewise free to bargain and contract at will. Both of these required a reduced state, although one still empowered to provide a basic income floor and maintain a monopoly on the currency. Again and again, Friedman's research culminated in a portrait of government inefficiency and market stability that dovetailed with his ideological preferences. In the words of the economic historian Beatrice Cherrier, was it all just a "lucky consistency"?[35] Or was Friedman seeing only what he wanted to see?

But what, really, is at stake in this question? Surely it would matter if Friedman suppressed evidence, faked his results, or refused debate and argument on his central points. Does it matter that a clear set of ethical and political commitments guided his work? After all, it wasn't these ethical and political values that made his ideas persuasive to others—in fact the opposite was true. Liberal economists resisted many of Friedman's ideas simply because they clashed with their own preconceptions. As Larry Summers remembered, "He seemed, with his emphasis on individualism, freedom, and markets, to be so unconcerned with fairness and the needs of the collective."[36] Over time, Summers came to see Friedman's ideas as another route to the same goals. Nor did Friedman try to minimize his differences with others. To the contrary, he reveled in provocation and conflict, looking for the contrast, not the concordance. It took the sheer force of events to convince other economists that his ideas about consumption, money, and history were worthy of respect. Ultimately, this work would transform Friedman from an outsider into a pillar of the established order, a foundational influence on monetarists, new classical economists, and new Keynesians alike.

Similarly, it was not Friedman's persuasive powers, impressive though they were, that transformed his political ideology from a minority position to one that defined an era. As Friedman put it: "I may be persuasive, but I'm not that persuasive."[37] As a young man, Friedman developed a particular view of his desired government, synthesizing the ideals of his teachers with his studies in economics. That vision remained largely static as the U.S. state grew, and over time it made increasing sense to others. By the late 1960s, as the Vietnam War raged, Friedman's warnings about the threat to liberty no longer seemed implausible, nor by the 1970s did his warnings about stagflation.

What matters is that Friedman's ideas and insights proved persuasive to many, both the powerful and the lowly, because they matched experience, offered new ways to tackle old problems, and predicted what would happen next. The list of ideas and policies he seeded bears repeating: the U.S. armed forces staffed by volunteers instead of conscripts, educational vouchers, floating exchange rates, the monetary interpretation of the Great Depression, the consumption function, universal basic income, monetarism. It is also worth remembering the sheer scope and scale of his work; first musings on universal basic income in the late 1930s, a rush of papers that roiled economics throughout the 1960s, a pivot toward the public realm that led to best-selling books and television fame in the 1980s. These are not the products of a mere ideologue, although they do reflect the power of a coherent worldview. They also reflect the enormous gains to be harvested when arbitrary barriers of prejudice fall, as they did so fortunately for Friedman. Most clearly do they manifest an extraordinary intellect, rooted in a family, university, and political culture that valued relentless, fearless inquiry for its own sake—and opened the space for it to become a lifelong pursuit.

We can understand Friedman's longevity by seeing how much of his work lies at the intersection of fundamental problems that will never be solved and ongoing tensions that will never be fully eased. In monetary economics, Friedman at once recognized the problems of the gold standard and the limitations of fiat currency. His work tried to stake out a middle road between inflation and deflation, and many of his markers on this path still stand. Policy rules were for Friedman a way to recognize the state's enormous power over economic activity, while mitigating the worst consequences of short-term thinking and human error. In other realms, he wrestled with the basic dilemma, expressed with his customary flourish: "How can we keep the government we create from becoming a Frankenstein that will destroy the very freedom we establish it to protect?" Friedman's response was to ask another question: What would it look like if the market decided? At first, using market mechanisms for governance seemed crazy. Then it seemed like common sense. Today, the concept is contested by both left and right. The method threatened to collapse two very different domains—the economic, bent on efficiency, and the governmental, forever balancing security, stability, equity, and a host of other priorities. But if the balance between economic efficiency and social stability is hard to find, that doesn't mean the attempt will ever stop. Friedman provided one set of answers—and raised another set of questions—that remain perennial, even to those who disagree with him.[38]

Simply put, Friedman is too fundamental a thinker to set aside. He was present at the creation of our modern world, from the fiscal revolution to the dying days of Bretton Woods. His theories and books were talismans for those who wanted to forge a new way forward. At critical moments he shaped the course of events and the possibilities on offer. It is fashionable to say we are at the end of neoliberalism or exiting the era of markets. Yet Friedman's ideas have so deeply shaped our current moment that they cannot be tossed away at will. Declaring the end of Friedmanomics does not make it so.

Whatever social and political order emerges next, it will not be, cannot be, a clean break with the past. It will not leap Athena-like from the head of Zeus, born of itself. It will instead be assembled out of inherited materials, retaining critical elements, re-marking boundary lines, weighing competing claims. If we are unlucky, the new order will form itself in blind reaction against all that came before, the good and the bad. If we are unlucky, the future will condemn and dismiss Friedman and all that he built. If we are fortunate, the future will look back across the twentieth century and find the questioning, curious, and singular mind that surfed the long waves of political and economic change.

A NOTE ON SOURCES

Endnotes serve to identify the sources of specific facts, interpretations, and direct quotations; if you find something I write startling or hard to believe, please check the notes. Beyond providing evidence for my claims and narration, the endnotes serve as a guide to the myriad bodies of scholarship I have drawn on in this biography. For ease of reading, in many cases a single endnote contains multiple references for a single paragraph.

Given the frequency with which they appear, I have not included specific citations to macroeconomic data such as unemployment, inflation, and monetary aggregates, but readers should know that unless otherwise noted, this data is taken from two main sources: FRED, a website maintained by the Federal Reserve Bank of St. Louis at https://research.stlouisfed.org/, and the U.S. Bureau of Labor Statistics website at https://www.bls.gov/. Throughout the book, I use "inflation" to refer to changes in the overall price level, not relative prices. The measure I employ is the Consumer Price Index (CPI), an official figure released by the BLS.

ARCHIVES CONSULTED

Hoover Institution Library and Archives

Collected Works of Milton Friedman (miltonfriedman.org/hoover/collections)

F. A. Hayek Papers

Fritz Machlup Papers
Milton Friedman Papers
Martin Anderson Papers
Mont Pelerin Society Records

University of Chicago, Hanna Holborn Gray Special Collections Research Center

Aaron Director Papers
Department of Economics Records
Frank Knight Papers
Henry Simons Papers
Margaret Reid Papers
Office of the President, Hutchins Administration
Theodore Schultz Papers, Department of Economics Records

Duke University, Economist Papers Project

Anna Schwartz Papers
Arthur F. Burns Papers
Paul Samuelson Papers

Yale University

Cowles Commission Archive

George Mason University

Clark Warburton Papers

Columbia University

Albert Gailord Hart Papers
Harold Hotelling Papers

University of Rochester

W. Allen Wallis Papers

Records of the Treasury Department

Office of Tax Policy

NOTES

INTRODUCTION

1. Interview with Lawrence Summers, April 24, 2001, available at https://www.pbs.org/wgbh/commandingheights/shared/minitext/int_lawrencesummers.html. William Breit, "Friedman in Louisiana," *Southern Economic Journal* 78, no. 3 (January 2012): 814–18. Michael Grunwald, "Biden Wants a New Stimulus," *Politico*, April 25, 2020, available at https://www.politico.com/news/2020/04/25/joe-biden-green-stimulus-207848. John Kenneth Galbraith, *Economics in Perspective: A Critical History* (Boston: Houghton Mifflin, 1987), 274.
2. Gary Gerstle, *The Rise and Fall of the Neoliberal Order* (New York: Oxford University Press, 2022). Elizabeth Popp Berman, *Thinking Like an Economist: How Efficiency Replaced Equality in U.S. Public Policy* (Princeton, NJ: Princeton University Press, 2022). Maurice Cottier, "'Dear Professor': Exploring Lay Comments to Milton Friedman," *Modern Intellectual History* (May 2022): 1, 23.
3. See, for example, Daniel Schiffman, Warren Young, and Yaron Zelekha, *The Role of Economic Advisers in Israel's Economic Policy: Crises, Reform and Stabilization* (Cham, Switzerland: Springer, 2017).
4. For a survey of changes, see essays in Niall Ferguson, Charles S. Maier, Erez Manela, and Daniel J. Sargent, eds. *The Shock of the Global: The 1970s in Perspective* (Cambridge, MA: Harvard University Press, 2010).
5. Interview with Summers, April 24, 2001.
6. For example, Nicole Hemmer, *Partisans: The Conservative Revolutionaries Who Remade American Politics in the 1990s* (New York: Basic Books, 2022). Various, "Against the Dead Consensus," March 21, 2019, *First Things*, available at https://www.firstthings.com/web-exclusives/2019/03/against-the-dead-consensus.
7. See papers and comments in Michael D. Bordo, John T. Cochrane, and John B. Taylor, eds., *How Monetary Policy Got Behind the Curve—and How to Get It Back* (Stanford, CA: Hoover Institution Press, 2022).

1. FROM RAHWAY TO RUTGERS

1. Milton Friedman, "Editorial: Higher Education," *Scarlet and Black* 2, no. 3 (June 1927): 4.
2. "Can You Imagine?," *Scarlet and Black* 2, no. 1 (1926): 3. "Can You Imagine?," *Scarlet and Black* 3, no. 1 (December 1927): 23.
3. *Rahway, 1665–1925: City of Homes and Industries* (Asbury Park, NJ: Schuyler Press, 1925), 64. Milton Friedman and Rose D. Friedman, *Two Lucky People: Memoirs* (Chicago: University of Chicago Press, 1998). Where possible, I have confirmed Friedman's recollections; discrepancies are noted.

4. *Rahway City Directory*, 1916–1917 (Rahway, NJ: 1917), 20. Tillie Friedman, "Rahway Hebrew Congregation," in *City of Homes and Industries*, 71–72.
5. Addresses noted in *Rahway City Directory, 1918–1919* (Rahway, NJ: 1918), 70.
6. "Klan in First Appearance Here at Church Service," *The Rahway Record*, February 10, 1925, 1; "Explosion of Bomb, Firing of Crosses Laid to K.K.K.," *The Rahway Record*, February 27, 1925, 1; Kathleen M. Blee, *Women of the Klan: Racism and Gender in the 1920s* (Berkeley: University of California Press, 1991), 72–76; "Arrest Mayor for Dousing a Radical," *The New York Times*, June 5, 1919, 2.
7. "Hebrews Prepare to Erect New Synagogue," *The Rahway Record*, March 4, 1919; "Hebrew Auxiliary Plans Card Party and Outing," *The Rahway Record*, April 24, 1925, 1; "Carteret Girl Tendered Party at Friedman Home," *The Rahway Record*, November 20, 1926, 6.
8. Friedman later stated his family "never had a family income that by today's standards would have put us above the poverty level." Friedman, "My Evolution as an Economist," in *Lives of the Laureates: Eighteen Nobel Economists*, eds. William Breit and Roger W. Spencer (Cambridge, MA: MIT Press, 1986), 68. Nonetheless, the family accumulated significant commercial and personal property, including a home valued at $14,000 in 1930. *Fifteenth Census of the United States, 1930*; Census Place: Rahway, Union, New Jersey; Roll: 1389; Page: 2B; Enumeration District: 0125; Image: 213.0; Bureau of the Census (Washington, D.C.: NARA, 1930).
9. Friedman and Friedman, *Two Lucky People*, 22.
10. Gerald Porter, a nephew of Milton Friedman, interview with author, November 21, 2014. Friedman also helped stage a Purim celebration and starred in a Hanukkah play, as recorded in *The Rahway Record*, March 13, 1925, and December 26, 1924.
11. Friedman and Friedman, *Two Lucky People*, 23. In a study of seven conservative Jewish intellectuals, George Nash finds a similar pattern. Nash, "Forgotten Godfathers: Premature Jewish Conservatives and the Rise of *National Review*," *American Jewish History* 87, nos. 2 and 3 (June and September 1999): 148.
12. Friedman erroneously remembered the death occurring when he was "getting ready to enter senior year in high school." Friedman and Friedman, *Two Lucky People*, 23. "Joseph Friedman, Main St. Merchant, Died This A.M.," *The Rahway Record*, November 1, 1927, 5. The address and listed survivors make clear this was Milton's father.
13. Beregszász is now located in Ukraine. His given name is also unclear. In Friedman and Friedman, *Two Lucky People*, he is identified as "Jeno Saul Friedman," but documents from his lifetime use Sol, Joseph, and Jacob; I use Sol, as it appears most frequently. No immigration records match the 1894 immigration date given in *Two Lucky People*. The closest is a 1892 arrival of an S. Friedman, sixteen years of age, on the ocean liner *Devonia*, his nationality listed as Roumania, Hungary, in Statue of Liberty—Ellis Island Foundation, Inc., Arrival Database, hosted at Ancestry.com.
14. Sarah Landau is listed on the manifest for the *Patria* on March 31, 1896; Statue of Liberty—Ellis Island Foundation, Inc., Arrival Database, hosted at Ancestry.com. Landau family details are from Gerald Porter interview with author.
15. Cherbourg, France, 1907. New York, Passenger Lists, 1820–1957, an online database, accessed through Ancestry.com. Their address was 502 Barbey Street. A 1906 photograph of Barbey and Arlington Streets is available through East New York Project, available at http://www.tapeshare.com/Barbey.html.
16. Gerald Porter, oral history interview, "Part 1: Personal Background and Academic Experience," available at http://www.math.upenn.edu/~gjporter/oral%20history1.pdf. "H.S. Graduation Was Held Tuesday Night; Prizes Are Awarded," *The Rahway Record*, June 22, 1928, 1.
17. Michael Greenberg and Seymour Zenchelsky, "Private Bias and Public Responsibility: Anti-Semitism at Rutgers in the 1920s and 1930s," *History of Education Quarterly* 33, no. 3 (Autumn 1993): 303, 301, 318.

18. For details on Friedman's education, see Daniel Hammond, "Columbia Roots of the Chicago School: The Case of Milton Friedman," in Julio H. Cole, ed., *A Companion to Milton Friedman* (Guatemala City: Universidad Francisco Marroquín, 2019), 157–91.
19. I capitalize "Progressive" to indicate the specific political and social movement spanning roughly 1880 to 1920. For defining Progressivism, see Daniel T. Rodgers, "In Search of Progressivism," *Reviews in American History* 10, no. 4 (December 1982): 113–32. For economists' role, see Thomas C. Leonard, *Illiberal Reformers: Race, Eugenics, and American Economics in the Progressive Era* (Princeton, NJ: Princeton University Press, 2016), and Bradley W. Bateman, "Clearing the Ground: The Demise of the Social Gospel Movement and the Rise of Neoclassicism in American Economics," in Mary S. Morgan and Malcolm Rutherford, eds., *From Interwar Pluralism to Postwar Neoclassicism* (Durham, NC: Duke University Press, 1998).
20. Dorothy Ross, *The Origins of American Social Science* (New York: Cambridge University Press, 1991).
21. Mary Furner, *Advocacy and Objectivity: A Crisis in the Professionalization of American Social Science, 1865–1905* (Lexington: University Press of Kentucky, 1975).
22. Thomas M. Humphrey, "Marshallian Cross Diagrams and Their Uses Before Alfred Marshall: The Origins of Supply and Demand Geometry," *Economic Review* (March/April 1992): 14.
23. For a dispute over the existence of a "marginal revolution," see Philip Mirowski, *More Heat Than Light: Economics as Social Physics, Physics as Nature's Economics* (New York: Cambridge University Press, 1989), 271; and Mark Blaug, "Was There a Marginal Revolution?," in R. D. Collison Black, A. W. Coats, and Craufurd W. Goodwin, eds., *The Marginal Revolution in Economics: Interpretation and Evaluation* (Durham, NC: Duke University Press, 1973).
24. Utility theory is comprehensively treated in Ivan Moscati, *Measuring Utility: From the Marginal Revolution to Behavioral Economics* (New York: Oxford University Press, 2019).
25. Mary S. Morgan and Tarja Knuuttila, "Models and Modelling in Economics," in Uskali Mäki, ed., *Philosophy of Economics* (Oxford: Elsevier, 2012), 6.
26. In situating marginal analysis as the transition point from classical to neoclassical economics, I follow a broad although not unanimous consensus among historians of economics. For a dissenting view, see A. K. Dasgupta, *Epochs of Economic Theory* (New York: Blackwell, 1985).
27. Ivan Moscati, "History of Utility Theory" (February 1, 2020), BAFFI CAREFIN Centre Research Paper No. 2020–129, available at http://dx.doi.org/10.2139/ssrn.3530949. Mirowski, *More Heat Than Light*, 234.
28. Mary S. Morgan, "Economic Man as Model Man," *Journal of the History of Economic Thought* 28, no. 1 (March 2006): 11.
29. Malcolm Rutherford dates institutional economics to the 1918 reading of a paper by Walter Stewart at the AEA. Malcolm Rutherford, *The Institutionalist Movement in American Economics, 1918–1947: Science and Social Control* (New York: Cambridge University Press, 2011), 3.
30. The term "neoclassical economics" was coined sarcastically by Thorstein Veblen, who opposed the new approach. Likewise, it was Marx who popularized the term "classical economics." Both terms were widely adopted and are used in historical scholarship without the pejorative cast.
31. Friedman and Friedman, *Two Lucky People*, 34. Kenneth Finegold, "From Agrarianism to Adjustment: The Political Origins of New Deal Agricultural Policy," *Politics and Society* 11, no. 1 (1981): 1–27.
32. Agricultural Adjustment Relief Plan: Hearings on H.R. 13991 before the Senate Committee on Agriculture and Forestry, 72nd Congress, 2nd Session (Washington, D.C.: U.S. Government Printing Office, 1933), 15.
33. Friedman and Friedman, *Two Lucky People*, 30.
34. Friedman and Friedman, *Two Lucky People*, 30, xi.

35. Robert Sobel, *The Worldly Economists* (New York: Free Press, 1980), 41, 38.
36. Arthur Burns, "Introductory Sketch," in Arthur Burns, ed., *Wesley Clair Mitchell: The Economic Scientist* (New York: NBER, 1952), 22.
37. Joseph Dorfman, *The Economic Mind in American Civilization, 1865–1918* (New York: Viking, 1949), 30, 223.
38. Wesley Mitchell, *Business Cycles* (Berkeley: University of California Press, 1913), 570.
39. Wesley Mitchell, "Statistics and Government," in Wesley Mitchell, *The Backward Art of Spending Money and Other Essays* (New York: McGraw Hill, 1937), 45.
40. Hammond, "Columbia Roots of the Chicago School," 9–10.
41. Alfred Marshall, *Principles of Economics*, vol. 1, 8th edition (New York: Macmillan, 1920; 1890), 14, 15.
42. Friedman's partner was Harold Harris, of Harris Department Store, "Rahway's Most Popular Store," advertisement in *Scarlet and Black* 4, no. 2 (February 1929). Their activities are described in Friedman and Friedman, *Two Lucky People*, 26–27.
43. Friedman and Friedman, *Two Lucky People*, 31. Hammond, "Columbia Roots of the Chicago School," 8.
44. Hammond, "Columbia Roots of the Chicago School," 4*n4*.
45. Knight defined profit as "a distributive share different from the returns to the productive services of land, labor, and capital," arguing that "the primary attribute of competition, universally recognized and evident at a glance, is the 'tendency' to eliminate profit or loss, and bring the value of economic goods to equality with their cost." Frank Knight, *Risk, Uncertainty and Profit* (New York: Arthur M. Kelley, 1964; 1922), 18.
46. Knight, *Risk, Uncertainty and Profit*, 61.
47. Knight, *Risk, Uncertainty and Profit*, 226, 311.
48. Knight, *Risk, Uncertainty and Profit*, 129, 248, 360, 349.
49. Friedman and Friedman, *Two Lucky People*, 32, 31.
50. Quoted in David Kennedy, *Freedom from Fear: The American People in Depression and War* (New York: Oxford, 2003), 160.
51. Friedman and Friedman, *Two Lucky People*, 34.

2. THE CHICAGO PLAN

1. Paul A. Samuelson, "Jacob Viner," in Edward Shils, ed., *Remembering the University of Chicago: Teachers, Scientists, and Scholars* (Chicago: University of Chicago Press, 1991), 543.
2. Milton Friedman and Rose D. Friedman, *Two Lucky People: Memoirs* (Chicago: University of Chicago Press, 1998), 36.
3. Quoted in Michael M. Weinstein, "Paul Samuelson, Economist, Dies at 94," *The New York Times*, December 13, 2009, A1.
4. Gabriel Almond interviewed by Gerardo Munck, in Gerardo L. Munck and Richard Snyder, eds., *Passion, Craft, and Method in Comparative Politics* (Baltimore: Johns Hopkins University Press, 2007), 67.
5. Edward Shils, "Some Academics, Mainly in Chicago," *The American Scholar* 50, no. 2 (Spring 1981): 180.
6. Frank Knight, "The Case for Communism: From the Standpoint of an Ex-Liberal," in Warren J. Samuels, ed., *Research in the History of Economic Thought and Methodology*, Archival Supplement 2 (Greenwich, CT: JAI Press, 1991), 58.
7. Knight, "The Case for Communism," 92. Angus Burgin argues that this critique of liberalism is the most salient message of Knight's talk. Angus Burgin, "The Radical Conservatism of Frank H. Knight," *Modern Intellectual History* 6, no. 3 (2009): 513–38.
8. Knight, "The Case for Communism," 89.
9. Friedman and Friedman, *Two Lucky People*, 37.
10. Friedman was twenty, and the voting age in Illinois was twenty-one. Rose was not at that time a U.S. citizen.

11. The Republican Party was linked to Prohibition and other laws often understood as anti-immigrant.
12. Malcolm Rutherford, *The Institutionalist Movement in American Economics, 1918–1947: Science and Social Control* (New York: Cambridge University Press, 2011), 7*n6*.
13. "Economics in the Rear-View Mirror," available at http://www.irwincollier.com/chicago-historical-enrollment-trends-economics-faculty-age-educational-background-1944–45. Samuelson, "Jacob Viner," in Shils, *Remembering the University of Chicago*, 546.
14. Details of the Director family's roots in Europe are taken from Friedman and Friedman, *Two Lucky People*, 2–6, and corroborated when possible by interviews with the family. Charterisk no longer appears on maps but is referenced in military accounts of World War I. See "Terrific Fighting East of Illukst," *The Dominion* (New Zealand), October 27, 1915, 6.
15. Author interview with David Friedman, the son of Milton and Rose Friedman, October 16, 2014.
16. Robert Van Horn, "Harry Aaron Director: The Coming of Age of a Reformer Skeptic," *History of Political Economy* 42, no. 4 (2010): 601–30; and James E. B. Breslin, *Mark Rothko: A Biography* (Chicago: University of Chicago Press, 1993), esp. chapters 2 and 3.
17. Author interview with David Friedman; Friedman and Friedman, *Two Lucky People*, 83, 11–17.
18. Friedman and Friedman, *Two Lucky People*, 17, 15, 9. This course may have been a "world history" course that was a forerunner to Reed's required humanities course, instituted in the 1940s.
19. Friedman and Friedman, *Two Lucky People*, 17. Information on Rose's name is from author interview with Janet Martel, the daughter of Milton and Rose Friedman, November 22, 2014. This was apparently a first attempt to get "papers"; later Rose became a citizen; *Two Lucky People*, 62–63.
20. In 1933, Mary Barnett Gilson was promoted from an instructor to an assistant professor. Gilson did not hold a Ph.D. or vote in department meetings. Overall, Chicago was known as a relatively hospitable place for women, graduating twenty-six women with a Ph.D. in economics between 1912 and 1932, second only to Columbia University. See Evelyn L. Forget, "American Women Economists, 1900–1940: Doctoral Dissertations and Research Specialization," in Mary Ann Dimand, Robert W. Dimand, and Evelyn L. Forget, eds., *Women of Value: Feminist Essays on the History of Women in Economics* (Brookfield, VT: Edward Elgar Publishing, 1995). During the 1930s, women received about 10 percent of all dissertations in economics, down from a high of nearly 20 percent in 1920; see 27.
21. The description in this chapter is focused on the ideas Friedman would have learned, as gleaned through syllabi, lecture notes, the published writings of professors, student work, and student recollection. For the full scope of price theory from 1890 to 1994, see the three-volume set, J. D. Hammond, Steven G. Medema, and John D. Singleton, eds., *Chicago Price Theory* (Northampton, MA: Edward Elgar Publishing, 2013).
22. Viner learned the technique at Harvard from Frank Taussig, sometimes called "the American Marshall." Arnold Harberger found his undergraduate courses at Johns Hopkins nearly identical to graduate price theory at Chicago. Arnold Harberger, "Sense and Economics: An Oral History with Arnold Harberger," conducted by Paul Burnett in 2015 and 2016, Oral History Center, the Bancroft Library, University of California, Berkeley, 2016.
23. Ronald Coase, "Aaron Director," in Peter Newman, ed., *The New Palgrave Dictionary of Law and Economics* (New York: Macmillan, 1998), 602.
24. Edmund W. Kitch, "The Fire of Truth: A Remembrance of Law and Economics at Chicago, 1932–1970," *The Journal of Law and Economics* 26, no. 1 (April 1983): 183. Gordon Tullock, "Foreword," in Ross B. Emmett, ed., *The Chicago Tradition in Economics, 1898–1946*, vol. 8 (New York: Routledge, 2002), 5.

25. Aaron Director, "Reproduction of the Syllabus for Economics 201: The Divisional Course in Economics," fifty-eight-page typescript, dated March 1958 [strike through], box 2, folder 1, "Drafts and Syllabus, 1937–1958," Aaron Director Papers, University of Chicago, Hanna Holborn Gray Special Collections Research Center.
26. Frank Knight, *The Economic Organization* (New York: H. Wolff, 1933; 1951), 31.
27. Ross B. Emmett, "Entrenching Disciplinary Competence in Chicago Economics," in *Frank Knight and the Chicago School of Economics* (New York: Routledge, 2009), 132. Melvin W. Reder, "Chicago Economics: Permanence and Change," *Journal of Economic Literature* 20, no.1 (March 1982): 8.
28. Milton Friedman, "Milton Friedman," in *Lives of the Laureates: Eighteen Nobel Economists*, eds. William Breit and Barry T. Hirsch (Cambridge, MA: MIT Press, 2004), 70. Friedman and Friedman, *Two Lucky People*, 35–36.
29. Philip Quincy Wright, ed., *Unemployment as a World-Problem: Lectures on the Harris Foundation 1931* (New York: Freeport Press, 1970; 1931).
30. Norman Wait Harris Memorial Foundation, *Reports of Roundtables 1931: Unemployment as a World Problem*, vol. 2 (Chicago: University of Chicago, 1931), 500. Chicago's response to the Depression has a significant scholarly literature; most recently, George S. Tavlas, *The Monetarists: The Making of the Chicago Monetary Tradition, 1927–1960* (Chicago: University of Chicago Press, 2023). See also David Laidler, *Fabricating the Keynesian Revolution: Studies of the Inter-war Literature on Money, the Cycle, and Unemployment* (New York: Cambridge University Press, 1999).
31. Andrew Mellon quoted in Herbert Hoover, *The Memoirs of Herbert Hoover: The Great Depression, 1929–1941* (New York: Macmillan, 1952), 30. Hoover may have been exaggerating Mellon's position to contrast it with his own. For an overview of debates on "liquidationist" responses to the Great Depression, see Lawrence H. White, "Did Hayek and Robbins Deepen the Great Depression?," *Journal of Money, Credit and Banking* 40, no. 4 (June 2008): 751–68.
32. Quincy Wright, ed., *Gold and Monetary Stabilization: Lectures from the Ninth Institute of the Norman Wait Harris Memorial Foundation, Held at the University of Chicago from January 27 to January 31, 1932* (Chicago: University of Chicago, 1932), 156.
33. University of Chicago, Department of Economics, Memorandum to Hon. Samuel B. Pettengill, April 26, 1932, *Hearings Before the Committee on Ways and Means, House of Representatives, Seventy-Second Congress, First Session, April 11 to 20, and May 2 and 3, 1932* (Washington, D.C.: Government Printing Office, 1932), 524. The memo's signatories were Garfield V. Cox, Aaron Director, Paul H. Douglas, Harry D. Gideonse, Frank H. Knight, Harry A. Millis, Lloyd W. Mints, Henry Schultz, Henry O. Simons, Jacob Viner, Chester W. Wright, and Theodore O. Yntema.
34. Milton Friedman, Economics 330: Money and Banking Notebook, box 120, folder 4, and "Syllabus, Economics 330: Money and Banking," box 5, folder 12, "Student Years—Syllabi," Friedman Papers. For more on Mints's views, see Tavlas, *The Monetarists*, which intervenes in a long-running debate about whether Friedman accurately characterized Mints's views on the quantity theory, concluding that Friedman's recollections were broadly accurate.
35. The price was fixed in 1834 by the Coinage Act, but the U.S. currency did not become fully convertible, with silver phased out, until the 1900 Gold Standard Act.
36. Irving Fisher, "The Business Cycle Largely a 'Dance of the Dollar,'" *Journal of the American Statistical Association* 18, no. 144 (December 1923): 1024–28. "Fisher Sees Stocks Permanently High," *The New York Times*, October 16, 1929, 8.
37. Irving Fisher, assisted by Harry G. Brown, *The Purchasing Power of Money: Its Determination and Relation to Credit, Interest, and Crises* (New York: Macmillan, 1911). John Maynard Keynes, *Treatise on Money*, vol. 2 (New York: Harcourt, Brace, 1930), vi, 149.
38. Quoted in Michael Kitson, "End of an Epoch: Britain's Withdrawal from the Gold Standard," in Randall Parker and Robert Whaples, eds., *Routledge Handbook of Major*

Events in Economic History (London: Routledge, 2013), chapter 12, also available at https://michaelkitson.files.wordpress.com/2013/02/kitson-gold-standard-june-2012.pdf, 8. In fact, Keynes argued Britain should not return to gold in the 1920s.

39. This account of Knight's classroom synthesizes Friedman's notebooks, detailed transcriptions of the same course from two other students of the era, and published reflections, in order to give the fullest possible reconstruction of Knight's teaching. I indicate textually when a statement was made directly to Friedman's class. Quoted material may be fragmentary or grammatically incorrect, in keeping with the original format of classroom notes.
40. Friedman, Economics 302, page 26, box 120, folder 8, Milton Friedman Papers. Notebook paginated by author for reference purposes; page numbers listed when no date is given.
41. James M. Buchanan, *Economics from the Outside In: "Better Than Plowing" and Beyond* (College Station: Texas A&M University Press, 2007), 205.
42. Author unknown, lecture notes, dated June 23, "Teaching—U of C-Econ. 302: History of Economic Thought," box 8, folder 1, ten-page typescript, Frank Knight Papers, University of Chicago, Hanna Holborn Gray Special Collections Research Center.
43. Milton Friedman, Economics 302, page 7, Milton Friedman Papers.
44. Knight, "The Case for Communism," 62.
45. Eric Rauchway, *The Winter War: Hoover, Roosevelt, and the First Clash over the New Deal* (New York: Basic Books, 2018).
46. Between 1931 and 1933, an estimated nine thousand banks failed nationwide; see https://www.fdic.gov/exhibit/p1.html#/10.
47. "Banking and Currency Reform, Appendix: Banking and Business Cycle," Undated thirteen-page typescript, page 3, box 1, folder 1, Aaron Director Papers, University of Chicago, Hanna Holborn Gray Special Collections Research Center.
48. Ellis Tallman and Eugene B. White, "Why Was There No Banking Panic in 1920–1921? The Federal Reserve Banks and the Recession," unpublished paper presented to the American Economic Association, available at https://www.aeaweb.org/conference/2020/preliminary/paper/F5KzBh4S.
49. Brian Balogh, *A Government Out of Sight: The Mystery of National Authority in Nineteenth-Century America* (New York: Cambridge University Press, 2009).
50. The Chicago Plan generally refers to a series of memos, authored largely by Simons and signed by Frank Knight, Lloyd Mints, Henry Schultz, Aaron Director, Paul Douglas, G. V. Cox, and A. G. Hart. The classic account is in Ronnie J. Phillips, *The Chicago Plan and New Deal Banking Reform* (New York: M. E. Sharpe, 1995). For a more detailed reconstruction, see Tavlas, *The Monetarists.*
51. Untitled Banking Memo, March 15, 1933, page 2, box 10, folder 1, "Drafts—'33 Banking," Aaron Director Papers, University of Chicago, Hanna Holborn Gray Special Collections Research Center.
52. Untitled Banking Memo, March 15, 1933, pages 3, 1.
53. The letter is reproduced in Phillips, *The Chicago Plan*, 198–99.
54. Sebastian Edwards, *American Default: The Untold Story of FDR, the Supreme Court, and the Battle over Gold* (Princeton, NJ: Princeton University Press, 2018).
55. Friedman, Economics 330 note card, box 120, folder 17, Milton Friedman Papers. The remainder of his notes for the class are found in a separate notebook, box 120, folder 4, Milton Friedman Papers.
56. On monetary policy by fiscal means, see Tavlas, *The Monetarists*, chapter 2, and George S. Tavlas, "Chicago, Harvard, and the Doctrinal Foundations of Monetary Economics," in Robert Leeson, ed., *Keynes, Chicago and Friedman*, vol. 2 (London: Pickering and Chatto, 2003), 175–99.
57. Harris Foundation, *Report of Roundtables 1931*, vol. 2 (Chicago: University of Chicago, 1931), 493–94. Mints also pressed Keynes as to why Federal Reserve banks could not

directly buy corporate and public utility bonds; when Keynes pointed out this was against the law, Mints suggested, "The law can be changed." Another participant accused Mints of "putting the government into business with a vengeance"; 479–80.

58. Accordingly, economists have struggled to fit these reforms into contemporary distinctions between fiscal and monetary policy, disagreeing over whether they represent nascent fiscal policy or merely fiscal means to monetary ends. See the back and forth essays between Tavlas, Davis, and Laidler in Leeson, *Keynes, Chicago and Friedman*, vol. 2, 27–251.
59. Friedman took four math classes in this first year, including three for credit: 306: Introduction to Higher Algebra; 341: Calculus of Variations; 324: Theory of Algebraic Numbers; and 310: Functions of Complex Variables. Milton Friedman, 15d Graduate Record, University of Chicago, 1932–1933, one-page typescript, box 5, folder 11, "Student years—transcripts," Friedman Papers.
60. Paul Douglas, "Henry Schultz as Colleague," *Econometrica* 7, no. 2 (April 1939): 104.
61. Friedman and Friedman, *Two Lucky People*, 48.
62. J. Daniel Hammond, "Interview with Milton and Rose Friedman," July 24, 1989, unpublished transcript in author's possession.
63. Friedman and Friedman, *Two Lucky People*, 41.

3. THE ROOM SEVEN GANG

1. Milton Friedman, "Social Economics," class note cards, ND, page 1, box 120, folder 13, Milton Friedman Papers. Friedman's note cards are inconsistently dated and unnumbered. Where available, a date is used to identify the location of a direct quote; otherwise page numbers, as reconstructed by the author, are employed. Figures for faculty and enrollment are from http://www.irwincollier.com/columbia-economics-department-in-wwii-excerpt-from-letter-to-president-butler-nov-1942/.
2. Milton Friedman, "Clark seminar," class note cards, January 15, 1933, box 120, folder 13, Milton Friedman Papers. "Readings for Economic Seminar Meetings on National Economic Planning," half-page typescript, ND, box 12, folder 5, "Student Years—Syllabi," Friedman Papers.
3. Marcia L. Balisciano, "Hope for America: American Notions of Economic Planning Between Pluralism and Neoclassicism, 1930–1950," in Mary S. Morgan and Malcolm Rutherford, eds., *From Interwar Pluralism to Postwar Neoclassicism* (Durham, NC: Duke University Press, 1998), 154.
4. Bradford A. Lee, "The Miscarriage of Necessity and Invention: Proto-Keynesianism and Democratic States in the 1930s," in Peter A. Hall, ed., *The Political Power of Economic Ideas: Keynesianism Across Nations* (Princeton, NJ: Princeton University Press, 1989).
5. Moses Abramovitz, "Days Gone By: A Memoir for My Family," unpublished manuscript, 2001, available at https://economics.stanford.edu/files/uploads/AbramovitzM_All.pdf, 50.
6. Abramovitz, "Days Gone By," 46.
7. Abramovitz, "Days Gone By," 48.
8. Abramovitz, "Days Gone By," 47.
9. Abramovitz, "Days Gone By," 44.
10. Adolf A. Berle and Gardiner C. Means, *The Modern Corporation and Private Property* (New York: Harcourt, Brace & World, 1968; 1932), xli, 356.
11. Song quoted in Robert S. McElvaine, *The Great Depression: America, 1929–1944* (New York: Times Books, 1984), 160.
12. Anthony J. Badger, *The New Deal: The Depression Years, 1933–1940* (New York: Hill and Wang, 1989), 90.
13. For continued debate over the 1933 recovery, see Margaret Jacobson, Eric M. Leeper, and Bruce Preston, "Recovery of 1933," NBER Working Paper 25629 (March 2019); Gauti B. Eggertsson, "Great Expectations and the End of the Depression," *American*

Economic Review 98, no. 4 (September 2008): 1477; Harold L. Cole and Lee E. Ohanian, "New Deal Policies and the Persistence of the Great Depression: A General Equilibrium Analysis," *Journal of Political Economy* 112, no. 4 (August 2004): 779–816.

14. Balisciano, "Hope for America."
15. Anne Mayhew, "How American Economists Came to Love the Sherman Antitrust Act," in Morgan and Rutherford, *From Interwar Pluralism to Postwar Neoclassicism*, 179–201. For a discussion of Adolf Berle's contribution to this consensus, see Nicolas Lemann, *Transaction Man: The Rise of the Deal and the Decline of the American Dream* (New York: Farrar, Straus & Giroux, 2019).
16. Schultz to Hotelling, August 3, 1933, box 1, Henry Schultz Correspondence, 1932–1937, Harold Hotelling Papers, Columbia University.
17. Abramovitz, "Days Gone By," 37–38.
18. Milton Friedman and Rose D. Friedman, *Two Lucky People: Memoirs* (Chicago: University of Chicago Press, 1998), 47.
19. Quoted in A. C. Darnell, "Life and Economic Thought of Harold Hotelling," in *The Collected Economics Articles of Harold Hotelling*, ed. A. C. Darnell (New York: Springer Verlag, 1990). Biographical details on Hotelling are from Darnell.
20. Irving Fisher, Ragnar Frisch, and Charles F. Roos, "Announcement of Econometric Society Founding," November 29, 1930, available at https://www.econometricsociety.org/society/about.
21. Friedman, "Statistical Inference," class note cards, September 2, 1933, box 120, folder 10, Milton Friedman Papers. J. M. Keynes, *A Treatise on Probability* (London: Macmillan, 1921). Robert Skidelsky, *John Maynard Keynes, 1883–1946: Economist, Philosopher, Statesman* (New York: Penguin, 2003), 290.
22. Friedman, "Math Economics," class notes, page 1, box 120, folder 11, Milton Friedman Papers.
23. J. Daniel Hammond, "Interview with Milton and Rose Friedman," July 24, 1989, unpublished transcript in author's possession, 15.
24. Darnell, "Life and Economic Thought of Harold Hotelling." Market socialism is generally defined as a system featuring publicly owned enterprises guided by market signals rather than government planners; it may also feature private enterprises.
25. Philip Mirowski and D. Wade Hands, "A Paradox of Budgets: The Postwar Stabilization of American Neoclassical Demand Theory," in Morgan and Rutherford, *From Interwar Pluralism to Postwar Neoclassicism*, 261.
26. Paul Samuelson, "Economics in a Golden Age," in Gerald Holton, ed., *The Twentieth-Century Sciences: Studies in the Biography of Ideas* (New York: W. W. Norton, 1972), 161.
27. Their debate is detailed in Avi J. Cohen, "The Hayek/Knight Capital Controversy: The Irrelevance of Roundaboutness, or Purging Processes in Time?," *History of Political Economy* 35, no. 3 (2003): 469–90.
28. W. Allen Wallis, "George J. Stigler: In Memoriam," *Journal of Political Economy* 101, no. 5 (October 1993): 775.
29. These sources belie Friedman's later statement to Hammond that he was uninterested in philosophy, although the reading list may have been aspirational. Friedman, "Philosophy 212: Spring Quarter, 1931," two-page typescript, box 5, folder 12, "Student Years—Syllabi," Friedman Papers. "Suggested Bibliography for Philosophy 327," one-page typescript, box 5, folder 12, "Student Years—Syllabi," Friedman Papers. Friedman took an incomplete in the class and turned the paper in late.
30. His notation of "individualistic" on the philosophy syllabus was likely intended to distinguish these writings from Mill's more socialistic *Principles of Political Economy*, which Friedman panned in a paper for Knight. Friedman, "Labor Theory of Value in the Classical School," paper submitted to Economics 302, winter quarter, with Professor Knight, thirty-one-page typescript, box 5, folder 13, "Student Papers," Friedman Papers, 1. Knight returned the paper with "Good" scrawled across the top.

31. John Stuart Mill, *On Liberty*, Norton Critical Edition, ed. David Spitz (New York: W. W. Norton, 1859; 1975), 98.
32. Wallis, "George J. Stigler: In Memoriam," 775, 777. Wallis quoted in "Wallis Years at the University of Rochester," transcript of interviews with William H. Meckling (Rochester, NY: University of Rochester Library, June 1982), 58. Paul H. Douglas, "Henry Schultz as Colleague," *Econometrica* 7, no. 2 (April 1939): 106.
33. Friedman and Friedman, *Two Lucky People*, 52. Transcript of interviews with Meckling, 58, 57.
34. George J. Stigler, *Memoirs of an Unregulated Economist* (New York: Basic Books, 1988), 24. Milton Friedman, "Professor Pigou's Method for Measuring Elasticities of Demand from Budgetary Data," *The Quarterly Journal of Economics* 50, no. 1 (November 1935): 163. Friedman and Friedman, *Two Lucky People*, 52–53.
35. A. C. Pigou, Milton Friedman, and N. Georgescu-Roegen, "Marginal Utility of Money and Elasticities of Demand," *The Quarterly Journal of Economics* 50, no. 3 (May 1936): 532, 533, 534. Later, Friedman decided that Georgescu-Roegen had been right, even introducing him at the University of Chicago as the only economist who had proven him wrong. Kozo Mayumi, "Nicholas Georgescu-Roegen: His Bioeconomics Approach to Development and Change," *Development and Change* 40, no. 6 (2009): 1236.
36. Samuelson quoted in David C. Colander and Harry Landreth, *The Coming of Keynesianism to America: Conversations with the Founders of Keynesian Economics* (Brookfield, VT: Edward Elgar Publishing, 1996), 149.
37. Henry Simons, *A Positive Program for Laissez Faire: Some Proposals for a Liberal Economic Policy* (Chicago: University of Chicago Press, 1934), 1.
38. Simons, *A Positive Program for Laissez Faire*, 3.
39. Simons, *A Positive Program for Laissez Faire*, 24, 3, 40, 3.
40. Simons, *A Positive Program for Laissez Faire*, 4.
41. Although scholars have not probed the connection, Simons's advocacy of taxation and expanded state programs in order to underwrite free competition and markets is reminiscent of Henry George's single tax, an intellectual tradition that still held considerable power during the teens and twenties when he was a young man, and influenced an early generation of libertarians. For Georgism, see Christopher William England, *Land and Liberty: Henry George and the Crafting of Modern Liberalism* (Baltimore: Johns Hopkins University Press, 2022).
42. Simons, *A Positive Program for Laissez Faire*, 26, 39. John F. Witte, *The Politics and Development of the Federal Income Tax* (Madison: University of Wisconsin Press, 1985), 96–101. In 1935 Roosevelt pushed what the press called a "wealth tax."
43. Simons, *A Positive Program for Laissez Faire*, 37.
44. Allen Wallis and George Stigler, "Letters to the Editor: Problems of Competition," *The New York Times*, December 7, 1934, 22.
45. Wallis, "George J. Stigler: In Memoriam," 777.
46. Undated note card, box 18, folder 11, W. Allen Wallis Papers, University of Rochester.
47. Frank H. Knight, "Ethics and the Economic Interpretation," in *The Ethics of Competition* (1935; repr. New Brunswick, NJ: Transaction Publishers, 1997), 25, 26, 28.
48. A classic statement of economics imperialism is George Stigler and Gary Becker, "De Gustibus Non Est Disputandum," *American Economic Review* 67, no. 2 (March 1977): 76–90. Previous discussions of Knight have missed his contribution to "imperialism" in economics, focusing instead on the influence of Lionel Robbins's 1932 *Essay on the Nature and Significance of Economic Science*. In part, this is because the most extensive examination of the Robbins definition to date, Roger E. Backhouse and Steve G. Medema, "Defining Economics: The Long Road to Acceptance of the Robbins Definition," *Economica* 76, no. 1 (October 2009): 805–20, has focused on textbooks and published work, rather than archival material. Even this account, however, betrays some uncertainty as to how the Robbins definition spread and contains suggestive hints of Knight's possible influence

in the ideas of Samuelson and Stigler. Focusing on Robbins neglects the way in which Knight's 1922 essay presaged Robbins's conclusions by offering an analytical rather than a subject matter definition of economics.

49. Milton Friedman, Homer Jones, George Stigler, and Allen Wallis, "Preface," in *The Ethics of Competition*, 1–2.
50. Joan Robinson, *The Economics of Imperfect Competition* (New York: Macmillan, 1933). Edward Chamberlin, *The Theory of Monopolistic Competition* (Cambridge, MA: Harvard University Press, 1933).
51. William W. Bratton, "*The Modern Corporation and Private Property* Revisited: Gardiner Means and the Administered Price," *Seattle University Law Review* 42 (2019): 602.
52. Milton Friedman, "Program of Study: Plans for Ph.D. Thesis," undated typescript, box 38, folder 1, doctoral thesis, Milton Friedman Papers. Friedman did not ultimately write a dissertation on this topic, and his proposal has largely vanished from the historical record.
53. Hammond, "Interview with Milton and Rose Friedman," 55.
54. First introduced in a 1927 conference paper, the Cobb-Douglas formula would be published in its final form in 1936 and is still used today. Paul H. Douglas, "The Cobb-Douglas Production Function Once Again: Its History, Its Testing, and Some New Empirical Values," *Journal of Political Economy* 84, no. 5 (October 1976): 903–16.
55. For a discussion of Douglas's role in the Chicago plan, including how it was shaped to accommodate his views, see George S. Tavlas, *The Monetarists: The Making of the Chicago Monetary Tradition, 1927–1960* (Chicago: University of Chicago Press, 2023), esp. chapter 3.
56. Douglas's myriad activities during this time are described in his *In the Fullness of Time: The Memoirs of Paul H. Douglas* (New York: Harcourt, Brace, Jovanovich, 1971), esp. chapters 6 and 7.
57. Douglas to Knight, January 3, 1935, box 41, folder 5, Department of Economics Records, University of Chicago, Hanna Holborn Gray Special Collections Research Center.
58. Knight to Douglas, January 9, 1935, and Douglas to Knight, January 10, 1935, box 41, folder 5, Department of Economics Records.
59. Knight to Douglas, January 5, 1935, box 41, folder 5, Department of Economics Records.
60. Douglas to Knight, January 3, 1935, box 41, folder 5, Department of Economics Records.
61. Edmund W. Kitch, "The Fire of Truth: A Remembrance of Law and Economics at Chicago, 1932–1970," *The Journal of Law and Economics* 26, no. 1 (April 1983): 166–67.
62. According to Rose in 1991, "He had not received tenure at the university, thanks to his having transferred his allegiance from Paul Douglas to Frank Knight." Friedman and Friedman, *Two Lucky People*, 34.
63. Stigler, *Memoirs of an Unregulated Economist*, 180–81.
64. Central to my understanding of the first Chicago school is the idea of a "research program" centered upon a "hard core" of irrefutable central theses (price theory and the quantity theory of money) as elaborated in Imre Lakatos, "Falsification and the Methodology of Scientific Research Programs," in Imre Lakatos and Alan Musgrave, eds., *Criticism and the Growth of Knowledge: Proceedings of the International Colloquium in the Philosophy of Science, London, 1965*, vol. 4 (Cambridge: Cambridge University Press, 1970), 133, and Martin Bulmer's ideal-typical school of social science, with a founder/leader, followers, and unifying ideas (opposition to economic planning) at odds with the discipline. Martin Bulmer, *The Chicago School of Sociology: Institutionalization, Diversity, and the Rise of Sociological Research* (Chicago: University of Chicago Press, 1984), 2.
65. Angus Burgin argues that faculty at Chicago in the 1930s had "limited affinity for one another and little sense that they considered themselves members of an ideological community." Angus Burgin, *The Great Persuasion: Reinventing Free Markets Since the Depression* (Cambridge, MA: Harvard University Press, 2012), 41.

66. Friends like A. G. Hart who broke ranks subsequently disappeared from reminiscences of the 1930s. For Hart's disagreements with Friedman, see Hart to Friedman, August 29, 1947, and February 28, 1953, box 1, Albert Gailord Hart Papers, Columbia University.

4. THE FISCAL REVOLUTION

1. Although not as prestigious as Harvard, Columbia, Wisconsin, or Chicago, as home of the "Ames school," Iowa State College had a strong reputation. The longtime Chicago department chair T. W. Schultz came from Iowa State College, as did Margaret Reid. It was a significant coup for Stigler to secure a faculty position there in 1936, amid the Depression. A decade later, the ruinous "Butter-Margarine War" erupted when the college administration, bowing to the wishes of Iowa's powerful butter producers, attempted to suppress a study authored by economists that found margarine to be equivalent to butter in taste and nutrition. Fourteen faculty members, including Schultz, left in protest; the department never recovered its former reputation. Stigler was by then long gone. See https://www.promarket.org/2021/05/23/iowa-butter-margarine-schultzs-academic-freedom/.
2. The Banking Act of 1935 ultimately rejected the 100 percent money solution promoted by Simons, which fell victim to political horse-trading and the hostility of bankers. Irving Fisher, assisted occasionally by Simons, carried on the crusade fruitlessly for many years afterward. See Ronnie J. Phillips, *The Chicago Plan and New Deal Banking Reform* (New York: M. E. Sharpe, 1995), 126–128, 153–164.
3. Thomas A. Stapleford, *The Cost of Living in America: A Political History of Economic Statistics, 1880–2000* (New York: Cambridge University Press, 2009), 172, 159. The study was administered by three agencies: the Bureau of Labor Statistics, National Resources Council, and Bureau of Home Economics. The final list of principal investigators included the Department of Labor, Department of Agriculture, U.S. Central Statistical Board, and Works Progress Administration.
4. Warburton to Mr. Thompson, "Report of Work for Week Ending December 12, 1936," December 14, 1936, box 12, Clark Warburton Papers, George Mason University. Thanks to David Levy for the reference.
5. Thomas A. Stapleford, "Market Visions: Expenditure Surveys, Market Research, and Economic Planning in the New Deal," *The Journal of American History* 94, no. 2 (September 2007): 432–33. Examples are taken from survey questionnaires, available at https://www.icpsr.umich.edu/web/ICPSR/studies/8908/publications#.
6. Stapleford, "Market Visions," 419. Leaders included Gardiner Means, Isador Lubin, and Lauchlin Currie.
7. A useful recent summary of Friedman's approach, comparing it to other analysis of ranks tests used today in statistical programming, can be found at https://gdmdata.com/media/documents/Test%20Cases/Knowledge%20Base/AnalysisOfRanks.html.
8. Allen Wallis and Dorothy Brady, "Memorandum to Technical Sub-committee of the Study of Consumer Purchases, Subject: Analysis of the Variability Between Cells (testing the significance of the factors used as controls)," June 24, 1937, page 1, box 97, folder 7, NRC Studies "Consumption" Memoranda; and Hyper-Technical Subcommittee of the Steering Committee for the Study of Consumer Purchases, "Memorandum to Technical Sub-committee of the Steering Committee for the Study of Consumer Purchases, Re: Adjustment of Random Weights to Take Account of Cell Shifts Shown by Expenditure Schedules," April 2, 1937, box 97, folder 7, Milton Friedman Papers, Hoover Institution Library and Archives.
9. Milton Friedman, "The Use of Ranks to Avoid Assumption of Normality Implicit in the Analysis of Variance," *Journal of the American Statistical Association* 32, no. 200 (December 1937): 675–701. See Hotelling to Kneeland, August 11, 1937, and additional correspondence, box 37, folder 6, Milton Friedman Papers. Milton Friedman and Rose D. Friedman, *Two Lucky People: Memoirs* (Chicago: University of Chicago Press, 1998), 69.
10. Simon Kuznets, *National Income, 1929–1932* (Washington, D.C.: U.S. Government Printing Office, 1934). Kuznets's legacy is described in Timothy Shenk, "Inventing the

American Economy," Ph.D. dissertation (Columbia University, 2016), available at https://doi.org/10.7916/D8NZ87N1; Thomas Piketty, *Capital in the Twenty-First Century*, trans. Arthur Goldhammer (Cambridge, MA: Harvard University Press, 2013), 14; the appreciative Robert William Fogel et al., *Political Arithmetic: Simon Kuznets and the Empirical Tradition in Economics* (Chicago: University of Chicago Press, 2013); and Dirk Philipsen, *The Little Big Number: How GDP Came to Rule the World* (Princeton, NJ: Princeton University Press, 2015), chapter 4.

11. Discrimination against female researchers and professors, along with nepotism rules, is documented in Margaret W. Rossiter, *Women Scientists in America: Struggles and Strategies to 1940* (Baltimore: Johns Hopkins University Press, 1982), esp. chapter 7. "$471 a Year," *Time*, December 9, 1938, 12.
12. All publications from this project were coauthored, but Friedman did most of the writing and took the lead in the dispute that followed. For this reason, I treat him as the solo author in most of what follows. Kuznets was Friedman's boss at the NBER, not his doctoral supervisor, as Edward Nelson suggests. Edward Nelson, *Milton Friedman and Economic Debate in the United States, 1932–1972*, vol. 1 (Chicago: University of Chicago Press, 2020), 68–69. Friedman explained his choice of Columbia in J. Daniel Hammond, "Interview with Milton and Rose Friedman," page 5, July 24, 1989, unpublished transcript in author's possession.
13. Simon Kuznets and Milton Friedman, "Incomes from Independent Professional Practice, 1929–1936," *National Bureau of Economic Research Bulletin*, nos. 72–73 (February 5, 1939): 11.
14. Kuznets and Friedman, "Incomes from Independent Professional Practice, 1929–1936," 17.
15. Mills to Friedman, October 25, 1938, box 226, folder 10, "Income from Independent Professional Practice," pages 5–6, Milton Friedman Papers.
16. Mills to Friedman, October 25, 1938, box 226, folder 10, "Income from Independent Professional Practice," Milton Friedman Papers. Riefler to William J. Carson, August 10, 1942, box 37, folder 24, "Income from Independent Professional Practice" replies, Milton Friedman Papers. C. Reinhold Noyes, "In re: Income from Independent Professional Practice, by Milton Friedman and Simon Kuznets," twenty-page typescript, October 27, 1941, box 37, folder 24, pages 1–2, Milton Friedman Papers.
17. Noyes, "In re: Income from Independent Professional Practice," pages 12, 17, 13, 11, Milton Friedman Papers.
18. Friedman and Kuznets to Mills, November 3, 1938, box 37, folder 24, page 3, Milton Friedman Papers.
19. Mills to Friedman, October 25, 1938, box 37, folder 24, pages 3, 6, Milton Friedman Papers.
20. Patricia Spain Ward, "United States versus American Medical Association et al.: The Medical Antitrust Case of 1938–1943," *American Studies* 30, no. 2 (September 1, 1989): 123–53. Noyes, "In re: Income from Independent Professional Practice," page 10, Milton Friedman Papers. Friedman and Kuznets to Dr. Frederick C. Mills, November 3, 1938, box 37, folder 24, Milton Friedman Papers.
21. Friedman cited both resolutions as an example of a "deliberate policy of restricting the number of entrants in order to keep down the total number of physicians, that is, to prevent so-called 'overcrowding.'" Kuznets and Friedman, "Incomes from Independent Professional Practice, 1929–1936," 16*n40*.
22. Eric D. Kohler, "Relicensing Central European Refugee Physicians in the United States, 1933–1945," in *Simon Wiesenthal Center Annual*, vol. 6 (Chappaqua, NY: Rossell Books, 1997).
23. Mitchell to Burns, August 27, 1945, box 2, "Correspondence: Wesley Clair Mitchell 1911–1945," Arthur F. Burns Papers, Duke University, Economist Papers Archives.
24. Friedman and Friedman, *Two Lucky People*, 54, 87, 79. Given inconsistencies in the memoir, I follow the most specific account.
25. Janet Martel, interview with author.

26. The full letter does not survive, but this passage is quoted in Friedman and Friedman, *Two Lucky People*, 81.
27. Friedman and Friedman, *Two Lucky People*, 112. Sylvia Nasar, for example, implausibly claims Friedman "numbered among Keynes's American disciples," relying on this section of Friedman's memoir. Sylvia Nasar, *Grand Pursuit: The Story of Economic Genius* (New York: Simon and Schuster, 2011), 369. See also Stapleford, "Market Visions," 430; William Ruger, *Milton Friedman* (New York: Continuum, 2011), 16, 34. More recently, Nelson extends the argument in *Milton Friedman and Economic Debate in the United States, 1932–1972*, vol. 1, 88, calling him "a Keynesian theorist" in the early 1940s.
28. In an interview with Lanny Ebenstein, Friedman could not "definitively remember for whom he voted, but thinks that it was Roosevelt." Lanny Ebenstein, *Milton Friedman: A Biography* (New York: Palgrave Macmillan, 2011), 34.
29. Alan Brinkley, *Voices of Protest: Huey Long, Father Coughlin, and the Great Depression* (New York: Random House, 1983); Richard Breitman and Allen J. Lichtman, *FDR and the Jews* (Cambridge, MA: Harvard University Press, 2013), 93.
30. Following Herbert Stein's classic definition, "'fiscal' in the 'fiscal revolution' refers to policy about the large aggregates in the budget—total expenditures and total receipts and the difference between them—as directed toward affecting certain overall characteristics of the economy, such as employment and unemployment, price levels, and the total share of government activity in the economy. It is the change in policy about such matters that constitutes the revolution." Herbert Stein, *The Fiscal Revolution: Policy in Pursuit of Reality*, second revised edition (Washington, D.C.: American Enterprise Institute Press, 1996; 1969), 4.
31. Lauchlin Currie's memo, "Causes of the Recession," described in William J. Barber, *Designs Within Disorder: Franklin D. Roosevelt, the Economists, and the Shaping of American Economic Policy, 1933–1945* (New York: Cambridge University Press, 1996), 108.
32. Hansen's thinking on Keynes is traced in William J. Barber, "The Career of Alvin H. Hansen in the 1920s and 1930s: A Study in Intellectual Transformation," *History of Political Economy* 19, no. 2 (1987): 191–205.
33. This concept was extended later into the liquidity trap.
34. Hansen quoted in "Investigation of Concentration of Economic Power," in *Hearings Before the Temporary National Economic Committee, Congress of the United States, May 1939* (Washington, D.C.: U.S. Government Printing Office, 1940), 3546.
35. F. H. Knight, "Unemployment: And Mr. Keynes's Revolution in Economic Theory," *The Canadian Journal of Economics and Political Science* 3, no. 1 (February 1937): 123. Jacob Viner, "Mr. Keynes on the Causes of Unemployment," *The Quarterly Journal of Economics* 51, no. 1 (November 1936): 147.
36. Currie quoted in Barber, *Designs Within Disorder*, 109.
37. Stein, *The Fiscal Revolution*, 156.
38. David C. Colander and Harry Landreth, *The Coming of Keynesianism to America: Conversations with the Founders of Keynesian Economics* (Brookfield, VT: Edward Elgar Publishing, 1996), 13.
39. Paul Samuelson, "Economics in a Golden Age: A Personal Memoir," in E. Cary Brown and Robert M. Solow, eds., *Paul Samuelson and Modern Economic Theory* (New York: McGraw Hill, 1983), 166.
40. Franklin D. Roosevelt, "Fireside Chat," April 14, 1938, Gerhard Peters and John T. Woolley, the American Presidency Project, available at http://www.presidency.ucsb.edu/ws/?pid=15628.
41. Friedman later offered a monetary explanation, the Fed's raising of reserve requirements in 1937. Milton Friedman, *A Program for Monetary Stability* (New York: Fordham University Press, 1960), 1, 45. Since then the debate over relative weighting of monetary and fiscal factors in the 1937 recession has been ongoing. For a recent installment that also summarizes the literatures, see Doug Irwin, "Gold Sterilization and the Recession of 1937–38," NBER Working Paper 17595 (November 2011).

42. Hansen testimony in "Investigation of Concentration of Economic Power," 3546, 3548.
43. Hansen testimony in "Investigation of Concentration of Economic Power," 3503. Secular stagnation is described in Alvin H. Hansen, "Economic Progress and Declining Population Growth," *American Economic Review* 29, no. 2 (March 1939): 4.
44. Stein, *The Fiscal Revolution*, 167–68.
45. "Outline of Course Given at Columbia by M. Friedman Entitled 'Structure of Neoclassical Economics,'" two-page typescript, "Wallis" in script at top, box 75, folder 1, Milton Friedman Papers.
46. Unknown author, "Notes on Friedman's lecture," October 5, 1939, twenty-page typescript plus one handwritten page, box 75, folder 12, University of Minnesota B.A. 102, Milton Friedman Papers. These notes were occasionally corrected in Friedman's hand, suggesting he checked them for accuracy.
47. "Notes on Friedman's lecture," Milton Friedman Papers.
48. Friedman to Burns, September 22, 1940, box 2, "Correspondence: Milton Friedman, 1940–1946," Arthur F. Burns Papers, Duke University, Economist Papers Project. Further correspondence from Friedman to Burns cited in this chapter is from this folder and collection.
49. Milton Friedman, "An Objective Standard for Determining a 'Minimum Standard of Living,'" seven-page typescript, box 37, folder 8, Objective Standard of Living, Milton Friedman Papers.
50. Sterner to Friedman, June 9, 1939, box 37, folder 8, Milton Friedman Papers.
51. Daniel Zamora, "Basic Income in the United States, 1940–1972: How the 'Fiscal Revolution' Reshaped Social Policy," in Peter Sloman, Daniel Zamora, and Pedro Pinto, eds., *Universal Basic Income in Historical Perspective* (New York: Palgrave Macmillan, 2021), traces how this early idea evolved into Friedman's later proposals. Also see Brian Steensland, *The Failed Welfare Revolution: America's Struggle over Guaranteed Income Policy* (Princeton, NJ: Princeton University Press, 2008), chapter 2.
52. Alfred Marshall, *Principles of Economics*, vol. 1, 8th edition (New York: Macmillan, 1920; 1890), 10.
53. Groves to Friedman, February 20, 1940, box 226, folder 7, Friedman at the University of Wisconsin, 1940–1941, Milton Friedman Papers. Groves's initial offer was of an associate professorship.
54. Friedman and Friedman, *Two Lucky People*, 85. For Rose's connection to the Corporate Bond Project, see David Levy and Sandra Peart, "Prudence with Biased Experts: Ratings Agencies and Regulators" (September 23, 2010), available at http://ssrn.com/abstract=1681609. John Davenport, "Where Arthur Sits," *Fortune* 80 (December 1, 1969): 62.
55. For a nuanced discussion of Samuelson's hire, see Roger Backhouse, *Founder of Modern Economics: Paul A. Samuelson, Becoming Samuelson, 1915–1948*, vol. 1 (New York: Oxford University Press, 2017), chapter 15. While documenting extensive anti-Semitism at Harvard, Backhouse concludes that was not the sole factor pushing Samuelson to MIT.
56. Malcolm Rutherford, "Wisconsin Institutionalism," in *The Institutionalist Movement in American Economics, 1918–1947* (New York: Cambridge University Press, 2011), 186–222.
57. Friedman to G. C. Sellery, April 11, 1941, box 226, folder 7; and Friedman to Robert J. Lampman, December 5, 1990, box 226, folder 8, Milton Friedman Papers.
58. Friedman to Burns, September 22, 1940, box 2, correspondence, Milton Friedman to Burns, 1940–1946, Arthur F. Burns Papers, Duke University, Economist Papers Project.
59. "New Faculty Wives Added to U. Social Circle," *The Capital Times*, October 13, 1940, Society News, 1.
60. Friedman to Burns, September 22, 1940, and Friedman to Burns, November 17, 1940, box 2, Arthur F. Burns Papers.
61. Milton Friedman, "Proposed Program in Statistics at the University of Wisconsin with Special Reference to the Social Sciences," box 205, folder 10, Statistics at the University of Wisconsin, Milton Friedman Papers.

62. The comment is repeated in multiple sources, including Walter A. Morton, "The Friedman Affair of the Economics Department in the Spring of 1941," September 18, 1979, four-page typescript, 1, 8–11, box 226, folder 8, Milton Friedman Papers.
63. "Fireworks in U.W. Department as Instructor May Get $3500 Prof's Job," *The Capital Times*, May 14, 1941, 1. "Milton Friedman Becomes Object of Controversy," *The Daily Cardinal*, May 16, 1941, 1. "Econ Profs Oppose Promoting Lecturer: Teaching, and Experience Are Cited in Protest," *The Daily Cardinal*, May 15, 1941, 1. The headlines inaccurately stated Friedman's title: he was a visiting professor, and had originally been offered a position as an associate professor.
64. Friedman to Burns, May 29, 1941, box 2, Arthur F. Burns Papers. The decision was also front-page news: "Friedman Drops Job Application," *The Daily Cardinal*, June 5, 1941, 1. "Friedman Drops UW Application," *The Capital Times*, June 5, 1941.
65. Friedman to Robert J. Lampman, December 5, 1990, box 226, folder 8, Milton Friedman Papers.
66. Friedman to Burns, November 17, 1940, box 2, Arthur F. Burns Papers.
67. Friedman to Burns, May 29, 1941, box 2, Arthur F. Burns Papers.
68. Friedman to Burns, May 29, 1941, box 2, Arthur F. Burns Papers.
69. Rose's scattered recollections suggest forceps were used and that she at some point unsuccessfully requested a cesarean delivery. The infant apparently died during labor. Friedman and Friedman, *Two Lucky People*, 104, 108, 124.

5. QUESTIONING KEYNES

1. Testing the consumption function was a concern for the emerging field of econometrics in places as far-flung as Geneva, Switzerland, and Cambridge, Massachusetts. J. J. Thomas, "The Early Econometric History of the Consumption Function," *Oxford Economic Papers* 41, no. 1 (January 1989): 136.
2. John Maynard Keynes, *The General Theory of Employment, Interest, and Money* (New York: Harcourt, 1964; 1935), 96.
3. Robert Dimand, *James Tobin* (New York: Palgrave Macmillan, 2014), 49.
4. Currie memo quoted in William J. Barber, "The Career of Alvin H. Hansen in the 1920s and 1930s: A Study in Intellectual Transformation," *History of Political Economy* 19, no. 2 (1987): 204.
5. David Bunting, "The Consumption Function 'Paradox,'" *Journal of Post Keynesian Economics* 11, no. 3 (Spring 1989): 347–59. See Thomas, "The Early Econometric History of the Consumption Function," for the argument that Kuznets's findings were less significant than presumed.
6. Richard Easterlin, "In Memoriam: Dorothy Stahl Brady, 1903–1977," *The Journal of Economic History* 38, no. 1 (March 1978): 301. Brady's papers do not survive; her career is described in Evelyn L. Forget, "Dorothy Stahl Brady," in Robert William Dimand, Mary Ann Dimand, and Evelyn L. Forget, eds., *A Biographical Dictionary of Women Economists* (Northampton, MA: Edward Elgar Publishing, 2001), 80–81, and Margaret Reid, "Brady, Dorothy Stahl," in *The New Palgrave: A Dictionary of Economics* (London: Palgrave Macmillan, 1987).
7. Dorothy S. Brady and Rose D. Friedman, "Savings and the Income Distribution," in *Studies in Income and Wealth*, vol. 10 (New York: National Bureau of Economic Research, 1947), 247.
8. James Tobin, "Relative Income, Absolute Income, and Saving," in *Money, Trade, and Economic Growth; in Honor of John Henry Williams* (New York: Macmillan, 1951), 135–136, 152. James S. Duesenberry, *Income, Savings, and the Theory of Consumer Behavior* (Cambridge, MA: Harvard University Press, 1940). Brady and Friedman's paper is often omitted even from detailed discussions of the topic. A full accounting of the oversights is in Mary Ann Dimand, Robert W. Dimand, and Evelyn L. Forget, eds., *Women of Value: Feminist Essays on the History of Women in Economics* (Brookfield, VT: Edward Elgar Publishing, 1995), 13–14.

9. Milton Friedman, *A Theory of the Consumption Function* (Princeton, NJ: Princeton University Press, 1957), 237, 5.
10. Duesenberry, for one, admitted his book "began as a critique of the Keynesian consumption function," while hastening to underscore, "It is not, of course, intended to argue that nothing needs to be done about depressions." Duesenberry, *Income, Savings, and the Theory of Consumer Behavior,* 1, 116.
11. J. Allan Hynes, "The Emergence of the Neoclassical Consumption Function: The Formative Years, 1940–1952," *Journal of the History of Economic Thought* 20, no. 1 (1998): 29.
12. Brady's other publications during this time were applications of the ideas laid out in her paper with Rose, analyses of various data sets, or discussions of how to teach home economics. Her publications in economic history, authored later in her career, are discussed in Easterlin, "In Memoriam: Dorothy Stahl Brady, 1903–1977."
13. Federal government finances—revenue, expenditures, and debt: 1940–1999, series Ea679-682, *Historical Statistics of the United States* (*HSUS*), https://hsus.cambridge.org/HSUSWeb/index.do. Amounts are in nominal values (not adjusted for inflation).
14. Friedman to Burns, November 17, 1940, box 2, Arthur F. Burns Papers, Duke University, Economist Papers Project.
15. John Maynard Keynes, *How to Pay for the War: A Radical Plan for the Chancellor of the Exchequer* (New York: Harcourt Brace, 1940), esp. chapter 2.
16. Friedman to Burns, September 23, 1942, box 2, Arthur F. Burns Papers.
17. Presented in December 1941, the papers were later published together. Walter Salant, "The Inflationary Gap: I. Meaning and Significance for Policy Making," *American Economic Review* 32, no. 2, part 1 (June 1942): 308–14. Milton Friedman, "The Inflationary Gap: II. Discussion of the Inflationary Gap," *American Economic Review* 32, no. 2, part 1 (June 1942): 314–20. See also Carl Shoup, Milton Friedman, and Ruth P. Mack, *Taxing to Prevent Inflation: Techniques for Estimating Revenue Requirements* (New York: Columbia University Press, 1943), 141–146, for a critique of Keynesian analysis used by the Bureau of the Budget, National Resources Planning Board, OPA, Department of Commerce, and Department of Labor.
18. "Example of computation of compulsory savings, prepared by the Division of Tax Research, March 3, 1942," twelve-page typescript, author indicated as "MF," box 38, CA 12, folder 1, Compulsory Lending 1940–67, Entry 682, Office of Tax Policy, RG 56, Records of the Treasury Department. "Tentative plan for supplementary individual income tax," Study by Mr. Friedman, November 7, 1941, three-page typescript, box 54, GA 6, folder 1, "Collections and Payment," Office of Tax Policy, Records of the Treasury Department.
19. "Statement" by Milton Friedman, U.S. Congress, Committee on Ways and Means, Data on Proposed Revenue Bill of 1942 (Revised), 171–175, May 7, 1942, House of Representatives, 77th Congress, 2nd Session, April 24–June 27, 1942.
20. Milton Friedman and Rose D. Friedman, *Two Lucky People: Memoirs* (Chicago: University of Chicago Press, 1998), 115. Morgenthau's campaign is detailed in Eric Rauchway, *The Money Makers* (New York: Basic Books, 2015), 209–26, 188–91.
21. Figures from Bureau of Labor Statistics, "Employment status of the civilian noninstitutional population, 1940 to date," available at data.bls.gov.
22. Aaron Director, "The 'Ceiling' Method for Controlling Prices," twelve-page typescript, July 23, 1941, pages 8, 9, box 2, folder 1, "drafts and syllabus, 1937–1958," Aaron Director Papers, University of Chicago, Hanna Holborn Gray Special Collections Research Center.
23. Director, "The 'Ceiling' Method for Controlling Prices," pages 1, 4–5.
24. Aaron Director, "Does Inflation Change the Economic Effects of War?," *American Economic Review* 30, no. 1, part 2 (March 1940): 354.
25. Director, "The 'Ceiling' Method for Controlling Prices," 12.
26. Allan Meltzer, *A History of the Federal Reserve, Volume 1: 1913–1951* (Chicago: University of Chicago Press, 2023), 415, 579. Lloyd W. Mints, "Monetary Policy," *The Review of*

Economics and Statistics 28, no. 2 (May 1946): 64. Director, "The 'Ceiling' Method for Controlling Prices," 2.

27. Director, "The 'Ceiling' Method for Controlling Prices," 2.
28. Director, "Does Inflation Change the Economic Effects of War?," 354, 355, 361.
29. Friedman to Burns, January 10, 1942, box 2, Arthur F. Burns Papers. I use the descriptor "monetarism" for continuity and clarity, although the term was not widely used in reference to Friedman's ideas until after 1968. Michael D. Bordo and Anna J. Schwartz, "IS-LM and Monetarism," NBER Working Paper 9713 (May 2003), 2, available at http://www.nber.org/papers/w9713.
30. Unnamed congressman quoted in John Morton Blum, *From the Morgenthau Diaries: Years of War, 1941–1945* (Boston: Houghton Mifflin, 1967), 40. "Summary of plan for collection of individual income tax at source," Memo by Mr. Friedman, May 7, 1942, box 54, GA 6, folder 1, Collections and Payment, Office of Tax Policy, Records of the Treasury Department. "Collection at Source in Great Britain," Memo by Mr. Friedman, May 19, 1942, box 54, GA 6, folder 2, Collections and Payment, Office of Tax Policy. T. C. Atkeson and Milton Friedman to Mr. Norman D. Cann, July 16, 1942, box 54, GA 6, folder 2, Collections and Payment, Office of Tax Policy.
31. Signed on October 1, the Revenue Act of 1942, which one historian describes as the "core of a new tax regime," reduced exemptions, raised rates, and established a progressive, broadly based tax system. W. Elliot Brownlee, "Tax Regimes, National Crisis, and State-Building," in W. Elliot Brownlee, ed., *Funding the Modern American State, 1941–1995* (Cambridge: Cambridge University Press, 1996), 91. Withholding was authorized almost a year later in the Current Tax Payment Act (known alternatively as the Ruml plan), signed on June 9, 1943. Stanley S. Surrey and William Clements Warren, *Federal Income Taxation: Cases and Materials* (Brooklyn, NY: Foundation Press, 1953), 15.
32. The most recent, and most nuanced, claim of Friedman as Keynesian comes from Edward Nelson, *Milton Friedman and Economic Debate in the United States, 1932–1972*, vol. 1 (Chicago: University of Chicago Press, 2020), which is discussed in notes that follow.
33. Friedman and Friedman, *Two Lucky People*, 113.
34. Friedman to Burns, January 20, 1942, box 2, Arthur F. Burns Papers. Most Treasury proposals assumed that limited price controls or rationing on goods was essential to war production; nonetheless high taxation was considered a way to minimize price controls. In *Milton Friedman and Economic Debate in the United States*, Nelson chastises other historians for assuming Friedman's statements as a Treasury employee represented his personal views (84), but then makes similar claims (90), while also treating published work that grew out of Friedman's Treasury research as equivalent to his academic research, calling a report from the Study of Consumer Purchases his "first book" (91) and *Taxing to Present Inflation* his "second book." Friedman naturally wanted credit for work he had done that was published; this is not the same as the product of independent inquiry. Even an *American Economic Review* article from this time was an outgrowth of a policy dispute between the OPA and the Treasury Department. Salant, "The Inflationary Gap: I. Meaning and Significance for Policy Making," 308–14. Friedman, "The Inflationary Gap: II. Discussion of the Inflationary Gap," 314–20.
35. Shoup, Friedman, and Mack, *Taxing to Prevent Inflation*, 3. I disagree with Nelson's contention in *Milton Friedman and Economic Debate in the United States* that Friedman intended his work in this volume to be "a general analysis" (96). Friedman, "The Inflationary Gap: II. Discussion of the Inflationary Gap," 320. See also *Taxing to Prevent Inflation*, 141–46, for a critique of the Keynesian analysis used by the Office of the Budget, National Resources Planning Board, OPA, Department of Commerce, and Department of Labor.
36. On monetary policy by fiscal means and the influence of the Chicago monetary tradition on Friedman, see George S. Tavlas, *The Monetarists: The Making of the Chicago Monetary Tradition, 1927–1960* (Chicago: University of Chicago Press, 2023), and Tavlas, "Chicago, Harvard, and the Doctrinal Foundations of Monetary Economics," in Robert

Leeson, ed., *Keynes, Chicago and Friedman*, vol. 2 (London: Pickering and Chatto, 2003), 175–99. The counterargument for Friedman as Keynesian is in Nelson, *Milton Friedman and Economic Debate in the United States*, especially 88–96. Nelson has a strong case to argue that Friedman's monetarism was nascent in the 1940s, yet this does not mean he should be understood as a Keynesian economist. The discrepancy can be reconciled by a fuller contextual understanding of Friedman within American economics in the 1940s.

37. Abba P. Lerner, "Monetary Policy and Fiscal Policy," *The Review of Economics and Statistics* 28, no. 2 (May 1946): 77–78.
38. Milton Friedman, "*Saving, Investment, and National Income* by Oscar L. Altman," *The Review of Economics and Statistics* 26, no. 2 (May 1944): 101. Milton Friedman, "Review of *Monopolistic Competition and General Equilibrium Theory*," *Journal of Farm Economics* 23, no. 1 (February 1941): 390.
39. It is less meaningful to use "Keynesian" as a synonym for "New Deal liberal" in the early 1940s, given that many of the ideas later understood as Keynesian had American roots that predated Keynes, and many New Deal policy-makers may not have had any familiarity with Keynes. Regardless, none of these terms applied to Friedman. On Keynes and price controls, see Zachary Carter, *The Price of Peace: Money, Democracy, and the Life of John Maynard Keynes* (New York: Random House, 2020), 327, 331. The Washington network is described in Roger Backhouse, *Founder of Modern Economics: Paul A. Samuelson, Becoming Samuelson, 1915–1948*, vol. 1 (New York: Oxford University Press, 2017), chapter 19.
40. Henry Simons, *Personal Income Taxation: The Definition of Income as a Problem of Fiscal Policy* (Chicago: University of Chicago Press, 1938), v.
41. Simons to Hart, October 5, 1942, and Simons to Hart, December 7, 1942, both in box 3, folder 36, Henry Simons Papers, University of Chicago, Hanna Holborn Gray Special Collections Research Center.
42. Nelson's claim that Friedman moved away from and then "moved back to a free-market position" is not supported by the archival record. See Nelson, *Milton Friedman and Economic Debate in the United States, 1932–1972*, 83.
43. Copious notes from Friedman's class are available, but have not been used by historians who have nonetheless quite confidently dated Friedman's limited government views to a later time. "Wisconsin, University of, notes taken by an unidentified student in a course on business cycles taught by Milton Friedman in the fall of 1940," seventy-six-page handwritten notebook, box 226, folder 8. Henceforth cited as "Wisconsin business cycles course notes." Every other page of the notebook has been numbered by the student; I cite either the numbered page or its unnumbered opposite side as verso. Quote is from October 14, 1940, 8.
44. "Wisconsin business cycles course notes," January 24, 1940, 47. Milton Friedman, *A Program for Monetary Stability* (New York: Fordham University Press, 1960), 45.
45. "Wisconsin business cycles course notes," January 24, 1940, 47.
46. "Wisconsin business cycles course notes," January 24, 1940, 47.
47. J. Daniel Hammond, "Interview with Milton and Rose Friedman," 5, July 24, 1989, unpublished transcript in author's possession.
48. Kuznets to Mitchell, July 10, 1942, box 37, folder 24, Milton Friedman Papers.
49. W. Allen Wallis, "The Statistical Research Group, 1942–1945," *Journal of the American Statistical Association* 75, no. 370 (1980): 325, 321, 329.
50. Wallis, "The Statistical Research Group," 326, 325.
51. Wallis, "The Statistical Research Group," 325–26.
52. Wallis, "The Statistical Research Group," 326.
53. Wallis, "The Statistical Research Group," 326.
54. Wallis, "The Statistical Research Group," 326. Wald wrote: "I wish to express my indebtedness to Milton Friedman and W. Allen Wallis, who proposed the problem of sequential analysis to me in March, 1943. It was their clear formulation of the problem that

gave me the incentive to start the investigations leading to the present developments." Abraham Wald, *Sequential Analysis* (New York: John Wiley and Sons, 1947), v. The Semmelweis example is in Robert H. Riffenburgh, *Statistics in Medicine*, 3rd edition (London: Elsevier), chapter 24.

55. Milton Friedman and Simon Kuznets, *Income from Independent Professional Practice* (New York: National Bureau of Economic Research, 1945).
56. Mitchell to Burns, August 27, 1945, box 2, "Correspondence: Wesley Clair Mitchell 1911–1945," Arthur F. Burns Papers.
57. Mitchell to Burns, August 27, 1945, box 2, Arthur F. Burns Papers.
58. Mitchell to Burns, August 27, 1945, box 2, Arthur F. Burns Papers.

6. CONQUERING COWLES

1. Stigler later recounted these remarks to Allen Wallis. Stigler to Wallis, June 19, 1946, box 10, folder 1, W. Allen Wallis Papers, University of Rochester.
2. "U. of C. Professor Killed by Goof Pills," *Chicago Herald-American*, June 19, 1946, 1. Friedman to Director, June 23, 1946, box 12, folder 3, Henry Simons Papers, University of Chicago, Hanna Holborn Gray Special Collections Research Center. For a convincing argument that Simons's death was a suicide, see Robert Van Horn, "Henry Simons's Death," *History of Political Economy* 46, no. 3 (2014): 525–35.
3. For a broad historical background, see Mary S. Morgan, *The History of Econometric Ideas* (New York: Cambridge, 1990). A historical account more focused on Cowles is Roy Epstein, *A History of Econometrics* (Amsterdam: North-Holland, 1987).
4. For the differences between formalism, abstraction, axiomatization, and mathematization, see E. Roy Weintraub, *How Economics Became a Mathematical Science* (Durham, NC: Duke University Press, 2002).
5. Carl Christ, "History of the Cowles Commission, 1932–1952," 22, available at https://cowles.yale.edu/sites/default/files/2022-08/history-cowles.pdf.
6. Jacob Marschak, "Memo to Chancellor Hutchins on Friedman and Samuelson," February 28, 1946, box 73, folder 2, Office of the President, Hutchins Administration, University of Chicago, Hanna Holborn Gray Special Collections Research Center.
7. A detailed account of Friedman's return to Chicago, along with an invaluable appendix of relevant archival findings, is David Mitch, "A Year of Transition: Faculty Recruiting at Chicago in 1946," *Journal of Political Economy* 12, no. 6 (December 2016): 1714–734, available at http://www.journals.uchicago.edu/doi/suppl/10.1086/688878/suppl_file/mitch.onlineapp.pdf. The phrase from Marschak conveys negative impressions Samuelson will have to overcome to be hired. Marschak to Samuelson, March 20, 1946, Unspecified, Paul A. Samuels Papers, David M. Rubinstein Rare Book and Manuscript Library, Duke University. Reproduced in Mitch, "A Year of Transition," Online Appendix.
8. Friedman to Burns, March 3, 1946, box 2, Arthur F. Burns Papers, Duke University, Economist Papers Project. Marschak, "Memo to Chancellor Hutchins on Friedman and Samuelson," February 28, 1946.
9. Votes are reproduced in tables 1 and 2 in Mitch, "A Year of Transition," 1719–720.
10. Milton Friedman and Rose D. Friedman, *Two Lucky People: Memoirs* (Chicago: University of Chicago Press, 1998), 143.
11. Milton Friedman, "Review of *Business Cycles in the United States of America, 1919–32*, by J. Tinbergen," *American Economic Review* 30 (September 1940): 657–60.
12. J. M. Keynes, "'Professor Tinbergen's Method,' review of *A Method and Its Application to Investment Activity*, by J. Tinbergen (Geneva: League of Nations, 1939)," *The Economic Journal* 49, no. 195 (1939): 586.
13. Milton Friedman, "Lange on Price Flexibility and Employment," *American Economic Review* 36 (September 1946): 613. How a model could or should mediate between theory and data was indeed a central tension of econometrics at the time. Eventually, econometrics would move farther from Friedman's position, with "no data anywhere in sight." Morgan, *The History of Econometric Ideas*, 262–63.

14. Robert M. Solow, "Cowles and the Tradition of Macroeconomics," paper presented at the Cowles Fiftieth Anniversary Celebration, June 3, 1983, 5, available at https://cowles.yale.edu/sites/default/files/files/conf/50th/50th-solow.pdf.
15. Employment Act of 1946, Pub. L. 79–304, ch. 33, 60 Stat. 23 (1946).
16. J. R. Hicks, "Mr. Keynes and the 'Classics': A Suggested Interpretation," *Econometrica* 5, no. 2 (April 1937): 156–58. Hicks originally called his model IS-LL; the LL curve was later christened LM in Alvin Hansen, *Monetary Theory and Fiscal Policy* (New York: McGraw-Hill, 1949).
17. There is a robust literature on the distinction between Keynesianism and Keynes. For a recent survey, see Bradley W. Bateman, "Keynes and Keynesianism," in Roger Backhouse and Bradley Bateman, eds., *The Cambridge Companion to Keynes* (Cambridge: Cambridge University Press, 2006), 271–90. The impact of Keynesian ideas on New Deal liberalism is described in Alan Brinkley, *The End of Reform: New Deal Liberalism in Recession and War* (New York: Knopf, 1995), chapter 10.
18. Paul Samuelson, *Foundations of Economic Analysis* (Cambridge, MA: Harvard University Press, 1947). A full account of the book's influence is in Roger Backhouse, *Founder of Modern Economics: Paul A. Samuelson, Becoming Samuelson, 1915–1948*, vol. 1 (New York: Oxford University Press, 2017), 475–78.
19. Roger Backhouse, "The Transformation of U.S. Economics, 1920–1960, Viewed Through a Survey on Journal Articles," *History of Political Economy* 1, no. 30 (December 1, 1998): 92. The survey sampled from three journals: *American Economic Review*, *Journal of Political Economy*, and *The Quarterly Journal of Economics*.
20. By the end of the war Samuelson's style of policy analysis "can legitimately be called 'American Keynesianism.'" Backhouse, *Founder of Modern Economics*, 431.
21. Malcolm Rutherford, *The Institutionalist Movement in American Economics, 1918–1947: Science and Social Control* (Cambridge, MA: Cambridge University Press, 2011), 277–79.
22. Olav Bjerkholt, "Lawrence R. Klein 1920–2013: Notes on the Early Years," *Journal of Policy Modeling* 36 (2014): 767–84. Lawrence Klein, *The Keynesian Revolution* (New York: Macmillan, 1947), 169.
23. Klein to Samuelson, December 10, 1948, quoted in Timothy Shenk, "Inventing the American Economy," Ph.D. dissertation (Columbia University, 2016), 323, available at https://doi.org/10.7916/D8NZ87N1.
24. Ross B. Emmett, "Sharpening Tools in the Workshop: The Workshop System and the Chicago School's Success," in Robert Van Horn, Philip Mirowski, and Thomas A. Stapleford, eds., *Building Chicago Economics: New Perspectives on the History of America's Most Powerful Economics Program* (New York: Cambridge University Press, 2011), 93–115.
25. Don Patinkin, "Reminiscences of Chicago, 1941–47," *Essays on and in the Chicago Tradition* (Durham, NC: Duke University Press, 1980), 16. For a contemporary explanation of the naïve model concept applied to weather forecasting, see Nate Silver, *The Signal and the Noise* (New York: Penguin, 2015), 131.
26. C. F. Christ, "A Revised Klein Econometric Model for the United States, 1921–1947," in *Discussion Paper Ec269, Cowles Commission* (1949), 51, available at cowles.yale.edu.
27. Eventually Cowles would move away from macroeconomic models toward game theory, and econometricians would increasingly use models to test economic theory. Philip Mirowski, *Machine Dreams: Economics Becomes a Cyborg Science* (Cambridge: Cambridge University Press, 2002). Morgan, *The History of Econometric Ideas*, 264.
28. Tjalling Koopmans, "Measurement Without Theory," *The Review of Economics and Statistics* 29, no. 3 (August 1947): 163, 167. Koopmans ousted Rose from an office when the two overlapped on a temporary appointment at the War Shipping Board during World War II. Friedman and Friedman, *Two Lucky People*, 110, 198.
29. The relationship between the Rockefeller Foundation and the NBER is detailed in Rutherford, *The Institutionalist Movement in American Economics, 1918–1947*, chapter 10. For details on the NBER's funding of Cowles, see Mirowski, *Machine Dreams*, 216–19.

30. Friedman to Burns, February 10, 1946, box 2, Arthur F. Burns Papers.
31. The presentation on October 23, 1947, was a joint seminar with the Statistical Techniques Group of the Chicago Chapter of the American Statistical Association. Cowles Commission for Research in Economics, *Report for 1947* (Chicago: University of Chicago, 1948), 10.
32. Savage left Chicago in 1960 and died young in 1971. For a discussion of Savage's influence on Friedman, see Gerald P. Dwyer, "Milton Friedman: A Bayesian?" (August 27, 2014), available at https://ssrn.com/abstract=2488101 or http://dx.doi.org/10.2139/ssrn.2488101.
33. Milton Friedman and L. J. Savage, "The Utility Analysis of Choices Involving Risk," *Journal of Political Economy* 56 (August 1948): 282.
34. Frank Knight, *Risk, Uncertainty and Profit* (New York: Arthur M. Kelley, 1964; 1922), 311. J. Daniel Hammond, "Interview with Milton and Rose Friedman," 20, July 24, 1989, unpublished transcript in author's possession.
35. Beatrice Cherrier and Andrej Svorenčik, "Defining Excellence: Seventy Years of the John Bates Clark Medal," available at https://osf.io/preprints/socarxiv/bacmj/. Details on Friedman's selection are not available in surviving documents.
36. Paul A. Samuelson, "Reflections on the Merits and Demerits of Monetarism," in *Issues in Fiscal and Monetary Policy: The Eclectic Economist Views the Controversy*, ed. James J. Diamond (Chicago: DePaul University, 1971), 11. Paul Samuelson, *Economics* (New York: McGraw Hill, 1948), 338.
37. Quoted in Backhouse, *Founder of Modern Economics*, 360.
38. Howard Ellis, ed., *A Survey of Contemporary Economics* (Philadelphia: Blakiston, 1948), 314. For a fuller discussion of the context, see George S. Tavlas, *The Monetarists: The Making of the Chicago Monetary Tradition, 1927–1960* (Chicago: University of Chicago Press, 2023), chapter 5.
39. Ellis, *A Survey of Contemporary Economics*, 314.
40. Friedman to Burns, August 15, 1946, box 2, "Correspondence: Milton Friedman to Burns," Arthur F. Burns Papers.
41. Friedman to Burns, August 15, 1946, box 2, Arthur F. Burns Papers.
42. For institutionalist approaches to money, see Perry Mehrling, *The Money Interest and the Public Interest: American Monetary Thought, 1920–1970* (Cambridge, MA: Harvard University Press, 1997), and Rutherford, *The Institutionalist Movement in American Economics, 1918–1947*, 112–16.
43. The best source for Schwartz's early life and career are three interviews, from which this account draws: "An Interview with Anna J. Schwartz," *The Newsletter of the Cliometric Society* 10, no. 2 (July 1995): 3–7; David Fettig, "Interview with Anna J. Schwartz," *The Region* (September 1993), available at https://minneapolisfed.org/publications/the-region; and Edward Nelson, "An Interview with Anna J. Schwartz," *Macroeconomic Dynamics* 8 (2004): 401. Arthur Gayer, W. W. Rostow, and Anna J. Schwartz, *The Growth and Fluctuation of the British Economy, 1790–1850: An Historical, Statistical, and Theoretical Study of Britain's Economic Development* (Oxford: Clarendon Press, 1953).
44. Nelson, "Interview with Anna Schwartz," 399.
45. Gayer died in a car accident in early 1951. Schwartz to Friedman, November 20, 1950, box 90, folder 3, Milton Friedman Papers, Hoover Institution Library and Archives.
46. Nelson, "Interview with Anna J. Schwartz," 403–404.
47. Nelson, "Interview with Anna J. Schwartz," 404.
48. Nelson, "Interview with Anna J. Schwartz," 401.
49. Friedman to Schwartz, March 3, 1948, box 90, folder 1, Milton Friedman Papers.
50. Friedman to Schultz, "Economics: Work for the academic year July 1, 1948 to July 1, 1949," typescript memo, June 7, 1949, box 79, folder 1, Academic Career: University of Chicago Minutes Economics Department 1946–1949, Milton Friedman Papers.
51. Friedman to Schultz, "Economics: Work for the academic year July 1, 1948 to July 1, 1949," typescript memo, June 7, 1949, Milton Friedman Papers.

52. Clark Warburton, "Monetary Control Under the Federal Reserve Act," *Political Science Quarterly* 61, no. 4 (December, 1946): 505–34, reprinted in Warburton, *Depression, Inflation, and Monetary Policy: Selected Papers, 1945–1953* (Baltimore: Johns Hopkins Press, 1966), 301. Schwartz to Friedman, April 5, 1948, box 90, folder 1, Milton Friedman Papers. I have not been able to locate a copy of this reading list. For Warburton's influence on Friedman, see James R. Lothian and George S. Tavlas, "How Friedman and Schwartz Became Monetarists," *Journal of Money, Credit and Banking* 50, no. 4 (June 2018): 757–87. For Warburton's career overall, see Michael D. Bordo and Anna Schwartz, "Clark Warburton: Pioneer Monetarist," in Anna J. Schwartz, ed., *Money in Historical Perspective* (Chicago: University of Chicago Press, 1987), 234–54.
53. "Banking and Currency Reform," undated thirteen-page typescript memo, box 1, folder 10, pages 1, 4–5, Aaron Director Papers, University of Chicago, Hanna Holborn Gray Special Collections Research Center. Contextual clues date the memo to the early 1930s and establish Simons as its author. Like many of Simons's writings, the memo was preserved in Director's papers.
54. Jacob Viner, "International Aspects of the Gold Standard," in Quincy Wright, ed., *Gold and Monetary Stabilization: Lectures from the Ninth Institute of the Norman Wait Harris Memorial Foundation, Held at the University of Chicago from January 27 to January 31, 1932* (Chicago: University of Chicago Press, 1932), 28. See Tavlas, *The Monetarists*, for a discussion of Viner's stance on the Fed and its potential influence on Friedman.
55. Henry Simons, "Rules Versus Authorities in Monetary Policy," *Journal of Political Economy* 44, no. 1 (February 1936): 3.
56. Milton Friedman, "A Monetary and Fiscal Framework for Economic Stability," *American Economic Review* 38, no. 3 (June 1948): 248.
57. Friedman, "A Monetary and Fiscal Framework for Economic Stability," 259.
58. For a summary of the debate over whether this article can be considered part of monetarism, and an argument that it is not, see Edward Nelson, *Milton Friedman and Economic Debate in the United States, 1932–1972*, vol. 1 (Chicago: University of Chicago Press, 2020), 138–43. For the article as a transition between a Simons-Mints framework and monetarism, see Tavlas, *The Monetarists.* The alternative institutional structure advocated in the framework makes it difficult to repurpose Friedman's thinking here for contemporary debates, as is done in Randall Wray, "A Monetary and Fiscal Framework for Economic Stability: A Friedmanian Approach to Restoring Growth," available at https://ssrn.com/abstract=1010174.
59. Friedman to Schultz, "Economics: Work for the academic year July 1, 1948 to July 1, 1949," typescript memo, June 7, 1949, Milton Friedman Papers.
60. Friedman to Joseph Willits, Rockefeller Foundation, September 26, 1947, reproduced in Robert A. Cord and J. Daniel Hammond, eds., *Milton Friedman: Contributions to Economics and Public Policy* (New York: Oxford University Press, 2016), 585–604. Further detail on Rockefeller funding of Cowles and Friedman is in Rutherford, *The Institutionalist Movement in American Economics, 1918–1947*, 280–81.
61. Milton Friedman, "The Methodology of Positive Economics," in *Essays in Positive Economics* (Chicago: University of Chicago Press, 1953), 2. Friedman's essay has inspired an enormous literature, fueled in part by his refusal to comment on the essay after publication. See Uskali Mäki, ed., *The Methodology of Positive Economics: Reflections on the Milton Friedman Legacy* (New York: Cambridge University Press, 2009).
62. Friedman, "The Methodology of Positive Economics," 6, 11.
63. Marcel Boumans, "Friedman and the Cowles Commission," in Robert Cord and J. Daniel Hammond, eds., *Milton Friedman: Contributions to Economics and Public Policy* (New York: Oxford University Press, 2016), 597.
64. Robert Solow, "Cowles and the Tradition of Macroeconomics," *The Cowles Fiftieth Anniversary Celebration* (New Haven, CT: Yale University Press, June 3, 1983), 9. In fact, Friedman's criticisms were taking a toll. Driven in part by new developments in mathematics, and in part by the inadequacies Friedman stressed, Cowles would shift from macro models to game theory in the coming years. Mirowski, *Machine Dreams*, 247–48.

65. Cowles Commission Conference 2, "Minutes for Saturday Afternoon, September 21, 1946," in "Staff Meetings, Minutes and Papers, Statistics, 1946–47," Cowles Commission Digital Archive, Yale University. Further details on the clash between Friedman and Cowles are in Epstein, *A History of Econometrics*, chapter 4.
66. Franco Modigliani quoted in Arjo Klamer, *Conversations with Economists: New Classical Economists and Opponents Speak Out on the Current Controversy in Macroeconomics* (New York: Rowman and Littlefield, 1983), 120. Friedman is quoted in "Minutes: No. 129, Liquidity of Assets Under Complete Information, by Jacob Marschak," December 22, 1948, in Cowles Commission, Staff Meetings, Minutes and Papers, 1947–49.
67. Milton Friedman and Anna Schwartz, "Alternative Approaches to Analyzing Economic Data," *American Economic Review* 81 (March 1991): 11. Friedman and Friedman, *Two Lucky People*, 197.
68. Koopmans to Joseph Willits, February 23, 1953, box 42, folder 4, Department of Economics Records, University of Chicago, Hanna Holborn Gray Special Collections Research Center.
69. Personal communication to the author from Philip Mirowski, July 17, 2019. The "considerable pressure" Koopmans felt and his attendance at a "composer's conference" are noted in Herbert E. Scarf, "Tjalling Charles Koopmans, August 28, 1910–February 26, 1985," Cowles Foundation Discussion Paper No. 1029, 24. Secondary accounts of the Cowles-Friedman battle have misrepresented the relationship between Koopmans and Friedman as cordial, often citing as their primary evidence a February 1947 letter of recommendation Friedman authored for Koopmans. See Lanny Ebenstein, *Milton Friedman* (New York: Palgrave Macmillan, 2007), 57–59, and Boumans, "Friedman and the Cowles Commission," 597. Both accounts omit entirely the issue of Rockefeller funding. Aside from that one letter, written before the publication of "Measurement Without Theory," Friedman's confidential assessments of Koopmans were far from positive and their relationship became increasingly difficult.
70. Friedman and Friedman, *Two Lucky People*, 208. See also Rutherford, *The Institutionalist Movement in American Economics, 1918–1947*, 276–79. Burns to Friedman, May 12, 1954, and Friedman to Burns, undated, box 22, folder 16, Milton Friedman Papers.
71. Friedman's memos to Schultz support these hires and express his opposition to closely linking Cowles and the department. See various letters from Friedman to Schultz, box 42, folder 10, Department of Economics Records.
72. Leonard Silk, *The Economists* (New York: Basic Books, 1976), 18.
73. T. W. Schultz, "Notes for a Memorandum for Mr. Cowles and Mr. Kimpton on the Cowles Commission," nine-page typescript, August 22, 1954, 6–8. No author, handwritten notes, September 21, 1954, box 41, folder 1, Theodore Schultz Papers, Department of Economics Records, University of Chicago, Hanna Holborn Gray Special Collections Research Center.
74. Milton Friedman, "The Marshallian Demand Curve," *Journal of Political Economy* 57, no. 6 (December 1949): 490.
75. Quoted in Shenk, "Inventing the American Economy," 334.
76. Tesler and Arrow quoted in Ebenstein, *Milton Friedman*, 56.
77. Friedman to Burns, October 9, 1954, box 2, Arthur F. Burns Papers.

7. LAW AND ECONOMICS

1. Hayek to Director, July 10, 1946, box 73, folder 14, Correspondence with Aaron Director, F. A. Hayek Papers, Hoover Institution Library and Archives.
2. Quotes are, respectively, from Wesley J. Liebeler and Benjamin Klein in Edmund W. Kitch, "The Fire of Truth: A Remembrance of Law and Economics at Chicago, 1932–1970," *The Journal of Law and Economics* 26, no. 1 (April 1983): 184.
3. The best account of Hayek's life and times in this period is Bruce Caldwell and Hansjoerg Klausinger, *Hayek: A Life, 1899–1950* (Chicago: University of Chicago Press,

2022). For a discussion of Hayek's views and the American "real bills" doctrine, see Lawrence H. White, "Did Hayek and Robbins Deepen the Great Depression?," *Journal of Money, Credit and Banking* 40, no. 4 (June 2008): 751–68. For the Austrian school reaction to the Great Depression, and the slide in Hayek's reputation, see Janek Wasserman, *The Marginal Revolutionaries: How Austrian Economists Fought the War of Ideas* (New Haven, CT: Yale University Press, 2019), chapter 4, 162–63.

4. F. A. Hayek, *The Road to Serfdom: Text and Documents, the Definitive Edition*, ed. Bruce Caldwell (Indianapolis: Liberty Fund, 2007; 1944), 106, 107.
5. Hayek, *The Road to Serfdom*, 85, 87, 148, 87. F. A. Hayek, "The Intellectuals and Socialism," in *The Collected Works of F. A. Hayek, Socialism and War: Essays, Documents, Reviews*, ed. Bruce Caldwell (Indianapolis: Liberty Fund, 1997), 237.
6. Marschak's comment is reproduced in Hayek, *The Road to Serfdom*, 251–52. The American reception of *The Road to Serfdom* is detailed in Angus Burgin, *The Great Persuasion: Reinventing Free Markets Since the Depression* (Cambridge, MA: Harvard University Press, 2012), 87–94.
7. Meg Jacobs, "'How About Some Meat?': The Office of Price Administration, Consumption Politics, and State Building from the Bottom Up, 1941–1946," *The Journal of American History* 84, no. 3 (December 1997): 910–41. Andrew H. Bartels, "The Office of Price Administration and the Legacy of the New Deal, 1939–1946," *The Public Historian* 5, no. 3 (Summer 1983): 5–29.
8. *PM Magazine*, quoted in Bruce Caldwell, "Introduction," in Hayek, *The Road to Serfdom*, 22.
9. Hayek to Luhnow, May 3, 1945, box 58, William Volker Funds, 1939–1948, F. A. Hayek Papers, Hoover Institution Library and Archives.
10. Henry Simons, Memorandum I on a proposed Institute of Political Economy, box 8, folder 9, Free Market Study, Henry Simons Papers, University of Chicago, Hanna Holborn Gray Special Collections Research Center.
11. Hayek's divorce is covered in part 6 of Caldwell and Klausinger, *Hayek: A Life*.
12. Director to Executive Committee of Free Market Study, October 30, 1946, four-page typescript memo, and Friedman, "A Program of Factual Research into Questions Basic to the Formulation of a Liberal Economic Policy," five-page typescript, undated, pages 1, 2, box 79, folder 4, "Free Market Study," Milton Friedman Papers, Hoover Institution Library and Archives. Although the memo is unsigned, it is unmistakably the work of Friedman, given its vocabulary, tone, and content.
13. Milton Friedman and George Stigler, *Roofs or Ceilings? The Current Housing Problem* (Irvington-on-Hudson, NY: Foundation for Economic Education, 1946), 13. Stigler to Wallis, undated, circa 1946, box 10, folder 1, Correspondence with George Stigler, W. Allen Wallis Papers, University of Rochester. Friedman to Burns, January 10, 1942, box 2, Arthur F. Burns Papers, Duke University, Economist Papers Project.
14. Details on FEE's founding are in Kim Phillips-Fein, *Invisible Hands: The Businessmen's Crusade Against the New Deal* (New York: W. W. Norton, 2009), 16–19, 26–30, and Henry Hazlitt, "The Early History of FEE," available at https://fee.org/articles/the-early-history-of-fee/.
15. Rose Wilder Lane, untitled review essay, *Economic Council Review of Books* 4 (August 1947): 1–8. The textbook controversy is described in David Colander and Harry Landreth, "Political Influence on the Textbook Keynesian Revolution: God, Man, and Lorie Tarshis at Yale," in O. F. Hamouda and B. B. Price, eds., *Keynesianism and the Keynesian Revolution in America: A Memorial Volume in Honour of Lorie Tarshis* (Cheltenham, UK: Edward Elgar Publishing, 1998), 59–72, and is given full coverage with documents in David M. Levy, Sandra J. Peart, and Margaret Albert, "Economic Liberals as Quasi-Public Intellectuals: The Democratic Dimension," in *Research in the History of Economic Thought and Methodology*, vol. 30-B (Bradford, UK: Emerald Group Publishing, 2012), 1–116. For Lane's libertarian views, see Jennifer Burns, "The Three 'Furies' of Libertarianism: Rose Wilder Lane, Isabel Paterson, and Ayn Rand," *The Journal of American History* (December

2015): 746–74. For the MIT investigation, see Roger Backhouse, *Founder of Modern Economics: Paul A. Samuelson, Becoming Samuelson, 1915–1948*, vol. 1 (New York: Oxford University Press, 2017), 557–75.

16. Phillips-Fein, *Invisible Hands*.
17. Quoted in John Patrick Diggins, *Up from Communism: Conservative Odysseys in American Intellectual History* (New York: Harper and Row, 1975), 387. Arthur Schlesinger Jr., "The Need for an Intelligent Opposition," *The New York Times*, April 2, 1950, 13, 56–58.
18. William F. Buckley Jr., *God and Man at Yale: The Superstitions of "Academic Freedom"* (Washington, D.C.: Gateway Editions, 2002; 1951), 64.
19. Read's views are covered in Mary Sennholz's appreciative biography *Leonard Read: Philosopher of Freedom* (Irvington-on-Hudson, NY: Foundation for Economic Education, 1993).
20. Wasserman, *The Marginal Revolutionaries*, 210. John O'Neill, "Who Won the Socialist Calculation Debate?," *History of Political Thought* 17, no. 3 (Autumn 1996): 431–42.
21. Paul Milazzo, *Henry Hazlitt: A Biography*, draft manuscript, chapter 1, 28.
22. Stigler to Wallis, undated, circa 1946, box 10, folder 1, Correspondence with George Stigler, W. Allen Wallis Papers.
23. Friedman and Stigler, *Roofs or Ceilings?*, 10.
24. On Watts's antidemocratic views and Carter's eugenics, see Levy, Peart, and Albert, "Economic Liberals as Quasi-Public Intellectuals," 1–116.
25. Friedman, notes on the back of an envelope postmarked August 6, 1946, box 38, folder 5, Milton Friedman Papers. These notes were a draft of a telegram Friedman sent to FEE, reproduced in J. Daniel Hammond and Claire Hammond, eds., *Making Chicago Price Theory: Friedman-Stigler Correspondence 1945–1957* (New York: Routledge, 2006), 21.
26. Friedman and Stigler, *Roofs or Ceilings?*, 10. Friedman and Friedman, *Two Lucky People*, 151. Stigler to Friedman, undated, in Hammond and Hammond, *Making Chicago Price Theory*, 20.
27. Stigler to Friedman, Tuesday, and V. O. Watts to Stigler, August 28, 1947, in Hammond and Hammond, *Making Chicago Price Theory*, 32, 36. Friedman to Martin Bronfenbrenner, October 8, 1946, box 38, folder 6, Correspondence 1946–1948, Roofs or Ceilings, Milton Friedman Papers. Friedman to Burns, August 15, 1946, box 2, Arthur F. Burns Papers.
28. Friedman and Friedman, *Two Lucky People*, 151. Read's role is described in Caldwell and Klausinger, *Hayek: A Life*, 656.
29. Adam Smith, *Wealth of Nations*, ed. Edwin Cannan (New York: Modern Library, 2000), 148. Henry Simons, *A Positive Program for Laissez Faire: Some Proposals for a Liberal Economic Policy* (Chicago: University of Chicago Press, 1934), 19.
30. Friedman, "A Program of Factual Research into Questions Basic to the Formulation of a Liberal Economic Policy," page 1, Milton Friedman Papers.
31. Ellis Hawley, *The New Deal and the Problem of Monopoly: A Study in Economic Ambivalence* (Princeton, NJ: Princeton University Press, 1966). A more recent take is Matt Stoller, *Goliath: The 100-Year War Between Monopoly Power and Democracy* (New York: Simon and Schuster, 2019).
32. "The TNEC Report," *The New York Times*, April 1, 1941, 22. The study was authored by the Swarthmore College economist Clair Wilcox, *Competition and Monopoly in American Industry* (Washington, D.C.: U.S. Government Printing Office, 1941). Aaron Director, ed., *Defense, Controls, and Inflation: A Conference Sponsored by the University of Chicago Law School* (Chicago: University of Chicago Press, 1952), 306.
33. Gordon Tullock, *The Simons Syllabus* (Fairfax, VA: Center for the Study of Public Choice, 1983), 5.
34. Stigler to Friedman, December 20, 1946, in Hammond and Hammond, *Making Chicago Price Theory*, 49.
35. Scholars have mistakenly stated that Hayek removed names at Luhnow's request; for a full discussion, see Caldwell and Klausinger, *Hayek: A Life*, 646–48, 647*n8*.

36. Milazzo, *Hazlitt: A Biography*, chapter 3.
37. "Contra-Cyclical Measures, Full Employment, and Monetary Reform, April 7, 4:30," pages 6, 7, Minutes of the Mont Pelerin Society, box 5, folder 12, Mont Pelerin Society Records, Hoover Institution Library and Archives. The minutes, understood to be private, are not comprehensive or verbatim. Page numbers are indicated when included.
38. "Discussion on Agenda, Etc., April 4, 4:30," Minutes of Discussion at Mont Pelerin Conference, April 1st–10th, 1947, box 5, folder 13, Mont Pelerin Society Records.
39. "Free Enterprise or Competitive Order," April 1, 4:30, III, pages 3, 5, Minutes of the Mont Pelerin Society, box 5, folder 12, Mont Pelerin Society Records. Although included in the meeting minutes, from their length and structure these remarks seem to be a written paper or address delivered by Director.
40. "Income and Taxation," Tuesday April 8th, 8:30 p.m., pages 1, 3–4, box 5, folder 12, Minutes of the Mont Pelerin Society, Mont Pelerin Society Records.
41. "Income and Taxation," Minutes of the Mont Pelerin Society, Mont Pelerin Society Records.
42. Friedman and Friedman, *Two Lucky People*, 161.
43. "Minutes, Mont Pelerin Conference, Tuesday, April 1st, 4.30," box 5, folder 12, Mont Pelerin Society Records.
44. "Wages and Wage Policy," Minutes of the Mont Pelerin Society, April 8, 9:30, box 5, folder 12, Mont Pelerin Society Records.
45. "Present Political Crisis," Minutes of the Mont Pelerin Society, April 9, 8:30, II, box 5, folder 12, Mont Pelerin Society Records.
46. Milton Friedman, "Neo-Liberalism and Its Prospects," *Farmand* (February 17, 1951): 89–93. This article was Friedman's only use of the term "neoliberal," most likely reflecting his audience in Europe, where "liberal" still referred to ideas in the tradition of Adam Smith, not the New Deal. For a brief discussion of this shift, see Gary Gerstle, *The Rise and Fall of the Neoliberal Order* (New York: Oxford University Press, 2022), 82.
47. Friedman and Friedman, *Two Lucky People*, 179, 180. Friedman to Stigler, November 15, 1950, in Hammond and Hammond, *Making Chicago Price Theory*, 116. The hometown of Friedman's parents, Beregszász in present-day Ukraine, was both a work camp and a central node for transports to Auschwitz. Families from Rose's nearby birthplace, Charterisk, were likely taken there.
48. Later published as "The Case for Flexible Exchange Rates," in Milton Friedman, *Essays in Positive Economics* (Chicago: University of Chicago Press, 1953), 157–203.
49. Many believed Eisenhower had stolen the nomination from Taft, aided by nefarious Eastern elites; the classic statement of "the big steal" is in Phyllis Schlafly, *A Choice Not an Echo* (Washington, D.C.: Regnery, 1964; 2014), chapter 8.
50. Friedman to Machlup, October 26, 1952, box 38, folder 25, Correspondence, Friedman, Milton and Rose, Fritz Machlup Papers, Hoover Institution Library and Archives. Burgin misreads this correspondence as indicating Friedman's support for African American civil rights. However, in 1952 both Friedman and Machlup used the term "civil rights" in reference to McCarthyism and issues of free speech and association. Burgin, *Great Persuasion*, 202.
51. Friedman to Machlup, October 26, 1952, Fritz Machlup Papers.
52. Friedman to Machlup, October 26, 1952, Fritz Machlup Papers.
53. Friedman to Machlup, October 30, 1952, Fritz Machlup Papers.
54. Kitch, "The Fire of Truth," 181–82. This influential account of law and economics at Chicago omits Levi's and Director's participation in the Free Market Study.
55. Wesley Liebeler and Robert Bork quoted in Kitch, "The Fire of Truth," 183.
56. Under Director's guidance, John McGee would later write up this argument in an influential article: John S. McGee, "Predatory Price Cutting: The Standard Oil (N.J.) Case," *The Journal of Law and Economics* 1 (October 1958): 137–69. Kitch, "The Fire of Truth," 209.
57. Warren Nutter, *The Extent of Enterprise Monopoly in the United States, 1899–1939* (Chicago: University of Chicago Press, 1951).

58. Solomon Fabricant, "Is Monopoly Increasing?," *The Journal of Economic History* 13, no. 1 (Winter 1953): 93. A second Director-supported project reached similar conclusions: J. Fred Weston, *The Role of Mergers in the Growth of Large Firms* (Los Angeles: University of California Press, 1953). The reception of Nutter's dissertation is covered in Eric Schliesser, "Inventing Paradigms, Monopoly, Methodology, and Mythology at 'Chicago': Nutter and Stigler," available at http://philsci-archive.pitt.edu/id/eprint/5423.
59. Stigler also noted the influence of the Harvard professor Joseph Schumpeter's "creative destruction" on his understanding of monopoly. George J. Stigler, *Memoirs of an Unregulated Economist* (New York: Basic Books, 1988), 98.
60. Robert S. Thomas, "Enlightenment and Authority: The Committee on Social Thought and the Ideology of Postwar Conservatism (1927–1950)," Ph.D. dissertation, Columbia University, 2010.
61. Hayek to Luhnow, March 11, 1950, box 58, folder 17, William Volker Fund, 1949–1952, F. A. Hayek Papers.
62. Research linked to the Antitrust Project is listed in George Priest, "The Rise of Law and Economics: A Memoir of the Early Years," in Francesco Parisi and Charles K. Rowley, eds., *The Origins of Law and Economics: Essays by the Founding Fathers* (Northampton, MA: Edward Elgar Publishing, 2005), 353–54.
63. Quoted in Kitch, "The Fire of Truth," 205–206.
64. For a recent account integrating the Harvard school, see Elizabeth Popp Berman, *Thinking Like an Economist: How Efficiency Replaced Equality in U.S. Public Policy* (Princeton, NJ: Princeton University Press, 2022).
65. Important to this change was the Antitrust Project member Robert Bork. For a critical summary of the change, see Robert Van Horn, "Reinventing Monopoly: The Roots of Chicago Law and Economics," in Philip Mirowski and Dieter Plehwe, eds., *The Road from Mont Pelerin: The Making of the Neoliberal Thought Collective* (Cambridge, MA: Harvard University Press, 2009), esp. 223–28, and Robert Van Horn and Matthias Klaes, "Intervening in Laissez-Faire Liberalism: Chicago's Shift on Patents," in Robert Van Horn, Philip Mirowski, and Thomas A. Stapleford, eds., *Building Chicago Economics: New Perspectives on the History of America's Most Powerful Economics Program* (New York: Cambridge University Press, 2011), 180–204. For a broad and critical overview of shifts in antitrust over the twentieth century, see Stoller, *Goliath*.
66. Simons, *A Positive Program for Laissez Faire*, 19.
67. Stigler, "The Economists and Equality," 1, 2, 1, 4.
68. George Stigler, *Five Lectures on Economic Problems* (New York: Macmillan, 1950), 1, 2, 4, 9. Karl Polanyi, *The Great Transformation: The Political and Economic Origins of Our Time* (New York: Farrar and Reinhart, 1944).
69. Friedman to Stigler, Saturday, February 7, 1948, in Hammond and Hammond, *Making Chicago Price Theory*, 78.
70. Jason L. Riley, *Maverick: A Biography of Thomas Sowell* (New York: Basic Books, 2021), 111.
71. Milton Friedman, "The Role of Government in a Liberal Society," lecture transcript, Wabash College, June 1956, Collected Works of Milton Friedman (miltonfriedman.hoover.org/collections), Hoover Institution Library and Archives.
72. Milton Friedman, "The Distribution of Income and the Welfare Activities of Government," lecture transcript, Wabash College, June 20, 1956, Collected Works of Milton Friedman.
73. Frank Knight, "The Case for Communism: From the Standpoint of an Ex-Liberal," in Warren J. Samuels, ed., *Research in the History of Economic Thought and Methodology*, Archival Supplement 2 (Greenwich, CT: JAI Press, 1991), 89. Piketty cites Kuznets's work, along with Robert Solow's growth model, as critical influences on previous economic research, in Thomas Piketty, *Capital in the Twenty-First Century*, trans. Arthur Goldhammer (Cambridge, MA: Harvard University Press, 2013), 11–17.

74. Friedman, "The Distribution of Income and the Welfare Activities of Government," Collected Works of Milton Friedman.
75. Friedman, "The Distribution of Income and the Welfare Activities of Government," Collected Works of Milton Friedman.
76. Friedman, "The Distribution of Income and the Welfare Activities of Government," Collected Works of Milton Friedman.
77. Simons to Hayek, December 18, 1934, box 3, Henry Simons Papers.
78. Frank Meyer, *In Defense of Freedom: A Conservative Credo* (Chicago: Henry Regnery, 1962), 6–7. George Nash, *The Conservative Intellectual Movement in America Since 1945* (New York: Basic Books, 1976), 161–65.
79. Watts to Mises, December 9, 1946, in Levy, Peart, and Albert, "Economic Liberals as Quasi-Public Intellectuals," 40, 116.
80. Friedman to Read, September 18, 1957, and Read to Friedman, September 11, 1957, in box 32, folder 2, Milton Friedman Papers.
81. For Stigler's hire, see David Mitch, "George Stigler's Career Moves: The Roles of Contingency, Self-Interest, Ideology, and Intellectual Commitment," in Craig Freedman, ed., *George Stigler: The Enigmatic Price Theorist of the Twentieth Century* (London: Palgrave Macmillan, 2020), 235–79.
82. Mitch, "George Stigler's Career Moves," 257, 262.
83. Stigler, *Memoirs of an Unregulated Economist*, 76.
84. Stigler, *Memoirs of an Unregulated Economist*, 76. A considerable literature has grown up around the Coase theorem, including arguments that it does not really exist. See Paul Samuelson, "Some Uneasiness with the Coase Theorem," *Japan and the World Economy* 7 (1995): 1–7; and Steven Medema, "A Case of Mistaken Identity: George Stigler, 'The Problem of Social Cost,' and the Coase Theorem," *European Journal of Law and Economics* 31 (2011): 11–38, available at https://doi.org/10.1007/s10657-010-9196-5. Examples cited are from Tatyana Deryugina, Frances Moore, and Richard S. J. Tol, "Environmental Applications of the Coase Theorem," January 14, 2021, available at arXiv:2004.04247.
85. Stigler, *Memoirs of an Unregulated Economist*, 103, 163, 119. For Stigler's empire as the "third pillar" of the Chicago school, see Edward Nik-Khah, "George Stigler, the Graduate School of Business, and the Pillars of the Chicago School," in Van Horn, Mirowski, and Stapleford, *Building Chicago Economics*, 116–48.
86. Stigler, *Memoirs of an Unregulated Economist*, 203.
87. Berman, *Thinking Like an Economist*, chapter 4.

8. HIDDEN FIGURES

1. Aaron Director, ed., *Defense, Controls, and Inflation: A Conference Sponsored by the University of Chicago Law School* (Chicago: University of Chicago Press, 1952), 329, 35.
2. Viner to Don Patinkin, November 24, 1969, in Don Patinkin, ed., *Essays on and in the Chicago Tradition* (Durham, NC: Duke University Press, 1980), 266.
3. Director, *Defense, Controls, and Inflation*, 12, 3, 15.
4. Schwartz to Friedman, April 5, 1948, folder 1, box 90, Milton Friedman Papers, Hoover Institution Library and Archives.
5. Friedman to Schwartz, April 22, 1948, and Schwartz to Friedman, May 12, 1948, folder 1, box 90, Milton Friedman Papers.
6. Friedman to Schwartz, October 11, 1948, folder 1, box 90, Milton Friedman Papers.
7. Friedman to Schwartz, March 17, 1949, July 19, 1949, and November 16, 1951, box 90, folder 2, Milton Friedman Papers.
8. Friedman to Schwartz, July 16, 1951, box 90, folder 4, Milton Friedman Papers.
9. Schwartz to Friedman, January 15, 1953, box 90, folder 4, Milton Friedman Papers.
10. Milton Friedman, ed., *Studies in the Quantity Theory of Money* (Chicago: University of Chicago Press, 1956), 17.

11. Milton Friedman, "Prices, Income, and Monetary Changes in Three Wartime Periods," *American Economic Review* 42 (May 1952): 612–35. Friedman acknowledged the research assistance of two students but not of Schwartz, while noting figures were derived from "a larger and still unfinished study."
12. Allan H. Meltzer, *A History of the Federal Reserve, Volume 2, Book 1, 1951–1969* (Chicago: University of Chicago Press, 2009), 93.
13. For an insider's account of the drama, see Allan Sproul, "The 'Accord'—A Landmark in the First Fifty Years of the Federal Reserve System," *Economic Policy Review* 58, no. 11 (November 1964): 22–31.
14. Meltzer, *A History of the Federal Reserve, Volume 2, Book 1, 1951–1969*, 35.
15. Not to be confused with the Depression-era "real bills" doctrine, restricting lending to durable goods, which was heavily criticized by Mints, Friedman, and many others.
16. See https://www.federalreserve.gov/monetarypolicy/fomc_historical.htm.
17. Figures are in Meltzer, *A History of the Federal Reserve, Volume 2, Book 1, 1951–1969*, 95.
18. Robert E. Weintraub, "Some Neglected Monetary Contributions: Congressman Wright Patman (1893–1976)," *Journal of Money, Credit and Banking* 9, no. 4 (November 1977): 518, 519.
19. Douglas's role in the accord is covered in George S. Tavlas, *The Monetarists: The Making of the Chicago Monetary Tradition, 1927–1960* (Chicago: University of Chicago Press, 2023).
20. Joint Committee on the Economic Report, Subcommittee on General Credit Control and Debt Management, *Monetary Policy and Management of Public Debt* (March 1952), *Congressional Record*, 691, text in Proquest Congressional.
21. *Monetary Policy and Management of Public Debt*, 740, 692, 741, 693.
22. "Address of Wm. McC. Martin, Jr., Chairman, Board of Governors of the Federal Reserve System, Before the New York Group of the Investment Bankers Association of America," October 19, 1955, available at https://fraser.stlouisfed.org/title/448/item/7800.
23. Carl Christ, "Report of the Bailey-Christ-Griliches Committee," November 29, 1957, ten-page typescript memo, folder 8, box 42, Department of Economics Records, University of Chicago, Hanna Holborn Gray Special Collections Research Center.
24. Ross B. Emmett, "Sharpening Tools in the Workshop," in Robert Van Horn, Philip Mirowski, and Thomas A. Stapleford, eds., *Building Chicago Economics: New Perspectives on the History of America's Most Powerful Economics Program* (New York: Cambridge University Press, 2011), 93–115.
25. "Outline for Discussion with Dr. Schultz re Dept of Econ," October 29, 1952, three-page typescript, 2, box 41, folder 1, Theodore Schultz Papers, Department of Economics Records, University of Chicago, Hanna Holborn Gray Special Collections Research Center.
26. Edith Kermit Roosevelt, "Men of Science: Dr. Milton Friedman, a Specialist on Theory of Earnings and Savings," February 22, 1959, *Newark Sunday News*, NP.
27. Gregory C. Chow, "Remembering Milton Friedman," in Robert A. Cord and J. Daniel Hammond, eds., *Milton Friedman: Contributions to Economics and Public Policy* (New York: Oxford University Press, 2016), 28–29.
28. See http://www.becker-posner-blog.com/2006/11/on-milton-friedmans-ideas—becker.html and http://www.latimes.com/local/obituaries/la-me-gary-becker-20140505-story.html. Friedman to Becker, May 24, 1954, box 20, folder 30, "Correspondence with Gary Becker, 1953–1983," Milton Friedman Papers.
29. Gary Becker, "Milton Friedman," in Edward Shils, ed., *Remembering the University of Chicago: Teachers, Scientists, and Scholars* (Chicago: University of Chicago Press, 1991), 145.
30. James Buchanan, *Better Than Plowing and Other Personal Essays* (Chicago: University of Chicago Press, 1991), 75.
31. See http://www.irwincollier.com/chicago-hms-pinafore-parody-for-milton-friedman/.
32. Emmett, "Sharpening Tools in the Workshop," 93–115.

33. Emmett, "Sharpening Tools in the Workshop," 110–11.
34. Friedman, *Studies in the Quantity Theory of Money*, 1.
35. Rodney D. Peterson and Ronnie J. Phillips, "In Memoriam: Lloyd W. Mints, 1888–1989: Pioneer Monetary Economist," *The American Economist* 35, no. 1 (March 1991): 79–81. Hansen quoted in Tavlas, *The Monetarists*, 294; Harry Johnson quoted in Tavlas, *The Monetarists*, 352.
36. Aaron Director, "Full Employment," June 20, 1956, 10. I believe this address was given to the Wabash College Volker Fund conference held on this date, not the Institute of Humane Studies as indicated on archival material. The transcribed speech is available at https://sites.google.com/site/georgetavlasresearch/book-manuscript.
37. My discussion of these changes is informed by the extended treatment in Tavlas, *The Monetarists*.
38. Friedman quoted in Tavlas, *The Monetarists*, 543.
39. Michael D. Bordo and Anna Schwartz, "Clark Warburton: Pioneer Monetarist," in Anna J. Schwartz, ed., *Money in Historical Perspective* (Chicago: University of Chicago Press, 1987), 234–54. Thomas F. Cargill suggests the pressure came from Treasury; Thomas F. Cargill, "A Tribute to Clark Warburton, 1896–1979," *Journal of Money, Credit and Banking* 13, no. 1 (February 1981): 89–93.
40. Friedman, *Studies in the Quantity Theory of Money*, 172, 25.
41. Friedman, *Studies in the Quantity Theory of Money*, 20–21.
42. Robert V. Roosa, *The Review of Economics and Statistics* 40, no. 1 (1958): 84–86. James Angell, *Journal of the American Statistical Association* 52, no. 280 (1957): 599–602.
43. Karl Brunner identified and defended "the Monetarist position," which then became known more generally by critics and supporters alike as monetarism. Karl Brunner, "The Role of Money and Monetary Policy," *Federal Reserve Bank of St. Louis Review* (July 1968): 9–24.
44. Michael Bordo, interview with author, February 21, 2018.
45. Schwartz to Friedman, February 5, 1954, box 90, folder 7, Milton Friedman Papers.
46. Friedman to Schwartz, February 10, 1954, box 90, folder 4, Milton Friedman Papers.
47. Schwartz to Friedman, October 31, 1951, and Friedman to Schwartz, October 5, 1951, box 90, folder 3, Milton Friedman Papers. The student was likely Eugene Lerner, who authored a chapter on the Confederacy in Friedman's *Studies in the Quantity Theory of Money*.
48. Schwartz to Cagan, February 23, 1956, box 91, folder 1, Milton Friedman Papers.
49. Friedman to Schwartz, April 5, 1956, box 91, folder 1, Milton Friedman Papers.
50. Friedman to Schwartz, July 14, 1957, box 91, folder 2, Milton Friedman Papers.
51. Schwartz to Friedman, February 19, 1958, box 91, folder 2, Milton Friedman Papers.
52. Friedman to Schwartz, February 26, 1958, box 91, folder 2, Milton Friedman Papers.
53. Friedman to Schwartz, October 30, 1958, box 91, folder 2, Milton Friedman Papers.
54. Schwartz to Friedman, April 9, 1959, box 91, folder 2, Milton Friedman Papers.
55. Milton Friedman, *A Theory of the Consumption Function* (Princeton, NJ: Princeton University Press, 1957), 3. For an extended treatment, see Jennifer Burns, "Hidden Figures: A New History of the Permanent Income Hypothesis," in *New Historical Perspectives on Women and Economics*, Cléo Chassonnery-Zaïgouche, Evelyn L. Forget, and John D. Singleton, eds., *History of Political Economy* 54 (2022): 43–68.
56. Friedman to Brady, May 4, 1948, box 21, folder 18, "Brady, Dorothy S.," Milton Friedman Papers.
57. Brady to Friedman, May 13, 1948, box 21, folder 18, "Brady, Dorothy S.," Milton Friedman Papers.
58. Margaret Reid, diary entry, July 19, box 53, folder 1, Margaret Reid Papers, University of Chicago, Hanna Holborn Gray Special Collections Research Center.
59. Friedman to Brady, November 8, 1948, box 21, folder 18, "Brady, Dorothy S.," Milton Friedman Papers.

60. Reid to Kathryn V. Burns, acting head, home economics department, January 19, 1949, box 1, folder 15, Margaret Reid Papers. Reid's contributions have received new attention in recent years; see Claudia Goldin, *Career and Family: Women's Century-Long Journey Towards Equity* (Princeton, NJ: Princeton University Press, 2021), 46–49, and a dedicated issue of the journal *Feminist Economics* 2, no. 3 (1996). Her early career is covered in this issue in Evelyn Forget, "Margaret Gilpin Reid: A Manitoba Home Economist Goes to Chicago," 1–16.
61. Milton Friedman and Rose D. Friedman, *Two Lucky People: Memoirs* (Chicago: University of Chicago Press, 1998), 164.
62. David Friedman, interview with author. Richard Easterlin, "In Memoriam: Dorothy Stahl Brady, 1903–1977," *The Journal of Economic History* 38, no. 1 (March 1978): 301–303.
63. Alvin Hansen, "The General Theory (2)," in Seymour E. Harris, ed., *The New Economics: Keynes' Influence on Theory and Public Policy* (New York: Alfred A. Knopf, 1943), 133–44.
64. Friedman, *A Theory of the Consumption Function*, 6. For a history of the concept that covers the contributions of Rose Friedman, Dorothy Brady, and Margaret Reid, see J. Allan Hynes, "The Emergence of the Neoclassical Consumption Function: The Formative Years, 1940–1952," *Journal of the History of Economic Thought* 20, no. 1 (1998): 25–49.
65. Margaret Reid, diary entry, July 19, box 53, folder 1, Margaret Reid Papers.
66. To T. W. Schultz from Margaret G. Reid and Dorothy S. Brady, memorandum, March 12, 1951, subject: proposed research project on the consumption and savings of families, page 4, box 21, folder 18, "Brady, Dorothy S.," Milton Friedman Papers. Friedman later rewrote this memo; the original that is quoted was written without his input.
67. Minutes, Meeting of the Department, May 23, 1951, box 41, folder 2, Theodore Schultz Papers, Department of Economics Records, University of Chicago, Hanna Holborn Gray Special Collections Research Center.
68. Minutes, Meeting of the Department, May 28, 1951, box 41, folder 2, Theodore Schultz Papers.
69. Friedman to Brady, June 14, 1951, box 21, folder 18, "Brady, Dorothy S.," Milton Friedman Papers.
70. Friedman to Brady, July 15, 1951, box 21, folder 18, "Brady, Dorothy S.," Milton Friedman Papers.
71. Brady to Friedman, July 17, 1951, box 232, folder 12, Writings, a Theory of the Consumption Function, 1951–1965, Milton Friedman Papers.
72. Friedman to Schultz, March 29, 1954, box 42, folder 10, Theodore Schultz Papers.
73. Reid to Friedman, February 7, 1954. The paper was S. J. Prais, "An Exegetical Note on Some Recent Work on Income Variations," eight-page typescript. Both in box 232, folder 13, Theory of the Consumption Function, 1951–1956, Milton Friedman Papers.
74. Franco Modigliani, "Life Cycle, Individual Thrift, and the Wealth of Nations," *American Economic Review* 76, no. 3 (June 1986): 297–313.
75. Friedman to Mack, August 31, 1954, box 109, folder 8, Notes, Drafts, Statistics C. 1954, Milton Friedman Papers.
76. Friedman to Reid, August 7, 1953, box 6, folder 1, Margaret Reid Papers.
77. Brady's name appeared as belonging to a "Red Front" in a report of the Dies Committee, likely the original source of the investigation. "Government Employees Listed by Dies as in Red Front," *New York Herald Tribune*, October 26, 1939, 8.
78. Schwartz to Friedman, January 19, 1954, box 90, folder 7, Milton Friedman Papers.
79. Friedman to Schwartz, February 1, 1954, box 90, folder 7, Milton Friedman Papers.
80. Tobin to Friedman, July 25, 1954, and Friedman to Tobin, July 24, 1955, box 109, folder 10, Consumption Statistics + Correspondence 1954–1956, Milton Friedman Papers.
81. Fabricant to Friedman, October 26, 1954, box 232, folder 12, Writings, a Theory of the Consumption Function, 1951–1956, Milton Friedman Papers.
82. Guy H. Orcutt, in transcript of "Conference on Consumption and Economic Development," Princeton University, October 21–22, 1955, in Eugene Lerner to Friedman, October 28, 1955, box 232, folder 13, Milton Friedman Papers.

83. Friedman, *A Theory of the Consumption Function*, ix. Reid's unpublished paper was presented at the 1953 AEA Annual Meeting. See "Papers and Proceedings," *American Economic Review* 44, no. 2 (May 1954): xi–xiv.
84. Friedman, *A Theory of the Consumption Function*, ix.
85. Friedman wrote most of *Income from Independent Professional Practice* (New York: NBER, 1945), which listed Kuznets as coauthor. The book served as Friedman's Columbia University doctoral dissertation.
86. Easterlin, "In Memoriam: Dorothy Stahl Brady, 1903–1977," 301–303.
87. James Tobin, transcript of "Conference on Consumption and Economic Development," Princeton University, October 21–22, 1955, 6, box 232, folder 12, Milton Friedman Papers.
88. Friedman, *A Theory of the Consumption Function*, 237, 235.
89. Brady to Friedman, Friday, ND, two-page handwritten letter, box 21, folder 18, Milton Friedman Papers.
90. Friedman, *A Theory of the Consumption Function*, 237.
91. David Friedman, interview with author.
92. Janet Martel, interview with author.
93. David Friedman and Janet Martel, interviews with author. Jonathan Peterson, "The Captain of Capitalism," *Los Angeles Times*, December 14, 1986, AD12. Edward Nelson, "An Interview with Anna J. Schwartz," *Macroeconomic Dynamics* 8, no. 3 (June 2004): 405.
94. Jerry Porter, Friedman's nephew, interview with author, 2014.
95. Janet Martel, interview with author; David Friedman, interview with author.
96. Friedman and Friedman, *Two Lucky People*, 157.
97. The Friedmans recounted a sanitized version of this incident in *Two Lucky People*, 266–68. Numerous sources, including Janet Martel, corroborate the assault described here.
98. U.S. Congress, Joint Economic Committee, "Hearings on Employment, Growth, and Price Levels Pursuant to S. Con. Res.13, part 4: The Influence on Prices of Changes in the Effective Supply of Money," 86th Congress, 1st Session, May 25–28, 1959, 611.
99. Milton Friedman, *A Program for Monetary Stability* (New York: Fordham University Press, 1960).
100. U.S. Congress, Joint Economic Committee, "Hearings on Employment, Growth, and Price Levels Pursuant to S. Con. Res.13, part 4," 610–11.
101. U.S. Congress, Joint Economic Committee, "Hearings on Employment, Growth, and Price Levels Pursuant to S. Con. Res.13, part 9A," 86th Congress, 1st Session, October 30, 1959, 3042.
102. U.S. Congress, Joint Economic Committee, "Hearings on Employment, Growth, and Price Levels Pursuant to S. Con. Res.13, part 4," 624.
103. Henry Simons, "Rules Versus Authorities in Monetary Policy," *Journal of Political Economy* 44, no. 1 (February 1936): 3.
104. Aaron Director, "Full Employment," June 20, 1956, 4, transcript in author's possession.
105. Peterson and Phillips, "In Memoriam: Lloyd W. Mints, 1888–1989," 80. Director, "Full Employment,"12.
106. U.S. Congress, Joint Economic Committee, "Hearings on Employment, Growth, and Price Levels Pursuant to S. Con. Res.13, part 4," 612.

9. POLITICAL ECONOMIST

1. John F. Kennedy, "Acceptance of Democratic Nomination for President," July 15, 1960, available at https://www.jfklibrary.org/learn/about-jfk/historic-speeches/acceptance-of-democratic-nomination-for-president.
2. "Friedman Comments on Conservative's Liberalism," *The Chicago Maroon*, February 16, 1962, 31.

3. Milton Friedman, "How to Tell a Conservative from a Reactionary," address to the Conservative League, University of Chicago, October 30, 1958, box 216, folder 6, "Unpublished Talks and Lectures, 1957–1959," Milton Friedman Papers, Hoover Institution Library and Archives.
4. Warren Kornberg, "Sen. Clark Is Booed at C. of C. Debate," *The Washington Post*, May 4, 1961, A2.
5. "Chambers . . . For attacks on . . . ," *Philadelphia Daily News*, May 4, 1961, NP.
6. The third member was Kermit Gordon, a former Rhodes Scholar and Williams College professor. Tobin is quoted in "Council of Economic Advisers Oral History Interview, JFK #1," August 1, 1964, available at https://www.jfklibrary.org/archives.
7. James Tobin, *The New Economics One Decade Older* (Princeton, NJ: Princeton University Press, 1972), 7.
8. John F. Kennedy, "Commencement Address at Yale University," June 11, 1962, available at https://www.jfklibrary.org/archives.
9. *The Economic Report of the President, January 1962, Together with the Annual Report of the Council of Economic Advisers* (Washington, D.C.: U.S. Government Printing Office, 1962), 17.
10. *The Economic Report of the President, January 1962*, 48.
11. A. W. Phillips, "The Relation Between Unemployment and the Rate of Change of Money Wage Rates in the United Kingdom, 1861–1957," *Economica* 25, no. 100 (November 1958): 283–99. James Forder provides an extended discussion of the ways the Phillips curve has been misremembered in the history of economics in his *Macroeconomics and the Phillips Curve Myth* (Oxford: Oxford University Press, 2014).
12. Paul A. Samuelson and Robert M. Solow, "Analytic Aspects of Anti-inflation Policy," *American Economic Review* 50, no. 2 (May 1960): 177–94. Tobin, *The New Economics One Decade Older*, 17.
13. *The Economic Report of the President, January 1962*, 92.
14. *The Economic Report of the President, January 1962*, 189, 185.
15. Don J. Lenhausen, "Inflation, Not Bust Held Biggest Threat," *Sunday Journal Star*, January 29, 1956, NP.
16. Chesly Manly, "Inflation—An Appraisal," *Chicago Sunday Tribune*, January 11, 1959, NP.
17. *The Economic Report of the President, January 1962*, 69.
18. Director, Friedman, and Stigler to Buckley, November 14, 1961, box 22, folder 13, Milton Friedman Papers.
19. Buckley to Friedman, January 25, 1962, and Friedman to Buckley, February 13, 1962, box 22, folder 13, Milton Friedman Papers.
20. Paul F. Healy, "The Glittering Mr. Goldwater," *The Saturday Evening Post*, June 7, 1958, 38.
21. Barry Goldwater, *The Conscience of a Conservative* (Shepherdsville, KY: Victor Publishing, 1960), from the foreword.
22. Russell Baker, "Republican Old Guard Rallying to Goldwater as Its Last Hope," *The New York Times*, July 23, 1960, 8. Richard J. Whalen, "Here Come the Conservatives," *Fortune* (December 1963), 107.
23. Goldwater, *The Conscience of a Conservative*, 12.
24. Rick Perlstein, *Before the Storm: Barry Goldwater and the Unmaking of the American Consensus* (New York: Hill and Wang, 2001), 156.
25. Friedman to Goldwater, December 12, 1960, and Goldwater to Friedman, January 17, 1961, box 27, folder 23, Milton Friedman Papers. The debate over exchange restrictions eventually yielded the Interest Equalization Tax, passed in 1963 as part of a larger effort to remedy the U.S. balance of payments.
26. Milton and Rose Friedman, "Greetings from Jerusalem and Best Wishes for 1963 from the Friedmans," two-page typescript, box 38, folder 25, Fritz Machlup Papers, Hoover Institution Library and Archives. In their memoirs, the Friedmans referred to these annual letters as a "Christmas letter." Milton Friedman and Rose D. Friedman, *Two Lucky People: Memoirs* (Chicago: University of Chicago Press, 1998), 302.

27. "And Friedman Chose a Rose . . . ," *The Straits Times*, October 18, 1980, NP.
28. Friedman and Friedman, *Two Lucky People*, 331.
29. Milton Friedman with the assistance of Rose D. Friedman, *Capitalism and Freedom: Fortieth Anniversary Edition* (Chicago: University of Chicago Press, 1962; 2002), xv.
30. Friedman with Friedman, *Capitalism and Freedom*, xvi.
31. Friedman with Friedman, *Capitalism and Freedom*, 2.
32. Friedman with Friedman, *Capitalism and Freedom*, 35–36.
33. *The Economic Report of the President, January 1962*, 110.
34. "Economist Friedman Speaks at Collection: 'The Road to Hell,'" *Haverford News*, April 13, 1962, NP.
35. Lawrence Fertig, "Barry's Answer to Heller," *New York Post*, August 24, 1964, NP.
36. Friedman to Roger Shugg, March 12, 1964, box 232, folder 3, Milton Friedman Papers.
37. Jeannette P. Nichols, "Friedman and Schwartz, 'A Monetary History of the United States' (Book Review)," *The Journal of American History* 51, no. 1 (June 1, 1964): 102. Herman E. Krooss, "Monetary History and Monetary Policy: A Review Article," *The Journal of Finance* 19, no. 4 (1964).
38. Milton Friedman, *A Program for Monetary Stability* (New York: Fordham University Press, 1960).
39. Donald L. Kemmerer, review of *A Monetary History of the United States, 1867–1960*, by Milton Friedman and Anna Jacobson Schwartz, *The American Historical Review* 70, no. 1 (1964): 197.
40. Milton Friedman and Anna Schwartz, *A Monetary History of the United States, 1867–1960* (Princeton, NJ: Princeton University Press, 1963), 413, 412.
41. Harvey H. Segal, "Economic Scene: Some U.S. Monetary Blunders," *The Washington Post*, November 25, 1963, D11.
42. Schwartz to Friedman, December 3, 1963, box 91, folder 3, Milton Friedman Papers.
43. Friedman to Barger, January 7, 1964, box 20, folder 13, Correspondence with Harold Barger, Milton Friedman Papers.
44. James Tobin, "The Monetary Interpretation of History," *American Economic Review* 55, no. 3 (June 1965): 464–85.
45. "Theorizing for Goldwater?," *Business Week*, November 23, 1963, 108.
46. Segal, "Economic Scene," D11.
47. "Theorizing for Goldwater?," 108.
48. Goldwater to Friedman, July 13, 1962, box 27, folder 24, Milton Friedman Papers.
49. "Theorizing for Goldwater?," 106.
50. Friedman to Royster, December 6, 1963, box 32, folder 15, Milton Friedman Papers.
51. "Right Face," *Newsweek*, January 13, 1964, 73.
52. "Economist Cites Peril of Central Planning," *The Daily Northwestern*, February 18, 1964, NP. "U.C. Economic Experts Advise Goldwater," *The Chicago Tribune*, April 12, 1964, NP.
53. Robert E. Weintraub, "Some Neglected Monetary Contributions: Congressman Wright Patman (1893–1976)," *Journal of Money, Credit and Banking* 9, no. 4 (November 1977): 518.
54. Patman is described as a "rural populist" in "The Fed Remodels Itself," *Business Week*, May 16, 1964, 64–76, and as a "populist" in "The Money Supply," *The Washington Post*, June 8, 1964. The prevalence of Friedman's views is stated in "The Money Supply," A18.
55. Brunner and Meltzer's differences with Friedman are treated throughout Edward Nelson, *Milton Friedman and Economic Debate in the United States, 1932–1972*, vols. 1 and 2 (Chicago: University of Chicago Press, 2020), esp. vol. 2, 163–71.
56. Paul Hoffmeister, "The Fed, the Financial Crisis, and Monetary History: An Interview with Dr. Allan Meltzer," July 25, 2012, Forbes.com. Michael Bordo, "Karl Brunner and Allan Meltzer: From Monetary Policy to Monetary History to Monetary Rules," prepared for "Karl Brunner and Monetarism," a conference hosted by the Swiss National Bank, Zurich, Switzerland, October 29–30, 2018, 6.

57. "The Fed Remodels Itself," *Business Week*, May 16, 1964, 64–76.
58. Chalmers Roberts, "The Men Around the Big Men," *The Washington Post*, November 10, 1963, E1.
59. Frank C. Porter, "Blunt Views from a Barry Aide: Everybody May Talk About Free Enterprise, but Hardly Anyone Wants It, He Says," *The Washington Post*, September 11, 1964, A10.
60. Harvey Segal, "Economic Front: Back to a Beggar My Neighbor Policy?," *The Washington Post*, November 18, 1963, B6.
61. Milton Friedman, "The Role of Government in Education," in Robert A. Solo, ed., *Economics and the Public Interest* (New Brunswick, NJ: Rutgers University Press, 1955), 123–44. Friedman also likely encountered the idea of vouchers in John Stuart Mill's *On Liberty*, which he had read as a graduate student.
62. By one accounting, between 1954 and 1964 Southern states had passed an estimated 450 laws and resolutions "attempting to block, postpone, limit, or evade the desegregation of public schools, many of which expressly authorized the systematic transfer of public assets and monies to private schools." See https://www.southerneducation.org/publications/historyofprivateschools/. For a history of vouchers emphasizing the role of "liberal educational reform movements, the civil rights movement, and black nationalism," see James Forman Jr., "The Secret History of School Choice: How Progressives Got There First," *The Georgetown Law Journal* 93, no. 1287 (2005): 1287–319.
63. Friedman, "The Role of Government in Education," 131*n2*. Friedman's correspondence with the editor Robert Solo makes clear he understood the segregationist interest in his proposal; the footnote specifically responds to this issue. See Friedman to Solo, October 15, 1954, and Solo to Friedman, October 28, 1954, and related correspondence, box 33, folder 20, Robert Solo Correspondence, Milton Friedman Papers.
64. Friedman with Friedman, *Capitalism and Freedom*, 117.
65. For Friedman's influence on the University of Virginia professors James Buchanan and Warren Nutter, his former student, see Dan Kuehn, "Accommodation Within the Broad Structure of Voluntary Society: Buchanan and Nutter on School Segregation," available at https://papers.ssrn.com/sol3/papers.cfm?abstract_id=3308162.
66. Friedman with Friedman, *Capitalism and Freedom*, 117.
67. Along with Stigler, Friedman recommended Sowell for an Earhardt Fellowship, noting he was "a socialist although too smart to remain one." See Jason L. Riley, *Maverick: A Biography of Thomas Sowell* (New York: Basic Books, 2021), 34.
68. William F. Buckley, "Why the South Must Prevail," *National Review*, August 24, 1957, 148–49. George Stigler, "The Problem of the Negro," *New Guard* 5 (December 1965): 11–12. Friedman with Friedman, *Capitalism and Freedom*, 117.
69. Milton Friedman, undated, "To the Committee of the Council," five-page typescript plus exhibit, box 41, folder 1, Department of Economics Records, University of Chicago, Hanna Holborn Gray Special Collections. There is no record of how this controversy was resolved.
70. Friedman, undated, "To the Committee of the Council."
71. Scranton quoted in Geoffrey Kabaservice, *Rule and Ruin: The Downfall of Moderation and the Destruction of the Republican Party, from Eisenhower to the Tea Party* (New York: Oxford University Press, 2011), 107. Kabaservice covers in detail the moderate Republican position on civil rights, and its differences with the conservative approach.
72. Friedman with Friedman, *Capitalism and Freedom*, 110, 109. Gary Becker, *The Economics of Discrimination* (Chicago: University of Chicago Press, 1957). Recent research on consumer discrimination in the segregated South finds "limited firm responses to market conditions," concluding that "ending racial discrimination in public accommodations required federal intervention." See Lisa D. Cook, Maggie E. C. Jones, Trevon D. Logan, and David Rosé, "Competition and Discrimination in Public Accommodations: Evidence from the Green Books," Inclusive Growth Fall 2021 Research Conference, Federal Reserve Bank of Minneapolis, available at www.minneapolisfed.org.

73. Friedman with Friedman, *Capitalism and Freedom*, 110, 112.
74. For a fuller discussion of Friedman's views on Judaism and capitalism, see Jeff Lipkes, "'Capitalism and the Jews': Milton Friedman and His Critics," *History of Political Economy* 51, no. 2 (2019): 193–236; and Nicolas Vallois and Cléo Chassonnery-Zaïgouche, "'There Is Nothing Wrong About Being Money Grubbing!': Milton Friedman's Provocative 'Capitalism and the Jews' in Context (1972–1988)," *History of Political Economy* 53, no. 2 (April 2021): 313–45.
75. Friedman with Friedman, *Capitalism and Freedom*, 113.
76. The changing fate of American anti-Semitism after World War II is noted in Mark Silk, "Notes on the Judeo-Christian Tradition in America," *American Quarterly* 36, no. 1 (Spring 1984): 65–85.
77. Friedman with Friedman, *Capitalism and Freedom*, 188*n2*.
78. "GOP's Goldwater: Busting Out All Over," *Newsweek*, May 20, 1963, 29.
79. Perlstein, *Before the Storm*, 222, 337.
80. "Friedman Cautions Against Rights Bill," *The Harvard Crimson*, May 5, 1964, NP.
81. "U.C. Economic Experts Advise Goldwater," *Chicago Tribune*, April 12, 1964, NP.
82. Sen. Goldwater (AZ), "Civil Rights," *Congressional Record* 110, Pt. 11 (June 18, 1964), 14319.
83. "How Whites Feel About Negroes: A Painful American Dilemma," *Newsweek*, October 21, 1963, 62, 17.
84. Perlstein, *Before the Storm*, especially chapter 19.
85. T. George Harris, "Rampant Right Invades the GOP," *Look*, July 16, 1963, 19–24. See also Kabaservice, *Rule and Ruin*.
86. The group also included Baroody's right-hand man W. Glenn Campbell, the Chicago Graduate School of Business professor Yale Brozen, and Karl Brandt from Stanford's Food Research Institute.
87. "Goldwater's Economists: The Senator and His Staff Want to Get Educated," *Newsweek*, August 31, 1964, 62–64.
88. "Goldwater's Economists," 62–64.
89. Friedman and Friedman, *Two Lucky People*, 270.
90. Milton Friedman, "The Goldwater View of Economics," *The New York Times Magazine*, October 11, 1964, 35, 113–37.
91. James Reston, "What Goldwater Lost," *The New York Times*, November 4, 1964, 23.
92. Richard H. Rovere, "The Conservative Mindlessness," *Commentary* 39, no. 3 (March 1965), 39.
93. Perlstein, *Before the Storm*, xv.
94. John Chamberlain, "Goldwater Economist," King Features syndicate, 1963. Herbert Stein, "New York, Chicago, Main Street . . . Three Conservative Brands of Economics," *The Washington Post*, November 29, 1964, NP.

10. THE PHILLIPS CURVE

1. A third economist, Henry Wallich, was also in the rotation. "The 'Academic Scribblers': Economists Achieve Greater Status but Statutory Theme Still Eludes Them," *The National Observer*, August 15, 1966, 22.
2. Daniel Patrick Moynihan, *The Politics of a Guaranteed Income: The Nixon Administration and the Family Assistance Plan* (New York: Random House, 1973), 51. For a recent exploration of this theme, see Gary Gerstle, *The Rise and Fall of the Neoliberal Order* (New York: Oxford University Press, 2022), esp. 98–104.
3. James Tobin, *The New Economics One Decade Older* (Princeton, NJ: Princeton University Press, 1972), 5.
4. Elizabeth Popp Berman, *Thinking Like an Economist: How Efficiency Replaced Equality in U.S. Public Policy* (Princeton, NJ: Princeton University Press, 2022). Berman focuses primarily on the 1970s, but notes "it was in the 1960s that the economic style really began to spread." She emphasizes the role of center-left technocrats. See also Binyamin

Appelbaum, *The Economists' Hour: False Prophets, Free Markets, and the Fracture of Society* (New York: Little, Brown, 2019).

5. James Tobin, "On Improving the Economic Status of the Negro," *Daedalus* 94, no. 4 (Fall 1965): 891.
6. "New Subsidy Plan for the Poor," *Chicago Tribune*, December 16, 1965.
7. Milton Friedman, "A Plan for Guaranteeing a Minimum Income to All," undated one-page typescript fragment, box 37, folder 8, Objective Standard of Living, Milton Friedman Papers, Hoover Institution Library and Archives. The paper is filed with correspondence indicating a likely date of 1939.
8. Friedman, "A Plan for Guaranteeing a Minimum Income to All."
9. Milton Friedman, "An Objective Method of Determining a 'Minimum Standard of Living,'" undated seven-page typescript, box 37, folder 8, Objective Standard of Living, Milton Friedman Papers.
10. George Stigler, "The Economics of Minimum Wage Legislation," *American Economic Review* 36, no. 3 (June 1946): 358–65.
11. Milton Friedman with the assistance of Rose D. Friedman, *Capitalism and Freedom: Fortieth Anniversary Edition* (Chicago: University of Chicago Press, 1962; 2002), 192.
12. Transcript available at https://millercenter.org/the-presidency/presidential-speeches/january-4–1965-state-union.
13. Walter Lippmann, "Principle of the Great Society," *Newsweek*, January 18, 1965, 13.
14. *The Report of the White House Conference "To Fulfill These Rights"* (Washington, D.C.: U.S. Government Printing Office, 1966), 37.
15. Alice O'Connor, *Poverty Knowledge: Social Science, Social Policy, and the Poor in Twentieth-Century U.S. History* (Princeton, NJ: Princeton University Press, 2001).
16. Michael Harrington, *The Other America: Poverty in the United States* (New York: Macmillan, 1962).
17. Steven B. Wolinetz, "Friedman, Harrington, and Poverty," *The Cornell Daily Sun*, December 16, 1964.
18. Austin C. Wehrwein, "'Upside Down' Income Tax Helps the Poor," *Decatur Sunday Herald and Review*, ND, NP. Moynihan, *The Politics of a Guaranteed Annual Income*, 67. Similarly, Brian Steensland, *The Failed Welfare Revolution: America's Struggle over Guaranteed Income Policy* (Princeton, NJ: Princeton University Press, 2008), points out it was not until the 1970s that the Republican Party and conservative movement developed a parallel policy apparatus to address poverty.
19. Richard L. Strout, "Negative Income Tax Argued," *The Christian Science Monitor*, December 12, 1966, NP.
20. Jenkin Lloyd Jones, "Three Economists Are Advocates of Paying Men for Doing Nothing," *El Sereno Star*, December 29, 1966, NP.
21. Steensland, *The Failed Welfare Revolution*, 36. Daniel Zamora, "Basic Income in the United States, 1940–1973: How the 'Fiscal Revolution' Reshaped Social Policy," in Peter Sloman, Daniel Zamora Vargas, and Pedro Ramos Pinto, eds., *Universal Basic Income in Historical Perspective* (New York: Palgrave Macmillan, 2021), 44. Relatedly, Melinda Cooper characterizes the mid-1960s as a unique moment giving rise to a "vision of social welfare that sought to completely transcend the poor-law tradition of private family responsibility." Melinda Cooper, *Family Values: Between Neoliberalism and the New Social Conservatism* (New York: Zone Books, 2017), 99. See also Daniel Zamora Vargas, "'Welfare Without the Welfare State': Milton Friedman's Negative Income Tax and the Monetization of Poverty," *Modern Intellectual History* (2022): 1–27.
22. Herbert Stein, "New York, Chicago, Main Street . . . Three Conservative Brands of Economics," *The Washington Post*, November 29, 1964, NP.
23. Friedman with Friedman, *Capitalism and Freedom*, 191–92.
24. Strout, "Negative Income Tax Argued."
25. Frank C. Porter, "Incentive Unresolved and Income Debate," *The Washington Post*, December 10, 1966, NP.

26. Friedman with Friedman, *Capitalism and Freedom*, 192.
27. It also anticipated contemporary discussions of resilience and the cognitive load of poverty. For example, see Anandi Mani, Sendhil Mullainathan, Eldar Shafir, and Jiaying Zhao, "Poverty Impedes Cognitive Function," *Science* 341, no. 6149 (August 30, 2013): 976–80.
28. Austin C. Wehrwein, "Economist Says Negative Tax Should Replace All Poverty Aid," *The New York Times*, December 19, 1965.
29. Jones, "Three Economists Are Advocates of Paying Men for Doing Nothing." Strout, "Negative Income Tax Argued."
30. "The Public Trough," *Sunday Star*, December 11, 1966.
31. Milton Friedman and Yale Brozen, *The Minimum Wage: Who Pays?* (Washington, D.C.: Free Society Association, 1966), 11.
32. Rose D. Friedman, *Poverty: Definition and Perspective* (Washington, D.C.: American Enterprise Institute for Public Policy Research, 1965), 17, 38.
33. Michael Bordo, interview with author, February 21, 2018. Janet Martel, interview with author.
34. Edward Nelson, *Milton Friedman and Economic Debate in the United States, 1932–1972*, vol. 2 (Chicago: University of Chicago Press, 2021), 77–78.
35. Milton Friedman, *Price Theory: A Provisional Text* (Chicago: Aldine Publishing, 1962).
36. D. E. Moggridge, *Harry Johnson: A Life in Economics* (Cambridge: Cambridge University Press, 2008), 123.
37. "Money Values—A Tangled Web," *New York Herald Tribune*, January 10, 1965, NP.
38. "Money Values—A Tangled Web." Friedman first elaborated the idea in "The Case for Flexible Exchange Rates," in *Essays in Positive Economics* (Chicago: University of Chicago Press, 1953).
39. Harvey Segal, "Economic Front: Back to a Beggar My Neighbor Policy?," *The Washington Post*, November 18, 1963, B6.
40. One example of a policy patch is the Gold Pool, an international syndicate to stabilize the price of gold. M. Bordo, E. Monnet, and A. Naef, "The Gold Pool (1961–1968) and the Fall of the Bretton Woods System: Lessons for Central Bank Cooperation," *The Journal of Economic History* 79, no. 4 (2019): 1027–1059. The potential challenge to maintaining Bretton Woods was noted by Robert Triffin, *Gold and the Dollar Crisis* (New Haven, CT: Yale University Press, 1960). Triffin's proposed solution, which gave more responsibility to the IMF, was the opposite of Friedman's.
41. Moggridge, *Harry Johnson*, 347.
42. The incident is covered in Moggridge, *Harry Johnson*, 204.
43. Harry Johnson, "A Keynesian's Impression of Chicago," October 28, 1960, excerpted in Moggridge, *Harry Johnson*, 205–206.
44. Arjun Jayadev, "Interview with Deirdre McCloskey, May 16, 2017," interview transcript, 4, available at https://www.ineteconomics.org/uploads/transcripts/McCloskey-Interview-Transcript.pdf.
45. Details on Tobin's background are available at https://www.nobelprize.org/prizes/economic-sciences/1981/tobin/biographical/ and https://www.tobinproject.org/about/james-tobin#_ftn7.
46. Tobin, *The New Economics One Decade Older*, 5.
47. Robert Hall, paraphrased in Nelson, *Milton Friedman and Economic Debate in the United States, 1932–1972*, vol. 2, 99.
48. Jonathan Peterson, "The Captain of Capitalism," *Los Angeles Times*, December 14, 1986, 14, AD12.
49. George P. Shultz and Robert Z. Aliber, *Guidelines, Informal Controls, and the Market Place: Policy Choices in a Full Employment Economy* (Chicago: University of Chicago Press, 1966), 63. Solow's regret over this remark is recorded in Nelson, *Milton Friedman and Economic Debate in the United States, 1932–1972*, vol. 2, 84.

50. Milton Friedman, "Statement, Testimony, and Comments," in U.S. Congress, Committee on Banking and Currency, Hearings on the Federal Reserve System After Fifty Years, Before the Subcommittee on Domestic Finance, Part 2, House of Representatives, 88th Congress, 2nd Session, March 3, 1964, 1133–78.
51. Friedman, "Statement, Testimony, and Comments," 1220–22. For a history of aggregates, see Richard G. Anderson and Kenneth A. Kavajecz, "A Historical Perspective on the Federal Reserve's Monetary Aggregates: Definition, Construction and Targeting," *Federal Reserve Bank of St. Louis Review* (March–April 1994), available at https://files.stlouisfed.org/files/htdocs/publications/review/94/03/9403rg.pdf.
52. Milton Friedman and David Meiselman, "The Relative Stability of Monetary Velocity and the Investment Multiplier in the United States, 1897–1958," in *Stabilization Policies: A Series of Research Studies Prepared for the Commission on Money and Credit* (Englewood Cliffs, NJ: Prentice Hall, 1963), 166. For a thorough technical account of the conflict, from which my account draws, see Nelson, *Milton Friedman and Economic Debate in the United States, 1932–1972*, vol. 2, 90–95.
53. Friedman and Meiselman, "The Relative Stability of Monetary Velocity and the Investment Multiplier in the United States, 1897–1958," 188.
54. Friedman and Meiselman, "The Relative Stability of Monetary Velocity and the Investment Multiplier in the United States, 1897–1958," 166, 169, 187.
55. Milton Friedman and Walter Heller, *Monetary vs. Fiscal Policy: A Dialogue* (New York: W. W. Norton, 1969), 27.
56. Robert J. Sales, "Nobel Laureate Franco Modigliani Dies at 85," *MIT News*, September 25, 2003, available at https://news.mit.edu/2003/modigliani.
57. Albert Ando and Franco Modigliani, "The Relative Stability of Monetary Velocity and the Investment Multiplier," *American Economic Review* 55, no. 4 (September 1965): 693, 707. The issue also featured a critique by Michael DePrano and Thomas Mayer, a thirty-four-page rejoinder to both by Friedman and Meiselman, and further separate responses to the rejoinder by Ando and Modigliani and DePrano and Mayer. Separately, in 1964 Donald Hester published a critique in *The Review of Economics and Statistics*, which also published a reply from Friedman and Meiselman.
58. Ando and Modigliani, "The Relative Stability of Monetary Velocity and the Investment Multiplier," 715, 716.
59. Friedman-Meiselman was eventually superseded by other scholars, but debate about its findings stretched over twenty-six separate papers, even birthing a second-generation St. Louis model. Peter V. Bias, "A Chronological Survey of the Friedman-Meiselman/Andersen-Jordan Single Equation Debate," *Research in Business and Economics Journal* 10 (October 2014): 1–21.
60. David Meiselman, "Discussion: How Feasible Is a Flexible Monetary Policy?," in Richard T. Selden, ed., *Capitalism and Freedom—Problems and Prospects: Proceedings of a Conference in Honor of Milton Friedman* (Charlottesville: University of Virginia Press, 1975), 294–302.
61. The 1967 address, published as a paper in 1968, has developed its own mini-literature. For overviews, see Robert J. Gordon, "Friedman and Phelps on the Phillips Curve: Viewed from a Half Century's Perspective," *Review of Keynesian Economics* 6, no. 4 (Winter 2018): 425–36; Robert E. Hall and Thomas J. Sargent, "Short-Run and Long-Run Effects of Milton Friedman's Presidential Address," *Journal of Economic Perspectives* 32, no. 1 (Winter 2018): 121–34; N. Gregory Mankiw and Ricardo Reis, "Friedman's Presidential Address in the Evolution of Macroeconomic Thought," available at https://scholar.harvard.edu/files/mankiw/files/friedmans_pres_address.pdf; and Beatrice Cherrier and Aurelien Goutsmedt, "The Making and Dissemination of Milton Friedman's 1967 AEA Presidential Address," November 27, 2017, available at https://beatricecherrier.wordpress.com/2017/11/27/the-friedman-legacy-on-the-making-and-dissemination-of-milton-friedman-1967-aea-presidential-address/. For a contrarian view on its importance, see James Forder, "What Was the Message of Friedman's Presi-

dential Address to the American Economic Association?," December 12, 2016, SSRN, available at https://papers.ssrn.com/sol3/papers.cfm?abstract_id=2884116.

62. Quotes are from the published version of the address: Milton Friedman, "The Role of Monetary Policy," *American Economic Review* 58, no. 1 (March 1968): 17, 15.
63. Friedman, "The Role of Monetary Policy," 1.
64. The term "stagflation" was coined by Iain Macleod in 1965, as discussed in Edward Nelson and Kalin Nikolov, "Monetary Policy and Stagflation in the UK," Bank of England Working Paper, 2002, available at www.bankofengland.co.uk/wp/index/html. Friedman, "Inflationary Recession," *Newsweek*, October 17, 1966, reprinted in Milton Friedman, *There's No Such Thing as a Free Lunch* (LaSalle, IN: Open Court, 1975), 61.
65. Friedman, "The Role of Monetary Policy," 10.
66. Friedman, "The Role of Monetary Policy," 11.
67. Friedman, "The Role of Monetary Policy," 9, 17.
68. Friedman, "The Role of Monetary Policy," 12.
69. Friedman, "The Role of Monetary Policy," 8.
70. Paul A. Samuelson and Robert M. Solow, "Analytic Aspects of Anti-inflation Policy," *American Economic Review* 50, no. 2 (May 1960), 192, 185. The authors noted wartime and Depression-era exceptions to the general pattern; see 188–89. James Forder provides an extended discussion of the ways the Phillips curve has been misremembered in the history of economics in his *Macroeconomics and the Phillips Curve Myth* (Oxford: Oxford University Press, 2014).
71. Phelps's first article was published in a British journal; Friedman did not cite it in the published version of his address. Edmund S. Phelps, "PCs, Expectations of Inflation, and Optimal Unemployment over Time," *Economica* 34 (August 1967): 254–81. Edmund S. Phelps, "Money-Wage Dynamics and Labor-Market Equilibrium," *Journal of Political Economy* 76 (July–August 1968): 678–711.
72. See, for example, "Inflation: Its Causes, Consequences, and Control," *A Symposium Held by the Department of Economics*, New York University, January 31, 1968, and Thomas J. Sargent, "A Note on the 'Accelerationist' Controversy, *Journal of Money, Credit and Banking* 3, no. 3 (August 1971): 721–25.
73. Friedman, "Inflationary Recession," in *There's No Such Thing as a Free Lunch*, 62.
74. Samuelson and Solow, "Analytic Aspects of Anti-inflation Policy," 186.
75. Friedman, "The Role of Monetary Policy," 12.
76. Kabaservice notes that the passage of the Voting Rights Act changed the dynamics between moderate and conservative Republicans, largely because the "civil rights acts freed conservatives from the need to defend the most morally objectionable and politically radioactive aspect of their philosophy." Geoffrey Kabaservice, *Rule and Ruin: The Downfall of Moderation and the Destruction of the Republican Party, from Eisenhower to the Tea Party* (New York: Oxford University Press, 2011), 152. For its similar impact on the Christian right, see Dan Williams, *God's Own Party: The Making of the Christian Right* (New York: Oxford University Press, 2010), 86–87.
77. Moynihan, *The Politics of A Guaranteed Income*, 52.
78. Irving Bernstein, *Guns or Butter: The Presidency of Lyndon Johnson* (New York: Oxford University Press, 1996), 360, 364. Deborah Shapley, *Promise and Power: The Life and Times of Robert McNamara* (Boston: Little, Brown, 1993), 369–75.
79. Draft figures are from https://www.sss.gov/About/History-And-Records/Induction-Statistics.
80. Newton quoted in Stephen Shames and Bobby Seale, *Power to the People: The World of the Black Panthers* (New York: Harry N. Abrams, 2016), NP.
81. A detailed account of Friedman's involvement in the issue is in John Singleton, "Slaves or Mercenaries? Milton Friedman and the Institution of the All-Volunteer Military," in Robert A. Cord and J. Daniel Hammond, eds., *Milton Friedman: Contributions to Economics and Public Policy* (New York: Oxford University Press, 2016), 499–522.
82. Friedman with Friedman, *Capitalism and Freedom*, 36.

83. Jennifer Burns, *Goddess of the Market: Ayn Rand and the American Right* (New York: Oxford University Press, 2009), 229. The Young Americans for Freedom convention is covered in multiple accounts, including Gregory Schneider, *Cadres for Conservatism: Young Americans for Freedom and the Rise of the Contemporary Right* (New York: New York University Press, 1999).
84. David Friedman, *The Machinery of Freedom: Guide to a Radical Capitalism* (LaSalle, IN: Open Court, 1973).
85. Quoted in Sol Tax, ed., *The Draft: A Handbook of Facts and Alternatives* (Chicago: University of Chicago Press, 1967), 366.
86. Oi's role in the establishment of a volunteer military is detailed in Appelbaum, *The Economists' Hour*, 29–45.
87. Walter Oi, "Costs and Implications of an All-Volunteer Force," in Tax, *The Draft*, 247.
88. Unidentified speaker quoted in Tax, *The Draft*, 371.
89. A detailed history of the policy change is found in Bernard Rostker, *I Want You! The Evolution of the All-Volunteer Force* (Santa Monica, CA: RAND Corporation, 2006). In 1980, Jimmy Carter reinstated the Selective Service System, opening the door to the future possibility of a draft.
90. Differences between Friedman, Hayek, and Mises on conscription are discussed in Singleton, "Slaves or Mercenaries?," 502–503.
91. Rostker, *I Want You!*, iii.
92. Milton Friedman, "A Volunteer Army," *Newsweek*, December 19, 1966, 100. Milton Friedman, "The Case for Abolishing the Draft—and Substituting for It an All-Volunteer Army," *The New York Times Magazine*, May 14, 1967, 114–19. Milton Friedman, "The Draft," *Newsweek*, March 11, 1968, 82. Singleton, "Slaves or Mercenaries?," 510. R. T. Stafford et al., eds., *How to End the Draft: The Case for an All-Volunteer Army* (Washington, D.C.: National Press, 1967).
93. Wallace's career is covered in Dan T. Carter, *The Politics of Rage: George Wallace, the Origins of the New Conservatism, and the Transformation of American Politics* (Baton Rouge: Louisiana State University Press, 1995).
94. Nixon is popularly characterized as following a "Southern Strategy" in the 1968 election that sought to bring segregationist voters into the GOP. Several generations of scholarship have challenged this premise. For the importance of the suburbs and the upper South and border states, see Matthew Lassiter, *The Silent Majority: Suburban Politics in the Sunbelt South* (Princeton, NJ: Princeton University Press, 2007). For emphasis on religion, see Joe Crespino, *In Search of Another Country: Mississippi and the Conservative Counterrevolution* (Princeton, NJ: Princeton University Press, 2009), and Williams, *God's Own Party*. Angie Maxwell and Todd Shields shift the timeline away from the 1960s and emphasize gender; see their *The Long Southern Strategy: How Chasing White Voters in the South Changed American Politics* (New York: Oxford University Press, 2019). Gerard Alexander emphasizes the three-candidate dynamics of the 1968 race, arguing that Nixon worked to assemble a complex national coalition in which Southern voters were not the essential voting bloc. *Race and the Republicans*, forthcoming, chapter 4.
95. Michael W. Flamm, *Law and Order: Street Crime, Civil Unrest, and the Crisis of Liberalism in the 1960s* (New York: Columbia University Press, 2005).
96. Milton Friedman and Rose D. Friedman, *Two Lucky People: Memoirs* (Chicago: University of Chicago Press, 1998), 387.
97. Shultz and Aliber, *Guidelines, Informal Controls, and the Market Place*, 27.
98. Martin did eventually succeed in raising real interest rates; Meltzer documents his significant delay as he sought consensus on the board and attempted to maintain policy coordination with the administration. Allan H. Meltzer, *A History of the Federal Reserve, Volume 2, Book 1, 1951–1969* (Chicago: University of Chicago Press, 2009), esp. chapter 3.

99. The 1968 tax surcharge is further discussed in Nelson, *Milton Friedman and Economic Debate in the United States 1932–1972*, vol. 2, 119–22.
100. Bernstein, *Guns and Butter*, 369, 358.

11. THE INFLATIONARY FED

1. "The Rising Risk of Inflation," *Time*, December 19, 1969, 66–72.
2. "The Rising Risk of Inflation," *Time*, December 19, 1969, 66–72.
3. The Burns memo, "Investing in Human Dignity," laid out his alternative vision. Quoted in Daniel Patrick Moynihan, *The Politics of a Guaranteed Income: The Nixon Administration and the Family Assistance Plan* (New York: Random House, 1973), 181. A comprehensive history of the FAP in its various guises, from which my account draws, is in Brian Steensland, *The Failed Welfare Revolution: America's Struggle over Guaranteed Income Policy* (Princeton, NJ: Princeton University Press, 2008).
4. Daniel Geary, *Beyond Civil Rights: The Moynihan Report and Its Legacy* (Philadelphia: University of Pennsylvania Press, 2017), highlights the many ways the report was interpreted in the decades after its 1965 release.
5. Moynihan, *The Politics of a Guaranteed Income*, 50.
6. The name of the Family Assistance Plan was not devised until later in the political process, but I use it here as shorthand for the swiftly evolving set of proposals that circulated during this time.
7. Arthur Burns, *Inside the Nixon Administration: The Secret Diary of Arthur Burns, 1969–1974*, ed. Robert H. Ferrell (Lawrence: University of Kansas Press, 2010), 22.
8. This is Moynihan's summary of the infamous Speenhamland memo, which largely excerpted Karl Polanyi's *The Great Transformation* and marked a turning point in the history of the FAP. Moynihan, *The Politics of a Guaranteed Income*, 179–80. Steensland, *The Failed Welfare Revolution*, 93–94.
9. Steensland characterizes the Shultz plan as the "laissez-faire paradigm" in *The Failed Welfare Revolution*, 107–108.
10. The Burns memo is quoted in Steensland, *The Failed Welfare Revolution*, 110.
11. Milton Friedman, "Welfare: Back to the Drawing Board," *Newsweek*, May 18, 1970, 89.
12. In *The Failed Welfare Revolution*, Steensland emphasizes the "symbolic pollution" of welfare that Burns attached to the FAP.
13. Lyndon Baines Johnson, "Government and the Critical Intelligence," an Address Marking the Fiftieth Anniversary of the Brookings Institution, September 29, 1966 (Washington, D.C.: Brookings Institution, 1966), 12, available at https://www.brookings.edu/wp-content/uploads/2016/07/critical_intelligence_lbj.pdf. There were four Phillips curve papers published in the series over two years, along with other papers on different topics.
14. An extended history of the *Journal of Political Economy* debate is in Edward Nelson, *Milton Friedman and Economic Debate, 1932–1972*, vol. 2 (Chicago: University of Chicago Press, 2021), 198–210. See also Michael D. Bordo and Anna J. Schwartz, "IS-LM and Monetarism," NBER Working Paper 9713 (May 2003), available at http://www.nber.org/papers/w9713.
15. James Tobin, "Money and Income: Post Hoc Ergo Propter Hoc?," *The Quarterly Journal of Economics* 84, no. 2 (May 1970): 301–17. James Tobin, "Tobin Attacks Friedman's Theories of Money Supply," *The Washington Post*, April 16, 1967, G1. Robert Solow, "Recent Controversies in the Theory of Inflation," in Stephen Rousseas, ed., *Proceedings of a Symposium on Inflation* (Princeton, NJ: Princeton University Press, 1968).
16. Alan Blinder quoted in Nelson, *Milton Friedman and Economic Debate in the United States, 1932–1972*, vol. 2, 211.
17. Robert J. Gordon, "Inflation in Recession and Recovery," *Brookings Papers on Economic Activity*, no. 1 (1971).
18. D. E. Moggridge, *Harry Johnson: A Life in Economics* (Cambridge: Cambridge University Press, 2008), 339–40.

19. Harry G. Johnson, "The Keynesian Revolution and the Monetarist Counter-Revolution," *American Economic Review* 61, no. 2 (1971): 1–14.
20. Unemployment rate from https://www.bls.gov/cps/prev_yrs.htm.
21. Robert J. Gordon, "The History of the Phillips Curve: Consensus and Bifurcation," *Economica* 78, no. 309 (January 2011): 16. Also important were interventions by Thomas Sargent.
22. Milton Friedman, "The Role of Monetary Policy," *American Economic Review* 58, no. 1 (March 1968): 11.
23. Robert J. Gordon, "Wage-Price Controls and the Shifting Phillips Curve," *Brookings Papers on Economic Activity*, no. 2 (1972): 387, 415.
24. Gordon, "The History of the Phillips Curve," 13.
25. Gordon, "Wage-Price Controls and the Shifting Phillips Curve," 386.
26. "Transcripts and other historical materials" available at https://www.federalreserve.gov/monetarypolicy/fomc_historical.htm.
27. Martin's original phrase was "independent within the structure of the Government," in "Statement Before the Committee on Finance, United States Senate," August 13, 1957, available at https://fraser.stlouisfed.org/title/statements-speeches-william-mcchesney-martin-jr-448/statement-committee-finance-united-states-senate-7821.
28. Milton Viorst, "Friedmanism, n., Doctrine of Most Audacious U.S. Economist: esp., Theory 'Only Money Matters,'" *The New York Times Magazine*, January 25, 1970, 22–84.
29. The third measure, M3, also included deposits in noncommercial banks.
30. Friedman to Burns, March 17, 1970, box 138, folder 8, Milton Friedman Papers, Hoover Institution Library and Archives.
31. H. Erich Heinemann, "Burns's Incomes Policy: Reserve Chairman Uses Prestige to Take His Argument to the Public," *The New York Times*, May 20, 1970.
32. Friedman to Burns, May 18, 1970, box 138, folder 8, Milton Friedman Papers.
33. Friedman to Burns, May 18, 1970, box 138, folder 8, Milton Friedman Papers.
34. Friedman to Burns, May 18, 1970, box 138, folder 8, Milton Friedman Papers.
35. Friedman to Burns, undated letter, "Sunday" est. 1963, box 2, Arthur F. Burns Papers, Duke University, Economist Papers Project.
36. Friedman to Burns, undated letter, est. May 22, 1970, box 138, folder 8, Milton Friedman Papers.
37. Friedman to Burns, May 24, 1970, note attached, "Burns on Incomes Policy," box 138, folder 8, Milton Friedman Papers.
38. Friedman to Burns, May 29, 1970, box 138, folder 8, Milton Friedman Papers.
39. Friedman to Burns, May 29, 1970, box 138, folder 8, Milton Friedman Papers.
40. Leonard Silk, "Nixon's Gradualism Path," *The New York Times*, September 16, 1970, 63.
41. "Burns on Burns," *The Wall Street Journal*, May 20, 1970, 18.
42. Friedman to Burns, undated postscript, est. May 22, 1970, box 138, folder 8, Milton Friedman Papers.
43. Allen Matusow, *Nixon's Economy: Booms, Busts, Dollars, and Votes* (Lawrence: University Press of Kansas, 1998), 70.
44. Friedman to Burns, October 13, 1970, box 138, folder 8, Milton Friedman Papers.
45. "Problems and Principles: George P. Shultz and the Uses of Economic Thinking," interviews conducted by Paul Burnett in 2015, Oral History Center of the Bancroft Library, University of California, Berkeley, 2016, 21, 22, 26. Henceforth cited as Shultz Oral History.
46. *Newsweek*, August 18, 1969, 19.
47. Shultz Oral History, 50. Shultz served on the Cabinet Committee on School Desegregation and helped revive federal affirmative action. J. Larry Hood, "The Nixon Administration and the Revised Philadelphia Plan for Affirmative Action: A Study in Expanding

Presidential Power and Divided Government," *Presidential Studies Quarterly* 23, no. 1 (1993): 145–67.

48. Shultz Oral History, 87.
49. Friedman to Shultz, cc'd to Burns and McCracken, October 23, 1970, box 33, folder 15, Milton Friedman Papers.
50. Juan Acosta and Beatrice Cherrier, "The Transformation of Economic Analysis at the Federal Reserve During the 1960s" (October 1, 2018), 25, 26, available at SSRN, http://dx.doi.org/10.2139/ssrn.3258049.
51. Matusow, *Nixon's Economy*, 61–62, 88.
52. Friedman to Shultz, cc'd to Burns and McCracken, February 9, 1971, box 33, folder 15, Milton Friedman papers.
53. Burns to Friedman, April 29, 1971, box 139, folder 9, Milton Friedman Papers.
54. Burns to Nixon, June 22, 1971, reprinted as Appendix B in George P. Shultz and John Taylor, *Choose Economic Freedom: Enduring Policy Lessons from the 1970s and 1980s* (Stanford, CA: Hoover Institution Press, 2020), 73.
55. "Prescription for Economic Policy: 'Steady as You Go,'" address of George P. Shultz, the director of Office of Management and Budget, before the Economic Club of Chicago, April 22, 1971, Chicago, Illinois, Press Release, April 22, 1971, box 33, folder 15, Milton Friedman Papers. Shultz Oral History, 85.
56. Matusow, *Nixon's Economy*, 107.
57. Paul A. Volcker and Toyoo Gyohten, *Changing Fortunes: The World's Money and the Threat to American Leadership* (New York: Times Books, 1992), 76.
58. Described in William Safire, *Before the Fall: An Inside View of the Pre-Watergate White House* (New York: Routledge, 2005), 515.
59. Milton Friedman, "Why the Freeze Is a Mistake," *Newsweek*, August 30, 1971, reprinted in Milton Friedman, *There's No Such Thing as a Free Lunch* (LaSalle, IN: Open Court, 1975), 125–27.
60. Friedman's visit is recounted in Shultz Oral History, 87. His retort is in Milton Friedman and Rose D. Friedman, *Two Lucky People: Memoirs* (Chicago: University of Chicago Press, 1998), 387.
61. Milton Friedman, "A Proposal for Resolving the US Balance of Payments Problem: Confidential Memorandum to President-elect Richard Nixon," in Leo Melamed, ed., *The Merits of Flexible Exchange Rates: An Anthology* (Fairfax, VA: George Mason University Press, 1988), 429.
62. Friedman to Shultz, September 21, 1971, box 33, folder 15, Milton Friedman Papers.
63. Friedman to Connally, cc Shultz, September 30, 1971, box 33, folder 15, Milton Friedman Papers.
64. Friedman, "Keep the Dollar Free," *Newsweek*, December 20, 1971, reprinted in Friedman, *There's No Such Thing as a Free Lunch*, 178.
65. Friedman to Connally, cc Shultz, September 30, 1971, box 33, folder 15, Milton Friedman Papers.
66. With some disagreements about timing, scholars consider Bretton Woods to have ended between 1971 and 1973; see the essays in Naomi Lamoreaux and Ian Shapiro, eds., *The Bretton Woods Agreements: Together with Scholarly Commentaries and Essential Historical Documents* (New Haven, CT: Yale University Press, 1991).
67. Milton Friedman, "The Case for Flexible Exchange Rates," in *Essays in Positive Economics* (Chicago: University of Chicago Press, 1953), 187, 200.
68. Friedman to Shultz, November 5, 1971, box 33, folder 15, Milton Friedman Papers.
69. Burns, diary entry dated November 6, 1971, *Inside the Nixon Administration*, 59. Friedman to Burns, November 6, 1971, box 138, folder 8, Milton Friedman Papers.
70. Allan H. Meltzer, *A History of the Federal Reserve, Volume 2, Book 2, 1970–1986* (Chicago: University of Chicago Press, 2009), 790.
71. Friedman to Burns, December 13, 1971, box 138, folder 9, Milton Friedman Papers.

72. Sherman Maisel quoted in Meltzer, *A History of the Federal Reserve, Volume 2, Book 2, 1970–1986*, 794.
73. Meltzer also notes that Burns wanted to avoid direct controls on interest rates; if they were kept low, this was less likely to happen.
74. Burns, diary entry dated October 14, 1972, *Inside the Nixon Administration*, 80.
75. Thomas Byrne Edsell and Mary Edsell, *Chain Reaction: The Impact of Race, Rights, and Taxes on American Politics* (New York: W. W. Norton, 1992), 90–95, 298–99.
76. Burns, diary entry dated October 14, 1972, *Inside the Nixon Administration*, 80.
77. Volcker and Gyohten, *Changing Fortunes*, 90, 61.
78. Volcker and Gyohten, *Changing Fortunes*, 25.
79. Shultz's account is confirmed by Volcker, in Volcker and Gyohten, *Changing Fortunes*, 118.
80. Volcker and Gyohten, *Changing Fortunes*, 82.
81. Shultz Oral History, 98–99.
82. Volcker and Gyohten, *Changing Fortunes*, 120. Friedman's papers also contain an undated, unsigned alternative proposal that he critically marked up and sent back to Shultz.
83. Volcker and Gyohten, *Changing Fortunes*, 123.
84. Volcker and Gyohten, *Changing Fortunes*, 123. Oil price increases predated the 1973 embargo. There were also significant rises worldwide in food prices. For an analysis tying these factors together, see Robert Barsky and Lutz Killian, "Do We Really Know That Oil Caused the Great Inflation? A Monetary Alternative," in Ben S. Bernanke and Kenneth Rogoff, eds., *NBER Macroeconomics Annual 2001*, vol. 16 (Cambridge, MA: MIT Press, 2002), 137–60.
85. Barry Eichengreen, *Exorbitant Privilege: The Rise and Fall of the Dollar and the Future of the International Monetary System* (New York: Oxford University Press, 2011).
86. Bretton Woods Agreement, Article 4, Amendment 2, available at https://www.imf.org/external/np/pp/eng/2006/062806.pdf.
87. Jeffry Frieden, "The Political Economy of the Bretton Woods Agreements," in Lamoreaux and Shapiro, *The Bretton Woods Agreements*, 21–37.
88. Michael Bordo, interview with author, February 10, 2020.
89. Inflation is the annual change in CPI; according to the Federal Reserve, the CPI annual rate of change was 6.1 percent for 1973, and 11.1 percent for 1974.
90. Milton Friedman, "Interest Rates and Inflation," *Newsweek*, August 23, 1976, in Milton Friedman, *Bright Promises, Dismal Performance: An Economist's Protest*, ed. William R. Allen (New York: Harcourt, Brace, Jovanovich, 1982), 261.
91. Allan H. Meltzer, "The Shadow Open Market Committee: Origins and Operations," *Journal of Financial Services Research* 18 (December 2000): 119–28.
92. Allan Meltzer, "Anna Schwartz," *CSWEP News* (Fall 2013): 7.
93. Meltzer, "The Shadow Open Market Committee."
94. Lawrence Noonan to Friedman, July 16, 1973, box 138, folder 9, Milton Friedman Papers.
95. Friedman to Noonan, cc Arthur Burns, August 1, 1973, box 138, folder 9, Milton Friedman Papers.
96. Edwin L. Dale, "Humility at the Fed: Inflation Brakes Don't Work So Well Amid Banking and Commodity Changes," *The New York Times*, August 1, 1973, 51, 60.
97. Friedman, "The Inflationary Fed," *Newsweek*, August 27, 1973, reprinted in Friedman, *There's No Such Thing as a Free Lunch*, 84.
98. Friedman to Burns, circa early August 1973, handwritten letter dated April 8, 1973, stamped received by Federal Reserve System 8/13/1973, box 138, folder 9, Milton Friedman Papers.
99. Friedman to Burns, circa early August 1973, handwritten letter dated April 8, 1973, stamped received by Federal Reserve System 8/13/1973, box 138, folder 9, Milton Friedman Papers.

100. Lutz Killian, "Oil Price Shocks, Monetary Policy and Stagflation," in *Inflation in an Era of Relative Price Shocks* (Sydney: Reserve Bank of Australia, 2010), 61. Brad DeLong, "America's Peacetime Inflation: The 1970s," in Christina D. Romer and David H. Romer, *Reducing Inflation: Motivation and Strategy* (Chicago: University of Chicago Press, 1997), 259. Economists have generally concluded that while the oil shocks of 1973 and 1979 created at least temporary price bulges, they would not have caused sustained inflation or recession without an accommodative monetary policy. Ben Bernanke et al. find that monetary policy is the main influence on the depressing effects of oil price shocks. See Ben Bernanke, Mark Gertler, and Mark Watson, "Systematic Monetary Policy and the Effects of Oil Price Shocks," *Brookings Papers on Economic Activity* (1997): 1.
101. For an extended defense of Burns, see Wyatt C. Wells, *Economist in an Uncertain World: Arthur F. Burns and the Federal Reserve, 1970–78* (New York: Columbia University Press, 1994). Even Wells admits that "it is hard to deny in hindsight that monetary policy should have been tighter during Burns' tenure at the Federal Reserve"; Wells, 246.

12. SIX DAYS IN SANTIAGO

1. Documented in *The Shock Doctrine: The Rise of Disaster Capitalism* (Renegade Pictures, 2010).
2. R. C. Longworth, "Protests as 7 Yanks Take Nobel Prizes," *The Chicago Tribune*, December 11, 1976, n2.
3. Franco Modigliani, "The Monetarist Controversy: Or, Should We Forsake Stabilization Policies?," *Economic Review* (Spring Supplement 1977): 27.
4. Modigliani, "The Monetarist Controversy," 34.
5. Robert Hall, "Notes on the Current State of Empirical Macroeconomics," unpublished manuscript (1976), 1, available at https://rehall.people.stanford.edu/all-publications.
6. Arjo Klamer, *Conversations with Economists: New Classical Economists and Opponents Speak Out on the Current Controversy in Macroeconomics* (New York: Rowman and Littlefield, 1983), 1.
7. Thomas Sargent, "Notes on the 'Accelerationist Controversy,'" *Journal of Money, Credit and Banking* 3, no. 3 (August 1971): 721–25. Robert Lucas, "Expectations and the Neutrality of Money," *Journal of Economic Theory* 4, no. 2 (April 1972): 103–24. Good general introductions to rational expectations are Daniel T. Rodgers, *Age of Fracture* (Cambridge, MA: Harvard University Press, 2011), 64–67, and Michel De Vroey, *A History of Macroeconomics from Keynes to Lucas and Beyond* (Cambridge: Cambridge University Press, 2016).
8. Thomas Sargent and Neil Wallace, "Rational Expectations and the Theory of Economic Policy," *Journal of Monetary Economics* 2, no. 2 (April 1976): 169–83.
9. "High Hopes, High Prices," *Newsweek*, September 29, 1975, 68.
10. Hall, "Notes on the Current State of Empirical Macroeconomics," 1.
11. For a 1978 explanation and defense of rational expectations for a lay audience, see Clarence W. Nelson, "Rational Expectations: Fresh Ideas That Challenge Some Established Views of Policy Making," Federal Reserve Bank of Minneapolis, January 1, 1978, available at https://www.minneapolisfed.org/article/1978/rational-expectationsfresh-ideas-that-challenge-some-established-views-of-policy-making.
12. Robert Lucas and Thomas Sargent, "After Keynesian Macroeconomics," *Federal Reserve Bank of Minneapolis Quarterly Review* 3, no. 2 (Spring 1979): 1.
13. Harberger's interview is quoted in Edward Nelson, *Milton Friedman and Economic Debate in the United States, 1932–1972*, vol. 2 (Chicago: University of Chicago Press, 2021), 311. Becker's interview is quoted on 452. Nelson also provides a thorough accounting of Friedman and the development of rational expectations on 297–318.
14. Milton Friedman, "The Monetarism Controversy: A Seminar Discussion," Federal Reserve Bank of San Francisco, *Economic Review Supplement* (Spring 1977): 12–13.

15. "Eight Room Home Planned to Save Energy and Maintenance in Surroundings of Unspoiled Beauty," box 109, folder 23, Milton Friedman Papers, Hoover Institution Library and Archives.
16. Robert J. Gordon, ed., *Milton Friedman's Monetary Framework: A Debate with His Critics* (Chicago: University of Chicago Press, 1974).
17. Michael D. Bordo and Anna J. Schwartz, "IS-LM and Monetarism," NBER Working Paper 9713 (May 2003), 3, available at http://www.nber.org/papers/w9713.
18. Milton Friedman and Rose D. Friedman, *Two Lucky People: Memoirs* (Chicago: University of Chicago Press, 1998), 420–23.
19. The student was Rolf Luders, one of the only Ph.D. students from Chile who had Friedman as a dissertation adviser. Friedman's connection to Chile has been widely discussed, most notably in Naomi Klein, *The Shock Doctrine: The Rise of Disaster Capitalism* (New York: Picador, 2007), but most accounts provide scant coverage of his actual time spent in the county. A recent detailed account of his 1975 and 1981 trips, drawing on Chilean sources, is Sebastian Edwards and Leonidas Montes, "Milton Friedman in Chile: Shock Therapy, Economic Freedom, and Exchange Rates," *Journal of the History of Economic Thought* 42, no. 1 (March 2020): 105–32.
20. "Salvador Allende's Chile: Marxist Threat in the Americas," *Time*, October 19, 1970.
21. The most comprehensive history of the Chile-Chicago program is Juan Gabriel Valdés, *Pinochet's Economists: The Chicago School in Chile* (Cambridge: Cambridge University Press, 1995).
22. The classic statement of ISI is in Raul Prebisch, *The Economic Development of Latin America and Its Principal Problems* (New York: United Nations Department of Economic Affairs, 1950).
23. John Waterbury, "The Long Gestation and Brief Triumph of Import Substitution Industrialization," *World Development* 27, no. 2 (1999): 324.
24. "Sense and Economics: An Oral History with Arnold Harberger," interviews conducted by Paul Burnett in 2015 and 2016, Oral History Center of the Bancroft Library, University of California, Berkeley, 2016. Henceforth cited as Harberger Oral History.
25. Harberger Oral History, 38.
26. Harberger's views on Chile are captured in a 1956 memo he sent to colleagues, republished later as Arnold Harberger, "Memorándum Sobre La Economía Chilena," *Estudios Públicos* 77 (Verano 2000): 401, 402. English translation by Deepl.com.
27. Harberger, "Memorándum Sobre La Economía Chilena," 412, 413.
28. Valdés, *Pinochet's Economists*, 13.
29. Mark Falcoff, *Modern Chile, 1970–1989: A Critical History* (New Brunswick, NJ: Transaction Publishers, 1989; 2004), 15. Valdés, *Pinochet's Economists*, 7.
30. Figures on nationalization are from Felipe Larraín and Patricio Meller, "The Socialist-Populist Chilean Experience, 1970–1973," in Rudiger Dornbusch and Sebastian Edwards, eds., *The Macroeconomics of Populism in Latin America* (Chicago: University of Chicago Press, 1990), 191. The treasury official is quoted in Valdés, *Pinochet's Economists*, 7.
31. For an analysis that connects Chile to broader populist trends, see essays in Dornbusch and Edwards, *The Macroeconomics of Populism in Latin America.*
32. M1 growth in 1971 was 119 percent. The 600 percent figure of annual inflation is from the consumer price index and is likely understated given price controls; wholesale prices show 1,000 percent inflation. Larraín and Meller, "The Socialist-Populist Chilean Experience, 1970–1973," 200. For the role of state-owned enterprises, see Larraín and Meller, 206, 217, and Falcoff, *Modern Chile, 1970–1989*, chapter 5.
33. Tanya Harmer argues that U.S. policy-makers perceived Allende in a regional context, with particular attention to Cuba. Tanya Harmer, *Allende's Chile and the Inter-American Cold War* (Chapel Hill: University of North Carolina Press, 2011).
34. The role of Nutter within this policy-planning process is covered in Daniel Kuehn, "'We Can Get a Coup': Warren Nutter and the Overthrow of Salvador Allende,"

Research in the History of Economic Thought and Methodology, vol. 39-A (Bingley, UK: Emerald Publishing, 2021).

35. Harmer, *Allende's Chile and the Inter-American Cold War*, 10, 249.
36. Figures are from the National Commission on Political Imprisonment and Torture Report, colloquially the Valech Commission, revised most recently in 2011. "Chile Recognizes 9,800 More Victims of Pinochet's rule," *BBC News*, August 18, 2011, available at https://www.bbc.com/news/world-latin-america-14584095. Figures on exile are found in Thomas Wright and Rody Oñate Zúñiga, "Chilean Political Exile," *Latin American Perspectives* 34, no. 4 (2007): 31–49.
37. Harberger, Oral History, 206. Karin Fischer, "The Influence of Neoliberals in Chile Before, During, and After Pinochet," in Philip Mirowski and Dieter Plehwe, eds., *The Road from Mont Pelerin: The Making of the Neoliberal Thought Collective* (Cambridge, MA: Harvard University Press, 2009), 319.
38. *The Brick: The Economic Policy Foundations of the Chilean Military Government* (Santiago: Centro de Estudios Publicos, 1992). English translation in author's possession.
39. *The Brick*, 11, 17.
40. Valdés, *Pinochet's Economists*, 13, 238. Fischer notes sympathies between the Chicago Boys and the Chilean *gremialista* movement; ultimately she concludes "neoliberalism in Chile (and elsewhere) cannot be equated with authoritarianism and military dictatorship." See "The Influence of Neoliberals in Chile Before, During, and After Pinochet," 338.
41. *The Brick*, 7.
42. Details on the travel arrangements are in Edwards and Montes, "Milton Friedman in Chile."
43. Details on Friedman's trip are taken from a tape recording he made only a few days after leaving the country. Milton Friedman, "Record of a Week in Chile, March 20–27, 1975," unpublished typescript transcribed from a tape, March 29, 1975. Collected Works of Milton Friedman, miltonfriedman.hoover.org/collections, Hoover Institution Library and Archives.
44. Larraín and Meller, "The Socialist-Populist Chilean Experience, 1970–1973," 197.
45. Milton Friedman, *Un Legado de Libertad: Milton Friedman in Chile* (Santiago: Instituto Democracia y Mercado, 2012), 24. Friedman to Pinochet, April 21, 1975, reprinted in Friedman and Friedman, *Two Lucky People*, 592.
46. Friedman quoted in Edwards and Montes, "Milton Friedman in Chile," 11.
47. Edwards and Montes, "Milton Friedman in Chile," 9, 10.
48. Friedman, "Record of a Week in Chile," 13.
49. Quoted in Edwards and Montes, "Milton Friedman in Chile," 8.
50. Friedman, "Record of a Week in Chile," 5, 15.
51. Friedman, "Record of a Week in Chile," 16.
52. For example, Seymour Hirsch, "CIA Chief Tells House of $8 Million Campaign Against Allende," *The New York Times*, September 8, 1974, 1, 26.
53. Friedman's comment to Pinochet is noted by Luders, who was present in the meeting, quoted in Edwards and Montes, "Milton Friedman in Chile," 7. A surviving transcript of one of Friedman's talks documents a fairly technical address about inflation, with no critique of the regime or mention of political freedom. Friedman, *Un Legado de Libertad: Milton Friedman in Chile*, 24.
54. The original text of Friedman's address in Chile does not survive. Transcripts of the same address, published and delivered on other occasions, are quoted here. Friedman's contemporaneous notes reveal that the main focus of his address was "the role in the destruction of a free society that was played by the emergence of the welfare state," as in the other speeches. See Friedman and Friedman, *Two Lucky People*, 400.
55. Milton Friedman, "The Fragility of Freedom," in *Milton Friedman in South Africa*, eds. Meyer Feldberg, Kate Jowell, and Stephen Mulholland (Cape Town and Johannesburg: Graduate School of Business of the University of Cape Town, 1976), 3–10. Friedman, "The Fragility of Freedom," *BYU Studies Quarterly* 16, no. 4 (Summer 1976): 568.

56. Samuel Moyn, *The Last Utopia: Human Rights in History* (Cambridge, MA: Harvard University Press, 2010).
57. Rosenstein-Rodan to Tintner, June 26, 1975, enclosing Rosenstein-Rodan to Valdés, UN Development Program, March 26, 1974, box 189, folder 1, Milton Friedman Papers.
58. Paul Rosenstein-Rodan, "Why Allende Failed," *Challenge* 17, no. 2 (May–June 1974): 7–13.
59. Jeffrey Sommers, "The Contradictions of a Contrarian: Andre Gunder Frank," *Social Justice* 32, no. 2 (2005): 7–12. Andre Gunder Frank, "Economic Genocide in Chile: Open Letter to Milton Friedman and Arnold Harberger," *Economic and Political Weekly* 11, no. 24 (June 12, 1976): 880–88.
60. Tinter to Friedman, June 16, 1975, box 189, folder 1, Milton Friedman Papers.
61. "Two Years of Pinochet," *The New York Times*, September 22, 1975, 32. Bruce Handler, "Chile's Economy Improves: Conditions Still Grim for the Poor," *The Washington Post*, November 28, 1975, A4. The Chicago student government also established a "Commission of Inquiry on the Friedman/Harberger Issue," which both professors vigorously disputed. Milton Friedman and Arnold Harberger, "Letter to Editor," *The Chicago Maroon*, November 3, 1975, box 188, folder 10, Milton Friedman Papers. Maryann Mahaffey, "Chile Suffers in Friedman Economy," *Detroit Free Press*, July 3, 1978, NP.
62. Orlando Letelier, "The 'Chicago Boys' in Chile: Economic Freedom's Awful Toll," *The Nation*, August 1976.
63. Letelier, "The 'Chicago Boys' in Chile."
64. Letelier, "The 'Chicago Boys' in Chile." Letelier's essay was an early version of the blockade thesis, which attributed Chile's economic problems to U.S. action. It was also a first version of an argument elaborated in Naomi Klein's *The Shock Doctrine*, of an intrinsic link between free market policies and authoritarian governments.
65. Friedman, "The Fragility of Freedom," in *Milton Friedman in South Africa*. Figures are from Larraín and Meller, "The Socialist-Populist Chilean Experience, 1970–1973," 208. Harberger became controversial in academia, eventually turning down a Harvard offer due to protests; Harberger Oral History, 202. "Bok Opposes Ideological Test for Posts at Harvard," *The New York Times*, April 13, 1980, 22.
66. Peter Kornbluh, *The Pinochet File: A Declassified Dossier on Atrocity and Accountability* (New York: New Press, 2013).
67. "Two Years of Pinochet," *The New York Times*, September 22, 1975, 32.
68. Union for Radical Political Economics, "The Economics of Milton Friedman and the Chilean Junta," box 188, folder 12, Milton Friedman Papers.
69. Rosenstein-Rodan, "Why Allende Failed," 7.
70. Estimates of worldwide deaths caused by Communist regimes range from 85 to 100 million. Mark Kramer, ed., *The Black Book of Communism: Crimes, Terror, Repression* (Cambridge, MA: Harvard University Press, 1999).
71. Milton Friedman, "Response to Letter from Unnamed Professor Printed in *Chicago Maroon*," October 3, 1975, reproduced in Friedman and Friedman, *Two Lucky People*, 595. Hayek's elaboration of the difference between authoritarianism and totalitarianism is in F. A. Hayek, "Principles of a Liberal Social Order," in *Studies in Philosophy, Politics and Economics* (London: Taylor & Francis, 1967), 160–77.
72. Milton Friedman, "Liberal McCarthyism: A Personal Experience," *The Commonwealth*, 490–95, available at https://www.commonwealthclub.org/blog/2010-11-30/milton-friedman-commonwealth-club-reader-part-i.
73. Janet Martel interview with author.
74. Although, given the runaway inflation, real wages began declining in the third quarter of 1972 and by the third quarter of 1973 had fallen to half their 1970 level. Larraín and Meller, "The Socialist-Populist Chilean Experience, 1970–1973," 202–203.
75. From 1975 to 1982, the Chilean economy grew rapidly and inflation declined considerably. A foreign debt crisis in the mid-1980s discredited some of the original Chicago Boys and led to changes in the financial sector. In 1990, after Pinochet left the presi-

dency, successive governments expanded social spending and services but retained the basic architecture of policy, including liberalized markets and international trade. Subsequent decades saw a rise in the middle class, while the percentage of people living below the poverty line fell from 53 percent in the mid-1980s to 6 percent in 2019. "In terms of income and other economic statistics, by 2020 Chile looked more like a southern European country, such as Portugal or Spain, than a Latin American nation"; see Sebastian Edwards, *The Chile Project: The Story of the Chicago Boys and the Downfall of Neoliberalism* (Princeton, NJ: Princeton University Press, 2022), 3. Nonetheless, as late as 2007 Klein could claim that "a war of the rich against the poor and middle class—is the real story of Chile's economic miracle"; see Klein, *The Shock Doctrine*, 105. Street protests in 2019 and the popular rejection of a new constitution in 2022 suggest the country's political direction remains unclear.

76. Edwards and Montes, "Milton Friedman in Chile," 18–19.
77. Friedman to Pinochet, August 7, 1976, box 188, folder 12, Milton Friedman Papers.
78. Hayek's remarks on Pinochet have been roundly condemned. Greg Grandin, *Empire's Workshop: Latin America, the United States, and the Rise of the New Imperialism* (New York: Henry Holt, 2006), 172–73; Fischer, "The Influence of Neoliberals in Chile Before, During, and After Pinochet," 327–28. For a more sympathetic treatment of Hayek's visit, setting it within his theoretical interest in limited democracy, see Bruce Caldwell and Leonidas Montes, "Friedrich Hayek and His Visits to Chile," *The Review of Austrian Economics* 28 (2015): 261–309.
79. Buchanan's two visits to Chile, like Hayek's, are the subject of their own mini-literature. Nancy MacLean, *Democracy in Chains: The Deep History of the Radical Right's Stealth Plan for America* (New York: Random House, 2017), argues for Buchanan's decisive influence on the Chilean constitution. A rebuttal of these claims is given in Andrew Farrant, "What Should (Knightian) Economists Do? James M. Buchanan's 1980 Visit to Chile," *Southern Economic Journal* 85, no. 3 (2019): 691–714. For another strand of scholarship highlighting different influences, see Kirsten Weld, "The Spanish Civil War and the Construction of a Reactionary Historical Consciousness in Augusto Pinochet's Chile," *Hispanic American Historical Review* 98, no. 1 (February 1, 2018): 77–115.
80. Friedman to Ernesto Fontaine, August 1, 1980, box 200, Milton Friedman Papers.
81. Pedro Ibáñez, "Welcome to Chile . . . ," box 167, folder 1, Mont Pelerin Society Records, Hoover Institution Library and Archives.
82. "Milton Friedman Praised Chile's Monetary Policy," *La Tercera*, November 20, 1981, 4.
83. Milton Friedman, "Free Markets and the Generals," *Newsweek*, January 25, 1982.

13. MONEY MATTERS

1. Hoover's battles with Stanford are chronicled in George Nash, *Herbert Hoover and Stanford University* (Stanford, CA: Hoover Institution Press, 1988). The statement that is quoted is on 154.
2. Steven Teles, *The Rise of the Conservative Legal Movement: The Battle for Control of the Law* (Princeton, NJ: Princeton University Press, 2008), 97.
3. Campbell's memoirs offer little insight into Friedman's arrival at Hoover. W. Glenn Campbell, *The Competition of Ideas: How My Colleagues and I Built the Hoover Institution* (Ottawa, IL: Jameson Books, 2000), 18. The windfall came after a rocky ten-year period for the Volker Fund, including a disastrous transformation into the pro-Nazi Center for American Studies. During this time, the Hoover Institution rejected a $10 million bequest. After CAS had closed, in 1978 the Volker Fund was revived and then liquidated, with $7 million coming to the Hoover Institution. Michael J. McVicar, "Aggressive Philanthropy: Progressivism, Conservatism, and the William Volker Charities Fund," *Missouri Historical Review* 105, no. 4 (July 2011): 191–212.
4. Campbell, *The Competition of Ideas*, 18. Lois Romano, "Reagan's Ranking Couple," *The Washington Post*, November 29, 1981, H4. Campbell's appointment coincided with a rapid proliferation of conservative think tanks and a related embrace of partisan identi-

ties; see Andrew Rich, *Think Tanks, Public Policy, and the Politics of Expertise* (New York: Cambridge University Press, 2004), and Jason Stahl, *Right Moves: The Conservative Think Tank in American Political Culture Since 1945* (Chapel Hill: University of North Carolina Press, 2016), with only brief mentions of the Hoover Institution. A fuller discussion of the Hoover Institution's history is found in James Allen Smith, *The Idea Brokers: Think Tanks and the Rise of a New Policy Elite* (New York: Free Press, 1991), 184–89. Rich, Stahl, and Smith all argue that increased numbers and partisanship served to dilute think tank influence. Contrariwise, Thomas Medvetz argues that think tanks crowded out independently produced knowledge; Thomas Medvetz, *Think Tanks in America* (Chicago: University of Chicago Press, 2012).

5. John Taylor, personal communication to author, February 19, 2021.
6. Thatcher's ideological studies are described in Charles Moore, *Margaret Thatcher: From Grantham to the Falklands* (London: Allen Lane, 2013), 253–55, 341–42.
7. Thatcherism blended Tory conservatism and the economic liberalism of the Liberal Party, which one historian calls the "twin inheritance" or the "essence of Thatcherism." Richard Cockett, *Thinking the Unthinkable: Think-Tanks and the Economic Counter-Revolution, 1931–1983* (London: Harper Collins, 1995), 250, 137. For the longevity of monetarist beliefs, see E. H. H. Green, *Thatcher* (New York: Oxford University Press, 2006), 59.
8. The phrase initially referred to policies of the Conservative chancellor Reginald Maulding, but came to be more broadly applied to any expansionary economic policy.
9. Dominic Sandbrook, *Seasons in the Sun: The Battle for Britain, 1974–1979* (London: Allen Lane, 2012), 45; and Dominic Sandbrook, *State of Emergency: The Way We Were, Britain 1970–1974* (London: Allen Lane, 2010), 74.
10. Heath's premiership and the attendant economic upheavals are covered in Sandbrook, *State of Emergency*.
11. Monica Prasad, *The Politics of Free Markets: The Rise of Neoliberal Economic Policies in Britain, France, Germany, and the United States* (Chicago: University of Chicago Press, 2006).
12. For in-depth coverage of Friedman, inflation, and the British press in the 1970s, see Wayne Parsons, *The Power of the Financial Press: Journalism and Economic Opinion in Britain and America* (Aldershot, UK: Edward Elgar Publishing, 1989), esp. chapters 4 and 6. For a discussion of Friedman in Britain up to 1979, see Edward Nelson, "Milton Friedman and UK Economic Policy," *Federal Reserve Bank of St. Louis Review*, part 2 (September–October 2009): 465–506.
13. Samuel Brittan quoted in Cockett, *Thinking the Unthinkable*, 184.
14. Sandbrook, *The Battle for Britain*, 226–27. The revival of monetarism in the British academy is summarized in Gordon Pepper, *Inside Thatcher's Monetarist Revolution* (New York: St. Martin's Press, 1998), 3–5.
15. James Forder argues that increased attention to Friedman's ideas did not mean a corresponding influence on policy. According to data compiled by Anne Williamson, from 1968 to 1989, Friedman was mentioned more than 500 times in Parliament, with 330 citations from Labour and 130 from Conservative MPs. James Forder, "Friedman's Lack of Influence on British Economic Policy," Economics Series Working Papers, Paper 802, University of Oxford, Department of Economics, 2016, 14.
16. Denis Healey quoted in John Lloyd and Christian Tyler, "Healey Backs Moderation But Denounces Howe Policy," *Financial Times*, May 23, 1980, 13.
17. These and other colorful examples are cited in Forder, "Friedman's Lack of Influence on British Economic Policy," 14.
18. Richard Kershaw, "Professor Milton Friedman Prescribes a Medicine for Britain," *The Listener*, November 18, 1976, 632–33.
19. Friedman to Harris, December 4, 1978, available at https://www.margaretthatcher.org/archive.
20. Stephen Erickson, *A Conversation with Harris and Seldon* (London: Institute of Economic Affairs, 2001), 56.

21. Thatcher to Friedman, May 11, 1979, available at https://www.margaretthatcher.org/archive.
22. Lawson to Thatcher, "Visit of Milton Friedman," February 22, 1980, available at https://www.margaretthatcher.org/archive.
23. Thatcher to Friedman, March 17, 1980, available at https://www.margaretthatcher.org/archive.
24. Milton Friedman, "Friedman on Britain," *The Observer*, June 7, 1980, NP.
25. His specific advice was to eliminate multiple reserve currencies in favor of Bank of England notes, rely on gilts (open market operations), and index long-dated bonds.
26. Allan H. Meltzer, *A History of the Federal Reserve, Volume 2, Book 1, 1951–1969* (Chicago: University of Chicago Press), 82.
27. Terry Burns, "Confidential: Chequers Luncheon for Academic Economists," fifteen-page typescript memo, July 11, 1980, available at https://www.margaretthatcher.org/archive.
28. The distinction between genuine, pragmatic, and political monetarists comes from Gordon Pepper and Michael J. Oliver, *Monetarism Under Thatcher: Lessons for the Future* (Northampton, MA: Edward Elgar Publishing, 2001), xvii.
29. Nigel Lawson, *The View from No. 11: Memoirs of a Tory Radical* (New York: Bantam Press, 1992), 81. Pepper and Oliver nonetheless declare Lawson was not a monetarist by their definition in *Monetarism Under Thatcher.*
30. Milton Friedman, "Friedman on Britain," *The Observer*, June 7, 1980, NP.
31. For details on the aggregate selection, including Friedman's opposition to M3, see Prasad, *The Politics of Free Markets*, 108.
32. Moore, *From Grantham to the Falklands*, 624.
33. A letter opposing the budget was signed by 364 economists. In retrospect, one of the open letter's two sponsors admitted an important motivation was retribution for a humiliating television debate with Friedman some years prior. Robert Nield, "The 1981 Statement by 364 Economists," in Duncan Needham and Anthony Hotson, eds., *Expansionary Fiscal Contraction: The Thatcher Government's 1981 Budget in Perspective* (Cambridge: Cambridge University Press, 2014), 1, 4.
34. Nield, "The 1981 Statement by 364 Economists," 4.
35. John Fforde, "The Dilemma of the Liberal Central Banker in 20th-Century Britain (a fragment for Easter)," April 30, 1981, internal Bank of England document, reprinted in Needham and Hotson, *Expansionary Fiscal Contraction*, 93.
36. Conservative Research Department, cited in Duncan Needham, "The 1981 Budget: 'A Dunkirk, not an Alamein,'" in Needham and Hotson, *Expansionary Fiscal Contraction*, 174.
37. "Speech by the Rt. Hon. Margaret Thatcher MP at the Center for Policy Studies AGM, St Stephen's Club, SW1," February 9, 1981, available at https://www.margaretthatcher.org/document/121409.
38. B. Ingham, "Minute to MT: Radio New Zealand, Annex A," July 29, 1982, available at https://www.margaretthatcher.org/archive.
39. Milton Friedman and Rose D. Friedman, *Two Lucky People: Memoirs* (Chicago: University of Chicago Press, 1998), 388.
40. Friedman and Friedman, *Two Lucky People*, 389. Reagan staffer Lew Uhler went on to found the still-active National Tax-Limitation Committee; see www.limittaxes.org.
41. For a history of 1970s tax limitation set within a longer history, see Isaac Martin, *Rich People's Movements: Grassroots Campaigns to Untax the One Percent* (New York: Oxford University Press, 2013), chapter 7.
42. John A. Lawrence, *The Class of '74: Congress After Watergate and the Roots of Partisanship* (Baltimore: Johns Hopkins University Press, 2018).
43. Friedman's activities are described in Kelly Goodman, "Don't Spend It Faster Than I Can Make It," paper presented to the Policy History Conference, Tempe, Arizona, May 16–19, 2018.
44. William F. Rickenbacker and Lewis K. Uhler, *A Taxpayer's Guide to Survival: Constitutional Tax-Limitation* (Loomis, CA: National Tax Limitation Committee, 1977), 4.

45. "Tax Cuts and Recession," *Newsweek*, May 12, 1975, reprinted in William R. Allen, ed., *Bright Promises, Dismal Performance: An Economist's Protest* (New York: Harcourt Brace Jovanovich, 1983), 296.
46. Rickenbacker and Uhler, *A Taxpayer's Guide to Survival*, 4.
47. Milton Friedman and Rose D. Friedman, *Free to Choose: A Personal Statement* (New York: Harcourt Brace Jovanovich, 1980), ix.
48. For Knight's influence on public choice, see David C. Coker and Ross B. Emmett, "Frank Knight and the Origins of Public Choice," American Economic Association Annual Meeting paper, January 3, 2020, available at https://www.aeaweb.org/conference/2020/preliminary/paper/SzTZ6F9s. Nancy MacLean, *Democracy in Chains: The Deep History of the Radical Right's Stealth Plan for America* (New York: Random House, 2017), situates Buchanan's public choice on the political right, specifically in resistance to desegregation and civil rights. For an alternative history that flags the importance of Herbert Simon and the longer tradition of public administration scholarship, along with the role of Buchanan, see Vincent Ostrom and Elinor Ostrom, "Public Choice: A Different Approach to the Study of Public Administration," *Public Administration Review* 31, no. 2 (March–April 1971): 203–16.
49. James Buchanan, "Public Choice: Politics Without Romance," *Policy* 19, no. 3 (Spring 2003): 17.
50. The term "rent-seeking" was coined by Anne Krueger in a paper on tariffs in the developing world, a good index of how public choice concepts became widely applied in economics. Krueger had no Chicago connection and did not cite Gordon Tullock, who is generally credited with the first formulation of the concept. Anne O. Krueger, "The Political Economy of the Rent-Seeking Society," *American Economic Review* 64, no. 3 (June 1974): 291–303. In 2014 Krueger's article was judged one of the top twenty most influential papers published in the journal's first century. See https://econthoughtdotorg.wordpress.com/aers-top-20-articles/.
51. James M. Buchanan and Gordon Tullock, *The Calculus of Consent: Logical Foundations of Constitutional Democracy* (Ann Arbor: University of Michigan Press, 1962). F. A. Hayek, *The Constitution of Liberty* (Chicago: University of Chicago Press, 1960).
52. For the role of Buchanan's students as consultants to California Proposition 1 and other tax limitation measures, see Kelly Goodman, "Tax the Rich: Teachers' Long Campaign to Fund Public Schools," Ph.D. dissertation, Yale University, 2021, chapter 5, 31–35. Milton Friedman, "Balanced on Paper," *Newsweek*, June 23, 1980, reprinted in Friedman, *Bright Promises*, 121.
53. Milton Friedman, "What Is Wrong with the Welfare State?," lecture at Roberts Wesleyan College, Rochester, New York, February 23, 1978, 4, 3. Friedman's language and argument echoed W. Allen Wallis, a Chicago classmate who, as the president and chancellor of the nearby University of Rochester, helped arrange the lecture. W. Allen Wallis, *An Overgoverned Society* (New York: Free Press, 1976), 184.
54. Friedman, "What Is Wrong with the Welfare State?," 11–13.
55. Friedman, "What Is Wrong with the Welfare State?," 14. This argument about bureaucracy had broader currency at the time. Joseph E. Hower, "'The Sparrows and the Horses': Daniel Patrick Moynihan, the Family Assistance Plan, and the Liberal Critique of Government Workers, 1955–1977," *Journal of Policy History* 28, no. 2 (2016): 256–89.
56. Friedman, "What Is Wrong with the Welfare State?," 16.
57. The evolution of what became Proposition 13 and its linkages to other tax reduction movements is covered in Martin, *Rich People's Movements*, 161–63.
58. Robert W. Crandell, "The Migration of U.S. Manufacturing and Its Impact on the Buffalo Metropolitan Area," Brookings Institution, paper prepared for Manufacturing Matters Federal Reserve Bank of New York, Buffalo Branch, June 6, 2002, available at https://www.brookings.edu/wp-content/uploads/2016/06/20020622.pdf.
59. For depreciation, see Monica Prasad, *Starving the Beast: Ronald Reagan and the Tax Cut Revolution* (New York: Russell Sage Foundation, 2018), 125–26.

60. Morton Kondracke and Fred Barnes, *Jack Kemp: The Bleeding-Heart Conservative Who Changed America* (New York: Sentinel, 2015), 29–30.
61. Laffer's career, and the origins of supply-side in his work with Mundell, is covered in Brian Domitrovic, *The Emergence of Arthur Laffer: The Foundations of Supply-Side Economics in Chicago and Washington, 1966–1976* (New York: Palgrave Macmillan, 2021). The napkin, currently on display at the Smithsonian, may in fact have been Wanniski's invention. For overviews of supply-side theory, see Stahl, *Right Moves*, chapter 3, and Wayne Parsons, *The Power of the Financial Press: Journalism and Economic Opinion in Britain and America* (Aldershot, UK: Edward Elgar Publishing, 1989), chapter 5.
62. "What Kemp-Roth Would Really Do," *The Washington Post*, October 10, 1980.
63. Dennis J. Ventry Jr., "The Collision of Tax and Welfare Politics: The Political History of the Earned Income Tax Credit, 1969–99," *National Tax Journal* 53, no. 4 (December 2000): 983–1026.
64. Quoted in Kondracke and Barnes, *Jack Kemp*, 40.
65. Dana Rohrabacher, "An Economist Against the Government: An Interview with Milton Friedman," *Santa Ana Register*, December 23, 1979, Collected Works of Milton Friedman, miltonfriedman.org/hoover/collections, Hoover Institution Library and Archives.
66. Martin Anderson, *Revolution: The Reagan Legacy* (Stanford, CA: Hoover Institution Press, 1990), 161–63, describes the exchange as a "political deal." Kondracke and Barnes note the rumors in *Jack Kemp*.
67. Rowland Evans and Robert Novak, "Reagan Talks Out of School," *The Washington Post*, October 12, 1979, A15. Quoted in Kondracke and Barnes, *Jack Kemp*, 46.
68. Friedman and Friedman, *Two Lucky People*, 496, 498. Further details on the series are in Angus Burgin, "Age of Certainty: Galbraith, Friedman, and the Public Life of Economic Ideas," *History of Political Economy* 45 (2013): 191–219.
69. *Free to Choose Volume One: The Power of the Market*, transcript available at www.freetochoose.net.
70. *Free to Choose Volume Three: Anatomy of a Crisis*, transcript available at www.freetochoose.net.
71. Friedman and Friedman, *Two Lucky People*, 504.
72. "GOP Wins Senate Control for First Time in 28 Years," in *CQ Almanac 1980*, 36th edition, 7-B-10-B (Washington, D.C.: Congressional Quarterly, 1981), 9
73. Dan Williams, *God's Own Party: The Making of the Christian Right* (New York: Oxford University Press, 2010); Robert O. Self, *All in the Family: The Realignment of American Democracy Since the 1960s* (New York: Hill and Wang, 2012).
74. John Kenneth Galbraith, *Economics in Perspective: A Critical History* (Boston: Houghton Mifflin, 1987), 274. Kevin D. Hoover, personal communication to author, January 15, 2021.

14. THE VOLCKER SHOCK

1. Martin Anderson, *Revolution: The Reagan Legacy* (Stanford, CA: Hoover Institution Press, 1990), 266, 172.
2. Friedman to Anderson, "The Importance of the Fed," December 13, 1980, three-page typescript memo, box 296, folder 5, Martin Anderson Papers, Hoover Institution Library and Archives.
3. William Niekirk, *Volcker: Portrait of a Money Man* (New York: Congdon and Weed, 1987), 9.
4. For the 1979 shock, see Meg Jacobs, *Panic at the Pump: The Energy Crisis and the Transformation of American Politics in the 1970s* (New York: Hill and Wang, 2017), chapter 7.
5. Monica Prasad, *Starving the Beast: Ronald Reagan and the Tax Cut Revolution* (New York: Russell Sage Foundation, 2018), 197.

6. Volcker is quoted in Allan Meltzer, *A History of the Federal Reserve, Volume 2, Book 2, 1970–1986* (Chicago: University of Chicago Press, 2009), 1010.
7. Charles H. Brunie, "My Friend, Milton Friedman," *City Journal*, April 11, 2007, available at https://www.city-journal.org/html/my-friend-milton-friedman-10239.html. Mary Farrell, *Beyond the Basics: How to Invest Your Money, Now That You Know a Thing or Two* (New York: Simon and Schuster, 2000), 66–67. Charles L. Fahy, *The Streetwise Investor: Steering Clear of Investment Traps, Pitfalls, and Other Dangerous Lures* (Chicago: Probus, 1993), 34, describing a conversation in the mid-1970s.
8. "Transcript of Press Conference with Paul A. Volcker, Chairman, Board of Governors of the Federal Reserve System," October 6, 1979, Washington, D.C., 11, 3, available at http://fraser.stlouisfed.org.
9. Paul A. Volcker with Christine Harper, *Keeping At It: The Quest for Sound Money and Good Government* (New York: PublicAffairs, 2018), 105.
10. "Transcript of Press Conference with Paul A. Volcker," 3, 7, 10, 8.
11. Milton Friedman, "Volcker's Inheritance," *Newsweek*, August 20, 1979, 65.
12. Remarks by Paul A. Volcker, Chairman, Board of Governors of the Federal Reserve, before the National Press Club, Washington, D.C., January 2, 1980, 6. On taxation as an additional influence on interest rates that was not acknowledged by the Fed, see Martin Feldstein, "Tax Rules and the Mismanagement of Monetary Policy," *American Economic Review* 70, no. 2 (May 1980): 182–86.
13. Arthur Burns, "The Anguish of Central Banking," 1979 Per Jacobsson Lecture, 21, 22, available at http://www.perjacobsson.org/lectures/1979.pdf.
14. Paul Volcker and Toyoo Gyohten, *Changing Fortunes: The World's Money and the Threat to American Leadership* (New York: Crown, 1991), 167.
15. Volcker with Harper, *Keeping At It*, 117–18.
16. Quoted in Meltzer, *A History of the Federal Reserve, Volume 2, Book 2, 1970–1986*, 1034.
17. William L. Silber, *Volcker: The Triumph of Persistence* (New York: Bloomsbury Press, 2012), 148–49.
18. Milton Friedman, "Has the Fed Changed Course?," *Newsweek*, October 22, 1979, 39.
19. Milton Friedman, "The Fed and Inflation," *Newsweek*, December 29, 1980, reprinted in Milton Friedman, *Bright Promises, Dismal Performance: An Economist's Protest*, ed. William R. Allen (New York: Harcourt, Brace, Jovanovich, 1982), 265.
20. Recounted in Silber, *Volcker*, 194–95, from an interview with Volcker. Burns may have been worried about a "constitutional" solution to monetary policy, along the lines of the tax reform movement.
21. Quoted in Prasad, *Starving the Beast*, 127, which also details business opposition to ERTA and Reagan.
22. Milton Friedman, "Closet Keynesianism," *Newsweek*, July 27, 1981, reprinted in Friedman, *Bright Promises*, 299.
23. Milton Friedman, "The Kemp-Roth Free Lunch," *Newsweek*, August 7, 1978, 59.
24. Milton Friedman, "Prosperity Without Inflation," *Newsweek*, December 15, 1980, reprinted in Friedman, *Bright Promises*, 195.
25. Milton Friedman, "Deficits and Inflation," *Newsweek*, February 23, 1981, reprinted in Friedman, *Bright Promises*, 221.
26. William Greider, "The Education of David Stockman," *The Atlantic*, December 1981, 39.
27. Prasad, *Starving the Beast*, 101.
28. Steven V. Roberts, "The Roth of Kemp-Roth Fights for His Tax Plan," *The New York Times*, May 12, 1982, A26.
29. "What Kemp-Roth Would Really Do," *The Washington Post*, October 1, 1980, A17.
30. Quoted in Silber, *Volcker*, 212.

31. Milton Friedman, "Monetary Instability," *Newsweek*, June 15, 1981, reprinted in Friedman, *Bright Promises*, 217. "Monetary Policy and Open Market Operations in 1981," *Federal Reserve Bank of New York Quarterly Review* (Spring 1982): 34. Meltzer, *A History of the Federal Reserve, Volume 2, Book 2, 1970–1986*, 1060.
32. Greider, *Secrets of the Temple*, 377. Meltzer, *A History of the Federal Reserve, Volume 2, Book 2, 1970–1986*, 1084. For a detailed background on the legislation, see Greta Krippner, *Capitalizing on Crisis: The Political Origins of the Rise of Finance* (Cambridge, MA: Harvard University Press, 2012), chapter 3.
33. Krippner, *Capitalizing on Crisis*, chapter 3.
34. See https://www.macrotrends.net/2015/fed-funds-rate-historical-chart.
35. "Remarks by Paul A. Volcker, Chairman, Board of Governors of the Federal Reserve System at the National Association of Home Builders 38th Annual Convention and Exposition," Las Vegas, Nevada, January 25, 1982, 4, available at https://fraser.stlouisfed.org/.
36. Michael Mussa, "U.S. Monetary Policy in the 1980s," in Martin Feldstein, ed., *American Economic Policy in the 1980s* (Chicago: University of Chicago Press, 1994), 109.
37. Paul A. Volcker, "Statement Before the Joint Economic Committee," June 15, 1982, available at fraser.stlouisfed.org.
38. Sector-specific statistics on recession are from https://www.federalreservehistory.org/essays/recession-of-1981–82. For an early use of the term "the Volcker shock," see David Warsh, "Inflation and the Economists," *The Boston Globe*, February 26, 1980, 13.
39. Volcker with Harper, *Keeping At It*, 109.
40. Milton Friedman, "The Yo-Yo Economy," *Newsweek*, February 15, 1982, reprinted in Friedman, *Bright Promises*, 253. For the monetarist critique of lagged reserves, see Meltzer, *A History of the Federal Reserve, Volume 2, Book 2, 1970–1986*, 834–35.
41. Greider, *Secrets of the Temple*, 354, 379–80.
42. Ronald Reagan, *Economic Report of the President 1982* (Washington, D.C.: U.S. Government Printing Office, 1982), 10. David Hoffman, "'Stay the Course' on Economy, Reagan Urges," *The Washington Post*, October 14, 1982, A1.
43. Milton Friedman, "An Aborted Recovery?," *Newsweek*, August 23, 1982, 59.
44. Milton Friedman, "Memorandum to the President's Economic Policy Advisory Board on Monetary Policy and Economic Conditions," January 14, 1983, Collected Works of Milton Friedman, miltonfriedman.hoover.org/collections, Hoover Institution Library and Archives. Milton Friedman, "The Yo-Yo Economy."
45. Frank Morris, "Do the Monetary Aggregates Have a Future as Targets of Federal Reserve Policy?," *New England Economic Review* (March–April 1982): 5.
46. Milton Friedman, "More Double Talk at the Fed," *Newsweek*, May 2, 1983, 72.
47. Milton Friedman, "The Needle Got Stuck," *Newsweek*, July 25, 1983, 66.
48. Inflation in the United States remained low until 2021, when the annualized CPI passed 7 percent. Inflation remained a relatively common problem in Latin America.
49. Nigel Lawson, *The View from No. 11: Memoirs of a Tory Radical* (New York: Bantam Press, 1992), 457.
50. Paul A. Volcker, *The Triumph of Central Banking? The 1990 Per Jacobsson Lecture* (Washington, D.C.: International Monetary Fund, 1990), 11.
51. The most influential statement of this argument is in Greider, *Secrets of the Temple*. Friedman also subscribed to this view. See John Taylor, "An Interview with Milton Friedman," *Macroeconomic Dynamics* 5 (2001): 107.
52. For accounts based on these minutes, see Silber, *Volcker*, especially chapters 9–12, which note Volcker's belief that long-term interest rates would decline with monetary tightening. Krippner, *Capitalizing on Crisis*, chapter 5, elaborates the veil argument and shows it emerged retrospectively.
53. Lawson, *The View from No. 11*, 1049.

15. TWO LUCKY PEOPLE

1. Milton Friedman, "Lessons from the 1979–1982 Monetary Policy Experiment," *AEA Papers and Proceedings* (May 1984): 397. Milton Friedman, "What Could Reasonably Have Been Expected from Monetarism: The United States," paper for Mont Pelerin Society meeting, Vancouver, Canada, August 29, 1983, available at Collected Works of Milton Friedman, miltonfriedman.org/hoover/collections, Hoover Institution Library and Archives.
2. Daniel T. Rodgers, *Age of Fracture* (Cambridge, MA: Harvard University Press, 2011), 55.
3. For a retrospective and summary, see Neil R. Ericsson, David F. Hendry, and Stedman B. Hood, "Milton Friedman as an Empirical Modeler," in Robert A. Cord and J. Daniel Hammond, eds., *Milton Friedman: Contributions to Economics and Public Policy* (New York: Oxford University Press, 2016), chapter 6.
4. Christina D. Romer, "Anna Schwartz Memorial," *CSEWP News* (Fall 2013): 11.
5. Michael Bordo, "Anna Schwartz: My Mentor," *CSEWP News* (Fall 2013): 4.
6. Anna J. Schwartz, "Reflections on the Gold Commission Report," in Anna J. Schwartz, ed., *Money in Historical Perspective* (Chicago: University of Chicago Press, 1987), 329. In 1985 the Gold Bullion Act restored gold coinage, in response to the rising popularity of South African and Canadian gold coins.
7. "And Friedman Chose a Rose . . . ," *The Straits Times*, October 18, 1980, NP.
8. Anne Keegan, "Close-Up with Anne Keegan," *Chicago Tribune*, October 15, 1976, NP.
9. "And Friedman Chose a Rose . . ."
10. Polly Ullrich, "The Other Economist in the Friedman Household," *Chicago Sun-Times*, October 31, 1976, 3. Milton Friedman and Rose D. Friedman, *Two Lucky People: Memoirs* (Chicago: University of Chicago Press, 1998), photo insert, NP.
11. Friedman and Friedman, *Two Lucky People*, 544, 550.
12. Monica Prasad, *The Politics of Free Markets: The Rise of Neoliberal Economic Policies in Britain, France, Germany, and the United States* (Chicago: University of Chicago Press, 2006), chapter 2.
13. Robert M. Collins, *Transforming America: Politics and Culture in the Reagan Years* (New York: Columbia University Press, 2007), 131–32. Robert L. Bartley, *The Seven Fat Years: And How to Do It Again* (New York: Macmillan, 1992).
14. Quoted in Jonathan Levy, *Ages of American Capitalism: A History of the United States* (New York: Random House, 2021), 604.
15. Levy, *Ages of American Capitalism*, 619.
16. Milton Friedman, "The Social Responsibility of Business Is to Increase Its Profits," *The New York Times Magazine*, September 13, 1970, SM 17.
17. Brian R. Cheffins, "Stop Blaming Milton Friedman!," University of Cambridge Faculty of Law Research Paper No. 9/2020, European Corporate Governance Institute-Law Working Paper No. 523/2020, available at http://dx.doi.org/10.2139/ssrn.3552950. Andrei Shleifer and Robert W. Vishny, "The Takeover Wave of the 1980s," *Science* 249, no. 4970 (August 17, 1990): 745–49.
18. "America's Money Master," *Newsweek*, February 24, 1986, 46–53.
19. Daniel Patrick Moynihan, *The Politics of a Guaranteed Income: The Nixon Administration and the Family Assistance Plan* (New York: Random House, 1973), 65.
20. Dylan Gottlieb, "Yuppies: Young Industrial Professionals and the Making of Postindustrial New York," *Enterprise & Society* 22, no. 4 (2021): 962.
21. For a social history of trucking deregulation, see Shane Hamilton, *Trucking Country: The Road to America's Wal-Mart Economy* (Princeton, NJ: Princeton University Press, 2008).
22. Paul Samuelson, "Some Uneasiness with the Coase Theorem," *Japan and the World Economy* 7 (1995): 5.
23. On the pre-Reagan roots of postindustrial policy, see Brent Cebul, "Supply-Side Liberalism: Fiscal Crisis, Post-Industrial Policy, and the Rise of the New Democrats," *Modern American History* (2019): 2, 139–64.

24. David Greenberg, "The Reorientation of Liberalism in the 1980s," in Gil Troy and Vincent Cannato, eds., *Living in the Eighties* (New York: Oxford University Press, 2009).
25. Quoted in William Greider, *Secrets of the Temple: How the Federal Reserve Runs the Country* (New York: Simon and Schuster, 1988), 543.
26. Greenspan to Friedman, October 14, 1986, box 149, folder 9, and Friedman to Greenspan, July 13, 1983, box 149, folder 9, Milton Friedman Papers, Hoover Institution Library and Archives.
27. Friedman to Greenspan, February 24, 1988, October 24, 1991, and June 23, 1998, box 149, folder 9, Milton Friedman Papers. Robert Hetzel, "Too Big to Fail: Origins, Consequences, and Outlook," *FRB Richmond Economic Review* 77, no. 6 (November/December 1991): 3–15.
28. Friedman to Greenspan, October 22, 1982, box 149, folder 9, Milton Friedman Papers. Greenspan as quoted in Owen Ullmann, "So, What's New? The 'New Economy' Looks Like the Same Old Economy to the Nobel Laureate, Milton Friedman," *The International Economy* (March/April 2001): 14–17.
29. "Interview: Choices for Freedom and the Future," *The Chicago Maroon*, April 10, 1992.
30. For the counterargument, see Charles G. Leathers and J. Patrick Raines, "Friedman, Schumpeter, and Greenspan's Financial Policies," *International Journal of Social Economics* 40, no. 5 (2013): 504–20.
31. Francis Fukuyama, "The End of History?," *The National Interest*, no. 16 (Summer 1989): 3.
32. Service in Memory of Milton Friedman, 1912–2006, January 29, 2007, University of Chicago, available at https://www.youtube.com/watch?v=yjemk7SEfzA.
33. Richard Tomlinson, "From Genghis Khan to Milton Friedman: Mongolia's Wild Ride to Capitalism," *Fortune*, December 7, 1998.
34. John Williamson, "What Washington Means by Policy Reform," in John Williamson, ed., *Latin American Adjustment: How Much Has Happened?* (Washington, D.C.: Institute for International Economics, 1990).
35. John Williamson, "The Washington Consensus as Policy Prescription for Development," January 13, 2004, lecture delivered at World Bank, available at https://www.piie.com/commentary/speeches-papers/washington-consensus-policy-prescription-development. Moises Naim, "Fads and Fashion in Economic Reforms: Washington Consensus or Washington Confusion?," October 29, 1999, Working Draft of a Paper Prepared for the IMF Conference on Second Generation Reforms, Washington, D.C., available at https://www.imf.org/external/pubs/ft/seminar/1999/reforms/Naim.HTM.
36. Naim, "Fads and Fashion in Economic Reforms."
37. Robert Lenzer, "Lower Taxes, Kill the IMF, Say US Experts," *Forbes*, November 9, 1998, NP.
38. Milton Friedman, "'No' to More Money for the IMF," *Newsweek*, November 14, 1983, 96.
39. Milton Friedman interview by Nathan Gardels, "Free Markets and the End of History," *NPQ* (Winter 2006): 41.
40. Rahm Emanuel, "The China Trade Vote: Free Trade Is a Winner," *The Wall Street Journal*, May 23, 2000, A26.
41. Milton Friedman, "Preface: Economic Freedom Behind the Scenes," *Economic Freedom of the World: 2002 Annual Report* (Vancouver, BC: Fraser Institute, 2002), xvii, xviii, available at https://www.fraserinstitute.org/sites/default/files/EconomicFreedomoftheWorld2002execsum.pdf.
42. Friedman, "Preface: Economic Freedom Behind the Scenes," xvii.
43. "Transcript: Milton Friedman," *The Wall Street Journal*, September 3, 2004, available at https://www.wsj.com/articles/SB109415897030708399.
44. John B. Taylor, "An Interview with Milton Friedman," *Macroeconomic Dynamics* 5 (2001): 105. Friedman was not alone in this confusion. "The visible success of monetary policy during the past half-decade is therefore all the more puzzling," concluded Benjamin M.

Friedman (no relation). Benjamin Friedman, "Lessons on Monetary Policy from the 1980s," *Journal of Economic Perspectives* 2, no. 3 (Summer 1988): 52.

45. Evan F. Koenig, Robert Leeson, and George A. Kahn, eds., *The Taylor Rule and the Transformation of Monetary Policy* (Stanford, CA: Hoover Institution Press, 2012).
46. Frameworks as a compromise between rules and discretion is defended in the introduction to Ben S. Bernanke, Thomas Laubach, Frederic S. Mishkin, and Adam S. Posen, eds., *Inflation Targeting: Lessons from the International Experience* (Princeton, NJ: Princeton University Press, 1999), 6. For the relationship between monetary and inflation targeting, see "German and Swiss Monetary Targeting: Precursors to Inflation Targeting," in *Inflation Targeting*, chapter 4.
47. Michael Woodford, "Doing Without Money: Controlling Inflation in a Post-Monetary World," NBER Working Paper 6188, September 1997, available at http://www.nber.org/papers/w6188. Michael Woodford, *Interest and Prices: Foundations of a Theory of Monetary Policy* (Princeton, NJ: Princeton University Press, 2003).
48. Robert E. Lucas, "Money Neutrality," Nobel Prize Lecture, December 7, 1995, available at https://www.nobelprize.org/uploads/2018/06/lucas-lecture.pdf.
49. N. Gregory Mankiw, "Real Business Cycles: A New Keynesian Perspective," *Journal of Economic Perspectives* 3, no. 3 (Summer 1989): 87–88.
50. A pithy, critical overview of financial economics in the 1970s is John Cassidy, *How Markets Fail: The Logic of Economic Calamities* (New York: Farrar, Straus and Giroux, 2009), chapter 7.
51. Friedman to Fama, April 17, 1978, and Fama to Friedman, May 24, 1978, box 145, folder 2, Milton Friedman Papers. Friedman was dismissive of Fama's sometime collaborator Fischer Black, who was also at Chicago during this time. See Perry Mehrling, *Fischer Black and the Revolutionary Idea of Finance* (New York: John Wiley and Sons, 2005), chapter 6.
52. Cassidy, *How Markets Fail.* Friedman to Fama, May 31, 1990, box 145, folder 2, Milton Friedman Papers. Friedman cited as a rejoinder to criticisms of rational economics is in Arjo Klamer, *Conversations with Economists: New Classical Economists and Opponents Speak Out on the Current Controversy in Macroeconomics* (New York: Rowman and Littlefield, 1983), ix.
53. Gauti B. Eggertsson and Michael Woodford, "The Zero Bound on Interest Rates and Optimal Monetary Policy," *Brookings Papers on Economic Activity* 1 (2003): 147.
54. This unpublished quote has wide circulation online. For an excerpt and fuller context, see Michel De Vroey, "Lucas on the Lucasian Transformation of Macroeconomics: An Assessment," July 2010, IRES Discussion Paper, Catholic University of Louvain. Lucas used "Keynesian" both as a conceptual apparatus and shorthand for a particular vision of the market system.
55. For a technical account of the imprint left by rational expectations, see John B. Taylor, "How the Rational Expectations Revolution Has Changed Macroeconomic Policy Research," February 29, 2000, revised from a lecture presented at the 12th World Congress of the International Economic Association, available at https://web.stanford.edu/~johntayl/Papers/IEALecture.pdf.
56. Bradford DeLong, "The Triumph of Monetarism?," *Journal of Economic Perspectives* 14, no. 1 (Winter 2000): 83–94.
57. Friedman to Greenspan, June 6, 1994, box 149, folder 9, Milton Friedman Papers.
58. Friedman to Greenspan, February 11, 1988, and Greenspan to Friedman, October 25, 1988, box 149, folder 9, Milton Friedman Papers.
59. "Milton Friedman," in Brian Snowden and Howard Vane, eds., *Modern Macroeconomics: Its Origin, Development, and Current State* (Cheltenham, UK: Edward Elgar Publishing, 2005).
60. Alan Greenspan, "Monetary Policy Under Uncertainty," remarks by Chairman Alan Greenspan, August 29, 2003, Jackson Hole, Wyoming, n1, available at https://www.federalreserve.gov/boarddocs/speeches/2003/20030829/default.htm. Friedman to Greenspan, February 24, 1998, box 149, folder 9, Milton Friedman Papers. Simon London, "Milton Friedman—The Long View," *Financial Times*, June 7, 2003, 12.

61. Milton Friedman, *Monetary Mischief: Episodes in Monetary History* (New York: Harcourt, Brace, Jovanovich, 1992), ix, 249, 253.
62. Friedman and Friedman, *Two Lucky People*, 396. Friedman interviewed by Gardels, "Free Markets and the End of History," 41. Friedman and Friedman, *Two Lucky People*, 588.
63. Milton Friedman, "Letter to the Editor: Our Unlegislated Tax Increase," *The Wall Street Journal*, August 13, 1999, NP. Milton Friedman, "Preface: Economic Freedom Behind the Scenes," *Economic Freedom of the World: 2002 Annual Report* (Vancouver, BC: Fraser Institute, 2002), xx, available at https://www.fraserinstitute.org/sites/default/files/EconomicFreedomoftheWorld2002execsum.pdf.
64. Friedman and Friedman, *Two Lucky People*, 391.
65. The phrase is from Herbert Stein, "The Fiscal Revolution in America, Part II: 1964–1994," in W. Elliot Brownlee, ed., *Funding the Modern American State, 1941–1995: The Rise and Fall of the Era of Easy Finance* (Cambridge: Woodrow Wilson International Center for Scholars and Cambridge University Press, 1996), 266.
66. Friedman interviewed by Gardels, "Free Markets and the End of History," 39.
67. Milton Friedman interviewed by David Isaac, "To Keep U.S. Economy Growing, Curb Gov't, Take Risks," *Investor's Business Daily*, April 15, 2004, NP.
68. Milton Friedman, "Pay It Backwards: The Federal Budget Surplus," Uncommon Knowledge interview, December 13, 2000, available at https://www.hoover.org/research/pay-it-backwards-federal-budget-surplus.
69. The metaphor was suggested by Jude Wanniski, "Taxes and a Two-Santa Theory," *The National Observer*, March 6, 1976, available at https://wallstreetpit.com/26546-jude-wanniski-taxes-and-a-two-santa-theory/.
70. Friedman, "Pay It Backwards."
71. James Peron, "What Milton Friedman Actually Said About Illegal Immigration," Radical Center, April 21, 2018, available at https://medium.com/the-radical-center/what-milton-friedman-actually-said-about-illegal-immigration-6b19efaf7a5. Friedman rightly noted that undocumented migrants rarely used federal and state welfare programs, for which they were largely ineligible. His comments reflected a larger dialogue about immigration and welfare. See also Ana Minian, *Undocumented Lives: The Untold Story of Mexican Migration* (Cambridge, MA: Harvard University Press, 2018), 63–67.
72. "Transcript: Milton Friedman," *The Wall Street Journal*, September 3, 2004.
73. Brian Rosenwald, *Talk Radio's America* (Cambridge, MA: Harvard University Press, 2019).
74. Friedman interviewed by Gardels, "Free Markets and the End of History," 43.
75. Charles Goodhart, "Obituaries: Milton Friedman," *The Guardian*, November 16, 2006; Tom Van Riper, "Milton Friedman Dies," *Forbes*, November 16, 2006; Holcomb Noble, "Milton Friedman, the Champion of Free Markets, Is Dead at 94," *The New York Times*, November 17, 2006, A1; Nassim Kadem, "Milton Friedman, Patron Saint of Free-Market Economics," *The Age*, November 18, 2006, 5.
76. All subsequent quotes are from "Service in Memory of Milton Friedman, 1912–2006," January 29, 2007, University of Chicago, available at https://www.youtube.com/watch?v=yjemk7SEfzA.

EPILOGUE: HELICOPTER DROP

1. Ben S. Bernanke, *The Courage to Act: A Memoir of a Crisis and Its Aftermath* (New York: W. W. Norton, 2015), 30, 65.
2. Brian Carney, "Bernanke Is Fighting the Last War," *The Wall Street Journal*, October 18, 2008, NP.
3. Adam Tooze, *Crashed: How a Decade of Financial Crises Changed the World* (New York: Penguin, 2018) 206–208.
4. "Open Letter to Ben Bernanke," November 15, 2010, *The Wall Street Journal*, NP. Allan H. Meltzer, "Quantitative Quicksand," June 6, 2013, Project Syndicate, available at https://www.project-syndicate.org/commentary/why-quantitative-easing-has-failed

-to-boost-us-investment-and-jobs-by-allan-h—meltzer. Schwartz quoted in Michael Bordo, personal communication to author, February 24, 2022.

5. Explanations of IORB can be found at https://www.federalreserveeducation.org/about-the-fed/archive-structure-and-functions/archive-monetary-policy/.
6. Summarizing numerous findings, Michael Belongia and Peter Ireland, "The Demand for Divisia Money: Theory and Evidence," *Journal of Macroeconomics* 61 (2019), available at https://doi.org/10.1016/j.jmacro.2019.103128.
7. For updated historical analysis of M2 through the great financial crisis, see Richard G. Anderson, Michael Bordo, and John V. Duca, "Money and Velocity During Financial Crises: From the Great Depression to the Great Recession," NBER Working Paper 22100, March 2016. Meltzer, "Quantitative Quicksand," June 6, 2013.
8. Charles Goodhart and Manoj Pradhan, *The Great Demographic Reversal: Ageing Societies, Waning Inequality, and an Inflation Revival* (London: Palgrave Macmillan, 2020). Tooze, *Crashed*, 15.
9. Stephanie Kelton, *The Deficit Myth: Modern Monetary Theory and the Birth of the People's Economy* (New York: PublicAffairs, 2021).
10. Changes to the strategic document are highlighted at https://www.federalreserve.gov/monetarypolicy/guide-to-changes-in-statement-on-longer-run-goals-monetary-policy-strategy.htm. Mickey D. Levy and Charles Plosser, "The Murky Future of Monetary Policy," October 1, 2020, Hoover Institution Economic Working Paper 20119.
11. Adam Tooze, *Shutdown: How Covid Shook the World's Economy* (New York: Viking, 2021), chapter 6.
12. Milton Friedman, "The Optimum Quantity of Money," in *The Optimum Quantity of Money and Other Essays* (Chicago: Aldine Publishing, 1969), 4–5, v.
13. Bernanke, *The Courage to Act*, 64.
14. Martin Sandbu, "Coronavirus: The Moment for Helicopter Money," *Financial Times*, March 20, 2020.
15. See https://www.cnbc.com/2020/03/16/coronavirus-stimulus-romney-proposes-1000-for-every-american.html. https://www.cotton.senate.gov/news/press-releases/cotton-releases-coronavirus-response-plan-to-give-cash-directly-to-american-families-and-businesses. Jennifer Burns, "Granting Cash Payments Is a Conservative Principle," *The Hill*, March 30, 2020, available at https://thehill.com/opinion/finance/490222-granting-cash-payments-is-a-conservative-principle.
16. Peter Brimelow, "Interview: Milton Friedman at 85," *Forbes*, December 29, 1997.
17. John Greenwood and Steve H. Hanke, "Too Much Money Portends High Inflation: The Fed Should Pay Attention to Milton Friedman's Wisdom," *The Wall Street Journal*, July 20, 2021, NP.
18. The Semi-Annual Monetary Policy Report to Congress, February 23, 2021, 24, available at https://www.govinfo.gov.
19. Alan S. Blinder, "When It Comes to Inflation, I'm Still on Team Transitory," *The Wall Street Journal*, December 29, 2021. "Yellen Says 'I Was Wrong' Last Year on the Path of U.S. Inflation," *Bloomberg News*, May 31, 2022. Jerome H. Powell, "Monetary Policy and Price Stability," August 26, 2022, available at https://www.federalreserve.gov/newsevents/speech/powell20220826a.htm.
20. Tyler Goodspeed, "How Monetary Policy Got So Far Behind the Curve: The Role of Fiscal Policy," and Larry Summers, "A Labor Market View on Inflation," in Michael D. Bordo, John T. Cochrane, and John B. Taylor, eds., *How Monetary Policy Got Behind the Curve—and How to Get It Back* (Stanford, CA: Hoover Institution Press, 2022), 115, 17–32.
21. Tyler Cowen, "Inflation Is Best Explained by This Underrated Economic Theory," *The Washington Post*, September 21, 2022.
22. Barry Eichengreen, *Exorbitant Privilege: The Rise and Fall of the Dollar and the Future of the International Monetary System* (New York: Oxford University Press, 2011), 111–12. See also Gary Gerstle, *The Rise and Fall of the Neoliberal Order* (New York: Oxford University

Press, 2022), 215. For the contrary view, see J. Bradford DeLong, *Slouching Towards Utopia: An Economic History of the Twentieth Century* (New York: Basic Books, 2022), 497.

23. Bordo, Cochrane, and Taylor, *How Monetary Policy Got Behind the Curve*, x.
24. Monika Piazzesi, "Inflation Blues: The Fortieth-Anniversary Revival?" in Bordo, Cochrane, and Taylor, *How Monetary Policy Got Behind the Curve*, 357–72.
25. Nancy MacLean, "How Milton Friedman Exploited White Supremacy to Privatize Education," INET Working Paper No. 161, September 2021, available at https://www.ineteconomics.org/research/research-papers/how-milton-friedman-exploited-white-supremacy-to-privatize-education. Zachary D. Carter, "The End of Friedmanomics," *The New Republic*, June 17, 2021. Larry Kramer, "Beyond Neoliberalism: Rethinking Political Economy," April 26, 2018, Public Board Memo, available at https://hewlett.org/library/beyond-neoliberalism-rethinking-political-economy/, 6. Jeffrey Sachs, "The Bolivian Hyperinflation and Stabilization," *AEA Papers and Proceedings* 77, no. 2 (May 1987): 279. "Friedman's Influential Essay on Business, 50 Years Later," *The New York Times*, September 13, 2020.
26. Gerstle, *The Rise and Fall of the New Deal Order*, 2.
27. For an influential statement, see Ezra Klein, "The Economic Mistake the Left Is Finally Confronting," *The New York Times*, September 19, 2021. For a roundup of UBI experiments, see https://basicincome.stanford.edu/research/ubi-visualization/.
28. Eric Alterman, "Cruisin' with Miltie," *The American Prospect*, November 17, 2006, available at https://prospect.org/article/cruisin-miltie/.
29. Milton Friedman, "Public Schools: Make Them Private," *The Washington Post*, February 19, 1995.
30. Deirdre Nansen McCloskey, *Bourgeois Equality: How Ideas, Not Capital or Institutions, Enriched the World* (Chicago: University of Chicago Press, 2016).
31. Quoted in "Notable and Quotable: Milton Friedman," *The Wall Street Journal*, June 14, 2015, available at https://www.wsj.com/articles/notable-quotable-milton-friedman-1434318595. Friedman, "Public Schools: Make Them Private."
32. Milton Friedman, "A Comment on CSWEP," *Journal of Economic Perspectives* 12 (Autumn 1998): 197–99.
33. R. Glenn Hubbard, "Even My Business School Students Have Doubts About Capitalism," *The Atlantic*, January 2022, available at https://www.aei.org/articles/even-my-business-school-students-have-doubts-about-capitalism/. Marco Rubio, "Inaugural Henry Clay Lecture," December 8, 2021, available at https://www.rubio.senate.gov/public/index.cfm/2021/12/rubio-delivers-lecture-on-how-the-bipartisan-economic-consensus-is-destroying-american-greatness.
34. See https://www.romney.senate.gov/romney-offers-path-provide-greater-financial-security-american-families/.
35. Beatrice Cherrier, "The Lucky Consistency of Milton Friedman's Science and Politics," in Robert Van Horn, Philip Mirowski, and Thomas A. Stapleford, eds., *Building Chicago Economics: New Perspectives on the History of America's Most Powerful Economics Program* (New York: Cambridge University Press, 2011), 335–67.
36. Interview with Summers for the PBS series *Commanding Heights*, April 24, 2001.
37. "Two Lucky People," *The Commonwealth*, September 4, 1998.
38. Milton Friedman with the assistance of Rose D. Friedman, *Capitalism and Freedom: Fortieth Anniversary Edition* (Chicago: University of Chicago Press, 1962; 2002), 2.

ACKNOWLEDGMENTS

I am grateful to Janet Martel and David Friedman, the children of Milton and Rose Friedman, for meeting with me at an early stage in this project, maintaining scholarly access to the Friedman archive, and to Janet for generously granting publication permissions. Jerry Porter, Milton Friedman's nephew, gave me invaluable insight into the Friedman family. Rose and Milton's grandson Patri Friedman showed me how Friedman's ideas continue to evolve. It must be fraught to have a scholar tackling the life of a family member; in the end, I hope all of Rose and Milton's relatives will find something to appreciate in this book.

When I arrived at the Stanford history department, this book was little more than a glimmer in my eye (and a job talk), but happily I had landed in the ideal environment to launch an ambitious second project as a junior historian. A series of extraordinary department chairs ensured I could manage the tenure track and a growing family; thanks especially to Kären Wigen for arranging a critical research leave, to Paula Findlen for wise counsel, and to Matt Sommer for exemplary EQ. Caroline Winterer has smoothed the path ever since my first interview. I was privileged to learn from and be inspired by a formidable roster of senior colleagues in the U.S. field, including Al Camarillo, James Campbell, Clay Carson, Gordon Chang, Estelle Freedman, David Kennedy, Jack Rakove, Richard White, and Caroline Winterer.

I hope to do the same for the brilliant scholars who have joined the U.S. field since: Jonathan Gienapp, Destin Jenkins, Kathryn Olivarius, and Pedro Regalado. J-FROG buddies Allyson Hobbs, Ana Minian, Yumi Moon, Edith Sheffer, Laura Stokes, Jun Uchida, and Mikael Wolfe were an invaluable support group. I've appreciated the chance to advise Rowan Doran (who hardly needs my help), and to field questions from other colleagues in the hallway, after faculty meetings, and at Historical Conversations. The incredible teachers, staff, and families of the Children's Center of Stanford Community were a critical support, especially in this project's early years.

Throughout the writing of the book, I've been motivated by dozens of Stanford undergraduates whose questions in lecture, requests for classes on the history of capitalism, serendipitous encounters at coffee and doughnuts, and willingness to "get lost" in the archive have continually refreshed my faith in intellectual life. I wish I could name you all; rest assured you made a difference. Many thanks to the hardworking history staff for creating a strong departmental culture for our students. I've also been pushed by innumerable graduate students; particular thanks to Claire Arcenas, Austin Clements, Theresa Iker, Natalie Larah, Glory Liu, Austin Steelman, and Alastair Su for keeping me sharp. Along the way, I've benefited from audience comments and questions at the U.S. History Workshop, Gender History Workshop, Political Theory Workshop, Approaches to Capitalism Workshop, Symbolic Systems Forum, Social Sciences History Workshop, and Economic History Workshop, and have been enriched by the conferences, workshops, and events sponsored by Juliana Bidanure's Basic Income Lab. Other valued interlocutors on the Stanford faculty include Ran Abramitzky, Dan Fetter, Emily Levine, Florencia Torche, Fred Turner, Gavin Wright, and Sylvia Yanagisako.

My research and thinking have benefited significantly from connections to Stanford's Hoover Institution, the custodian of Friedman's papers, where I have been appointed a Research Fellow for much of this project. In addition to providing access to Friedman's papers under ideal circumstances, the Library and Archives' visionary director, Eric Wakin, supported an annual Political Economy Workshop that allowed me to test out my developing ideas amid a rotating community of more than fifty visiting scholars pursuing research in the archives. Chris Marino and Emily Gibson stepped in at critical moments with key primary sources. I could always count on the archives staff to be professional, conscientious, and motivated to provide an unparalleled research environment. Charles Palm shared his encyclopedic knowledge of Friedman's archive and made my task far easier in countless ways. Friedman himself seemed to come alive in Hoover's Economic Policy Working Group and the annual Monetary Policy Conference, affording me an exceptional opportunity to see how his legacy lives on in the work of John Taylor and the late George Shultz. Regular conversations with visiting fellows George Tavlas and Michael Bordo, along with their written work, were indispensable. John Cochrane gave generously of his time to read a draft, along the way helping me understand what it must have felt like to be in a Chicago workshop. Niall Ferguson's arrival opened up new space for publicly engaged history and biography in the Hoover History Working Group; the group also provided rigorous feedback on two chapter drafts. I received helpful comments and questions from Annelise Anderson, Michael Boskin, Niall Ferguson, Bob Hall, Erik Wakin, and Kevin Warsh. Friedman's longtime secretary, Gloria Valentine, was a valued guide.

A number of colleagues outside of Stanford have been essential. Meg Jacobs encouraged me to write a biography of Friedman. I am thankful to Angus Burgin for helping me get over an early case of nerves as I headed outside my comfort zone; Steve Teles has been an indispensable conversationalist from the start. Steve, Tim Shenk, and Angus Burgin workshopped a first draft via Zoom, giving me a much needed boost as the pandemic closed in. An early invitation to Harvard's Joint Center for History and Economics, courtesy of David Armitage and Jo Guldi, helped kick-start my research. The Society for United States Intellectual History community was a welcome source of camaraderie. I was glad to stay in touch with David Hollinger and Nils Gilman through the Bay Area Consortium for the History of Ideas in America, and to make new Berkeley contacts, including Mark Brilliant, Desmond Jagmohan, Daniel Sargent, and Nathan Sayre.

Desmond Jagmohan and Jacob Levy helped me see Friedman through the lens of political theory. Cléo Chassonnery-Zaïgouche and John Singleton encouraged me to write about the women in Friedman's life and career, as did the organizers of the Women in Intellectual History Conference. Daniel Zamora connected me to global debates over universal basic income. I am grateful for feedback, questions, and comments from audiences at the following venues: Rutgers Economic History Workshop; HOPE Conference on Women and Economics; Duke University History of Political Economy Seminar; Center for Study of Work, Labor, and Democracy at UCSB; a Stanford regional meeting of the Mont Pelerin Society; American Historical Association Annual Conference; New Directions in American History Conference; Policy History Conference; Organization of American Historians Annual Conference; and Berkeley Political Theory Workshop. I also benefited from several anonymous reviews of the manuscript and related work. I would never have attempted this book without the long-ago encouragement of Ray Fisman, who cheered me through Ec 10 problem sets in Cabot House. Also long ago, at Harvard Business School, Debra Spar and Forest Reinhardt gave me a crash course in writing about economics and interpreting macro data.

Among the most rewarding aspects of this book has been joining the exile community of historians of economics, who have been extraordinarily welcoming. Philip Mirowski, the madcap dean of the field, provided critical readings and critical information; his passion and archival tenacity inspire awe. Bruce Caldwell's Center for the History of Political Economy at Duke has given hope to legions of scholars across the globe who believe we ought to know our economic history, and our history of economics, for all our sake. Bruce remains the essential source for all things Hayek. A 2015 conference, the Legacy of the First Chicago School of Economics, organized by Doug Irwin and held at the Becker Friedman Institute for Economics at the University of Chicago, was a much appreciated chance to meet the scholars whose books helped me get oriented in the field. At various points, Steven Medema provided trenchant comments and questions. I enjoyed comparing notes with Roger Backhouse as he completes the second volume of his monumental Paul Samuelson biography. My understanding of Friedman has been immeasurably deepened by the pathbreaking work of Edward Nelson, the author of two comprehensive volumes on Friedman's economic thought, and George Tavlas, who has painstakingly reconstructed the origins of Chicago monetary economics. Those wanting to further pursue the history of Friedman's economics are encouraged to read their work.

For sundry primary sources, sharing of unpublished work, and other helpful assistance I am indebted to Paul Burnett, Bruce Caldwell, R. W. Dimand, Sebastian Edwards, Ross Emmett, Kelly Goodman, Doug Irwin, Daniel Hammond, Kevin Hoover, Daniel Immerwahr, Daniel Kuhn, David Levy, Paul Milazzo, Philip Mirowski, David Mitch, Leonidas Montes, Edward Nelson, Eric Rauchway, John Singleton, Stephen Stigler, George Tavlas, and Robert Van Horn.

A fleet of research assistants, all of them Stanford students, helped with this work. Spencer Nelson was critical to the early stages and made several East Coast research trips on my behalf. Alastair Su dug out Friedman's Treasury Department memos, while Ian Miller kept the project moving at several key moments. Other essential research assistants include Brandon Aponte, Austin Clements, James Hanley, Ali Karamustafa, Jack Kimmel, Michel Lee, Brian Moran, Brendan O'Byrne, Eilaf Osman, Sunil Rao, and Austin Steelman. I also relied on the independent researchers Joan Cavanaugh and Diane L. Richards. Thanks to John Koo for advice on statistics. Jerry Marshall helped with permissions.

Al Shipley, Rahway City Historian, helped me excavate Friedman's earliest writing and understand his family history. Archivists and librarians at the University of Chicago Special Collections (especially Christine Colburne), Berkeley Oral History Center, Duke University Economist Papers Project, and George Mason University Special Collections have been exceedingly helpful.

I have received financial support from the Stanford University School of Humanities and Sciences, the National Endowment for the Humanities, and the Hoover Institution.

At Farrar, Straus and Giroux, Alexander Star artfully served up compliment sandwiches that kept my writing engines fueled. The book was vastly improved by his scrupulous editing of several lengthy drafts. The rumors that he has a photographic memory are true, as far as I can tell. Andrew Wylie has been a valued advocate and strategist, with an unerring eye for detail and the big picture. Thanks to Ian Van Wye, Scott Auerbach, Karla Eoff, Vivan Kirklin, and Rima Weinberg for expert copyediting and production guidance.

Debts to family and friends are deepest of all; I've gone on long enough, but you know who you are. I have dedicated this book to Nick, my indefatigable cheerleader, statistical consultant, and first reader—I could not have done it without him. Likewise, Iris and Anton provided a thousand reasons to step away from the office and my computer, and a million moments of joy and wonder preserved not in a book but in my heart.

INDEX

Page numbers in *italics* refer to illustrations.

ILLUSTRATION CREDITS

PHOTOGRAPHIC INSERT

1. Milton Friedman Papers, Hoover Institution Library and Archives, http://digitalcollections.hoover.org/objects/64144.
2. Milton Friedman Papers, Hoover Institution Library and Archives, http://digitalcollections.hoover.org/objects/64143.
3. University of Chicago Photographic Archive, apf2-07467, Hanna Holborn Gray Special Collections Research Center, University of Chicago Library.
4. University of Chicago Photographic Archive, apf1-03515, Hanna Holborn Gray Special Collections Research Center, University of Chicago Library.
5. Milton Friedman Papers, Hoover Institution Library and Archives, http://digitalcollections.hoover.org/objects/64142.
6. University of Chicago Photographic Archive, apf1-07615, Hanna Holborn Gray Special Collections Research Center, University of Chicago Library.
7. Milton Friedman Papers, Hoover Institution Library and Archives, http://digitalcollections.hoover.org/objects/58175.
8. David M. Rubenstein Rare Book & Manuscript Library, Duke University.
9. Milton Friedman Papers, box 90, folder 3, Hoover Institution Library and Archives.
10. Courtesy of Maximiliane Hunold.
11. University of Chicago Photographic Archive, apf1-07023, Hanna Holborn Gray Special Collections Research Center, University of Chicago Library.
12. Photograph by Lloyd Eldon Saunders.
13. University of Chicago Photographic Archive, apf1-06232, Hanna Holborn Gray Special Collections Research Center, University of Chicago Library.
14. University of Chicago Photographic Archive, apf1-07023, Hanna Holborn Gray Special Collections Research Center, University of Chicago Library.
15. Photograph by Truman Moore / Getty Images.
16. © 1969 TIME USA LLC. All rights reserved. Used under license.
17. Photograph by Bettmann via Getty Images.
18. Milton Friedman Papers, Hoover Institution Library and Archives, http://digitalcollections.hoover.org/objects/64149.
19. Milton Friedman Papers, Hoover Institution Library and Archives, http://digitalcollections.hoover.org/objects/64150.
20. AP-Photo / Reportagebild.
21. University of Chicago Photographic Archive, apf7-03480, Hanna Holborn Gray Special Collections Research Center, University of Chicago Library, © The Chicago Maroon.

22. © George Tames / *The New York Times* / Redux.
23. © Teresa Zabala / *The New York Times* / Redux.
24. The Heritage Foundation.
25. Photograph by Steven N. S. Cheung, Milton Friedman Papers, Hoover Institution Library and Archive, http://digitalcollections.hoover.org/objects/64152.